AP Foreign Correspondents in Action

World War II to the Present

Based on extended interviews conducted from the Pakistani countryside to Washington, *AP Foreign Correspondents in Action: World War II to the Present* reveals for the first time what it takes to get the stories that bring the world home to America. It gives new frontline insights into major events from the Japanese surrender in 1945 to the 2010s Syrian civil war, and it helps understand the impact of news on international affairs by revealing foundational journalistic practices.

Both successes and failures through eight decades of foreign correspondence from Afghanistan to Zimbabwe show that public discourse has been best served by correspondents who, at great risk, challenged accepted narratives, exposed omnipresent lies, gave a voice to the voiceless, and stymied the frequently violent efforts of those who feared truth-telling eyewitnesses.

Giovanna Dell'Orto is an associate professor at the University of Minnesota's School of Journalism and Mass Communication. She teaches and researches the interplay between news, journalistic practices, and international affairs – topics she has lectured about to academic and professional audiences from China to Chile. A former newswoman with The Associated Press and fluent in four languages, she is the author of *American Journalism and International Relations*, also from Cambridge University Press, which analyzes the impact of foreign correspondence on American foreign policy from 1848 to 2008. She is also the author or editor of three other books on journalism and foreign affairs. She holds a PhD in Mass Communication from the University of Minnesota.

AP Foreign Correspondents in Action

World War II to the Present

GIOVANNA DELL'ORTO
University of Minnesota

CAMBRIDGE
UNIVERSITY PRESS

CAMBRIDGE
UNIVERSITY PRESS

32 Avenue of the Americas, New York, NY 10013-2473, USA

Cambridge University Press is part of the University of Cambridge.

It furthers the University's mission by disseminating knowledge in the pursuit of education, learning, and research at the highest international levels of excellence.

www.cambridge.org
Information on this title: www.cambridge.org/9781107519305

© Giovanna Dell'Orto 2016

First published 2016

Printed in the United States of America by Sheridan Books, Inc.

A catalog record for this publication is available from the British Library.

ISBN 978-1-107-10830-1 Hardback
ISBN 978-1-107-51930-5 Paperback

To the memory of Anja,
and to Kathy, Terry, and all foreign correspondents
who give so much to tell the stories

Contents

Figures

Acknowledgments

While I was researching wire copy for my *American Journalism and International Relations* book at AP's Corporate Archives in New York, their invaluable director, Valerie Komor, suggested that, given my interest in foreign correspondence, I should give a call to George Bria, a "former correspondent." I did, asking for a meeting the next morning before my flight home. George said he would be delighted, but could we make it before his doubles tennis match since, having just turned 95, he might be a bit tired afterward? I knew I had a story. After interviewing George, whose career in foreign news began with covering the end of World War II, and 60 other AP foreign correspondents, I have this book – and thousands of pages of notes, historical photos, plus warm memories of my own – so my biggest, profoundest debt of gratitude goes to all of them, for their time, candor, insights, and unfailing, exceptional graciousness.

Beyond the interviews, I am grateful to many of them for continued conversations over unforgettable meals, from a multicourse dinner party in Islamabad to a potent herbal pick-me-up in Bethlehem; from breakfast at the Royal Bangkok Sports Club to refried beans in Tucson; from Casablanca beer in Rabat to late-night cocktails in Jerusalem; from a sushi roll in Tokyo to a cheese plate in Silver Spring, Maryland; from dumplings in Beijing and Shanghai to steak in Mexico City; and even heritage-homage Italian dishes in suburban New York and Washington as well as Edinburgh and Denver. To Donna, George, Kathy, Tad, Tony, and Vicki – and their families – a heartfelt thank-you for hosting me for a night, a weekend, or a month, an extraordinarily generous welcome that made irreplaceable insights possible. Beginning with John Daniszewski, AP's international editor and also interviewee, I am admiringly grateful to the supervisors and editors who allowed, even facilitated, my unfettered access to their staff – a true model of free expression values – as well as to the many photographers who donated their stunning shots (special thanks to Domenico Stinellis, who found the cover image). Without the great store of knowledge, and reliably prompt and cheerful help, of Valerie and archivist Francesca Pitaro over four years, this project would have never taken off.

Nor would it have maintained altitude without the University of Minnesota, its College of Liberal Arts, then led by Dr. Bud Duvall, and its School of Journalism and Mass Communication, with its stellar staff, and led by Director Dr. Albert Tims, which provided grants and research leaves that made it possible for me to travel to conduct the interviews as well as to hire two fabulous research assistants, Stephen Bennett and Rodrigo Zamith, who helped prepare for them and then transcribed dozens of hours of recordings (for the latter, thank you also to Alyssa Anderson, Marcheta Fornoff, and Devan Grimsrud). The SJMC's IT and digital media team, Scott Dierks and Wally Swanson, offered their limitless expertise with tireless kindness at every stage. I have greatly benefited from the suggestions by Donald Ritchie, Historian of the United States Senate; Professors Hazel Dicken-Garcia and Mitchell Stephens; and colleagues at the meetings of the American Journalism Historians Association, International Communication Association, International Studies Association, and Joint Journalism and Communication History (AJHA/ AEJMC). The anonymous reviewers for Cambridge University Press provided crucial encouragement and advice. Cambridge senior commissioning editor Robert Dreesen has supported and sustained this book from the initial idea – it is our second book, a partnership I tremendously treasure.

As always, my parents, Dario and Paola Dell'Orto, have been with me on the whole journey – and my father even took me to one interview, in Santiago de Chile. While traveling, and beyond, the warm and generous friendship of Jacques and Georgia Billeaud, Samer Farha, Lutz Görgens, Francis Hwang, Bruno and Mafalda Melica, and Art and Debby Rotstein gave me safe harbor from Tokyo to Tucson. On Friday, April 4, 2014, two email messages, from Jacques and Steve Elliott, our bureau chief when all three of us worked at AP Phoenix, jumped out as I opened my mailbox – one's title read "relevant to your book" and the other "tragedy." Having just returned from a book tour in Arizona talking about journalism and immigration, I assumed they were notifying me of the latest deadly border incident.

Their emails contained only a link: http://www.ap.org/Content/AP-In-The-News/2014/AP-photographer-killed-reporter-wounded.

Anja Niedringhaus had been murdered and Kathy Gannon horribly wounded by a policeman who fired his automatic weapon at them as they sat in their car in Afghanistan, on assignment to cover the country's pivotal elections. Anja and Kathy – I could see them, less than a year earlier, peering through the crowds at Benazir Bhutto International Airport arrival hall, and then smiling, laughing, discoursing in every now infinitely precious moment of the weekend they welcomed me to Pakistan, taking time for interviews even as they were getting ready for another Afghanistan assignment. As I was writing this book, another AP foreign correspondent, video journalist Simone Camilli, was killed (together with an AP translator) covering war in the Gaza Strip – and I hate keeping this count, fully aware of how many more are in harm's way as I type this.

Telling stories to better understand others – it is what AP foreign correspondents put their lives on the line to do and, in my small, privileged way, it is what this book is intended to do. Humbly and gratefully, I dedicate it to them.

I

Introduction

They have had lamb chops with Pope John Paul II, tea with Osama bin Laden's bodyguard, pizza with Fidel Castro, and canned tuna with Zapatista fighters. The world's most and least powerful have alternately tried to cajole and evade them. They have been bombed, kidnapped, held at gunpoint, and have come under all kinds of fire from Beirut to Khost, Afghanistan, to Tamaulipas, Mexico. They have filed all continents' major stories – from U.S. warships, on keyboards shaking during record earthquakes, and by thrusting film and papers at random passengers in airports' international departure lounges whom they deemed trustworthy enough to become "pigeons."

Anybody who has followed foreign news in U.S. media over the past eight decades is certain to have read their stories – and most likely not to know their names, or anything else about them. These global news agenda-setters are the foreign correspondents of The Associated Press, the most significant unknown shapers of Americans' worldview. How they have brought the world to America from the 1940s to today is the core of this book – providing not only an entirely new firsthand history of the major sociopolitical junctures of the 20th and 21st centuries, but shedding new light on the connection between journalism and international affairs at a time of turmoil for both.

With the end of the Cold War paradigm, the splintering of the "war on terror," and profound, insularity-inducing economic trouble, American foreign policy in the mid-2010s appears to be struggling to define its priorities and direction in a world bursting with violence. U.S. news media – facing a crisis that, far from being simply a failure of traditional business models and platforms, is threatening the very existence of a mediated public sphere – are increasingly disengaging from international coverage. Assuming that foreign correspondence helps frame the box within which ordinary Americans and policymakers alike think of the world, and therefore delimits the range of possible foreign policy options, today's disengagement is both paradoxical and dangerous.

It also highlights the growing importance of the news organization that provides the bulk of foreign news to the American public (and beyond) – The Associated Press. Neglected by scholars but practically dominant, since the early 20th century the New York–based news cooperative has gathered and brought world news not only to the nation's leading media, but also to the remotest weeklies in the U.S. countryside. For every celebrated journalist in the spotlight, dozens of AP reporters have toiled, often anonymously, to bring the world to millions of readers. The organization, founded in 1846, estimates that today half the world's population sees AP news every day: In 2013, AP published 2,000 stories a day and a million photos a year, and served 1,400 newspapers and thousands of broadcasting outlets in the United States, plus thousands more in more than 100 other countries.

As one historian of foreign news put it, "No one expected the *New York Times* [or any other newspaper] to have a correspondent everywhere a coup might break out, but they did expect the AP to have someone there" (Hamilton 2009, 278). And yet, aside from an internal history that devotes one chapter to its foreign correspondents (Reporters of The Associated Press 2007; Heinzerling 2007), the story of these global storytellers has not been told – until this book. Based primarily on new oral history interviews with 61 correspondents who covered virtually every continent from 1944 to today, the book's central aim is to document the evolution of foreign correspondence practices at AP in eight decades of U.S. dominance in global affairs, and therefore it focuses on the U.S. connection, even though AP's audience is far wider. The emphasis here is on practices: The book is neither hagiography nor satire, as many biographies, autobiographies, and spoofs of foreign correspondents are, nor a snapshot of a particular time or place, as are ethnographies of the correspondents as a "tribe" (such as Pedelty's 1995 study of the press corps in El Salvador and Hannerz's 2004 one of reporters in Jerusalem, Johannesburg, and Tokyo).

The extended interviews – conducted almost exclusively in person in locales ranging from the Pakistani countryside to the Washington AP bureau – reveal, in all but a couple of cases for the first time publicly, *why* the stories that brought the world home to America were written the way they were. Thus, the book not only creates a document of untold history and gives new eyewitness insights into major events ranging from the Japanese surrender in 1945 to the 2010s Syrian civil war, but it also advances scholarship both on a severely threatened journalistic profession and on the evolving relationship between news media and U.S. policymaking over time. As will be elaborated in the next section, the underlying assumption is that, to understand news content's impact on international affairs, we must discover the journalistic practices that made content what it is (and is not).[1]

---

[1] A point made by some correspondents themselves – e.g., Rosenblum (2010), 9.

With extensive quotations that allow the interviewees' own voices to freshly and clearly emerge, the book reveals and analyzes the major themes in foreign correspondence processes from the first story idea to reactions to the published copy – or to put it in journalistic terms, how correspondents have figured out what the story was, how they got the story, and how they got it onto the wire. At the story's inception, themes revolve around the preparatory work (including needed skills such as language and the original interest in journalism) and the story selection and news judgment processes. At the reporting level – arguably the most critical – the central themes are the development, maintenance, and ethical protection of sources; the fundamental act of reporting from the scene and the related, disturbingly universal exposure to dangers, violence, and trauma; the overseas perception of journalists; and the team and competition dynamics with fellow journalists both within and outside AP.

Once correspondents are back in the office (or wherever a writing device with some connectivity for filing has been available), the analysis focuses on their standards, including objectivity; the potential impacts on content of their relationship with foreign governments (and opposition groups), ranging from access to censorship, as well as with the U.S. government, including its military; and the filing of copy, especially through gigantic changes in communication technologies. Story production also involves the interaction with editors at AP headquarters (including any clashes over news values, selection, and salience of coverage), and ultimately the reactions from audiences, and, last but perhaps most crucial, the impact on the U.S. public, reflecting the correspondents' beliefs in the purpose and influence of their profession.

The development over time of each of these themes is also analyzed, since interviews span eight decades – the oldest interviewee, or narrator, turned 101 in November 2014 – elucidating the evolving professional and public understandings of foreign correspondence as well as changes in the ethical, institutional, political, and technological constraints on journalistic practices. Professional practices will be evidenced by the discussion of news judgment (the evaluation of what to cover) as well as of the actual coverage, while the explanation of how correspondents dealt with their editors will illuminate institutional constraints. Ethical and political constraints are spotlighted in both reporting practices and the interaction with U.S. and foreign governments. The changing technological constraints represent an underlying thread throughout the book that emerges vividly in filing routines.

Covering most major international events from World War II to today, the correspondents candidly describe counting bodies in Marine Corps barracks in Lebanon, the killing fields in Cambodia, and Japan's tsunami-devastated provinces; fighting censorship and surveillance in the Soviet Union, China, and Brazil; challenging Washington's storylines from Sarajevo, Baghdad, and Pyongyang; and agonizing over public responses from South Africa to Afghanistan. Professional storytellers all, they vividly portray their core responsibility across the years – getting to the right sources at the scene, from

Mao Zedong, Salvador Allende, and Margaret Thatcher to Vietnamese widows, Polish resistance fighters, Syrian rebels, and North Korean children. Before turning to the selection of the correspondents as well as the use of interviews as a methodology for both oral history and political science, the next section provides the underlying theoretical assumptions about journalism and international affairs as well as a brief overview of the history of foreign correspondence.

FOREIGN CORRESPONDENCE AND INTERNATIONAL AFFAIRS

Bringing a long-term historical perspective to the study of the connection between journalism and international affairs is sorely needed to better understand the evolution of this dynamic. Communication history has seen an increased interest in foreign reporting and international media developments (e.g., Hamilton 2009; Chapman 2005). Journalism historians, however, have hardly engaged the significant body of literature, in the fields of both communication and political science, that explores the role of the news media in shaping foreign policy and international relations either directly, in what some critics see as Western news media's "neo-imperialism" (Boyd-Barrett and Rantanen 2004, 32), or through their influence on public opinion. Those studies of media and foreign policy, on the other hand, are rarely historical or even interdisciplinary, so that theories drawn from international relations and communication hardly ever interact productively, and the field has struggled to determine causality or even directionality of influence between alternatively watchdog and lapdog journalism and policymaking (for a review of this literature, see Miller 2007; Baum and Potter 2008).

In previous research (Dell'Orto 2008 and 2013), I brought together history, mass communication, and international relations to focus the scholarly discussion (and its professional implications) on a new model of media effects on international systems: the functioning (and malfunctioning) of the news media, particularly foreign correspondence, as the public arena where literally foreign concepts become understandable realities, which in turn serve as the basis for policy. My conclusion (Dell'Orto 2013) stressed three major points: First, while discourse A should not be understood to lead directly to foreign policy B, the more simplistic, stereotypical, and detached discourses about the world are, the less public debate can occur over policies and the more restricted is the range of policymaking options – making it imperative to study what are the practice constraints on those discourses, as this book does. If we assume, as I and others do (see especially Delli Carpini and Keeter 1996; Williams and Delli Carpini 2011; Bollinger 2010; Baum and Potter 2015), that a democracy needs some level of informed citizenry, and that the news media are one of the essential sources of information as well as a space of negotiation over meaning, then the second point is that the news media must engage foreign affairs as a pivotal responsibility. Third, the news media serve, for better or worse, as "irreplaceable mediators" between the world and Americans, especially those who have little direct experience of it, by creating select images of nations' identities – and AP correspondents, almost invisible in the historical record, have borne a large share of this mediating role. Finally, normatively, the implication is that foreign correspondence is a necessary investment for news media, even – perhaps especially – today, in the age of social media and user-generated content.

Both scholars and news organizations are increasingly positioning professional journalists in the role of expert fact-checker, interviewer, eyewitness, and analyst amid the onslaught of global online information – finally heeding Walter Lippmann's call, as one proponent of "knowledge-based journalism" put it (Patterson 2013; also Terzis 2015). Another proponent of "wisdom journalism" argues for conceptualizing most journalists as analysts and interpreters, leaving reporting, including foreign reporting, to others – from locals to wire services such as AP that, being "fast, dogged, and reasonably reliable" "can get an initial, workmanlike, accurate summary up within an hour of a news event … a condensed, clear news story" (Stephens 2014, xviii, 65). AP itself appears to be both reinforcing its reputation as "the definitive source" of "the fastest, most accurate reporting from every corner of the globe," and adding something akin to knowledge and wisdom journalism, which it called "impact," as discussed in the next chapters.

AP's 2012 annual report, for example, highlighted as one of the agency's crucial services "authenticating user-generated content," particularly from the world's most dangerous hot spot for journalists, civil war-torn Syria. Its 2013 report traced the company's continuing efforts to protect its content from "misappropriation" online, including getting revenue from aggregators. A 2013 report on the impact of digital technologies on news found that "trusted news brands" are the preferred sources for 82 percent of Americans (Newman and Levy 2013, 13) – which might be reassuring given that another study showed that distrust in institutional news media pushes people, paradoxically, toward more partisan sources, producing "an overall information loss for the citizenry" (Ladd 2012, 138). The whole reason for having foreign correspondents – and for that matter, any professional journalist – reporting from the front lines is that they can provide unique perspectives unlike those proffered by local media, the various actors, and U.S. policymakers. Analyzing foreign correspondence by AP and major U.S. newspapers from 1848 to 2008 (Dell'Orto 2013), I found a highly suggestive connection between oversimplified, U.S.-centric, reductive stories about locales as different as Japan and Israel and stalemated (or worse) policies toward those countries, as well as between perceptive writing grounded in local realities and realistic assessments enabling effective leadership.

If we accept those premises, it becomes imperative to understand the evolution of the institutional, professional, ethical, and technological practices of foreign correspondents – in other words, what exactly makes foreign correspondence what it is – which is the purpose of this project. It is also an urgent task. Foreign correspondence is widely considered one of the most endangered forms of newsgathering today, both in the United States and in other Western countries, and both in print and broadcasting (Paterson and Sreberny 2004; Perlmutter and Hamilton 2007; Sambrook 2010; Willnat and Martin 2012; Wu and Hamilton 2004).

Because of the news industry's faltering business model, the multimillion-dollar cost of foreign bureaus is a glaring temptation for a cut, and most U.S. news organizations have vastly retrenched their foreign service in the post-Cold War era, though some digital-only, entertainment-oriented organizations such as Vice Media and BuzzFeed are expanding overseas (State of the News Media, 2014, 5). Because of news managers' increased attention to audience responses, the proven, wide gap between journalists' preferences for news in the public interest and the public's actual interest in entirely less weighty matters (Boczkowski and Mitchelstein 2013) means that conflict in the Central African Republic pales into insignificance next to a starlet's indiscretion that lights up Twitterdom. Intriguingly, a 2013 survey of audience interest in types of news found a respectable 56 percent of Americans saying "international news" was important to them, while a meager 14 percent chose "entertainment and celebrity news" (Newman and Levy 2013, 31) – raising the question of whether our good intentions, or perhaps our socially conscious survey answers, are later betrayed by our actual clicks.

Many argue that, in quantity, there has never been more foreign news available to anyone interested enough to seek it, thanks to the plethora of online sources – from obscure bloggers to small local media to the massive foreign services of non-U.S.-based professional organizations such as the BBC or Al Jazeera. "Yes, but" – as the *New York Times* former executive editor (and former foreign correspondent) put it – the thinning of the ranks of professional correspondents has meant increasing, often appalling, risks for stringers and freelancers, and again the majority of the uninterested public is left with a cacophony of voices and little authority to tell apart competing claims to the truth.[2] Furthermore, the online news environment is highly imitative – original sources of content are few, and those snippets reverberate through infinite variations with few substantial new facts or analyses. A collection of essays by some of journalism's most prominent scholars is tellingly entitled *Will the Last Reporter Please Turn Out the Lights* (McChesney and Pickard 2011) – before the lights do go out, it is vital that the history and practices of America's foreign correspondents be recorded and analyzed, but with rare exceptions, they are absent from existing literature.

In journalism history scholarship, as well as in memoirs, foreign correspondence is generally treated only as war correspondence – tracing the steps of such notable reporters as Ernie Pyle and Khmer Rouge survivor Sydney

---

[2] Bill Keller, "It's the Golden Age of News," *New York Times*, November 3, 2013.

Schanberg (Knightley 2004; Schanberg 2010; Sweeney 2006; Patton 2014) – to the extent that a recent study of UK and U.S. television coverage of wars from Vietnam onward argued that the lack of a "peace correspondent" reveals "a news obsessiveness with conflicts between dominant extremes [that] tends to reinforce rather than challenge the path to violent conflict" (Spencer 2005, 1). The only two historical surveys of U.S. and other Western foreign correspondence and foreign correspondents highlight compelling stories of distinguished and notorious reporters, but they are not systematic analyses of professional practices (Hamilton 2009; Hohenberg 1995). Although many correspondents for the best-known organizations have written about their experiences abroad, those books tend to either be analyses of the foreign countries and events (such as Robert Fisk's thousand-page tomes on the Middle East, 2002, 2005) or "war stories" memoirs. As one of the correspondents I interviewed put it, those accounts should be balanced with older spoofs of the profession where bumbling, hard-drinking, entirely unprepared journalists stumble through the news, such as William Boot in Africa (Waugh 1938) or the "IP" wire reporter in Paris who is the protagonist of *Kansas City Milkman* (Packard 1950). Satire aimed at foreign correspondence continues today: The online magazine *Slate* ran an article on the eve of the 2013 U.S. government shutdown "using the tropes and tone normally employed by the American media to describe events in other countries" that even quoted that most anathema of sources, the cab driver [3]

Contemporary studies of foreign correspondents tend to focus on who they are (through demographic data obtained from surveys; e.g., Hess 1996) and, less prominently, on their work routines (Terzis 2015; Willnat and Martin 2012; Gross and Kopper 2011; Hahn and Lönnendonker 2009). U.S. foreign correspondents, estimated to number around 200 to 300 throughout most of the 20th century, were predominantly white and male (women reached a peak of about one-third of the total in the 1980s, which has remained unchanged, while minorities inched up but still hovered around less than 20%, even including foreign nationals), highly educated (more than 90% had a college degree), and had a stronger presence in Europe than anywhere else. A 2001 survey of 354 foreign correspondents found that those traits continued at the dawn of the 21st century, with a new pessimism about the lack of audience interest in serious foreign news and more interest on the part of correspondents in trends rather than breaking news (Wu and Hamilton 2004).

As to work routines, studies based on surveys, interviews, or observation have focused on news selection, producing evidence of who correspondents are and what they think of what they do (Willnat and Martin 2012, 502–503) and, in the ethnographic studies, touching upon practice concerns that are essential to this book – the relationship between editors and correspondents and the

---

[3] Joshua Keating, "If It Happened There . . . . The Government Shutdown," *Slate*, September 30, 2013. Interviewing the taxi driver as a "well-placed source" is a recurrent joke in journalistic circles; several of the correspondents mentioned it – as worth a shot as a "well-tuned" local voice, but certainly not the only or even a prominent source (Belkind, 7).

latter's autonomy (Hannerz 2004, 149; Pedelty 1995, 24, 91); the importance of language skills in gaining access to sources (Hannerz 2004, 88–89); the trauma-coping mechanisms (Pedelty 1995, 2, 58); and the struggles with objectivity (Pedelty 1995, 178). But those observations are limited to interviews with sets of journalists who happen to be there when the anthropologists do their fieldwork. The actual practices throughout the news process are not extrapolated from coverage of actual events during eight decades, an analysis that forms the core of this book. That is the crucial missing link in the connection between practice and content – explored as it happened across time and around the world.

Paradoxically, the most neglected area of study, historical or otherwise, is that of reporters for The Associated Press, whose bylines AP members and clients often do not even publish and whose organization does not carry the cachet of the *New York Times* or the BBC – even the autobiography of one of AP's most consequential leaders, Kent Cooper, starts with a self-deprecating anecdote about the utter lack of AP name recognition, and it was Cooper who first recognized by name an AP international correspondent in the preface to his 1925 reporting from the Arctic (Cooper 1959, 3, 109). But AP stories often serve as the agenda setters for more visible correspondents and constitute the entire diet of original foreign reporting for an increasing number of media outlets worldwide, dominating, albeit "inconspicuously," even the apparently free-for-all online news world (Paterson 2005, 145; Boyd-Barrett 1980; Hohenberg 1995).

By virtue of their more pervasive presence, larger numbers, and the far wider public distribution of their stories, AP correspondents have helped shape Americans' understanding of the world even more profoundly than far better-known colleagues. Given the retrenchment elsewhere, and its new ability to reach audiences directly through the app AP Mobile, AP's role in foreign newsgathering seems destined to only grow larger, despite the industry-wide financial challenges. In 2007, Rick Hall, the managing editor of Salt Lake City's *Deseret Morning News*, an AP member, had this to offer on AP's extensive coverage of the war in Iraq: "Nobody mentioned the costs, but it was clear the extent AP was going through to cover the story. It's horribly expensive, and bless AP for being there. . . . . We don't use as much international as we did 20 years ago, but I'm not so sure it's a bad thing that we help pay for that" (Ricchiardi 2008). In fact, in the 2010s, AP has continued what some call its Marine Corps tradition – first in, last out – by becoming the first international news organization to open permanent, full-time, multimedia bureaus in Pyongyang, North Korea (in January 2012), and in Yangon, Myanmar (in March 2013).

AP's very roots as a not-for-profit news cooperative are in international newsgathering. In the 1840s, a group of New York editors pooled their resources to get faster news transmission from the Mexican war front as well as from Europe (via Canada, because transatlantic ships with European newspapers docked in Nova Scotia before coming down the shore to U.S. ports). Until the early 20th century, however, AP foreign newsgathering was almost exclusively through a cartel arrangement with other news agencies, such as Reuters, rather than original reporting (Heinzerling 2007, 262), though the agency made a profound mark on U.S. journalism by institutionalizing the "inverted pyramid" style of leading with the most important information, most succinctly put. In the early 20th century, after expansion in the major European capitals, bureaus were opened around the world, and AP started distributing its wires to numerous international clients (Cooper 1959, 67, 263–270; Morris 1957, 177), breaking the "cartel" dominated by European agencies. In addition to a 1960s peak of 12 foreign-language wires, through most of the 20th century, two central foreign news editing desks existed in New York, one charged with editing copy from abroad for American media, the other with filing stories for international outlets. (In the 2000s, both desks were decentralized, and "regional" hubs were established in London, Mexico City, Cairo, Bangkok, and Johannesburg.)

The AP foreign service came of age in the World Wars era that, with the early Cold War period, is considered "a golden age for foreign correspondence" (Cole and Hamilton 2009, 174), with news from overseas occupying a growing, even dominant place among an American public whose opinion was closely studied by policymakers. AP competed with another U.S. wire agency, United Press (later UPI), for breaking news, even as both newspapers and, later, broadcasters expanded their foreign newsgathering. The Vietnam War served as a turning point in the relationship between the media, the public, and the government: Many in Washington blamed correspondents for turning the public against the war, and the backlash resulted in increasingly adversarial positioning both between journalists and government officials, who sought more and more to bar access, as well as, paradoxically, between media and a public disenchanted with "the establishment." In the 1990s, the sudden collapse of bipolar world politics and the digital revolution – combined with an existing shift in media companies' priorities from public service to consolidated corporate bottom line – altered correspondence, and journalism overall, in dramatic ways still playing out 20 years later.

Professional foreign correspondence by all but a handful of U.S. outlets disappeared, while social media became a crucial aspect of fragmented global power dynamics. All eyeballs seemed to focus on the dizzying rise of new communication technologies, creating among the public and many scholars the dangerously complacent illusion that newsgathering might be left to anyone with a smartphone, a wireless signal, and a Twitter account. On the distinctly positive side, digital technologies did make the flow of news across the world unprecedentedly instantaneous and cost-effective, as this brief timeline illustrates: AP's service began with the Pony Express and, three decades later, its first leased telegraph wire enabled it to transmit stories without competition. A major breakthrough came in 1933, with the first teletype circuit transmitting

60 words per minute – a punched-tape relay that endured overseas for half a century. In the mid-1970s, satellite started to allow text to move at 1,200 words per minute, and computerized advances quickly followed, culminating in the 2008 launch of the AP Mobile app.[4]

AP'S FOREIGN CORRESPONDENTS

Already before World War II, AP foreign correspondents began to earn a reputation for popping up everywhere, trying even Gandhi's patience. Finding an AP reporter waiting for him as he was released from prison in the middle of the night in the 1930s, the Mahatma reportedly shook his head and professed that he would likely run into AP even at heaven's door (Heinzerling 2007, 266) – and some 15 years later, Max Desfor, one of the interviewees in this book, was on hand to photograph Gandhi's history-making 1946 meeting with Jawaharlal Nehru. In one measure of the particular importance of international news, as of 2015, 30 of AP's 51 Pulitzer Prizes were won on foreign assignments (both reporting and photography – since the 1990s, AP has also had a video news service). AP correspondents repeatedly paid the highest price for this global presence: From the Spanish-American War in 1898 to conflict in the Gaza Strip in 2014, 33 died while on duty overseas – five in the span of a year, 1993–1994, and three as this book was written in 2014.[5] Many more were expelled from various countries, though AP was usually the first to restore its bureaus as political conditions changed – forced to close its Shanghai bureau in 1949, it reopened one in Beijing in early 1979 as soon as China and the United States began diplomatic relations. Similarly, AP's correspondent was the last American resident reporter booted out of Cuba in 1969, and Fidel Castro did not allow the agency to reopen in Havana until 1998, joining CNN as the only other U.S.-based news organization with a permanent presence on the island.[6] Africa, as for most agencies, was the weakest link – the first bureau there did not open until 1957 (in South Africa). In addition, a handful of roving correspondents reported from hundreds of countries, specializing in "trend" stories, from lighter features to global problems such as climate

---

[4] AP Technology, 1846–2013, unpublished reference guide, The Associated Press Corporate Archives, New York.

[5] The list was provided by AP archivist Francesca Pitaro in February 2014, and it includes staff correspondents as well as local hires and stringers on assignment for AP overseas. (For 1994, see Nicholas K. Geranios, "Foreign correspondents discuss dangers," The Associated Press, April 25, 1994.) The three AP staffers killed in 2014 are: in April, 48-year-old Anja Niedringhaus, when an Afghan police officer – supposed to be protecting the convoy she and AP reporter Kathy Gannon were traveling in to cover Afghanistan's national elections – turned his AK-47 on them; in August, 35-year-old Simone Camilli in an ordnance explosion while covering the war in the Gaza Strip; in November, 39-year-old Franklin Reyes Marrero in a car crash while returning from an assignment in Cuba.

[6] Anita Snow, "Cuban government approves re-opening of AP Havana bureau," The Associated Press, November 13, 1998.

change. Women had a harder time breaking into the foreign service – the first female foreign chief of bureau was not appointed until 1975, in the wake of a class-action lawsuit charging discrimination against female and nonwhite employees (Reporters of The Associated Press 2007, 214).

AP's foreign service, active in approximately 110 countries, comprises several types of professionals posted overseas, although their roles are becoming increasingly blurred due to resource constraints as well as new delivery and technological necessities. The majority of reporting and writing has been the province of "correspondents" (a mix of both international correspondents and local hires), though photographers and, in recent decades, videographers often traveled together with "text reporters" on assignments. Foreign bureaus also include managers, such as bureau chiefs and news editors (who to some extent have overlapped with correspondents, being in charge of both the editorial processes as well as administrative and commercial tasks), and technical/support staff.

This research selected as interviewees 61 international correspondents, though they often mentioned working with photographers and local hires, and some started as local hires and were then moved to the category of "New York hires." Several also assumed administrative duties in their career, but the focus of the interviews was on their reporting, not their editing or managing practices. This selection does not imply any merit ranking, but rather sought to concentrate on the practices of expatriate, usually American correspondents who dealt principally with text as their means of storytelling. Local hires – a category that has been steadily increasing and blurred, amounting to as many as 69 percent of American news organizations' employees abroad in 2004 (Wu and Hamilton 2004, 521) – and still and video photographers deserve their own study and are a compelling area for further research.[7]

Of these 61 correspondents, in line with the design and the historical expectations, most are American men; seven are not U.S. citizens (hailing from Great Britain, Bolivia, Canada, Chile, and Germany), and 16 are women. Their ages ranged, at the time of the interviews (March 2012–June 2014), from the upper 30s to 99, and they had worked for AP from six to 49 years, the vast majority of which in overseas assignments. Cumulatively, the 61 correspondents worked for AP for over 1,710 years – or nearly 30 years on average – representing an exceptional trove of institutional and professional knowledge. At the time of the interviews, 28 were still working for AP in a variety of positions in the United States and overseas; the others had either retired or were working in different jobs, including other media, nonprofits, and education. When I interviewed them, 13 of them were residing in the New York City area; eight in the Washington, DC, area; three in Florida; two in Hawaii; and one each in Arizona, California, Colorado, Minnesota, Missouri, Oregon, and Washington. Overseas, four were living in China, Japan, and Mexico each; three in the United Kingdom; two in

---

[7] Murrell (2015) explains the impact of "fixers" on TV foreign correspondence practices.

Israel (and the West Bank); and one each in Bolivia, Chile, France, Germany, Italy, Morocco, Pakistan, Portugal, South Korea, Spain, and Thailand.

Their education and experience in journalism prior to a foreign posting, their language skills, and other factors that prompted the choice of a foreign correspondent career are discussed in Chapter 2 insofar as these details are relevant to their approach to the practice of foreign correspondence. No other biographical details were solicited, because, again, the emphasis in this research is on practices, not the personal characteristics of each correspondent, though interviewees sometimes volunteered information about their upbringing or families as it impacted their coverage of foreign news.

As far as postings, in the interviews, the correspondents discussed reporting from Australia, the Arctic, and Canada, as well as at least 19 countries in Latin America and the Caribbean (from Argentina to Venezuela); 19 countries in Europe (from Albania to the Vatican); 22 countries in Africa (from Algeria to Zimbabwe); 11 countries in the Middle East (from Bahrain to Yemen); and 23 countries in Asia (from Afghanistan to Vietnam); plus a smattering of countries that no longer exist (Czechoslovakia, East Pakistan, Rhodesia, the Soviet Union, Yugoslavia). Two were roving "special correspondents" based in New York and Paris, respectively, and they each reported from more than 100 countries. Such geographical breadth of coverage was necessary to build a comprehensive sample, and so was the vast variety of the major world events that the correspondents covered, such as: in the 1940s and 1950s, from World War II to China's civil war; in the 1960s and 1970s, from the Castro regime to the many conflicts in the wake of African decolonization, from the Vietnam War to the Iranian Revolution, from the Khmer Rouge takeover of Cambodia to civil war in Nicaragua. In the 1980s, the interviewed correspondents covered the fall of Communist regimes across Eastern Europe and the prodemocracy protests in Beijing's Tiananmen Square, plus coups from Bolivia to Tunisia. The 1990s saw them cover continued violence between Israelis and Palestinians, the wars in the former Yugoslavia, the election of Nelson Mandela, and devastation in the aftermath of Hurricane Mitch, as well as civil wars in Afghanistan, Algeria, El Salvador, Nicaragua, and Somalia. With the 21st century came the global impact of 9/11 but also the Indonesian tsunami and the economic rise of Brazil. The second decade of the century saw no dearth of turmoil: the Japanese tsunami and nuclear crisis, the eurozone economic crisis, continued violence in Afghanistan and Iraq, the second intifada, the cartel wars in Mexico, and the uprisings in North Africa and the Middle East dubbed the "Arab Spring."

INTERVIEWING INTERVIEWERS: METHODOLOGICAL AND THEORETICAL NOTES

Correspondents were selected for oral history interviews in part with the aim of discussing reporting practices – and their impact on public opinion as well as policymaking in foreign affairs – around some of the major international events from 1944 to today. The use of in-depth interviews in political science and mass communication research, particularly, has been recognized as helping "identify causal mechanisms that are not evident in other forms of data" (Mosley 2013, 5) – and nowhere is this truer than in the case of oral history, which in fact is both a method of preserving historical testimony and the narrative that that process produces for analysis. Essentially qualitative and therefore interpretivist (Jensen 2012, 266), interviewing as a methodology gains in nuance what it loses in replicability and generalizability. In the case of oral history (unlike the "snapshot in time" that shorter interviews provide studies such as Hahn and Lönnendonker 2009), an added advantage is the very creation of a set of data that goes well beyond what could be contained in a single book and that might otherwise disappear (two interviewees died months after the interviews, and several are in their 80s and 90s).

The most important caveat in the use of oral history interviews to illuminate specific processes (in this case, foreign correspondence practices) is that oral histories, at their core, are memories – and "memory is not a passive depository of facts, but an active process of creation of meanings" (Portelli, quoted in Thomson 2011, 77). Furthermore, notable experiences tend to be memorized as stories, which form a crucial part of the narrators' identity while also reflecting collective memories and social, cultural, and professional norms (Ritchie 2011). Interviewing journalists for an oral history is particularly self-reflective, because journalists are both interviewers themselves (though for notably different uses; Feldstein 2004) and storytellers – the interviewees' photographic recall of events up to 70 years prior, down to the spelling of names, is one of the most striking features of my data set.

The methodology of oral history has been particularly effective in restoring to history's record the voices of ordinary people – those who might have left no other records of their experiences of the past – and books based on it have focused on groups as diverse as American Catholic nuns and Vietnam Veterans Against the War (Garibaldi Rogers 2011; Stacewicz 1997). At least five recent oral histories focused on journalists, either as a group (African American journalists and the Washington press corps; Terry 2007 and Ritchie 2005) or because of their coverage of a specific region (China, in MacKinnon and Friesen 1987) or event (the terrorist attacks on 9/11 in Gilbert et al. 2002; the Iraq War in Hoyt et al. 2007). The oral histories that come closest to this project are those of American correspondents in China in the 1930s and 1940s, and those of war reporters in Iraq, because they focus on how journalists operated and their influence on American understanding. Some of the themes in the Iraq stories, in particular, echo those by my interviewees. In these volumes, however, as in most oral history studies, the emphasis is on the interviewees' own narratives, with minimal intervention by the historians except for thematic or chronological arrangement, thus achieving a more documentarian than analytical focus. This book, on the contrary, mined the narratives for an analysis of the evolution of professional practices in foreign correspondence.

By necessity, the sample for this research was not random but purposive. The choice of The Associated Press is based on the long-established, enduring, and pervasive dominance of the news organization's foreign service, coupled with its near-total obscurity in the scholarly historical record. Although for part of the period under study AP competed with other wire services (most directly United Press Associations, then United Press International), from the early 1980s onward it has been the dominant American wire service, a necessary qualification for this study because of the intent to contribute to the understanding of the interplay between U.S. media and U.S. policymaking. One significant peculiarity of studying AP's foreign coverage is that not all stories on its wires are either published or broadcast by AP members and clients, particularly before AP launched its online presence, nor are they necessarily published in their original form (editors often shorten AP stories and change the headlines). Nevertheless, given AP's crucial role as the first gatekeeper of foreign news and the increasing scarcity of professional competition, it can be safely assumed that most of AP's international content reaches a large audience.

The interviewees were selected based on their "type" (international correspondents with substantial experience working for AP overseas and mostly, if not always exclusively, writers) and the countries and events they covered (determined by a previous scrutiny of their bylines), to achieve maximum breadth across time and geography. To the original sample, a handful of correspondents were added through the "snowball" effect, on the recommendation of other interviewees, but only if they fit the above criteria. Although an esprit de corps certainly exists among foreign correspondents, and several interviewees had strong bonds with one another, this was by no means a pattern, and many did not know most of the others – thus minimizing the possibility of homogenous findings due to a self-selecting sample.

Because the research focus was on foreign correspondence practices, not on either the correspondents or the organization per se, this selection method resembles the "elite informants" discussed by Beckmann and Hall (2013, 198) as "designed to extract systematic information about practitioners' *actual behaviors* on *specific cases* in the *recent past*." Only one (retired) correspondent I pursued declined to participate. I conducted the interviews, all audio-recorded digitally, between March 2012 and June 2014; because of the crucial clarity and nuance gained by face-to-face interaction (see Mosley 2013, 7), 52 interviews were conducted in person and only nine via telephone or Skype.[8] The average length is just under two hours per interview. The shortest interview lasted 37 minutes, and the longest five hours and 19 minutes; in both cases, interviewees were still working for AP at the time. I also analyzed AP's Oral History Collection

---

[8] The complete list of locations and dates is available from the author.

for four interviews of correspondents who had passed away before the start of this project and for further detail on some of my interviewees.[9]

The semi-structured interviews centered on variations of four main questions: How did foreign correspondents evaluate foreign news in different periods from the 1940s to today? That is, what news judgment did they exercise in selecting what to cover? How did foreign correspondents cover selected events, and what sources did they choose? How did foreign correspondents interact with the "international" desk at AP headquarters in New York (and, more recently, with the regional editing desks that have replaced it)? And, lastly, how did foreign correspondents interact with government officials, both U.S. and foreign? Did they experience feedback, broadly defined, from the U.S. and foreign governments on their coverage? How did they envision their reporting in the context of U.S. foreign policy?

As the questions prompted, correspondents responded using their own actual experiences, not speculating about general trends (unlike most interviews and surveys conducted with journalists – e.g., Hahn and Lönnendonker 2009). Beyond those general thrusts, the interviews were open-ended, in line with the expectations of oral historians that there is a "conscious intention" on the part of both interviewer and interviewee "of creating a permanent record to contribute to an understanding of the past" (Oral History Association). The interview agreement that each interviewee signed allowed them to review the transcripts and to excise any parts they wanted – the latter provision was ethically essential for the informed consent of journalists still employed overseas, whose ability to work (and even security) might have been compromised. Only a handful of sentences were thus cut from thousands of pages of transcripts; in no case did these deletions change the essential analysis or findings, and most concerned either unsolicited political opinions or mentions of colleagues irrelevant to the research. No other request for confidentiality was either made or granted. All interviewees agreed to be identified by name (unlike the anonymous ones in Pedelty 1995 and Hahn and Lönnendonker 2009), and it should be noted that the supervisors of those interviewees still employed by AP granted permission freely and raised no questions of review or oversight.

When fact-checking transcripts, I used histories as well as a sample of over 330 stories by the correspondents, out of the several hundreds to thousands that each published. Analysis of, and quotations from, those stories accompany the interview excerpts in order to further reveal how practices impacted news content. Additional contextual material includes books and self-reflecting articles the correspondents wrote, especially a dozen highly unusual first-person stories on AP wires in which correspondents described their personal responses to experiences as varied as one's first visit to his Czech hometown

---

[9] The Oral History Collection in The Associated Press Corporate Archives in New York contains approximately 160 interviews conducted since 1972, at least 62 with foreign correspondents or foreign editors.

after fleeing it at the height of the Cold War four decades before, sending the first cell phone tweet from North Korea, riding with Libyan rebels into Tripoli, witnessing the U.S. bombing of Baghdad and Kabul, eating only the food rations allowed by the Cuban government, and transporting a grievously wounded colleague and another's corpse out of under-siege Sarajevo.[10] Other foreign correspondents' selected biographies and books of reportage were also studied for any mentions of AP correspondents, as well as for convergence and divergence between the practices of AP correspondents and those of other reporters covering the same events.

Perhaps the strongest caveat about the reliability of interviews is the effect that the interviewers have on the narrators' answers (and even on the access to narrators; Mosley 2013, 12), which is akin to the concern of anthropologists in their participant observations (Hannerz 2004, 8). Other oral historians have noted that, because of the extensive contact that this methodology necessitates, personal involvement is high – and there is the unacknowledged but evident fact that oral historians inherently believe in the importance of giving their interviewees a place in history, often because they admire either them or their cause (see Garibaldi Rogers 2011; Stacewicz 2007). A brief personal disclosure is therefore necessary: At various periods between 1999 and 2007, I worked as an AP newswoman in the United States and in Italy, though I only briefly met five of the interviewees then and worked directly with one (Victor Simpson, then news editor in Rome).

My familiarity with AP practices was a significant advantage in understanding the basic routines and dynamics that correspondents mentioned (the overnight shifts, the AM/PMers, "dealing with New York," etc.). Furthermore, the shared ethic of professional journalism framed all interviews in the understanding that this book would be strictly objective and would reflect both the successes and failures of foreign correspondence – in fact, a few correspondents declined to provide any changes to the transcripts, arguing that they would not have allowed their sources to do the same and thus should not avail themselves of that advantage. Nevertheless, it would be intellectually dishonest not to state openly that I developed tremendous professional admiration for the work that these correspondents performed, often at huge personal cost, and gratitude for the exceptionally candid and extensive access I was granted. All interviewees kept our

---

[10] Denis D. Gray, "Dramatic changes in Eastern Europe are reuniting families long-separated by the Iron Curtain, including one of an AP correspondent," The Associated Press, February 21, 1990; Jean H. Lee, "Tweets, pics give real-time peek into North Korea," The Associated Press, February 28, 2013; Ben Hubbard and Karin Laub, "AP reporters ride with rebels into Libyan capital," The Associated Press, August 22, 2011; John Rice, "Fear and awe as bombs fell on Baghdad," The Associated Press, March 18, 2003; Kathy Gannon, "Analysis: First-person view of Afghan collapse," The Associated Press, October 7, 2011; Anita Snow, "Living on rations in Cuba: Meals made up of rations and goods from farmers' markets," The Associated Press, May 31, 2007; Tony Smith, "Tearful farewell, then a drive past desperate refugees," The Associated Press, May 21, 1992.

interview schedule even in the face of news breaking or a death in the family hours before, and the research won further depth and nuance from the impromptu strolls through history that many correspondents led me on – at sites ranging from the latest mass kidnapping in downtown Mexico City to the precise spot where Yitzhak Rabin was gunned down in Tel Aviv. Close to midnight on a nearly deserted sidewalk off Beijing's Chang'an Avenue, we tried to identify the exact spot where "tank man" had defiantly stood, under the bored stare of young security officers who likely had no idea what Tiananmen had witnessed in 1989.

Such shared moments afforded unique glimpses not only into the correspondents' personalities and character, but – essentially for this project – into how they approached their work. Take that vignette from Beijing: I had met Terril Jones at the Reuters bureau where he worked in the early evening, after a very long day of coverage during a particularly newsworthy week for China (the National Party Congress was in session down the street). The interview lasted nearly three hours, and when we left Reuters around 10 p.m., neither of us had had a bite to eat. Nevertheless, Jones insisted – and I eagerly agreed – that we take a bus to Tiananmen Square and walk beyond, where he pointed out many of the sites we had discussed in the interview when he had recalled his coverage of the turmoil in 1989. Over dumplings, we were still going at it well past 1 a.m. (and the next night, the interview with AP China bureau chief Charles Hutzler also ended close to midnight):[11] Anecdotal evidence, certainly, but corroborated throughout this book, that correspondents felt tirelessly invested in their jobs – and that their foremost perceived responsibility was to be eyewitnesses to history, no matter the cost.

In AP's multimedia London headquarters, overlooking Camden Lock, Europe editor Niko Price told me about covering the devastating aftermath of Hurricane Mitch in mud-buried villages in Nicaragua in 1998. Price also wrote about the traumatizing experience for the wire:

A sea of thick mud stretches as far as I can see on all sides, and sucks me in up to my thighs. Three feet away, a woman's body lies face-up in the sun. Salvation – in the form of a clump of branches that would provide a foothold – is just 5 feet ahead. It might as well be 5 miles. Each step requires a Herculean effort to extricate a waterlogged leg from the muck, then the horror of squishing it down in again and praying it doesn't fall on one of the hundreds of bodies buried beneath. A week ago, before coming to Nicaragua to cover a mudslide unleashed by Hurricane Mitch, I had seen one dead body. On Tuesday I saw 22, on Wednesday about 30. After that, I stopped counting. . . . [A hospitalized survivor, 23-year-old Ricardo Garcia] cries when he tells me how he dribbled water from his mouth into that of a total stranger, a 2-year-old girl named Selena who . . .. was too weak to lift her head. . . . That was Monday. So far, I haven't cried.[12]

---

[11] Throughout this book, professional titles refer to the position held either at the time of the interview or at the time been recalled, depending on context, and not current titles.

[12] Niko Price, "Reporter deals with rotting bodies, screaming children," The Associated Press, November 8, 1998.

FIGURE 1.1. Mexico City–based correspondent Niko Price struggles to pull himself through a field of mud left by a mudslide that wiped out the town of Rolando Rodriguez, Nicaragua, in the aftermath of Hurricane Mitch, on November 6, 1998. (AP Photo/John Moore)

In the sunlit conference room, Price (26) said covering that story was a highlight of his career. I asked him why. He answered without hesitation: "Because I had the feeling that if I wasn't there, nobody would care."

Whether the readers of Price's stories, and those of the other five dozen AP correspondents who have covered the world for eight decades, care about the rest of the world is a question beyond the scope of this book. That if AP's foreign correspondents were not there they would have little reliable foreign news to care about, however, is increasingly true, and it has major implications for Americans' worldview and, consequently, policymaking. This book, for the first time, tells from idea generation to public reaction how the stories were made – how the correspondents got there, stayed there, and brought the world to the public, so that it stood a chance to care.

2

Getting Ready, Getting Started, and Getting Lost in Translation

[AP's head of personnel] had phoned me in, and he said, "Well, how would you like to go to Vietnam?" And it took me a minute to see what he was thinking – I didn't know what he was talking about. And I said, "Yeah, absolutely." So I hopped on the subway, went back to the office . . . getting myself really geared up to go to Vietnam in my head, what am I going to do . . . it's a war, and blah blah. . . . I go to his office, and we spent like an hour talking, telling me about the stuff, about the details. . . . I stand, I shake his hand, and he says, "Well, I know you're going to do a good job," blah blah. "By the way, what are you going to do with your apartment?" And I said . . . "[My roommate and AP colleague] Barry Kramer will take it over." . . . He looks at me and he says, "Wait, you're not going to Vietnam. Kramer is!" He confused the two of us. And so I had my hands on his – he had this huge, massive wooden desk – and my knuckles were like white. And I think he kind of thought he was going to . . . get talked backward out of his seventh-floor window, and he looks at me and says, "You're going to Africa." To this day, I don't know if he just pulled it out of his ass or what, but sure enough. . . . I didn't say anything about Africa [before]. It never even occurred to me. I didn't know anything about it. . . . I thought, "Cool! I don't give a shit – send me anywhere." (Rosenblum, 1–2)[1]

The trajectory for most AP foreign correspondents until recently followed the same blend of ritual path and serendipitous opportunity that 38-year veteran,[2] roving correspondent Mort Rosenblum experienced when he joined in '65. After jobs in newspapers and domestic AP bureaus, a stint on the foreign desk (initially called the cable desk, later international, recently merged) was followed by the first assignment abroad. The posting choice was often predicated on area or

---

[1] All quotations are verbatim from the transcripts of the author's recordings; repetitive expressions such as "you know," "I mean," and "sort of" have been deleted for ease of reading unless germane to the meaning. Quotations within these extracts (e.g., above, "Well, how would you like to go to Vietnam?") are not meant to indicate speakers said those words verbatim, but rather to reflect the correspondents' best recollection of those conversations.

[2] Throughout this book, years and dates reflect those at the time of the interview; years comprise those working for AP overseas, unless otherwise noted.

language expertise, but even more often apparently random, and usually very sudden; with several notable exceptions of correspondents who spent decades in one location, this continued throughout most careers. This chapter opens the narrative of foreign correspondence practices over eight decades at the beginning of the journalists' careers, starting with the preparatory work. What drew correspondents to the job? How did they get the assignment and prepare for it? How did they get started once they landed overseas? What skills did they need? The last section details arguably the most impactful of those skills – language. While correspondents ran the gamut from a few weeks of Berlitz to fluency in half a dozen idioms, they all agreed that news content changed dramatically depending on whether they were reporting with or without translators. This posed a particular challenge given that most correspondents moved around the world throughout their careers. Though their backgrounds vary widely, and so to a lesser extent do their paths, what drew the interviewees to AP was the hope to do foreign correspondence. And what spurred that dream was that its mixture of challenges, adventure, variety, and idealism represented the "pinnacle" of journalism.

BASKETBALL SCORES, CABLE EDITING, AND GLOBAL HOPSCOTCHING: THE RITUAL PATH

From the 1940s to the 2000s, three-quarters of would-be AP foreign correspondents I interviewed were hired in a U.S. bureau, after passing the current events and writing "AP test," and then moved to New York headquarters. So they had covered high school sports and state legislatures, and worked everything from broadcast to the overnight shift, before first handling international news as editors on either the foreign desk, which managed copy from overseas destined for AP members in the United States, or the world desk, which edited copy for AP subscribers overseas. The paradox of relative rookies fresh from Syracuse or Charlotte, Bismarck or Carson City, even Honolulu, editing the copy of seasoned foreign correspondents and chafing while "waiting and praying" to be sent overseas underscores one of the institutional strains – the often tense dynamic between reporters in the field and "the desk," discussed in Chapter 11.

Only half a dozen correspondents remained in the location of their first posting for the majority of their multi-decade careers, such as Kathy Gannon covering Pakistan and Afghanistan since the late 1980s and Victor Simpson covering the Vatican since the early 1970s. Most hopscotched around the globe. Dan Perry's 24-year itinerary includes Romania to Israel to the Caribbean, back to Israel, then London and back again to Jerusalem and Cairo. In 44 years with AP, Bob Reid (35) was assigned overseas to "Bonn, Berlin, Cairo, Beirut, Damascus, Dubai, Baghdad, Khartoum, Tripoli, Delhi, the Punjab, Manila, Bangkok, Phnom Penh, Hong Kong, Tokyo."

Throughout the Sunday we spent talking in a sunny Berlin courtyard, Reid's phone pinged with the constant updates that came with his responsibility as AP chief of bureau for Germany, Austria, and Switzerland, a few days after President Barack Obama's visit to the capital. But Reid's (1–3) career, like that of most correspondents until recently, began humbly enough. While freelancing sports stories in college, he got a call from the AP chief of bureau in Charlotte, North Carolina, to come take the test and landed the first night rewrite job. Years later, his next move to the New York desk nearly crashed, literally:

I borrowed the bureau car to go cover a Jimmy Carter speech, when he was a candidate, and on the way back I got rear-ended by this woman. Didn't hurt me, didn't hurt the woman, screwed up the bureau chief's car. All night, all the way back to Charlotte and all that night, I was sweating, what am I going to tell this guy? Even though I had a piece of paper from the highway patrol exonerating me, even though they charged the woman because I was stopped at a light, nonetheless, you're a little bit nervous. So I got into the office, early that morning after having rehearsed my speech all night. The bureau chief comes in, and he walks behind me, and as he passes me, he mutters, "See me in my office." Oh, here it comes. So I walk in; he closes the door. And without a word, he picks up a piece of paper and throws it at me. I grabbed it. And it was a letter from New York offering me a job on the world desk.

From the domestic bureau, the "boot camp" (as Mark Porubcansky [2], later the *Los Angeles Times* foreign editor, put it) continued on the desk in New York. Nearly 40 years after his "breaking in" on the desk before being sent to Tokyo, Terry Anderson (1–2) recalled the pressure vividly:

You had an index printer then that would show the first three lines of every story being filed by the foreign bureaus, and you had to decide whether it was worthwhile to go look at that story and maybe pick it up, or just let it go, and it would pass out of the system and nobody would ever see it. And when things are busy, that thing would be going zip, zip, zip, zip, and if you took one story, opened it up on the computer, started editing it, and that thing's still going zip, zip, zip, zip, and by the time you've finished, you're behind. Now you got to triage the rest of the stories. ... And then finally one day ... [the desk supervisor] says, "Taking a vacation, you got the desk." That's it. ... The first night was a total disaster. I got so far behind. ... And it's a real balancing act for young journalists to be rewriting some senior correspondent's story in such a way as to improve it without changing it, because it's not your story. ... You're supposed to help, you're supposed to bring in background, you're supposed to check and ask questions, but ... you're not the writer. It's his name on it, and you're dealing with very senior correspondents who hated the desk for pissing in their stories.

Charles Hutzler (1–2), who had joined AP hoping to land in China, spent only a few months on the foreign desk, enjoying his exposure to major international news and dreading the wait time until the call came for Beijing:

I started to sort of count the heads of people who were interested in going to China. And I thought, "My God, I'm going to be here forever!" And I got lucky ... China's economy

FIGURE 2.1. China bureau chief Charles Hutzler poses in the AP Beijing bureau on March 8, 2013, in front of a photo featuring twice Pulitzer Prize–winning AP photographer Horst Faas in Beijing in 1972, when he was covering President Nixon's door-opening trip to the country. (Photo by Giovanna Dell'Orto)

began to really take off [in the early 1990s] . . . and the people who were in line to come to China ahead of me, fortunately, didn't speak Chinese all that well.

Several broke this mold, however. Vicki Graham (2), who helped reopen the bureau in China in 1979 and was back writing in Shanghai 34 years later, was plucked from the feature department (the "poets' corner") precisely ahead of all the Chinese speakers on the desk:

I know there was a lot of resentment: "Who is she? We studied Chinese. We slaved on the night desk. We slaved on the international desk. Who is she? She comes in from San Francisco, special writer, moves upstairs, and you give her this assignment." . . . I could only say that they wanted a writer and that's who I am, and a reporter. . . . I would be, probably, the person with enthusiasm they just sent in.

In the middle of the Iraq War, Sally Buzbee (1–2, 14–15, 5), then assistant bureau chief in Washington, moved to Cairo for five years as Middle East regional editor because she wanted to understand the reality on the ground affected by the policies she covered inside the Beltway:

I thought, there's no way I can be a well-rounded journalist going forward unless I see the Iraq War firsthand . . . you can't miss the seminal event of your generation. . . . I'm very much a believer in, you can't talk about U.S. policy unless you have someone on the ground who can tell you what's really going on. . . . I understood the policy of the Iraq War, but the only way that I actually understood the nitty-gritty Iraq War was to just go there and spend three weeks in the [Baghdad] bureau and report myself. There was just no other way to get up to speed on a story like that.

Charles Hanley was based in New York for most of his 43 AP years, but as a "full-time globetrotter," while Denis Gray never got to headquarters – he volunteered to go to Vietnam straight from the Albany, New York, bureau in 1973 and covered not only Southeast Asia, but also Somalia, Rwanda, Kosovo, Iraq, Afghanistan, Pakistan, and Australia for the next four decades. (As Richard Pyle [1], who was Saigon bureau chief from 1970 to 1973, explained, Vietnam was a voluntary assignment – but one that, being "the story of the time . . . almost left someone like me without a choice but to do that.")

Over the decades, most of the non-U.S. citizens, and a few American correspondents too, started their AP careers directly overseas before moving to the better salary, benefits, and prestige of expatriate "New York hires." Two multi-decade Latin America hands started in the 1960s in their native Chile and Bolivia, while Hebrew-speaking Marcus Eliason went from messenger to writer in the Tel Aviv bureau the day the Six-Day War broke out in 1967. Gannon, on the contrary, could not have been farther from her native Ontario when AP hired her – in Peshawar, where she had gone as a freelancer to cover the Soviet-Afghan conflict. Robin McDowell, whom I interviewed as she relaxed at her home in the Minnesota woods before taking off for Burma, began part time in Cambodia, where she had helped start the country's first English-language daily. Matthew Pennington's first AP stories covered American soldiers on an MIA-finding mission helping children maimed by old U.S. ordnance in Laos, where he had gone from the UK as volunteer with the United Nations Development Program.

Paul Schemm's (2) 2007 move from Agence France-Press in Egypt best exemplifies the blurred nature of "local hiring":

[AFP] put me in the Cairo bureau, but they cut my salary in half because they said I was now a local hire. And I'm like, I'm an American who just came from Baghdad to work in Cairo for the French news agency. What aspect of that is local? There's nothing local there at all. . . . The amount I was cut to, it was basically what they paid a local – an Egyptian hire. Even though you had to be practically trilingual for the job. So that, let's just say that left me dissatisfied so that when the AP approached me . . . about moving to the editing desk, I was very much up for it.

The Big Draw

The paths to foreign correspondence might have been diverse, but getting there was nearly everyone's wish from early on, the goal of journalistic and linguistic efforts started often as school kids. Jean Lee (1), who opened the AP's first bureau in Pyongyang, recalled writing that she "wanted to be a foreign correspondent" in her high school yearbook, inspired by her Korean grandfather, a journalist in Seoul who would buy her notebooks and ask her to write daily "reports" of her childhood visits to the country. Steven Hurst (2) had attended university in Vienna, lived with Hungarian refugees, studied Russian – so "every time somebody asked me, when I finally went to go work for the AP in Columbus, Ohio, 'What do you want to do?' I said that I wanted to go to Moscow" – where he got to cover the collapse of the USSR.

The allure seems to have been double: living in specific foreign countries – from Germany to Russia to Japan, where some had family roots, young memories as soldiers or extensive academic background (foreign correspondents from all U.S. organizations tend to have spent a significant part of their youth abroad; Hess 1996, 14) – and doing what many called the most "challenging" journalism. Paul Alexander (2–3; also see this chapter's box), who would cover some of the worst hotspots of the post–Cold War era, thus explained his pining to get away from his first posting in quiet Australia for any war-torn country:

[E]verybody sort of considered that war correspondents were the best, to be able to deal with the challenges of being in a place where it was inherently dangerous, and to be competing against the best of everybody else. . . . We used to have a saying that when you were in, you counted the days until you were out; and when you were out, you counted the days until you went back. And that you were never more alive than when you could be killed at any time. A very sick way of thinking about things, but if you are into adrenaline, it doesn't get any better than that. Plus, you were where history was being made.

Even those on whom war reporting cast no special spell – "I didn't have any real desire to go out and see people getting killed and maimed," Buzbee (8) said – still felt it was necessary to cover conflict firsthand. In fact, though many mentioned the ambition, curiosity, and excitement of covering the "big stories," the underlying drive that emerged from all interviews was being present before humanity's horror and glory – "understanding what people's human connections are . . . and to do that, you really have to get out and talk to people" (Bryson, 51). And in addition to being present, the correspondents could write it up and share it with everyone. Tad Bartimus (3), one of the first women AP assigned to cover Vietnam during the war, self-mockingly described her early drive to get to that country:

My mother was a person who was really very much against the war, and my father was a pilot flying to the war, my brother was in ROTC and knew that he was going to be involved in it. And so I had to have a role to play, of course. And I was going to be the journalist that sorted it out and explained it to the world.

In-depth reflections on the correspondents' sense of purpose are the core of Chapter 13, but one more quote is relevant here. Less than a year before being gravely wounded when an Afghan police officer opened fire with his AK-47 on her and Pulitzer Prize–winning AP photographer Anja Niedringhaus during a reporting trip to cover Afghanistan's elections from its provinces,[3] Gannon (83, 6) shared her sheer joy about a job that allowed her to explore that deep connection with people of all kinds:

I've been really tired, where I didn't sleep for three years or something, and something sets me off. . . . But mostly, I'm hugely fortunate. . . . I get to do big stories, I get to go and spend days on a story, really days on a story, to then come back and have it put out with really amazing pictures that Anja does . . . to see so much and do so much on somebody else's dime. What a dream, really, let's be honest here.

READY? YOU'RE OFF

Despite the desires and routines, many first overseas assignments came out of the blue. As Gray (AP Oral History, 2005, 4) put it, "I was in Albany, New York, covering . . . basketball and fatal car crashes. And four days later, I was in the middle of Saigon, my first day as a war correspondent." Gray, at least, had already been to Vietnam as a soldier; 23-year-old Sam Summerlin (2) went from Raleigh to New York to covering the Korean War, of which he knew, he said, "absolutely nothing." Terril Jones (34) was still looking for an apartment after transferring from Asia to Paris when he was sent off to cover the Liberian civil war: "[W]ithin two or three weeks I was in a Land Rover, negotiating with a very shadowy figure of how to smuggle myself and a photographer and a Land Rover across the river into deep Liberia." Just outside Buchanan, the country's second-largest city, Jones met a rebel singing to himself "as he carried a skull down a dirt road toward a rebel checkpoint . . . taking it back to decorate his guard post."[4]

Language knowledge did not always moderate the randomness, as Perry (9) remembered of his first posting:

[International editor] Tom Kent saw my CV – it said I spoke Romanian on it – and said, "How does Bucharest sound?" I eyed him quizzically. [chuckles] . . . I remember I knew nothing about Romania and trying to sound like I knew something, I suppose. I said if I were based in Bucharest, could I also do reporting out of Braşov, which is a city perhaps 50 miles north of Bucharest, which I happened to remember existed. And Kent said sure.

Nick Tatro (2) had been studying Arabic on his own when foreign editor Nate Polowetzky – who held that position from 1973 to 1990 – "came up to me and said he was going to send me to Iran, and I said, 'But I've been studying Arabic.' He said, 'Oh, it's all the same squiggles, Farsi and Arabic.' And I said, 'Well, I don't know about that.' Anyway, he wound up sending me to Egypt instead of Iran for reasons he never told me." Joe Frazier, who would go on to cover revolutions across Central America for 30 years, had specialized in French and Russian, while a few years later John Rice (1), a Spanish-speaker, was assigned first to South Africa and then, when he told the foreign editor that he had

---

[3] "AP photographer killed, reporter wounded," The Associated Press, April 4, 2014.

[4] Terril Jones, "Liberia's No.2 city ruled by ragtag rebels," The Associated Press, June 25, 1990.

"been in an antiapartheid group kind of perfunctorily" in college, switched to Jordan.

In some cases, too much knowledge raised red flags: Alan Cooperman's (1–2) assignment to the Soviet Union was nearly derailed when AP President Lou Boccardi feared he might be "too much of a Russia guy," if his knowledge of the country and its language meant he had "a point of view on the story." John Fenton Wheeler (2; 2008, 25), the last American correspondent kicked out of Cold War–era Havana, was asked whether he had any Cuban connections, to which he answered, "My dad smoked cigars, and I think he smoked Roi Tan, and I think it was partially made in Cuba." Claude Erbsen (1), who would eventually oversee AP's business outside the United States and was fluent in Spanish and Italian, first got sent off to cover the Bay of Pigs invasion, and although correspondents would not make it past Florida, AP arranged a formal "good-bye" from his wife – "in a room with the portraits of the AP correspondents killed in action in wartime." Later, Erbsen (7–8) had been reading up on Andean countries for his first assignment to Lima when he ran into general manager Wes Gallagher:

[H]e said, "Come to my office." So I went in. He said, "I've changed my mind. You're not going to Lima." I knew it. And he said, "You're going to Brazil." And you know Brazil is as big as all of Latin America, the rest of it put together, and then some. And I said, "Okay, who am I replacing?" and he told me who I was replacing. And I . . . stammered, "But-but-but he is the bureau chief." And he says, "So are you." At this point, I really wanted to faint again. . . . When I made that remark about "B-b-b-b-but . . ." he said to me, "The operation is so screwed up down there, you can't make it any worse." . . . [T]hat's cheerful.

Seven months later, Erbsen was in Rio de Janeiro – a long lead time compared with the suddenness with which many others found themselves overseas. When Max Desfor (1) was assigned to the Korean War – for which he would win the 1951 Pulitzer Prize for Photography – within 15 minutes of being called to his editor's office, "my passport was on its way for military accreditation and I had tickets to go to Seattle, and I was to wait there for the passport to arrive."

Sending female correspondents to war zones took a bit more deliberation, as Vietnam War correspondents Edie Lederer and Bartimus illustrate – but hardly more time to pack. In 1971, San Francisco newswoman Lederer (1–3) stopped in Saigon on a Pan Am around-the-world vacation, because she and a girlfriend had decided "we were going to go see this war that everybody hated and not tell our parents," and AP staff there took her on helicopter rides over the Mekong Delta and to the notorious "5 o'clock follies" news conferences. Pyle, then Saigon bureau chief, started petitioning AP to send her back full time:

And so out of the blue . . . in 1972 I get this phone call from the president of the AP, asking me if I wanted to go to Vietnam for six months. And that was sort of a shock, because every year you would get this form from the AP asking, "What do you want to do when you grow up?" And I said that I wanted to be a foreign correspondent. But it was impossible. So the first thing I said was … "If I do this, am I going to have to go to New York to work on the foreign desk?" And he said, "No, you're just going to go to Vietnam." So I actually became a war correspondent never having worked on the foreign desk, because [foreign editor] Ben Bassett still wouldn't have a woman on the foreign desk.

In 1973, Bartimus (7–9) went to Saigon to replace Lederer:

I was badgering the hell out of [AP's international editors] … [UPI Southeast Asia correspondent Kate Webb] was getting on the front page of the *Miami Herald* day after day after day, and I would take that front page and take a red grease pencil and tear off a whole tear sheet and circle Kate's byline and say, "If she can be there, I can be there. This rule of no women in a war zone is not working for me," or words to that effect. And I would put [these tear sheets] in an envelope … and send them directly to Wes Gallagher. And I did that for two years. … And then [Gallagher's deputy] Keith Fuller just turned up at the AP bureau [in April 1973] and threw down the [green international air travel] credit card and said, "You've got a week to get there."

Correspondents had far more say in their subsequent assignments, but most continued to test unknown waters – often precisely because they craved new challenges. Five years after assigning her to Vietnam, Fuller sent Bartimus (34–35) on a roving tour to cover guerrilla movements in Latin America, after wearily inquiring, "What's this new wrinkle?" while pointing at the man whom Bartimus had married a week before and telling her she would be on her own "except, we will try to come and get you if you're dead." Both Bryson in postapartheid South Africa and Otto Doelling in reconstruction Germany agitated to get to new places they had no background in – respectively India and the Middle East – precisely because they felt they were beginning to know the story too well where they were. Graham (19) passed up Paris for India because, after China, she "really wanted another big story." David Crary (10) used the base in Paris for "fireman duty" during the Bosnian War, traveling to Sarajevo eight or nine times: "I kept kind of raising my hand to go back there, after being very scared the first time." Alexander (1) wrote his way out of Australia after a temporary assignment to the war in Somalia in 1993:

During that period in the country, out of 102 days, I had 99 bylines. Halfway through, I was told, "Yes, you're still going to have to go back to Australia." Two-thirds of the way, "Yeah, you're going to have to go back, but it won't be for very long." And then, towards the end of my first three months, "Well, why don't you stick around Nairobi for a little while?"

Anderson (11) also pushed to be relocated from "quiet" South Africa to cover the 1982 Israeli invasion of Lebanon – where he would be kidnapped by extremists and held hostage for nearly seven years:

I knew they were going to be sending dozens of correspondents because it's a war, it's what you do – can I go? I said, "There's nothing going on here, man, nothing." And [the manager] said, "Terry, remind me how many languages you speak," and I said two. He said, "What are they?" I said, "English and Japanese." He said, "That's not likely to be of much help in this situation." I said, "I don't know, but everybody else speaks English, anyway – what the hell." So he said, "Okay, get on the plane."

Others did not quite get their wish. After three years in Nigeria, Arnold Zeitlin (14) had put in a request for "the East": Gallagher said, "'We're going to send you to Pakistan.' About which I knew nothing. And I said, 'Is there an alternative?' And he said no. So I went to Pakistan." And whereas some managed to stay put for decades – Laub in Israel and the West Bank, for example, where she got married and raised two children – many other senior correspondents continued to have long-term assignments dropped in their lap.

Reid (55), who had been helping anchor post-9/11 coverage from Pakistan for a year virtually nonstop, recalled taking a week-long break in the mountains in September 2002 and listening on his shortwave radio to a Voice of America discussion of U.S. plans in Iraq:

I had always thought, Iraq? This is just nonsense. They're not going to go to war in Iraq. This is just pure garbage. But after I listened to that program, I began to think, I'll be damned, they are going to go to war in Iraq. ... So when I got back to Islamabad, I called the foreign editor and said I had listened to this thing, and I wonder, are we really going to go to war against Iraq? And she said well, we didn't think so ... [but] we better start thinking about how to plan the war. Fine. So I finished up in a couple of days and went back to Brussels. ... I got another call from New York ... the news editor in Cairo has a vacation to China planned. She's already paid for it ... Could you go over there and just be there for two weeks? Two weeks ended up – I got out like in the middle of December, went back to the States for Christmas, flew back on New Year's Eve from Atlanta to Frankfurt, spent one night in that, I guess the Radisson ... adjacent to the airport terminal, left at something like 2 a.m. the following day or the day after – you know with the time difference – flew to Kuwait, and then we started planning for it.

Rosenblum's (3) actual deployment to the Congo, discussed at the beginning of the chapter, was also fast-tracked by political crisis – in the middle of a night he had spent up with food poisoning:

[T]he phone rang ... "our guy just got thrown out of the Congo ... you got like four hours to get the shuttle to Washington, pick up your visa at the Congolese Embassy, and then catch the night flight to Brussels and then, on the next day, to the Congo." And it was totally out of my mind that I was going to go anywhere ... I just grabbed a few things, gave the rest to my roommate, and went off on a 45-year assignment overseas with a suitcase, a little suitcase.

HITTING THE GROUND RUNNING (OFTEN FOR COVER)

Given the little prep time, the often unknown destination, and the rushed transfer, how did correspondents start functioning once they arrived at their posting? By wasting no time in setting up logistics, scraping acquaintances with colleagues, scoping out sources, and diving headfirst into the news, as Rosenblum (3–4) recalled:

And I landed at like 5 o'clock in the morning in Kinshasa at this crazy fucking airport, total mayhem. … French, spoke about four words of it, and not very well. … Everybody's pushing and shoving and screaming, and I finally get through, and I get out and I find this driver who looks like he's relatively good in this falling-apart, old vehicle … I have no idea where I'm going to stay. I hadn't even thought about that part. And the two hotels were totally jammed because there was a mercenary war going on [Congo's war of independence and related civil unrest]. … So I stopped some European-looking guy on the street and he said, "Yeah, there's this guesthouse that the Sabena Airline uses, and maybe we can get you a room there." And I have no idea what I'm doing. … [Congo's President] Mobutu [Sese Seko], who had just been in power for a short time and he was just consolidating, and he made this major address. … I went down to the Congolese news agency and I met someone, a really nice guy, and he explained to me what it was, and he showed me the text. And I could actually read it, and I went through it and I took some notes and went around and called some people. I found a really good guy at the U.S. Embassy, who became a very good source the rest of my life.

When he later traveled to Lagos, some of the bewilderment made it into a story about how the Nigerian civil war was affecting the sprawling city, such as in this paragraph: "Lagos island itself, a few square miles, is an incredible tangle of slums and modern buildings where a newcomer can find himself lost minutes off a major road."[5]

In more established postings, from India to Poland to Saigon, many correspondents recalled being met on the airport tarmac by the bureau chiefs, who helped them find places to live and oriented them around the city – for a few hours at least, before putting them to work. In war zones especially, correspondents would get "right into the fighting," Desfor (1) recalled – even if it meant "somehow or other manag[ing] to forget" what his boss had told him about prepping in Tokyo before going into Korea. The only other surviving AP correspondent to have covered World War II, George Bria (2), had a term for what it felt like to arrive in the middle of "very rough fighting" in Italy in 1944: "very green." Before landing in Vietnam, Bartimus (10–11) had all of two days in Hong Kong – waiting for her credentials, for provisions to carry to the Saigon bureau, and trying to soak up whatever knowledge she could from Vietnam correspondents decompressing on R&R, who "tried to tell me in two days how to stay alive."

Pyle (7) had been handling Vietnam copy on the New York desk before transferring to Saigon, but still felt thrown off the deep end when he was first sent to the press center in Da Nang and onward to the battle zone:

---

[5] Mort Rosenblum, "Nigerian Civil War Altered Life in Lagos," *Los Angeles Times*, August 17, 1969, c19.

FIGURE 2.2. Ten days after arriving in Vietnam in May 1973, Saigon-based correspondent Tad Bartimus rode in a helicopter to Pleiku with Canadian peacekeepers following the ceasefire. (Photo courtesy of Tad Bartimus)

They say, "Go to Da Nang," and you say, "Oh, well, okay." So I ... got in this goddam C-130, fly to Da Nang. I have no idea what I'm doing, go up there ... to the Da Nang press center, AP. This is an old French brothel ... had all these little rooms, like a hotel. And every news organization that was permanently in Vietnam had a reserved room there, so we had one. And we had like four bunks in it, a whole bunch of military gear that we used when we went in the field. ... And I went out in the field, and I learned – I got shot at for the first time ... it was a learning experience right from the get-go. And that's the way you had to do it. ... You wanted to have some kind of a distinction applied to what you were doing. And one distinction was that you were doing this and other people couldn't do it. Wouldn't do it. They wouldn't think of doing it.

Arriving in Lagos in 1966, in the middle of a coup d'état, as the AP's West Africa correspondent responsible for 17 countries, Zeitlin (7–8) recalled feeling "petrified," "extremely insecure," and wondering if in fact he could do this:

And at one point I had to go down to the Congo ... and the censor demanded all dispatches be written in French and I could speak some French, but to write in French was beyond my capacity and I had to run around and find somebody who could help me put my dispatches in French. ... The cable head was to Brussels. I was writing about "le looting and le shooting." [chuckles] And Brussels, "What the hell is this guy writing about?" And I really felt very bad. And I finally wrote to Gallagher. I said, "I think you better take me out of here – I don't think I can do it." And he was very nice. He said, "No, you stay." And gradually ...

Nearly 50 years later, a 22-year-old Angela Doland (2), newly arrived in Paris, found herself occasionally alone on the desk, writing some stories directly for the world wire: "It was so terrifying, it literally kept me up at night afterwards ... so often getting up and checking my computer afterwards to make sure that everything I had written was okay." Occupying that same "very lonely seat" in Paris had been Elaine Ganley (4–5), also newly arrived, one night in 1984 when the government fell: "But I was talking to New York. They knew I was brand new, and they were going, 'Okay, just calm down and do it.' And so one does." Debbie Seward (8), assigned to the Soviet Union in its waning days, listed off a few of the subjects one had to understand for that assignment – "Russian history, Soviet history, ballistic missiles, what's going on in Washington" – and that was just to cover the Kremlin, while "the next day you're off in Nagorno-Karabakh covering a conflict there ... you're a small team with a very big story with very big stakes."

To deal with breaking news situations in new places, correspondents relied on AP's global infrastructure, cramming through the archives and polling the local staff, as both Alexander and Reid recalled:

You try to do as much reading as you can before you go in. The AP archives has always been a huge resource. You print out the previous two to three weeks' stories. ... There would almost always be a one- or two-day handover between the previous person giving you sources, giving you a little tour of where to go, how to do things. That was always one of the benefits, I felt, of working for AP ... you weren't just someone from a newspaper dropping in for a week or two. (Alexander, 6–7)

You never have enough time. But you got to read, you got to study. If you go into a place completely cold, you're doing a disservice to everybody. You are wasting the local assistant's time, you're wasting your time, and you're blowing a wonderful opportunity to do something that will make a mark. ... And you always have to engage, you have to make friends with the locals that you're there with ... they have a lot to teach you if you'll take the time to learn from them. (Reid, 38–39)

THE CORRESPONDENTS' TOOLKIT

Past the furious cramming and the initial skydive, what skills have correspondents needed overseas? "Guts, sheer guts ... in amplitude" was the universal consensus as expressed by Doelling (28–29), who wrote the AP's Handbook for International Correspondents in 1998 and who added that correspondents often put their lives on the line "for the duration, and wouldn't think of being anywhere else, except there, where the story was." Basic survival, then, is a primary skill (Chapter 7 details the daunting dangers correspondents have braved). Many of the journalists working in the 1940s through the 1980s credited their military training, either through ROTC programs or in actual battle zones, for helping them not only assess dangers but also understand how the U.S. military functioned as they covered its wars. Anderson, a Marine Corps Vietnam veteran, had perhaps the most dramatic opportunity to rely on his training during his years as a hostage, but many other journalists, including non-AP and non-Americans, have argued that their "fieldcraft" saved lives, among them the BBC's Martin Bell in Bosnia (1995, 7). Two long-term roving correspondents, Rosenblum (29) and Hanley (8), mentioned their "war bag," containing everything from a flak vest to wads of cash, "stuff to patch together somebody," a small pair of binoculars, and maps – which, Hanley recalled, he and Rosenblum once fought over in Iraq. In the 2000s, most reporters assigned by major news organizations to wars such as Iraq and Afghanistan had to undergo "hostile environment training" courses (Reynolds 2010, 10), though some questioned their value in case of chemical, biological, or terrorist attacks.[6] And as many put it, you could never tell how correspondents would fare in dangerous assignments based on gender or on appearance – or even experience. Who could have guessed that Gray (33–34), who has covered scores of countries at war since Vietnam, has a "phobia about flying"? And yet he did overcome it, over and over again:

I've logged hundreds of hours in helicopters, sometimes under fire ... flying in the backseats of jets on air raids ... and with ... a T-28, a World War II plane, piloted by a Cambodian pilot in 1974, going on a bombing attack in Cambodia. You can imagine how I felt. [chuckles] ... Or ... covering the tsunami off Indonesia [in 2004]. ... [T]he USS *Lincoln* was nearby, so they steamed in within 24 hours or 48 hours. And I flew on a small plane from Thailand and landed on the deck of the USS *Lincoln* and then spent the next 10 days flying helicopters off of the USS *Lincoln* to drop supplies to these horrendously stranded, dying tsunami victims who were still scattered along the shore of Banda Aceh. So I hate flying, but [chuckles].

Beyond physical and psychological survival, the skill that topped most correspondents' lists is the nonstop willingness, and openness, to see, listen to, and learn about all manners of cultures, people, and events with genuine and humble curiosity – so that you can uncover meaning, not just cover breaking news, as two leading international editors, and former correspondents, phrased it:

I think it's the ability to feel empathy for the people you're covering and at the same time to be somewhat of a hard-headed realist about the bigger picture: The economic currents of the day, the big geopolitical currents, the big realpolitik, the big issues of national interest that were driving the stories that you're observing up close. To be able to bounce back and forth from the zooming in and the zooming out, and in an effective way, and to tie the zooming in to the big picture. I think those are the best correspondents. (Daniszewski, 19)

You're not just writing about what happened, what would visibly happen. You're also trying to get at what is really going on. What it really means. ... The ability to think analytically ... is of incredible value. Much more, more even than writing, more than anything else. ... Thinking about what's happening, seeing what lies beneath the surface,

---

[6] The *New Yorker*'s Jon Anderson, who took one such course before covering the Iraq War, wryly noted that by the end of the day's training, neither the journalists nor the instructor appeared to have any confidence that they would in fact survive (Jon Lee Anderson, *The Fall of Baghdad*. New York: Penguin Press, 2004, 29–31).

thinking ahead several steps like a chess game and saying whoa, if this happens, then that might happen and that might happen; here's the possible outcome. Now, as long as it's not too far-fetched, that is a legitimate way to approach the achievement of distinctive journalism. (Perry, 16–17, 20)

Several correspondents compared this to covering "the lava while it's bubbling under the surface" before a volcanic explosion (Rosenblum, 12), to layer on enough context and historical perspective that a story explains not only what happened, but why it is happening (Frazier, 39), so that people who know very little about it learn, care (Graham, 39), and maybe even share the news with others (Jones, 37) – and of course to do all this more speedily than the competition. Over time, these skills have been threatened across the industry by the pressures to tweet every little breaking news as well as by the tendency to parachute reporters all over the world without enough time to truly develop a sense for any country, its quirks, but also its trends over time.

Most correspondents highlighted the need to learn as much as possible, because "a better knowledge and more feeling" for the story go together – "and you try to get it all; otherwise winging it is pretty good, but I think you're better off if you know what you're doing," as 99-year-old Desfor (13–14) put it, chuckling. Reid (61) argued that "everything you do has to be designed for 'How is this going to help me understand this place I'm in the most,'" or, in Erbsen's (21) words, "A journalist should be on duty 24/7." Pyle (7) remembered how George McArthur, called into the Saigon office the day Ho Chi Minh died in 1969, sat down at his typewriter, banged out the definitive story on the meaning of the North Vietnamese leader's demise, handed it to the desk, and left – "he knew what he was doing."

But many also mentioned that knowing too much might take off the necessary inquisitive edge, so that the ideal skill is combining in-depth knowledge with fresh eyes – "being in that sweet spot between knowing the region and having a compassion for its people, and interest and knowledge about it, but also still maintaining the distance so you don't get too native and not thinking anything is a story or being bored," according to Mike Weissenstein (18), who in 12 years reported from the Middle East and Latin America. A veteran of covering Central America's guerrilla wars, Frazier (32) remembered his shock when he first landed in Haiti – and the even more disturbing lessening of that shock with time:

I got off of the plane [in Port-au-Prince], and the first thing I said was, "*Oh my God*. How could human beings live like this?" That was poverty like I didn't know could exist, and to this day, oh, it was just grinding and grating. Awful, awful, awful living situation. It wasn't even living. And so I went in and got hit with that right away … But then, of course, you start getting used to it, like we did in El Salvador. It's what you see day in and day out, and the impression left after a time … the shock value disappears, or at least diminishes. [W]hile you need people down there who are experienced, you need fresh eyes in there too, so that you don't get inured to the stuff that shouldn't be going on, and you begin to think it's the norm. … Yeah, people are getting shot in the street every day – yeah, yeah, yeah. And that kind of dehumanizes you in some certain way some-times. I started to realize that it was happening to me. This should have a huge impact on me every time it happens, but after a point it no longer did. And I said, maybe this isn't right. Maybe I shouldn't be seeing things like this. But news is the unusual, right? And that wasn't the unusual. That was the day-to-day life.

This balance between the depth of local knowledge, a fresh approach and the ability to see the "big picture" translates in three functions, each discussed in depth in other chapters. The first is the ability to "recognize a story," to "follow your nose" to an interesting tip – instant news judgment:

There was a very good story that [Mexico-based AP writer] Adriana [Gómez Licón] did about Twitter getting upset because somebody in Guadalajara saw a blonde child beggar at a street corner and immediately called child welfare authorities saying, "This had been kidnapped."[7] And . . . it opened this whole debate about race in Mexico, which Mexicans would normally rather have a root canal than talk about race. Because the official line is "We're all some layer of brown," and it's like no, no you are not. . . . [T]hat's skill number one. You can give me somebody who's a terrible writer but is kind of gossipy and kind of knows what the story is, and I can make them into a reporter. And if you just can't recognize what a story is, you might as well give up right now, because that's basic. (Stevenson, 30)

The second fundamental skill is the willingness to go out to where the story is happening – often at grave personal danger. "Being on the ground" underlies all that correspondents do, and it relates to having an eye for the telling detail, for "visualizing" (Belkind, 6) in addition to contextualizing a story. There is a massive mudslide in the Philippines? A good foreign correspondent will write "what it's like to walk around . . . how you go up to your knees in mud with every step that you take. You can smell the decay starting to set in. It's still incredibly humid. There's a threat of storms coming in while the rescue workers are still trying to find possibilities of survivors" (Alexander, 30).

Finally, finding and developing the right sources is critical: "Curiosity is the main thing. I'm a born snoop," Korean and Vietnam Wars correspondent McArthur (21) put it. "The more people you meet, the more you know, the better you get," Seward (4) said. Two distinct if paradoxical skills govern the relationship with sources: constant verification of what they say, according to the journalistic dictum that "even if your mother says she loves you, check it out," accompanied by inherent respect for those speaking, no matter how abhorrent their views might be. Reflecting on covering Afghanistan and Pakistan during the "war on terror," Gannon (84–85) warned against treating them as a "freak show":

What would you do if you were going to go to cover your own country? What kind of information do you need? What . . . would you want to know? Same kind of thing. Which then to me reflects your respect for people and where you're going. . . . Not

7 Adriana Gómez Licón, "Case of blonde girl beggar strikes nerve in Mexico," The Associated Press, October 27, 2012.

everybody's deserving it, but respect, period . . . and I'd say be curious and interested about them. Not about them as it affects you. But about them. . . . I mean for sure the terrorism and everything, and it's far reaching and everything, but you have to be here to tell the story of here.

SPEAKING IN TONGUES OR LOST IN TRANSLATION

But following stories on the ground through local sources entails one more set of skills – the ability to communicate in foreign languages. Throughout the decades, AP was more likely than other organizations to pay correspondents to study or practice other idioms (Hess 1996, 81). Outside Europe, language requirements were often flexible: Although AP's coverage of the Vietnam War won unprecedented accolades, for example, "almost nobody could speak Vietnamese" among U.S. correspondents in Saigon (The Associated Press and Hamill 2014, 21). Europe editor Niko Price (14) recalled that in Los Angeles in the early 1990s, he was one of a couple of bureau staffers who spoke Spanish in the heavily Latino city, whereas he said it would be "unconscionable" today for AP to send non-Spanish-speakers to Latin America or to the border.

AP has the advantage of a widespread network of bureaus: For organizations where one reporter has to cover a dozen countries at a time, it is virtually impossible to match assignment to idiom. Even at AP, though, and even with fluency, fast-moving correspondents can run into trouble. North Africa correspondent Paul Schemm's (10) Egyptian-accented Arabic was hit or miss across the region during the Arab Spring. Lee (11) had to master the nuances of the Korean used in the North as opposed to the South: "They call their country Choson. South Koreans call North Korea Bukhan. So they have different words for themselves, and they consider it a bit offensive for us to be using the South Korean words to describe them." Seward (12), for whom Russian was the fourth language, saw it change as the Soviet Union started to collapse: "The references on posters in demonstrations, the songs they were referring to, the books they were referring to, it's changing. And so people who thought that they had really good Russian, they did, but they had really good Soviet Russian."

The proficiency levels of the interviewed correspondents vary greatly – ranging from barely able to hail a cab to fluent in half a dozen foreign languages, with most mastering two or three – but all argued that it made all the difference when they could understand enough "to do interviews and not get trapped" (Erbsen, 6), and be understood enough to earn trust, whether at the highest government ranks or on the street. The Japanese-language press briefings at Tokyo's Imperial Palace were far more detailed than the English ones (Talmadge, 2), for example, while the ability to pose a clear, concise, fluent question they had "no way out of answering" helped get past Mexican officials' penchant for "circumlocution" (Stevenson, 30). (Though some leaders still manage to create a language barrier:

Pope Benedict first announced his historic resignation during an obscure meeting on Italian saints – in Latin [Simpson, 38].)

Fluency is also key to understanding local media, both for background and breaking news. Maureen Johnson (17), helping out in Tehran during the hostage crisis without a word of Farsi, still shuddered more than 30 years later recalling how "horrible, awful" it was to feel so helpless: "There would be this old Khomeini booming on the television and . . . I would say, 'For all we know, he's just said he'd shot them all.'" Also recalling the Iranian Revolution, Reid (27–28, 24–26) reflected on how language stumbles, including multiple translations, compounded lack of knowledge about an enigmatic phenomenon:

[F]irst Khomeini comes back and he immediately appoints Mehdi Bazargan [as prime minister] . . . with some big ceremony. The world's media was there. . . . Khomeini . . . didn't speak anything but Farsi and Arabic, so he's sitting there talking in Farsi and we have one guy taking quotes in Farsi. Then [Bazargan] would give the quotes in French – we had one guy taking French. And then I was taking the English, and three of us had all the quotes totally different. There was no idea what the guy had said, how much was elaborated by the two translators, who were very political and had their own political views. Total nightmare.[8] . . . We noticed that the Tehran English dailies never gave full names of religious figures. They would give their title and their family name. So we had no idea what Khomeini's first name was, and no one else we could ask had any idea of what it was either. . . . So the foreign editor calls one day – and this is a big deal because it was hard to get calls through internationally, especially places like Iran – so he says (he was a sarcastic character), "Tell me, . . . there certainly seem to be a lot of Iranians around named Ayatollah." [laughs] "Well, the name is Ruhollah." "I think we should start using it – we use everybody's first name." But see, the point of that story is just to show the depth of ignorance. We had no clue. We had no clue how anything worked.

Being able to strike up a conversation with regular people in their language has also been essential, as Hutzler (13) recalled about his reporting in China during the major corruption scandals of the late 1990s, including one involving a trading company smuggling goods tax-free into the country:

Before this scandal broke, I was just really lucky enough to get introduced to somebody who did security work at the time for the Central Committee of the Communist Party. And . . . he was a very, very sort of garrulous person; he's just one of these guys who wanted to talk. He didn't have an agenda. . . . And so another journalist who didn't speak Chinese had actually been introduced to him, but never was able to sort of capitalize on the source. . . . [T]his contact then introduced me to this person. And he became a really good source. It was sort of a slow-building relationship. And then when this scandal broke, he was able to provide really great information.

English is increasingly widely spoken, but correspondents are wary of relying on English speakers as sources because, obviously, they are not easily

---

[8] But the story still got on the wire: Robert H. Reid, The Associated Press, February 5, 1979.

identifiable when "working the street" (Reid, 72) and tend to hail from particular sociopolitical and urban backgrounds that inevitably color their perspectives. In addition, as Bryson (46) put it, ignoring the language means "You can't eavesdrop. And it's so important to be able to hear people when they're not trying to present themselves to you." So when language fails, most correspondents have worked with translators who, when trusted and experienced, can become invaluable interview partners, articulating questions linguistically and culturally so as to get at the core of the inquiry – not "just a vehicle, like a Google translator" (Reid, 34).

Correspondents know, however, that relying entirely on translators – usually not professional linguists but local staffers, fixers or government-provided interpreters – means risking that they will filter the information, either to deliberately spin a point or simply because they are trying to guess at the meaning instead of translating verbatim. They also might not have sufficient fluency in English to capture nuances. The trickiest environments tend to be a double whammy – precisely where local languages are difficult for many Westerners to be proficient in (such as the Middle East, China, Haiti), conflict and government surveillance (often in the form of official translators and "minders") make it crucial to understand what sources are saying directly, instead of what is being "translated." In Baghdad between the two U.S. wars, Eileen Powell (18) knew enough Arabic to realize what her government minder left untranslated:

I was out interviewing people about – there were sanctions, there were all sorts of things, what was life like. . . . And I asked a woman, and I said it in English, and then he translated, I said, because she was working at a vegetable stand, I said, "Can you get meat here?" And he asked her something, and she shook her head no, and then he said to her, "You better say you can or you'll be in trouble." So she talked about sheep and whatever, something like that. . . . Or someone would say, "It's really difficult; we're just having a horrible time because the utility system isn't working, we don't have enough electricity at home, and . . . we're losing children in the hospitals," that never got translated.

Gannon (66), who studied Urdu and Persian in addition to French, had enough Pashto to see the runaround another correspondent was given in post-9/11 Peshawar: He "was supposed to be interviewing an Arab – the guy was speaking Pashto. And his interpreter was telling him that it was Arabic." Snow (10–11) had no Creole at all while covering the military intervention to restore President Jean-Bertrand Aristide in Haiti in 1994, but even so it was evident that her driver/translator was not quite getting all the details:

You would go somewhere like Cité Soleil, which was this horrible slum, and there would be a dead body on the ground. And you would say, "Sam, ask him what happened to that man." So he would ask him in Creole, and the man would talk for like five minutes, and then Sam would say, "He say Macoute [paramilitary forces] come, shoot man, now he dead."

Gray (5–6), who is fluent in French, German, Czech, and Thai and studied several other languages, similarly regretted having unknowingly missed, in translation, not only "great quotes" but "so many great insights even, because insights often come from sort of phrases people use or the kind of language or the way they speak":

I went to do a story in Cambodia about a village where – it's been about 20 years – they uncovered a huge amount of bones from the Khmer Rouge massacres. Probably one of the biggest burial sites in Cambodia. I mean, thousands of bones. . . . What does this do to this village? The old people, the young people, how do they react? So I went there, and it turned out to be one of the nicest, most moving stories I've done recently, but I really wanted to do it well. I had a very good interpreter, but once again, I knew that he wasn't telling me, so I really, this time, I really pressed him. I pressed him, I pressed him. And because of it, the quotes turned out to be absolutely marvelous. And I knew that if I didn't press him an extra bit, out of laziness or out of whatever, he would have just given me the paraphrase. And again, that made me realize, how often in my life have I missed something.

Gray's resulting story reveals the survivors' chilling memories, such as the leading anecdote of a woman "breastfeeding her baby with her hands and feet shackled; her husband thrown into a pit to be turned into human fertilizer" – details that the 63-year-old Cambodian conjured "in powerful pantomime" – as well as her reflection: "'Whenever I think of the Khmer Rouge time I don't feel hunger or thirst,' she says, sinking into her chair in a ramshackle hut open to the rains and mosquitoes. 'I feel nothing except the feeling that I am already dead.'"[9]

CONCLUSIONS

Language, then, can be a challenge for hopscotching correspondents often sent abroad suddenly and somewhat haphazardly, but it is also one of the most critical skills for them to do what has drawn them to this career, and to AP as the means to get there: getting out and deep into the world to meet the people, learn the cultures, and tell what and why history is happening, from the ground up. The personal risks of this kind of reporting are undeniable, and a high tolerance for danger emerged from all interviews – not for the sake of a mindless adrenaline rush, but while in the pursuit of what the correspondents saw as a mission. Basting chicken in his Florida kitchen, Anderson (13) coolly assessed the enormous risks he had run covering the Lebanese civil war – and why he had loved it:

There were many people covering the Lebanon war who never got near the front, and I never would criticize such a person, because when you think about it, it's crazy. Not wanting to be shot at or shelled is a perfectly normal and acceptable human feeling, and being willing to go out into very extreme situations is not necessarily an admirable trait,

[9] Denis D. Gray, "Mass grave raises ghosts from the past," The Associated Press, August 25, 2012.

Civil War in Rwanda, 1994

Paul Alexander: I was there ... when [the refugees] started pouring across. ... There had been a lot of gunfire that we could hear from the border [in Zaire]. ... I remember going to the UN Rwandan office and saying, "These people are coming across." "Oh, we heard about a few coming across the jungle crossing north of the city. We'll go check it out." "No, you don't understand – the borders are open. They're just throwing everything open, and people are just pouring across." ...

[Rwanda] was, for me, the most challenging story. One of the reasons I liked doing all this was because I liked to stretch myself. I liked to find what my limits were. And in just a matter of a couple of days there, I found every one: physical, intellectual, and emotional. Physical, you're working 18, 20 hours a day covering this story, in hot, steamy conditions. There is a volcano that is erupting north of this city, so there's volcanic ash in the air. People are coming across, they're carrying down trees and using them as firewood, so you have green smoke. The sun was disappearing an hour before it got down to the horizon because of all the crap in the air. I ended up having to leave basically because I had lost my voice towards the end. ... Intellectually, you got 500,000 people crossing the border in just like a three-day period. Just getting to the border was like swimming upstream. And plus, it was kind of dicey. I had a gun pointed at me from some guy who, like, smiles, "I could kill you right now and nobody would do anything." Seeing all these machetes and everything else. And just trying to get a feel for just the numbers, and plus, you just had over 500,000 people killed in Rwanda. Your mind is just boggling from both of these things. And then emotionally, the dichotomy of wanting to feel sorry for these people, not really knowing if that's right. ...

I got robbed at gunpoint by Zairian soldiers there, who would fire in the air every time I would hesitate to cooperate. Six times, it turned out. I did get them to give me my passport back. So I got to do an expense account from there: 500 dollars, robbed at gunpoint by Zairian soldiers. And I put in parentheses, "no receipt" (Alexander, 15–16).

but it is useful for a correspondent, and [*The Times*' Robert] Fisk and I and a few other correspondents were very willing to get right out there just as far as we damn well could, and it was dangerous. ... It's an enormously complicated situation. Admirable people, the people who are ordinary people, just trying to get through these terrible circumstances and most of the time doing it with a little grace and dignity, trying to help each other; a lot of vicious people, some evil people who would make your skin crawl just to talk to. But you're operating at absolutely top capacity – mental, physical, and psychological. You're covering a story that is going in 2,000 newspapers a day in the front page. You are at the peak of why you're doing this, and yes it takes a toll ... not just a physical toll, it's a psychological toll, and it doesn't make you an admirable person, often. It emphasizes some unadmirable traits. You need aggression, you need total focus, you need a certain amount of coldness, if you will, to be able to function after you've seen some of those things, but by God, I have to say that's the most exciting, interesting job I've ever had.

Whether they had come up through the ranks deep in America or had stumbled upon AP in far-flung locales, correspondents shared a unique trait – an almost incredulous gratefulness to be allowed a front seat to history, which they demonstrated with near-obsessive dedication to their story, the story they loved, no matter how harrowing the circumstances. Tony Smith drove out of besieged Sarajevo carrying AP photographer David Brauchli, who had been grievously wounded by a mortar shell, while another correspondent followed in a separate car transporting the corpse of his photographer colleague, killed in the same attack. Brauchli, "shoeless, wearing hospital pajamas and wrapped in blankets," looked out the car window at the hundreds of forlorn refugees along the road and "heaved a despairing sigh: 'If we hadn't been hit, we'd still be reporting this,'" Smith wrote.[10]

The "dirty secret," as Rosenblum (7) told me, "is that any of us who have foreign correspondent stuff in our blood, we'd all do it for free if we could." As Price (26) put it, foreign corresponding "is wonderful, it's noble, it's fulfilling ... it's a gift and then they pay you for it." A colleague who covered the fall of the Berlin Wall echoed, "sometimes you'd pay them to let you do the job" (Johnson, 20). Just how they did it, across all continents and eight decades, is the subject of the next chapters.

---

[10] Tony Smith, "Tearful farewell, then a drive past desperate refugees," The Associated Press, May 21, 1992.

3

What's the Story? News Judgment, News Pitches

Faced with covering a whole country, if not half a continent, the correspondents' first, essential task is deciding what is news – and then fighting for it to become a slice of the global newshole. This responsibility with crucial effects on the American public's awareness and understanding of the world often starts with AP, because of its agenda-setting role for other media, which is so strong that one study called AP "the de facto determiner of most of the international news that appears in the US press" (Hess 1996, 93), even though of course the cooperative cannot determine if and how its material is used by its members and clients. Gatekeeping decisions about what foreign news to publish rest with news editors and, increasingly, algorithms, under influences ranging from personal idiosyncrasies to ideology to readers' preferences – so that nuanced stories provided by AP are sometimes ignored or truncated.

Journalists' "news values" in selecting what to cover and publish have been criticized as enduringly too domesticated (focusing mostly on effects for the United States rather than actual foreign countries), too biased toward cultural proximity and economic and military strength (thus disproportionately focusing on developing nations' "coups and earthquakes" only), and too willing to follow the old maxim that "if it bleeds, it leads," with a growing exception for cute pandas, sexy celebrities, and such soft feature stories (for a review, see Chang et al. 2012; Westwood et al. 2013). A study of television news in 17 countries in 2008 found that U.S. public and private channels had a far higher percentage of hard news and a far lower percentage of soft news than other nations', although they also carried a significant amount of "sensational" foreign news; it further found that American TV news mentioned three dozen nations only, the second-lowest total in the sample, and that the most covered countries paralleled U.S. foreign policy interests, with U.S. channels tying Taiwan's for the lowest number of "purely foreign" news percentages (Cohen 2013, 57, 316, 30). Although timeliness has also long been a criterion for newsworthiness, it assumes worrisome aspects in the digital environment's overarching quest for "immediacy" (Usher 2014), and its consequences are discussed in Chapter 11. The other bulging elephant in the newsroom – what journalists believe their audience wants covered – is addressed in more detail in Chapter 12.

The need to cover "revolutions, earthquakes, the usual stuff," as 41-year veteran Denis Gray (20) put it, has not changed over the decades, and studies suggested such "official" news was the bulk of coverage in U.S. media in the 1970s and 1980s, to the detriment of more social and cultural approaches (Gans 1979; Wilhoit and Weaver 1983). Newsworthiness standards, however, have shifted as AP evolved from the news agency of record for the American public to a more global approach and, recently, to emphasizing investigative journalism in an effort to carve a niche for itself when bare-bones breaking news appears to have migrated to social media in the digital age. These changes worry some correspondents and critics, who argue that too few are left to cover what might not be trendy (and therefore unprofitable) today but could turn out to be "big stuff" tomorrow (Garber 2009).

This chapter clarifies how choices have been made by correspondents on the ground, around the world, and across time, through real examples of practices that emerged across the interviews – the latter particularly important because the direct question "How do you decide what to cover/what is news?" often elicited a rather blank stare and variations of, "Well, it is obvious." After all, correspondents listed as a basic professional skill knowing what is the story. As Otto Doelling (19), the author of one of AP's correspondence guides, self-deprecatingly argued, "I was cocky enough to think I knew which stories would be of general interest. I didn't worry too much about what people might think of what should be the story or not be the story. I figured I knew what the story should be and I pursued it."

THE OBVIOUS NEWS

> If you're working for the news wire, partly those decisions are made for you. Because if there's news happening, if there's big news happening ... if there's breaking stories or whatever ... which is always the most exciting thing to do, like if there's a hostage situation or a bomb or something, it's obvious what you're going to cover. (Pennington, 7)

All correspondents agreed with Matthew Pennington, who reported on South and Southeast Asia since 1999, that major stories of violence, conflict, disasters, government overthrows, and the like are covered reflexively. They are "obvious stuff": "Wherever the fire bell went off, that's where you went off to" (McArthur, 8). In the late 1960s, West Africa correspondent Arnold Zeitlin (8–9, 11) had to juggle the "primary story" of Nigeria's civil war with lighter fare from there (e.g., a story about the prevalence of polygamy being such that

FIGURE 3.1. West Africa correspondent Arnold Zeitlin (center) crosses the Niger River after a Nigerian Army operation in Onitsha during the Biafra civil war in the late 1960s. (Photo courtesy of Arnold Zeitlin)

one of the fastest-selling cars in the country, a compact, was advertised "as exactly what 'a man with four wives needs'").[1] He also had to "at least make the rounds" in the dozen other countries on his beat, trying to cover something other than the coups everyone wanted – and could understand:

We went to all the coup d'états. ... Because they were the only thing that London and New York were interested in. If there was a coup d'état, it had to be. Okay. So I struggled. ... I had happened to be in the country, and I was driving back to Nigeria next door when on the car radio I heard martial music. That was the signal that there was a coup d'état. And I turned around the car and went back. And did a story on this coup d'état [in Dahomey]. ... So I had the coup d'états sewed up. You didn't have to explain much about coup d'états – everybody knew.

What makes conflict a must – drama, deviance, impact – also works for natural disasters, especially from countries that might otherwise be off the radar. Another West Africa correspondent called the devastating four-year

[1] Arnold Zeitlin, "Second Nigerian Region Declares Independence," *Washington Post*, September 21, 1967, A26; Arnold Zeitlin, "Unconcern, Arms Prolong Nigeria War," *Chicago Tribune*, November 3, 1968, A17; Arnold Zeitlin, "Multiple Marriage Issue in Nigeria," *Los Angeles Times*, December 15, 1968, D23.

drought in the Sahel "the biggest story" he covered there in the 1970s (Heinzerling, 2). Correspondents in both Indonesia and Latin America called disasters their "bread and butter" that made their countries "get onto the front pages" (Price, 15). The same logic applies just as well to the least foreign of locales, the United Kingdom, where one reporter's three-decade career started with the Lockerbie disaster, followed by a plane crash and a stadium crush: "A lot of people died the first couple of months that I was here. Then it got quieter" (Barr, 3).[2] Most journalists have rules even for body counts, quantitative measures of newsworthiness: Eduardo Gallardo (12), who covered Latin America for four decades, figured that more than six or seven people dead in a single highway crash is news, but two in a small plane not really – unless one needs a Web filler. Ditto for earthquakes: "6.2 or 6.3 [on the Richter scale], you use it. Then. Now, over 4 we can use." For one Mexico City–based correspondent, that country's violence in the 2000s was so widespread that "there's not a need to, every time there's four bodies that show up, to write a story about it," leaving more time for events that are "representative of the bigger trends and changes" (Weissenstein, 10).

Many recognized that even the most straightforward of breaking news – an earthquake or the assassination of a prime minister – should be an opportunity to tell a larger story: "the challenge is to write the stories that actually can capture the complexities of life in a way, but are still topical and important stories. . . . Like, how do you write an earthquake story that is not just a death toll story? . . . Because it's not" (McDowell, 21). Dan Perry's (12) first assignment to Israel in the 1990s coincided with Yitzhak Rabin's murder:[3]

And of course the assassination here was incredibly interesting because it had been done by an extremist Jew, and it really underscored the more interesting story of Israel, which is the unbelievable fissures and divisions internally between the different kinds of Jews, which is something that people outside of Israel don't always know about very well. And therefore it's a theme that you can explore[4] . . . what makes something interesting is multifaceted, and one of them is things that people don't necessarily know.

In fact, most correspondents tried to balance the steady diet of bad news with stories that could give a more nuanced impression even of those countries mired in deadly violence. Pennington (16), in Afghanistan in the mid-2000s, wrote about a Kabul entrepreneur refashioning the burqa into a "flowing gown" as an example of women going into business:[5]

---

[2] In January 1989, 47 people were killed and more than 70 severely injured when a British Midland flight crashed just outside the airport near Kegworth. In April 1989, 96 people were killed and more than 700 injured in a crush at the football stadium in Sheffield during a match.

[3] Perry was one of the AP writers who covered the assassination; see, among many stories, Dan Perry and Dianna Cahn, "Joyous scene turns to stunned grief," The Associated Press, November 4, 1995.

[4] Perry started to do so the day after the assassination; Dan Perry, "Israelis agonize as Rabin assassination shatters illusions," The Associated Press, November 5, 1995.

[5] Matthew Pennington, "Refashioning the burqa: Women go into business in post-Taliban Afghanistan," The Associated Press, April 11, 2005.

But my sort of overriding feeling is that there's a lot of negative news that comes out, and I think … that's what people want to read about. They don't want to read about sunny stories, they want to read about what's really affecting people's lives, and I think you can end up with a very negative impression of the country just from reading the news. And I'm aware of that, so we try and do upbeat stories when we could, but it's kind of hard work.

Correspondents noted that the real skill consists in turning "the truly extraordinary," as well as the endemic, into stories that could showcase larger trends. In Cairo covering the late 1970s peace process between Egypt and Israel, Nick Tatro (19, 2) felt that the major "storylines define themselves," but insight would come well beyond the diplomatic circles:

I remember doing interviews along the Nile with boatmen, and they have these feluccas with one sail, and they made their living shuttling people, goods, or heaven knows what, up and down the Nile. And one of them said, "Yeah, when there's peace with Israel, I'll be able to buy a TV set and a refrigerator." So that's what peace meant for him, and that was really the story when I was there, that change of Egypt leaping out of its isolation, breaking the taboo on dealing with Israel, and changing the whole nature of life in Egypt.

Digging beyond breaking news, while also covering it, has been a great challenge both in ongoing situations, like under-siege Sarajevo – "For three and a half years of siege, there were a lot of days when there really wasn't much that was new, and you might get a feature about this going on, or that going on" (Porubcansky, 15) – or when a correspondent has a giant beat, like Larry Heinzerling (20–21) with the whole of West Africa:

[I]n Nigeria, when I went back in '71, the civil war was over, but a lot of soldiers still had their weapons and so there was a lot of armed robbery going on. And to discourage this there would be public executions at the beaches in Lagos. And these turned out to be like carnivals. Thousands of people would show up and vendors were selling stuff to these people and they were all watching while these guys were tied up to oil drums and shot. And I wrote a story about that and took a picture and got incredible play – it was all over the place – because it seemed brutal, but it was a good way to send a message to the rest of the country that this wasn't going to be tolerated. So, things out of the ordinary like that. Corruption is so endemic there that after you bump into it 17 times, you say, okay, I've got to write about this. Whether it's just petty – that the policeman wants a bribe to let you go. There's a marvelous story where I got stopped once coming from Dahomey, which is now Benin, to Nigeria by car. And the [Nigerian] customs guy stopped me … at the border, told me to open my trunk, looked in, saw some apples that I had got in Benin – because it was a former French colony and you could get apples in Benin – confiscated the apples, closed the boot of the car, let me go. I get to the next checkpoint, they want to see inside the boot again. I open the boot, and here is this guy's automatic weapon. [laughs] Because he had put it down to take out the apples. So, that took me three hours of talk until they finally got the other guy to come collect his weapon and say, "Yeah, I'm at fault." So, amusing, funny, but it was a good little story to tell.

This "little light stuff to make up for the heavier-duty stuff" – as Claude Erbsen (2) put it, the future World Services executive who, in 1967 from Rio de Janeiro, wrote both about Copacabana beach and stumbles in the U.S. aid program to Brazil[6] – reflects another enduring and "obvious" type of news: "human interest" stories. Based in Key West during the Bay of Pigs era, Erbsen (2) recalled "writing a feature on the fact that, even though Cuba and the U.S. were not exactly on the best of terms, every afternoon there were old Oswald the Rabbit cartoons playing on Cuban television." A colleague allowed as resident correspondent in Havana a few years later also wrote about the "crowds of enraptured adults" who gathered in hotel lobbies every afternoon "to follow the adventures of Bugs Bunny, Porky Pig and Felix the Cat."[7] Still, some of the stories are hardly substantial – virtually all Brazil correspondents mentioned they had to cover its "unmissable" carnival (Olmos, 9; Erbsen, 15; Clendenning, 10). Gallardo (23) ruefully noted that his "last big story" before retiring had been "a U.S. governor in some state who got a mistress in Argentina": "Can you believe I was ordered to fly to Buenos Aires to find the woman, try to talk to her, and I spent hours just standing at the main entrance of the building where the woman lives." The absurdist story itself left little doubt about Gallardo's feelings on reporting it:

It's a wild scene outside the luxury apartment building where Gov. Mark Sanford's mistress reportedly lives, where dozens of journalists have camped out, interviewing every passerby in hopes of finding Sanford's elusive "Maria." But with at least five Marias living in the building, the mystery persists ... [with journalists] scrambling for clues and complaining about their stakeout duty on one of the coldest days of the Argentine winter. Is it Maria the soy and fruit exporter or ... maybe the Maria who poses next to an Argentine flag on her Facebook page? Hopes briefly rise as one woman walks out saying "Yes, I'm Maria!" "But I'm not the one you're looking for!" she quickly adds, giggling her way down the sidewalk.[8]

Iberia bureau chief Al Clendenning (21) argued that what AP wants from him is "the biggest story in Spain every day that's going to go international" and sell well – even if it happens to be a short but "massive" story about the 87-year-old billionaire Duchess of Alba marrying a man 25 years her junior.

In other words, from carnage to momentous political change to day-in-the-life features, "AP wanted everything," as Vicki Graham (4) recalled as we sat in her apartment in Shanghai's French Concession, cookies on the table and laundry flapping off the small balcony. Her mandate when she helped reopen the first bureau in Beijing in 1979, after 30 years of broken diplomatic relations, was

---

[6] Claude E. Erbsen, "It's Summer at Copacabana," *Washington Post*, January 15, 1967; Claude E. Erbsen, "Billions in Aid, Yet Brazil Lags," *Chicago Tribune*, July 23, 1967.

[7] Isaac M. Flores, "Havana Enjoys Itself, Despite Red Controls," *Los Angeles Times*, April 3, 1966, C16.

[8] Eduardo Gallardo, "Mystery of Sanford's mistress deepens in Argentina," The Associated Press, June 25, 2009.

all-encompassing: "How do people look? What does the food look like? How do they smell [the foods]? What do they say? What's going on? Is there a cat on the roof? Persimmon growing in the courtyard? How many patches on their clothes? What happened to them in the Cultural Revolution?" And when the request evolved toward deeper stories, her mandate became: "We want what's really meaningful, not just every bus plunge in India. But, you know, don't miss one" (Graham, 39). Listening to Japan bureau chief Malcolm Foster (10–11) rattle off the big stories his bureau was covering in 2013, "everything" still seemed the order – including a new nationalistic prime minister and the impact on the tense relationship with China over uninhabited islands;[9] the dropping numbers of bluefin tuna, which makes prime sushi, that "typical Japanese kind of cultural thing" (though the story, beginning with "the king of sushi," quickly turned into a deep environmental, cultural, economic dive);[10] the impact of Japan's public debt on its aging population; and the lack of post-tsunami rebuilding as "a way to highlight some of these deep-seated problems in Japan: The bureaucracy, the inability to be flexible and make important decisions quickly."[11]

Another longtime Japan hand also found that, especially in the 1980s, "the world was very interested in quirky Japanese stories" – like the first craze for energy drinks for salarymen or for gold flakes on desserts for the new bubble millionaires – which raised the challenge of writing stories that have something important to say about the society "and they're not just catering or pandering to kind of the weird Japan stereotype" (Talmadge, 3). In fact, one caveat to the "obvious" news for many correspondents was not to fall into stereotypes, reader-grabbing as they are, or at least to move beyond them: "People love to read about all the faces of Italy, from the mafia to cuisine, you know? From Venice to the pope . . . those are the stories themselves that you have to be careful or they become cliché" (Simpson, 32–33). Stereotypes can be a danger even in the least-known, most closed-off countries, like North Korea, where Lee (14–15) found herself balancing the stories "that will appeal" – "a performance with Mickey Mouse characters"[12] – with those she felt "a certain responsibility as a journalist to write":

The first time I went there, it was a very Soviet method [of shopping]. . . . You take this little paper to the cashier, pay for it, she gives you another slip back, you take it back to the counter, and they give you what you asked for. . . . But in 2011, they were introducing a new form of shopping, which is, they put things on a shelf and you browse and you pick

---

[9] Tokyo and Beijing escalated tensions over, and military presence around, the Japanese-administered, unoccupied islands called Senkaku in Japan and Diaoyu in China. Japan bought three islands in the chain from a private owner, and China accused it of colonialism on Chinese territory.

[10] Malcolm Foster, "Tuna collapse fears fail to curb Japan's appetite," The Associated Press, March 1, 2013.

[11] Elaine Kurtenbach, "Tsunami-hit towns still barren as rebuilding lags," The Associated Press, March 8, 2013.

[12] "Small world: Show for N. Korea's Kim goes Disney," The Associated Press, July 9, 2012.

and choose what it is you want, there's a price on it, you take it to the cash register, they ring you up. ... I did think it was really important to write about this, this emerging consumer culture, because it's part of the evolution. But the stories that tend to be really popular are much more about not how the country is changing, but the kind of stereo-typical stories about how weird they are.

Lee's story on "a decidedly un-communist development in North Korea: A new culture of commerce" centered on the Kwangbok-area supermarket in downtown Pyongyang, which displayed "lime green frying pans, pink Minnie Mouse pajamas, popcorn and a line of silvery high heels" and featured saleswomen in red "gently" advising perplexed shoppers to "pick the items yourself and put them in the basket."[13] One shopper chastised her nephew, "trying to wrest a cellphone from his mittened hands" while admonishing him to thank her for all the "tasty goodies" – but also "to give thanks to the fatherly general as well," an "obligatory comment" about Kim Jong Il.

Conflict, and Beyond

Of all the "obvious news," conflict, never in short supply, remains the mainstay. In the midst of chaos, keeping up is hard enough: "the first six months of the war [in the former Yugoslavia], when it was really, I mean *really* hectic and not controllable, we were just running after the story," one of the leading correspondents in that conflict, Tony Smith (6), said. But, contrary to many media criticisms, correspondents consistently tried to go beyond violence in their coverage, as exemplified by Joe Frazier's (5, 6, 21–22, 33) account of his search for deeper truth behind the daily horrors of guerrilla wars and coups across Central America and the Caribbean:

We spent a lot of time covering the fight [during the Sandinista revolution] and so forth, which I didn't really like to do because I didn't think it was really what was going on. It was part of what was going on, but it didn't tell the whole story. So I tried to get out and do people stories about how this is affecting Nicaraguans of various persuasions ... general life in the country and the divisions in families ... which to me was the story going on there. But there was enough combat going on all around us that we couldn't ignore it, because it was too a part of the story. ...

[W]e would get into small towns that had really had their living crap knocked out of them ... and you'd spend a couple of days there just talking to the people who lived there through the sides changing back and forth, and nobody knew who was going where, happening all around us. ... And to me that was the story of El Salvador, and I tried to write that story. ... It wasn't about who's in charge of this town this week or that town the next. It was what it did to the everyday poor Salvadorans who all they wanted to do was wake up alive in the morning. ...

[In Haiti,] they were throwing out [President Jean-Claude] Duvalier, so we had a peg. The hard story was there, so we could piggyback the stuff in there very easily. You go to a

---

[13] Jean H. Lee, "China brings supermarket concept to North Korea," The Associated Press, February 25, 2012.

hospital up in Cap-Haïtien, and you find out they have no doctors in that hospital – you have to bring your own. If you want surgery, you have to bring two gallons of gas to run the generator to run lights in the operating room. ... Things that people in the United States simply cannot comprehend. ... And to me, that remains the story of Central America. What it did to the people who lived there. The political factions were interesting, the fighting was interesting, but I got stuck on the human effect of the war, all of them.

Reflecting on coverage of the first Palestinian intifada, editor Nick Tatro (22) wished the comprehensive "roundup" stories of the violence had been less about "the day's body count" and more eyewitness accounts "giving readers an idea of what actually happened." In the second intifada, one correspondent who was then on the desk regretted that the more than 100 suicide bombings came with such regularity that the bureau developed "a sad routine" triggered by radio or police scanner reports:

[S]omeone would shout the Hebrew word for bombing, which is *pigua*, or it could be a bombing or a shooting. And then this machine just clicked into motion. Our guys in the West Bank and Gaza knew to check for claims of responsibility; the Israeli channels started bringing pictures from the scene. We'd send a reporter there, to hospitals. ... Even writing the story ... it was like painting by numbers in some ways. "It was the deadliest since" or – a few hours after it happened, you'd have like the scope of it and you have the context and then the first victims' quote and the survivors' quote, color, political stuff. It's sad, but that's the job sometimes. (Laub, 22)

Especially when covering conflicts, correspondents know the challenge is to write beyond the formulaic body count – "hard to do on a wire story when you're covering the whole thing," Mark Porubcansky (20) recalled of reporting from Bosnia. So they stay attuned to sudden insights even from the most obscure interviewees, such as a small-town Croat grocer:

I went into the interview ... with just very modest expectations. I just wanted to talk to people about what was going on in this place at this particular time. ... And he wanted to say that, "Look, I'm guilty for this, and a lot – and everybody else in my village is guilty. The best people in my village have some responsibility for this, because we saw it coming, we didn't think it was going to happen, we did nothing." He just had to get it off of his chest. It sort of came flooding out of him. ... It was something that *he* wanted to tell *me* about what he had learned. (Porubcansky, 20)

Porubcansky's story described the Balkans as a "tangle of victimization, self-pity and self-justification. Victimized by history, by ideology, by their leaders, people have victimized each other during the past three years in the hope of avoiding more victimization themselves. ... What makes today's Vukovar so typical – and terrifying – is the few thousand sad souls who remain, living on self-justification, monotony and nobody-asked-me-anyhow hopelessness."[14] The story closed with the grocer's quote:

[14] Mark J. Porubcansky, "Yugoslav history lesson: 'Do unto others' first," The Associated Press, June 25, 1994.

"I could understand how my grandfather, who couldn't read, could be seduced to make war on someone," Ivica said. "But I can't believe people now would do it." They did. The past and present live concurrently in the Balkans, and the future is hard to change.

To find that balance between the necessary combat coverage and the larger sociopolitical and humanitarian story has been especially challenging when the combat involved Americans – in Korea "we covered the armistice talks in the morning, and the war in the afternoon," one correspondent deadpanned (AP Oral History, Summerlin 2004, 6) – particularly during dramatically politicized wars such as in Indochina or Iraq. Denis Gray (34), who covered both, argued for the fighting snapshot – "the sort of daily, 'We bombed this, we did that, this unit attacked here, we overran that position'" – as well as the two big-picture stories: "what is war like from the average soldier fighting it? And, on the other side, what is the impact of war on civilians?" After conflict subsides, the media spotlight leaves – but the civilian impact and the resumption of normal life loom ever larger, making them the chosen storyline for many correspondents trying to write beyond body counts. George Bria (10) in late 1940s Germany focused on a 30-year Ruhr coalminer in a story about disagreements between the British and American military governments over socializing the mines,[15] and when he went to Nuremberg, Bria wrote about its famous toy factory, not just the Nazi trials:

And the [toy factory] manager showed me a toy he had, he had a little car that he put on a table, and it went zoom to the end of the table, and as soon as it got to the end would turn around, come back, and not fall off the table. So I wrote this story about the resurgence of Nuremburg toys, and it got a very good play, and the executive editor ... said, "This is the kind of story we want." [laughs] You know? People story. Also, reawakening, resurgence, the hell with the trials. I covered the trials, but it was a routine thing by the time I got there.

Even decades after the Khmer Rouge massacres, Gray (56) tried to find a creative way to explain what it was like for him as a journalist to travel to Anlong Veng, a former Khmer Rouge haven led by Ta Mok "the butcher" – and for their victims who still lived there:

[W]e were doing this story on atrocity tourism, and as I always do whenever I can, I go for a jog after the day's work is done. So I went for a jog and I thought, "Wow, maybe there's a story ..." ... Two things came together: jogging through this surreal place, past the school that Ta Mok, the butcher, built. These kids are waving to me, saying, "Hi, how are you?" And everybody is very friendly. And again, this surreal juxtaposition of what happened there and this joyous jog I had. And then remembering the people that I knew in Cambodia who were killed by the Khmer Rouge.

---

[15] George Bria, "Ruhr Digger Willi Works for Anybody," *Washington Post*, July 4, 1948, B8.

Over morning coffee across from one of Bangkok's parks popular with joggers, Gray showed me the "Jogging in hellholes" story, which began and ended with Cambodia:

Anlong Veng, in the sticks of northwest Cambodia, ranks high on the surreal scale among the many places on four continents where I've laced up my running shoes. But then there was one of Saddam Hussein's pleasure palaces in Baghdad, Rwanda just after the tribal massacres ... Now, I'm on the homeward stretch in Anlong Veng, forced to peer into the well of memory, and out of it rise images of the executioners – some likely these very smiling citizens around me – and their shattered victims. Among those were many friends, perhaps the bravest and most loyal ones I've ever known. We covered the Cambodian War together, before they perished at the orders of Anlong Veng's killers in the reign of terror that followed. In mid-stride, I raised my right hand to salute them.[16]

Terry Anderson (9), in South Africa toward the end of the apartheid regime, struggled with it personally through the "Kafkaesque world" of the white suburb he lived in with his black household staff – and also struggled with his articles because he often "didn't know how to express it really," unlike the more traditional armed conflicts he was covering in the Caprivi Strip and Zimbabwe. Trying to find a different angle to cover the ongoing slaughter in 1990s Rwanda, Gray (59–60) heard a tip from another journalist about a hotel in a national park that had been taken over by baboons:

So we ... started rolling through the beautiful, lush countryside – but as I said, some really horrible stuff, we literally ran over bones of some of the people who had been slaughtered ... it was absolutely madness. Anyway, we reached this national park, totally deserted, nobody there, and this hotel which was once a fancy hotel where all of the tourists from all over the world would go to see wildlife, totally deserted. And we were met, literally at the reception counter, with a big baboon sitting on the desk. [chuckles] ... I'll just read you, just to give you the gist of the story: "Visitors once called this hotel a little corner of paradise, but these days they break into your car when you pull up on the driveway, the management is surly, and the guests have atrocious table manners. They defecate right in the dining room."[17] ... So it was sort of a metaphor for this animalistic behavior of Rwanda at that time.

Mark Stevenson (14–16), who has covered Mexico since the 1990s, described the danger of turning a human story into a conflict narrative that deadens the deeper currents – as he argued happened to immigration in the past decade, when stricter border enforcement and the brutal takeover of smuggling by the cartels changed the narrative from the old "cat-and-mouse game":

[16] Denis D. Gray, "Jogging in hellholes," The Associated Press, August 29, 2006.
[17] Denis D. Gray, "Primates replace tourists amidst the anarchy of Rwanda," The Associated Press, August 26, 1994.

2005–2006, when the immigration debate was going, you would regularly go up to Sasabe or Altar, the migrant jumping-off points, where it was obvious this was a cottage industry ... people loping off, marching off, often in columns following their pollero, with their big water jugs and their old plaid jackets and their cans of sardines and launching across the border. ... [I]t was like ... trying to cover a semi-legal activity that everybody knows is going on ... and it's made into a human interest story about what's forcing you to make this terrible trip, into what becomes a criminal situation. ... And before ... you would get the occasional mass death story ... it was still a human interest story. Now it's become a largely criminal story.

NOTHING HAPPENS HERE

For all the difficulties of covering conflict, the bigger challenge is covering countries where "nothing happens." That phrase, recurring in interviews, reveals the correspondents' standards of newsworthiness, and it debunks some of the scholarly arguments that "core" countries like Europe attract the most attention. In fact, while the indicted countries ranged at different times from Jordan to Japan, European nations – and the "incredibly tedious" European Union (Johnson, 10) – often made the correspondents' list.

In his spare office in Rabat, a Gadhafi poster ironically hung on the wall and a demonstration rumbling in the square around the corner, North Africa correspondent Paul Schemm (3, 13–14, 24–25) remembered how he had applied just before the "Arab Spring" for this "very sleepy job that kind of no one wanted":

And back then, Morocco, Algeria, Tunisia ... there was this terrorism story in Algeria, but it was hard to report on. Tunisia, nothing happened. And Morocco was, you know, the king. There was some politics, but very minor. Tourism stories. ... It's very easy to come up with article ideas when you're in a big situation like [Libya's uprising]. The stories are all around you. Everything is the story, every element. It's much harder to work in a quiet place like Morocco and find a story that people want to hear. ... The Middle East always seems to sort of write itself. ... [After the 2011 demonstrations in Morocco] this is not a very dramatic story to tell – Morocco's slow-motion return to the status quo ante. Yeah, it's one of these watching-paint-dry stories. ... So it's a difficult story to tell. And frankly, if you want to sell a story about Morocco, you find a way to talk about the Humphrey Bogart movie and Casablanca ... people want the exotic, they want the desert trips, the camels, things like that. But there are very real stories here. It is a despotic government, it is an out-of-control police force. But just, it's not on the same level as Egypt, and so it's a harder ... it's a softer hegemony, a softer dictatorship. So ... it's difficult to find ways to tell that story.

Schemm did write about Morocco's "pro-democracy protests" petering out while popular King Mohammed VI "appears to have co-opted much of the dissatisfaction."[18] But camels and clashes make for more popular stories, while

---

[18] Paul Schemm, "Morocco's democracy protests restart after hiatus," The Associated Press, September 18, 2011.

deeper sociopolitical movements are hard to uncover and cover, especially if there is a lack of access, and to sell to an easily distracted public – a sentiment echoed throughout the decades, though the locales changed. Jordan in the 1980s and 1990s was a "jumping-off point" for coverage of wars in the region but in itself was "fairly boring, fairly peaceful and tranquil" – note the qualifiers of boring (Rice, 1–2). The belief that Central America was "so safe and so backyard of ours" meant that the eruption of guerrilla wars there in the 1980s caught many organizations "pretty flatfooted" – and one longtime correspondent in the region worried that any future unrest would do the same, since the perception that the story "moved on" resulted in shuttering most bureaus (Frazier, 39). One correspondent lived four years in the late 1990s in Canada, "where you spend a week trying to hatch some clever plan [for an original story] and basically not need to file any spot news story in the meantime, because Canadian politics was not like the antiapartheid struggle" (Crary, 9). In southern Africa in the 1990s, the end of apartheid dominated, while the rest of the region quickly fell off the radar:

Angola I'm sure didn't get the attention it deserved, which was also in our coverage area. Namibia, it was very hard to find time to write about Namibia. You could say nothing ever happens there, but I'm sure that's not true. But in the scale, compared to what was happening in countries like South Africa, where apartheid was ending, or Mozambique where there was a civil war, or Angola where civil war was ending, some things just kind of fall by the wayside. I always say that as a foreign correspondent that the hardest stories to tell are the ones that go against people's preconceptions about the place where you are. And so, you can either be contrarian and try to tell those stories or get lazy and tell the stories that people are most likely going to say yes to and are going to want to read. I suppose I would go back and forth between those two things. (Bryson, 9)

Some of the former European colonies in Africa were at least far more newsy than their colonizers. Based in Lisbon in the late 1960s, Ike Flores (10, 18), fresh from Cuba, found "there was nothing happening really in Portugal at that time," so whenever he could he made quick jaunts to the decolonization wars in Angola, Mozambique, and Guinea Bissau, and "otherwise I would travel from one end of the country to the other . . . write about what I saw, the people I talked to and I did soft pieces." Some of the most difficult countries for foreign correspondents seem to have been the major industrial powers with big tourism draws – perhaps because of the public's perception that their political and social stories no longer mattered. In Tokyo in the mid-1970s, Anderson (3) had a hard time finding stories with "spark" because all editors seemed to care about was the booming economy (especially cars). In Japan's capital 40 years later, comparing it to China or India, Foster (11) asked, "How do you write about a country that's kind of slowly in decline? It's a challenge." Victor Simpson (1–2, 6) noted a drastic change in Italy's coverage from when he arrived in the 1970s – "every afternoon the streets of Rome were filled with tear gas," plus reporters covered movies, fashion, "the quirky brilliance of the Italian people" – to today's pale focus on dry Euro troubles:

There were a lot of elements to any story you wrote. . . . Little Italy is just a small player in Europe . . . but always an important one because 12 of the U.S. bases are in Italy and there's the center of East-West espionage. A lot of great stories to write about. . . . Western Europe in fact has become a business story, with various spin-offs, immigration, things like that. But the story has changed very much for Western Europe.

Do Some Countries Just Matter More?

AP correspondents' assessment of what made countries newsworthy, therefore, seems to run contrary to the recurrent criticism that foreign news follows basic economic and policy interests, privileging "core" countries over the "peripheral" ones (Chang 1998; Koh 2013) and only provides negative, conflict coverage of less developed nations (Behr 1981; Wilhoit and Weaver 1983). Nevertheless, correspondents did sense that some countries mattered more than others – to editors and to the American public – either based on familiarity or extreme unfamiliarity, cultural affinities, or enduring, sometimes trite, storylines that were difficult to change. At the happy end of the spectrum, Brazil has always had "stories that sold themselves. Pelé and samba. . . . You could walk down the street and pick up stories like cigarette butts" (Erbsen, 9). The same applied to France, fashion destination and "eternally identified with good food and good wine and gastronomy . . . as much as I think these are eternal subjects for France, they are occasional subjects for us" – for example, in a 2013 story about how "even the French" "head to the microwave at night after work to zap frozen meals" (Ganley, 13–14).[19] Israel is perhaps the most extreme example of a tiny country drawing outsized attention: "What was a story in Israel was not a story in Jordan, because there was more interest in Israel in the United States than there was in Jordan" (Rice, 4). In the Middle East in general, "there's always another big story going on. . . . The Mideast is . . . a place of, not really triage, but of enormous need to be flexible, because all of a sudden . . . you're focused on Iraq and Iran, and Sudan can spin off news with absolutely no warning" (Buzbee, 3).

The popularity of a country's particular storyline, though, can also impede the development of alternatives, particularly for a wire service that cannot skip breaking news. One correspondent remembered how New York editors spiked "an animal story of some sort" from South Africa, arguing "You can't do that in South Africa. You can't have a non-apartheid, sort of soft feature story" (Crary, 6). From Jerusalem, Perry (29) recalled his time in the Caribbean as when "you could write whimsical stuff that was interesting . . . something I rather miss, because there's not a lot of whimsy right now in the Middle East." A longtime

---

[19] Elaine Ganley, "French eat both frozen meals and fine cuisine," The Associated Press, February 21, 2013.

Israel hand, Marcus Eliason (6–7), remembered how he had been stuck in conflict mode and blind to diverse coverage until the foreign editor called asking why stories were no longer coming fast and furious after fighting had "died down" – and what else might be going on:

"Well, it's kind of domestic stuff, there's a big fuss about . . . an Israeli [who] has written an anti-Zionist play. There's a big fuss about the price of cigarettes, they've just raised the traffic fines, there's a huge scandal about an Orthodox religious man who snatched his son from the mother and took him to Canada, and now the police . . ." He said, "Hold it, hold it. Sounds like there's a story here, isn't there?" I said "What story?" He said, "What else is going on in Israel, that's a story. You put Israel in the headlines, day in and day out, day in, day out, people want to know what this place is all about!" And that was one of the most fun stories and most important stories, I think, that I ever wrote, because it told people there's a whole society going on here besides the headlines you read every day. . . . That's also a matter of time: Do you have the time? Do you have the staff to do it? . . . The *New York Times* can, always knows that the AP will cover them on the big news if their correspondent chooses to go out and do a feature about life on the kibbutz. But the AP, we've got to be doing it all. And that's hard.

Interest in non-breaking news stories could drive coverage in countries that had not seen correspondents for a long time, either because they were ignored by U.S. journalists (such as Canada) or closed to them (such as China):

So I had a whole country [Canada] that we hadn't paid attention to for years [in the late 1970s]. And anything I wrote would be fresh and new. . . . I would just do as much reading preliminarily as I could, and following the Canadian Press, and things would catch your eye and intrigue you. . . . I could hop from here to there to the other place and would be the first AP reporter there in a couple of decades, probably. (Hanley, 5)

Something like China, which had been so closed for so long and then opening back up, is going to be a subject of great curiosity to curious, thinking people. And any story that makes people say, "Wow, I didn't know that" or "Who would have thought that?" is going to get good play when you're writing for the kind of audience that AP was writing for – American newspaper readers or international newspaper readers. . . . "Wow, Chinese village, what's that like?" You wouldn't really say that about a German village. . . . But, for the reporters in the '80s in China, now it's easy to say, "Oh, yeah, look at the fluffy stories that they wrote." But that was what they had access to . . . and that's what people were eating up so much. (Jones, 14–15)

HOW DOES IT ALL AFFECT US?

As many of the excerpts above imply, a major factor driving news selection, among and within countries, is relevance to the United States and, more recently, to global issues like the fight against terrorism. Drawing connections to foreign audience interests is natural, even necessary: a hospital for elephants maimed by land mines is more interesting than the opaque "minutiae of Thai politics," for example (Pennington, 7), and a Brazilian tree-killing frost became reason to open a multi-country "coffee desk" when the beverage's prices skyrocketed

(Gallardo, 11).[20] One of the early correspondents in West Africa scoured local women's magazines for story ideas "about the way people lived ... and you try to write it so that whoever reads it in the United States or anywhere will say, 'Hey, they do it differently' or 'and we do the same thing.' ... How does a family live on a dollar a day? I think Americans respond to that kind of story" (Zeitlin, 11). Still today, one correspondent managed to spend a week in Ecuador and write about its massive flower industry because of speculation that former NSA contractor and whistleblower Edward Snowden might seek asylum there (Weissenstein, 11). One story began, "Gino Descalzi used to fret about things like aphids, mildew and the high cost of shipping millions of roses a year from Ecuador to florists in the United States. These days he's worried about a 30-year-old American thought to be stuck in the transit area of the Moscow airport, and he can't believe it."[21]

Earlier correspondents recalled how up to the early 1990s, AP's main mission was to cover the globe for its U.S. members – "Don't forget, Denis, that you're writing for the *Miami Herald*, not the *Manila Times*," Gray (21) recalled longtime foreign editor Nate Polowetzky admonishing him. Graham (4) shuddered at the time she wasted going "to the Great Wall with, like, the governor of Ohio, handing out balloons" when China reestablished relations with the United States, and nearly two decades later, her successor in Beijing still found that his "bread and butter" was "the diplomatic crisis" with Washington over Taiwan (Hutzler, 3). U.S. interests could be noble – American regard for press freedom meant "they kill a reporter at a small radio station in a remote Guatemala city, it's news" (Gallardo, 16) – or callous, as in the scarcity of stories on the South Vietnamese casualties during the war: "But whereas we would write about almost every American death, in order to write a story about the impact of the war on the South Vietnamese military I had to go and find a woman, a South Vietnamese mother who had ... lost three or four sons and had one still fighting and he was the last. ... I remember her wailing to me, 'If my last son dies, who's going to take care of me in my old age?'" (Lederer, 3–4).

Given the United States' geopolitical dominance from the 1940s to today, the major global storylines have been automatically America-centric – especially such paradigmatic themes as the Cold War and then Islamist terrorism. Earlier correspondents working across the world remembered how the U.S.-USSR conflict was always there: "Foreign governments were described as pro-Western or pro-Communist. You didn't just say the such-and-such government," and the emphasis was on "whatever a particular story meant in Cold War terms" (Erbsen, 19; also Johnson, 19). Today, it is Muslim extremism that functions as an overarching news principle in many regions – to the regret of correspondents based in critical countries like Egypt, Indonesia, or Pakistan, who felt the terror focus often obscured the foreign reality itself.

---

[20] See, for example, a story from Rio de Janeiro on a cold wave damaging plants in the Brazilian state of Parana; Eduardo Gallardo, The Associated Press, May 17, 1977.

[21] Michael Weissenstein, "Ecuador flower growers in Snowden shock," The Associated Press, June 30, 2013.

Recalling early 2000s coverage of bombings in Bali, Robin McDowell (10) believed that the changing face of Indonesian terrorism was often misunderstood as the media struggled "to be willing to see it as something other than just al-Qaida and this is all linked to 9/11." Kathy Gannon (25), who has covered Afghanistan since the late 1980s, felt that the news is rarely "focused on the people of the places as opposed to the people who have come *into* the places, such as the NATO, ISAF [International Security Assistance Force], U.S. ... Their [local] voice has not really been heard or told in a strong way, other than in relations to the war on terror." In order to make those voices heard, Gannon (25–27) went where no Western reporters had dared – embedding with the Pakistani and Afghan armies:

We had to ... climb three hours in the snow, knee-deep in the snow, to get to a military outpost across the border from Afghanistan, in Pakistan, to spend time with the Pakistani soldiers. And ... it was wonderful. You're sleeping in a little container like them, freezing to death ... and kerosene lamps, that you wake up in the morning with this headache the top of your head wants to come off. ... At night you're all living together, and they're singing their songs, and you're trying to have a conversation about – and they're from Punjab, where it's 80 degrees most of the time and 130 in the summer. And they're stuck up in frigid weather and barely see in front of you because there's a snowstorm on, and the poor guys are thinking, "What the hell am I doing here?" And their frustrations – their frustrations with their own military leadership, their frustrations with the expectations of the West, and, "What do you mean I'm not doing enough, what are you trying to say?" ... [I]t was a wonderful story and we had to really work to get it. It was the first time they had ever done it, and really when they started off, they really had no intention of taking us up to the outpost. But I just kept pressing, pressing, and they said, "Oh, it's winter, it's not good." I said, "I don't care, I'm from northern Canada, please." ... It's sometimes difficult for editors to just want to hear that voice and not have the American input. And it's hard and I understand that post-2001. But I think it's just so important. ... And I have to say, and really in respect to AP ... they give me this freedom to go out. And that's not to say that I don't have to really push and push and push to get a story. There's all kind of constraints, financially and otherwise, security, and then you have to justify it vis-à-vis your security.

The story about Pakistan's 20th Lancers armored regiment, bedding down over woolen blankets on frigid floors as the wind howled around their "bullet-pocked bunker" 8,000 feet "up a mountain on one of the world's most inhospitable borders," showed the men cheering themselves up by singing and clapping along to Punjabi love songs among the choking kerosene fumes while their commander gazed "at photos of his 4-year-old daughter on his computer. But as the men chatted, it became clear that they were feeling a bit underappreciated. Why did the West accuse Pakistan of not pulling its weight in the war on terror? ... Why else were they in this hellish place if not to keep the Taliban at bay?" No wonder that, as the story pointed out, it was an "unprecedented step" for the army to allow the journalists frontline access.[22]

---

[22] Kathy Gannon, "Pakistani troops feel West undervalues their war," The Associated Press, March 11, 2012.

In much the same way, Gannon (3–4) took post-9/11 reporting trips around Central Asia's "stans" that, while focusing on Islamism, shone a light on countries normally off the radar. For example, she wrote about the religious radicalization of youths happening in unlikely places like Internet cafés in Azerbaijan and Uzbekistan, a country where former al-Qaida–affiliated men "told The Associated Press they used the terrorist trails to return home," including one interviewed in his "dusty compound hidden behind high walls, living with his four children, sitting on a colorful cushion as he rocks his infant son."[23] Donna Bryson (39–40, 43–44), who was based in Cairo in the early 2000s, also struggled to write about the place of Islam in Egyptian daily life beyond the dominant terrorism narrative that had been evident since the instant the Cairo newsroom, watching the Twin Towers fall, "knew it was going to come back to Cairo. . . . [T]here was just that sense that day that it's going to come back to the Middle East, and did." But she did write a story about the rebuilding of an ordinary "mosque down the street" in an average Cairo neighborhood:

I talked to people in the neighborhood about what that mosque meant to them . . . and just how it was the center of the community. And I was able to do that story after 9/11. And . . . it wasn't a story about anything, so much. But it was a story about Islam, really, about what Islam meant to the neighbors, to the people – we lived downtown, so to the kind of people that I would see walking back and forth from work, the people who ran grocery stores and who shined shoes and who sold apples. . . . [M]aybe that's why that story worked, because people didn't feel that they were talking to me about Islam. They were talking to me about what happened the day that the roof collapsed, and how lovely their new mosque was, you know? And I think we kind of talked around it, and maybe the story in a way talked around it, so maybe no one really understood why I did that story, but I'm also glad [I did]. . . . But then at the same time I interviewed the sheik of Al-Azhar, which was really much more a story about political Islam, and maybe that one probably got read much more. But I'm not sure it was as illuminating.

The story about Cairo's Al-Azhar University centered on the respected place it had in the Muslim world as "the ultimate Islamic institution," as one professor there said "in a sonorous tone he likely uses to good effect as a weekend preacher in his neighborhood mosque." The "barely distinguishable" Sam ibn Nuh mosque, on the contrary, was described as a living monument, one where members of its congregation – poor shopkeepers and peddlers – "sleep, eat and quarrel" and where one man died in peace, "brought to his beloved mosque by neighbors when he fell ill."[24]

---

[23] Kathy Gannon, "Uzbeks find their way home through network of terrorist trails," The Associated Press, June 8, 2005, and Kathy Gannon, "AP Exclusive: Uzbeks across Central Asia secretly picked up, jailed for Islamic militancy," The Associated Press, June 12, 2005.

[24] Donna Bryson, "Al-Azhar's philosophy influences Muslims bombarded with religious advice, bin Laden's railings," The Associated Press, June 28, 2004; Donna Bryson, "Community, experts work together to rebuild humble, beloved mosque," The Associated Press, February 26, 2002.

The danger with overarching narratives – the Cold War, Islamism, even globalization – is that they can miss not only foreign realities but other festering problems, leaving less discerning correspondents "surprised" when the faddy stories die down and the enduring, ignored ones explode. In more than 44 years with AP, Bob Reid (60–61) saw all three simplified narratives fail:

The Soviet Union collapses, the world is one – [Francis] Fukuyama and the … *End of History* [book]. News organizations are struggling at this time to find relevance, especially in foreign reporting. So in an attempt to find something, we're doing all these boring wonky globalization – missing, I might add, all the point of how globalization played out – but … just one big Kumbaya world. The public didn't care about this crap. We didn't want to write it. It was just terrible. News organizations were almost thrashing around for a raison d'être, before Mr. Bin Laden breathed new life into our struggling business. … So then, all of the sudden, in the dull, dead Middle East – "It hasn't changed in eons. It's the same people doing the same thing. … So what? Let them rot." News organizations weren't investing in the area anymore. It wasn't considered a prime bit of real estate. The world is going to be where? Europe? Developing economies? Asia! How many times have I heard, in one way or another … "the pivot to Asia." Horseshit. I heard this 40 years ago, and then when the Japanese were going to rule the world … And Japan's economy has been flat now for what? Who studies Japanese anymore? Who thinks Japan is going to be the model for the planet? Now it's China. Whoa! China!

What Is This Country Again?

Some correspondents noted that another paradoxical danger in selecting stories based on global trends, big themes, and foreign (often, still, U.S.) audience preferences is that it can obscure analysis of the foreign country per se – that correspondents are covering "home news abroad," as one study of post-9/11 U.S. press practices in Europe put it (Hahn and Lönnendonker 2009, 511). Over four decades in Rome, Simpson (13) saw interest in both Italian and Vatican news decline drastically, with editors only wanting stories about Pope Francis "if he's going to change anything" – a nearly impossible bar for religious doctrine – and declining a follow-up story about Italy's momentous 2013 elections: "I have never seen, in my life, the results, okay, and the next day they didn't want a story."[25] Paris-based Elaine Ganley (38, 16–17) doubted that today she would be allowed to fly to Tunisia, which she has covered for decades, simply "to kind of see what was going on" (as she had done in the 1990s, producing a story highlighting the criticism that "this North African nation of gentle smiles and jasmine-scented sun is a picture-postcard police state") or that she could write a big takeout on France as she had done in 1990 for a story

---

[25] A search for "Italy election" stories on the AP wire (through LexisNexis) beginning on election day, February 24, 2013, found more than a dozen business wire stories on the repercussions of the election on the Euro crisis and the world economy but only one story on election day: Victor L. Simpson and Colleen Barry, "Italians vote in polls seen key to finance crisis," The Associated Press, February 24, 2013.

called "Uncertain France." That story described how France, "once great, still grand, always fiercely proud" was "suffering an identity crisis" as it adapted to united Europe and divisive immigration:[26]

The topic hasn't changed. And yet, this is not a story that I would write today, because it's a real look at France and ... it's too French, France-centered ... would this have a readership, who would the readership be? ... and what's the hook? The hook is there's a lot of problems, that these problems still exist. ... We would have to do something European, well, let's narrow it down and get the angle. Let's do the Far Right, the Far Right in Europe. I've actually done that story, because I do follow the Far Right. But just France? Probably not. [In fact, AP writers from five countries contributed reporting on Ganley's story of how "far-right parties from the Mediterranean to Scandinavia are gaining momentum among the populace and a foothold in their nations' power structures."][27]

Country-exploring times were the "luxury days," as Ganley (38) called them. Charles Hanley (5), a New York-based roving correspondent, recalled Polowetzky "taking me by the hand and leading me to his world map on the wall and saying, 'What haven't we done?'" and sending him off to Pacific Rim islands and on an 11,000-mile journey through the Arctic to see "what's happening out there and report, with no specific story in mind or whatever" – which produced stories ranging from a U.S. antimissile base in the Marshall Islands to seal hunting with Polar Eskimos in Qaanaaq, Greenland.[28] Veteran correspondent and editor Larry Heinzerling (7, 11–12) also recalled a "flush" AP, when he could roam western and southern Africa and write beyond the obvious Cold War storylines peddled by sources, such as Soviet support for liberation movements in Portuguese colonies:

I went to cover the guerrilla war in Guinea Bissau,[29] the PAIGC was fighting a guerrilla war there, and ... I went with them for two weeks into the jungle, and they were showing me the villages and the village councils that they had set up and how they were trying to operate in the, quote, "liberated" area. But there were Portuguese warplanes flying overhead every day. ... I completed that trip, and then I went back on the Portuguese side. And we actually went back to one of the villages I had been to previously with the guerrillas. And the villagers welcomed them as if everything was fine. So, here I was, I had been in the village with the two different sides. ...

[I]t was no big problem to say I'm going to go to Ghana for two weeks and look around without any specific story in mind. And ... after you had done several of these

[26] Elaine Ganley, "Tunisia: Peaceful haven or police state?" The Associated Press, July 23, 1994; Elaine Ganley, "AP Newsfeatures: Uncertain France," The Associated Press, November 18, 1990.

[27] Elaine Ganley, "Europe's far-right in steady crawl toward power," The Associated Press, May 4, 2012.

[28] Charles J. Hanley, "Secretive islands at heart of strategic debate," The Associated Press, January 10, 1985; "Tomorrow encroaches on land of 'The People,'" The Associated Press, October 4, 1987.

[29] Larry Heinzerling, "Guerrilla War Goes On in 'Guinea-Bissau,'" *Christian Science Monitor*, November 15, 1973, 10.

countries, you began to build up a notebook of examples of corruption or examples of progress or examples of crime or something that you could then start writing broader stories because you had all the string for it. But you would go to the embassies and they'd say, "Oh, there's this interesting new dam project they're building up north." You would get ideas from dinner conversations with fellow correspondents or diplomats or businesspeople. And then wait for an opportunity to go and cover them. If we went to Senegal, you could write about Gorée Island, which was the takeoff point for slaves going to the Americas. And then do a thing about the peanut industry or the fishing industry on the coast, or the Muslim Brotherhood in the south and the Casamance. Once you got there, you got to hear things and say, "Okay, I'm going to spend two days and go look at that." And you might hear things about other countries in one country and say, "I need to go next door and see what's going on in Liberia."

Many correspondents around the world and across the decades argued for the time to immerse themselves in a country so that they could literally sniff around for news – and build illustrative stories about foreign peoples, from Cambodia to Brazil, Poland to Egypt, out of in-depth descriptions and apparently non-news items that nobody else noticed:

I remember once going to a kindergarten in China [on an arranged trip] and they put on a show for me. . . . people are out in the country and they discover an enormous turnip or a carrot or something. [. . .] And it's just wonderful and, oh, there's so much. . . . [O]ne little kid tries and tries and can't do it. Can't do it. Tries again and fails. Individual cannot do

FIGURE 3.2. After three days of marching through rough terrain with rebel forces in 1972 in "liberated areas" of then Portuguese-ruled Guinea-Bissau, West Africa correspondent Larry Heinzerling has blisters treated by a medic of the African Party for the Independence of Guinea and Cape Verde (PAIGC). (Photo courtesy of Larry Heinzerling)

it, but only when the child goes back and brings everybody – they, all together, get the turnip. ... That was the play (Graham, 33–34). [The story began critically before detailing the "ideology skit": "In kindergartens across this nation of a billion people, China's youngest citizens are the model toddlers of a society that rewards discipline above all. But some parents say the price of such youthful good behavior is stifled creativity. For 9 million children in state-run kindergartens, the powerful and primary lesson is: Don't be an individual, be a team player. ... In vain a 4-year-old girl tries to pull up a monumental turnip in a kindergarten morality play. 'I can't do it alone,' she wails in defeat."][30]

I saw a small advertisement in the Polish newspaper ... it was a tour agency advertising a trip to Katyn [in the USSR]. Nobody had been to Katyn since the massacre [in 1940 of thousands of Poles by Soviet secret police]. ... And the Soviet Union had not collapsed yet, the Berlin Wall wasn't down. ... We went with a photographer and some others, and we took the train with these families to the Katyn Forest and ... it was viscerally one of those moments. ... But it's the kind of story that you could have put aside, and nobody would have ever noticed if you had never done it (Seward, 6). [Seward's story brimmed with that visceral emotion, beginning thus: "Jerzy Rudzisnki took one look at the Soviet memorial at Katyn dedicated to 'Victims of Fascism – Polish officers shot by the Nazis in 1941.' Then, the 53-year-old sculptor turned away bitterly, quickly climbed 15 feet up a pine tree, and nailed in a small wooden plaque inscribed with his father's name and true date of death: 1940. Uniformed and plainclothes Soviet police watched him from afar but did nothing."][31]

[W]e were driving past Tahrir Square [in Cairo] and there was this enormous picture of [President Hosni] Mubarak's son, a big billboard like I had never seen before. And a lot of discussion then was whether Mubarak was trying to order the succession in favor of his son, and I wrote a story about this and about how amazing it is that this huge billboard is on. ... And as a result of that story, they took it down. And I think that the regime was amazed that anyone would see it as worth a story. ... I don't know how they would think that people would not notice it, but they didn't think it was noticeable in that sense, they didn't think it was newsworthy (Bryson, 36–37). [The story, aside from a tongue-in-cheek lead and ending featuring a shoeshiner across the billboard who had missed the connection between Mubarak's son and the Olympians he was portrayed with, described in depth the history of Gamal Mubarak's behind-the-scenes rise to power.][32]

[In Recife] I learned about a slave leader, who was called ... Zumbi. ... And [in the 1600s] he set up a small group of local farmers, former slave farmers, on the top of a hill. ... And they competed with the sugarcane and other tropical products, and ... these Portuguese farmers, they felt threatened economically by this group. ... At some point the colonial army stepped in ... and destroyed the whole settlement, and either arrested or killed the runaway slaves. ... They found Zumbi and – this is the story – he was so badly tortured that it spread terror among the black population down here. ... It seemed to me a very interesting story because of the background we have about Brazil as not having this

---

[30] Victoria Graham, "China's model toddlers learn life's requirements early," The Associated Press, March 16, 1981.

[31] Deborah G. Seward, "In Katyn's dark woods, relatives mourn murdered officers," The Associated Press, October 31, 1989.

[32] Donna Bryson, "Billboard evokes questions about presidential aspirations of Mubarak's son," The Associated Press, September 10, 2004.

kind of turbulence or being exemplary – it is, but there are some not-so-beautiful chapters in its history. . . . The idea was that on the top of the hill everything looked like how they looked 400 years earlier. . . . Humble people were still working the way they did 400 years ago . . . you could find an explanation why that happened . . . with [President Luiz Inácio] Lula da Silva and the Partido dos Trabalhadores [Workers' Party] coming to power and trying to rescue all that population of excluded from the social and economic life of this country (Olmos, 27–29). [The story began with Zumbi's granite statue "in a clearing high in these green hills, a lonely tribute to a broken dream . . . equality remains a distant dream for millions of black and mixed-race Brazilians."][33]

After the Khmer Rouge collapsed, people who had been killers would return to the same villages where they (a) grew up, and (b) were killing people. . . . These are like agrarian communities, you go to the market and you see the guy that you saw kill somebody or who was responsible for killing your family, and how do you deal with that? And the reason I became interested in it was because, when it comes to someone stealing a motorcycle or stealing something from you, you kill them. It would be like a mob attack of people. But when it came to this guy walking in the market, it's like, "Hi." "Hi, Pak." . . . So then it becomes more of a why, anthropologically speaking or sociologically speaking, what's going on here? Why are people reacting this way? (McDowell, 2–3). [Her story answered, in part, "out of tolerance, fear, fatigue or a sense of powerlessness" – especially if the horrors were committed by someone in authority, like Ta Karoby, a former prison commander who survivors said ate his victims' livers and McDowell found still living in the same village, "treated no differently than any other resident."][34]

[P]robably one of the biggest projects that I've ever done [was] basically looking at the original route of the Pan-American Highway . . . and traveling to every country along that route and driving not all of the highway but a big chunk of it . . . trying to capture how societies were changing there. . . . And looking at the places where it was supposed to have been built but never got there, and how people are living very differently there from the ways that they live in the places that the highway's come to (Price, 4). [Price's story opened with a "bare-chested 19-year-old mother," "painted chin to toe with the black juice of the jagua fruit," wondering how long it would take her to reach her country's capital, Panama City, by canoe and bus – even though her village of thatched-roof huts on stilts was supposed to be "at the center of the most ambitious development scheme in the Western Hemisphere," the Pan American Highway.][35]

PEOPLE STORIES AND BIG PEOPLE STORIES

Full country immersion facilitated doing those "people stories," but in all countries a recurring choice has been balancing covering the people and the "big people" (presidents, princes, popes, and pop stars). Even though the "basic news of affairs of state, commerce, and politics" cannot be missed, AP's

[33] Harold Olmos, "Brazil's self-image as 'racial democracy' a myth, blacks say," *The Associated Press*, January 2, 1996.
[34] Robin McDowell, "Cambodia's killers and victims live side-by-side," *The Associated Press*, February 14, 1998.
[35] Niko Price, "Unfinished road a tribute to dashed dream of unified Americas," *The Associated Press*, November 16, 2002.

mission to include how foreign peoples lived outside a few circles of power can be said to start with this 1925 directive by general manager Kent Cooper (Cooper 1959, 94–95):

To acquaint American newspaper readers with life as it is lived by the hundreds of millions on the other continents, the foreign staffs ... shall tell what is happening in and what interests the people of the countries to which they are assigned. They shall continue to report the news of governments, of course, but they also shall present fully for American readers a picture of the lives of the people, their varied activities and interests, their joys and their sorrows, their amusements and their devotions, their work and their play. ... To do this they must go out of the beaten paths of travel to observe and write of life in the towns and villages of which readers in this country may never have heard. We are to have date lines from wherever spot news or features can be found, not just from the capitals of a few countries.

Cooper's strategy aimed to convince AP members to pay more for expanded services, as well as to attract stronger journalists to the cooperative. It seemed to work, given that one December 1925 Kansas City *Star* editorial on AP foreign correspondence gushed: "The Associated Press has begun to live up to the Greek philosopher's saying that nothing human was alien to him. It has not lowered its standards. ... It is striving to report every phase of the human spectacle" (quoted in Cooper 1959, 96–97). The same directive applied to World War coverage, when Cooper urged AP correspondents to bring the war home to Americans by getting a story "about a boy from each home town where The Associated Press had a member paper" (Cooper 1959, 244–245) – and war correspondents from World War II to Iraq have covered that personal view from the trenches.

In his sunny apartment overlooking New York's East River, Bria (16) vividly remembered his stories about the end of World War II in Italy nearly 70 years earlier – not "the headquarters story about advancing 10 miles" but how American soldiers had taught Italians to say "okay" but not quite to eat canned corn (despite leaving behind "an unshakable conviction that Americans eat only out of cans"), and how Romans, when not making a brisk trade "selling England and America" (black market cigarettes produced there), lined up at public fountains with German-issued jerry cans because the water supply was iffy but Trevi and its kin kept gurgling.[36] From "somewhere in Korea" – actual dateline – one correspondent wrote of how GIs liked the "new, light, all-metal prefabricated bunker" they called "Old Baldy," which could give them "quick cover from thunderous Communist shelling."[37] Chain-smoking in his suburban Virginia home, George McArthur (4, 23) remembered his proudest story from the Korean War 60 years before, a 400-word take that "practically wrote itself" on an unlikely and unassuming hero, "Worm":

[A] little kid who was sitting in ... the regimental headquarters, one night at 3 a.m., and the perimeter of his outfit was raided and this kid was all alone. But as always at that

---

[36] George Bria, "GIs Are Leaving Mark on Italy," *Washington Post*, Mary 25, 1947, B2; George Bria, "You Can Blow Rings around Rome for $2.50," *Washington Post*, December 2, 1945, B3.

[37] Sam Summerlin, "'Old Baldy' Tests Metal of Bunkers," *Washington Post*, October 5, 1952, M8.

time, there are a lot of rifles around and that kid went over and picked up three loaded M-16s with the magazines full and went outside and stood off a goddamn squad or platoon of the bad folks and shot up some. There were a lot of dead around there the next morning. And he did it all as a matter of course. And the kid's nickname, I always remember, was "Worm." He was tall and skinny. And the kicker of my story was one of the reasons he did as he did, "I didn't like being called Worm, but I guess they'll do it anyway."

When she helped cover U.S. combat troops leaving Vietnam in 1973, Edie Lederer (6; 2002, 169) zoomed in on Vietnamese civilians who were certain to feel the lack of GIs – "the hundreds and hundreds of bar girls," most of whom were "pretty stoic, though many wondered how they, and their half-American children, would survive":

And I got a couple of guys who were friends of mine to take me barhopping [for three nights], so I interviewed bar girls. . . . [Being] the newest person in the bureau, I knew that the guys would do all the big military stuff. And I tried to think of something that would be really interesting and show a different side of the war and sort of the impact on the people, the South Vietnamese.

Beyond conflict, choosing the "little people" often meant following the lead of an official pronouncement to explore a country's daily rhythm, instead of focusing on ultimately inconsequential politicking. Covering Brazil's economic boom in the early 2000s, Clendenning (2–3) traveled twice to one of the poorest towns, Guaribas, to analyze the impact of President Lula da Silva's "zero hunger" initiative, which gave monthly money handouts to female heads of household:

I remember talking with one family where basically they didn't have to worry as much about money for food, so now they were starting to save some money . . . they were having the kind of debate to purchase things that had never been options for them before. . . . When Lula was up for reelection, his big claim to fame was "Okay, I've lifted all these people out of poverty." So we went back to revisit the place we visited before, to see, hey, how are things now here, three years later. And this town, which actually hadn't been a Lula supporter too much the previous time we went, was now totally in support of him *and* they had running water in the town now. They'd created a huge cistern system, and basically we were going around and people were showing us . . . turn on a tap and show us how they had running water.

The first story opened with a trip "a thousand miles from Rio de Janeiro's beaches and not far from the Mountains of Confusion," down "a dirt road with potholes big enough to swallow cars," to interviews with "rail-thin" Isaias Conrado Alves, who kept in a "grimy sack" "his most valuable possession: A yellow ID card entitling him to 50 reals, or about $17, every month for food," and Valdenos Alves, whose dream with the money saved for food was to buy a table and four chairs so his wife and children could get "off the packed dirt floor at dinnertime." Three years later, we hear from both Alveses again: Isaias, whose crop failed but who avoided starvation thanks to the "Zero Hunger" program, showing Clendenning "with a toothless grin" the strong flow from the water tap outside his house, and Valdenos now fighting with his wife over the new disposable income, which he spent on a 26-channel satellite TV system when she wanted a refrigerator and a new roof.[38]

In China in 1999 during the Y2K craze, another correspondent found an even more off-the-beaten-road window into Chinese society – UFO sightings, "treated with unexpected seriousness in this country usually straightjacketed by its communist leaders":[39]

I noticed that in the Chinese newspapers there started to be all these little reports about UFO sightings, over a period of a couple of months . . . and in different parts of China. It was kind of odd. It's not the sort of thing that state media usually reported on. . . . So I went and found this little village [outside Beijing] where supposedly they had found it and it was a really brutally cold December day, which was not good because it meant nobody was outside. And my experience back then was, again, you wander around a village and you're very visible and the next thing you know, the Communist Party secretary is telling you you can't be there. . . . So I go over to this hall where these workers are working on the roof and I tell them, "I'm a reporter from AP and I saw the report about the UFO." And they said, "Oh, we don't know anything about that, but you should ask Party Secretary Chen." And I kind of roll my eyes and think, "Oh no, this is doomed." But then, Party Secretary Chen appears and he's like, "You want to know about the UFO! Well, let me tell you!" And he says, "Some people think it was a UFO and some people think it was a ray of light of the Buddha, but I don't want people to say that, because then they might think that we're Falun Gong. So we're just going to call it an auspicious sign." . . . I actually had spent so much time reporting on it that I began to dread turning this story in, because I knew that New York was going to sort of think I had just really lost my mind. (Hutzler, 30–31)

Nevertheless, officialdom and "big people" still have their place. McArthur (18) did not rely solely on "Worm" and his brothers-in-arms to cover the wars in Korea and Vietnam:

The GI will, once you establish some friendship with him . . . kinship, he's told you all he knows at about 15 minutes. . . . [Y]ou don't interview the GI for information until you get down to the level of where they mix the cement. . . . I have tremendous respect for the American soldier, and enjoyed talking to them, and always established a rapport. But if I wanted some information, I went to the fucking colonel. And to the general if I had to, and to the four-star if I had to.

Beyond generals, other global names hog a disproportionate share of the spotlight – few more consistently than popes and British royals. From the 1940s to today, Rome gets a large foreign press corps because of the Vatican,

[38] Alan Clendenning, "Remote farm town is test case for anti-hunger campaign introduced by Brazil's president," The Associated Press, April 21, 2003; Alan Clendenning, "Running water, money for food: 'Zero Hunger' augurs easy re-election for Brazil's Lula," The Associated Press, September 16, 2006.

[39] Charles Hutzler, "China sees UFOs and calls it science, not superstition," The Associated Press, January 3, 2000.

but how much coverage the Vatican gets depends on how popular the pope is (Bria, 8; Simpson, 7–8). The "quirky" Windsor house is also a "natural," according to two correspondents who spent decades in London – one of whom ironically added that in those stories "you don't add a paragraph saying this is all of course totally irrelevant in the real world" (Barr, 9–10, 4; Belkind, 19). Larger-than-life political figures that got oversize coverage included Soviet leaders and, more "locally," such opposites as Nelson Mandela and Augusto Pinochet – and Chile-born Latin America correspondent Gallardo (12) wondered about the vagaries of notoriety, how Pinochet had become "*the* name of Chile":

> He became sort of a symbol of brutality and abuse. [Marxist President Salvador] Allende was very well-known also, but then he had the competition from Castro and Guevara. But Pinochet is all by himself, and that's really strange because the first Brazilian military dictators were probably as brutal as Pinochet or even more. Argentina! I mean they killed tens of thousands of people, thousands of people . . . Would you remember the names of the Argentine dictators? [Jorge Rafael] Videla, [Emilio Eduardo] Massera – but Pinochet? Ask anybody anywhere.

WHO GETS TO CHOOSE THE NEWS?

One of the inherent tensions in choosing what is news, as all the sections above suggest and Chapter 11 discusses, centers around who makes the decision – the correspondent on the ground or editors elsewhere? The majority of correspondents said they usually got to pick what to write about instead of receiving direction, but their sense of the story depended on how long they had been on assignment. Frazier (32), shocked by the poverty and despair in Haiti, wrote about "rooms full of babies" in the morgue and "men with open sores on their legs washing them off in sewer ditches . . . this was the fresh eye going in. Somebody who had lived there for five years probably wouldn't write about it, but I did." Other reporters new to Beijing or Paris found quirky stories that old hands might have passed over in the pursuit of meatier news, such as the famously risqué Lido nightclub doing a Christmas show for children – including one toddler in the front row who "waved frantically as Santa burst onto the stage, joining a dance line with showgirls in feather headdresses and G-strings" (Doland, 1).[40] The non-breaking news stories just need a bit more convincing of editors, as McDowell (20–21) found out when she offered an unexpected take on the plight of Southeast Asian female migrant workers in the Persian Gulf, many of whom are abused by their employers and, in a few high-profile cases, react by killing them and are then sentenced to beheading. One woman was rescued from death row after Indonesians

---

[40] Angela Doland, "Paris club goes from topless dancers to Christmas for the kids," The Associated Press, December 8, 1998.

raised enough money to buy her freedom – only to find herself "rich and hated," accused of having become "like a nut that forgot its shell":[41]

They raised more money than the blood money needed, so she got the rest, and it wasn't a huge amount, but it was enough to make her super-rich in her village. And it created so much jealousy and hatred, she's totally ostracized because she built a new house, she's now wearing a nice golden necklace . . . It was kind of just to me an interesting story on: If you give money to somebody, a charity or anything like that, do you really have a right to judge how it's spent? . . . It's not like a natural story. It's not a story that ends up in the front of the *New York Times*, necessarily. But it is a real moral dilemma story. . . . I can always get those stories through, but . . . I have to have a lot of other good stories to – [editors] have to kind of trust you, and you have to be able to really argue for it.

The arguing can also go the other way. Veteran correspondent Reid (51–52), with AP for three decades when he was sent to work on the Afghanistan war desk, had to fight against a few inopportune story ideas from New York:

And frankly, [after the war started] they demanded some stories that I said, we run this, they're going to throw us out in a heartbeat, and [AP Afghanistan local reporter] Amir Shah's so deep into a Taliban jail there's no way he'll ever get out. So there was a lot of back and forth and debating, what are the limits, how far can we go? Should we really do a story that says there are plenty of targets left and there's this and this and this – whoa!!! That was actually a request. . . . Yeah, ministries that had not been bombed out. In the mind of an American, this isn't a great secret. . . . But you start writing this stuff in Taliban-controlled Afghanistan, you're a spy. And the truth of the matter is most of the Taliban gunmen didn't want us in there anyway. So that had to be discouraged. . . . So you had one story, one story comes and goes, and you lost your person inside . . . it took a lot of arguments.

Opportunities and Challenges of Writing for "Impact"

Some arguments also greeted AP executives' early 2010s new news selection focus on "impact" journalism – border-spanning, big-theme, exclusive, unique, groundbreaking stories – dictated by shrinking resources and the imperative to distinguish AP, in the audience's eyes, from professional (and amateur) competition. In the best cases, this "deep, explaining" approach can move a stalled, often repetitive narrative forward, as in coverage of the Israeli-Palestinian conflict (with, for example, an analysis of the "default outcome of doing nothing in Israel-Palestine being one state that will not be what the Israelis want" because of demographics; Perry, 19)[42] or the unrest across North Africa:

I had proposed this unemployment story because just from living here [in the West Bank], I know how frustrating it is. I know lots of young, especially young men, who

---

[41] Robin McDowell, "New ordeal for Indonesian who escaped Saudi sword," The Associated Press, September 6, 2011.

[42] See, for example, Dan Perry and Josef Federman, "AP Analysis: In Mideast, partial deal tantalizes," The Associated Press, March 19, 2013.

don't have work. Some of them are high school dropouts, others are university gradu-
ates, but there is not just enough jobs around. And if they don't have a job, they can't get
married . . . here you have to go to the father of the bride and ask for her hand, and then
the father will say, "Well, do you have the house, do you have the gold, do you have the
dowry, do you have etc." . . . all these young lives are on hold, and I just thought that this
is a really interesting way of looking at the post–Arab Spring situation. And the Arab
world still has on average the highest youth unemployment in the world . . . And then we
thought of how to present it. . . . Tunisia came up and the incredible figure of 178 self-
immolations – out of those I think 143 deadly – and then we got the plan together and
this involved planning with our international features editors and Mideast chief and big,
big collaboration. Then I got to go to Tunisia for five days, follow the case. I'd done the
sort of the macro, the World Bank and all of these things already previously. . . . It's again
sort of to stand out, not just with AP's credibility, but also with the insightful stories that
carry a bit of weight. In this sea of opinion and not very well-documented or pseudo-
journalism that some people produce – I'm not talking about my colleagues, I'm talking
about the people who just have a laptop and an opinion – so you really need to produce
this kind of quality stuff to stand out. (Laub, 38–39)

Laub's story centered on 27-year-old Adel Khedri, who one morning in 2013
went to the busy Tunis boulevard where he peddled cigarettes, had an espresso
with milk, stopped in front of a theater, and set himself on fire – just like the other
"high school dropout-turned-street vendor [who] launched the Arab Spring.
These two book-ends of a revolution that toppled four Arab dictators show
how little has changed in between for millions of jobless, hopeless 20-
somethings across the Middle East and North Africa. The difficulty of finding a
job, which helped spark the unrest, is now a prescription for continued turmoil."
The story then wove trends and figures with Adel's experience, including the
details that remained "fuzzy" despite AP interviews with two dozen people, from
his family to burn center doctors to witnesses to his suicide.[43]

But several veteran correspondents, some still working for AP, worried that
finding an impactful story that nobody had done – particularly in countries with
competitive, independent local media – is such a high bar that it might mean
missing the less attention-grabbing events that can define a country: "sometimes
when you do those little stories, it leads you to see a pattern of a more important
story, or to understand a more important story in greater depth, because you're
following it" (Rice, 15). It also appeared like a major reinterpretation of the
mission of being "the wire service of record," when "we'd do stories because we
thought, even though hardly anybody's going to read this story, probably, it's
something that we just need to have a record of" (Talmadge, 13). Eric Talmadge
(14–15), who spent nearly 25 years in Japan before transferring to the Pyongyang
bureau, offered the example of reports about a Japanese family starving to death:

I had an editor in Bangkok [regional desk] say, "Shouldn't we do this story? I mean a
family starving in Japan, in an affluent country like Japan." I thought about it, and I had

---

[43] Karin Laub, "Vendor's suicide reflects despair of Mideast youth," The Associated Press, May 11,
2013.

read the story, of course, and considered it. ... It was that particular family's situation that led them into that, and it doesn't really say anything about the country, it doesn't say anything about a trend. It's just a sad thing that happened, but it really doesn't mean anything in a bigger sense of where Japan is going. So we just passed it. ... [T]hat would be the good interpretation. The other interpretation is that I don't have time for this story. If the family has starved to death, you could probably write a very compelling piece about what happened to them as individuals. You'd have to really get into it, though, and we just don't have the resources for that. So, in that balance, that story was not the kind of thing that we're looking at to do so much. And we're passing a lot more stories like that, that aren't really breaking news, that are developments. People who aren't interested in Japan probably aren't going to care all that much about this. If that's the case, we just don't do it. ... You have to be a lot more intelligent, and you have to take a lot more responsibility for what you do write because you're not writing a lot of stuff. So you can't just fall back on, "Well, we did that 200-word story the other day about that." You don't have that 200-word story to say, "We covered that." You actually have to cover it in a significant and meaningful way now.

PREDICTING THE BIG STORIES – AND MISSING A FEW

The high-wire act of covering significant breaking news while also producing in-depth "impact" pieces stresses perhaps the hardest news judgment skill correspondents have needed over time – not only to know a story when they see one, but to predict where and how it might develop. As award-winning Vietnam correspondent Malcolm Browne put it, the "daily work ... consisted mostly of trying to guess where news would break and being on the spot when it did" (Browne 1993, 126). Many correspondents noted how local contacts, shoe-leather reporting, and the experience-acquired sixth sense that "something is wrong here" are critical alert systems. Some correspondents in the Soviet Union and Eastern Europe in the 1980s up to 1991 had keen eyes for jarring daily life details that hinted at Communism's disintegration, though others felt it still caught them unawares (see more in this chapter's box):

One of my earlier stories was about the popularity of a country music festival with American country music in Poland, but translated into Polish. But it was a story that said a bit about how Poles, in spite of martial law and being under the boot of Moscow, really were longing to affiliate with America, so they would find something like a country music festival that wouldn't easily be banned (Daniszewski, 3–4). [The story about "the foot-stompingest tribute to American country" "this side of the Vistula" began, "Although some Communist officials criticize it as 'Ronald Reagan music,' more than 15,000 Polish good ole' boys and girls braved rainy skies one weekend last month to swing to Nashville-style music at a rollicking country *piknik*."][44]

There were other parts of the Soviet Union that ... within people's memory, had suffered famine and food shortages ... but in Moscow ... there had always been bread in the stores. [B]read was subsidized, was unbelievably cheap – it was literally kopecks per

---

[44] John Daniszewski, "Country-Western May Be 'Ronald Reagan Music,' but the Good Ole' Poles Like It," *Los Angeles Times*, September 13, 1987.

loaf. And it was always there, and then in 1990, there was one day when there were bread lines, and there just wasn't bread in the stores. . . . I went to a friend's apartment for a very humble, but delicious, dinner of roasted potatoes with cheese and his wife . . . said, "there's no bread in the stores today." And I left dinner early to run back to the bureau (Cooperman, 2). [Cooperman's story featured many Muscovites in line, speaking darkly about what this shortage portended.][45]

Soviet society was literally near collapse while we were there. It was in its death throes as a system, we had no inkling of this. . . . You just couldn't quite grasp how the thing really worked, how a society could be so deprived and be a world power. . . . I personally was always a little amazed that people put up, how they could put up with this. But of course they were under terrible surveillance, and if you complained you'd lose your job. Or worse. . . . [K]nowing what we know now, I think we may have . . . not emphasized enough how precarious that system was. [W]e as correspondents couldn't really see behind the facade deep enough. And that's because the government was in total control. (Minthorn, 5, 10)

Ironically, the experience with Soviet Communism led correspondents in Cuba to prepare for the sudden demise of the Castro regime – "this big story, which still hasn't happened," as Anita Snow (20), who reopened the AP bureau in Havana after decades, put it. Cuba's political story has continued to be one of controlled, incremental change instead of a sweeping "new generation" that many had expected would replace revolutionary leaders.

Other stories have defied predictions, such as the perennially stalled Middle East peace process, which correspondents have covered waiting for a breakthrough for decades (Rice, 1), and, in contrast, South Africa's 1994 first post-apartheid election, where parachuted war correspondents found peaceful change instead of civil war (Bryson, 3–5). When the world, and the media, is not watching – when something happens "outside the flow of events as you perceive them" (Reid, 60) – sensing a big story is even harder, as Mideast regional editor Sally Buzbee (13) found out in the mid-2000s when Sudan imploded in civil war and AP "basically peeled" a reporter off to focus on the conflict, with no logistical support from local regimes and "always in danger of getting robbed or killed." Predicting where American bombs will fall has also been necessary not only to position AP for war coverage, but to assess what stories are needed before conflict erupts, as two veterans of war reporting recalled. Richard Pyle (3–4b), who had been in Bahrain following the low-intensity naval conflict over oil supplies, figured, correctly, not only that Iraq's 1991 invasion of Kuwait would mean a U.S. war, but also that information about the war would be controlled by U.S. General Norman Schwartzkopf's headquarters in Saudi Arabia, where AP set up its Gulf War operations. Right

---

[45] Alan Cooperman, "Bread in short supply in Moscow for first time since Khrushchev," The Associated Press, September, 3, 1990; John Daniszewski had written in a similar vein about bread and other food shortages in Communist Poland, quoting one shopper staring at bare shelves and saying, "Maybe there's a war coming"; "For Polish consumers: Bare shelves, long lines," The Associated Press, July 31, 1989.

after 9/11, Reid helped direct coverage of how Afghanistan and Pakistan were preparing for war and, after the United States attacked, of the action itself, coordinating stories ranging from Washington to refugee camps in Chaman.

But even experienced correspondents admitted sometimes missing the signs of crucial sociopolitical shifts in the scram of breaking news ("too close to the trees to see the forest," as several correspondents put it) and, far more troubling, due to the persistence of set narratives. Reid's examples are worth quoting at length, because they reveal how defining stories were hard to see before they exploded – from the Arab Spring's sudden rise and drastic turn to Islamist radicalization to Iraq's self-combustion in sectional violence, realities that smashed the rosy lens of a "democratic Middle East" that had tinted much initial U.S. coverage:

I'd been hearing about the Egyptian people are fed up and are about to rise up ... since 1982. And it had never happened. And no one could really explain why it had never happened. ... I went to Thanksgiving dinner with some friends, the Thanksgiving before [the 2011 uprising] started in Egypt ... and there was this one young guy there ... from a connected family ... and he was just convinced that it was all going to blow up, and imminently, and people are just fed up with this, blah blah. I kind of dismissed him as, number one, he's young and anxious, plus he's been in the States for a long time getting his education ... so he's coming in with an American sense of frustration, and the Egyptians who had been here and put up with this for 5,000 years haven't reached quite that level. Well of course he was right. ... Again, it's really hard to predict how this stuff develops. Sometimes it develops differently when all the combustibles are still there. God only knows why this one blew up and the last dozen passed in the night[46] (Reid, 71–72).

It was too broad, and too big, and too rolling. ... Who would have thought there would have been a two-and-a-half-year war with more deaths than the Iraq War as a result of Syria? Who would have ever thought that the U.S. would have sanctioned the crackdown in Bahrain and backed off from any pressure of significant amount, to the point that senior diplomats were complaining to me that "you should write more about Bahrain so we can leverage that"? ... I think there was one common theme we could have written and predicted, but we would have had trouble defending it, and the story would have been seen as too Israeli – which is, all the stuff at the end of the day is going to do nothing but play into the hand of Islamists. And that's all you're going to get. ... Had we done that, though ... we would have been challenged as being set in designing this line, and how would we have defended against it before the events had played out that way themselves? (Reid, 75)

Iraq broke relations with the United States in 1990, or vice versa, and there wasn't really a lot of knowledge about Iraq ... not only within the U.S. government, but in the press corps either. ... Saddam Hussein got hanged for an event that got this much copy in *The Times* of London, and [a] LexisNexis search proved that was the only mention of it.[47] ... Because there were people who did know Iraq, many of them Iraqis, and they had been talking about

---

[46] Among many stories chronicling Egypt's failed protests, see Paul Schemm, "Egypt's workers battle police amid rising economic discontent," The Associated Press, April 7, 2008.

[47] In December 2006, Saddam was executed by hanging after being convicted on charges of having ordered the killing of 148 men and boys after an assassination attempt against him in 1982.

this and warning about this, but people didn't listen to them. That first of all, it'll be a bloodbath, too many scores to settle, and then it will break down along tribal lines, and then it will break down along Shia/Sunni lines, and no one will agree with anyone and blah blah blah blah. And when this began to happen, it was almost like it was a bit of a surprise. (Reid, 57–58)

Steven Hurst (7), who like Reid was Baghdad bureau chief, argued that by the mid-2000s, the story of the Iraq War consisted of "trying to tell what was going on in Iraq across society ... a war inside of Iraq which the United States was standing watching and trying to keep the sides apart and getting killed by both, a hated occupation force." But it was a story whose early signs were often hard to recognize, even when reporters happened to be in the middle of portentous events and had an inkling of their vast significance, as in Reid's (58–59) retelling of the assassination of Imam Al-Khoei, who had returned from exile to advocate for Iraqi Shiites to cooperate with American forces and was murdered by a mob apparently incited by the al-Sadr clan:[48]

So at one point this [reporter] in Kuwait said, "The military has invited us on a trip to Najaf tomorrow, should I go?" "Well, yeah, but what's it about?" "Well, something about a reconciliation meeting." These things are a dime a dozen. Nobody thinks much of them. But it's not going to cost us any money, and the guy's got nothing else to do; his job is to sit there and wait by the phone until he's invited to go see something. What am I going to do, tell him no, the one time he gets an offer? So yes, go up there. But the local military people didn't have a clear idea of who was going to attend the meeting, and it was a little bit vague, and security, and we can't tell you too much until you get there. So then, lo and behold, in the afternoon, we get this call from the same guy, who was a very sharp guy ... [but] he's no Middle Eastern hand, he's been thrown into this thing. ... [H]e calls and says, "Something has gone wrong with this meeting, we're not sure ... we think there was a falling out and one of the guys may have gotten killed." ... What did this set in motion? All the fighting with Muqtada, the battle of Najaf, the battle of Karbala, the various terrorism, the backlash on the destruction of the Golden Dome [Al-Askari Mosque] in Samarra that plunged the nation in civil war. All that was rooted in this one little meeting in one little town that we weren't sure even who the participants were, much less sensed the significance of what was at play here.

Stretched resources, lack of in-depth local knowledge, the attempts of many actors to keep media away, sheer lack of time – all led to missed opportunities to tell more prescient stories, or to tell some stories at all. Charles Hutzler (29–30), a longtime China correspondent, said one miss

---

[48] As the AP story added, "The bloodshed underscored how difficult it will be to bridge deep enmities and political rivalries in Iraq as the American military and interim administration led by retired U.S. Gen. Jay Garner tries to fill the power vacuum left by the collapse of Saddam's regime. The U.S. military had been eager to display the meeting at the shrine of Imam Ali, considered by Shiites the successor to the prophet Muhammad. The military flew two helicopters of journalists to the holy city of Najaf to see it. But the group arrived at the site too late to witness what happened." Patrick McDowell, "Two Islamic clerics die in attack at Shiite shrine at meeting meant to promote peace, witnesses say," The Associated Press, April 11, 2003.

from his first trip to Xinjiang continues to "nag" him because he did not "know the story well enough to clue in to the signals" that could have given him a rare early insight into Muslim separatism. In the regional capital of Urumqi, after wrapping up an interview, his Uighur "handler" from the Foreign Affairs Office took him to lunch and, after an "elliptical" conversation about the Uighurs' relationship with the separatist movement, offered to show him a shopping mall:

And it's one of these, a multistory, ugly, nondescript concrete building in which retailers rent little different spaces, right? ... There are places like this all over China. And ... he said, "This was started by a woman, by a Uighur woman who really wants to help her people." And I kind of didn't think anything of it, and I didn't do anything with it. And that woman ... was in fact this Rebiya Kadeer, and it was in 1994, 1995, she was really being celebrated as this model Uighur entrepreneur and very much seen as being sort of supportive of the government. But she then actually, later, has gone on to be ... their best-known advocate of separatism and ... was forced into exile, basically. ... [The handler] was running quite a risk, and I just didn't know how to assimilate the information.

Another challenge for correspondents is to see behind the "commonsense" narratives, often popular in U.S. political and diplomatic circles, that can obfuscate reality, with dire consequences for U.S. public opinion and policymaking. Rosenblum (11) felt media missed how African conflicts were at heart fought as a proxy Cold War, "a huge, international, great game going on at the level of these individual little countries." Frazier (40–41) wished he could have spent more time studying just whom the guerrilla wars were substituting for "dreadful" regimes in Central America:

We say well this guy here is no good, and he needs to go, and we don't pay any attention to who is going to come in and take over. Who do they think is going to come in, the Girl Scouts? I don't think so. ... Governments founded in violence tend to stay violent and remain by violence, or the threat of it, and I'm not sure we looked at that, at the time, as hard as we should have. ... I don't know how you do that on the spot. History is about change. Change happens in strange, different ways, over time sometimes and sometimes rapidly. We considered ourselves trying to do a fast read on history during those years, because nobody else was doing it.

Three veteran correspondents – in the Middle East, Mexico, and South Asia, respectively – discussed how event-oriented coverage of the Arab Spring, Mexican politics, and the war in Afghanistan could hew too close to simplified Western narratives like "democracy" or "winning hearts and minds," and how they tried to explore the local sensibilities that better explained what was happening – or would happen:

I think at the time we were really very much wrapped up in the day-to-day, because sometimes the developments were so huge that you try to keep up. ... What I've seen in retrospect, I think, is that the Arab Spring is just so much more than what I think sometimes is the Western perspective of people rising up against dictatorships. Because as part of my current research, it's so much about young people rising up or protesting the lack of a real future. ... So I think it's too simple to just say an uprising against dictatorship ... because that's kind of a neat but very simplified narrative. And once you're done catching up with the spot developments, I think the challenge then is to try to write more about what really motivated or what still motivates people and what the concerns are and so forth. But when it's a huge story like the Libyan Revolution, seriously, as an agency reporter you just, "Oh, I got to do this, and I got to say that," and you try to catch your breath and then maybe later you think about it. (Laub, 32–33)

[Reporting on the end of Mexico's PRI reign in 2000] was also something where having covered it for a long time helped, because ... you understood how long, how far back it went. ... After Fox won, there were people saying, "Thank you, Vicente Fox, for democracy." Well, it wasn't Vicente Fox who brought democracy; democracy brought Vicente Fox. ... But as you watch that, you start to understand the arc of how things are moving (Rice, 16). [One of Rice's dozens of stories about the 2000 election traced the "long struggle" to end the PRI rule, opening with a vignette of Fox when he had been a freshman congressman protesting another rigged election by hanging fraudulent ballots on his ears and the then president-elect asking his aides, "Who does he think he is?"][49]

I met with family members [in Wardak Province] who said that their relatives had been taken and talked about how heavy-handed and abusive the U.S. special forces were and gave incidents ... like where they've been stopped and beaten up and humiliated and then sent on their way, because no, they're not Taliban, but they were accused of it. ... [An earlier story I did] was dated September 2002.[50] Almost exactly the same. And this was from Uruzgan and "Okay, they should leave now, they don't understand our culture, there are no more Taliban here, it's finished, goodbye." ... And here was 2013, and I had written in 2002, September, about this. ... You could tell that you had disenfranchised a whole section of the population, the Pashtuns. ... I did a story about how 2,000 had come ... to join the police and the army, which was being run by the Northern Alliance. They were humiliated. Everybody said, "Oh, Taliban. You're Pashtuns, you're Taliban, you're nothing." And so they all went back, and the deputy police chief said ... "All but four joined the Taliban." He says, "I have four, but all the rest ran up into the hills." ... In a way it sort of vindicates what we were writing back in 2002, and it's taken this long. (Gannon, 67–68)

Gannon's story from Wardak's capital, Maidan Shahr, relied on dozens of interviews to portray the "hostility," including a story from Mohammed Nabi, whose son had also been picked up by U.S. special forces and who told of how he and about 80 other men were detained after Friday prayers at their village mosque: "'For two hours, we stood in the snow,' Nabi said. 'One old man wanted to go to the bathroom and they said: "Go in your pants."'" His brother nodded in agreement, and other men started shouting about their own experiences."[51] Even more bluntly, and glumly, on the 10th anniversary of

---

[49] John Rice, "Long struggle led to Mexico's opposition victory," The Associated Press, July 8, 2000.

[50] Kathy Gannon, "Cultural gap causing friction between Americans and one-time Afghan allies," The Associated Press, September 17, 2002.

[51] Kathy Gannon, "Angry Afghan villagers want US special forces out," The Associated Press, March 11, 2013.

the U.S. war in Afghanistan, Gannon wrote an analysis of why "the warning signs of chaos to come were there right from the start," arguing that the effort to back anyone opposing the Taliban had turned power over to the hardly better warlords who "stoked ethnic fighting, corruption and lawlessness" – an outcome that "shouldn't have surprised anyone":[52]

The U.S. had been reassured by its allies, known as the Northern Alliance, that their heavily armed ethnic militias would not storm Kabul when the Taliban left. So I called Abdul Rasool Sayyaf, a powerful Afghan warlord, to ask where his men would go instead. He laughed at the naivete of the Americans. "We will all be there," he said. "No one can keep us out." And indeed, within hours after the Taliban left, Kabul was swarming with militia. They took over houses, rampaged through the streets looking for Taliban and killed a few stragglers, throwing their bodies into a park. It was the beginning of a pattern of deception and misunderstanding that plagued Operation Enduring Freedom, which has endured longer than virtually anyone in the U.S. had feared.

In Vietnam, Bartimus (12; 2002, 189) argued that the emphasis on the Americans' fight against Communism overshadowed Vietnamese nationalism: "I really felt that we were missing the point as reporters by not doing more on the Vietnamese people, except every time a village got burned up, or My Lai, or the casualty count, or the occasional widow." Her predecessor in Saigon, Lederer (9), regretted spending too much attention on peace talks and not enough time in the field, where random villagers might have given her more insight into the diplomacy itself: "We stopped in all these little villages to talk to villagers, to see if they thought this peace agreement was going to last. And almost everybody we interviewed said no. They were smarter than a lot of people in this country." A Saigon bureau chief, Pyle (18), regretted not hitting "hard enough" the stories of internal Vietnamese politics (again, because they "were so esoteric nobody gave a damn") and of how "the U.S. military was being eroded from within by morale problems, tensions, and racial tensions, and drugs," also because it was hard to witness and public interest in Vietnam was flagging by this point.

Even the most momentous historical changes and the most heart-wrenching human tragedies, when covered reactively as breaking news and "just everyday events" (Gallardo, 7), might not do enough to advance understanding of deeper stories like human rights, radicalization, and migration:

We were prompted to cover [human rights violations in Chile] because something happened. I did write a couple of stories, sort of feature-like, including, for example, a profile on these women who devoted their lives to searching for their father. It was very well used all around. But it was exceptional. We normally covered stories prompted by something. They found bodies there. Okay, we'll go there, cover it, follow it for a few days or whatever. (Gallardo, 21)

---

[52] Kathy Gannon, "Analysis: First-person view of Afghan collapse," The Associated Press, October 7, 2011.

A lot of people who became active jihadis in the late '90s and 9/11 had cut their teeth in the Bosnian War. . . . I remember at one time someone from Gorazde told us how disappointed they were when they raced out into a field after an airdrop and opened it up, expecting to find food, and it was weapons, probably Iranian. But the Bosnian Muslim army was sensitive to this, and they basically kept a lot of the jihadis in areas where we couldn't get to, simply because it was too dangerous and the situation was unstable. . . . By the time some of this stuff emerged, it was too late to track it or do much with it. The Serbs undercut this; they talked about their jihadis out there, and they overstated the jihad angle to it, so people tended to discredit that as propaganda. (Reid, 96–97)

There was a sense that we were doing, in some cases, I hate to say it, but set pieces . . . in the sense that okay, another group of immigrants has died up in the States. You go down, you do the funeral. You talk to the relatives, you talk to the local officials, you talk to the police, you talk to the advocacy groups and . . . you usually tried to find out what the economic trigger was that sent them up. . . . It was becoming a little bit like a hurricane story, where we have a very definite formula of preparations, hurricane parties, hurricane hits, search and rescue, recovery . . . do the reconstruction story on day two, which is a "and I began to hear boulders falling off the mountain." Funerals, mourning relatives. There is a grocery list of things you're going to do on one of these stories. (Stevenson, 16–17)

Sitting in a café in Bethlehem's Manger Square, church bells competing with muezzin calls and cars honking in the background, Karin Laub (11–12) listed the themes that she felt most people still missed about the Israeli-Palestinian conflict that she has covered for nearly three decades – and what made it hard to convey them in stories:

I think they don't understand the feeling that I think a lot of the Palestinians have of this continuous sense of being deprived of freedom of decisionmaking. . . . [A]t the height of the second intifada, they could not turn anywhere without being stopped at a check-point. Often they could not make any plans. . . . Even now if you are a West Banker you need permits from the Israeli military to enter Jerusalem or to enter Israel. So this sense of being restricted, of being boxed in, and someone else making decisions for you, it's a horrible feeling, and I don't think people understand how difficult that is. And the other thing I don't think people understand is the urgency that is required to solve this problem, this conflict. I think that there is kind of a perception that "Yeah, Middle East, they all hate each other, it's always going on, and we lived with this until now and we'll continue to live with it." But that is actually a very dangerous approach. . . . We [as journalists] walk a fine line because we're here to report and not to preach. So, for example, a colleague of mine – we sort of figured this out together – he spent five days at the largest West Bank checkpoint into Jerusalem, at Qalandia, and basically the idea was he just took notes: "At 8:05 there were 500 people" or whatever, "and the waiting time was" – I think that's the best way to explain things,[53] to be close to the ground, color,

---

[53] Ben Hubbard, "Checkpoint misery epitomizes a Mideast divide," The Associated Press, February 21, 2010. The story begins: "The journey to Jerusalem, for tens of thousands of Palestinians, begins in a dank, trash-strewn hangar. They move through cage-like passages and 7-foot-high turnstiles to be checked by Israeli soldiers from behind bulletproof glass. The soldiers often yell at them through loudspeakers. . . . The Qalandia crossing, say the Israelis, is where potential attackers are filtered out before they can reach Jerusalem on the other side. Palestinians

people's voices, and then provide a lot of context. And that's what we sort of try to do every day. Sometimes there are the political stories that you also have to do – [Palestinian Prime Minister Salam] Fayyad resigns and what does it mean. That's also part of our job, it's not just all human interest. There's a whole range of things, but try to be as fair as possible, try to explain, try to have the real voices in the story, and hope for the best.

CONCLUSIONS

Choosing what is news marks the first task for AP correspondents overseas, who largely determined what countries, and what stories in them, the American public, and increasingly a global public, would come to know. Throughout the decades, some types of news remained so "obvious" that in their absence "nothing happened" – violent conflict especially, an easier (if extremely dangerous) story to tell even from places routinely off the radar, though correspondents tried to shed some light on the causes and impacts of fighting instead of just keeping score of the deaths. The tension between providing a daily record of breaking news – the standard for a wire service – and offering insightful, unexpected analysis – the premise of today's "impact" journalism, with roots in the "people story" dating back nearly a century – has long complicated news judgment. But correspondents also discussed another tension, between what they would like to write because it reveals larger truths, even though it might not be considered "news," and the stories that appeal, often meaning stereotypical ones that perpetuate set narratives familiar to editors and audiences.

Although not surprising given Washington's geopolitical dominance, the recurrent strategy of selecting news based on its U.S. impact can lead to missing the story of foreign countries themselves as more than bit players in America's global enterprises, such as the Cold War or the "war on terror." So the way correspondents described being able to unravel some of those hidden, truer meanings – with long-term exposure to a country, the ability to sniff around and follow unlikely tips – should not be jeopardized despite today's shriveling resources. The emphasis on pursuing big themes over record keeping leads to a paradox: Correspondents' ability to write stories that advance knowledge of major movements instead of formulaic, disconnected pieces is hindered by the constant requests for breaking news updates but also helped by following how events evolve over time with the kind of widespread presence overseas that no other U.S. media organization now has the infrastructure for. In fact, the cause of missed stories seemed to be not just the time pressure but, more disturbingly, the persistence of simplified, Western tropes like democracy and empowerment that correspondents had trouble authoritatively contradicting within objective journalism. A few correspondents regretted not having written enough about how the Arab Spring might engender radical Islamism instead of liberation, or how the U.S. policy of bringing down "bad

say it's a daily humiliation they must endure to reach jobs, family, medical appointments and schools. ... For five days, an Associated Press reporter waited with them."

guys" without worrying too much about who would replace them – whether in Kabul or Managua – might mean added misery for foreign peoples.

Even when some correspondents did try to change the tune – scouring Taliban-controlled areas or West Bank checkpoints at great personal risk – they could only "hope" that their challenging explanations would make a dent in the public's understanding. And of course, as AP reporters, they never wrote opinion pieces – so their narratives have been largely dependent on choosing not only their stories but their sources, which Chapter 4 discusses.

USSR Collapse, 1991

Deborah Seward: I was on the night shift the night that the coup happened, and had written a ... PMer [AP story for afternoon-edition newspapers], about how Gorbachev was due back in Moscow in order to firm up the union treaty which would give greater autonomy to this, that, and the other thing. And I went home, it was between 1 and 2 – the bureau usually closed at midnight, but I didn't ever manage to close it then. Early in the morning, sometime between 4 and 5, since I was the overnight desk person, the phone rang, saying Radio Russia is reporting this. ... It was different than let's say Poland, where the opposition told you this is what we intend to do. ... [T]here was a great deal of uncertainty. And that's a very interesting thing, because as a reporter you're not expected to be uncertain (Seward, 11).

Mark Porubcansky: That was a period [the August 1991 putsch] where it was clear that just incredible things were happening. ... [T]o be there and be writing about the statue of [Soviet revolution leader Felix] Dzerzhinsky coming down in front of the Lubyanka, the KGB headquarters, was like, "Really?" ... [T]hink about it. A *coup* in the Soviet Union. It was incredible (Porubcansky, 8–9). [Porubcansky's analysis of the turmoil during the failed coup began: "The 24 hours that ended with the toppling of a monument to the man who first unleashed 'Red Terror' on this troubled land were arguably the most dramatic in six years of reform. Those hours were also fraught with clues to the future. ... The word 'Russian' was on everyone's lips. The word 'Soviet' was nowhere."][54]

Alan Cooperman: [I]n retrospect, people say, "Oh, it was inevitable. It was inevitable the Soviet Union was going to fall apart." You know, as someone who was there, I never thought any of these steps were necessarily inevitable. At the time, I saw a lot of different ways that things could go. ... [T]he day

---

[54] Mark J. Porubcansky, "24 hours that shook the Soviet Union," The Associated Press, August 23, 1991.

before the coup, I could have walked around Moscow and interviewed people in any line, anywhere. I just said, "I'm an American correspondent," and they would have been glad to talk with me. ... [The day of the coup] I wanted to see whether there was suddenly a big line of people at the American Embassy. ... I started interviewing the people in the line, and they wouldn't talk to me. And I remember one young man who wanted to say something, and his father turned to him and he said, in Russian, "We don't need trouble." And it was just a [complete] turnabout [in the public mood]. ... I could just see it in people's faces. ... People didn't know ... who was going to come out on top and they went right back to the old Soviet mindset. Don't make any trouble for yourself. Don't say anything. Don't talk to anybody....

[T]hey told us, "No pictures! No pictures during – while Gorbachev is giving his [14-minute resignation] speech." So [AP photographer] Liu [Heung Shing] was crouched down by the television camera legs, the tripod, and the moment – the moment! – that Gorbachev finished the speech, Liu snapped this photograph ... Liu caught, actually, the papers coming down from Gorbachev's hand ... there was a certain, almost, a little bit of disgust, maybe mixed with relief, but there was real emotion in the way that Gorbachev dropped those papers. And Liu was a great photographer, captured that instant.[55] One shot – he wasn't like click-click-click-click-click-click – it was one shot. And got up, and as he got up from behind the thing, one of the KGB guards slugged him, right in his stomach. Because he had taken a picture. They'd said, "No pictures!" So they slugged him, and it was hard, knocked his breath out (Cooperman 3, 15–16, 24).

---

[55] Liu and four other AP photographers shared the 1992 Pulitzer for Spot News Photography for their photos of the coup and the collapse of the Communist regime.

4

Getting to the Sources (and Keeping Them Alive)

I'm awfully persistent, you know. . . . I was always there . . . over and over and over again. . . . I need all the time to ask people about what the situation is like and what are you thinking, even if I'm not doing a story. . . . I'm genuinely interested in having the conversations. . . . I genuinely want to go and sit there, whether you're sitting in a nice backyard like this or whether you're sitting on the floor, sharing a meal with somebody who lives in the Christian colony over here. . . . So I think that has assisted my access for all those reasons. And I go all the time. I mean, people see me everywhere. "Oh yes, Kathy, we know Kathy. Oh yeah, Kathy, for sure." It's not because Kathy is any great shakes, it's just that Kathy's always there. (Gannon, 37)

In the shaded garden of her Islamabad home on a cicada-filled spring evening, Kathy Gannon was describing how she develops sources on one of the most challenging foreign beats – reporting from Pakistan and Afghanistan since the late 1980s, work that nearly cost her her life less than a year later, when Gannon was severely wounded and AP photojournalist Anja Niedringhaus killed on assignment in Afghanistan. But on that peaceful Sunday, we had taken a walk through the mud-houses neighborhood across an unpaved alley from her villa, and a man getting a shave at the street-stand barbershop, the women strolling in their brightest saris, and the children busy with a pickup cricket game had all smiled and waved at us. Journalists like to say they are only as good as their sources – and Gannon's persistence, which has gained her access from top government leaders to children in tribal areas, is the main trait shared universally across time and space by AP correspondents who have developed strong sources at the Holy See, among the Taliban, and everywhere else.

Access to "the man on the street," rulers, and insurgents is the foundation of foreign reporting, and each source presents unique challenges in different cultures and political systems. This chapter details how correspondents have found and kept their sources, from North Korean children to the anonymous spokespeople (yes, there is such a thing) for the Élysée in Paris. It also delves into twin ethical responsibilities: verifying sources, not an easy task when faced with daunting tales of horrors, and protecting those who dare speak to journalists. All correspondents named six types of sources as necessary, to varying degrees, to build their coverage: U.S. and other diplomats and, in wars, military personnel; local leaders; dissidents and activists; local journalists and media; NGOs; and "man on the street" ordinary citizens. Many also highlighted the current dilemmas posed by sources speaking through social media. Several themes emerged: the crucial importance of cultivating sources around the clock, in every avenue possible, and showing genuine interest in everybody, no matter how obscure or unpalatable; the difficulties of putting ordinary citizens on the record for world publication, especially but not exclusively in repressive regimes; the often quixotic standards for verifying information; and the necessity to protect sources, sometimes well beyond their own awareness of dangers.

FINDING SOURCES: A TYPOLOGY IN PRACTICE

Although all reporters have to develop sources, foreign correspondents face several additional hurdles, not only language and perceptions (discussed in Chapters 2 and 5), but starting from scratch, among millions of strangers. In 1966, for example, Myron Belkind (7–8) was assigned to cover India and started with sources in "politics, in the government, among newspaper editors, among people that you just network with at dinner parties or that you go out and meet at universities. And next thing you know ... they'll say, 'Let me take you to my village'":

I was lucky that within a week of my arriving ... I was sent ... to what is considered probably among the poorest states in India, Bihar ... by 24-hour train journey, to cover the famine, not from the statistics that the Indian government was giving out in terms of how many tons of food they were sending and how many people were affected, but seeing it through my own eyes. So, then, you start developing contacts in Bihar, you start developing contacts wherever you travel. ... [I]t never stops.

Sources high and low are even more critical during major breaking news, such as the 1979–1981 Iran hostage crisis – especially the end, when AP correspondents had been ordered to leave Iran, as recalled by Charles Hanley (2–3), the special correspondent who had been writing the "round-up story" from New York:

[W]e all knew they would be released on that day, it had become apparent. But again, we had to rely on our little list of sources. ... I'm in New York, and I had to call the control tower in Tehran, at the airport, to find out whether wheels were up and whether they had taken off. And I just couldn't get it confirmed and it was frustrating as hell, and nobody could speak English. "Parlez-vous français?" and nobody could speak French. "Habla español?" and nobody could speak Spanish. And I even said, "Sprechen sie Deutsch?" and I don't know a word of German other than that. [laughs] But if I found a German speaker, I would scream out, "Who speaks German? Come over here!" And finally they passed the phone around the control tower and someone spoke English and confirmed to me, they had taken off at such-and-such time . . . we got the bulletin out at that point.

Bob Reid (88–89), 44 years with the AP reporting from Tehran to Berlin, from Bosnia to Iraq, argued, "You can't lock yourself up in your room with your laptop and basically just rewrite what you're spoon-fed or vague interpretations from the general flow of media. You have to get out." First stop are "established organizations" like universities or the U.S. Embassy, not to rely on them but "to use what resources they have." Then "any personal encounter with people in this gets you something": tea at the family home of local employees (one never knows who might have a relative in the government); a quick visit to a local shop ("Nine times out of 10, all this gets you is whatever you bought, but that one time in 10 . . . maybe the guy turns out to be a local leader in the block and other people solicit his advice and opinions and he has some view of what's going on, who's engaged in this"); and the local journalists, "because they may be under censorship and . . . may see you as their way to get something out that they can't get out themselves."[1]

The Diplomats

The U.S. Embassy was a standard first stop for AP correspondents until the late 20th century – the recent drop-off of this practice intriguingly paralleling the hesitations of U.S. diplomacy in this century. These interactions, the core of foreign correspondents' relationships with the U.S. government, are discussed in more detail in Chapter 10, but they long were crucial in getting the newly arrived journalists grounded (see also Roderick 1993, 116; Pedelty 1995, 7). Rosenblum (4), whose 38-year career in more than a hundred countries started with the out-of-the-blue assignment in Kinshasa discussed in Chapter 2, made friends with an embassy political officer there who remained a source throughout both men's rise up the ranks. Correspondents brought along the same skepticism that applied to all sources, using "a counter-source to double-check it out with" (Belkind, 8) – such as other embassies. In Beijing when U.S.-Chinese relations restarted, Graham (6) split her diplomatic time between the American compound and a variety of others:

[T]he American Embassy was very helpful to American journalists, because they knew how bad it was [for journalists trying to collect information]. . . . The Americans would give you some insight on what the Americans were doing, but as for what things meant, maybe what's going on in China, I did have to rely on political secretaries in other embassies. And East Europeans tended to be very helpful. Other Communists, they had a lot of Party visits and those were important visits, and then we got some insight.

---

[1] The last point, about local journalists under censorship being eager to get information to foreign reporters, was also cited, in her autobiography, by Georgie Anne Geyer, a *Chicago Daily News* correspondent in Latin America and elsewhere beginning in the 1960s (Geyer 1998, 66).

Similarly, Erbsen (14–15), fluent in multiple languages, sought out Yugoslav diplomats at the inevitable functions across Latin America in the 1960s and 1970s "because they had their feet in both camps":

The bureau chiefs of the AP, Reuters, UPI, AFP were ex-officio on all the invitation lists. Which was useful when you wanted to grab a lot of people in one place ... you're working on an issue or something, and you wanted to have one room where you could work your way through the room in half an hour, get a sense of what was going on.

In Africa during decolonization, Larry Heinzerling (5, 14), who had followed in his father's footsteps as AP correspondent in the least-covered continent, found piecemeal sources in a variety of embassies, starting with the U.S. one, then the former colonizers like the French and British, and even the newcomer Chinese:

Communist China was trying to expand its influence in the early '70s and open up an embassy in Nigeria. It was the first one, I think, in black Africa. And so I decided I'd go see the ambassador just to see what he was up to and what he wanted, why he was there. They wouldn't answer the phone, so I went to the embassy. I knocked on the door and someone came there and they said, "What do you want?" And I said, "I want to set up an appointment with the ambassador." And I said, "It's just a courtesy visit." And he said, "Everyone is very friendly in Nigeria, but we don't have any time for interviews." [laughs] ... But by and large, the diplomatic community was the main source, I think, for most correspondents in Africa for years.

Heinzerling still wrote his story on China's influence from Lagos:

The crimson flag that flies over China's new embassy compound on Ahmadou Bello Road droops in the sultry air of this West African capital. But for diplomats and China watchers alike, it is alive with meaning in a continent divided on Peking's growing activity and involvement.[2]

Another perk of diplomatic compounds was that different sources would gather there, a precious chance to talk with them for correspondents who might have had little access to them otherwise. At the U.S. Embassy in Kabul during the Soviet invasion, Reid (12) found missionaries, including one who "lived out near the presidential palace and he's telling me about the attack that night ... I'm just filling my notebook." Diplomatic receptions in 1950s Moscow ended up "with Khrushchev bantering with us and a circle of correspondents around him, and the ambassadors and other diplomats in a circle around us and listening in," so that right on arrival correspondents sent their drivers with visiting cards to "the hundred or so different ambassadors" to get on the invitation list (AP Oral History, Essoyan, 1997, 19). In Somalia and Bosnia, both wrecked by vicious wars, Paul Alexander (11), who had multiple war zone assignments in the 1990s, used diplomatic and military briefings as the jump-off point for his never-ending source collection:

---

[2] Larry Heinzerling, "China Resurging in Africa," *Washington Post*, April 3, 1972, A12.

In Somalia, you'd have a morning briefing by the UN. Then right before sunset, you'd have an afternoon briefing by the U.S. military. So you get an idea of what was coming up for the day, and what had happened towards the end. So that was of help to set your agenda, but you also talk to other journalists. You talked to your Somali staff. You got, just, ideas for stories here and there. You had one-day embeds ... the military would put on trips to outlying towns so you could see what the Canadians were doing, what the Australians were doing. ... So every time you heard something that sort of caught your ear, you'd think, file that away as a possible story later.

Foreign Government Officials

Continuing with officialdom, an essential on-the-record source has been foreign governments – their leaders, ministries, etc. With them too, tenacity pays, and so does the practice of keeping correspondents on-site for enough time to become known, and unavoidable, in a country's corridors of power. From her earliest days covering Pakistan's "interrupted attempts at democracy," Gannon (32, 27) spent a lot of time interviewing Benazir Bhutto (also once she was not in power, not only because she was more available but because "you're saying that you're still a value"). She had access to the powerful politician with her hair down – in a 1989 interview, the then first female leader of a Muslim nation spoke with her dupatta scarf "draped over her shoulder" instead of covering her head.[3] Gannon also cultivated Prime Minister Nawaz Sharif:

I used to go and make a point of going to Lahore to see him, to see his ministers. I got to know his ministers, we'd go out for tea. I don't do dinners and stuff like that, nighttime stuff. First, I don't want to; second, you're still a woman in this environment and ... I go to dinner parties all the time, and I go to receptions and this kind of thing at all these places. But I'm not hanging out drinking until four in the morning with them.

Cooking a multicourse fusion dinner of spaghetti, matzo balls and Asian salads for his wife and me, Arnold Zeitlin (15–16, 13), who opened the first AP Pakistan bureau in Rawalpindi in the 1970s, discussed the same approach:

I made it a point of visiting every prominent politician in Pakistan in the few months that I was first there. ... I came to the conclusion that the man who was going to play a major role in Pakistan during my time was Zulfikar Ali Bhutto, who was then out of office. ... I made it a point to appear at every meeting of his that I could get to and make sure that he saw me. And once he saw that I was quite interested in what he was doing, flattery is a wonderful tool. ... It was very beneficial to me. Because what I earned through that was access.

Well beyond Pakistan, that persistence – "the ability to wait and outwait," as another correspondent called a journalist's most essential skill (Geyer 1998, 259) – has been necessary to break through to leadership sources. Niko

---

[3] Kathy Gannon, "In interview, Benazir Bhutto says she's fighting evil in Pakistan," The Associated Press, September 12, 1989.

Price (5), covering Central America in the 1990s as it settled down after revolutions and civil wars, found that the lack of foreign press made it an unusual "playground for a journalist" "because you could show up on a Monday and by Tuesday, the minister of the interior was sitting down for an interview with you." As fans whirled over our heads in the open breakfast room of the Royal Bangkok Sports Club, Denis Gray (40–41) recalled how, newly arrived in Thailand in the mid-1970s, he cultivated representatives of King Bhumibol, who eventually let him travel to the countryside with them, even scoring rare interviews with "stunning beauty" Queen Sirikit:[4]

I didn't ask for an interview with the king, because they said it'd be really impossible, but they said, "Well, if you come along on one of these trips that the king takes, perhaps you can talk to him or at least get a feel for him." So, at that time, the king was still fairly young. ... And he made hundreds of trips into the Thai countryside, every corner of Thailand, often walking, going on jeeps to meet with villagers, to look at development projects, to deal with everything under the sun. ... So on one of these trips, when the king was going up north, we asked if AP could come along to just accompany him. They said, "Okay, fine," finally. So we went up to Chiang Mai and we spent several days with the king's retinue, going around to the villages and climbing up mountains and seeing what the king was able to do. ... [W]e had a really eyeball-to-eyeball, it was a really sweaty experience right there with the king. ... We may have exchanged one or two words, but I don't think we even quoted him in the story, if I remember, so it couldn't have been too great. But I figured ... this was a story worth not just a one-shot deal, but worth continuing. So I kept my contacts up at the palace.

When Egyptian president Anwar Sadat suddenly announced his willingness to travel to Israel to jumpstart the peace process in the 1970s, having done the rounds of all the "right ministries" (especially the foreign ministry, daily) paid off for Nicolas Tatro (3–4), who had arrived in Cairo only a month earlier:

[A]ll gave me access, at least once or twice a week, for Q&A and whatever I had on my mind and background stories. ... [T]hey knew me on a first-name basis. Sadat would go to his Mit Abu al-Kum, his hometown, and I'd go with him ... I wouldn't travel with him but I'd be there. And then he'd see me and he'd come over and say a few words. Now, these were not grand exclusives, but you know how the wire service of the day was always temperature-taking. So things are up, they're down, they're sideways. You'd always get a comment, and I think there was always a story. ... [I]t is the access that you need to do real reporting.

Around the same time, on a Saturday afternoon in New Delhi, Belkind (9–10) similarly knew where to go when he got the call from a colleague in the bureau that "India just exploded a nuclear device":

I went right to Mrs. Gandhi's office and got there just in time for a briefing they had called for Indian correspondents. ... I was there to see her first, and with my own eyes,

---

[4] Denis Gray, "Beloved Queen Sirikit Talks with Affection about the Rural Poor," *Bangkok Post*, May 24, 1979.

FIGURE 4.1. New Delhi bureau chief Myron Belkind with Indian prime minister Indira Gandhi when she spoke to the Foreign Correspondents' Association of South Asia, of which Belkind was president, in New Delhi in 1972. (Photo by Rangaswamy Satakopan, courtesy of Myron Belkind)

using the words "that the world should not be bothered; this is a peaceful nuclear explosion." I still remember the headlines the next day: "India explodes PNE [Peaceful Nuclear Explosion]." ... If we were waiting for Mrs. Gandhi, me and my colleagues would wait outside her residence in Number 1 Safdarjang Road. ... When I was in Kuala Lumpur, you get the proverbial message from the AP headquarters: "Get reaction from your prime ministers and presidents" to whatever happened. So I would go out to the 18th hole of the Selangor Golf Club in Kuala Lumpur and wait for Tunku Abdul Rahman, the first prime minister and leader of Malaysia, to come off his golf – he loved to play golf – and he would give us the quotes.

Correspondents in China as in Brazil, in the late 1970s as in the 2010s, found that developing personal relationships was essential to get behind the facade, whether it entailed inviting ministry officials to the AP apartment for dinner "for a little nugget of this, a nugget of that" (Graham, 3) – keeping up "personal relationships" because "the more times you meet with them, generally the more revealing they are" (Hutzler, 14) – or "waylaying" government or business leaders at events "for them to know you by face, because in the future that way they'll return your phone calls" (Clendenning, 4). During the Nigerian civil war in the 1960s, Zeitlin (10) went to the chief of army staff's home because "he would tell me all sorts of things that he would never tell me if I went to his office." During the historic 2000 Mexican election that ended the Partido Revolucionario Institucional's 70-year rule, AP's correspondents sought more inside access to Mexican politics than they had ever had:

We assigned a reporter to cover each of the candidates and . . . we didn't necessarily travel on every campaign trip with them; we chose our campaign trips – but we did work sources within the campaign. We got them to understand who the AP was and our reach. . . . We got better access than we'd ever had before. . . . I think it allowed us to get people, especially back in the U.S., excited about the election. I think it was a very closely followed election outside of Mexico, in part because of the drama of the election itself, but also in part because of the access that we were able to get. . . . It was at least a day a week of hanging out with the campaign people and taking them to dinner and really making sure that they knew who you were and would give you what they were giving the Mexican reporters, who were following them around every day. (Price, 8–9)

Some political leaders might not be the kinds of people one would want to get close to, but all correspondents said that getting the correct, full-picture story trumped any personal feelings:

I would go to see the Taliban, I would go to see the Northern Alliance. I talked to everybody. Everybody, everybody, everybody. Because to me that is what we do, is we talk to everybody and we ask questions. That's our job. No judgment, I ask questions, full stop, and report. . . . [At a post-9/11 news conference by former Taliban interior minister Mullah Khaqzar] I asked a question at one point, and he was so relieved to see a face he knew. . . . Suddenly [some of] the journalists . . . were a little bit nasty to me that I knew this person, and some were just sort of like, "How could you talk to him?" . . . And I was just like, are you insane? Give me a break . . . step back and have a little bit of balance (Gannon, 20, 46). [In the story about Khaqzar's news conference, Gannon noted that a few months earlier, Khaqzar had told AP that the Taliban's blowing up two historic, giant Buddha statues was worse than if they had cut his son's throat – but he had "refused to be quoted by name for fear the comment would cost him his life."][5]
It was an important thing to convey that, if the Soviet Union falls and the Soviet people can elect their leaders, they aren't necessarily going to elect all wonderful folks. They may elect people like Vladimir Zhirinovsky, who . . . was corrupt in various ways and certainly was saying unbelievably vile things about people with dark skin and religious minorities and Jews and all that kind of stuff. . . . I didn't really particularly care for Vladimir Zhirinovsky, and it was not very easy for me to penetrate his inner circle. But I did. I managed to spend a fair amount of time with him, enough to see him in action, hang out in his clubhouse. . . . I got close enough that I could do this profile (Cooperman, 24–25). [In his story, Cooperman explained that even outrageous comments, such as calling AIDS "a plague from the United States," "delight and excite many Russians, releasing deep resentments and soothing wounded pride like a magic ointment."][6]

The massive time investment does not always pay off, of course: "people who want to give you the runaround . . . they'll give you the runaround no matter

[5] Kathy Gannon, "Senior Taliban member defects, blames al-Qaida for turning Afghanistan into a terrorist haven," The Associated Press, November 24, 2001. Gannon followed up with a one-on-one interview with Khaqzar, "Weary of war, charter member of the Taliban leaves the movement, appeals for peace," The Associated Press, November 26, 2001.
[6] Alan Cooperman, "Nationalist offers magic balm for Russia's wounded pride," The Associated Press, February 6, 1994.

how long you spend," Gannon (88–89) said, adding that she would still pursue the outer circle around stonewalling sources. World War II correspondent Bria (3) still chuckled at how he had gotten in with Italy's postwar leaders some 70 years earlier – not quite telling Marshal Pietro Badoglio that the purpose of the interview was writing an advance obituary, for example. Red tape and consequent patience were needed for source-making in post-Soviet Russia: "If you wanted to visit a factory, if you wanted to visit a jail, if you wanted to go and talk with a bureaucrat someplace – it was easier to talk with Gorbachev than it was to talk with some tax authority someplace or some prison warden someplace. You had to fax these letters asking for things and get faxes back and back and forth" (Cooperman, 9). One longtime business reporter in Asia joked that the unresponsive state-owned Chinese companies must have kept "the telephone in the file drawer in the basement with the door locked" – so the strategy was to keep an assistant just working the phones while the correspondent rounded up the rest of the story (Kurtenbach, 9–10).

Despite all stratagems, some leaders remained largely off limits for interviews, like Chinese leaders in the immediate post-Tiananmen era (Hutzler, 4) and Fidel Castro a few years after the Cuban Revolution (Flores, 5). Access to leadership appears more ad hoc than clearly linked to sociopolitical systems. When we talked a couple of blocks away from Salvador Allende's house in Santiago, Eduardo Gallardo (8–9, 13) told me he had found the Marxist president far easier an interview than Augusto Pinochet or even his successors:

You have to be on their side to be close to them [today]. ... [On the contrary,] we were having dinner with Allende, all the foreign correspondents one night, and Allende said, "I'm going to ask you something" – to the Chileans, there were six or seven Chileans – "Who didn't vote for me?" I raised my hand, and he said, "I knew it. Anybody else?" No, nobody else. The *New York Times* correspondent ... also raised his hand, and he said, "I'm not a Chilean but I would not have voted for you, Mr. President." It was a joke, and it was very funny. ... [After the end of Allende's reign] generals wouldn't talk to reporters. Pinochet himself, well, he had some news conferences, and he recanted about anything he said. The famous sentence when he was told by a reporter that at the Santiago central cemetery they have found coffins with two bodies inside. And his reaction, "Well, that's a good way to save space at the cemetery." A couple of days [later] ... he said he was misinterpreted.

But the "space-saving" quote survived Pinochet. Gallardo repeated it in his obituary of the general "who overthrew Chile's democratically elected Marxist president in a bloody coup."[7]

And of course, correspondents might need to refuse promises of access – to Mexican cartel heads, for example, who effectively control large parts of the country and have waged a brutal murder campaign against journalists:

---

[7] Eduardo Gallardo, "Augusto Pinochet, long-time strongman in Chile, dies at age 91," The Associated Press, December 10, 2006.

We don't speak directly to the cartels. But we've been contacted by people who know people, saying would you like to talk to X? And almost always that's come from the Caballeros Templarios. And up to now, we've decided not to do that ... mainly because it's out of a security concern. ... If it's a meeting in a public place – which I can't imagine they would ever agree to – we'll do it, but we're not going to take a blind tour. We're not going to get into your car and be blindfolded, and we're not going to go someplace we don't know. ... What guarantees do you have? Zero. We don't bet our lives. No story is worth dying for. (Stevenson, 27)

Dissidents, Insurgents, and Activists

When societies are falling apart or deep in conflict, and different dissident groups are vying for supremacy, access can be easier to various leading political figures as well as activists of all stripes. Correspondents in Libya and Tunisia during the Arab Spring noted the change: "wartime makes people act differently, so they're much more willing to share. A lot of these guys [rebels], they wouldn't know if they were going to see tomorrow ... it changes behavior in a big way" (Laub, 31). Ordinary people would stop journalists to say, "My name's Mohammed and I have a declaration to make" (Ganley, 35) – such a

FIGURE 4.2. Middle East correspondent Nicolas Tatro interviews Shiite sheikh Sayyid Ali Ibrahim, one of the leaders against the Israeli occupation of south Lebanon, in Aadloun, Lebanon, on February 20, 1984. (Photo by Max Nash, courtesy of Nicolas Tatro)

stark change for "muzzled" nations that one story from Tunis detailed how it felt to "speak your mind in public for the first time and make a difference."[8] Benghazi was a "wide-open city," where correspondents would find lines of colleagues at the courthouse "interviewing some guy. And then you'd wait in line and interview them next" (Schemm, 10). Similarly, the Iranian Revolution was "one of those situations where all of the rules were unhinged and into that stepped journalists, who were able to get access they wouldn't have otherwise" – ranging from Ayatollah Khomeini's opposition to radical terrorist organizations to clerics in the holy city of Qom (Tatro, 10).[9]

Even in high-surveillance states, dissidents sought out AP bureaus: In Solidarity's Poland, correspondents first met many of the future post-independence leaders when they came to the AP office to drop off underground newspapers, and used them as "prescient" sources to understand broader developments across the Soviet world, together with the information they gathered firsthand from the chants and placards at protests before "they were dispersed by the police with tear gas" (Seward, 10; Daniszewski, 3). In Beijing, Moscow, and Havana, activists kept the AP phones (and fax machines) buzzing:

By fax, we would get these notices from Hong Kong from a guy . . . [who] had a network of sources, mostly in the political activist community, but all over China. . . . [P]eople were always contacting us. . . . Problems were changing as Chinese society became more open and mobile. Health problems, AIDS, became issues. So it wasn't just the run-of-the-mill typical dissidents who were contacting us. . . . [P]eople who were living, sort of, artistic, Bohemian lives in a village near the Old Summer Palace . . . called the bureau, and I just happened to be the one who answered the phone. And they were being kicked out of this village . . . because many of them didn't have the proper documentation to be living in Beijing and the authorities just didn't like people who were sort of forming voluntary communities like that. And so we got a call saying, "Can you meet with them?" So I went and met with a couple of these people in a restaurant and they told me that they were under pressure to move and that the police were coming to clear out the village the next morning. . . . We were . . . walking in the alleys of the village when the police arrived, which was really not great timing. Because the police drove up and the first thing they saw were these foreigners, and we sort of stood out, and we immediately got . . . detained in a building off to the side of this village for about four or five hours. (Hutzler, 4–5)

You'd have people [in Moscow] who were trying to get you, to hand off their latest tracts to you, which were typically . . . written on a manual typewriter with carbon paper, or in some cases they actually photographed the pages one after the other. . . . And then all of a sudden, all the Soviets wanted to fax you something. (Porubcansky, 5)

[Cuban] dissidents, we would get on their list, their call lists, they'd call us. Those were really like the main thing. . . . The dissidents . . . had taken that decision so they would talk, and so would the human rights people who were kind of part of the dissident

---

[8] Elaine Ganley, "Tunisians speaking out as shackles of silence fall," The Associated Press, January 19, 2011.
[9] Nicolas B. Tatro, "Iran Struggles with Freedom," *Chicago Tribune*, June 5, 1978, 14; "Peaceful Iran Protest Breaks Six-Month Cycle of Violence," *Washington Post*, June 18, 1978, A20.

group. ... They were often scared. ... A lot of this stuff, they wouldn't have gone to jail for, but somebody would have given them a hard time. Somebody would have come to their house, and maybe they couldn't leave for a day or two. (Snow, 26–27)

In a bustling Sanborns cafeteria off one of Mexico City's main boulevards, Anita Snow (7–8) told me how, trying to interview guerrilla groups like the Zapatistas, she used to chase them to remote jungle outposts – sometimes, incongruously, in a high-clearance VW Kombi – and AP even rented a house in San Cristóbal de las Casas, the center of the Chiapas revolt, for easier access:

I was out 10 days once ... and my news editor was very kind of upset that I had been gone for so long without contacting, but there was no way to contact. And we were waiting for the interview of [rebel leader Subcomandante] Marcos, and I got the interview with Marcos. ... He was a big flirt. He really liked to flirt with women. He wore a ski mask, so you never really saw his face, but he had beautiful green eyes and all the women were swooning over him. ... We got an AP house there, because it was getting really expensive ... everybody lived in it, photographers, everybody. So we saved a lot of money and we always had a place to stay, and it was a good idea. ... Chiapas is hard to get around. ... Very isolated. It takes like eight hours in a jeep to get somewhere.

The Marcos interview story, datelined "Lacandon jungle, Mexico," said that it was his first with a U.S. news organization since the rebels had "suspended consultations on a government peace proposal" and "tightly limited access to the zone they control." The story described Marcos arriving "on horseback for the interview at the house overlooking a lush green valley. He wore his trademark black ski mask and held a sawed-off shotgun with a shiny wooden handle. Two bandoleers of red shotgun shells crossed his chest. Puffing on his pipe, Marcos said Mexicans from all social sectors are hungry for change in a corrupt one-party system."[10]

The trail to rebel groups was similarly convoluted, and mediated, when Snow (14) interviewed Guatemala's URNG comandantes "in a clandestine camp cleared from the dense jungle along the slopes of a volcano."[11] Stevenson (4–5), who covered much of the unrest starting from his base in Mexico, also cultivated activists as a conduit to the rebels' "very guarded" core:

You very seldom penetrated that, and you would do it only with blind contacts and phone calls in the old "go wait in the parking lot, and somebody will observe you, and if they think you're alone, they'll tell you and then they'll give you a call, and you find a note in the tree telling where." That old blind trail kind of thing that we did with rebels in Mexico. ... [W]hen you reported on the Zapatistas, or on the Acteal massacre, you would quickly find the Jesuit priest who knew all the players ... and I just remember the Jesuits because they were the best. ... [O]bviously there's a way they want you to write

---

[10] Anita Snow, "Rebel leader says failure to reform system could spark national movement," The Associated Press, April 2, 1994.

[11] Anita Snow, "From mountain hideout, rebels say new accord could mean peace," The Associated Press, May 8, 1996.

the story in the end, and who's the good guys and who's the bad guys, but they're not going to push that. They're smart enough to know that you're smart. But a lot of that would be, you're out in the outback or on the side of the road, and you see a Jesuit you know in a passing pickup truck, and you'd be like, "Is something happening up the road?" And he would be like, "Yes, get your photographer. Come with me. Meet me in 15 minutes." And they're going to raid this town, because they think there's a paramilitary force there. So you would literally be drawn into that, never by the army, never really by the government, never really by the rebel forces themselves ... [who only say] "Yes, we will welcome you in for a weekend or for a day when we choose, when everything is all set up. But if you want to come back or if you want a contact or if you want to come on a specific story, I'm sorry you're shit out of luck. We're not here to serve the press." And they quite obviously aren't. So a lot of that, back in those days, was making contact with the outer circle.

Most correspondents found the easiest access in one of the most contested, conflict-ridden zones of the past 70 years – Israel and the Palestinian Territories, "a reporter's paradise because everyone is accessible," West Bank correspondent Laub (3, 7) said:

You just can't shut people up basically, because they are in such a competition to get their narrative across. . . . [T]hey are basically handing it to you, in some ways. You could just go into any refugee camp and talk to people and people are eager to talk, they see that the world is taking an interest. Especially on the Palestinian side, they want to be heard, and whenever we would enter a camp or any neighborhood, immediately people would gather, and if I talked to a couple of people, then others would come and they would volunteer their opinion.

Israeli settlers could be a bit harder to convince – another veteran Middle East reporter was kicked out of a non-sanctioned settlement in the mid-2000s and had to get "permission" to return, after which people were "falling over themselves to tell me their part of the story" (Eliason, 8). The openness – when matched with persistence – can also get correspondents onto a story that does not fit the typical frame of this much-covered conflict:

I went myself and interviewed former Palestinian Prime Minister Ahmed Qurei, known as Abu Alaa.[12] I asked him about this, I was like, "Well, what about a default outcome?" and he just immediately went with it and said, "Yes, basically if the Israelis insist on occupying us, we will stop talking about two states and start talking about one state, that's fine." No one else thought to go to them and ask them this. (Perry, 19)

The Local Press (and Local Hires)

From Nigeria in the late 1960s to the Middle East or Mexico today, and whether it is underground activist publications, state-run media, or the big sellers, local journalism is mined for sources and information. Rosenblum (18)

---

[12] Dan Perry, "AP Interview: Palestinian doubts 2-state solution," The Associated Press, April 23, 2012.

said he could still hear the Radio Biafra voice as it had come decades earlier through his "little Sony shortwave radio" at 6 a.m. in the morning repeating "The price of liberty is eternal vigilance! Biafra, be vigilant!" One correspondent recalled staffers in the Middle East whose main job was monitoring local broadcast and newspapers, and even in Mexico the public's interest was so high that reporters scoured furiously five newspapers a day for stories – and also for confirmation, since for any incident "five of them would have the same story and they would all ... have significantly different facts" (Rice, 13–14).

In closed regimes, the official state media, such as TASS in the Soviet Union or Xinhua in China, published de facto government news releases – except of course where they silenced news detrimental to the regimes, as all Polish media except Gdańsk Radio did of the Solidarity-led strikes there (Reid, 19). Whether in Moscow right after Stalin died or in Beijing 40 years later, reporters faced the necessary but grim "drudgery" of sorting through piles of copy for an inkling of news breaking across vast countries, for "bulletins" that might be "buried in the 31st paragraph of a long communiqué":

[O]ne of the drills all of us had to follow, was you turned up ... late every night to wait for the morning editions because, the first year or so, that was about the only source of news ... and to be ahead of the competition you had to get the newspapers when they came off the press. And it ... ended up the whole press corps was at [Moscow's] Central Telegraph grabbing the papers, and reading them, and trying to find what was news-worthy ... then typing it on three or four carbons and then ... you kept one carbon and you handed three carbons into the censor through a little – you never saw who was behind the green, green glass wall – and eventually your copy was returned, blue-penciled if they didn't like it, or words cut out and if it was straightforward, it was clean. (AP Oral History, Essoyan, 1997, 16, 22–23)

And we had ... close to 50 newspapers a day that were delivered to the bureau, because that was the way you found out what was going on in all parts of China. So every province or major urban center had its own newspaper. ... [I]f we wanted to have an inkling of what was going on in places like Xinjiang or Tibet, ... you'd find it in the *Xinjiang Daily*, or the *Tibet Daily* ... delivered days later. ... And of course not just the sensational, violent stuff, but what people's concerns were, consumer trends. (Hutzler, 3)

Having a core of independent, professional local journalists could be enabling, so much so that a recent study of press freedom argued that "Americans must ... see the foreign press as our press" and its censorship as an unacceptable violation of Americans' rights (Bollinger 2010, 112). Different forms and traditions of reporting, however, can also be a hindrance, as in Japan, where all mainstream media belonged to "kisha clubs" at the various ministries, which then granted permission to attend press conferences and controlled access (Kurtenbach, 9). Anonymity, a practice that AP has tried to avoid more assiduously than many other organizations (Duffy 2014), troubled reporters in London as in New Delhi – "they would write stories without the sources. 'It is understood,' which used to drive me crazy" (Belkind, 19) – or in Bonn and Berlin, where the widely used "aus Regierungskreisen" ["from government circles"] clashed with the U.S. rules where "you have to prove everything, like you're writing a legal brief" (Reid, 6). Even when reached directly, government or company spokespeople sometimes refused to be quoted by name, demanding instead that the quote be attributed, for example, as "Air France said" in France (Doland, 3) or "Just quote the press office" in Spain and Brazil (Clendenning, 4).

The local journalists and stringers working for AP are also essential conduits to sources, particularly when the correspondents do not speak the local language and on sensitive stories where either very ordinary or very elite access is needed. One reporter recalled "dowry deaths" in India, a news story where local media provided the initial tip and Indian staff would get police and family members to talk (Graham, 25–26). Another correspondent obtained an interview with Jordan's king the very day he arrived in the country because the AP stringer "had the real connections . . . our people on the scene who did the cultivation, and we were the beneficiaries of it" (Doelling, 16). A momentous break for AP international coverage – the first reporting trip to China since Mao's revolution, covering the 1971 "ping-pong" diplomacy – came through the combination of a connected local hire with a veteran correspondent, John Roderick, who had cultivated access decades earlier by living with Mao and his comrades in the caves at Yan'an when he covered China for AP in the late 1940s:

I was running the desk in Tokyo, and one of our reporters there who was Shanghainese Chinese . . . covering [the ping-pong tournament] . . . said, "Hey. The Chinese have invited the Canadians to Beijing to play exhibition games." So, of course, the natural reaction, I said, "Well, can you go and find out from the Chinese whether they'll also invite the Americans?" . . . [H]e knew them – became friendly with the Chinese officials. The Chinese said, "Well, why don't you people write to the foreign ministry in China?" . . . So I sent it [a cable message], and within 24 hours, John Roderick . . . was on his way to Hong Kong, going to China. (Liu, 3)

Zhou Enlai, whom I hadn't seen since the caves of Yan'an, met me at the Great Hall of the People, which is on the Square, Tiananmen Square . . . he shook hands with me and he said, "Mr. Roderick, it's been a long time, hasn't it?" . . . [W]hen we had the ping-pong teams all together in a kind of a tea and a press conference sort of thing . . . I said, "Please. We were allowed to come to China and we hoped it would be just a beginning," and all that sort of thing. And he leaned forward and said, through his interpreter, "Mr. Roderick, you have opened the door." A quotation I was quick to pick up and relay [laughs]. (AP Oral History, Roderick, 1998, 25)[13]

Roderick's first-person story of the trip brims with enthusiasm from the lead: "This is my first dispatch from China in 22 years. The news I have to report would have been incredible only a few weeks ago – Americans are welcome in the People's Republic. . . . Our assignment is to cover the [table tennis] team. But

---

[13] Roderick also described the event in his 1993 book, *Covering China* (140–164).

the biggest story of all – China – is all around us and crying to be told."[14] Roderick even poked fun at some of the tense rhetoric, like a quotation on his plane to Beijing that incited global citizens to unite against "the U.S. aggressors" – but the only aggressor to die in a confrontation was a fly next to his ear swatted by an "apple-cheeked stewardess in pigtails." After Roderick and Vicki Graham (7) reopened the AP bureau in Beijing in 1979, their photojournalist colleague Liu Heung Shing (who would later win a Pulitzer Prize) became essential to get Chinese citizens, many of whom had never seen a Westerner, over their shock in encountering the red-haired female foreign correspondent, and to tell their stories – though Liu also cut quite a figure, draped in cameras and with his fashionable Ray-Bans.

The Man (Woman, and Child) on the Street

"Vox pop," the classical Latin-inspired journalistic lingo for the voice of the people, the "street" opinion on whatever news is being reported, is a particularly important tradition for American journalism, which is steeped in personalized narrative much more than the politicized, structural genres elsewhere (Benson 2013). The insistence on raw individual emotion, though, often runs into cultural walls. Some correspondents struggled with translating their reporting needs in societies that prize reserve, such as Japan during the shattering 1995 Kobe earthquake, or in more communal societies, such as the Soviet Union:

> I remember meeting this guy, his home had collapsed, killing his entire family. The place where he had worked had collapsed. So he had no home and no place to go work, and I asked him, "How do you feel about this?" And he said, "Oh, I will persevere." ... I know there's got to be some emotion in there, somewhere. You've just gone through all this. ... So, on one hand, you're dealing with the physical devastation, and then you're watching a culture trying to cope with that, and cope with it in a very different way than how you would cope and how most of your society would cope. (Alexander, 25–26)
>
> If you're doing an interview with me, here, I'm going to say, "I did this. I think this." There, it's always, "We do this. We think this. This is our way." And ... you always get the feeling that they're trying to explain their culture rather than giving you the immediacy of an individual person. And individual circumstance is something that really translates to a Western reader, being able to make a connection to an individual. (Porubcansky, 21)

The imperative to get the pithy quote from a random person on the street – preferably a street Americans reading AP copy in Alabama or Wyoming would recognize by name – and to do so on deadline without the time to canvass potential sources for those comfortable with commenting on the record led some Paris correspondents to a last resort, the "café for quotes" across the street from the bureau:

---

[14] John Roderick, "Americans Warmly Greeted in Peking," *Los Angeles Times*, April 12, 1971.

And because ... our office is not far from the Champs-Élysées, we could say, "said someone in this café near the Champs-Élysées." ... Because if readers have been to France, they know the Champs-Élysées. They may know it if they haven't been. (Ganley, 10)

A professional constraint on finding sources among ordinary citizens abroad is that U.S. standards of journalism, unlike those in many countries, require a full name – and often age and occupation – for every person quoted. That is irritatingly incomprehensible to many foreign peoples, such as the French ...

Someone can have something brilliant to say, which you'd just love to put in your story, but then, "Well, you can just call me Jacques, that's okay, that's enough. Why do you need more?" (Ganley, 9; also Doland, 3)

and the Italians ...

God forbid you could ever use somebody's name, because basically everyone's afraid here ... a country where no one trusts anybody else. ... And try explaining [that you need attribution] to them and they think you're a jerk. (Simpson, 16–17)

and the Spaniards ...

You say who you are, what you're working on, start the interview, and say, "The first thing I need is I need to know your first and last name, your age, and your occupation." And if they ask you why, you tell them why – because we need to. People need to be convinced people we talk to are real. ... If we're getting general comments or examples of people, and they just don't want to give their names, that's really not good enough for AP. (Clendenning, 18)

But to get vox pop, and what one correspondent called to "curry the gossip" (Smith, 5), can pose a serious threat to ordinary citizens seen talking with foreign (particularly American) correspondents in oppressive regimes. A few years after the revolution, Ike Flores (6) found Cubans ready to chat on *almost* any topic – except "the regime ... they didn't want to implicate themselves." Fifty years later, another Havana correspondent reporting about Cuban street food like "pizza in a basket" (lowered from a building near the University of Havana) wrote that her sources refused to give last names, "uncomfortable talking with a foreign reporter about an issue as political as food."[15] In Syria under Assad, "there were people who would say things but you really, sometimes you would protect them for their own sake ... these people have to stay there, I'm leaving. Their homes are there, their families are there" (Powell, 17). One 2004 story from Tripoli profiled a former political prisoner covered in scars – some inflicted by Gadhafi's police, some his own "attempts to end his suffering" – who "said his speaking out imperiled him but he was beyond caring. He gave his full name, although his wife begged a journalist

---

[15] Anita Snow, "Cubans head to the street to augment food rations with pizza and 'pork rind' of macaroni," The Associated Press, June 12, 2007.

not to print it for the sake of their children." The correspondent did not use it, but detailed what it took to interview dissidents like Fouad in Libya:

Government minders accompany journalists on most forays out of their hotel, and police question journalists seen conducting interviews or taking photographs unaccompanied. Most of the dissidents spoke in hurried conversations on Tripoli streets, glancing over their shoulders to see who was watching. One man alternated between praises for Gadhafi and talk of arbitrary imprisonment as a minder wandered away and back. ... Fouad and another dissident approached AP discreetly in a city square when no minders were present, then walked away one by one, telling the journalists to follow after a few minutes. Fouad's friend, walking a block ahead, led the journalists through a maze of streets before ducking into Fouad's doorway.[16]

Interviewing ordinary Chinese, many reporters found, remains a challenge to this day, because of the repercussions for those who dare go against the party line – for attribution and worldwide publication – on "any sensitive topic," especially in the wake of failed movements like the 2011 Jasmine Revolution (Kurtenbach, 9). In the words of China bureau chief Charles Hutzler (4), who spent decades in the country, getting the Chinese "man on the street" is "easy but tough" because people do talk, but eventually the police will start watching them, disrupt interviews, "or at least stand there and be obvious about it and make it uncomfortable for the interview subject." And then there are countries where any unauthorized interaction between locals and foreigners is literally illegal, as Jean Lee (4–5), who opened AP's bureau in Pyongyang in 2012, found out – making time and persistence even more critical:

I spent a lot of time mapping out who it is that we would like to speak to, where it is that we would like to go. Most of it needs to be arranged in advance. ... Say you want to get some vox pop – I might just go to a local store and start asking some questions to get some local color. That would technically be illegal in North Korea. So it requires a lot of advance planning. And that's not to say that I don't do it; there are times when I find an opportunity to just chat with people. ... [P]eople really have to watch what they say. They're very conscious of what they say.

Success in making contact with ordinary people also depends on the perception of journalists as such and as foreigners, Americans, and other characteristics, as Chapter 5 details. Donna Bryson (82) – an African American female correspondent in South Africa, India, and Egypt in the 1990s–2000s – found that she could take advantage of "role playing":

You can see that they respond to the idea that you're American, so you really play that up. ... Or you can see that they really want to explain things for you, so you really play dumb. Or you can see that they don't have time for someone who doesn't understand, so you really try to show them that you've done some homework.

---

[16] Niko Price, "AP Exclusive: Dissidents tell of torture, secret prisons, executions under Libyan regime," The Associated Press, February 26, 2004.

Correspondents from the Soviet Union to Egypt would play up or down their "foreignness":

[As the USSR was breaking up,] you could walk down the street and if you merely told someone you were a foreign correspondent, and especially [an] American [correspondent], they would stop in their tracks, whatever they were doing, and they would talk with you. They were so interested in the West, in foreigners. ... The only risk was that your interview would become hijacked because they would ask you more questions than you would ask them. But it was great, and, yes, you could get virtually anybody – [any] ordinary person – to stop. But also ... I would say to a Russian friend – this is a literal story of how I said it – "So, tell me, who's your favorite comedian? Who's the best comedian in the Soviet Union?" And they said, "That's Gennady Khazanov, he's hysterical!" And I said, "I want to talk to Gennady Khazanov." And he said, "Okay." And within 20 minutes, I had Gennady Khazanov on the telephone.[17] ... *If* I could get the number, which was sometimes difficult because there still weren't phone directories ... I can't remember anybody ever turning me down [for an interview]. (Cooperman 5–6)

I went and spent a lot of hours with the Muslim Brotherhood. I went to their speeches at night and their tent meetings and met their young radicals and ... they, too, were trying to get involved in the information game ... I got to know them, and I got to know what they thought and how they thought it. ... They had little cassette tapes that were very popular, sold in the market, of various sheikhs who were giving speeches about the political events of the day and putting it in religious terms. ... I made a huge effort to get those tapes and get them translated and take the key parts of them and report on it or, at least, understand what was being said. So certainly from the religious part and then just interviewing ordinary Egyptians from different walks of life, whether it'd be at the Zamalek club or something, where the elite would gather, or you're talking down with the felucca guy on the Nile, in Bulaq or some other godforsaken neighborhood in Egypt with no running water and no paved streets and stolen telephone lines and electric and so forth. ... I lived in an Egyptian house ... in the downstairs, and the family lived upstairs ... and it wasn't much, but it was definitely part of the neighborhood. (Tatro, 5–6)

Sometimes intermediaries like NGOs would help reach the "man on the street," particularly in Africa where correspondents might have half a continent on their beat or when communications infrastructures were in lockdown. "Parachuting" from Miami throughout the Caribbean and Central America, Tad Bartimus (6) often started with the youngest parish priest (more likely to be liberal) and moved on to the "concierge at the best hotel," the "cop on the beat," and even "the madame of the local whorehouse," who could provide a neutral "sanctuary" in combat zones. Seeking access to indigenous villages in rebellion against the government across Central America in the 1980s, Frazier (25) would find a "human rights guy there whom we knew or who knew somebody we knew who would introduce us: 'This guy is okay. You can talk to him.'"

---

[17] Alan Cooperman, "Soviets keep sense of humor in trying times," The Associated Press, June 8, 1991.

In the 1980s during the Ethiopian famine, David Crary (3) sought out "the NGOs who had already been on the ground and established local contacts ... [and were] willing to get out in the field, get away from their offices, who knew the local people and the lay of the land" – like those working at the Korem camp who became protagonists of a story about rains giving a "tinge of green" and a sign of hope to the desperate thousands there.[18] Covering Sarajevo on multiple assignments during the siege in the Bosnian War, however, Crary (13–14) was more than happy to shed all officialdom – and feel closer to the story through the "real" families he kept visiting:

> If I compare my stints in Sarajevo with day-to-day reporting in Paris, it was completely different in terms of spending time with ordinary people and doing stories about them and much less of going to news conferences and talking to the government bureaucracy – actually the government bureaucracy was pretty shattered and shambled and pretty hard to reach on the phone anyway. ... [I]t did deepen the bond, definitely, because you were writing about the citizenry and not the officialdom ... made you feel more like you wanted to help things get better for them.

Lastly, sources are not always face-to-face – correspondents have used a range of media from communiqués to graffiti to online posts. In Vietnam, where U.S. media competition was intense, one correspondent picked up mail early at the PX station and found a news release about a group of Green Berets, including the commanding officer of U.S. special forces in Vietnam, charged with murdering a Vietnamese man. He scored a scoop that made front pages from the *New York Times* to the *Los Angeles Times*, especially since the army immediately instructed those charged not to talk to the press:[19]

> [Correspondent George Esper] wrote this story. And all hell broke loose about this thing. And then the briefing comes up and everybody's demanding to know ... "Where the hell did the AP get this goddamn story?!" ... This news release was in everybody's mailbox. But George went over early ... and we owned that story from the beginning. (Pyle, 23)

Over the past decade, often anonymous sources online and on social media have added another form of access both to leaders breaking news through them and to ordinary citizens, but one laden with practical and ethical dilemmas. As Perry (22) put it, vox pop used to be something that the journalists pulled: "This is vox pop that is pushed. Very different dynamic." Bryson (40), Middle East news editor in Cairo around 9/11, had some particularly distasteful online voices pushed toward her – execution videos:

---

[18] David Crary, "Tinge of green on once-parched land is sign of hope in Ethiopia," The Associated Press, September 22, 1985.

[19] "Green Beret Chief Held in Slaying of a Vietnamese," *New York Times*, August 6, 1969, 1; "7 Ex-Green Berets and Leader Charged with Viet Murder," *Los Angeles Times*, August 6, 1969, 1; "Army Secretive on 'Beret' Murder," *Washington Post*, August 7, 1969, A3.

I was telling myself, well, this is in Arabic and my Arabic-speaking reporters are going to have to be the ones who have to report on this. But then one day I said, I should really watch one, because my people are watching these things, and that was just horrific. And then I began to wonder why. Do we really need to watch these? What are we really contributing to the reporting by having anyone watch that kind of stuff? You're not authenticating it by watching it.

Stevenson (27–28), whose coverage of Mexico's narcotrafficking cartels is one of the most dangerous assignments in the world today, found a different type of "social media" message directed at correspondents – roadside banners commenting on AP stories:

[I]n Ciudad Juárez we ran a story saying that the Sinaloa cartel was winning there. It's the Sinaloa against the Juárez cartel ... for control of that route. [W]hat U.S. officials were telling us was that Juárez still controlled the level of street killings and local drug gangs, but then all of the drug shippings they were seizing across the Juárez-El Paso border were all Sinaloa. ... So based on tips and the markings [on shipments], they were saying everything that's coming through is Sinaloa. We publish that story and immediately the next day there were graffiti and signs and postings saying, "It's not true. Sinaloa hasn't won."[20] And there were some killings related to that. And so the mayor came out and said, "Look, these kinds of stories are causing violence, they're causing deaths." That's a nasty position to be in. ... [W]e don't really think that's true. We don't think we caused any deaths.

CULTIVATING SOURCES: TIME, PATIENCE, AND CARE

While each type of source demands a slightly different approach, they clearly call for aggressive pursuit and persistence. But politeness and genuine interest also go a long way in keeping the sources so eagerly sought, from the pope, whom "you can't slander ... as you would a politician," joked Victor Simpson (40), who covered the Vatican since the late 1970s, to the reclusive Ernest Hemingway, who had hung a sign on the chain blocking the road to his Cuban finca, "'Do not come in unless you have a prior appointment,' in English and in Spanish":

So being a good Southern boy, I went around to the local bar and called up and Mary Hemingway answered. It was about 10 or 11 o'clock in the morning. She said, "Thank you for calling, Mr. Hemingway is working. He works from 5 a.m. to 1 o'clock, and nobody interrupts him." ... So he gave me the courtesy of giving me an interview. So common courtesy does pay off. ... Because that got me one of the great beats of my life. Because a little time later, I got the bulletin from Sweden that Hemingway had won the Nobel Prize. ... I called him up, and I said ... "You won the Nobel Prize." ... So he said, "Well what do you want?" I said, "Give me 850 words and don't talk to anybody else for 15 minutes." So he said "You got a deal." And then he called back, and he said,

[20] Alicia A. Caldwell and Mark Stevenson, "AP Exclusive: Sinaloa cartel wins Juarez turf war," The Associated Press, April 9, 2010.

"Sam, why don't you arrange a press conference out here?" So it dragged on for another hour, and I got the front page of the *New York Times*. (Summerlin, 9)

With "ordinary" sources, politeness and interest matter even more. Among indigenous Central American rebels, "you don't just start asking questions":

It's not considered polite. ... You just talk about things in general and work into it slowly. ... It helps if you go in there three or four times and they get to know you a little bit, they start to recognize you. They know you're not just in on a whirlwind tour. You may actually care about them, which I did. ... They said, "Look, there is a lot of bad stuff, and we want our story told." And there was an assumption that we'd do it in a balanced and fair manner, and I think we did. ... Both sides wanted their stories out, and we were basically the only way it was going to get there. ... There were times where we weren't trusted and people wouldn't give us the time of day – "Get out, we don't want trouble here." That happened not infrequently. (Frazier, 25)

Fearlessly and gently, Gannon (71, 7) sought out reactions among Afghans to the American military presence a decade after 9/11 in Lashkar Gah, in the country's unsettled south, and to Israel's bombing among Lebanon's Hezbollah militants:

[W]e went to a bus stop, which was going out to different parts of Helmand [province]. ... [T]here was some that were really angry, you could tell. And nicely I stayed kind of a little bit, asked them and let them yell a little bit, and then went on to somebody else or whatever, because it was just the same ranting. But it was such a joy again for me to go into the teahouses – and the teahouses are like platforms, you sit on there and you have your tea and your food and everything and everybody's coming in – and just to talk about what they were doing.

I had made friends with this woman who worked at the hospital in Tyre, and so when they had a two-day ceasefire, I asked her if we could go to her village, and so she said, "Yeah." And so I went to her village. It turns out her uncle was a big Hezbollah guy in the village. How nice was that?[21]

All correspondents said that cultivating sources takes a combination of two skills that are often in short supply in an increasingly fast-paced, cash-strapped profession – patience and time. Gray (51–52) invested long preparations – and backbreaking 11-hour mule rides through the Burmese jungle – to nail a rare interview with Khun Sa, the biggest opium warlord in the Golden Triangle, the drug's top global production area:

[W]e got ahold of his middleman in Mae Hong Son and he said, "Okay, come on up." ... In the morning, we were picked up by a pickup truck, went for a couple of hours through Thailand up to the border. ... And we thought we would have to walk, which would have been bad enough, but even worse ... they mounted us on mules, and every time I see a mule, I still get a backache. ... Within about a kilometer from this camp, ... all our mules started to charge, and they sort of charged two or three times their normal speed,

[21] Kathy Gannon, "Halt in fighting sends Lebanese streaming back to war-ravaged regions," The Associated Press, August 14, 2006.

went straight into their sort of paddock, and stopped, they refused to go anywhere. . . . [T]he next morning, we met the "Prince of Darkness," and I think the first quote I have opening my story was, "They said I have horns and fangs."

Gray's story opened with Khun Sa laughingly "curling fingers next to his temples" to illustrate how American narcotics officials had branded him as devilish, while he wanted "the world to see him . . . as a rebel general fighting the Burmese government to liberate the Shan, one of the many ethnic minority groups who suffer under an autocratic regime," a claim the rest of the story questioned.[22] Gray had also been in the same region to interview a very different leader – Thailand's King Bhumibol, who traveled there to persuade hill tribesmen to switch to more benign, if less lucrative, crops.[23]

Spending time with sources – "talking, talking, talking, and in the first hour nothing happens" (Gannon, 88) – becomes essential to see through the breaking news and into the deeper transformations of society, as noted in Chapter 3. During the mid-1990s Afghan civil war that led to the establishment of the Taliban regime, Gannon (20) found herself on the front lines, drinking tea for "ages" and eventually, having covered the war action, gently probing the devout Muslims about their treatment of girls:

"I don't understand you guys. . . . You know God really loved the Prophet, he loved the Prophet and he only had one child that lived, and it was a girl. Now how precious must a girl be if God has given it to him, his favorite?" . . . Oh, one guy, he says, "No, no we put our girls in the corner." I said, "I know! . . . You want to have a beard like the Prophet, you want to have a turban, and then you go and put your girls in the corner. What is that all about?" And they'll laugh. . . . And if they would say they had four boys and one girl, I'd say, "Well, I'm so sorry. That's too bad, just one girl?" . . . And then if somebody had like five girls and one boy, I said, "You're such a lucky man, five girls, that is so nice." And there'd be kids around, because then they'd be listening, and they'd all be laughing.

Those contacts – painstakingly developed one lung-busting, missile-dodging mountain hike after the other "on my hands and knees crawling to the top to finish" – gave Gannon name recognition and a reputation for fairness among the different mujahedeen groups, which paid off more than a decade later, when Osama bin Laden catapulted Afghanistan into the biggest international news story of its time. Shortly after the U.S. war started, having obtained a coveted permit to get into Afghanistan from Pakistan, Gannon was arguing with the border officials when one remembered her from a trip with a Pashtun leader 15 years earlier. Although she never met bin Laden, Gannon (14–16, 4–6) had contacts just a few degrees of separation from his inner circle – and thus got unique information when she interviewed his bodyguards in Yemen:

---

[22] Denis D. Gray, "Warlord tries to retain control of narcotics trade, claims to be fighting for oppressed minority," The Associated Press, September 18, 1990.

[23] Denis Gray, "The Many Roles of King Bhumibol," *Singapore New Straits Times*, March 10, 1977.

Because I was there at the time when the Russians were there ... a lot of people I know like Gulbuddin Hekmatyar and that, but also ... fighters from different groups. And [one bodyguard would] say, "You know this person?" I said, "Yeah, are you kidding me?" And we got such interesting information from him, and I spent a lot of time, kept going back and forth. ... He was just a treasure trove of information about what Osama had been doing from 1996 to at least when he was there at the end. ... [W]hether you use it as a story or not, to me, I'm just so fascinated to talk to people who have this close relationship with someone that you can't have access to and just to hear their stories and try to understand what is that person like and what was the environment like, what was the thinking like, how does he react to things.

One of Gannon's stories from Sana'a focused on the bodyguard and other convicted al-Qaida operatives, whom Yemen had allowed to go free as long as they signed an agreement to obey the law, although they neither apologized for nor regretted their sympathies or jihadi acts. "The West looks at Sheik Osama as a terrorist, but for us he is a saint," one bodyguard, Naseer Ahmed al-Bahri, told her. Another former operative, Ali Mohammed al-Kurdi, sitting "on the floor of a second-story apartment," told her about two suicide bombers he had sent to Iraq "with the pride of a teacher speaking of his students, showing no trace of regret for the blood he helped to spill."[24]

In South Africa as it emerged from apartheid, Bryson (12–13) cultivated sources by doing the rounds over and over again, literally knocking on all doors until someone talked to her – even if it took a mini-election to determine the source of the day:

[The African National Congress] prided itself on being a democratic organization and being an inclusive organization. Often, when you're dealing with people on the ground who are local members of the ANC, when you arrive they would say, "Well, let's get all of the neighbors together, let's get all of the members of our local ANC, and we'll vote on who's going to be interviewed for you today." And you really just have to wait while people discuss, and then they make sure that it's going to be fair and everyone gets a turn. And it could take a very long time ... you really did have to have the patience to wait it out. ... The Truth and Reconciliation Commission hearing started when I was in South Africa, and they were going to start in the Eastern Cape. ... I can remember going to a township in Eastern Cape and knocking on doors. And every single door that I knocked on, somebody in that household had either disappeared or died. ... I didn't go with introductions. I just went to a neighborhood and started knocking on doors.

Mark Stevenson (21) also went knocking on doors in Mexico, and often found that an impromptu encounter born of "talking to everyone you meet" might reveal far more than an interview set up with "weeks of prep" – for example, on the mystery surrounding the more than 100 murdered women in Ciudad Juárez who "just vanished into thin air and their bodies were abandoned in the desert later":

---

[24] Kathy Gannon, "Yemen signs pacts with al-Qaida militants to swear off attacks, but they still love bin Laden," The Associated Press, July 4, 2007.

I remember walking into the state police headquarters at one point ... we weren't supposed to be in there, so we sort of snuck in, and we were just walking from cubicle to cubicle. And I walked into this one office and there was a little letrero, a little sign over his cubicle, saying "servicio médico forense," which means he was part of the medical examiner's team ... and, cold, I say, "Hi, I'm a journalist, can you talk about the women's killings?" He reaches into his desk drawer and he pulls out a skull and he plops it on his desk. And he says, "You want to know why they're not solving these killings? This is why. This was bouncing around in a police precinct headquarters, and it was never tested and there was no crime scene evidence preservation, and they just bundled these things, they find these things in the desert and they're smoking and they throw a cigarette butt down and 50 policemen have been in there, and they dump it into a bag, into a sack with bones from other crime scenes, and then just – and that's why this is never going to be solved." "And can I quote you on that?" "Yes, because I'm quitting tomorrow."

The story quoted "one top investigator for Chihuahua state police, who asked to remain anonymous until his resignation is made formal." It also explained that the warden of the prison where two murder suspects were held – who had told AP that the men had come in with "bruises," hinting at police brutality in getting confessions, and had agreed to allow AP to interview them – was replaced the same day with no public explanation, and the interview canceled.[25]

Many correspondents, for AP and beyond (see Fisk 2002, 107), echoed a sentiment of gratitude, even close to awe, for ordinary people, particularly in tragic circumstances like wars or natural disasters, who opened their hearts and homes to the journalists:

I literally lived with people for days on end for some stories [about hurricanes] – and people who had very, very little – and they would open up their doors and share their food and be very happy to take in a complete stranger who wanted to learn about what their life was like. ... I wonder whether I would do the same. (Price, 5–6)

Kashmir, going up to Kashmir to talk about violence again and again, people want to sit down and talk to you as one human being to another. And part of that is tea again ... very pale, honey-colored tea. And the result becomes – it doesn't seem like business, it's not – it's a sharing. And for them, your questions are acknowledging that what happened to them is significant and not just being ignored. Anyway, that's what I told myself, when I'm asking people, how does it feel? ... I think about that a lot because often, people will say, "How can they ask that? Don't they, don't you know how they feel?" And I think, well I can assume how it feels, but isn't it showing some respect to ask people to tell you what they feel as opposed to making an assumption? But it's still hard for that question not to sound stupid. Stupid questions are fine as long as the answer's not, right? (Bryson, 33–34)

To get that viscerally human perspective for a story about U.S. drones, Gannon and Niedringhaus traveled unaccompanied by military or security to Taliban-controlled areas, along highways "often booby-trapped by militants"

---

[25] Mark Stevenson, "Mexican border city doubts police have caught serial killers, despite official pressure," The Associated Press, December 31, 2001.

and across rock-strewn riverbeds, to interview Afghan refugees about their obliterated villages:

It took a lot of arranging because we had to get to the village. Khalis Family Village is on your way to Tora Bora. And the fellow who we went to in Khalis Family Village, who brought us to the families who had come from the drone-hit area, he said, "We never see any foreigners here, because the Taliban are here." ... [W]e just spent all afternoon talking to this old guy, and there's these kids, and ... he was angry about the drones, but he was smart, too, about it. ... I mean, it's a village. He said, "No, the Taliban never bother us, so why don't these people leave?" [I]t was a very sort of basic – and he was upset because he had to leave his three cows behind, and he had to hand the key to his house to his neighbor, and he didn't know. ... [A]t the end of the day, you have a story that tells what the Afghans are saying about drones. That's all. They're just telling me what they're saying about it. And it's lovely. (Gannon, 73, 26)

The story led with Ghulam Rasool, "barely able to walk even with a cane," padlocking his front door and handing his keys and cows to a neighbor to flee the "relentless airstrikes from U.S. drones," which he and fellow villagers called "benghai," Pashto for "buzzing of flies," scrunching their faces and trying to make the sound as they explained to Gannon. Rasool's 12-year-old grandson intervened to tell her he also recalled the attack and had walked to the next village to see the three dead bodies his friends had told him about.[26]

  Elaine Ganley (26–27), who in more than 30 years in Paris has made her beat France's tense racial and ethnic dynamics – particularly with immigrants from its former colonies – vividly recalls finding a source who would describe, for the world to read, her experience with genital mutilation:

I got all those figures, I got information, I got the experts, etc., and then I found a young lady who was willing to talk about it. And she told her story, from when she was a little girl, 6 years old, how she and her sister were taken to a lady with tattoos on her mouth and smell of incense, and they were told they were going to a party. And they were taken to some place, and taken to a basement, and she said ... "Mommy, why are we – there's no party here, there's just garbage, why are we here?" And then ... each of the sisters was separately ... mutilated ... and how they tried not to get blood on their party dresses.[27]

Covering the collapse of the Spanish economy in the 2000s, Clendenning (16) had to overcome some Spaniards' understandable reluctance to announce to the world they were broke and facing eviction. After attending a bunch of early-morning protests, he found a 45-year-old mother of two willing to share her life story. Irene Gonzalez, "desperately waiting to hear if she'll benefit from an emergency government decree that protects Spaniards such as her from being evicted for failing to make their mortgage payments" on her "cramped

---

[26] Kathy Gannon, "Afghan villagers flee their homes, blame US drones," The Associated Press, March 28, 2013.

[27] Elaine Ganley, "Despite tougher laws, an ancient custom remains a secret horror for some girls in Europe," The Associated Press, September 7, 2007.

apartment in a working class neighborhood," already stacked with cardboard boxes should the reprieve not come, became the lead on the evictions story.[28]

VERIFYING SOURCES: IN PERSON AND ONLINE

After all the time-consuming, delicate, often dangerous work to get to sources, and get them talking on the record, correspondents still have to undertake a basic but formidable task: determining whether any of the information they were given is true, especially harrowing stories of torture and murder that could not be independently verified or, at the other end of the spectrum, interviews conducted under the clear threat of intimidation when sources most likely self-censored.

First of all, AP does not "kill people off," many correspondents proudly said, meaning that even news of deaths, no matter how official or urgent, must be double-checked. Matthew Pennington (4–6) was taking dictation over the phone from Pakistani staff covering a 2007 campaign rally for former prime minister Benazir Bhutto when an explosion went off, killing several supporters:[29]

[A]fter [the local reporter] counted the bodies, he met someone there who told him, "You don't want to be here, you want to be at the hospital." Because it wasn't clear at this point whether Bhutto had been hurt or not, because her spokesman had spoken to us and basically said she's okay. ... So our guy, Zarar Khan, went to the hospital, where there was security people blocking the way, and he blagged his way in ... all these times he was ringing stuff in, but he'd lost his telephone along the way, so he was just [grabbing] telephones from people and ringing stuff in. And then eventually ... people came out of the operating theater and they were crying and they were close associates of Benazir, and he managed to get two people to confirm that she was dead. ... A lot of Bhutto's people are from Karachi, and our stringer was from Karachi. He knew these people, he had known them for years, and he's there at the scene, they come out, and you've got named people saying that she is dead. ... I would never sort of kill someone off, as it were, with an anonymous source ... it's the ultimate sort of judgment that you can make on some factual event. So you just have to be cast-iron sure and name sources who know, whom you are convinced know what they're talking about. ... I remember once, there was some Pakistani military operation to go after ... a senior militant in a tribal area, and we had a brigadier who I'd spoken to, and he said, "Yeah, this guy is dead." And it turns out that he wasn't dead. And this guy was a brigadier, he's very senior, he was the number two in the sort of information hierarchy. But ... he wouldn't give his name. ... [E]ven if you have someone of considerable stature and authority ... you can't be sure they're always going to tell the truth or even ... more than he knows.

During the military regime in the late 1970s, Terry Anderson (5–6) rushed to the Seoul bureau in the middle of the night, despite a curfew, when reports came

[28] Alan Clendenning, "Spaniards hope for eviction reprieve amid crisis," The Associated Press, December 10, 2012.
[29] Sadaqat Jan and Zarar Khan, "Pakistani opposition leader Bhutto killed in suicide attack on campaign rally," The Associated Press, December 27, 2007.

in that President Park Chung-hee had been "wounded in a shooting accident," and then had to make the same call:

It becomes apparent that the president is dead, he's been assassinated. And the question is, at what point do we call that? Because it's all coming in from sources, and nobody knows what the hell is going on, the troops were in the street, the tanks were in the street, and he's dead, and [local Korean reporter K. C. Hwang] said I know he's dead ... [but] you don't want to go on the wire with something like that unless you're dead solid. Do you have it? Are you sure? Do you have two sources, who's telling you this? And of course I'm entirely with him because he's Korean and he speaks Korean and he knows everybody in the government, all the dissidents, and finally we call it.

That burden of proof – multiple sources, official accounts, independent verification – might be too high when dealing with the worst atrocity stories or death counts that are hard to bear. Stevenson embarrassedly recalled when engrained mistrust in the political agendas of official sources made him bury the lead – forego the most important information – in a story about the devastation wrought by Hurricane Mitch on Nicaragua and Honduras, both countries afforded special emergency U.S. immigration privileges.[30] When both doubled their death tolls to 10,000, Stevenson (25) believed one because of what AP correspondents in the field were reporting, but put the other "in the third paragraph because I didn't believe it. And I got this very friendly note back from the New York desk, saying, 'Very nice story, Mark. Please, when it involves *thousands* of deaths, could you please keep that in the lead?'" Allegations of torture pose particular challenges, especially when both sides have well-oiled communication strategies, as Hutzler (19–20) found out covering China's repression of the Falun Gong group:

[W]e would try to verify by contacting officials, but they were just denying everything. ... [The Falun Gong's] stories were not outlandish. They were very consistent with what a lot of other political prisoners had told us over the years. So I think we did go on faith. And they were willing to provide details, they were telling about themselves. Often, if they knew the names of the police officers, they were providing the names of the police officers. So yeah, it was one of those things that couldn't be verified that way, but it was consistent.

Gray (11–12) said he was still "very, very upset" that, four decades earlier, AP editors had spiked one of the pathbreaking stories on the horrors in Pol Pot's Cambodia that he had written after interviewing refugees at the border:

There were no second sources; it was the refugees. There was nobody in Cambodia to verify it. You could get some CIA guy to say, "Yeah, we've heard that there's some bad stuff" or whatever, but – so we had to go with refugee sources. But I knew Cambodians well enough to know that these were ordinary villagers ... simple villagers telling me what they saw. ... I didn't ask them, "What do you think about the Khmer Rouge?" No.

---

[30] In late 1998, the destructive hurricane generated record flooding and devastated Central America, killing at least 11,000 people and leaving thousands more missing.

"What happened to you when you got pushed out of Battambang? Where did you live? Who was your commander? What did he do to your wife? What did he do to your children?" And they came out with just graphic stories. So I felt that they were basically 99 percent true. And they were.

That same close questioning led Laub (34, 7–8), covering the economic distress in North Africa and the West Bank, to grill the relatives of Adel, the Tunisian cigarette peddler who burned himself alive ("you just have to keep asking, and sometimes you cannot arrive at a truth, but you try to at least present all the different sides of it"), and to poke her head, figuratively, in refrigerators across the West Bank – their contents telling a more accurate story than many a pronouncement:

I think the serious problem for any journalist is to get past the slogans and actually get to people's opinions ... [T]he West Bank was in big financial trouble, and people weren't getting their salaries. So I'm trying to figure out what people really feel about this; whom do they blame for it and so forth. And then you get a lot of inshallahs first, and people don't want to stick out their necks too far. And you just have to keep asking, "How do you make ends meets, what is in your refrigerator?" ... But ... this cannot be done in 10 minutes. So basically grab people out of the crowd, go home with them, sit with them, have a cup of coffee, be patient, and in the end you'll get a better sense.

Perhaps no society in the world today is more secretive, isolated, and censored than North Korea. Over fruit smoothies in a hip café in Seoul's Itaewon neighborhood, Lee (7–8), who had just wrapped up a meeting with a contact from the North, candidly shared how hard it was to get anything close to "the truth" – but also the difference that being on the ground made:

[T]here's so many competing interests and politics, there's so much obfuscation, and that you just need to try to sort through all of it and ... exercise judgment to try to figure out what's going on. ... I've been going there now almost on a monthly basis for the past two years. ... I'm seeing things outside of those big sort of staged events. I'm seeing things happening on the street at a daily life level. ... And so I'm starting to understand how the society ticks, at least a certain part of it. But I still don't know what the truth is when it comes to what's going on. So it's part of a process. In putting together a story on North Korea, we speak to a lot of people. It's not just the people in North Korea. We speak to people outside the country, experts, and people from NGOs who live there, and they have a certain perspective. So it takes a lot of work to put one story together.

Lee noted that stories made clear whether an interview was conducted without oversight or selection by officials. This is a concern also in war zones, where correspondents who traveled with military escorts or were embedded with U.S. forces questioned how much civilians would feel free to say – though sometimes it was the only way to encounter them within an acceptable risk level, as during the worst days of the Iraq War:

So you were almost caught in the embed process, and then you tried very hard, as much as you could ... to talk to Iraqis. And you could do it, but you were often accompanied by American troops, and obviously the Iraqis are, some were honest, perhaps, and some were in fact critical with the American troops standing next to you. But others ... what could they say? If they had pro-al-Qaida or pro-insurgency or pro-Taliban leanings, they obviously would not spill them out to you with an American troops next to you. ... And, sometimes, I think we may have gotten honest interviews, sometimes probably not ... very difficult to judge. (Gray, 32–33)

Even traveling alone, at terrific personal risk, to remote villages in Afghanistan – as Gannon (72–73) did on the drone story discussed earlier – meant a tremendous amount of verification, again using decade-old sources, before even starting on the road. Assuming that Afghans might legitimately have an ax to grind, after all, could she find two places where Western officials would confirm strikes despite the secrecy surrounding drone programs? A source related to some of her old contacts from the civil war, and a friend of a friend, gave her dates and locations for two villages in Nangarhar that had been struck relatively recently:

ISAF [International Security Assistance Force] or NATO will tell you if there's been an air strike. They won't tell you whether it was a drone. ... So I got all the details, where and everything, and I said, "Could you please confirm that there was a strike? Preferably drone?" ... [I]t went back and forth, back and forth: "Exactly where? Where's the village?" Na na na. ... So I got them to confirm that yes there had been an air strike on the day that they said. So great, perfect, and I had it. Which was critical to the story, because if they would've said, "No, we didn't have an air strike on that day. I don't know what the hell they're talking about." It wouldn't have mattered whether lying or not lying, if their records say ... so when he came back and said, "All I can say is that yes." Ah, yay! So I made arrangements.

Reading between the lines, and verifying, official information from both U.S. and local sources also became a frustrating but necessary routine for Reid (71, 63–64), who headed the Baghdad bureau when some of the worst violence spread across the expanse of Iraq:

[Multi-National Forces, Iraq] had a funny way of coming in with the most boring-sounding releases that later blew up into all kinds of things. One ... came rather late, but that "the commander has decided that pursuant to article such-and-such of the Uniform Code of Military Justice, the investigation ... has been initiated in regard to detention policy." Mistreatment of detentions. At the time, the U.S. had like five of them around the country, so detaining a lot of people. And so my first reaction was, I was kind of irritated because I had almost finished the story for the day and now I have to recast the thing. ... Called the military and which camp are we talking about? They wouldn't say and we didn't have another way to track it. ... So later we found out it was mistreatment at Abu Ghraib, you know how that played out.

The Pulitzer Prize–winning account of the massacre of an estimated 400 civilians by U.S. troops at No Gun Ri in 1950, five weeks into the Korean War, required some of the most extensive digging and verification by an AP team, as Hanley (14–18), who co-authored it, recalled.[31] A writer in the Seoul bureau, Sang-Hun

---

[31] Sang-Hun Choe, Charles J. Hanley, and Martha Mendoza, "After half-century's silence, U.S. vets tell of killing Korean refugees," The Associated Press, September 30, 1999. Choe, Hanley

Choe, started reporting on allegations by survivors in the mid-1990s, eventually joined by Hanley and the AP investigative unit, who focused on a relatively simple point: Survivors had claimed the troops had been with the 1st Cavalry Division, but the U.S. military denied that this division was in the area at the time. AP reporters "papered the walls of the office" with 1950 U.S. Army topographical maps and confirmed the division had been there, after tracing all units' movements, based on the twice-daily reported coordinates found in the archives, as well as spottings of refugees and North Korean combatants. Having obtained 2,000 soldiers' names through a Freedom of Information Act request, Hanley and reporter Martha Mendoza started making "cold calls" "to try to find someone who knew something about this":

[W]e're getting nowhere except we're learning a lot about the war front in July 1950, but nothing about this mass killing. And on the 34th call, Martha found a guy who said, "Yeah, I think there were some refugees killed under a bridge." And then we found another guy and then we realized, "Okay, it's the Second Battalion, Seventh Cavalry Regiment, First Cavalry Division," so we were able to focus on that battalion. And in the end, we got about 15 guys and I say about – and there was a big discussion about this at the time – because what they told us varied. There were guys who gave us some real detail about what happened. And other guys who said simply, "I know what you're talking about. It happened, but I don't want to talk about it." But you consider that a confirmation of a sort as well.

The soldiers' accounts – 130 interviews by telephone and in person – matched chilling details from the survivors' claims, like how "bodies were stacked up at the entrance to the tunnel so people could hide behind their relatives' dead bodies." Then one reporter also found written communications ordering the shooting of refugees. Finally, in fall 1999, the story hit the wire, noting that it revealed "a chapter of the 1950-53 Korean conflict that would remain unwritten until a dozen ex-soldiers, in interviews with The Associated Press, corroborated the allegations of South Koreans who say they survived a mass killing at the U.S. Army's hands."

The very "fog of war" makes it "difficult to tell what's real and what's not," many correspondents said: The internecine conflict between Bosnians, Croatians, and Serbs was a challenge that AP met by having correspondents with all sides reporting each version from the ground to a central editing desk in Vienna, which not only pulled together the "disparate threads" but also generated story ideas: "Hey, we're hearing this from this side, why don't you check this out?" (Alexander, 13). In El Salvador's civil war, Frazier (11–12, 13–14) had no difficulty finding the front lines – bodies were showing up outside the AP's Salvador office – but confirming who had control beyond the city required some creativity, as well as the sobering realization that only his eyewitness reports could be trusted:

[T]here was a very difficult time sorting out the truth and the fiction down there. We spent most of our time doing that. . . . This was still during the Reagan administration, so

and Mendoza, with research assistance by Randy Herschaft, shared the 2000 Pulitzer Prize for Investigative Reporting.

we had their spin on things. And in those years I was naïve enough that if I went to the embassy and they told you what was going on, you should believe it. ... If they say, "Well, we took these towns and we're controlling this, that, and the other," the only way to find out was to go out there and see. Sometimes you couldn't do that, because transportation would be blocked, access would be blocked. So we developed this little system, which I will confess to having thought up myself. Every town in El Salvador has what is called a *central*, which is a telephone operating station. And most houses didn't have any telephones, so the only interaction in and out of these places was through the *central*. So whenever one side or the other took over the town, they'd take over that office first, right, to control the communications. So if you wanted to know who's in charge, you'd just call and see who answered the phone, pretty much. [chuckles] But you really had to go out and put your nose in it, because it was very, very hard to trust any official source there. ... You didn't believe anybody face value. You couldn't.

Even in peace time, correspondents undergo painstaking checks before putting stories on the wire – a process entirely outside the public's view that eats up another big chunk of reporting time, which today is already under heightened competitive, technological, and audience pressures, as discussed throughout this book. The checks might be something as basic as the number of dissidents arrested in Cuba in 2003, with sources from Havana to Miami giving widely different totals (Snow 25–26),[32] or of hostages taken by Islamist terrorists deep in the Algerian desert in 2013,[33] who announced they had 41 prisoners:

And we thought it was like a smash-and-grab operation – they came in, grabbed some people, drove off. And we're like, "There's no way they have enough cars to take 41 hostages. That's ridiculous." What we didn't realize is that they'd gone in, occupied the place, and had 41 hostages. ... Once we'd realized that they had taken over the living quarters, then it was like, "Only 41 hostages?" As it was, it was much more than 41 hostages because ... they took the workers as well. It was just 41 *foreign* hostages. (Schemm, 17–18)

When correspondents jump the gun and skip the checks, the consequences are embarrassing corrections on the wire. Covering a meeting of the Organization of African Unity, Rosenblum (6–7) quoted Zambia's president calling the British prime minister a "traitor" – a pretty strong story of postcolonial conflict, until it turned out that he had said "trader." Fact-checking is even harder when it comes to whistleblowers, whose tips might be both true and driven by agendas far removed from freedom of information. A Mexican motor oil businessman who had contacted Stevenson (19) with allegations of illicit Pemex contracts effectively killed the story when he tried to bribe the correspondent, asking him, "So what will it take for you to write

---

[32] Anita Snow, "Cuban leaders round up dissidents, restrict American diplomats' movements," *The Associated Press*, March 19, 2003.

[33] In January 2013, terrorists took hundreds of people hostage in a remote desert gas plant in Algeria. More than three dozen foreign hostages died.

this story?" On the other end, investigating NGO reports of a spike in blood lead levels in a mining town in northern Mexico, where many houses had been built next to "a huge pile of lead tailings," Stevenson (24–25) found a local scientist at a protest march who told him that the company had known a decade earlier about the effects on children:

So [I] went in, interviewed the company, and they had their CEO at that point answering questions. And I'm ... starting it out with softballs like "Isn't it tragic that these people built their houses right next to your tailings?" And he was like, "Yeah, yeah, but we're thinking of doing something with the tailings, maybe building an ecopark to send out positive vibes." Totally flip. So we came out with that story. ... They did not let the CEO talk about that ever again (Stevenson, 24–25). [The story opened with the statement that "officials did nothing as poisonous lead seeped into the bloodstreams of thousands of children" from the "250-foot-tall mountain of slag towering over surrounding houses and schools." It closed with Met Mex Peñoles director Manuel Luevanos saying the company "had encased a small patch of the black mountain in concrete" – not that it would make any difference, but "it could become a landmark ... maybe we could use it to send ecological messages to the community."][34]

The widespread use of social media is creating a new set of ethical and professional dilemmas. Despite pressures to follow whatever is trending, most correspondents tend to err on the side of caution when bombarded with anonymous, often unverifiable user-generated content and use it sparingly or as "tip service" (Reid, 74). The paradox, of course, is that sources found through social media are most appealing when reporters cannot get to the scene – as in the Syrian conflict in the 2010s – which makes their information proportionately harder to check independently. Malcolm Foster (12), who headed the Japan bureau when the 2011 earthquake, tsunami, and nuclear disaster struck, turned down a too-good-to-be-true source found online because her story about working at the Fukushima plant could not be confirmed:

Basically we were desperate to try to talk with some of the workers at the plant, and we couldn't get access to them, because we didn't know how to get ahold of them and the company wouldn't let us talk to them. So we were desperately trying to search for people through the social networks. And we found one woman, and it sounded legitimate, but we ended up not using her, I believe, because we just could not verify that it was accurate. And I'm happy to do that. I err on the side of being certain.

Some correspondents were adamant that quoting someone off Facebook was worse than the anathema anonymous source ("at least an anonymous source, you actually met the person, you know something about them," McDowell 17). Veteran correspondents like Reid (74) argued that the delivery method – a

---

[34] Mark Stevenson, "Mexican children live a tragedy foretold in shadow of refinery," The Associated Press, May 5, 1999.

phoned-in tip, a faxed release, an online video – does not affect the need to pay attention but verify:

[In Iraq], some people started using [social media] to release [statements]. At first we were a little nervous about that, because there's always a possibility of bogus, hack accounts. But then, [groups] kept saying, "No, no, this is really us." And so you would start looking at them the way you would have looked at a fax machine 40 years ago. . . . And then people began to post pictures and videos. We ended up using some of that, but there would have to be some kind of vetting . . . is there anything in that that might raise suspicion? Is the foliage wrong? Is that building really there? Does this look like it was superimposed? Does this look like it was photoshopped?

In the end, some correspondents admitted that, despite the most rigorous efforts to verify both in-person and online sources, the whole point of naming a source is just that – it is what somebody said, not the reporter's firsthand knowledge:

[Post-Gadhafi Libya] is an incredibly random and strange place to operate . . . the government . . . said [former Gadhafi spokesman] Moussa Ibrahim had been captured one day while I was there . . . turned out it wasn't true. They were just reporting a rumor from the soldiers. . . . You can have stuff solidly from a source . . . from an official, and it turns out not to be true, which is incredibly frustrating (Schemm, 17).

If something purports to be from [Syrian provincial capital] Idlib, we would run it by Arabic speakers who would confirm that the accents of people around are indeed from Idlib. You look for signs of buildings that you know are iconic in the area. . . . [Y]ou try to run it by experts who would be able to verify things that you yourself could not, for example. And also certain sources have gained credibility. You try to deal as much as you can with the sources that you believe to be credible and that you are familiar with etc., etc. . . . Look, you come clean. You say, "This is from amateur video that has been verified to AP standards." . . . When you attribute something to a source, you say, "The source said." That fact will remain true even if what they said is untrue. That is not any excuse for running a statement that turns out to be untrue. . . . But you always cite the source. You never pretend as if you know something that you don't. Clearly you're citing the source because to the best of your ability to discern, the source is worth citing and very, very, very, very probably speaking the truth. But can you swear to it? You do your best. In the end a lot of what we do is judgment calls, which there is no escaping. (Perry, 23–24)

PROTECTING SOURCES' LIVES – AND DIGNITY

The needs to develop and verify sources are such deeply engrained constants in the professional practice of foreign correspondents that, despite the inherent dangers and struggles, they have become second nature. What all correspondents really agonize over is a profound ethical dilemma that, again, exists entirely outside the public's view – how to protect sources, not only from unnecessary pain and embarrassment, but from losing their lives because they talked to journalists. From China to Latin America, many correspondents faced the reality that sources were putting their lives on the line to speak:

But you think about all of these people who are in terrible places, like [Alfredo] Landaverde in Honduras, a former security minister who would meet with you on the streets of Tegucigalpa. You'd go into a restaurant, he'd have no security, carrying no weapon, and tell you all about police corruption and how this led up all the way to the top. And I'd be like, "Señor Landaverde, are you sure that you want to talk about this?" And he says, "Yes, this is what I believe. People know I say this and I say this." And then you go out the next time and ... two guys on a motorcycle pulled up next to him and shot him to death six months later.[35] So you're impressed by how people even in these terrible places are much more forthcoming than you have any right to expect them to be (Stevenson, 22).

Frazier (22, 16, 25), whose wife was killed by a bomb as they reported on guerrilla movements in Central America[36] and who therefore said he could more easily put himself in the place of traumatized civilians, had to explain sources' reticence to his editors, but still carried the burden 30 years later of what the consequences might have been for those who did talk to him:

I talked to this woman who had five kids, and she was exceedingly pregnant and she was standing by a fire, just throwing sticks under a pot of what I assumed were beans. And I asked her about it, and she said, "Well, los malos, the bad ones, came through and they carried away my husband because he was preaching the word of God. I haven't seen him since then." She said, "They would come and lay ambushes [for] us from when we were out cutting coffee," and then she just turned away and said, "But I saw nothing, I saw nothing at all."[37] People were just powdered with fear. ... [W]e used to get requests out of New York from people who knew better: "Well, go out in the street and talk to the average Salvadoran. How does the average Salvadoran feel about this?" And I would tell them that the average Salvadoran who has two working brain cells is keeping his mouth shut because you could become dead real easily out there. ... There would be people we would interview and several hours later they'd turn up dead. You'd have to hope that's coincidence, but you never know. We dealt with that all the time. ... It didn't take much.

Terril Jones (31–33) was still working as a reporter in Beijing when I met him at his office a few blocks west of Tiananmen Square, where he had been on the ground among the tanks reporting the uprising in June 1989 (see this chapter's box). Nearly a quarter century later, he could not forgive himself as he thought about what his stories, and those of a Western press heady with prodemocracy optimism, might have cost his fully identified sources when the Chinese regime

---

[35] Stevenson quoted Landaverde by name in a story about how "Honduras has become a main transit route for South American cocaine"; Mark Stevenson, "Honduras becomes Western Hemisphere cocaine hub," The Associated Press, October 30, 2011. Landaverde was gunned down less than two months later.

[36] Linda Frazier, a journalist on assignment for the *Tico Times*, was killed when a bomb was detonated at a press conference in Nicaragua in 1984.

[37] The story portrayed the identical vignette: Joe Frazier, "Refugee camps swelling in El Salvador," The Associated Press, January 18, 1981.

held – sources like Yang Zhisheng, "a junior from Inner Mongolia studying management at Beijing University of Science and Technology," who is featured in one of Jones' early stories saying he didn't fear the army and playing his accordion on top of his makeshift home, a commandeered public bus in Tiananmen Square:[38]

Were there people arrested because of AP stories or photos? Were people executed because of them or tortured or maimed – beaten so that they couldn't walk again? Or were they separated from their families? Were their families persecuted? It's all possible. ... And that is the real – the haunting legacy ... the people I have interviewed, and people I have met for just a brief moment, and today suffer really unspeakable consequences as a result. I'm certain there are those who did and we'll never know. ... And it does make me feel guilty sometimes when I'm just having a good time or if I'm enjoying traveling or being with my kids or taking them to see their grandparents or

FIGURE 4.3. Tokyo-based correspondent Terril Jones interviews student protesters in Beijing's Tiananmen Square in May 1989, days before the violent crackdown by the Chinese armed forces. (Photo courtesy of Terril Jones)

[38] Terril Jones, "Students living in makeshift city in Beijing's central square," The Associated Press, May 25, 1989.

taking them even to Beijing Zoo . . . I just don't know how lucky or fortunate I might be compared to what kind of misfortune I may have facilitated. That, I think, is the true tragedy that all reporters who were part of that coverage took part of. Unknowingly and unintentionally, but inevitably. . . .

[O]n the night of June 3rd [1989], when they were shooting their way into the square . . . I was stopped in the lobby of the Beijing Hotel, and . . . a young guy . . . said he was with the Gōng'ānjú, Public Security Bureau. He flashes his ID, says, "What do you got there, what were you doing?" . . . I pulled my video camera out. And he took the . . . tape . . . two hours' worth, and confiscated it. . . . I was hugely upset, and I argued a little bit, and then I was so angry that I stormed off to my room. What I should have done is that I should have followed him outside, and as soon as he hit the crowds, grabbed his arm and said, "This guy is from the PSB, he confiscated my film." The crowd would not have let him get away with what he had. . . . I don't even know or remember what was on that videotape. I do know that there were people who identified themselves and were talking about their hopes and their aspirations, and why they were taking part in this thing. I, to this day, I don't know what that may have facilitated, either.

China correspondents from the 1970s to today have needed similar caution in all interactions, with ordinary citizens and low-level officials, which they assume the government is monitoring – stealthily through electronics or blatantly with green Mercedes, which Graham recalled followed her whenever she set out to interview dissidents. (Not that inviting them to the bureau was easier, since it was housed in a compound with ID-checking guards; Graham, 12.) Nearly four decades later, "we have always assumed that the bureau is completely bugged," China bureau chief Hutzler (5–6, 14) told me – as we sat in the bureau's conference room – but the duty remained to protect sources:

And that's always been the most difficult part of the job here because, in the end, there's only so much you can do. . . . [W]e use pay phones to contact sensitive sources. But basically, if you're being followed, they can see that you've used such-and-such pay phone and then just get the number from the phone company. . . . And then there's intimidation against sources, right? That you talk to people and then they get visited by the authorities. . . . Most of the people who are dissidents or activists, sort of their family members, or even now ordinary Chinese who have run afoul of the authorities somehow, by the time they get to us, they're pretty desperate and they're mostly cognizant of the threats that they face and they've made the decision to risk those repercussions because they feel that getting their story out will benefit them in some way. . . . [Hutzler and a source who did security work at the time for the Central Committee of the Communist Party] had sort of a prearranged routine where, because I couldn't call him at his office because the phones would have probably been monitored – and actually, . . . when the journalists' offices were all in these diplomatic compounds, if we tried to call . . . many government offices, we were blocked. . . . [S]o I had this routine with this guy, where I would call him at his home and . . . I would say, "Oh, it's your old friend, lao pengyou" . . . And we had sort of a set meeting place, so all we ever had to do on the phone was talk about the time. And we would meet from time to time and sit and chat . . . that was a very valuable relationship for a time. And then, as so often happens with these kinds of relationships, he gets promoted to a certain level where it becomes too risky to meet with foreign reporters.

Despite her pride in AP's on-the-ground reporting from North Korea, Lee (7) also talked about the need to always ensure that she was causing no harm "to the people who are brave enough to speak to us," calling it "a good ... and necessary moral compass for any foreign correspondent to have, no matter where you're working." John Daniszewski (11), interviewed in his office as the head of AP's international coverage, espoused a similar principle while recalling his reporting in Eastern Europe as Communist regimes were falling:

I think [sources] of anyone were more sophisticated about what the government was doing, and so they were not likely to be caught unawares if they were being followed or anything like that. I think their homes also were monitored all the time. So if you had a confidential conversation, you would take it outside, talk to somebody in a park ... where you think there would be no monitors. No eavesdropping equipment. Even, you thought that somewhere in your car or a taxi or a waiter might be overhearing what you were talking about, so it was just sort of a fact of life there. ... It's true, we actually did turn the faucets on.

In the essentially lawless cartel fiefdoms along the U.S.-Mexican border, Stevenson (11–13) had to adjust his reporting practices so as not to endanger his life or that of his sources – including granting anonymity:

After 70,000 deaths in the drug war, if you say that they asked that their name not be used for fear of reprisal, that becomes much more credible. ... [P]eople in an area where there is a cartel conflict will talk the blue moon, will tell you everything about the cartel that doesn't control their town. And they will tell you absolutely nothing about the cartel that does. ... When we were up in Valle de Juárez, outside of Ciudad Juárez, people would say, oh yeah, the cartels hand out leaflets, with a typical, completely misspelled threat against the rival cartel ... you have tacos at Doña M's little restaurant, and when you come back through town, Doña M had gone out, gotten some of the leaflets to share with you. So people were helpful, people really want to get their story out. ... So it's putting together pieces to a puzzle where you're never going to walk up and have people, interview people about the cacique, the cartel boss who dominates their town. You put that together by going to the next town ... it's never a straightforward thing. ... [P]eople help you when they can. But often they'll develop their own little code words – like in Tamaulipas, nobody talks about the Zetas. You talk about "la letra" or "la última letra" [the letter, the last letter] – you don't even say the word has become so powerful.

Granting anonymity is one paradoxical practice: correspondents fought with all their might to get full information from people, only to fight harder not to reveal it to anyone else, particularly not the government. For Harold Olmos (22), refusing to reveal the source who had alerted him that the Bolivian military was mobilizing to quell uprisings in the mines in the mid-1970s – a sergeant related to another journalist – meant alienating the government in his native country, which eventually expelled him. Pyle (21–22), one of AP's Saigon bureau chiefs during the Vietnam War, and his colleagues risked provoking both U.S. officials and other journalists by protecting a U.S. pilot willing to disclose his refusal to bomb North Vietnam. They assumed responsibility, as it were, after some massive digging to unearth this exclusive source who had given AP blunt, front-page quotes like "Anytime you bomb on the massive scale we did up there ... there's bound to be bombs off target, no question about it" and "I can live with [years in military prison] easier than I can with taking part in the war":[39]

[A] little item came in from Washington that said that some pilot named Captain Michael Heck had been suspended from duty pending court martial because he had refused to fly a mission over North Vietnam [in 1972]. So George [Esper] said, "Well, that's a hell of a story." ... I'm sitting at the next desk trying to know what [George] is doing, on this otherwise quiet day, dialing, dialing, dialing, finally he gets an answer, tracks this guy down – a base in Thailand, which is where they flew from. ... They have this conversation which goes on for like 45 minutes. ... Esper, he was a fast sonofabitch. ... And he gets in the graces of this guy and he tells the whole story. ... George writes this thing ... this is on the front page of the *New York Times*. And all hell breaking loose, people calling the bureau, "Who is this pilot?! You got some pilot you talked to? Who is this guy?!" "Well we made an agreement with him, in order to talk with him we promised not to say where he's located." ... So the next day George calls ... Michael back. ... And he says, "Oh God, George, Jesus Christ. All hell's broke loose. They got me in the restricted here, and I can't go anywhere and they won't let me talk." "They won't let you talk?" He says, "No, they told me not talk to anybody, including you." And George says, "You mean they muzzled you, right?" Michael says, "Yeah, I guess you could say that they muzzled me." So George says, "Thank you." "The Air Force muzzled this guy," he writes, the roof falls in again.[40]

Out of regard for their sources and subjects, in Rhodesia in the 1970s as in Bosnia in the 1990s, correspondents said they did not report a striking detail – intriguingly in both cases about the dead – that felt disrespectful:

There was another awful [massacre] down in the east, down by Mutare it is now, where there were a bunch of Protestant missionaries ... and there was a baby of about three months, and we got down there pretty swiftly, and this child had an imprint of a boot across her forehead. ... I thought, I can't even think of anything to write about this. ... But then of course there were no mobile phones or anything in those days, so you went back to the office to write a story ... so you had time to consider. ... I was talking to a reporter who was sitting next to me, and I said, "This is awful, but it is a good story, and I know that it will play well, it will get on the budget." And he said, "You know, there are more things to life than getting on the budget, aren't there?" ... And indeed there are (Johnson, 3–4). [The story of the British missionaries and children "hacked to death by black raiders" noted that the youngest victim, a 3-week-old girl, "shared a coffin with her mother" and that one girl had placed her sister's favorite toy, a yellow owl, on her coffin.][41]

---

[39] George Esper, "B-52 Pilot Who Refused Mission Calls War Not Worth the Killing," *New York Times*, January 12, 1973, 1.
[40] The Captain Heck story is also told by Hugh Mulligan (AP Oral History, Mulligan 2005, 20–21).
[41] Maureen Johnson, The Associated Press, June 29, 1978.

I was in Bosnia, and we had heard about an incident where a family was having lunch and they all got killed. . . . The mother, they pulled her out from the morgue, and she still had an expression of "oh" – such shock. A mortar round had come right through while they were eating lunch, through the window. A detail that I never could use, never felt comfortable using: Her watch was still ticking. . . . Because there were a series of ads in the States at the time of Timex, "takes a licking and keeps on ticking." And I just felt that people – even though it wasn't a Timex – that it just didn't feel right to me, for some reason, to use that, even though it was such an incredible detail. (Alexander, 15, 29)

At the most personal level, correspondents also struggle with the demands of a dramatic, fully reported story when that entails intruding on people's suffering, thus perhaps provoking more pain, without offering any palliative stronger than a packet of crackers or publication, provided the harrowing quotes even make it on the wire. They never want to be the reporter who, according to a memoir, ran around the Kinshasa airport at the height of the 1960s Congolese conflict, perusing the evacuation flights and yelling, "Anybody here been raped and speaks English?"[42] And yet they need to probe:

[E]very Cambodian refugee had, guaranteed, two, three, four people or his whole family wiped out, to bring back those memories, sometimes asking great detail, "exactly how did they kill your father? Did they smash him over the head, or did they throw him alive into the pit? Or did they shoot him?" To get a real graphic story, you need that . . . sometimes it's very painful for them. Countless times, obviously, they start crying, and it's painful for you. . . . So I try, as best as I can, to show empathy and also to bullshit with them about other things, and not just go, two-minute sound bite, "Hey, how did they kill your dad?" . . . [W]hen somebody spends two or three hours with you and they're starving and all the rest of it, I don't pay for the interview, but sometimes I will give a donation to the village chief or to the mother, to buy some rice. Or, often, I will buy them something rather than give money. Recently, when we went to the villages here in Burma, Chin state is the poorest state in Burma . . . we asked our guide, "Obviously we don't want to pay these people, so what do you think?" And he said, "Why don't you bring some crackers for the kids?" (Gray, 16–17)

[Y]ou're in a small Mexican town and you want to get some real human case, you want to get a human voice, people who have relatives that have been kidnapped or disappeared . . . and this woman is telling me something but it doesn't really have all the elements and she doesn't know all the facts on this one. And you're standing there and all of the sudden a crowd gathers around you and they're all, "Did you write down my name? My brother is missing. Write down his name!" And I'm like, "Señor, yo no soy funcionario, yo soy periodista" [Sir, I'm not an official, I'm a journalist.] So you wind up writing down all their names, and that feels terrible because you're not going to do

---

[42] The sentence became the title of the memoir of Edward Behr, a correspondent for Reuters and other organizations. He described seeing "thousands of Belgian civilians" waiting to be airlifted out of the new independent Congo in 1960 and how "into the middle of this crowd strode an unmistakable British TV reporter, leading his cameraman and sundry technicians like a platoon commander through hostile territory. At intervals he paused and shouted, in a stentorian but genteel BBC voice, 'Anyone here been raped and speaks English?'" (Behr, 134).

anything, other than give a general impression that there's a problem out there. So that feels like crap. (Stevenson, 33)

They would bring [American POWs from Vietnam to the Philippines] and ... when they first arrived off the plane, we didn't contact them. We weren't permitted. So, whether the next day or the day after or whenever we encountered them – some of them – I don't know whether they were selected or whatever it is, but I'm sure that the ones that we communicated with, they were very good. They seemed okay. But, on the other hand, there were so many of them, planeloads and planeloads, that maybe they had already separated the ones that were there that might have ... required special treatment. ... And of course we would, on our side, understand that – what they had gone through (Liu, 5). [The stories noted it too, describing the "chalky-faced prisoners" hobbling and with arms dangling "limply."][43]

Gallardo was on the tarmac with the families of the victims of the 1972 plane crash in the Andes, waiting for the survivors to be brought in, more than two months after the disaster, and nobody knew who had lived, or how. The story's only hint at the gruesome truth that would emerge – that they had survived by eating the dead – was at the very end: "Reports at the time of the crash also indicated the aircraft did not carry much food."[44] More than 40 years later, Gallardo (3–4) still choked at the memory of that first meeting in San Fernando:

[T]he helicopter landed, and an air force officer opened the door, and he said, "I want to read the names of the people who survived." And I had been talking before with several relatives of the missing Uruguayans, and the guy started reading the names and ... after 16 names he said, "Well, unfortunately that's it. No more survivors." And the couple standing next to me fell to the ground, crying. They were the relatives of a man called Numa Turcatti ... and afterward I found out that Numa Turcatti had survived until ... three or four days before the rescue. And he just couldn't eat the flesh of ... those who died. ... I just didn't pay the attention I would pay now to the couple. Because the survivors emerged from the helicopter and they started talking to us. ... Right away, oh, embracing and smiling, they fell to the ground just crying, impressive, impressive. And the couple that was there, they – when I remember about it now, I should have talked to those people or said something ... DELL'ORTO: What do you wish you had said? GALLARDO: I don't know. I really don't know. I was very shocked.

CONCLUSIONS

Once they are in position in a foreign country and have made their news choices, foreign correspondents' first and most critical task is finding, developing, and maintaining sources across all strata of society. Perhaps no part of the journalistic enterprise is more immersive and time-intensive than convincing others – from world leaders to street children – to give their testimony, on the record, for global publication. The list of sources has remained constant across time and place: U.S. and foreign government leaders and officials; their

[43] "34 More POWs Freed," *Stanford Daily*, March 6, 1973.
[44] "16 Survivors of Oct. 13 Plane Crash Found in Andes," *New York Times*, December 23, 1972, 1.

opposition (including rebels, insurgents, and dissidents), some hard to find and others all too eager to spin their narrative; local media and journalists; and that most American of journalistic characters, the "man on the street," who in most countries wants to remain anonymous and, in some, is breaking the law to talk to a foreign journalist.

With all sources, correspondents needed time, patience, and respect – and a whole lot of leg work, whether it meant jungle muleback rides, mujahedeen-led mountain treks, or endless door-knocking in South African townships. Similarly intensive and necessarily on the ground is the task of independently verifying the information sources give – from official statements to harrowing accounts of tragedy to tweets. For vox pop sources, protecting them is an additional, agonizing responsibility for correspondents who cannot afford to buy into the set narratives discussed in Chapter 3, such as the expected "triumph of democracy" during the Tiananmen protests. Finding ways to protect sources' lives – from avoiding surveillance to granting anonymity – is something they are, disturbingly, called to do routinely in many areas where, across time, to be seen as talking to journalists, especially American journalists, has implied a clear danger, one that correspondents have not always been able to mitigate and that continues to haunt them after decades.

Chapter 5 explores the other side of this interaction between correspondents and sources: the reaction to the journalists' own personas, beginning with their being identified with the United States – an often unpopular, sometimes deadly calling card for all involved.

Tiananmen Square Protests, 1989

Terril Jones: AP quickly staked out the square 24/7. We took shifts. We had somebody on the square at all times. ... And it was just an incredibly exhilarating feel ... just a sense of absolute astonishment, saying, "Wow, this could happen. What's going on here?" Something – the only thing that can happen is a collapse of the Communist government. That's what everybody really thought was going to happen. ...

[O]n the night of June 2nd, I was in the AP bureau at Qijiayuan ... I was doing a nighter for the protests and ... I heard something outside the window ... and there were these large squares of soldiers jogging from the east to the west, toward Tiananmen Square. ... I took a car and I went down to the square. And what had happened was, the students who were there and the citizens ... tens of thousands of citizens had stopped the soldiers and talked them out of it. ... [W]e had these big cell phones that literally were bricks ... and I was phoning in stuff. And I remember [an AP editor] ... was incredulous, said, "What? They're just like, they're just turned around?"

And I said, "Yeah, they're just trudging back to where they came from. They were turned back by people power." ... That was, of course, the headlines, around the world the next day. That night is when the army came in – the night of June 3rd. ...

I was, actually, up in my hotel room, in the Beijing Hotel, overlooking Chang'an Boulevard in front of me and the square ... I just held the phone outside the window, and they could hear gunshots, they could hear ambulances, they could hear crowds shouting. ... [T]ens of thousands of people down here, around the Beijing Hotel and Wangfujing – and several times during the day, they were so curious, they would just come out and stare. And the soldiers would run forward and they would shoot. Often up in the air, but sometimes shooting at people. ... [E]verybody would just disperse and panic and run away and then come back. That happened at least three times on the morning of the fourth. ... Again, the Chinese have an expression: "kan renao" [literally, "watch the commotion"]. It means to go see what the fuss is about. And the Chinese love to go see what the fuss is about ... they just couldn't keep themselves away from the "renao." ...

Citizens were instructed to stay away from this square. And, in particular, there was one phrase that said ... "Anybody who is using cameras or binoculars or telescopic devices will be subject to being shot on the spot." And so June 5th ... I was just out there, looking around, and we heard gunshots coming from the square. And you could hear tanks coming, and they're pretty loud too. ... I could see tanks that were coming into view. ... I lift up my camera. People scatter. They run away from me because all of a sudden, now I'm a target. ... But that first picture that I took down there ... that's the picture that has the guy ["tank man"] in it. Who I didn't see. ... And I hid my film. I'd always keep my cameras and my film in a ... [bathroom] square hole to access the pipes and stuff like that. ... [In] my shot ... he was here and the tanks were way over here. ... He just didn't move. He stood there as these things were approaching. ... And it showed, to me, that – first of all, it was very premeditated ... it wasn't like the tanks were coming down here and he says, "dang," and then he jumps out like that. He's standing there as he sees these things coming. And they just keep coming and coming and coming and coming and coming until it finally goes up and stops here. ...

[In the aftermath] students went underground. There was a most-wanted list issued. The very shrill commentary returned to the airwaves. And the press muzzled, all over again. And certainly, I think, many people saw a chance – what they felt was a chance of a lifetime – snatched. Snatched is too weak of a word, but snatched away from them (Jones, 17–27, 31).

[The difference between Jones' stories on June 3 and June 5, 1989, illustrates the drastically altered mood after the military intervention.[45] The first story describes how "thousands of pro-democracy students and residents combined forces" to turn back soldiers, who "straggled away" in disarray. The second tells "a grim story of carnage" as newly reticent interviewees, lying in a hospital "on filthy mattresses caked with dried blood, their clothes torn, bandages hastily applied to bullet wounds," "recalled the People's Liberation Army shooting, clubbing and even strangling its way through a sea of unarmed protesters." One woman who said she had gone near the scene "to see what all the excitement was" was shot in the back as she fled soldiers – and like all the others, she "would not let her name be used." The story ended by saying that all patients "implored an American reporter to 'report the truth' about the Tiananmen violence."]

---

[45] Terril Jones, "Military turned back in advance toward Tiananmen Square," The Associated Press, June 3, 1989; Terril Jones, "Wounded say soldiers fired without provocation," The Associated Press, June 5, 1989.

5

Being an American Abroad – Perceptions of Journalists

> The thing about the [early 1980s] Lebanon war was you could go anywhere as a correspondent, even an American correspondent. You could show up and virtually every side would talk to you and respect your credentials – not the government credentials. The AP had very elaborate credentials made to look impressive in Arabic and English. ... We used to carry during the war at least a half a dozen press passes. You had one for the government, you had one for the major militias, each of them, you had one for the major PLO factions, you had a Syrian ... And then it started going all bad and ... those people ... were not interested in anything about who you were, other than that you were an American, the Westerner, etc. ... There were very few correspondents left when I was kidnapped. ... And I told [colleagues and relatives] they are not going to take me because right now ... I'm telling their story, I was covering the Israeli occupation of South Lebanon, struggling down to South Lebanon, doing stories about what the Israelis were doing, which was cutting down 500-year-old olive groves[1] and ... generally rampaging through South Lebanon. ... [I was] one of the few people who was covering the occupation of South Lebanon, but as it turned out they didn't care, it didn't matter. In fact, they thought I was a spy, so I was doubly on their list. (Anderson, 17–18)

Terry Anderson, an American AP correspondent, was kidnapped by Hezbollah militants in Beirut in March 1985 and held hostage – virtually always in tiny windowless rooms, chained hand and foot to walls – for almost seven years, longer than all other foreign hostages held periodically with him (see this chapter's box). Quietly recalling the ordeal nearly 30 years later in his plant-ringed south Florida rambler, Anderson (25) figured that his persona as a well-known U.S. journalist made him into the kidnappers' "poster boy," keeping him (and them) in the news, but might also have saved his life, because killing

---

[1] Anderson had begun reporting from southern Lebanon at least two years before his kidnapping; in a story datelined Karkah, he described how "villagers fear that their olive and orange trees will be cut down to eliminate hiding places favored by guerrillas," Terry A. Anderson, "Israelis building new defense line," The Associated Press, August 6, 1983.

him "was going to look bad." Albeit usually far less tragically, all foreign correspondents' practices, especially their ability to get access to both sources and scenes, are affected by who they are, beginning with foreigners and journalists – and as in Anderson's case, which of those identifiers comes first could mean life or death.

Across time and countries, correspondents have been hindered or helped in a great range of degrees by how people identify them. Being a journalist could mean immediate expulsion or open-armed welcome as someone capable of bringing help, whether or not the AP name carried any recognition. Being a Westerner could leverage the "foreigner discount" – the ability to push further than locals could – except of course where Westerners were the enemy in ongoing hot or cold wars. Given the predominance of U.S. global power in the eight decades traced in this book, Americanness is a unique challenge – not exactly a door-opening calling card in Fallujah or among FMLN fighters in El Salvador, it nevertheless carried a certain cachet in other contexts, like postcolonial Africa. In countries with government-run media, U.S. correspondents were routinely taken for U.S. officials – or, far more dangerously, spies. Especially in Africa, race has mattered too – for the nearly entirely white press corps as well as the rare African American correspondent. Beyond these perceptions, for the 16 women correspondents interviewed, gender has added a layer of scrutiny (and clothing), though hardly any restrictions. For better or for worse, other people's reactions to these multiple facets of identity have impacted how correspondents first encounter the world.

WE ARE THE (ASSOCIATED) PRESS

Despite the tremendous dangers inherent in bearing witness to violence, conflict, and corruption (detailed in Chapter 7), being identified as a journalist long provided a modicum of protection in many countries. All correspondents saw as a particular bonus being a journalist with AP – as a prestigious, trustworthy organization, but also, paradoxically, as a cloak of anonymity in some contexts. Correspondents in Europe, China, India, Japan, and the Middle East from the 1940s to the 2000s found the AP badge well known and prestigious enough to open doors and loosen tongues (Bria, 4, 17). An "AP man" in Egypt in the early 1960s was "a big deal," one such man recalled, even though he might have only been "a young kid from Valdosta, Georgia," because "the AP stood for something" (McArthur, 9). An AP woman brought even more reverential treatment, and it helped overcome gender barriers, Vicki Graham (17, 26) found as bureau chief in China and then in India in the late 1970s and early 1980s: "[In Beijing] they treated me like the representative of The Associated Press ... [in India] as far as the news went, I was treated like an AP bureau chief. And that's how the Indian government treated me, and that's how everybody else treated me. I didn't have any problems. If anything, they were impressed that I was a woman." Today, one correspondent in job-title-conscious Tokyo still said that his first identifier, even before American, was "the fact that I'm working for The Associated Press, and that does have a pretty good name value in Japan. People … figure they can trust you to a certain extent because of the company that you work for" (Talmadge, 17).

But others found that many ordinary people were not familiar with The Associated Press and its cooperative structure and vast reach, which are harder to grasp than a major newspaper like the *New York Times*, the 24/7 broadcasting of CNN, or even, to many correspondents' frustration, rival wire service Reuters – whose British connections rang closer to home in formerly colonized areas across Africa and the Middle East. To Stevenson (31–32), a longtime Mexico hand, having to explain to ordinary people what talking to AP will mean – especially in terms of global visibility – brings a special satisfaction that makes up for the "low rung" position:

We had a very nice story with a woman who owns a little tiny corner store in Mexico City, but got angry because Coca-Cola said, "You can only have my Coca-Cola refrigerator if you sell only Coke. If you sell anything else, I'm going take my refrigerator away." Which is in fact against Mexican antimonopoly law. This woman took Coca-Cola to court and won a huge damage settlement, millions of dollars in fines. So it was a little street corner lady storekeeper beats Coca-Cola.[2] And nobody else had done the story. … [Y]ou're sitting there with her, interviewing her in her store in [a] low-income neighborhood in the eastern slums and listening to her talk through methodically: "This is when I got fed up, and this is what they said to me." And talking to her and saying, "Señora, le quiero prevenir que Usted se va a volver muy famosa. ¡Prepárate!" [I want to let you know that you will become very famous, so get ready.] … And in fact, for the next few weeks she was all over the news, "tiny storeowner beats Coca-Cola." … And you don't really know how to prepare people for that. And that's one of the weirdest things about this job is that … we are not the highest profile, … we don't have big staffs and drivers … but everybody all around the world is reading us, and when you talk to me, it means *New York Times* editors reading this and everybody else is reading this. So it's kind of like you're operating under the radar screen.

In remote Afghan tribal areas targeted by U.S. drone strikes, villagers who "had no idea" about AP understood "we were journalists and we were going to tell their story" – and were happy to be interviewed, despite their anger at being caught in between the strikes and the Taliban:

[I]t wasn't like, "you tell the world that I hate drones" kind of thing. … I was the one that had to sort of make them understand that this was something that we wanted to just tell people and explain that this is what's happened. Please just tell your story. … Somebody came to his door, wanted to – couple of foreign women [Gannon and AP photographer Anja Niedringhaus]. And … we had tea and spent a lot of time sort of talking about it

---

[2] Raquel Chavez was described as "vigorous, fast-talking … as she sat on an upturned Coke crate outside her one-story brick shop"; Mark Stevenson, "Mexican shop owner pushed for big antitrust fine against Coca-Cola bottlers," The Associated Press, November 15, 2005.

and explaining, and he was quite happy to. He was angry as he told the story; he was angry. But he wasn't angry at me. (Gannon, 74–75)

On many occasions, downtrodden people are only too eager to talk, believing that the media come to their rescue – raising ethical dilemmas discussed in Chapter 4, since all correspondents can do is try to bring the world's attention to their plight, with no guarantees of help. From China to Chile, from ordinary Afghan villagers to besieged Bosnians to left-wing guerrillas, many have sought to publicize their cause through foreign correspondents who they believed powerful and sympathetic – or vulnerable to threats, as in the case of armed militants storming bureaus to get their statements on the wire. The pro-democracy narratives noted in Chapter 3, plus a reputation for independence and fairness absent from state-run media, made Soviet and Chinese citizens eager to talk to correspondents for domestic political gain: "If they got the story on the foreign media, it would get the attention of foreign governments and it would put pressure on [their] government" (Hutzler, 4; also Cooperman, 23). In Berlin when the Wall fell, a 55-year-old therapist from East Germany pulled the sleeve of an AP reporter and asked her, in halting English, whether she was from the BBC – thrilled to be understood for the first time by a native speaker of the language she had taught herself by listening to the broadcaster's TV series "Follow Me!", though the rest of the interview was in German, to "speed it up a bit" (Johnson, 20).[3] After an attempted coup against President Hugo Chávez in 2002, one AP correspondent was given a rare friendly welcome because "the Venezuelan leftists were so upset at the local press that they were overjoyed to see the foreign press, because the foreign press at least described it as being a coup. ... All these guys who would hate me now were thrilled to see me" (Rice, 11).

The sheer presence of foreign reporters in the Bosnian conflict was for many victims the first sign that anyone in the outside world cared, and might step in to help, though the original gratefulness turned sour as massacres continued: "There was more cynicism about what the foreign press corps could do because it had been two years and things hadn't changed. ... [P]eople [in Sarajevo] stopped expecting that somehow these dramatic reports from AP or CNN or the *New York Times* ... were going to help" (Crary, 14; also Bell 1995, 21–22). Tokyo-based correspondent Eric Talmadge (10) got an unusual view of the impact of U.S. war on civilians – and the perceived power of the press – when he went along with Japanese troops to Samawah, Iraq, in early 2004, renting his own house, with local AP staff, outside the base:

I remember one day ... I was like making lunch or something, and a bunch of local leaders ... from the town came by, unannounced, and there was maybe seven or eight of them and they're all dressed up very formally. And they said, "We want to talk to you

<hr/>

[3] Maureen Johnson, "East Berliner savors freedom, though it may be too late," The Associated Press, November 13, 1989.

about this Japanese base. We know you're with the AP, and we know that you're writing about the Japanese. And we want to talk to you about this." … So they had this impromptu powwow with me about, they were unhappy with the amount of rent that the Japanese were paying. They wanted the Japanese to pay more rent to them, and they wanted *me* to tell their story. They wanted me to put pressure on the Japanese by writing a story. So, of course, the story wasn't exactly what they were looking for, but it was a perspective that I got on the Japanese that I wouldn't have otherwise gotten.

One story from Samawah, after remarking that the number of journalists, especially Japanese, "is about equal to troops," quoted a local goldsmith and founder of the Samawah-Japan Friendship Association as complaining about the abundance of sewage and lack of infrastructure, including gardens, and added, "He hopes the Japanese will change that, and not be spooked into a retreat" by Iraq's instability.[4]

With the same purpose to influence coverage, but a violent strategy, left-wing South American guerrillas repeatedly stormed AP bureaus in the 1980s to get their propaganda on the wire while Eduardo Gallardo (14–15) was there. In Chile, he faced members of the anti-Pinochet Frente Patriótico Manuel Rodríguez:

[T]hey wanted us to send a communiqué, and also they wrote slogans on the walls of the office: Muera Pinochet, Luchar hasta el Final, Patria o Muerte [Death to Pinochet, Fight to the End, Fatherland or Death] … [W]e were under orders to send the communiqué to New York and they … never moved it, because the language they were using wasn't news language – "el pueblo invencible se levantará contra" [the invincible people will rise against], that kind of a thing. … [T]hey never mistreated any of us, they just wanted to send that communiqué, and they sprayed the walls with slogans. … [Editors in New York] knew; I think this happened in Beirut a lot. After the guerrillas left, we would send a real story to New York saying leftist guerrillas raided the AP bureau today, so the editors realized what was going on.

One story, describing a similar incident in Lima as part of an apparent new trend by urban guerrillas to attack U.S. targets, quoted one of the four young gunmen as saying that they wanted "to hit Yankee imperialism, strike where it hurts."[5] Technology has changed that interaction, accounting for some of the lack of access that correspondents had to Iraqi insurgents, for example (even beyond the obvious security issues), said Reid (98–99), who led the Baghdad bureau for parts of the 2000s war:

With the jihadis, I often thought, maybe they feel they don't really need us like they used to. They have their own means, they have their own websites, they have their own email distribution lists, YouTube accounts. They were far more hostile and inaccessible than, for example, the Taliban militia. The Taliban had regular journalist mailing lists … We never got this from the Iraqis.

---

[4] Eric Talmadge, "Troops from Japan spark hope in southern Iraq city persecuted under Saddam," The Associated Press, February 14, 2004.

[5] Eduardo Gallardo, "Urban guerrillas have U.S. targets," The Associated Press, October 4, 1984.

THE OUTSIDER: COVER AND TRAP

Journalist was a useful identifier in many contexts. In others, being a foreigner helped, but it could also spell danger. The advantages of foreignness ranged from the surprise element in isolated countries to the "foreigner discount." From the Soviet Union to newly reopened China to today's North Korea, the foreign reporter was so exotic that many ordinary citizens interacted out of sheer curiosity, including little children in Pyonyang "mobbing" an AP photographer who let them play with his three cameras (Lee, 13; also Graham, 17–18; Minthorn, 11–12). Showing up in Chochi, a remote Indian hamlet that had become stigmatized as "the AIDS village" and where villagers felt "ashamed" or even denied what had killed their relatives,[6] Donna Bryson's double "foreignness" as an African American helped overcome people's reluctance to discuss a topic of great suffering and humiliation:

> Maybe they thought that I'd be more likely to listen and not judge. They had already been judged by their neighbors, and now was their chance to tell their story to a real outsider. And I was kind of exotic as an African American in India. In some ways I suppose that helped too. People wanted to know my story, and then once they got talking about my story, they had to share theirs. . . . I wore saris and I wore salwar kameez, and I'm not sure what kind of impact that had on people . . . that was just part of my persona in India, was the African-American woman in a salwar kameez. (Bryson, 31–32)

Two other women correspondents with decades living in, and covering, Muslim countries, Kathy Gannon and Karin Laub (19), felt that being foreigners gave "a license to do things that maybe local women would not be able to do," like not wearing a headscarf:

> The only time I wore a headscarf . . . was doing a story about Salafis in Gaza, and they were very reluctant to speak to a journalist. After lengthy negotiations, this one sheik agreed to meet with me, but he said, "Only if she comes with her head covered." And I said, story, pride? Okay, I'll take the story.[7] So I put on something, but I did like a Benazir Bhutto where the hair is still showing. It was like my compromise. . . . Because on a very personal level, I do see how much Palestinian women and Arab women still sort of struggle under sort of these blanket restrictions. There are so many doors that are so closed to them, and for me somehow the headscarf is a symbol of that. . . . I found that particularly the Hamas leaders, they bend over backwards to show how open-minded they are, and so they've never ever asked me to put something on and . . . other than the Salafis where I made this one exception, those are usually the ones who are the sort of more fundamentalist people I would be dealing with, and they don't ask. (Laub, 20)

---

[6] Donna Bryson, "AIDS death brings panic and prejudice for Indian village," The Associated Press, November 10, 1997.

[7] Karin Laub, "Muslim firebrands challenge Hamas rule in Gaza," The Associated Press, February 15, 2010. The story, datelined Rafah, in the Gaza Strip, detailed how Jihadi Salafis "preach global jihad, or holy war, adhere to an ultraconservative form of Islam and are becoming a headache even for Hamas, the Islamic militant group that rules Gaza," by defying the informal truce between Hamas and Israel.

It's much easier for me than if I were Afghan. I'm not Muslim. And I don't pretend to be, and I always say that to them, but I know about the religion. . . . And I only wore a loose scarf on my head. I never wore anything more than that. And a long shirt. Always the same one. And one Taliban said to [AP correspondent] Amir Shah, "Your boss is so humble, she always wears the same thing." [laughs] Fashion show? This isn't. But I'd go to the front line all the time. So they also respect strength, and they respect people who look them in the eye. They respect people who have courage. (Gannon, 19–21)

Laub (31) also noted, wryly, that when NATO was bombing the Gadhafi military during the 2011 uprising, "Westerners were actually getting pretty good reception with the Libyan rebels." Particularly in the Middle East, a generic "foreigner" perception helps more than the specific American one, and so does outsider religious status. Whether in Muslim countries or Israel, some correspondents found that being identified as Christians lessened the perception of bias (Powell, 12). Specific personal backgrounds, however, are best kept off the public view for the same reason: whether it is Lebanese or Italian descent, U.S. reporters tried to keep it silent to avoid the assumption that they would be personally involved covering those countries (e.g., Bria, 10). On the other hand, Bolivia-born Harold Olmos (15) turned his non-Americanness to AP's advantage in Latin America during the 1970s peak years of discontent with the alleged cultural imperialism by U.S. media: "I address my colleagues and the people I interview in Spanish, I use the local jargon, and it was hard to tell that I was working for an American news agency, that I could be blamed of any bias, of any prejudice."

THE SHADOW OF THE STARS AND STRIPES

AP correspondents, regardless of their nationality, have often been perceived as Americans, which has carried a larger aura, positive and negative, than any other country across the 20th and early 21st centuries. Some correspondents found it made no difference in how they were treated, others that it helped. More still found it could translate into stony silence from possible sources and even death threats when the identification linked not only to the United States but to its government and intelligence services, a common mistake in countries with state-run media and pervasive surveillance. There seemed to be no evident geopolitical pattern. From Vietnam during the war, to India after Washington's tilt toward Islamabad during the India-Pakistan conflict, to post-9/11 Cairo, some correspondents who might have expected to take some flak for U.S. actions did not, as long as they were perceived as reporters – whereas others' lives were endangered when taken for spies.

Even covering massive protests outside the U.S. Embassy in New Delhi, for example, one correspondent never felt "threatened as [American]. The Indians who were opposed to the American policy weren't opposed to Americans" (Belkind, 14). Bryson (42) continued to walk from her home to the Cairo bureau after 9/11, and "I didn't feel like the 'Arab street,' so called, if it does exist, was chasing me down the street":

> If anything, the anger made people want to talk. I can remember going to Palestinian refugee camps in Syria and Jordan, and the fact that I was an American was a chance to rail against America. Or in some ways to express, if anything, more sadness than anger, but certainly not a, "We don't want to talk with you." As a reporter, I want people to talk to me, even if the people are shouting at me. It's much better than not getting at least a conversation going.

In Afghanistan, Gannon (28), who is Canadian, also often felt that her sources' anger at U.S. presence and actions in the country did not attach to her personally:

> And yeah, "Why don't these foreigners all leave and what are they doing?" Sure they want to have a chance to say that, but they're not angry at me. Sometimes I go into a situation where there's been a bombing and civilians had been killed or whatever, and there's anger for sure. ... There's an anger in the subject when you start to talk, but sometimes you'll have some who look at you a little bit belligerent. ... I know how to handle it and to be respectful. By the end of the conversation and as the tea, more tea is drunk, or you're sitting on the floor having food, slowly that person is starting to open up a little bit and a little bit more. ... I've never really experienced people who said, "I'm not going to talk to you because you work for an American organization."

Some correspondents even found that being American opened up special goodwill in countries like China or Poland during their late 1980s anti-totalitarian movements "because America was seen as the shining model that many wished to follow," as Jones said of the Tiananmen Square protests (Jones, 21; also Seward, 7). Another reporter in West Africa in the late 1960s found picture posters of the Kennedys in a hut where he slept in a Burkina Faso village, and overall felt American reporters were "considered more neutral than the British in the former British colonies and the French in the former French colonies" (Heinzerling, 11) – something that North Africa correspondent Paul Schemm (20) still experienced more than 50 years later: "Morocco and Algeria, they have a chip on their shoulder. They will tell you in French how much they don't like the French."

But Schemm's (20) wide-ranging experience from Morocco to Syria in the early 2010s illustrates how haphazardly Americanness was a plus or a minus for correspondents:

> In Egypt, it was generally a minus. But in my case, I could just say I've lived here for a very long time. I speak ... good Egyptian Arabic. It wasn't too hard to win people over. ... [W]hen I was doing man-on-the-street interviews a few days afterwards [the 2011 uprising] – and this is a time when journalists were getting attacked because ... the government had put out these stories saying journalists were trying to destabilize the country. ... You talk to your middle-aged, reasonable shopkeeper type and then ... once you've got his protection, then if someone comes in and wants to rabble-rouse, he'd be like, "No, no, no, this dude's fine." All you need is two or three guys to say you're fine

and then it keeps it from turning into a mob around you. And that happened to me, that worked in my favor a few times. The farther away I was from Egypt, the less able I was to do that. In Syria, obviously no one cared that I was American, it wasn't a problem. Except for if they were jihadists. In Libya, they loved all foreigners, especially Americans, because we helped with the airstrikes and stuff like that. They really loved the French. In Morocco, they don't mind Americans.

Given the looming presence of American policies, and armies, in the Middle East, the region has posed a special challenge for U.S. correspondents to get past this aspect of their persona. Reid (11) was in Kabul as the Soviet tanks rolled in during the late 1970s invasion, and a man cooking a meal outdoors looked at him, spit, and muttered "Russian." When Reid corrected him, the man replied, "Very nice!" Reid only half-jokingly told me, "It was the only time in the Middle East that it ever paid to be an American." As Moscow correspondent, Steven Hurst (10, 6) traveled to Afghanistan a dozen times during the Soviet war and saw, in an interview with "real hard-nose jihadists," "the look of hatred that these men sitting in a circle under the trees in this rather lovely lush garden of this compound way out in the countryside – I'll never forget that." And Hurst saw it again during the U.S. war in Iraq, making it "wise not to be out" when, after a relatively safe early period, the security situation deteriorated so rapidly into civil war that it became largely impossible for American journalists to report from the streets because they were identified as the "boogeymen":

[I]n the early days, you would hear an explosion in Baghdad and you'd jump in a car with a driver and go see what happened. But if you did that [in 2006–2007], you showed up looking like me, which is clearly not an Iraqi, and you happened to be in the presence of somebody who was really mad at the Americans, why, something bad could happen.

Covering Israel and the Palestinian territories since 1987, Laub (7) has found it useful to say that AP is "an international news organization" and that she is from Germany, to overcome "a bit of skepticism" that might attach to U.S. journalists since most Palestinians see the United States as "so completely biased and so completely siding with Israel." Laub (23) added that, "strangely," she has not "encountered any actual hostility of any sort" among Palestinians, only occasional complaints from officials about stories – as indeed we did not when she took me around the Aida refugee camp and along the Israeli barrier outside Bethlehem, where a fearsome-looking group of young men barreling down the narrow road in the opposite direction went out of their way to let our car squeeze through, cheerfully waving us on. Another reporter in Tunisia during the Arab Spring uprisings faced some official angst but did not take it personally. The woman in charge of "press minders" called up the reporter on her cell phone, "screaming mad about this, that, 'it's you and all of you foreign reporters.' [...] I didn't take offense, because I understood that the streets were just crazy and that everything she knew, understood, and believed in was gone" (Ganley, 39).

In Latin America, one American correspondent based in São Paulo in the 2000s found that many Brazilians considered the United States a model and treated him "very, very well," while elsewhere his Brazilian-accented Spanish allowed him to dodge some anti-Americanism because people would ask him if he was from Brazil and he responded "I live in São Paulo" (Clendenning, 8–9). In Asia, two correspondents with different personal histories had opposite experiences. Talmadge (16), who lived in Japan longer than in the United States and is fluent in Japanese, needed people to absorb that in order to go beyond the initial impression: "They automatically, when they see me or they talk to me, they think subconsciously, 'Whatever, this guy is an American.' And they don't deal with me necessarily the same way that they deal with another Japanese person." In North Korea, "a country where they've been told since childhood that Americans are the enemy and that Americans want to kill them," Jean Lee (4–5, 17) found being an ethnic Korean helpful – "I'm less intimidating, and I don't seem so much like a foreigner," although the cover is short-lived:

[Nationality] does come up because often when we ask for permission, if they find out we're American, they're very wary. But because they do know about the AP, they know that we have a presence there, people try to be as accommodating as possible. . . . We're the only Americans there. So . . . everywhere we go, we're very conspicuous.

Back in the Middle East, Reid (98) also found that Iraqi groups "didn't really want to cooperate with the Western media":

[Iraqis] looked upon American journalists as just extensions of the U.S. establishment . . . they imagined our society to be like theirs, where the media is part of the establishment. Why do anything for the press? That's just one arm of the monster.

From Government Mouthpiece to Spy

From World War II Italy (Bria, 17) to today's Middle East, that kind of equation – U.S. journalists as representatives of the American government at best, as spies at worst – is the most dangerous misperception that AP correspondents have faced, especially because it is most popular among the most virulently anti-American groups, which can be the most powerful in many countries, and among authoritarian regimes eager to blame outsiders for domestic unrest. Where the U.S. overtly intervened and attempted regime change, the official reception was especially frosty. Midcentury correspondents in Cuba found that what one called "the Yankee part" "came into play," and AP reporters were expected to represent an official U.S. government line (Flores, 14; also Wheeler, 19). After the Bay of Pigs and the missile crisis, the Havana bureau was briefly closed and initially allowed to reopen only with non-U.S. reporters. When Ike Flores was eventually let back in as resident correspondent, the Castro regime "considered me still a CIA informant . . . a difficult work" (Flores, 2–3; Flores 2007, 82). Castro, in a speech, called Flores' successor, John Fenton Wheeler

(2008, 2–9), either "extremely naïve or in cahoots with the CIA" for, at an earlier news conference, Wheeler said he was "a journalist, not a judge" when asked to declare that two exiles were CIA agents sent to kill the Cuban leader. Wheeler's minder, the same as Flores', later testified in the U.S. Senate that he had been ordered to try to implicate both journalists as "a nest of espionage" (Wheeler 2008, 55–59).

In Iran around the U.S. Embassy hostage crisis, AP staffers were thrown out of the country in apparent retaliation for the restrictions the U.S. government had put on the official Iranian news agency operating in America – a tit for tat whose repercussions continued for decades (Tatro, 11; Reid, 99). As recently as 2014, during the Ukrainian conflict, armed men in Simferopol accused an AP video crew of being spies, detained them for a few hours, and confiscated their equipment.[8] In Somalia during the U.S. intervention, the threat of death or kidnapping for all Americans, or all seen as "the U.S. clan," was so high that one roving war correspondent, Paul Alexander (10), lied for the only time about his nationality and said he was Canadian:

Just because it wasn't going to matter in the overall scheme of things, except for possibly reducing my risk, which I was all about reducing risks. Because there were going to be risks that you couldn't avoid taking. . . . I can't say that I would've gotten killed if I would have said I was American, but it was a potential escalator of tensions. So, for that matter, it was just not worth it to me.

In then-Zaire in the 1990s, Bryson (14) still felt the "baggage" that Americans had there because people remembered the 1960s execution of Congo's prime minister Patrice Lumumba, whom the United States had long opposed. Gray (35) used the same word, baggage, as a challenge especially for reporters in Iraq and Afghanistan:

[W]hen we talk to officials in any government and common people of every government, we try to get across the idea that we are not part of the American government. We are the AP, we're independent. . . . [O]ne day we may praise our government, the next day we may criticize them horribly. But . . . the idea of somebody that objective, because in their own countries they see their own press being one-sided, backing one political party, one insurgency movement or whatever. It's hard for many in many countries to see us as independent. . . . Certainly in Afghanistan and Iraq and Somalia, Rwanda, Vietnam, earlier on but even now . . . maybe less so, Cambodia, they would see you as, if not a tool, at least halfway siding with the U.S. government.

Even when this perception prevails, correspondents have found ordinary citizens more forbearing. In Phnom Penh right before it fell to the Khmer Rouge, after the United States "seduced" Cambodia into war and then "abandoned" it, Gray (9–10) had no "incident where [Cambodians] had anything negative to say to me . . . even though they knew that I was American and Americans were just about to cut the strings." In Central

---

[8] "Armed men confiscate AP equipment in Crimea," The Associated Press, March 7, 2014.

America, Joe Frazier (4) similarly believed that neither the villagers nor the guerrillas held against him the Reagan Administration policies – although the governments sometimes "would say that we're in the sack with the leftists ... because sometimes we wrote things that they didn't like, therefore we must be the enemy, right?"

The erroneous perception of AP as a conduit to the American government could even lead some sources to reach out to journalists, from Afghan and Pakistani officials occasionally asking Gannon (27) to "give the message to America that we're not terrorists, we are moderates" to a French foreign ministry spokesman, after a news briefing in Paris explaining the French opposition to the Iraq War, running after the AP correspondent "as I was walking out the door, going, 'Did you understand? Did you understand? Did you get that? Did you get that?'" (Ganley, 31) But when the perception moves from pseudo-diplomat to actual CIA spy – either because people are used to their own media serving intelligence functions or because they have a hard time understanding why American civilians would poke around so persistently in some of the world's scariest places – the results could be deadly.

Anderson (AP Oral History, 1997, 7) believes that one of the reasons for his kidnapping was some "very virulently anti-American" Hezbollah group's conviction that he was a spy:

I'd gone out to interview one of their top leaders immediately after the bombing of the Marine headquarters to ask him if he had done it. And anybody who would take chances to go around and ask questions has got to be a spy, right, particularly if he's an American.

Shortly before Anderson's kidnapping, another longtime Lebanon correspondent, Robert Fisk of *The Times* of London, witnessed this misperception in a tense encounter when both journalists at a checkpoint were questioned by Palestinian gunmen (Fisk 2002, 500):

"Why are you here?" Anderson produced his Lebanese press card. Journalists. American and British journalists. "America kills Palestinians." No, no. We are journalists, press, *sahafa*, reporters. There were more gunmen round us now, holding automatic weapons, draped with ammunition belts, none of them smiling. A man in black looked at Anderson. "America kills Muslims." This was getting worse. ... "Are you a spy?" I had been afraid of that. We protested. We had a duty to be there. We wanted their help. We wanted to talk to them. ... Anderson held out his press card again. Something had gone wrong. For years, gunmen like these – hostile, undisciplined though they might be – had respected our jobs, respected the word *sahafa*, press, on the windscreens of our cars. They had understood what we were doing. Suddenly the connection had dried up. We were no longer journalists to these people. Our jobs meant nothing to them. We were *foreigners*.

The identification with spies is a phenomenon that predates the CIA, and U.S. intelligence sources have approached American journalists to work as agents, to provide information, or to plant misinformation (as one former CIA analyst alleged had happened in Vietnam, for example).[9] In a more recent example, a *New York Times* reporter wrote about the CIA calling him into conference in Iraq for help in a kidnapping case (Filkins 2008, 285–286). John Roderick turned down a request from the Office of Strategic Services while reporting for AP in 1940s China, though many of his Chinese sources thought he was in fact a spy (Roderick 1993, 117; AP Oral History, Roderick, 1998, 17–18). Roderick also believed that some of his colleagues in other organizations collaborated with intelligence agencies, a belief shared by another well-known AP reporter, Malcolm Browne in Saigon (Browne 1993, 90–91), and a handful of interviewees. The question of this dangerous CIA practice was investigated in the 1970s by the U.S. Senate, putting an official end to the recruitment of journalists, though some argued it was "merely curtailed" (Houghton 1996; Loory 1974; Bernstein 1977; Daniloff 2008, 246).

None of the correspondents interviewed here said they had been approached to provide intelligence, adding they always sought to make the distinction between reporter and agent extra clear, whether by never carrying weapons even in chaotic conflict zones like Somalia (Alexander, 9) or by alienating important sources, as Rosenblum (9) did in Lagos when he "walked out" on a new political officer at the U.S. Embassy who had "made some real presumption" about Rosenblum's background information-sharing with his predecessor. But many said that the widespread misperception across the world was the "big bugaboo" that they found hard to dispel, beginning with fellow foreign correspondents from authoritarian regimes, and that could be used by those governments as a handy excuse for extra intimidation and surveillance.

In Beijing, Graham (13) found journalists for Soviet state-run agency TASS trying to "cultivate" her with an assiduity that evidenced their belief that she had special insight on U.S.-Sino relations. Running into an AP bureau chief at a 1980s reception at a military club, Nicaragua's Sandinista interior minister joked, "I wonder what's going on in Nicaragua that the CIA is in town?" (AP Oral History, Aguilar, 2009, 31). In Sierra Leone when Fidel Castro visited in the early 1970s, one correspondent was thrown out of a press conference by Cuban journalists, and that was just the beginning of his troubles:

I went back to my hotel room, and that night the police came to arrest me and seized my notebooks and everything else. And I think they were doing it . . . to show that they were in solidarity with the Cubans. And . . . there was a little marimba band at the hotel that was playing the night before, "It's cherry pink and apple blossom white time," and I wrote down in my notebook, "It's cherry pink and apple blossom white time in Sierra Leone." And the police interrogator said, "What is this code?" Well, what I had intended to do was write a cultural story about how in a continent where there are no apples or cherries they're playing this music as one example of the sort of cultural dissonance that you get, in the colonial, and independent, Africa. But anyway, finally the embassy rescued me and got me out, so it was alright. (Heinzerling, 18)

[9] The Associated Press, November 20, 1977.

In the waning days of the Soviet Union, Alan Cooperman's (10–11) friendship with an economics officer in the U.S. Embassy, who later turned out to be a CIA agent, got Soviet authorities "interested" in Cooperman too:

I did get some bizarre kinds of feelers, which were clearly provocative. Most specifically, somebody called the AP bureau looking for me, and wanting me and only me . . . and started talking to me about helicopter designs, and was I interested in these helicopter designs? And he would bring them to the bureau. . . . "Well, why are you calling me? Why are you telling me about this? I don't – is there a news story, is there something that's happened? What are you trying to . . . ?" "No, no, I have access to Soviet helicopter designs, and I'd like to show them to you." And I said, "That really doesn't interest me." And he said, "Well, don't you have a friend at the U.S. Embassy who'd be interested?" And at that point . . . I knew that this was a provocation to see whether I would bite. And I said, "I am not interested. I am a journalist. Do not call back. Do not send anything to me. I do not want to see it. I am *not* interested." . . . And I didn't hear that provocation again.

A BLACK-AND-WHITE DISTINCTION

If the journalist, foreigner, American layers of correspondents' personas required some clarification, two other layers are immediately visible and visceral – race and gender. The vast majority of correspondents interviewed, and U.S. foreign correspondents in general, has been white, and some who covered African and Asian countries said it had an impact – though both white and black correspondents said that ultimately they were still set apart by their Americanness too.

A few correspondents said that being perceived as white, and therefore immediately different, helped them. One reporter in Nigeria in the 1960s felt he "could knock on all doors and be accepted," perhaps as a "leftover from the colonial era" (Zeitlin, 10). A reporter whose mother is Chinese found that "being a large, white-looking guy" helped him both in China and in France to get interviews with random people on the street – that and being "generally friendly and can speak their language" (Jones, 7). Covering racially charged conflicts in 1990s South Africa and Somalia, white correspondents had dramatically different experiences. Those in South Africa toward the end of apartheid, when violence raged in many black townships, felt their being "there with your cameras and your notebooks and stuff, you were obviously there covering the story" (Daniszewski, 16) – and that made them safe, even welcome:

Over and over again I would be amazed at how in the townships the black activists and the ordinary people . . . as soon as they learned you were a foreign reporter, they seemed to view you as a potential ally, a potential sympathizer, and seemed to somehow want to incorporate you into their side. . . . I don't think I ever had an experience in a township where I felt people being hostile because I was white and they were black. I just didn't feel that. Whereas later, later visits, after the end of apartheid, I think the racial gap resurfaced, and I've heard that from other white reporters, that they didn't necessarily feel at ease going into the townships. (Crary, 5)

Alexander (22–24) also felt the "very difficult challenge" of being a white reporter among the deteriorating security situation in late 1990s South Africa, so he drove "an old Renault with a cracked windshield to cut down on the risk of being carjacked" and was mindful of where only reporters of color could safely go. But it was at a crowded rally in Somalia right after the Black Hawk Down incident that his "spider sense" got "working overtime":

[Warlord Mohamed Farrah] Aidid was going to be speaking, so we all had to be there. This was the first time I had been there after four journalists had been killed.[10] Basically the place had become almost off-limits due to just general chaos. I remember getting out of the car and seeing the crowd come between me and the car. I'm starting to get nervous. ... Aidid is speaking, and he actually mentions when the four journalists got killed. And I'm having this translated to me, and I'm watching the reaction of the people around me. Is he going to say, "That's a good idea, let's get rid of them all"? And it turns out, he said, "The journalists are our friends. What happened shouldn't have happened." ... And so people were smiling at me. And I can see my translator relax a little bit. But there were other times when you would be there, in the crowd, and you'd see the looks that you would get. It was disturbing to know that if the mood of the crowd changed quickly, that would be the last thing that you ever saw.

In Somalia, Alexander worked with one of the rare African American correspondents for the mainstream media then, Keith Richburg of the *Washington Post*. Trying to confirm casualties after a U.S. helicopter attack, Richburg and Alexander found a way to walk "into an emergency ward [at the city's main hospital] taking a body count" without inflaming rampant anti-Americanism: Richburg dressed up and barked orders, while Alexander trailed after him, taking notes "like an obedient underling" (Richburg 1998, 86–87). Richburg's analysis of being an African American reporter in Africa, *Out of America*, provokingly details his struggle to reconcile this dilemma for black journalists: which of these two identifiers demands more allegiance, critical and accurate journalism or "a black agenda" (Richburg 1998, 144; also Broussard 2013)? Bryson (68–71), as an AP correspondent in southern Africa, first in the early 1990s and again in the late 2000s, experienced some of the same tension and expectations:

I arrived in South Africa and 80 percent of the country looks like me. But ... each of those people who looks like me have their own histories, they speak languages that I don't speak, they make assumptions that I don't make. They are strangers. And I think in a way I learned that ... I owed them the dignity of understanding that they were strangers and that we had to have a conversation to understand each other. That just looking like one another isn't the end of the story or even the beginning of a particularly good story. ... I can remember when I was still at university and doing an internship in Oregon and interviewing ... a black man, and I started out my questions, and he said, "Those are just the kinds of questions that a white reporter would ask." As if I should have had more

---

[10] On July 12, 1993, four journalists – three working for Reuters and one for AP – were killed in Mogadishu by a mob while trying to cover a UN raid on a Somali command post.

understanding or asked other questions. ... [N]o one has ever asked me that outside America. Maybe outside America you're freer to be an American as a black American, perhaps. ... I don't think I was ever for very long mistaken as a South African. One person told me it was the shoes. I definitely had American shoes. ... I guess the perception is more that the Africans should support Africa, be pro-Africa, be pro-development and not criticize. As an American, I didn't really face that.

Some black interviewees would tell Bryson "Welcome back," but quickly add that "we're happy to have you here as a reporter, but we don't need to be told what to do just because you're a black American." So she had no "special entrée" there, and besides, South Africans were so eager to get their stories out that "you could have been green and had a pretty good chance of talking to black South Africans." Though she still encountered random racism – even in unlikely places like Kosovo – and some white South Africans, having "grown up

FIGURE 5.1. Johannesburg correspondent Donna Bryson covers South Africa's first multiracial national elections in Johannesburg on April 27, 1994. (Photo courtesy of Thery Ndopu)

not seeing blacks as someone that you'd acknowledge in greetings," "just would walk right by" her, others offered surprising, if not always pleasant, insights, perhaps out of defensiveness or assuming that with white reporters they could have left them unstated:

Sometimes when you get into conversation with a white South African, at some point they might say something like "black Americans are not like *our* blacks." ... I would find myself thinking, if they'll say that to me, what else would they say to me if I keep quiet? ... I guess I offered an opportunity for people. Just doing my job offered people an opportunity to have new experiences themselves. (Bryson, 14–16, 6–8)

NO BURQA FOR US

When she first arrived in South Africa, Bryson (15) was also outnumbered among correspondents as a woman, and received a bit of useful wardrobe advice from a female colleague – to wear a dress or a skirt "'so that they know that you're a human being' ... because a woman dressed in pants was just, 'What is that?'" From the 1970s to today, AP's female correspondents have found that gender affects some of their reporting practices, but even in the most male-dominated societies, being a woman has not always meant danger or exclusion. In many Middle Eastern countries, for example, even amid violent conflict, correspondents found advantages in being perceived as unthreatening, in having access to local women, and in being able, at times, to blend in.

As one Beirut editor put it, at the height of the civil war when "gunmen went nuts in the streets so no male reporter could go there for at least a while till they calmed down," "the women reporters could go ... because of the machismo, they just didn't look at women as threats at that time. ... [T]hey wouldn't necessarily talk to the women, but they could see what had happened more readily" (Tatro, 14). For Laub (21), being a woman in the West Bank also meant more intimate access to areas off-limits to male reporters: "Often if you go to a house of mourning or something, it's much easier, because they're separate, and if you want to talk to the mother of the victim or something like that, you can just slide in there and you can establish an immediate bond." Sally Buzbee (8–10), who worked several assignments in Iraq during the U.S. war, felt shielded wearing a concealing abaya and a loose headscarf disguising her hair color around Baghdad, "because I didn't want people to see who I was, especially in the bad times." All the while she was thinking, "no one is going to make me wear this forever. ... I chose to report there. I'm voluntarily putting myself in this situation and it's temporary" – and she was also acutely aware that "that superficial layer [of protection] could go away at any point ... and you would have been way more vulnerable." When covering the Maghreb, Paris-based Elaine Ganley (46) usually wore a scarf and a raincoat, and in taxis sat in front so she would look like a relative of the driver's, but did not otherwise find being a woman "troublesome."

FIGURE 5.2. Paris-based correspondent Elaine Ganley eats couscous with a Moroccan family while on assignment in Casablanca in 1997. (Photo by Abdeljalil Bounhar, courtesy of Elaine Ganley)

In many other cases, however, the very physical aspect of being a woman made correspondents stand out as a curiosity, as red-haired Graham (7) recalled of late 1970s China; blonde, pants-wearing Anita Snow (8) experienced among 1980s Central American villagers who "always wanted to braid our hair"; and Maureen Johnson (2) discovered around the same time when she stood out even at Downing Street for off-the-record briefings among the male crowds. Most importantly, being a woman sometimes affected access around the world, with men refusing to talk to a correspondent (Snow, 8) or addressing her male driver or translator instead (Buzbee, 10–11) – even though all women correspondents insisted on continuing to go to the "dicey" areas just like the guys (Powell, 4).

Perhaps nowhere has been dicier for women correspondents recently than Taliban-controlled areas, where the attempts to keep women reporters at bay has ranged from the farcical – asking them to stand behind window curtains at a press conference (Filkins 2008, 28–29) – to the deadly. Over nearly 30 years, Gannon (43) faced it all, winning far more acceptance than exclusion – such as from the Taliban chief justice who wanted to speak with her male photographer but finally consented to an interview because, after six hours, he "would have had to have slept there, because to have come out and to have left me sitting there, would've been shameful for him"[11] – and even challenging a UN special envoy negotiating with the Taliban in the 1990s to not cave in on women's rights (as further discussed in Chapter 9's box).

CONCLUSIONS

In source building and eyewitness reporting, AP correspondents have been affected by how foreign governments and ordinary citizens reacted to the different layers of their personas. Being foreigners and journalists both helped and hindered their practices, though being identified as press usually offered some protection if people thought the media could help (or be used). Unlike many of their counterparts at big-name newspapers or networks, AP correspondents could count on a reputation for neutrality – or even on anonymity. As Westerners, they also enjoyed the freedom outsider status conveys. Being perceived as Americans has been far trickier, because Washington has loomed larger than all other powers across the past eight decades. Anti-American anger could be a great resource if it got people to talk – but it could turn deadly if journalists were misperceived as U.S. government functionaries or spies, something correspondents had to battle, especially where it meant constant surveillance. Even in countries at war with the United States, most correspondents felt people distinguished them from the CIA, but occasional fudging came in handy where identifying as American was an unnecessary risk. Two more personal identifiers allowed for very little fudging – race and gender, which have cut both ways, especially as they were nearly immediately qualified by the overarching "foreigner" image. The female correspondents interviewed found that gender ultimately made little difference in their ability to get the job done – though they had to resolutely face down repeated attempts to discriminate against them.

All of these perceptions only come into play, of course, where correspondents can actually go and interact with locals. Some areas have been off-limits because it is simply too dangerous for journalists or foreigners or Americans to be there. Tragically, the lines of this deadly danger are unpredictable: In April 2014, Gannon and Niedringhaus traveled to southeastern Afghanistan – where they had reported frequently before – under the protection of Afghan forces to cover

[11] Kathy Gannon, "Chief Taliban justice refuses to meet diplomats seeking information about trial of foreigners," The Associated Press, September 5, 2001.

preparations for the first round of the country's presidential election. They were at a village police headquarters waiting for their convoy to move when an Afghan police unit commander "walked up to their hired car, yelled 'Allahu Akbar' – God is Great – and fired on them in the back seat with a Kalashnikov assault rifle."[12] Niedringhaus was killed instantly and Gannon severely wounded, while their translator and freelance videographer in the car were untouched. According to official accounts, the shooting was not planned, and at his trial, the shooter did not explain his action.

It might never be known if he decided to target Gannon and Niedringhaus because they were journalists, or foreigners, or Westerners, or women, or all of the above. But the shooting remains a devastating reminder of the price foreign correspondents pay simply for being there to bear witness and tell the stories, which to them is the most essential element of who they are, and what they do, as Chapter 6 explains.

Terry Anderson's Kidnapping in Lebanon, 1985–1991

Terry Anderson: I went out the next morning to play tennis at dawn, Saturday morning, with Don Mell, the photographer. ... And we finished the game ... I had volunteered to take him to his apartment, down the Corniche. And when I stopped to let him out ... they jumped out of their car and stuck a gun in my ear and said, "Get out." ... When they drove me away, he [Mell] jumped in the car and tried to chase them.[13] When I saw him years later, I asked him, "Don, what the hell were you going to do, hit them with your tennis racket?" He's saying, "Oh, just seemed like I could do it." And they took me off, and I was hidden for the next seven years, and you know it was all kinds of bad things happen but I survived. ...

One of my biggest advantages was – possibly out of my Marine Corps training, out of my combat experience, out of the analytical side of being a correspondent – it doesn't do any good to deny what's happening to you, it doesn't do any good to be mad about it – you are mad, it doesn't do any good to hate anybody, although you are fairly justified in hating somebody who kidnapped you and beat you up. ... I became a negotiator, to try to get things, change conditions, try to have an effect, which is very frustrating because you often can't affect anything; you're chained to the wall and nobody is listening to you. But that's how I coped with it, tried to persuade

---

[12] "Death sentence given in AP photographer's killing," The Associated Press, July 23, 2014. In early 2015, the sentence was changed to 20 years in prison.

[13] Mell was interviewed for the AP's story on the kidnapping, which ran on the wire, unbylined, on March 16, 1985.

them and give us a radio, which over the years we finally got. Try to get books, try to get magazines, try to get letters home ... just try to convince them ... we are your prisoners, we are not criminals, we didn't do anything, we haven't been sentenced to jail, you have no right to punish us. ...

Three years or so in, we were held in ... a bedroom that had steel put over the windows in an apartment house in Southern Beirut, in the slums. And they brought in a new guy; and we're all chained to the wall, blindfolded whenever the guards open the door. ... Guard comes in one morning ... boots me in the leg, "Get up!" Okay. He yanks me up, pokes me with his gun, unlocks some chains, shoves me out the door, it's the morning bathroom run; and we've been doing this for three and a half years, right? ... He pushes me in the bathroom, hauls me out, curses at me in Arabic, pokes me with the gun, kicks me again, chains me up. ... And I said, "Biddi [I want] Mahmoud!" Mahmoud is the chief guard. He spoke good English, very lazy man. "Biddi Mahmoud!" "Leesh?" [Why?] "Biddi Mahmoud hala [now]." ... I say, "Mahmoud take this guy away because if you don't, he is going to have to kill me. I've been out here three and a half years; I don't need this shit from him." And the guard never came back. ...

I was the last one [hostage to be freed]. I was alone for a couple of weeks, and they were treating me reasonably well. ... I said, you can take the chain off, it's not like I'm going to run away, I know I'm going home, we all know, so we can get rid of the chain. And they took the chain off, put it by the wall. And I stayed there waiting day from day to day, so it's the same. ... And then the last day, I turned on the radio in the morning and there's an announcement, I've been released and I'm on my way to Damascus. And I called Mahmoud again, and I said, "Mahmoud, listen to this: I'm not here, I'm gone, babes, I'm on my way to Damascus." And we laughed. He went away, and I spent the day playing cards and listening to reasons why I had not yet arrived, which included a snowstorm that had blocked the roads, there was no snowstorm. Late that evening they came in and gave me new clothes, a new watch to replace the one they'd stolen, oddly enough, and "trust me Ali" tried to get me in a political argument again and I just went, "Please go away, man, I don't want to deal with this." They gave me a half dozen carnations and said, "Tell your wife we're sorry." I didn't, by the way, I threw them away. And taped my eyes and put me in a car, drove me down the road. They said just stand outside and they drove away, and then obviously by previous arrangement, this car full of mukhabarat, Syrian secret police, drove up, put me in, took my blindfold off, and we drove to Damascus. We had to stop at secret police headquarters, mukhabarat, for a couple of hours. I didn't realize then, but they were trying to find a foreign minister who was off with his mistress and they couldn't find him.

So I get to Damascus, and it's a deputy foreign minister who's there for the press conference, and Gianni Picco [of the United Nations] – we knew he had achieved the release – and had a little press conference there. I remember being smothered by [AP correspondent] Alex Efty's beard (Anderson, 18, 20–21, 25–26).

6

Eyewitness Reporting: Getting to the Scene

I had a vacation to Indonesia, if you can think of any place that's farther away [from Egypt]. From January 25th to literally February 11th [2011]. I scheduled a three-week vacation that entirely matched up to the days of the revolution. I left knowing there were reports that there was going to be this big demonstration. But ... every other demonstration hadn't worked. Why would this one suddenly work? Why would this one spark the thing? ... We landed in Dubai, and I saw the news and ... my jaw dropped. And then every day for the next three or four days, in Indonesia, people are calling up, "Where are you? Are you going to be ... ?" I'm like, "I'm not in the country, I'm not there." ... And then one day I woke up and it was 2 in the morning Cairo time, 6 in the morning Indonesia time, and I saw the NDP [National Democratic Party] building on Jazeera burning. And I realized ... this just got real. ... [E]ventually, after some of the hardest days of my life, ... I quit the vacation. I left my wife and one-and-a-half-year-old child in Indonesia, in Bali. ... And then I was there for the last week. And I was in Tahrir Square when [President Hosni] Mubarak resigned. So that was something that was very important to me. (Schemm, 3–4)

Rushing straight into history-making mayhem, as Cairo-based correspondent Paul Schemm did when the Arab Spring erupted while he was vacationing in Bali, is a visceral instinct that all foreign correspondents share – and that sets them apart. The most basic reason for their job, after all, is reporting from the scene, even if it is a scene virtually everyone else is trying to flee, and the drive to be present never stops at office hours in a profession that most consider a calling. This chapter details how correspondents got to be eyewitnesses to some of the most pivotal moments of the past eight decades, what their stories gained from their presence, and the treacherous routes they took – hitchhiking with Libyan rebels and U.S. helicopter pilots, trudging over Afghan mountain passes and earthquake-crumbled roads, and talking their way past checkpoints manned by a gamut of international thugs. It also explains what correspondents do when they cannot get to a scene – when extreme violence, regimes that are secretive or hostile to the press, or just impassable routes have kept them away from the action and relegated to "listening posts," in some cases for decades.

SEEING WITH OUR OWN EYES

All correspondents consider essential to their jobs, and to the accuracy and impact of their stories, the ability to see with their own eyes – not just to cover breaking news events, which is a widely shared and central authority claim for journalism across history (Zelizer 2007), but to roam their countries searching for insights. The task has always been time-consuming, costly, and extremely dangerous – which has made it increasingly rare as news organizations struggle with budget cuts. But all correspondents vehemently argued that reporting cannot be done any other way than by getting close to the story, staying close to the story, and being there when something happens (Rosenblum, 46). Also critical is sniffing out what will happen: Before Iraq's civil war made it nearly impossible to travel around the country, "if you didn't have a story idea, if you just had time and went someplace, you were bound to come back with something," Reid (63) recalled. The alternative is to sit "in an office, just taking news from a national agency or monitoring the radio" (Belkind, 5), or sit "around in some press center being spoon-fed stuff" (Pyle, 24), which is the preference of governments and armies around the world, who have tried (and sometimes succeeded) in either keeping correspondents away or controlling their access.

Lost if correspondents cannot be eyewitnesses is the ability to gather enough visual details that can transport the audience into the foreign reality, reported with the authority coming from their knowing "you're on the ground" (Gannon, 79) as an independent, objective journalist. Covering the conflict in Somalia, roving correspondent Paul Alexander (30) tried to "get people to taste the dust in the air" (all the "different qualities of dust"), to smell "the decay of the shallow graves across from the hotel," to hear the daytime chaos and dark quiet of night – "that sort of grit." From World War II to the Korean War to Central American guerrillas, from Mother Teresa's death to Mexico's self-defense movements against drug cartels, correspondents found that visual images in their visceral immediacy can drive a story – and remain ingrained in memory. George Bria (6) paced down his living room mimicking the German officer he had seen – nearly 70 years earlier – surrender the troops in Italy in the same Florence park where Bria used to "roll a hoop" as a child:

[T]wenty-two years later, in a Quonset hut, a sizeable, long metal one, there was the surrender. General Mark Clark was the leader of the Allied troops, and all the brass . . . was there, lined up at the end of the Quonset hut. . . . Clark . . . had a dog, a fox terrier . . . that somehow was loose in the hut, and the German came in, stomping in with his field boots. And this dog at his feet – this was ridiculous, anyway, he was shooing the dog away, but finally the dog got away. And the general with his retinue came up to the brass, the Allied brass, and put out his hand, but nobody took it. There was his hand

FIGURE 6.1. George Bria shows a copy of the RCA cabled "flash" he sent saying that the German armies had surrendered unconditionally in Italy in World War II, as well as a collection of his press passes from the 1940s, in his New York City apartment on January 2, 2015. (Photo by Giovanna Dell'Orto)

outstretched. I thought, wow, what a symbol this was. . . . I was there, I saw it, I wrote the story. I don't know whether it ever got used, but I wrote it.

"Chasing North Korean troops" with an Allied outfit during the Korean War, Max Desfor (4) made a quick stop for "nature's call" and saw a pair of hands sticking up in a snowfield:

[B]ack of hand to back of hand, and right a couple of inches from the hands, sticking up through the snow, was a black hole. And of course the first thing I did was make a picture of it. . . . [T]he black hole obviously was where that body underneath there had breathed his last. But I immediately then called the commanding officer . . . they discovered there were about 100 bodies of men and women. . . . [T]he troops that we had been chasing, and were still chasing, were very much on the run, and the people that they had taken with them and started to take them all the way north with them, they just couldn't keep up with the troops, so the troops just shot them all and left them lying there. And then apparently the snow came down and covered all the bodies, and the only thing still visible was what I described of this one man and they found him. His hands were bound at the wrists, back to back. And it was very typical of what had happened.

In Nicaragua, the mother of a former Contra showed one correspondent a photograph of him "with [CIA director] William Casey's daughter framed on the wall – in this kind of little Podunk town in the middle of the jungle . . . hung alongside this big, strange, really cheesy tiger-skin carpet" (Rice, 12–13).[1] When a source told a colleague that some of her relatives were at a camp of child Sandinista soldiers, Joe Frazier (36) "said, Jesus, we better get out there" and did:

[W]e got in with some difficulty because it was a very conflicted area. And we ran into a camp of these kids, and it was set that their parents had to bring them food from home – the Sandinistas couldn't even provide that – and a lot of them were getting killed. ... [T]hey said they were very proud. ... These kids were basically not even as tall as their rifles (Frazier, 36). [The height detail became the lead of Frazier's story, followed by this description: "Sandra Sanchez Sandoval, 14, cradled her assault rifle in her lap, took a pensive slurp from a crimson 'raspado' of shaved ice and syrup and spelled out her duty. 'We are here to defend our homeland, because we want to stay free. The "contras" will not pass over this bridge,' she said."][2]

When Mark Stevenson (26) heard that the Mexican Army was moving into the area where self-defense forces, reputedly backed by a rival cartel, had been standing off the Caballeros Templarios, he decided to go in too, since it was "somewhat safer" and anyway the last chance "to see these towns under siege":

[T]hey had been literally barricading themselves in – dug ditches around their town and had put out signs, SOS in rocks on the local soccer field, so that the helicopters could see it as they flew over. ... If you were to drive towards these towns, you wouldn't see anything out of the ordinary, except for the fact that all the businesses on one side of the highway had been burned out. And in fact, when you go down to the last hamlet, Coalcomán, which is way down at the end of the highway, as you drove in you saw all the burned-out trucks and buses on the highway leading in. And as you come in, you see all their lumberyards – because that's a lumber town – burning. The Caballeros Templarios on their way out, after they've been expelled, just torched everything. [One story about self-defense movements in Michoacán stated that it was "burning" after the Knights Templar cartel "has set fire ... in a medieval-like reign of terror," adding that on a highway between two villages, "the ruins of three sawmills torched by the cartel still smoldered this week."][3]

Of a week spent in "hot, humid Calcutta" while Mother Teresa was lying in state before her funeral, Donna Bryson remembered the "physicalness of it," including one "terrible image":

Her feet were upright, parallel at the end of the bed, and as the days went by, they were just starting to collapse. ... I don't think it ever made it into the story. But that's a week of the same story, day after day.[4] And just trying to find something new to say – and maybe

[1] John Rice, "Renewed sounds of war in northern Nicaragua," The Associated Press, March 1, 1993.

[2] Joseph B. Frazier, "Nicaraguan children recruited to fight," The Associated Press, November 3, 1983.

[3] Mark Stevenson, "Mexico cartel dominates, torches western state," The Associated Press, May 22, 2013. Also Mark Stevenson, "In Mexico, self-defense squads battle violence," The Associated Press, January 21, 2013.

[4] Bryson was in Calcutta to report on the beginning of the lying in state ("Mother Teresa to lie in state for public homage in India," The Associated Press, September 7, 1997) and stayed there until after the funeral and burial ("Prayers offered at Mother Teresa's graveside," The Associated Press,

that's a strange thing, maybe it's a reporter's thing, because maybe readers don't want you to say something new every day? (Bryson, 28–29)

Being on the scene also allowed for new perspectives to emerge in ongoing stories of conflict, where one of the correspondents' "responsibilities is to keep that story alive during the quieter periods," as Alexander (20–21) put it. For that, to give a sense of what it felt like to be a Sarajevan during the city's siege, he wrote a profile of a 23-year-old gravedigger – an unexpectedly deadly profession:

Funerals were done at dawn and dusk because they were the most likely times to have a little fog in the air, because Serb snipers had a tendency to shoot at people attending the funerals. So there were like a couple of metal shipping containers where people would wait until it was just dark enough to be able to get out there to do it. ... I was having translation done of an interview with a gravedigger. And it turned out that three or four of his fellow gravediggers had been killed since the war started. So the lead on my story was that Haris Subasic has one of Sarajevo's most dangerous jobs – he's a gravedigger. So those things just hit you, everywhere.

Alexander's story quoted Subasic as saying, "Almost every day, the snipers shoot. They can see you like you're in the palm of their hand. ... I dive to the ground. You get used to it, like all the people of Sarajevo" – including those coming to bury their dead in the former soccer field.[5]

A keen eye for details could also help presage future developments. In Algeria right before the 1990s civil war, as elections that the Islamic Salvation Front was poised to win were canceled, Elaine Ganley (41–42) would go to "Friday prayers ... and it was fields of people, streets filled with people praying, you had to pick your way through ... finding rooftop terraces to be on, to be part of the prayer. ... [I]t is amazing to see, and then the sermons and the fiery sermons and people getting all riled up." In Amona, an unauthorized Israeli West Bank settlement in the 2000s, one correspondent interviewed a 27-year-old woman, dressed conservatively though planning a month-long holiday in Goa, who quoted to him "the actual chapter of the Bible where this place is mentioned ... stuff that you wouldn't get ... unless you actually went there" (Eliason, 8). The story read: "To [Orit] Caspi, the transcendent deed of ownership is Chapter 18 of the Book of Joshua: 'And Joshua said unto the children of Israel, How long are ye slack to go to possess the land, which the Lord God of your fathers hath given you?' Verse 24 mentions Kephar Ammoni, from which Amona's name is derived."[6] Traveling with Pope John Paul II on his first visit to Poland in 1979, Vatican correspondent Victor Simpson (10) was amazed by the reception in the Communist country – with "teary-eyed Poles" pleading for him to stay, the pope wincing "every time

September 14, 1997), writing daily stories about the ceremonies as well as Mother Teresa's legacy, her links to Calcutta, and the variety of people paying respects to her.
[5] Paul Alexander, "Bosnian gravedigger dodges death to bury the war's casualties," The Associated Press, December 16, 1993.
[6] Marcus Eliason, "Olmert's tough line heightens settlers' fears that Israel is leaving them behind," The Associated Press, January 22, 2006.

police pushed back" those seeking to greet him, and "Soviet-made armored vehicles in a show of disrespect trampl[ing] over flowers strewn on the motorcade route":[7]

Wherever he went hundreds of thousands, millions would turn out. ... The regime realized what was happening to them, they tried to fight against it, and at the end of the day they couldn't do it. You could feel the atmosphere, you could feel the Poles rising up, which they did, in a bloodless revolution. You could feel them, you could feel them. And I think he went to Poland seven times and I did all seven trips and you could feel the changes. ... [T]he pope came back after martial law, and everyone said, ah-ha, one word the pope is not going to use ... he's not going to mention the Solidarity labor union, right? Well, the pope stepped off the plane and proclaimed solidarity and said something about it the minute he was there, he didn't stop talking about Solidarity until he went back to Rome [in an apparent "test of wills" with Poland's government, Simpson's story noted].[8]

Obviously, an eye and ear for revealing details most help reporting when correspondents are "trying to understand this situation and then what it means, because anybody can stand out there and tell you what they saw," as Deborah Seward (13, 9) found out when she traveled around the imploding Soviet Union and Eastern Europe. She had sensed Mikhail Gorbachev's inability to hold the line when, on a visit to Krakow, flower-selling women also displayed his books: "This was so staged. And it was very clear that he just didn't get it ... that things had changed and that he wasn't going to get it." One of her predecessors in Moscow followed all politburo public appearances to study who might not be in the lineup – and try to deduce whose star was falling or rising at the Kremlin – so that "from your own observations, you could make ... reasonable, analytic comments. We always labeled it as such" (Minthorn, 6). Tasked with covering a similarly vast country, China, in the 1990s, Beijing-based Charles Hutzler (8) started to get a sense of the mass migration from the countryside to booming factory megalopolises when, on assignments for other stories in Henan or Sichuan, he went to villages "and you'd begin to realize that the families that were ... better off, were better off because they had someone who had migrated out and were working in these factories and they were sending money back home."

The second crucial result of eyewitness reporting has been to dispel myths – beginning with those correspondents themselves might harbor before seeing a country firsthand. As one Central America correspondent said, "There were things going on down there that I wouldn't have guessed as to how people had to live" (Frazier, 3). Most importantly, "looking around" allows correspondents to pierce through the rhetoric from all actors, whether the U.S. military, foreign

[7] Victor L. Simpson, "Globe-trotting pope making his 100th foreign tour despite age, infirmities," *The Associated Press*, June 4, 2003.

[8] Victor L. Simpson, "Pontiff and authorities in apparent test of wills," *The Associated Press*, June 20, 1983.

governments, or rebel leaders. Want to write about the expansion of Israeli settlements when the only sources giving numbers are inconsistent? "[W]e went to almost every settlement, or every one we could get access to, and tried to get the number of additional units that had been put in settlements" (Tatro, 22). When in the early 2000s the Taliban announced that they had eradicated opium, Gannon (47–48) decided not to dismiss the news but to investigate it on the ground, and found out how they had done it:

[T]hey went to the village, every village mullah and every village elder. And they said, "If anybody in this village grows poppies, I'm arresting you and the person who is growing it." Now the one thing with the Taliban, everybody knew that if they said it, they did it. . . . And so what happened was the village elder and the village mullah did the policing, not the Taliban. . . . [I]n that whole campaign, they eradicated all the poppies but for a half an acre or something. In all of that, four people were killed. . . . I was the first one who had written about it, and everybody said, "Ah, this is stupid, that's not true."[9] I had the UN, I had everything and I'd gone to all these places, and the day laborers, who had been picking, were in tears, because they were losing so much money. I went to Helmand, I went to Kandahar, I went to Nangarhar, I really wanted to see whether they had. [As the story noted, the farmers were indeed complying – not because they bought the Taliban decree that "it's not Islamic to farm poppies for heroin," but, they said, "because we are afraid."]

Faced with "all sorts of kind of slanderous and/or erroneous or just crazy theories" about "these strange masked rebels popping up and disappearing" in Mexico, John Rice (9–10) went "running off into the boonies, trying to find these guys, and not knowing if they're dangerous":

We got to one town . . . Ocosingo . . . when it was still mopping up, when there were still dead people in the street. . . . And then you'd go out and meet the guys on the roadblock and say "Hi" and "We'd like to talk to you." . . . [Juanita Darling of the *Los Angeles Times* and I] rented an airplane and we flew out to a place where we knew the Zapatistas were, and we landed there to see if somebody would talk to us. And we got lucky, because there was a town that was half Zapatista and half not Zapatista. . . . [W]e talked to the non-Zapatistas first, but they were all part of the same community, brothers and sisters . . . so they . . . took us to the other side. [T]hey hadn't really gotten their ideological line together very well. So we got to talk to people before they really imposed "this is what we want" kind of thing. And so it was a very collective thing. We'd asked, "Can we talk to you? What do you want?" "Wait – I must get other people; we can't do this alone." . . . They insisted on having like 40 people, and us two asking questions. Forty people responding . . . "We'd like a tortilla mill, I'd like not to have to wash clothes half the day, carry water from" – real human . . . you got to see what was behind a lot of the rhetoric that gets imposed when you get politics in the way.

---

[9] Kathy Gannon, "In war on heroin, Afghan rulers ban poppies, farmers know not to disobey," The Associated Press, November 16, 2000. She followed up the next spring with a UN report that the campaign had succeeded, "U.N.: Taliban virtually wipes out opium production in Afghanistan," The Associated Press, February 15, 2001.

"The dead still litter the streets of this little south Mexican town and vultures circle over the cornfields on its edge. . . . On Tuesday, the first group of reporters to reach the town since the fighting found 11 dead in the marketplace building, most in still-liquid pools of blood. Their bodies lay amid rotting vegetables, half-drunk soft drinks and stale tortillas," Rice's story read. Two days later, another AP story reported on attacks against journalists too in Chiapas – even those traveling in "a convoy of clearly marked press vehicles."[10]

Despite the risks, the need to get "the dirt under your fingernails" (Pennington, 17) is even more critical where, to the local spin, the U.S. government or military is adding its own. Correspondents considered "embedding" with U.S. troops (discussed in Chapter 10), one essential way to see one side of war – the actions of American soldiers, from heroics to atrocities. Desfor (10, 8–9), who covered U.S. troops in the Pacific in World War II, was on the tarmac in Saipan with his cameras as the Enola Gay landed after dropping the atomic bomb, and a few weeks later got a U.S. pilot to take him to Hiroshima to witness the "terrible gruesome sight." He also got very up close when he landed with assault troops at Yokosuka, near Tokyo, as World War II was ending – not knowing what welcome to expect:

When they came off the ships and took up machine gun positions on the land and pretty soon they sort of looked around and saw that there was nobody doing anything to them. . . . And the funny part was that over to the left I saw a group of Japanese, and I went close and they were waving us in. [chuckles] There was a welcoming party, sort of. And of course the American troops got up and took their machine guns out of position and life went on.

In Iraq, Gray (62), who did several embeds, recalled witnessing soldiers at a roadblock stopping a farmer on the way from the market, searching his vehicle, and putting a knife through his tires: "right there, that turned somebody against the Americans and it wasn't needed. So things like that you can report. Whereas if you weren't embedded, you might not see any of that." But correspondents also struggled to go out independently, in the countryside or in the heart of Baghdad, to seek voices on civilian impact as well as the sectarian strife:

Because at some point, the U.S. is going to pull out [of Iraq] and you've got to understand how those alliances are forming. . . . Because then the Americans say one thing, and then the Shiite emerging power structure says another, and if those don't match up, then . . . we really wrote our stories as two or three reporters who were finding things out, and then we put that information together. We had to, because no one person could get to all the sources of information in the country. (Buzbee, 7)

Covering the Lebanese civil war and the U.S. Marines' involvement, another correspondent found that street reporting was necessary to piece the stories

---

[10] John Rice, "Ocosingo emerges to scenes of death," The Associated Press, January 4, 1994; Anita Snow, "Attack on journalists raises concerns about reporters' safety," The Associated Press, January 6, 1994.

together – as long as the reporters had a reasonable chance of making it back to the office alive:

You don't pick up a phone and call somebody because the phone probably isn't working, there's nobody at the other end, and you get no sense of what it looks like. So we really were out on the street all the time, and, because of that, we had a certain rapport with basically all sides of this conflict. . . . [F]or example, a bunch of Marines had been killed at a checkpoint . . . and the Marines didn't want to talk about it. Well, we drove around to the militia on the other side and we asked them what had happened that morning and they told us. And then we drove back to the Marines base and we said, "Okay, here's what happened, how did this happen? Now you tell us, you talk to us." So that gave us a certain confidence, because we felt that we were neutral and we were out on the street and reporting all sides, that maybe they cut us a little slack, and essentially I think they did, until it got to the point of kidnapping, and then, different rules. (Powell, 2–3)

The fundamental importance that all correspondents attach to seeing the world firsthand drives their desire and ingenuity in getting themselves to the scene, as well as their near-awed happiness in doing so despite terrific risks. Some history-making occasions – pro-democracy revolutions, say – have the potential to be so joyous that it is easier to understand what got correspondents in on the run. Echoing Schemm's rush from Bali, Paris-based Rosenblum (42) also jumped into the story of the collapse of European Communism – from a vacation with his future wife in the Florida Keys:

I'm driving and I'm carefree and happy, with this beautiful blonde, and I'm listening to the radio, and the fucking Berlin Wall fell. And I'm in Miami on vacation, and I'm not in Paris and the Berlin Wall is like an hour away. . . . That was probably the worst moment [in my career]. . . . It got better because I immediately went back and went to Prague, and I was in Prague when . . . there's like a million people in Wenceslas Square and they're all waving their keys in the air. The Czechs have this thing that when they're protesting something, they wave the keys, meaning "Get the fuck out of here." And . . . you could just see Czechoslovakia go free, right? So there was this guy translating from Czech for me, and he's translating and I'm writing down, and I turn over and . . . he's just so broken into tears that he just can't . . . And I'm sitting there, just filled with this . . . just in the middle of all of these, this million of people that built their revolution.

But it is the critical need to bear witness, far more than the adrenaline, that would make virtually all foreign correspondents – and very few others – agree with this apparently astonishing statement by Tokyo-based Eric Talmadge (5) recalling the aftermath of Japan's 2011 tsunami-triggered nuclear meltdown: "I was out in Fukushima for almost all of the first 49 days of the crisis, and that's exactly where I wanted to be. I wanted to be out talking to people and seeing things, out there reporting and using my skills." After spending more than a decade on the desk in Jerusalem while her children were growing up, Karin Laub (18) got back to covering the West Bank and Gaza and said it felt "like I was in a candy store" to be able to write illuminating social stories such as the changes in dating and marriage mores.[11] Gannon (39–41) said she was "just really lucky" to be in Kabul right as the Taliban seized it in 1996, after most international workers had fled but Gannon had flown in from Pakistan before all flights were halted. She had "wanted to see because again, I always went to see" – even sights that included "an ex-president's bloated body" still dangling from a noose outside the palace while "shops re-opened and people walked the sunny streets":[12]

I went to cover the front lines and there was a lot of fighting and everything, and then did my story, went to sleep, woke up at 4 o'clock in the morning . . . and there, [the Taliban] had their tanks outside my door, saying the morning prayers. And then somebody said Najib, the former Communist [president of Afghanistan], was hanging in the town square. So I went out and . . . it was horrific.

RESPONSIBILITY THAT OUTWEIGHS DANGERS

Nearly 20 years earlier, the same responsibility to bear witness had driven Gray to Phnom Penh as the Khmer Rouge advanced, but, after a month, AP ordered him and another U.S. correspondent to evacuate by U.S. helicopter just before the city fell. Gray (8) called it "probably one of my greatest regrets in my life": "I should have stayed," he insisted, because the Cambodian staff turned down AP's offer to leave, despite the "horrendous" situation with the Khmer Rouge shelling the airport and poised to overtake the city with foreseeable brutality. As just about everyone was trying to get out of Saigon when the North Vietnamese closed in, Richard Pyle (16–17), who had been bureau chief there, kept "pleading" with managers to send him back, even to just mop "the goddamn floor": "Not that they needed me but I just wanted to be back there at the end, like I had an obligation to be there because I had felt so strongly about this whole experience in Vietnam itself that I just felt like I was betraying myself and betraying others by not being there."

From World War II to the Syrian civil war in the 2010s, all correspondents have had to weigh the deadly dangers of reporting on the ground against the responsibility to do their jobs according to their standards, often chafing at the safety arrangements proposed by their U.S. editors. The reason they often chose to go, or to stay, in perilous places has not changed: to have enough understanding for events so that they could get their audience to comprehend and care, as Laub (36) put it assessing her time in Maaret Misreen, a town emblematic of "the swath of rebel-controlled territory in northwestern Syria":

[11] Karin Laub, "Postcard from Palestine: In hard times, a university degree is a bride's biggest asset," The Associated Press, January 19, 2007.
[12] Kathy Gannon, "Afghan rebels seize capital, execute ex-president," The Associated Press, September 27, 1996.

There were still people, for example, who were government employees who lived in this rebel-controlled town, that they would cross a number of checkpoints, rebel and regime checkpoints, every day to go to government jobs in [Idlib], the nearest bigger city. So all these little absurdities, or the rebels trying to find cash to keep the town running, or how they are distributing the bread. . . . If a reader sees another story about "rebels took blah-blah-blah today" – we have to do these stories but . . . people can't relate to it as easily as to a story from the ground that says, here is Mahmoud So-and-so and . . . this is what he's up against while he's living in this little town. . . . Maybe this is not a huge story or something, but . . . you have to ask yourself again every day how much of this is worth that much risk.

Laub's story showed people outside the town's only bakery running for cover when a helicopter was heard, since breadlines had been bombed before – and others so desperate to get their maximum 24 pieces of flatbread that they "didn't budge."[13]

Conventional war reporting is inherently risky – as Desfor (5) discovered when his quest for good "hometown" stories on U.S. soldiers in Korea took him on his first parachute jump:

I proceeded with the paratroopers loading into the aircraft. As soon as I got inside, I started interviewing the kids on my left and right, the closest ones to me. . . . When I got finished, I knew that they would make good . . . "hometowners," and I wrapped up all my writing, all my interviews, and handed it to the pilot, since he was going to go around and go back out. . . . I had specifically told the commanding officer that I wanted to be in the first wave. It wasn't bravery, believe me, it was just that I figured out that the best place to be to be able to get the troops floating down in, under their parachutes, and I think that was the picture that was much needed. . . . [J]ust prior to [getting to the drop zone] one of the youngsters that I had interviewed asked me if I had ever jumped before. And I said, "No, never. Nowhere near it." He says, "Well, all you have to do is bend your knees when you hit the ground." It didn't make much sense to me, but that's what I call paratrooping 101. [chuckles] And I guess I must have remembered it, but what I had not done was tighten my helmet, because as soon as my parachute opened, my helmet came down and hit my nose and it kind of hurt. But I did remember to bend my knees when I landed.

Far riskier are the civil wars, rebellions, and guerrilla movements that correspondents cover. Traveling to the first Nicaraguan town Sandinistas controlled "to try to get some idea of what a Sandinista government might look like" resulted in confiscated equipment and 20 hours of detention under armed guard, where some people offered journalists food but "guerrillas in from the field poked their heads in the door and asked jokingly if we were CIA agents," as the story recounted (Frazier, 7).[14] Hours after a ceasefire in the 2006 war between Israel and Hezbollah in Lebanon, Gannon (8–9) and a

---

[13] Karin Laub, "No water, power, cash: Syria rebels run broke town," *The Associated Press*, December 16, 2012.

[14] Joe Frazier, *The Associated Press*, July 1, 1979.

photographer decided to leave other reporters and head off toward the border, "where most of the damage was." Despite a large "TV" sign on their car, they came under fire within sight of a UN compound by what turned out to be a "very nice and very apologetic" – but also "very nervous" – group of Israeli soldiers.[15] Alan Cooperman (13–14) did not budge from the Russian White House during the August 1991 putsch. His story described the "grave and a bit surreal" mood inside the building, with lawmakers slinging gas masks over their shoulders and sipping tea when not bumping into walls "as they groped through the hallways, which were plunged into darkness to reduce targets for snipers":[16]

I wanted to stay, and I was in there for two nights, including the night in which it later turned out that orders were given [to elite troops] to storm it. The orders were disobeyed. But I still have the gas masks that were handed out. ... The food ran out. ... [M]y cell phone there was like a brick thing that weighed about 25 pounds and was about a foot square – for as long as that thing held out, I reported on what was going on. ... I was so energized and on adrenaline by the story, and, by the way, was very lucky to be allowed to stay in there. ... [T]he head of the Foreign Affairs Committee of the Russian parliament took me into his office at the time that they ... forced all the foreigners out of the building. ... I did try to get around that night to interview people, but it was really hard. Again, all the corners were darkened. They set up barricades. And I was able to move around a little bit. But also, that was scary. Moving through the darkened corridors where these guys ... had guns that were loaded. They thought that they were going to be attacked, and they were jumpy.

Other correspondents also tried not to stand out at the scene, to minimize the dangers (discussed in Chapter 5) associated with being journalists and foreigners, thus maximizing their ability to move around and see, unmolested by either officials or crowds. Covering the banlieues around Paris where violent riots among the mostly immigrant, Arab, and North African population have erupted regularly in the 2000s, Elaine Ganley (20–22) tried to go into the projects "very discreetly" (only pencil and paper, and a cell phone for photos since "we have lost a lot of equipment out there"). Still, threatening hostility lingered:

[O]ne project in particular I kept visiting and visiting, it's really considered about the roughest in Paris area ... called Les Bosquets. ... [W]hen it was all the old projects [before attempts at beautification after the 2005 riots] ... the graffiti just was enough to scare you. And then in these hallways filled with graffiti, exposed to the outside, kids that hang out, doing whatever, and if you approach them, they can be very nasty. [...] There in Les Bosquets, there were two cafés. ... I did not realize what a taboo I was breaking by crossing the doorstep. ... I sat down and had a tea, and I eventually had two young men at the table with me, and just making the most, really obscene remarks, to which I ...

15 An account of the shooting is in Kathy Gannon, "Fragile peace could break down at any village or hilltop in southern Lebanon," The Associated Press, August 14, 2006.

16 Alan Cooperman, "Russian lawmakers prepare for potential assault," The Associated Press, August 21, 1991.

really didn't crack because I thought I cannot show that I am being intimidated, I simply can't. And I actually went in there a couple times ... but they kind of got used to me, because it was a place to meet inside another part of the population that you won't see outside, you won't see them anywhere else.

Two of Ganley's stories from Les Bosquets – from 1991 and 2007 – similarly introduced life in the "bleak high-rise tenements of Montfermeil [that] seem light years from the city of light," with "ragged pants and T-shirts" dangling from a tree, pigeons feasting on "garbage dumped from windows" and "streaks of graffiti blacken[ing] dank entryways like screams."[17] In the latter story, one 33-year-old electrician, "sipping coffee in a cafe where men and boys play rummy," told her that residents would nevertheless hesitate to leave: "What are they going to do somewhere else?"

Alerted by phone tips that Chinese state factories were being shut down, triggering protests across the country that the government was not even acknowledging, Hutzler (15–16) picked the demonstration where he stood a chance not to be immediately noticed by police and arrested while reporting – a protest by pedi-cab drivers not far from tourist-thronged Chengdu. Laid-off workers had tried to eke a living through pedi-cabs, only to have them confiscated by police because they were unlicensed, so Hutzler figured "I can sort of just hop from pedi-cab to pedi-cab, looking like a tourist, and interview the pedi-cab drivers as I went along. And that's what I did." Trying to experience firsthand the challenges for Central Americans "hoping to cross the border into the United States and grab a piece of the American dream," as the editor's note prefacing the story read, Niko Price (23–24) and a photographer shadowed a smuggler entering Mexico from Guatemala with a guide, a prostitute he brought along, and "13 Salvadoran peasants." They waded across a raging stream, ran through shoe-sucking mud fields, and finally were among the last six left behind in a coffee field with the empty promise that a pickup vehicle would arrive:[18]

[W]e were sort of asking around, as subtly we can, to try to find ... a people smuggler. Which was difficult as two Americans in a little Guatemalan town. It seemed a little bit odd. But after a couple of days, we were able to meet up with someone who was a smuggler and ... negotiated for some time, I think it took about a day, he wanted to charge us and we weren't going to pay smuggling fees to a smuggler. [chuckles] But eventually he said we could join. And so we waited around all day with a group of Central Americans who had all come up, in a safe house, and then finally in the evening we were bundled into a van and driven near the border. Spent the entire night running through fields and woods, and it was pretty grueling. ... And the next morning what we

---

[17] Elaine Ganley, "In high-rise suburbs, the French good life seems far away," The Associated Press, August 1, 1991; Elaine Ganley, "Residents of French slums suspicious of change as presidential election approaches," April 11, 2007.
[18] Niko Price, "Central Americans struggle to make the long road north," The Associated Press, May 6, 2001.

did after we left the group, we went back to the border. . . . So we were covered in mud, and our shoes were broken, and we looked in bad shape. But we needed to get our visas stamped, the entry stamp, so we just walked into the house and the guy [border officer] took one look at us and said, "Wow, you guys had fun last night."

KEEP OUT! (OR IN ON A LEASH)

Not all government officials have been as compliant as that Mexican border guard. In a tacit acknowledgment of the importance of eyewitness reporting to dispel myths and move international audiences, groups in power from Afghanistan to the Soviet Union have tried their hardest to keep correspondents away, or to only allow them close to the scene on staged, controlled tours (as further discussed in Chapter 9). After wrangling a rare permission from the Taliban to enter Afghanistan during the U.S. attack in October 2001, Gannon (60–61, 66) nearly cried when the border guard would not let her cross in from Pakistan. Then Amir Shah, who had driven to pick her up, roused the provincial governor and got him to okay the entry:

I was driving and I thought, "I cannot believe I am here. I am so lucky to be here." Because of course you had hundreds of people out here in Islamabad, and they were all up in the north and nobody was in Kabul, except me. And I went down to Chicken Street one day and one of the carpet dealers . . . came out and said, "Oh, are the foreigners back?" I said, "No, not yet. Just me." [chuckles] . . . I don't think I left Kabul until it was April I think, March/April. . . . Just following the story, because it was really so important for me to be there.

Another correspondent was not so "lucky" trying to get back into Iran after the U.S. Embassy hostage crisis began in November 1979. He made it to the airport but "was put on the next plane out of there" on a visa technicality (Doelling 14). Arriving in Algiers in early 2011, her press visa in hand, Ganley (53–56) was held up at the airport and did not get to the communications ministry in time to get the written "permission" to report from the country. The next morning, she skipped the bureaucracy to attend a demonstration she expected might herald the end of the decades-old state of emergency and sweep Algeria into the Arab Spring unrest. There, her cell phone was stolen out of her hands while she was taking photos of a human rights attorney and her glasses smashed on the ground.[19] Later, she heard chanting and, looking out from her hotel balcony, saw an "unauthorized" protest by the Communal Guards, "the eyes and ears of security forces fighting the terrorists," and ran out to cover that too:

But by the time I got down, the police . . . pulled them over to the side of the road, to get them off the street. And everybody was milling about, and more police were coming . . .

---

[19] Still, Ganley reported on the protests and the heavy police presence: "Algerian police break up crowd at pro-reform rally," The Associated Press, February 19, 2011.

I started talking to them, a lot of them don't speak French but I found one who did. . . . And then there was a tap on my shoulder and a gentleman goes, "Who are you"? And I said, "Oh, I'm a journalist." . . . I showed him my stamp in the passport, and then they asked for my piece of paper from the communications ministry. And I said I hadn't been there yet, they don't answer the telephone, and I'm busy. And they said, well you're not allowed . . . and they wanted to put me in . . . the police van, and take me to the police station. . . . [M]ore and more of them were crowding around me saying I had to, and eventually I said, I will go to the police station, but I will go on foot, because I did nothing wrong, and I'm not getting in the van like a criminal. And so they detached someone to . . . walk with me to the police station. And so I spent a couple hours there. . . . And so they have a file on me, I don't like that they have this file because . . . what impact does this have on me? I don't know. . . . What they succeeded in doing, of course, was taking me away from these Communal Guards.

But not in preventing her from filing a story about it: A few days later, Ganley's story described the Communal Guards' protest, "an eloquent example of the breadth of social unrest in this gas-rich North African nation," quoting guards as airing their grievances to her even "as police hustled the protesters to the side of the boulevard."[20]

Another correspondent also found that at protests, in Communist Poland, "you would be stopped and asked for your identification and then held for an hour or two, until the story you were going to cover had gone away, and then be let go" (Daniszewski, 11). Reporting on early antiapartheid struggles in black South African townships like Soweto also required a pass. Sneaking in a couple of times after the pass expired, one correspondent was briefly arrested with a group of other journalists: "We were in a church meeting with . . . some of the underground leaders, and the police came and surrounded the church and said they were going to teargas everybody if we didn't come out. So we came out. And then they released us shortly afterwards" (Heinzerling, 4).

Many governments have also tried to control journalists' access to scenes by taking them on controlled tours, something that correspondents resist but often have no choice but accepting. In Algeria during the 1990s civil war, Ganley (43) was taken "on a tour of some of these massacred villages in a little, kind of a minivan . . . [with] little curtains on it, and we went in a touring car to visit . . . the cemetery where the people massacred in Sidi Rais [in 1997] were buried. . . . It was very macabre." So was the story, starting with the names of the hundreds of dead "scratched on plasterboard sunken into freshly turned mounds of dirt," and later adding that the dazed residents' accounts remained "contradictory, and the horrors are still incomprehensible."[21] Tatro (19), on embeds with the Israeli Army when it occupied southern Lebanon, found them revealing in ways that sometimes defeated the purposes of the "controlled

[20] Elaine Ganley, "Algeria keeps lid on social unrest for now," The Associated Press, March 2, 2011.
[21] Elaine Ganley, "Mystery, contradictions plague site of largest Algerian massacres," The Associated Press, October 25, 1997.

environment" – including soldiers "riding down the highway shooting into the underbrush for fear" of ambushes, as well as suicide bombers attacking them. Also eager to get into Lebanon a decade earlier, Terry Anderson (11–12) first crossed the border in "a jeep driven by an Israeli press corps officer." But the arrangement quickly fell apart when his escort insisted on taking him only as far as Beaufort Castle, a historical hilltop fort over the border that Israeli paratroopers had just retaken from the PLO:

[I] said, "Oh, excuse me, Lieutenant, I'm not a tourist okay, I don't care about the Crusader castle. I need to get to the front line; I need to go to where there are battles." He said no, no, no, we're going to Beaufort, and I said, "Okay, you go to Beaufort," got out of the jeep and . . . hitched a ride with an army truck headed north. And I got upfront, and I spent the day trying to get as close as I could to the actual violence. Where are they, how fast are they going, what's their immediate goal, their tactical goal, because the Israelis were telling the world that it was a limited incursion, of limited length, and they had no intention of going for Beirut, which was all dead lying. . . . I went to the press center and they yanked my press pass. He said, "You left your press officer." I said, "No, he left me." And . . . we screamed and yelled and hollered and they gave me my press pass back. The next few days, a group of us would get in the car with the Israeli escort officer and drive for Beirut, drive as far as we can . . . figure out what we could, and drive back. And . . . after about a week, . . . I went to the Israelis and I said, AP is transferring me to the Beirut bureau. Then they said . . . you will never be permitted to come back. I said I don't want to go back. So they said okay well we're not going to furnish transportation. . . . I covered the war in East Beirut for about a week . . . and then I said I want to come over to the West because the West had constant bombing, bombardment. It was in isolation. The people then in the AP office there were working 20 to 22 hours a day and in danger. . . . You could still get through some of the checkpoints. We had shells coming over, but we did get through and went to the AP bureau, and I worked there for the next couple of months.

Even in peacetime, many governments restrict journalists' movements. Correspondents wanting to explore East Germany, Europe's Cold War front line, could get past Checkpoint Charlie, albeit with a hefty "fee." But if they wished to go beyond Berlin, they needed to secure an extra visa detailing their motivations and precise itinerary, which could not be changed – so restrictive that Reid (20–21) concluded, "We knew nothing of the way the country operated in and what it was like to live in the German Democratic Republic. And why? Because the state wouldn't let us." Today in Pyongyang, Lee (17) could not "walk around or move around at will. It's against their rules for us to – for any foreigner, frankly – to get to move around the city without what they call a guide." Even a visit to an ice-skating rink, swimming pool, or restaurant had to be arranged in advance and on days when foreigners were permitted, though once in, Lee still grabbed the rare opportunity to chat with locals. In both the Soviet Union and China, where journalists had to get permission to travel outside of the capitals, they went on government-organized trips to remote provinces, and tried to turn them into occasions to get behind the scenes of how people were living under, and rebelling against, authoritarian control. Mark Porubcansky (6–7) went on a 1988 trip to Magadan, the former "jumping-off point for the various Gulags," where the foreign ministry even organized a meeting with a survivor who told him he remembered "the interrogation, the death sentence never carried out and the tiny knots he tied in pieces of string to remind him of what he saw in a Stalinist labor camp."[22] That was a far cry from the usual "game," where correspondents had to give the ministry a detailed trip plan 48 hours before traveling anywhere and, since they depended on another government agency to book the travel, "they might say, 'Well everything is fine, but there don't happen to be any flights on that particular day.' They wouldn't get back to you within the 48-hour timeframe, so you're sunk." In 1996, Hutzler (20–22) traveled to Xinjiang on the "subterfuge" of talking about the oil industry and wanting to visit Kashgar, a celebrated historical trading city, when he was really interested in the separatist unrest simmering there that he had been reading about in the *Xinjiang Daily*. His minders said that after a nice banquet, they would take him to visit the main mosque's imam – whose name rang a bell:

I had brought a folder – pre-Internet days – of newspaper clippings, and I had all these reports from the *Xinjiang Daily*, and sure enough, this guy had been the target of an assassination attempt by separatists. They cut his throat and he lived. So the next evening, we're sitting on the floor in a part of the mosque and this very kind of dignified older gentleman with a turban comes out and he's got a big bandage on his throat. . . . And it was just one of these things that I couldn't believe that they were producing him. . . . I asked him a lot of questions about it, and he didn't really want to provide that many details, but he had another imam with him who would talk about the problems of separatism in general in Xinjiang. . . . [I]t ended up being a sort of very successful trip and kind of a model for using this cage that we had been put in. . . . [W]ith enough really good reporting done ahead of time, careful sort of plotting out of reporting, you could actually really get at stories. And in some cases, the government side of things is really indispensable.

Another means of getting to restricted areas, from Cambodia to Cuba to Hungary, was to go with European or American personalities like the evangelist Billy Graham, whom two correspondents in the 1970s accompanied in Communist-controlled Eastern Europe (Reid, 17–18) and the Indian state of Nagaland. On the border with Burma, the state required special travel permission and kept correspondents at arm's length (Bradsher 2013, 97) – so that when a small rebellion erupted just as Myron Belkind (15–16) was attending a Graham rally at a football field, he had a scoop with such eyewitness details as the 2,000 people who stayed in their seats only because Graham "appealed to them."[23] In 1979, Gray relied twice on U.S. humanitarians to get to heart-wrenching stories. Trying to return to Phnom

---

[22] Mark J. Porubcansky, The Associated Press, November 21, 1988.
[23] "Convoy Hit as Graham Preaches," *Chicago Tribune*, November 23, 1972, B26.

Penh right after the Khmer Rouge regime fell to report on its atrocities as well as widespread famine, Gray (45–46) was one of the first American journalists allowed in with a U.S. relief group, World Vision, and spent a "moving, shocking month" discovering that many friends had been killed and that Tuol Sleng prison, where many had been tortured, "still had literally blood on the floor." As the Vietnamese boat people crisis reached its height, with desperate refugees braving pirate-infested waters on makeshift boats, Gray (43–44) realized that going to refugee camps was not close enough to the action. He got permission to go onboard the *Seasweep*, a boat that World Vision had leased to mount an improbable search in the vast South China Sea:

> [I]t was quite a rickety ship, I must say, it wasn't exactly an ocean liner, and we sailed up and down the coast, from the top of Indonesia to off Hong Kong somewhere, or further up the coast, looking for these refugees. Two weeks, up and down . . . very frustrating, we didn't find anybody. But my photographer and I – there were so few crew on board that we actually also stood watch. We took turns, four hours at a time, standing at the prow of the ship looking for refugees using binoculars; didn't find them. . . . [T]hree o'clock in the morning, off an oil rig, about 200 kilometers off the Malaysian coast, there was a distress signal that came out from this oil rig saying, "We've got some Vietnamese boat people nearby. Can you help?" . . . Then we had this Vietnamese wooden boat approaching us with 46-some people on board. And we had this extremely dramatic rescue of hauling these refugees from the boat up to the *Seasweep*. . . . [T]he story is told from the two sides: our side, looking for them, and then interviewing the people who we rescued.

The story began by recounting the group's escape. As a typhoon was brewing, Vietnamese authorities had ordered "fleeing boats gunned on sight," and one man's "wife was drained of energy after giving birth to a baby boy":

> The timing could not have been worse . . . Vo Huu Minh, a former U.S. Government employee with a sick wife, thought to himself, "we have a 90 to 100 percent chance of failure." But the momentum of two months' planning and the intricate deceptions had passed the point of no return. The nine-metre boat, piloted by a fisherman who had never used a compass in the open sea, crept out of the resort of Vung Tau under cover of night, then headed for international waters as fast as its 20-horsepower engine allowed.[24]

TIME AND LOGISTICS: GROWING CHALLENGES

As all the examples above illustrate, reporting from the scene, especially in the hardest-to-reach places, requires substantial investments of time and logistical resources, which are increasingly endangered in today's money-tight, immediacy-crazed journalism. Several correspondents noted that the dark secret of journalism is the amount of time spent waiting – for sources, for events, for developments, for confirmation, for permits, for their place in the interviewers' line – sometimes only getting "spin and fabrication" after hours

---

[24] Denis D. Gray, "Refugee Drama on the High Seas," *Bangkok Post*, August 4, 1979.

"standing in the rain ... corralled into some pen outside some government office" (Perry, 36).

Bryson (11–12, 75–77) recalled how long it took to do just two spot feature stories in 1990s South Africa – one on a school desegregation court case and another on the return home of the first black South African who won Olympic gold – and why it was time well spent. For the first story, Bryson and a photographer arrived early enough to watch a little girl get ready to go to school, and then went with her, finding "what you would expect, a mob of shouting white South Africans, who didn't want to let the kids into school, shouting ugly things":

[T]here you have the very typical. That's the confrontation we all expect. And the next day, the police were still there, but at least the opposition parents had gotten tired and other white parents just wanted their kids to go to school, and it was a much quieter day. And, there was a little white girl that I spoke to that day ... who said she was very eager to meet the new students and show them around. For her it was a normal day at school, and I think it's good that we stayed two days. The first day was the story that you would expect, and the second day was maybe a little bit more normal.

The first-day story on school desegregation opened with the obvious historical parallel between Potgietersrus and American cities where black children, "protected by a police cordon," had walked into schools while many white students stayed home. It quoted 10-year-old Thabang Thula, sharing her happiness at being allowed in a school three blocks away with the "dozens of journalists waiting outside," but also a white man shouting in Afrikaans, calling black students "apes" and cursing journalists "after his daughter burst into tears when mobbed by reporters and cameramen." The second-day story quoted 8-year-old Rusel Wildeboer – whose parents had kept her home on the first day "because of the crowds of police and journalists" that had dwindled to a handful by the next day – as eager to help her black classmates "because they're new."[25] For the Olympian story, Bryson drove all day to the tiny village north of Johannesburg where the former miner lived. There, as the story reads, "It's easy to pick out Josia Thugwane's home from among all the other tin shacks on his dirt road. His is the place with the brass band, prancing drum majorettes and ululating matrons out front":[26]

I get to the house, and there's a line of reporters waiting to interview him. ... I don't think I was so particularly pleased with my job that day, but at least there was a band to entertain myself while waiting. ... [By the time I got to him] he was "very happy to have won." I might have even been able to write that from Johannesburg. ... But then you wouldn't have had ... the moment of, I wonder if I'm going to be able to find his house,

[25] Donna Bryson, "Heavily guarded black children knock down a vestige of apartheid," The Associated Press, February 22, 1996; Donna Bryson, "School peaceful on second day of desegregation," The Associated Press, February 23, 1996.

[26] Donna Bryson, "First black South African to win gold returns to hero's welcome," The Associated Press, August 11, 1996.

and then you look up and there's a marching band. .... If you take it off TV or you take it off the telephone, you're just going to get something so narrow. You are not going to be able to escape your own assumptions about it. But when you go out and you see the whole scene, it can change the story for you.

AP's international editor, John Daniszewski (5), highlighted the necessity of "actually [having] to go someplace to see what happened" as he recalled his days as correspondent in Communist Poland. There, to cover protests, "you would have to get in a car and drive for five or six hours in order to see it; otherwise you weren't going to get the information, or if you got the information, it wouldn't be verified because there was always a chance that a Solidarity activist or a union activist could call and tell you something had happened, but it wouldn't have the same credibility as if you had been there and seen it yourself and taken pictures – how big was the crowd, thousands or hundreds, or a dozen." The pressure to be everywhere and cover everything nearly got to Schemm (11), based in Benghazi as AP's sole text reporter during part of the Libyan uprising:

I kind of went a little crazy about trying to nail everything down. .... I just got very emotional about it at one point just because I couldn't cover everything. .... I was spending hours in the car every day going to the front line, and then I came back to Benghazi and there'd been a huge explosion in an ammo dump – 70 dead or something – and I just couldn't, I couldn't cover that too. And I'd missed it.

Having lone correspondents covering large areas means that some stories are missed out of sheer logistical impossibility (Liu, 6), especially when they are of the magnitude of Iraq or in a fast-breaking, unpredictable environment like the Arab Spring. Both challenged even a veteran like Reid (58, 73), who compared the first to "showering at the bottom of Niagara Falls: You go into the motions, but you're just being beaten down." Price (16), who covered many hurricanes in Central America, said natural disasters also required extra planning and some guessing:

We were taking what the forecasters were saying about the path, figuring out when that meant the airport would close and when you had to make the call of where to go. And sometimes sending people to two different places and knowing that one of them would get it but not knowing which, because you didn't have the luxury to wait until you knew where it was going to send them, because by then it would be closed.

Even in more normal circumstances, the vastness of countries like India or Brazil, plus usually congested roads, sometimes in disrepair, created hours of delay in getting to the scene of breaking news even in major cities (Powell, 16; Clendenning, 14). In contrast, in small Albania in the early 1990s, the lack of private cars and fuel made it imperative to drive only as far as half a tank would go (Porubcansky, 22). During China's mushrooming AIDS epidemic tied to a blood-selling scandal, Hutzler (7) tried to follow up the tips by the ministry of health: "They would say in the Hunan, but they wouldn't say which villages they were. Since Hunan has about 80 million people, that's very difficult." In January 2013, when terrorists took hundreds of people hostage at a remote gas plant in Algeria, Algiers released "nothing, and what they did release was not true in many cases," so correspondents had to balance the rare official pronouncements with what the militants were telling Mauritanian websites and what eventually released hostages from as far as the Philippines were revealing – all with the actual scene "800 miles away from the capital, deep in the desert, in a restricted zone" (Schemm, 23–24).

Crossing hostile borders takes even more effort: When the October 1973 war between a coalition of Arab states and Israel grounded flights into Egypt, Richard Pyle (27-28b), fresh from Vietnam, flew to Rome, then Tripoli, then Benghazi; from there, he was 24 hours on the road across the desert with "this 14-year-old kid, a driver, with his car." Getting in and out of Gaza and its crowded refugee camps used to be a day's work for Laub (3),[27] who only needed to avoid what the Israeli Army would cordon off as a "military area," whereas journalists' movements have been severely restricted recently. Borders can be impassable: In Sudan, which split into two during a bloody civil war, journalists from Cairo covered the north and those from Nairobi the south, and "never the twain shall meet" (Powell, 16); shuttling between Seoul and Pyongyang means a detour through Beijing, because there are no direct flights, and no border crossings for what would be a three-hour drive (Lee, 2). One of the most logistically challenging assignments was under-siege Sarajevo. Correspondents going in for short stints, like Vienna-based Mark Porubcansky (13), who first arrived with tires amassed in the car backseat to "absorb the bullets," had to carry all essential supplies, from peanut butter to water purification tablets, for the bureau lacked running water most of the time.

STRUGGLING TO GET IN

For many correspondents, getting to the scene was as dangerous as reporting there. Celebrated early 20th-century correspondent H. R. Knickerbocker wrote, "Whenever you find hundreds of thousands of sane people trying to get out of a place and a little bunch of madmen struggling to get in, you know the latter are newspapermen."[28] When I repeated this quote to Tony Smith (7) in his modernist villa perched above Douro Valley vineyards, he agreed it fit perfectly the image of him and a handful of colleagues standing in a Sarajevo suburb's car park right before the siege. They watched a convoy with all other foreigners evacuate, and got ready to travel into the city – a frightening trek they

[27] Among her first stories from the Jabalia camp, see Karin Laub, "Jabalia has become center of resistance to Israel," The Associated Press, December 19, 1987.
[28] From AP correspondent Mort Rosenblum's book on foreign reporting, entitled *A Little Bunch of Madmen.*

would undertake in reverse a few days later, carrying a gravely wounded photographer to safety and the body of a killed colleague to his family:[29]

So the press was there, the TV guys were there, and the ... European Community at the time, their monitors were there. And so when things started getting a little bit hairy around Sarajevo, the hotel was targeted. A couple of shells fell close by, nothing happened ... I'm sure this was done to scare us out. And it worked. ... European Community decided it was too dangerous for their monitors. They were unarmed and they had no mandate to do anything, they were just there to watch, so they pulled them back to Split.[30] And then of course the TV networks basically made their decision based on that and pulled everybody back to Split. And so when the TV guys go, then the press goes. ... Santiago Lyon and David Brauchli, two [AP] photographers, and myself ... decided that no, we shouldn't do this, we should go *in*, we should go into Sarajevo. The story was just really getting to its first climax, I would say, and yet people were all leaving to Split, and we figured, if everybody goes to Split, how are we going to follow the story? Nobody is going to be here, and we don't know what the local guys will be able to file or not. ... I do recall being on the car park of the hotel and everybody – this whole convoy of ... European Community jeeps and transporters and then the TV guys in their Land Rovers and everybody in this convoy heading back to Split, driving out of the car park, going back to Split. And we were the only guys there. [chuckles] There were two cars, it was this bashed-up old Golf which somebody had rented ... and I had this little, dreadfully damaged Toyota Corolla automatic shift, which I had run into a tank trap a few days earlier.

Correspondents repeatedly risked their lives to get to the scene "to follow the story," as Smith put it, and alert the world to what was really happening. Mirroring Schemm's and Rosenblum's experiences, *The Times*' Robert Fisk, who worked closely with AP correspondents in Lebanon, was on vacation in Ireland in 1982 when he heard the Israelis had entered West Beirut. His multiday, sleepless journey back – a mad drive to Dublin, flights to Geneva and Damascus, three taxis to Beirut, and a walk across a minefield – finally led him to the AP office, where news editor G. G. LaBelle was "cursing beside the telex machine, long, unrepeatable oaths because all the lines were now collapsing. ... He looked up at me with big, unsmiling red eyes. 'So you made it. About fucking time'" (Fisk 2002, 354–356). LaBelle's wife, correspondent Eileen Powell (5), described the hair-raising routine of reporting around Beirut, a spider's net of rival militia-controlled checkpoints and unpredictable violence:

[Y]ou come around the corner, you look, you sneak into a doorway, you look again, can you make it? Go a little farther. Because you had to get to somewhere where you could ask somebody a question. What happened, when did it happen, who did this? Who did you think did it? What did you see, what did it look like?

---

[29] Tony Smith, "Tearful farewell, then a drive past desperate refugees," The Associated Press, May 21, 1992.

[30] Tony Smith, "EC pulls its last observers out of Bosnia due to danger," The Associated Press, May 12, 1992.

When the U.S. Marine barracks in Beirut were bombed in 1983, killing more than 240 Americans, LaBelle, Powell, Fisk, and Anderson all rushed to the corpse-strewn, smoking rubble, and Fisk described how Anderson, a Marine veteran, threw "himself at the fencing. 'AP, AP, I gotta come in. You've *got* to let me in'" until a young guard pulled the wire aside for them (Fisk 2002, 513).

At times, correspondents have relied on soldiers to get to the scene, with some safety guarantee if they are American troops. In the Korean War, Desfor (4) hopscotched from outfit to outfit to ensure he was always with frontline U.S. combat troops – and learned how to "scrounge" the necessities for the freezing campaign with the help of "miniature bottles of whiskey": "[T]hat's how I acquired the clothing I needed and anything else I needed, whether it was food or transportation ... But I moved with them and was able to get the action pictures I needed." When a U.S. frigate hit a mine during the 1980s U.S.-Iranian feud in the Persian Gulf, Pyle and the handful of other journalists on a pool assignment aboard another Navy vessel were taken "lily padding," by helicopter from ship to ship, to a cruiser standing guard where the USS *Samuel B. Roberts* was sinking. There, Pyle wondered what the Navy would do with the journalists once it started retaliating. But the Navy let them stay right on the bridge for what he called "a one-day war with Iran," and he even filed copy directly:

[W]e'd fired all our chaff at these real or imagined Silkworm missiles being fired from Iran. ... [T]he sun is going down, the battle's all over, it's all resolved, and [officer of the deck Augie Ponturier] goes to the door of the bridge, going off duty, going off watch. He turns around and he says, "And now, it's Miller time." [laughs] ... Of course there's no booze allowed on American ships, so it was just a poetic statement, but it was beautiful, and there it was in the story. (Pyle, 8–10b)[31]

While covering the 2004 tsunami that killed nearly a quarter million people in Southeast Asia, Talmadge (6) worked off the safety and comfort of the USS *Bonhomme Richard* for three weeks:

Pretty much every day we'd just take a helicopter off of the ship, go into some of the worst-hit places that no one else had been able to get to yet, drop off some supplies, maybe wander around a little bit, kind of assess the situation, then get back on the helicopter and go back to the ship. ... I'd see some nasty stuff during the day, then I'd come back to the ship, write my story in a fairly nice room, I'd have three squares a day, then go to bed and start over again. And it was tough because we were seeing some really bad devastation there, but at the same time, it was kind of structured and I was clearly in the mode of doing my job.

In Vietnam during the war, after the U.S. military pullout, Bartimus (18) missed the easy access to helicopters that would take her closer to North Vietnam, but she managed to ride with peacekeepers going on inspection

---

[31] The "Miller time" quote ends the confrontation story; Richard Pyle, "Iran fired Silkworm missiles at U.S. ships," The Associated Press, April 19, 1988.

tours, so that her main worry once on the scene was "wandering around and try not to step on landmines." After the Taliban destroyed the two sixth-century monumental Buddha statues in Bamiyan in early 2001, generating worldwide outrage, Gannon (50–51) and a handful of other foreign reporters prevailed upon the Taliban to take them to the site – which they did, on an ancient Russian prop plane that barely landed on an outcropping scarcely long enough to allow for take-off. In 2012, Gannon (68–71) convinced the Afghan National Army to allow her and Niedringhaus to embed for two weeks ("they were so surprised to hear that we just wanted to hear their story"). All the Afghan Army representative offered to help them get to the embed location – near Gardez in the volatile Taliban-controlled border areas "where all the action is" – was "I don't know, take a car, I guess." So eventually they did, wearing burqas in the back of a car driven by AP Kabul newsman Amir Shah:

Amir Shah had to come back by himself. And if anybody did spot two foreigners, even if they didn't catch us, sure as shit they would've taken Amir Shah on the way back. And so, I'm not that interested in proving a point to anyone about "I don't wear a burqa." For me it wasn't about that, it was about Amir Shah's safety and then also about our safety. ... So we got to Gardez. ... And anyway we only stayed there for two days because we wanted to go out to a smaller post, and we went out and spent two weeks. One at a brigade and the other one at a 20-man post where you had 20 soldiers with only one helmet among them, they shared it, and one lantern, so that at night you'd have ... 10 soldiers down in one part of the post and 10 soldiers on the other part of the post. So you'd have the lantern for half the night, have your food, and then you walk it up to the guys on the top.

The helmet vignette made it into one revealing story from Chinari outpost: "In 2014 when the last U.S. and NATO forces are gone, Afghanistan's defense will fall to troops like these. President Hamid Karzai says his army is ready. The soldiers at Chinari outpost agree but feel seriously unequipped. Twenty of them share a single helmet, which they passed from one to another as they posed for photos." An earlier story from Gardez listed soldiers' complaints about ancient equipment and boots falling apart, though Gannon noted that she heard "a mix of messages from dozens of officers and enlisted men," including one soldier, "a squat man with piercing brown eyes," who did not want the international soldiers to leave but also felt disrespected – he "gave off a strange mix of resentment, envy and appreciation."[32]

Even rebels have been correspondents' impromptu escorts. During the Lebanese civil war, Pyle (16–17b) found some protection driving from Damascus to Beirut through militia-controlled territory by picking up hitchhiking armed militiamen and giving them rides. Covering the 2011 uprising against Gadhafi, Schemm sneaked over the border into rebel-held

---

[32] Kathy Gannon, "As army grows, a unit highlights the challenges," The Associated Press, June 11, 2012; Kathy Gannon, "From M16s to boots, Afghan troops feel slighted," The Associated Press, May 20, 2012.

FIGURE 6.2. North Africa correspondent Paul Schemm (center) is welcomed to revolutionary Libya on the morning of February 22, 2011, right after crossing into the country from Egypt a few days after the revolution broke out. The man on the left, wearing a sign saying "no to tribalism, no to sabotage, long live the Libyan youth," is a border guard. (Photo courtesy of Paul Schemm)

territories and rode with them through exhilarating advances toward Benghazi and frightening retreats that saw him dodge shelling and count bodies in desert morgues to find a kernel of truth. Laub (1–2) first went to Tripoli on a "government-sanctioned assignment" with a group of reporters largely kept in a five-star hotel with their minders and then, refused another visa as the regime crumbled, she "rode in with the rebels into Tripoli" – at night under sniper fire – something she called a highlight of her career (see this chapter's box).

The editor who suggested that Laub try the "back door" into Libya was Bob Reid, no stranger to creative and circuitous ways of getting to a tumultuous scene. On Christmas 1979, Reid (9–11) was on the desk in Bonn when news broke that the Soviets had entered Afghanistan and the one Ariana Airlines plane due to return to Kabul was on the ground ready to depart in Amsterdam, where nobody at the AP office was working. On a whim, Reid called the Frankfurt airport controller, and discovered that the plane was actually on the ground there – and "frantic messages" from New York told him to try to get on it:

I told [the agent] I wanted a ticket to Kabul, one-way – because one of the tricks you learn is that you never buy a two-way ticket because it's easier for them to throw you out if you got a round-trip ticket.[33] ... So I bought the ticket, paid in cash, and ... I sat there and waited and waited with a couple of other [journalists]. ... And right around 1:30 in the morning, door flies open and a collection of Afghan airways personnel in uniform, looking like they were going to their execution, just barrels through the waiting room, out the door, onto the bus. ... Ariana Airways, to their credit, gave us full service. They fed us a meal, they asked us about drinks, the whole bit. [laughs] So I fell asleep and I woke up and we were circling over Kabul. And I didn't have a visa, which wasn't such a big problem at the time because Americans could buy them at the airport at the time, Communist regime or no Communist regime. But this was a special case, so how would they treat me? We landed and got off the plane. ... I'm standing in this shack by myself with this guy and some visa police. They were all a little befuddled because apparently there was a communication screw-up and the ground crew in Kabul had no idea the plane is in the air. It had appeared! [laughs] ... The guy gives me a little sheet of paper, and I fill it out. And it gets down to profession. One of the first things you learn is don't write journalist. Anybody who doesn't speak any English somehow knows that word. I think I just put down writer, and wrote it a little bit messy, so there might be some confusion. Guy looks at it, bam, stamped. I get up and am in the streets of Kabul.

Just Go, Go, Go!

Rushing to the scene of breaking news – whether revolutions or earthquakes – has sometimes required correspondents, like Reid, to drop everything and get going before being able to fully assess the dangers or even the feasibility of getting through. The cascading anti-Communist uprisings across Eastern Europe and the Soviet Union in the late 1980s and early 1990s left little time for planning. Vienna-based Porubcansky (8) was keeping a live USSR visa just in case, so when he got a call from the foreign desk at 6 a.m. telling him to hightail it to Moscow because the 1991 putsch had just started, he ran to pick it up at the consulate and was on the scene the same afternoon. Just before Christmas 1989, with Romania the last Warsaw Pact country still resisting uprisings, Warsaw-based Daniszewski and Paris-based Rosenblum got going on instinct. Daniszewski (7–8), who would be shot in the unrest, noticed news

---

[33] Robert Fisk of the London *Times* also got into Kabul with a one-way ticket; Robert Fisk, *The Great War for Civilisation*. New York: Alfred A. Knopf, 2005: 51.

of anti-Ceauşescu demonstrations in Timişoara and decided it was time to make a run for it:

I went to the airport and booked a flight and went to Belgrade. And I rented a car and drove into Romania. I didn't have a visa, and Romania had always been one of the countries that was stingiest with visas. It was a really repressive police state. ... So I didn't really have a game plan for how I was going to get into the country, but when I arrived at the border, the uprising or the popular discontent had already sort of overwhelmed the border police, and with a small gift of cigarettes ... a drunken border guard – I was able to cross into the country.

Rosenblum (43–44) had decided to rent a charter to Romania after watching on TV as Ceauşescu gave a speech and, when the raging crowd surged toward him, took a step back:

I said, holy shit, the balance of fear has shifted. ... And we got clearance from the French Air Force to leave French airspace, but we didn't get anything from the Romanians. And so we just took a chance. ... Heading down toward the runway, it's pitch dark. All of the sudden lights come on. Plane lands. And we get out of the plane and we walk to this darkened airport building, and there's a window, and there's one guy behind the window ... stone-faced, big stare. And I walk up with my passport and I say, "Hey, how's it going?" And he says, "Better now." And he stamps me in. ... So we stop this guy in ... a little Dacia ... I'm saying, "What's going on here?" And the guy turns around and in this perfect English he says, "A small revolution in a small place." And then we get into town. ... [T]his TV tower ... and the Securitate, Ceauşescu's troops, were all around it, firing into it ... that's where the whole revolution was. So we got to the gate and these people ... were TV people, and so they barred the gate, and nobody was getting in. ... But they had a list of people who had been cleared. And so they said, "French television?" "Oui, oui, si, si!" So I kind of went in with them.

Smith (5), who had studied the former Yugoslavia and spoke Serbo-Croat, had been covering the "political collapse" of the region for a couple of years, but had no war reporting experience to prepare him for the conflict that exploded there. As the dominos started rapidly falling, he chased the war from Slovenia to Zagreb all the way to Sarajevo, setting up successive AP operations where none had existed – finding apartments to rent through friends, hiring local staff and security, getting cars and fuel – amid ethnic cleansing and heavy firefights.

Going in "cold" from a brand-new assignment in Paris to West Africa to cover the Liberian civil war, within hours of landing for the first time on the continent Terril Jones (35) was driving through the rubber plantations to Buchanan:

There were like human heads that had been severed, stuck on poles, by villagers of government soldiers, burned-out armored personnel carriers. Kids were playing soccer in Buchanan with a skull, a human skull ... it still had like brains inside it and stuff. It was not something that you'd buy on a shelf – it was very rugged and rough, and it was my first time in Africa. It was like, "Whoa! Welcome to Paris ... " kind of thing. It was quite a shock. But it was an incredible experience.

Earlier, from his base in Tokyo, Jones (10–11) had covered a volcanic eruption on the island of Miyake-jima that had left a local village "a smoldering, barren patch"[34] – with hardly more time to prepare or less danger amid dense fumes, and, instead of the Land Rover, with a car taken off the street whose unknown fate he was still regretting 30 years later:

> [T]he car had keys still in it and I was trying to get to the other side of the island, and I drove down around it and I was confronted by a massive wall of lava that was creeping down the mountainside. . . . It just totally blocked the road and was burning everything in its path . . . a land-mass of pumice. . . . I stopped the car and walked up to it and you could feel the heat. You could look inside, you could see it red-hot on the inside. And you could hear it move. It was just like, creeping very slowly down the side of this mountain. . . . I was trying to drive a stick-shift car for the first time, and it took me about 10 minutes, jerking around, just to get this car in 180 degrees so I could leave. . . . I was forced to leave it not where I found it. And I have also always regretted that.

When the Scene Gets to You

In March 2011, Tokyo bureau chief Malcolm Foster was at his desk and correspondent Talmadge was at home napping on his day off when the seventh-floor office and the house started shaking so violently that Foster could barely hold on to his keyboard. Suddenly, the scene of breaking news had come to them – one of the strongest earthquake and tsunami ever recorded killed more than 15,000 people and triggered a nuclear crisis. As we talked in the same skyscraper office, Foster (4–5) recalled that "Everybody jumped into action," feeding updates to AP's Asia desk, following the damage reports as they came in, and watching in horror as the tsunami alert came up and footage of the massive waves appeared live on Japanese national TV. Within three hours from the first tremor, AP correspondents were driving to the worst-hit provinces, navigating packed roads, shut-down highways, nuclear meltdown, and collapsed cell phone service – as well as worrying about the safety of their families.

Either suddenly through natural calamity or simply by living where the everyday is news itself – as in war zones like Vietnam, where "you covered the war as sort of an adjunct to your everyday life" (McArthur, 14) – eyewitness reporting has sometimes landed on a reporter's doorstep, highlighting the all-encompassing nature of the profession. In Saigon, a correspondent in his hotel room had just seen a plane bomb the presidential palace when the bureau chief phoned for confirmation. By the time he dressed and got to the office, "on the wire was an eyewitness story, with my byline!" (Zeitlin, 23) On his first day in Cambodia, Gray (7) was having "little fried fish from the great lake for lunch" at the Le Royal Hotel, home base for all correspondents, when a grenade was

---

[34] Terril Jones, The Associated Press, October 3, 1983.

thrown into a cinema down the street: "So we all ran there from this wonderful lunch. . . . People were coming out and there was blood all over the place . . . flip-flops people were wearing were just covered with blood."

As we sat on the patio of his Florida house, the only loud noise a gardener mowing a nearby lawn, Tatro (13) recalled being home in Beirut watching reruns of *Starsky & Hutch* when "suddenly the gunfire didn't seem to match the TV and big gun battles started right outside the apartment. . . . I crawled down and looked between the gap in the balcony and there were gunmen and stuff going on in the street" – members of some of the 99 different militias who were wreaking havoc in the Lebanese civil war – "[I]t was kind of the way it was, at almost any place in town on any given day there could be some battle." A friend's phone call woke up Latin America veteran Harold Olmos (11–13) before dawn and, rushing out to the balcony, he heard machine gun fire coming from Venezuela's presidential palace. A coup was under way, and Olmos spent the next few days holed up in the bureau, never hanging up the phone with New York lest the line go dead. The day the 1967 war broke out between Israel and a coalition of Arab countries, Marcus Eliason's (2) boss upbraided him for not rushing to work before his scheduled shift, so he started explaining:

"Look, I had to go to my mother and dig a trench for her in the garden in case the town got bombed, and then I had to take a whole bunch of soldiers to their mustering points, you couldn't just say no, you had to do it if they asked. And then I had to go and buy supplies, and then there was a lot of traffic, but –" "Hold it, hold it, hold it!" says one of the guys sitting at the desk. "Don't tell us about it, write this all down." And so I did . . . you typed on big sheets of paper, and then the editor with a big felt pen went through the story, and I just saw this slashing . . . cutting and swiping and reducing long-winded sentences to their essence and so on quite amazingly. At the end of it, there was a story and it got published. And my name was on the AP wire. I couldn't believe it . . . probably the first byline I ever had with them.

Also in Israel, during the second intifada one correspondent worried about how to get her children to school past multiplying roadblocks (Laub, 40), and, during the Gulf War, AP staffers worked out a system for covering the barrage of Scud missiles Iraq fired toward Tel Aviv, which many feared might be armed with gas:

[W]e literally would walk out onto our porch, watch a Scud come over, get into our car, drive to our office in Jerusalem, and file an urgent that a Scud was coming in. Our guys in Tel Aviv, after it hit, would then come out of their safe room and go to wherever it had hit and write the story. But it was just this really weird thing . . . you're standing there on your deck or your balcony watching a warhead come over and of course it could have hit in the yard next door. (Powell, 14)

Serendipitous opportunities for eyewitness stories can be far safer but no less illuminating. One correspondent traveling by train in postwar Germany recognized in the next compartment a former SS dentist who had just been acquitted in the so-called Second Auschwitz Trial, and immediately interviewed him, getting an exclusive (Doelling, 6). Edie Lederer arrived in Seoul to help cover the crisis after President Park Chung-Hee's assassination and walked into the bureau saying she had the lead – because she had flown in with the deputy secretary of state. "You haven't even sat down and you own the story already," a stunned correspondent greeted her (Anderson, 6).

Anita Snow (17–18) decided to live on the equivalent of Cubans' food rations for a month, and write about it, because in eight years as Havana bureau chief she "developed great friendships and deep respect" for Cubans, but "as a foreigner paid in U.S. dollars" she had never lived like them, "using their ingenuity to make sure there's enough to eat at month's end," as her first story said. Another story was more intimate, saying the "fragrant smell of onions and coriander wafting from the bubbling pot of beans" conjured the memory of her recently deceased mother, "a Southerner who would have recognized and appreciated many of the humble dishes I am cooking for my study on how and what Cubans eat" with the rations:[35]

[I]t's an extremely small basket of . . . heavily, heavily subsidized goods. So it includes like enough chicken for two meals maybe – this is for a whole month – it was something like 10 eggs, a few pounds of sugar . . . small amounts of coffee, some cigarettes, anyhow, so I acquired all of that stuff. I kind of assigned myself a salary, which is very small in Cuba, it's about $30 a month or something, the equivalent of. . . . I went out and I used my salary to buy some vegetables, and . . . I bought more eggs. You barter, you trade . . . It was the most fascinating thing I did when I was there . . . because it was about real people, and how people live.

MISSION IMPOSSIBLE: OFF-LIMITS SCENES

Those kinds of stories are of course impossible when correspondents are banished, as had happened in Cuba in the 1960s. In Kabul on 9/11, Gannon (57–58) and a handful of other reporters and Red Cross workers refused to leave – until Taliban leader Mullah Omar ordered all foreigners out and announced the border with Pakistan would close:

I thought, "That's it, now I have to go." . . . I had no choice, [I] had to leave, and as much as I hated to leave Amir Shah and that, but if the border closed then I was stuck there and there's nobody, we can't do the story. . . . So from the 13th [of September] to the 7th [of October], I went down to Quetta and did stories out of Quetta, because of course that's the closest you could get. You had the Pashtuns coming, you get to the border, you could do stuff. We did stories, good stories. But I just so much wanted to be in Afghanistan.

Like Gannon, correspondents have been kept away from a country or region, occasionally for decades, because of closed regimes, government prohibitions or visa denials, and excessive dangers. In each case, they struggled to find ways to

[35] Anita Snow, "Living on rations in Cuba: Meals made up of rations and goods from farmers' markets," The Associated Press, May 31, 2007; Anita Snow, "Cuban food project conjures up memories of family, Southern fare," The Associated Press, June 6, 2007.

continue to cover the story – at "listening posts" just across borders, tracking local media (and, today, social media), relying on local journalists, and doggedly continuing to try to get in. Given its rising power in international relations, the most extraordinary example of an off-limit area is China, where almost no Americans could go from 1949 to the 1970s.

Throughout that crucial time, correspondents and other "China watchers" set up in Hong Kong, where they relied most heavily on the U.S. consulate, which "spent millions of dollars on a staff of a hundred editors and translators busily engaged ... in gathering every scrap of information it could lay its hands on through its agents on the mainland," and on the official Chinese news agency, Xinhua, where "deep down in a deadpan, pedestrian account of a party conference or an official speech, one could, with patience, pull out nuggets: the promotion or demotion of a party, government, or army leader, a change in policy or an until-then-unreported death" (Roderick 1993, 120–21; also Topping 2010, 298). A livelier source was the Chinese refugees, some of whom had swum shark-infested waters to get to Hong Kong and could tell correspondents about life in China – though of course from a "somewhat more one-sided" perspective that required correspondents to carefully and over time corroborate details with multiple refugees and humanitarian groups (Liu, 18). Even a decade after the normalization of U.S.-Chinese relations, one veteran China hand and fluent Mandarin speaker, John Pomfret, had to relocate to Hong Kong temporarily when he was expelled for reporting on the post-Tiananmen martial law crackdown (Liu, 7).[36]

When other countries in the region became, or stayed, hermetically closed (such as post-1975 Vietnam or North Korea), Tokyo was AP's Asia headquarters. There, reporters monitored those nations' English-language news agency reports, trying to read between the lines and feel where the "tempo" deviated from the ordinary to glimpse a kernel of a story, as longtime Asia editor Bob Liu (6–7) explained:

[T]he rhythm ... was broken once when I was reading a Vietnam report. There was a big celebration and ... somehow you've got this inward thing in your mind that says, "Hey, something is not right here" – and this time I noticed that Ho Chi Minh was missing from that gathering, you see. So we put out a story saying that they had this celebration ... the Vietnamese leadership was there, but Ho Chi Minh ... no explanation why he was absent, but he's been sick, he's old. And I think it was two days later, something like that, they announced that he had passed away.

After China opened up in the late 1970s, Beijing in turn became a "listening post" for sealed-off North Korea. In the 1990s, after obtaining permission from the Chinese government to travel to the border, Hutzler (11) and a couple of colleagues were trying to investigate how China was attempting to develop the

---

[36] Jim Abrams, "Two students arrested, U.S. journalists expelled," The Associated Press, June 14, 1989.

FIGURE 6.3. Tokyo-based correspondent Elaine Kurtenbach stands at the North Korean-Russian border in the Tumen River Delta in 1992, during a trip to the usually off-limits country to report on Pyongyang's development efforts. (Photo courtesy of Elaine Kurtenbach)

region, without the cooperation of its neighbor, which was in the grasp of a deadly famine. Their minders kept preventing them from interviewing ordinary citizens, until one driver unexpectedly relented:

[W]e saw a guy farming on a field ... at the river that divides the North Korean and Chinese borders. And we yelled at the driver, "Stop! Stop! Stop!" And he stopped, miraculously, and we all just ran and went to interview this farmer. It was about 15 minutes of sort of unscripted, unmediated conversation with this guy who talked about North Koreans coming over in the winter, and the hungry North Koreans. It was hardly in-depth reporting, but it was what we could get at the time.

Into the 2000s, North Korea stories were done from the outside, with sources in Seoul, Washington, and the United Nations and only the rarest Pyongyang-sanctioned (and controlled) trip, as well as by watching North Korean state media "like a hawk", which required special permission in South Korea, said Jean Lee (11), who opened AP's first North Korean bureau in 2012. A year later, AP opened a full bureau in another cordoned-off state, Myanmar, which had been monitored from Bangkok, where editors wrote up notes sent from the local staffer, and occasionally could go in for "reporting stints" (Pennington, 8). Bangkok had also been the watch post for Cambodia, Laos, and Vietnam after they were taken over in the 1970s by Communist regimes that expelled U.S.

correspondents, who only managed to sneak in on short trips. As in Hong Kong, coverage relied on two local people hired to monitor those three countries' radios, an operation they called "Bamboo Service"; U.S. and other diplomats, who also set up intelligence-gathering in Bangkok; NGOs; and "huge streams of refugees" in camps along the Thai-Cambodian border, a four-hour drive that Gray (3, 14–15) and others frequently took.

Another long-inaccessible country was Khomeini's Iran. Shortly after the U.S. Embassy hostage crisis, AP correspondents were expelled from Tehran, so that the "full-time job for 444 days" of putting together the hostage story from information from around the Middle East fell to Charles Hanley (1), a special correspondent in New York.[37] Still in the 2000s, two Cairo-based editors noted that correspondents could rarely get into Iran, so coverage relied on the Iranian staff – which required trying to protect their safety too, even if it meant fudging a bit with the dateline:

Dubai was kind of what watched Iran for us. We did have people [in Iran], but there were things you just had to have under a Dubai dateline. We had done this story, and then I had gone on holiday to my hometown in San Diego, and there was a commentary in the San Diego paper about how the AP had written a story out of Dubai because ... Dubai is such a fun place to be, basically. That they were relaxing by the poolside in Dubai instead of getting in there and getting a story out of Iran. ... I didn't write a letter to the paper, but I just thought ... people [do not] always understand what the issues are. ... It is literally so that people won't get arrested. It really is. It often comes down to that. If you see a dateline that doesn't match with the story, it's not because the lazy reporter didn't want to leave the poolside in Dubai. It's probably because the reporter couldn't get a visa to get to the heart of the story or because it's dangerous to send a reporter to that place. You have to find ways to report it in other ways. (Bryson, 73; also Buzbee, 13)

Paradoxically, another unreachable country was right off the U.S. coast – Cuba. In the early 1960s, when Castro's regime jailed or expelled most reporters amid rising tensions, Claude Erbsen (1–3), figuring that "there was going to be a long period of having to watch Cuba from the outside," rented a room in a Key West motel and stuck a 30-foot steel antenna in the middle of it to monitor Cuban radio and especially television. (The latter provided crucial details unavailable to competitors in Miami, such as that the gunshot that silenced Castro during a speech to Bay of Pigs prisoners came from a guard who had accidentally dropped his weapon.) In the late 1960s, AP managed to reinstall another U.S. correspondent in Havana – who, the airport being off limits, resorted to taking turns with the Reuters correspondent, one trying to go through the main entrance and thus attracting security while the other peered through a crack at the bottom of a curtain in the room where plane hijackers

[37] In November 1979, in the aftermath of the Iranian Revolution, militants seized the U.S. Embassy in Tehran and held it, with 50 American hostages, for 14 months. The AP bureau chief, Nick Tatro, was expelled in November. His replacement was ordered out of the country in February 1980.

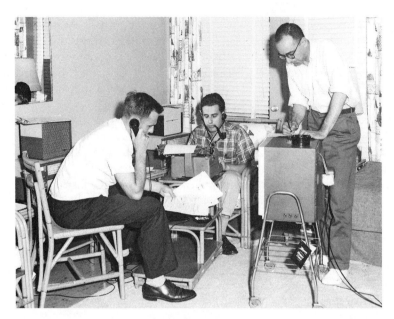

FIGURE 6.4. A few days after the Bay of Pigs invasion in April 1961, New York City desk editor Claude Erbsen (center) listens to Cuban radio through earphones as colleagues Neil Gilbride (left) dictates and Louis de la Haba (standing) edits copy in a Key West, Florida, motel where AP first set up shop to cover the news from Cuba. (Photo courtesy of Claude Erbsen)

were routinely taken (Wheeler, 6; 2008, 133). In 1969, he became the last U.S. journalist expelled from Cold-War Cuba.

Today's social media contribute to coverage of areas too dangerous to enter – most notably, in the early 2010s, Syria, where the Assad government rarely gave visas and Islamist militants captured and beheaded two U.S. journalists in 2014.[38] But three correspondents in the region – Laub (37), Perry (23), and Schemm (12) – noted that what an activist or a rebel is saying over a Skype interview, for example, cannot be enough for a story, nor is an amateur video posting, unless confirmed through other sources or verified independently – something largely impossible without being on the ground, as discussed in Chapter 4. The level of risk that correspondents tolerate to bear eyewitness, as evidenced throughout this chapter and the next, highlights how high the bar is for correspondents to declare some spots so uniquely dangerous that they simply cannot go there. Shortly after Anderson's kidnapping, AP moved its U.S. reporters out of Beirut and tried to operate the bureau from Cyprus (Powell, 8) – and it is ironic that a quarter century later, Beirut became the safe home base for

---

[38] The Islamic State in Iraq and Syria (ISIS) kidnapped and decapitated freelance journalists James Foley (40) and Steven J. Sotloff (31) in the summer of 2014.

AP's award-winning Syria coverage,[39] "bizarre because Beirut is one of these beautiful cities and very comfortable and then you spend your day watching horrible amateur video ... of death and destruction from Syria, and try to do your best to put together a decent story" (Laub, 36–37).

More frequently, it is only a region or even parts of a city where violence is so deadly or targeted that correspondents cannot venture there. As one *New York Times* correspondent in Baghdad during some of the worst times of the U.S. occupation put it, the "dissonance" for "cooped up" reporters can be "jarring" (Filkins 2008, 216) – he could hear bombs from the bedroom and see Iraqis from his rooftop, but he could not walk out. Reid (65), one of AP's wartime Baghdad bureau chiefs, had to battle the same security restrictions, at times leaving on-the-street reporting to Iraqi stringers, who also risked detention or worse.[40] During Somalia's civil war, when reporters risked their lives to make a run in the streets, press conferences were held on satellite phones. Alexander (8) recalled having "to call the UN office in Mogadishu, and ... you were using your sat phone to call a number in New York, which linked you back to a sat phone three blocks away." During the war in El Salvador, Central America veteran Joe Frazier (18) heard that guerrillas had mounted one of their most ambitious attacks against the small mountain town of Berlin, but the heavy fighting and shut-down roads made it unreachable. So he called the town's mayor, whose number another staffer had prudently gotten on an earlier visit – and what he got went straight to the top of the story: "His wife said, 'He can't come to the phone right now, he's shooting at guerrillas,'" and added, "there was house-to-house fighting in the city and the initial guerrilla attacks were directed at the military headquarters."[41]

Aside from wars, criminal organizations can also turn parts of countries or cities into no-go zones, forcing correspondents to develop ad hoc strategies to make quick runs in, while reducing the high chance of murder. When a month-long wave of gang violence "shut down" São Paulo, with "police stations getting sprayed with automatic weapons fire in broad daylight" (once a block from a correspondent's house) and "vigilante cops" retaliating by going on killing sprees in the slums, Alan Clendenning (5–7) knew he needed a story on "what it was like to live in the slums, not only on a day-to-day level, but what it's like to live there when you worried about vigilantes coming in and killing you just because of the color of your skin."[42] But he also knew that going into the favelas would be deadly without "the tacit permission of the gangs":

[39] In 2013, AP won the breaking news photography Pulitzer Prize for a series of photos from Syria and was a finalist in international reporting for multimedia reporting in Syria.

[40] Bilal Hussein, an Iraqi photojournalist working for AP, was arrested by U.S. forces in 2006 and detained until 2008 on suspicion of aiding insurgents in Iraq. One of his photos was among a group of AP images that won the 2005 Pulitzer Prize for Breaking News Photography.

[41] Joseph B. Frazier, "Guerrillas launch attack on mountain town, government reinforcements sent," The Associated Press, January 30, 1983.

[42] Alan Clendenning, "Killings of young men in Sao Paulo raise specter of police death squads," The Associated Press, June 4, 2006.

I found . . . a Spanish Catholic priest who worked in the area, and he worked with a lot of people. And I called him up and I said, "Hey, I want to go in and talk to people." And he was sympathetic to the story idea, thought it was a story that needed to be told . . . and he said, "Well, you just come to my church, which is on the edge of the slum, and your taxi driver stays there, and then you are going to go around inside the slum with me . . . You'll be fine in the day, we can't do it at night." . . . And the priest had a bright red Fiat Punto car, really basic but really bright red. And we got into it and we drove all around the slum and went around interviewing people. And the reason I could do it is because all the gang people, they knew what the priest's car looked like and they knew who he was, and anyone who was in his car was okay. There were times, though, where we would stop and he would point up a street and he'd say, "We can't go up that street." . . . We used to get kind of requests from New York as soon as something would happen: "Hey, let's go get reaction from the slums." Well, you can't just go into the slums.

In Mexico, "no-go zones" appeared around 2010, when in cartel-controlled Tamaulipas mass graves emerged with migrants "or bus passengers who simply crossed through that territory" – "You were literally going out past the last army or police roadblock, and who knows who's in charge there" (Stevenson, 7–10). An AP photographer and a colleague who had gone to shoot Hurricane Alex, about 100 miles from where the mass graves would be found, were confronted in a restaurant by a group of armed men who responded to the journalists' press passes by pulling out "a gold medallion with a Z on it" as their "credentials." Unable to count on police or army protection, correspondents were on their own to cover that story and the "mass exodus" that cartel warfare forced from one Rio Grande Valley town, Ciudad Mier:

[W]e were the first ones to go in on our own. . . . We don't generally travel with army convoys, because they don't want us . . . army convoys are tactical units, you're not going to get inside that, they don't want you inside that. And in fact, when we first saw the army in Ciudad Mier, they are sort of raiding the house at the end of the block, and we're like, "Hi!" Obvious, evidently press, non-Mexican. And boom, it was automatically "Stay back, go back." So they held us at distance with their guns pointed at us. And you just realize, the army you're not going to get any help [from]. The police you might get help from, but you don't know who their friends are. So that's always kind of a dubious proposition. . . . The federal police are often sent in, they know the area less than even you do, because they're dispatched from Mexico City. (Stevenson, 7–10)

Stevenson's story from Ciudad Mier, on the Texas border, minced no words, or images from the details gathered as far as the reporters were able to go:

Shell casings carpet the road outside a bullet-riddled subdivision on the outskirts of this colonial town . . . the most dramatic example so far of the increasing ferocity of war between rival drug cartels, and the government's failure to fight back. The state and federal governments say it's safe to go back and that people are returning. One official even invited tourists to return. The scenes witnessed by The Associated Press say something else. Even during daylight hours, a Mexican army squad patrols the town nervously. A bullet-riddled army pickup truck lies in the yard of the local military outpost, a metallic casualty of an ambush last weekend that locals say killed four soldiers. The

Army does not officially recognize it even happened. . . . Perhaps most frightening of all is what is happening farther up the road. . . . Even those brave enough to sneak back into Ciudad Mier won't take the road to Guerrero, where 11 Zeta gunmen were killed in a clash with soldiers days before. In more than an hour's time, not a single vehicle passes in that direction.[43]

CONCLUSIONS

Reporting from the scene is the fundamental reason for the correspondents' job, the drive that fuels their calling, and the most extreme source of danger – which they willingly face because it is necessary to write stories that have accuracy, authority, and enough "grit" for impact. Visual details, like rocks spelling SOS on a soccer field in a cartel-besieged Mexican town, grab readers, and by being on the scene, correspondents get to know enough about their country that they can then analyze and explain the underlying, invisible currents beyond preconceptions held by outsiders, and find stories they were not even looking for. From the demands of masked Central American rebels to how U.S. soldiers treat Iraqis at roadblocks, only correspondents on the ground have a chance to see through the spin. That crucial responsibility to bear witness in a way that will make audiences care so outweighs most risks that correspondents say there is no other place they would rather be than where the action is. Given that conflict, violence, and disasters are "obvious" news, this news judgment comes at a high cost for correspondents who want to go beyond the daily death toll – or even accurately report that, as Chapter 7 details.

In war and peace, correspondents have had to circumvent the efforts by groups in power to keep them away from the scene, which range from visa denials to forcible removal from the streets, as well as to constrain them to narrow, controlled peeks like organized tours, which journalists then subvert to grab fleeting occasions for real, unobserved reporting – even only 15 minutes with a farmer along the China-North Korea border. Just as with source development, a necessary skill for eyewitness reporting is patience and time, and some stories are missed because single correspondents cannot be everywhere – much as they try, true "madmen" struggling to get to mayhem. To "follow the story," correspondents might attempt to drive a tank trap–dented car into besieged Sarajevo or sneak around corner after corner in militia-controlled Beirut to get "where you could ask somebody a question." Soldiers and rebels have at times provided logistical protection, but breaking news often forces correspondents on the road to a scene with little more than a one-way ticket to Soviet-occupied Kabul – not that it is easier if the scene gets to the correspondents, whether an earthquake or an outburst of shootings.

---

[43] Mark Stevenson, "Refugees: No return to town hit by Mexico drug war," The Associated Press, November 22, 2010.

In a few cases, correspondents have been left out – for three decades from China, for example – stuck in listening posts or trying to glimpse news from state-run or social media. But even where being on the scene means risking death, as in Syria's civil war or São Paulo's slums, they never give up attempts to get in, because that is the essence of correspondence:

[T]here is no substitute, be it the Internet or whatever, for being in a place. . . . I understand the budget necessities, but I don't care what you say, going there to the spot, not only, first of all, is it more accurate because you're actually there, you're not on the phone, they can fake things over the phone, you're not obviously doing it thirdhand on the Internet, you're actually there, seeing people's reactions, seeing, really, the way they live. So it's obvious: If our mission is to report the truth, then we have got to be on the spot. (Gray, 17–18)

As Chapter 7 analyzes, being on the spot has subjected correspondents to constant levels of threat and the trauma of spending a disturbingly vast amount of time counting bodies of victims of unspeakable violence – at the ever-present risk of becoming one.

Libyan Civil War, 2011

Paul Schemm: They'd spray-painted the whole post, saying "Welcome to Free Libya." And they let us, like, pose with their guns and stuff . . . because it was just random tribesmen who had taken over. . . .

[W]e stopped at an army base where there were a bunch of missiles, antiaircraft missiles. And there were just a bunch of dudes there with guns. They're like, "Yeah, look around." . . . [B]eing in the Middle East so long, where everything to do with the military is completely off-limits, being able to just wander around an army base, it was like, we were like kids in a candy store, we'd never seen anything like this. And then we went to Tobruk, and there everyone's cheering, firing guns in the air, having little parties . . . then they saw us and they were like, "Western journalists!" And they're rushing to us to tell us their story. . . .

Sirte was a big Gadhafi stronghold; there were serious army units there. So everyone just sort of started piling off in that direction; we all went piling off after them in our cars [with local drivers]. . . . And up until this point, everyone had in their mentality, "It's going to be like Egypt, it's going to be like Tunisia," sort of peaceful revolution, the government falls apart. . . . And basically the Libyan Army started firing back, with artillery. . . . [W]e also changed our location, we lived in abandoned houses or rent houses from families closer and closer to the front. And suddenly we realized that the front was moving back. And you'd talk to people, and you wouldn't want to go too far because you didn't want to get caught. . . .

You were desperately looking for somebody with, like, a bit of gray in their hair. . . . "Do you have ranks?" "No, we have no ranks in this army." It's just like, "Who's in charge?" "We're all in charge." . . . And so when there would be clashes, it was like, you didn't know who to believe. I remember one rumor ran around, "Sirte has fallen!" . . . So you drove as far as you could and then realized, Sirte hadn't fallen. And so, yes, there was a clash – 10 people dead, we had to go to the morgue and count the bodies to make sure it was true. So I spent a lot of time looking at dead bodies during that time. Which was actually kind of horrible . . . [W]e slowly just started getting driven back. And it started happening faster and faster . . . we pulled out of Benghazi and went all the way back to Tobruk, which made it kind of hard to cover the conflict (Schemm, 8–12).

Karin Laub: Cars were scarce, because fuel was very scarce, so the APTN [AP television] stringer and I found ourselves hitchhiking to the front. . . . And before we knew it, we found ourselves in Zawiya, which is a coastal city about 50 kilometers west of Tripoli. . . . There were these guys had come out, and they looked horrible, they looked like they had just come out of a nightmare or something, and it turns out they were prisoners that had been sprung from a government base a few more kilometers ahead. So this whole adventure started with this prison break . . . and we just kept going with this [defected] officer. Then it turns out that at this huge base, the rebels had taken it and they were carrying out all the ammunition, boxes and boxes of ammunition. It was all just very dramatic and we're calling the office on the sat phone and reporting this. . . .

This is like, I think, 11 o'clock at night, 12 o'clock at night, [the officer] says, "I'm getting calls from people who say that the rebels are in Green Square." And so [AP correspondent] Ben [Hubbard] and I look at each other, "We got to go." So we drive back in with him, but now Tripoli's pretty dark and we don't really know yet who is holding what. As we approach Green Square, this group of people stops us and says, "Slow down, there are snipers." And then they kind of direct us in a safe way, and then all of a sudden we see Green Square, it's like illuminated and party time and people and commotion, and it was just incredible. So Ben and I did some quick interviews, grabbed some color, called in the stuff, and then just got out of there. . . . It felt like I was really, it's such a cliché, but I was really witnessing history. That was a pretty great day (Laub, 28–31).

[Hubbard and Laub's first-person story detailed some of the same scenes and enthusiasm as the rebels, and reporters, in a "mass of cars . . . like a rolling celebration" met little resistance "pulling through towns whose names we had only seen on maps because they had until that day remained in Gadhafi's grip." When "gunfire this time not celebratory erupted in front of our car" six miles outside Tripoli, the reporters took refuge with a local family, who served them juice and "fired up their generator so we could have electricity to use our computers and charge our phones." In Tripoli's main square, familiar from earlier minder-heavy trips, they found celebrations, noise, and two rebels lying "side by side in one corner on a row of steps . . . they commemorated their arrival in the capital with a nap."]44

44 Ben Hubbard and Karin Laub, "AP reporters ride with rebels into Libyan capital," August 22, 2011.

7

The Costs of Being There to Count the Bodies

I got my turn, filed my story [on anti-Ceauşescu demonstrations in Timişoara, Romania] to our Vienna office, and talked to my colleague there, who told me that they had had reports of more gunfire in the city, and I said, "Well, I have been inside, but I haven't heard much – but I'll go out and check." [chuckles] And then I did leave [the Yugoslav consulate, where journalists were filing stories on the single operating line] and . . . there was a shooting around us. And I fled with my Yugoslav colleague and spent some time trying to make my way back to our hotel, but most of the streets were blocked by pretty heavy fighting. And at one point I felt compelled to double back and I came on a checkpoint, and at the checkpoint the people across the street opened fire on our car and I was shot. . . . Obviously a lot of these stories are dangerous, but it is what we do. It's not unlike being a law officer or a member of the military, where you know that there's a possibility that in the course of doing your job you could suffer injury or death. But it is also the calling to try to bear witness to what's happening in the world. We always say, and we mean it, that no story is worth dying for. And that we won't take unreasonable risk. But we will take what we regard as reasonable risk in trying to tell a story. . . . [J]ournalists may be putting themselves in danger, but the danger they expose themselves to is usually much less than the people who are living in those places face . . . and sometimes it feels like the very least the journalist can do, if those populations are facing those dangers, is to be there to show it and to tell people about it. Because otherwise they're going to be killed or massacred or subjected to bombing or put in jail and no one's going to hear about it, and then we're really in a sad state. (Daniszewski, 8–9)

In his glass-walled office overlooking the open newsroom of AP's Manhattan headquarters, news from around the world scrolling constantly down the two or three computer screens at each desk, vice president and senior managing editor for international news John Daniszewski recounted getting shot and wounded while, nearly a quarter century before, he covered the collapse of the Communist regime in one of Eastern Europe's most repressive countries. A land of "fear, suspicion and retribution," his story had read – "I know, I became a victim of that chaos Saturday night."[1] His experience is dramatically widespread – the need to be on the scene, to "go out and check" firsthand reports of violence, has subjected nearly all foreign correspondents to deadly peril. They have braved it in the same self-effacing manner, not courting "bang-bang" but aware of the risks their calling to bear witness implies, and believing that, while no story is worth a life, they owed it to their sources, and audiences, that it be told. This chapter discusses the disturbingly universal experience of correspondents with dangers, violence, and mental as well as physical scars, and how it impacted reporting. According to the Committee to Protect Journalists, 1,135 journalists (foreign and domestic correspondents) were killed from 1992 through June 2015 because of their work, either in reprisal or on "dangerous assignments." "The AP office got shelled. I filed under fire, I got shot, mortared, screamed at, detained," Terry Anderson (15) recalled – and he was by no means uniquely risk-taking, though the price he paid, nearly seven years hostage to Hezbollah, is among the highest.

Far beyond conventional war reporting and its inherent dangers, all correspondents have had to contend with inhabiting horror, whether watching the smoke rise from the corpse of a phosphorus-burned child or being shown the bloodied scalps of raped and murdered women. For correspondents on the scene, one of the most repellent, and recurrent, tasks of digging for the truth is counting bodies. Whether in Korea or Libya, Mexico or Pakistan, making sense of the death toll – often in the face of outright lies by governments and militants – by literally numbering corpses is a major source of trauma, which until the 21st century was mostly swept under the rug by the movie-made image of the foreign correspondent as adrenaline junkie. Interviews, however, showed correspondents painfully aware of the costs, and accepting the inevitable consequences only because they believe that the risks to get to the action are necessary to report truthfully and give a voice to those for whom violence is inescapable.

WAR ZONE REPORTING

Since wars are the most "obvious news," correspondents' most inevitable risks come from battleground reporting, with nonconventional, civil, and guerrilla wars even more dangerous because violence permeates everyday life. In more than four decades with AP, Denis Gray (27–28) covered "three major wars and ... quite a few minor ones," sustaining a "slight wound" when embedded with a U.S. squad in Sadr City. Wars make for important stories and forge profound bonds, so covering them is "some of the most exciting journalism you can have," but "anyone who has seen war hates it," Gray said, tears welling up as he remembered his fallen colleagues and how all journalists are "very much

---

[1] John Daniszewski, "AP correspondent shot 3 times in early throes of Romanian revolt," The Associated Press, December 26, 1989.

vulnerable." In his estimate, Vietnam was dangerous because reporters "could roam around anywhere" and Cambodia far worse because they did not even have the logistical support and medical care of U.S. troops that, on the contrary, made correspondents somewhat safer in Iraq and Afghanistan. But each war assignment, even embeds, entails a constant risk calculation:

[I]f you want to find out what's going on, you want to go with that patrol who knocks, that goes into an Afghan house, and see how they operate and see how they treat women, . . . which I've done many times. If you're behind the colonel in the headquarters, you're not going to see whether the troops either did well or made some gross, racist remarks or mistreated a woman or didn't treat them properly. . . . [Y]ou are literally like one of the soldiers. And you take exactly the same risks. . . . [On an Iraq embed] we were ambushed . . . twice in 10 minutes going through Najaf, once from a rooftop and another one from the roadside. (Gray, 28–29, 62)

To be on the ground, whether in 1950s Korea or 2010s Afghanistan, correspondents find themselves among "bullets flying all over the place" (Summerlin, 2). Eric Talmadge (11–12) very nearly paid with his life only a couple of days after embedding with Canadian troops at a base in Kandahar that he had been told was safe – except that "every now and then you'd get a rocket attack on some peripheral or on the fence":

I was sitting in our . . . media tent . . . it was a cloth tent but it had actual doors. The door was open and it was a nice day and I'm working on my computer, and from the corner of my eye I see a flash, I hear a bang, and in an instant, we were sprayed by all the gravel from outside, it was spraying through the door. . . . [A]n RPG . . . hit the side of the C-can right in front of our door, so it was maybe 10 meters away, 15 meters away from where we were sitting . . . if it would have gone off, we would all be dead. And there were maybe three of us sitting in the tent, and after the fact, duh, we all hit the ground . . . and we're just kind of lying there and one of the Canadian officers comes in about five minutes later. He says, "We've all got to go down and get in the bunker." So we got in a bunker and . . . and we're all just kind of quiet. It's dark and the sun has just set and this [officer] is sitting there and his cell phone goes off. . . . Somebody had just called him, didn't realize where he was, and he just picks it up and he goes, "Hey, can I call you back? This isn't really a good time for me right now." . . . It just kind of summed it up, it was not a good time right now. . . . And every day for the next week was the same routine. Not quite so close, but every day we're getting shelled. And this was right in the middle of the base. And had I not been embedded, I would never have known that, because the military was not saying that they were getting such attacks.

Talmadge wrote a story about the rocket attack, including the phone call in the packed bunker, where soldiers, civilian workers, and journalists were "shoulder-to-shoulder, knee-to-knee," and found some "reassurance" in "sharing this strange moment" with each other. The story ends: "The siren wails again. 'All clear,' the voice [on the PA system] says. 'All clear.' A fighter roars off the flightline. Everyone goes back to work."[2]

---

[2] Eric Talmadge, "Rocket attacks fact of Afghan life," The Associated Press, January 29, 2010.

Also in Afghanistan, region veteran Kathy Gannon (61, 63–65) had it coming from all sides when the United States started bombing Kabul after 9/11: outside the AP house, the Taliban and their even more dangerously anti-American Arab supporters, and from the sky, constant house-shaking bombing from B-52s. The "reassuring" voices of her editors in New York and her husband, Pasha, in Islamabad were cut off when a missile fell right behind her, blowing in the windows and forcing her to evacuate the bureau:

It sent me flying across the room, and I lost my glasses, my shoes, and the phone. But my first thought was, "These idiots. Oh my God, they're going after the phone. They're tracking the satellite phones and they found ours." ... We got stopped at one intersection, and you can hear the planes and there was a lot of bombing and big groups of people. Arabs were going by on their motorcycles. And Amir Shah is trying to talk his way out of this and "what are these foreigners doing" and he's showing the papers. ... Finally ... they let us go ... and we got to the Intercon [Intercontinental Hotel] and we spent the night there. And then the next morning the – we didn't sleep much – I looked out and we went and could see everything was gone and the Northern Alliance were at the edge of the city.[3] ... And Pasha, he didn't know what, because one minute we're talking, the next minute I'm gone, and finally I got a line much, much later, so I could let him know that everything was okay.

Several of her colleagues also came under U.S. fire. John Rice (3) was in Baghdad during the Persian Gulf War, "sitting it out" with three Middle Eastern journalists in an upper-story room of the Al-Rashid Hotel as bombers took out Iraq's air force headquarters a thousand yards away – an experience he later wrote about as "terrifying" but also "appallingly beautiful" and "spine-meltingly impressive": "We watched the tracers rip into the sky and listened to the repeated thunder of bombs dismantling the base. Pieces of metal hurled by the explosions clanked off of the hotel's shaking walls. Gradually, a dense cloud of dust and smoke rose above the second story, the third, the fourth."[4] Reid and about 100 journalists staying in Baghdad's Palestine Hotel during the 2003 U.S. bombing fared far worse when a U.S. tank embroiled in a heavy fight nearby fired on the hotel, killing two reporters – prompting one U.S. commander to scream over military radio, "Did you just fucking shoot the Palestinian [sic] Hotel?" as one embedded AP reporter heard, according to the subsequent investigation (Katovsky 2003, 371–373). Ironically, one correspondent sent to Iraq to help cover the invasion stayed there a rare straight 100 days – and had a bad heart attack the day after returning to New York (Hurst, 6).

From Northern Ireland to Beirut, from Managua to Chechnya, urban warfare that turned everyday living into bullet-dodging also exposed

---

[3] "As the sun rose over the Hindu Kush mountains, Kabul residents celebrated the end of Taliban rule over the city," Kathy Gannon, "Taliban deserts Kabul as Northern Alliance moves into the capital," The Associated Press, November 13, 2001.

[4] Rice's story about his experience of the bombing of Baghdad during the Gulf War ran on the AP wire a day before the Iraq War began in 2003; John Rice, "Fear and awe as bombs fell on Baghdad," The Associated Press, March 18, 2003.

correspondents to deadly peril even on the way to the food market, as one reporter covering the first intifada put it – at least in "a war zone they don't fight every day all the time" (Powell, 12). The explosion of ethnic fighting as the Soviet Union disintegrated meant trying to avoid front lines without ever knowing where one might break out next, as Moscow-based Alan Cooperman (13) found out repeatedly:

I was in a field interviewing people in Nagorno-Karabakh when a helicopter flew over-head and the helicopter made one big circle and then it made a tighter circle and then it came down lower and then it opened its doors, and ... one of the people that I was interviewing said, "Oh, that's what they did yesterday before they started shooting." And I remember that [another correspondent] and I ... took off running. ... They did not open fire. If they would have fired at us, they would have killed us.

Joe Frazier (7–8), whose wife was killed by a bomb while covering Central American guerrilla wars, had a close call when he and a colleague (who would also be killed a few years later) left the hotel where they had been staying – on the main road into Managua, where they expected the Sandinistas to move in – to find a place to file their stories and photos:

So we went in separate cars, this was at night. And we always did that, so if somebody broke down, they weren't stuck out there. ... My windshield just exploded in front of me. I remember lying over on my side and bullets came flying through the side of the car. I counted seven bullet holes in my car and ... to this day we're not really sure who did that. Because right after the war everyone was packing weapons, everyone picked up thrown-away military gear. ... But I got my chest full of blasts of shrapnel that for months kept working its way out through various holes in my body. I was scared to death, but I wasn't hurt very bad.

The AP office in Beirut was near the Commodore Hotel – the correspondents' hangout during the civil war – where it was not unusual to have "major rockets flying over the hotel, machine guns all over the place," rocket-propelled grenades exploding down the street, and the occasional "own goal," a car bomb that would explode en route. "[T]hat's what the streets were like at the time," Tatro (13) said, matter of fact.

Streets in Sarajevo were no better. Tony Smith (8), who had gone into the besieged city when everybody else fled, drove around in his Toyota Corolla, "the beast of Bosnia":

I had to try and get away from sniper fire and ... I tried to change down, because I'm used to a manual, stick shift ... and I'm thinking, "Oh shit, it's an automatic." And so it didn't go around the corner, it went straight on. And I ran into a tank trap, so the whole front was like pushed in, it looked like this ... shark with indigestion, a really bad dent at the front. But the thing kept running, God bless Toyota, you know?

Not that staying in was much safer. The apartment that Smith had turned into AP's first wartime Sarajevo bureau, after renting it from the family of one of the fixers he had rescued in the suburban parking lot before driving into town, was

FIGURE 7.1. Correspondent Eileen Alt Powell (second to last against right wall) and AP colleagues take refuge in a hallway of the Commodore Hotel, where many in the media lived and worked, during shelling of West Beirut in the Lebanese civil war in 1985. (Photo courtesy of Eileen Alt Powell)

on a top floor near the hospital, a target of Serb shells – but convenient to "go find casualties and count them when things started getting bad" (Alexander, 11). Paul Alexander (10) vividly remembered his first day in Sarajevo, when he barely survived a group of Serbs "using an antiaircraft gun as a surface-to-surface weapon, just walking it up and down the street," while the street signs were "pocked full of holes" from combat as well as "snipers checking the windage each day."

Probably the closest call in Bob Reid's five-decade AP career came during the Bosnian War, as he and an AP Croatian photographer traveled in between assignments. Sipping sparkling water in a bird-filled Berlin courtyard 20 years later, he recalled how fighting had closed all normal routes, so they were driving down an unpaved road just past the last checkpoint and near a British base, making good time and dreaming they might arrive in Split in time for a "nice meal or even a swim in the pool," when they saw "these armed men in uniform running along the side of the vehicle, screaming and holding their weapons in a firing position." Thinking they must have missed a checkpoint, Reid (91–95) and his colleague stopped the car and put their hands up. But the men dragged them out of the car and into the woods, where three dozen militants milled around:

[T]hey asked us who we were, driver tells them in Croatian. And then they made us go deeper into the woods, and that's when we started to get scared, thinking they were taking us up there to shoot us, because the Bosnian War was vicious. You could be shot like this, disappear in those woods, they'd never find the body, no idea what happened to you. Missing people all over the place. So they made us sit down, and I noticed that Hrvoje [Knez, the photographer] was very nervous. And he was smoking a cigarette but he could barely get it into his mouth. And then it dawned on me, this isn't cowardice – he can understand what they're saying. So I remember kind of whispering, "Are they going to shoot us?" And he says, "I don't know. They're waiting for the commander to come to decide." So we sat there for about 25 to 30 minutes, it was a very long 25 to 30 minutes. And the way we were seated, there were guys who pointed weapons at us. They weren't really mean or hostile, but they were pointing the weapons at us. So all of a sudden, this guy – kind of tall, gray-haired guy in his maybe mid-40s, distinguished-looking, sharp uniform, very physically fit – shows up. And the guy who had been in charge of the operation mumbles something to him. He walked over and said, "Get the hell out of here."

After negotiating to get back their passports – but not the car, luggage, camera equipment, or thousands of dollars in cash – Reid and the photographer found themselves walking down the road in the late afternoon, laughing at their own relief, until an observer from the European Commission drove by in an armored car and offered to take them to Split. On the way there, they braved mortar fire, a checkpoint manned by drunk Croatian militia, driving with a compass "and more-or-less sense of direction" through woods, and even the efforts of the friendly observer to ride into Muslim villages being "cleansed" – all on the eve of Reid's birthday.

Deadly as Bosnia and Beirut could be, several correspondents with multi-war experience believed that Somalia was the grimmest and toughest, with little food, bad water, and constant violence that necessitated the permanent presence of heavily armed guards (when correspondents could even be there – into the late 2000s, Mogadishu would at times be considered a "no-go" zone). Alexander (7, 9) came under fire three times in a few weeks when fighting broke out around the hotel:

Our walls were getting peppered with bullets. Six went through walls and hit the rooms. We were playing Scrabble in the hallway, in bulletproof vests and helmets, because there was nothing else to do. ... So there was talk at one point about whether we should evacuate. ... [T]hese Pakistani peacekeepers showed up, ready to escort us out, and we're all going, "We're not going anywhere. This is the story, we're right in the middle of it." ... [O]ne of the times I was shot at was on the roof of the hotel in Somalia ... and a bullet hit the wall on the other side of my head and did not go through the wall, whereas, as I said before, several others did punch through the walls. That's where I'm talking about the luck.

The violence in Somalia, and elsewhere, could get so pervasive that many correspondents, like Alexander (10), talked about horrifying dangers with a nonchalance betraying how they had come to accept them as the new normal – and perhaps also how they disliked to focus on this aspect of their job:

[In Somalia] our bar was the roof of the hotel. So we would be sitting up there on the parapet, drinking at night, and you could tell somebody who was brand new to Somalia because there'd be gunfire off in the distance and they'd be like, hitting the deck. We'd be sitting up there, laughing at them. Ha-ha-ha-ha. Unless, of course, you had a burst of gunfire or a couple, then everybody would get down (also Richburg 1998, 70–71).

Alexander (18–19) did have another close call in Somalia, when he and a photographer went to North Mogadishu to interview rebel leader Ali Mahdi (after the *New York Times* correspondents finished their interview), whose staff offered to escort the journalists' two-vehicle convoy on their way out – to what they had hoped would be lunch at a cheap lobster restaurant nearby. Right at the first intersection, a gunfight broke out:

[W]e're in the third vehicle, a Land Rover. Our Cherokee is in the front, and the security car is in the middle. And you can hear gunfire hitting metal, and I can see someone from our car pointing his AK out and firing, so our driver just stops dead and backs right back up into the compound. And we see somebody get hit in the security guard car and fall off. "What the hell is going on?" And then we see our Cherokee just speed off. . . . [T]here's a big, hasty discussion and they say, "Okay, you have to go now." "What do you mean we have to go now?" "No, we scared them off in the intersection, but they won't be scared off for long. This is your window of opportunity to get away." So we pull out, the driver floors it. We're in the back seat, just sort of peering over the edge, don't really see anything there, so they were right. So we're sort of finally sitting up a little bit, and as we're getting close to the Green Line separating the two sides of the city, [the photographer] looks up at me and says, "I guess this means no lobster." . . . And the interpreter/bodyguard . . . was the only casualty – he had a burn on his arm from the barrel of his AK where he got 21 rounds off of his own.

Two correspondents who roamed West Africa during its decolonization wars minimized how much danger they had been in, despite riding with a guerrilla group under threat of attack in Guinea Bissau (Heinzerling, 18) and being "locked in some cell with blood marks on the wall and guys shak[ing] guns" – but the latter only happened "not for very long . . . you just get held in places," Rosenblum (26) told me, puffing on his after-lunch pipe in his desert Tucson home. A veteran Latin America hand, Eduardo Gallardo (4), was held by guerrillas three times in Chile and Peru, but it was such a common occurrence among correspondents that he did not find it "too impressive."

JOURNALISTS AS TARGETS

In addition to the risks inherent in being present at scenes of havoc, correspondents brave the danger of being targets of specific violence aimed at journalists or foreigners by a gamut of forces, from criminal organizations to national governments, as discussed in Chapter 5. Even before the 2014 attack by an Afghan police officer that left her seriously wounded, Gannon (29–31) had been told of threats against her in the "chatter" picked up by U.S. and Canadian intelligence from sources ranging from mujahedeen groups to Pakistan's Inter-Services Intelligence, the latter prompting her to build reinforcing walls, a bullet-proof guard house, and to leave her home in Islamabad for a week in – Afghanistan. Acutely aware of the dangers, she did not often feel threatened walking down the street or talking to people even deep in the volatile tribal areas – and that amounted to a conscious decision:

[E]ither you become hostage to your fears or you decide this is how I'm going to handle it or you leave. Those are your choices, really, basically. ... I think it's an amazing environment still, after all these years. ... And the people you meet, they want to talk to you. They're thrilled that you want to know what they think and find out what. And I don't say that there isn't hostility. ... If I feel that there is some anger there, just directed at the fact that I'm a foreigner, I nicely, quietly, walk away, leave and get into something else. Yes, you have to watch against kidnappings and target killings and stuff. ... Honestly, I have been in situations where I could see in the face this real sort of, kind of a smoldering – and I just sort of try to talk to somebody else and keep a conversation going. ... The dangers of being kidnapped, the dangers of being bombed, the dangers of being shot, the dangers of being – I know. ... This is the environment that I'm working in right now and where I've chosen to go to get this information.

Few correspondents have worked for decades in such a constantly high-risk environment as Gannon, or paid the same price, but many had open verbal or physical threats, especially by those interested in preventing witnesses to their actions, beginning with governments. In revolutionary Tehran, Nick Tatro (11) was summoned to the "guidance ministry" and told that all foreign correspondents were no longer accredited, had 24 hours to leave Iran, and officials "couldn't guarantee [their] security." Returning to his hotel to pack, he found that his passport had been stolen, but through contacts at the U.S. Embassy, Tatro managed to get a new one in a few hours and a ticket on one of the last British Airways flights out. The passengers applauded when it took off. Eduardo Gallardo (5–6), who left Chile for a decade of other assignments before the Pinochet coup, had read the writing on the wall when, during a large truck drivers' strike against the Allende government, the general called all foreign correspondents to army headquarters late at night:

General Pinochet comes in, in full combat gear, huge pistol, dark glasses, helmet, and he says, "Gentlemen, I've invited you to ask you to relay a message. ... The situation is becoming very unstable, very dangerous, so I call upon my compatriotas not to force me to take my army into the streets. If the army goes into the streets, it goes to do what it has been trained to do." That is kill. ... We didn't know what to say, because right after that he said, "Eso es todo, señores, buenas noches" [this is all, gentlemen, good night], he turned around, and walked away. ... We went and wrote the story, "Army Chief threatens ... "

During the civil war in El Salvador, traveling through the volatile countryside meant ambushes, mines, "accidental contacts with things you didn't want to get in touch with going on out there," and rolling into ditches waiting for sudden firefights to clear. But the greatest danger came from the government that, believing that foreign correspondents sympathized with leftist guerrillas, lost no occasion to intimidate them (Frazier, 14; also AP Oral History, Aguilar, 2009). Frazier (14–15) and a photographer had gone to check out rumors that leftists had taken over the labor ministry and were leaving the scene when "three national police showed up" and led them down an alley with guns in their backs. They also took Frazier's small recorder, whose tape had a "loud, raucous antigovernment demonstration" on one side and a news conference on oil prices on the other: "And the guy pressed the play button and there's some guy blowing his nose on the price of oil ... I used clean tapes after that." Even holing up at the Camino Real hotel, as most of the press did, was no safety guarantee, since less than an hour after checking in, the phone would ring and an anonymous voice would growl, "We know you're here, you son of a bitch" (AP Oral History, Aguilar, 2009, 35):

[W]e'd be sitting around in the lounges of the hotel and somebody would come up to us and ... he'd pull his jacket back and there'd be a nice 45 on his belt and he'd say, "I certainly hope nothing bad happens to you down here." ... [S]ometimes, like 2 and 3 in the morning, we'd get phone calls and we'd answer, and all you'd hear on the receiver was click, click, click – and it was a revolver, then silence, hanging up. Stuff like that went on fairly often. There'd be bodies that would show up in the parking lot, sometimes with decals on our cars saying, "Betray your country not ours" and "We know who you are and we know where you live." ... Intimidation was just constant, it really was. And pretty soon we just sort of blew it off and, it is what it is. ... And then we'd get pulled over and ... we'd be turned against the side of our car with a gun at our necks and ... we could usually blabber our way out of it, but it was this constant feeling ... that something horrible was about to happen. (Frazier, 15–16)

Frazier's memoir on El Salvador contains a copy of a typed hit list from 1982 that has "Joe Frazer [sic] de los Estados Unidos de la AP" as number 10 in "pseudojournalists in service of subversion" (Frazier 2012, 21).

In Syria's civil war, rebels aiming to control the coverage detained in locked rooms and threatened to imprison "blacklisted" correspondents like Paul Schemm (18–19), claiming he was "lying about Al-Qaida being present in northern Syria, which, of course, it was." And that was the milder run-in he had with extremists there:

[O]ne of these ... rebel groups with extremist Islamist tendencies surrounded our cars and wanted to take me away because I was an American. The rest of the group were Jordanian and Hungarian. And that was quite disturbing and ... I haven't decided yet whether the guy who was talking to us – who was an Iraqi, and the rest of his team was probably North African, but it was a lot of dudes with guns – I don't know if he was just trying to intimidate me, but they were quite threatening. And we were in the middle of a

FIGURE 7.2. San José correspondent Joe Frazier talks with guerrilla leader Edén Pastora at his rebel camp inside Nicaragua, near the Costa Rican border, in 1983, not far from where Frazier's wife, also a journalist, would later be killed when a bomb was detonated at a press conference held by Pastora. (Photo courtesy of AP Corporate Archives)

town and our driver was from that town and there were a lot of people from the town around us, and I think that's why we were able to talk our way out of it. But they'd heard that there was an American journalist moving around, so they apparently decided to come check it out.

From Europe to Latin America, secret police agents also intimidated correspondents. Covering one of the first student protests against Portugal's military regime, Ike Flores (10–11; 2007, 188) was beaten on the back by riot police while trying to show his press card, then jailed by the notorious PIDE until the U.S. Embassy came to the rescue. On his first foreign assignment, Dan Perry (9–11) was walking home in Bucharest – feeling that his "Americanness" made him "immune" to the swirling street demonstrations against Romania's first post-revolution leader, Iliescu – when one demonstrator shouted "him" and all of a sudden policemen were beating Perry with clubs and dragged him into a dark, windowless van full of drunk detainees as he screamed "I'm American," in fluent Romanian. One of the fellow prisoners asked Perry what he had done, and, when he responded, "Nothing, I'm a foreign correspondent," he seemed to like it – soon everyone in the van was shouting it too, all the way to the police station, where officers started beating the other men on the head. Perry protested to the station's chief:

And the guy's like, "Sit down, acreditare." So I showed him my blue foreign ministry accreditation. ... So he has me tell him what happened and he's writing it down, in person, [the station's] chief of police ... I say a civilian for some reason picked me out and instructed these cops to beat me ... and he writes down, "undercover Securitate officer picked me out and instructed the cops to beat me." And I read that and I say, "That's not what I said." And he looks at me and laughs and says, "Oh, okay. Do you want me to change it?" "Well, whatever you think is best." So he took my statement and then they took mug shots, which in retrospect I should have not agreed to, and then they released me.

In Peru, Gallardo (14, 17–19) had been in the AP office for all of 10 minutes, replacing a vacationing bureau chief, when guerrillas stormed in, put a pistol against his forehead, and ordered him to relay communiqués on the wires. After spraying the walls with leftist slogans, they left – to do the same at the UPI office – and Gallardo called the police. The Peruvian secret service came instead, and when Gallardo told them what the guerrilla had done, one officer took both of his pistols out of the holsters, stuck them in the reporter's face, and asked whether the guerrilla's weapon was "Like this or like this one?" Later that night, he got a call at his hotel: "Hey, chileno, you're still there? You better watch!" And in the mid-1980s, replacing correspondents in Colombia who were threatened, Gallardo received another late-night call to appear before the secret service, where he was grilled over his reporting. After listening to several more incidents as we talked in a sparkling Santiago hotel lobby, I asked Gallardo if he had always felt that the job was worth these risks: "Oh yes, yes, of course. I'd be happy to go back to do it."

A Chilean national working as an AP correspondent, Gallardo had a double level of threat, and many other correspondents noted that local journalists often faced even higher risks than foreigners. In Haiti's mid-1990s unrest, one correspondent saw the Haitian fixer/driver that a group of 30 foreign correspondents were using shot dead in front of their eyes by a Duvalierist (Snow, 10). Years later on the island, a reporter sent by editors to the slum of Cité Soleil to get reaction to Aristide's flight into exile was robbed at gunpoint three times on the way back to the hotel, "and you did see journalists screeching into the hotel compound with their back window shot out and then all of those flak jackets that you had sitting in the back of the car that nobody had put on, all of the sudden people would start to put their flak jackets on" (Stevenson, 7).

TAKING SAFETY SERIOUSLY

Faced with pervasive dangers, in war zones and specifically targeting journalists, correspondents have always tried to manage risk, but many said that in the 2000s safety considerations have increasingly impacted reporting, with management getting far more involved and requiring more security and training. At the most basic level, correspondents, while never bearing weapons, routinely wear body armor and helmets in violent conflicts or clashes – even in sweltering deserts, echoing Laub's (32) sentiment that "when you hear mortars and automatic gunfire going off, you kind of figure, I'd rather be warm than

FIGURE 7.3. Jerusalem bureau chief Dan Perry talks with Palestinian leader Yasser Arafat after interviewing him at his compound in Ramallah in December 2001. (Photo by Jacqueline Larma, courtesy of Dan Perry)

dead." Correspondents also adopt ad hoc measures. In Sarajevo as the siege was closing, violence was escalating and no formal government was at hand with information, Smith (9) and his five remaining colleagues split into pairs, changing partners daily, to "go out to patrol for an hour, an hour and a half, trying to pick up what was going on, get some sound bites, some vox pop, some photos, and then try and figure out what was going on on the ground and match that to what was being reported politically. ... And so this is what the scheme we had worked out was, to try to be safe and to try and get as much coverage as we could for what the desk needed, both photos and news."

Smith (13) also covered up the car plate, because "you don't want to be identified by anybody, so it doesn't give them the excuse to shoot at you before you've actually spoken to them," while Daniszewski (14–15) learned to move around Sarajevo "always trying to keep a building or something between you and the snipers," and he hoped that the big duct-tape "TV" on the car as he traveled down sniper alley would "deter someone from shooting at you, and at least alert friendly forces that they shouldn't be shooting at you as well." In fact, one ABC producer was killed going down sniper alley by a bullet that hit the back of his van between the taped *T* and *V* (Hess 1996, 36). In Israel around the time of the intifada, Perry (26) learned how to check under his car for explosives every day, avoided open spaces like restaurant terraces where suicide bombers might strike – exactly like the buzzing one where we were talking off Jerusalem's popular Jaffa Road, he noted – and decided on an interview with Arafat in his Ramallah headquarters days after Israelis had bombed all around it, "kind of [knowing] Israel didn't really want to assassinate Arafat at that point, so the building itself was probably safe."[5]

As two correspondents who covered dozens of hot spots put it, reporters need to constantly relearn how to protect themselves, physically and mentally, because each war has different traumas (Alexander 3, Hanley 8–9) – but conflict is far from the only danger. A few female correspondents said they had feared rape – which, for example in Haiti, might also have entailed exposure to HIV (Snow, 11) – so they tried not to go out alone. Suddenly hit with the Fukushima nuclear disaster, AP Tokyo had to scramble to learn about nuclear radiation dangers, keep up with the expanding (and conflicting) evacuation zones declared by Japanese and U.S. officials, and fly in a U.S. reporter who specialized in the nuclear industry with a dozen dosimeters for the staff on the scene, including Talmadge, who would call in three times a day with radiation readings (Foster, 6–7). While some reporters refused to go near the exploded reactors, Talmadge (8), who had been close enough to hear one go bust while waiting for what turned out to be a false tsunami alert, tried to talk New York editors out of ordering him to leave. When they insisted, he had to drive over mountains in a snowstorm, and hit a telephone pole (see this chapter's box for more on Japan's disaster).

Safety measures sometimes generate disputes between correspondents on the ground and editors thousands of miles away – if there is communication, since even today mobile phones might not work deep in jungles or deserts. Having entered Libya without body armor, expecting a calmer Arab Spring moment instead of violent civil war, Schemm (16) was asked to go into Tripoli to check again on a report he had determined was false, but his driver would only go so far, so Schemm called editors back: "I want to make clear what you want me to do. Because, right now, we don't have transportation. To do this, I would have to ride with rebels into the heart of a firefight. I just want you to tell me, in your own words, that you want me to do that." But after the editors backed off, Schemm and an AP photographer went anyway:

[W]e went building to building – at that time, I'm not sure how much people were shooting at us. The people we were with were doing lots of shooting, so it was . . . a lot of bullets and stuff. . . . [T]here's that point where you kind of think, "Wow, that was really stupid, and what did I really get out of that?"

The AP bureaus in Beirut in the 1980s and Baghdad in the mid-2000s struggled more than most with the desire to report versus the certainty of danger. Eileen Powell (7), who was in Lebanon when Anderson was taken, said the attitude of journalists there about security was "delusional" because,

[5] Dan Perry and Karin Laub, "Beleaguered Arafat says he'll face down militants, calls for peace with Israel," The Associated Press, December 8, 2001. The story noted: "Arafat was interviewed for an hour in his office in an imposing compound . . . yards away from the scene of an Israeli missile strike earlier in the week that was widely interpreted as a message that the Palestinian leader was no longer fully immune."

despite the increasing kidnappings of Westerners, they believed they would be okay since they were trying to give a voice to all sides. They did begin to sleep away from home, use drivers, work in pairs, be outspoken when some of the local staff was kidnapped and then released. In the few months before AP ordered all U.S. staff out after Anderson, a former Marine whom many other correspondents considered a tower of strength, was taken hostage while returning home from a tennis match, several of his frightened colleagues tried to negotiate his release, despite knowing they could be next. (Powell went around Beirut's militia offices, for example.) Several correspondents in Baghdad during the explosion of sectarian violence, kidnappings, and beheadings in the mid-2000s felt that all news organizations, including AP, had pulled back too much, allowing foreign correspondents to leave heavily fortified offices only rarely and with security guards, ultimately making reporting there not only most challenging for "street reporters" ("it's like being in jail but you have to work," Reid, 64; also Schemm, 1–2; Buzbee, 7) but prohibitively expensive.

In the mid-2010s, correspondents in Syria and Mexico faced the most restrictive safety measures, with violence so widespread and unpredictable from a variety of groups that large parts of those countries became no-go zones. "It's like the Bermuda triangle," Laub (35) said of Syria. Mark Stevenson (10–11), based in Mexico City for nearly three decades, said that the gruesome and enduring escalation of drug cartel violence made entire swaths of the country too dangerous to even travel down the highway, as noted in Chapter 6:

[Y]ou don't know what you're doing wrong . . . you could get stopped out in the middle of nowhere and that would be the end of you. . . . We got to the edge of Ciudad Mier and . . . literally there are spots where you're walking on shell casings and you're seeing . . . the back of flak jackets, bandoleers, tossed on the side of the road where somebody had obviously got hit and they tore his flak jacket off. You see that, you see cattle abandoned wandering over the road, and you see nobody coming up. You look at it for an hour and there is nobody coming up, and you're like, there is no way in the world we're going there. So you start to use security protocol. But that's basically, that's essentially security – the places you don't go.

In summer 2014, Stevenson and a photographer needed all the impromptu security they could devise when traveling deep into narco territory to investigate the latest Mexican government's report that 22 cartel members had been killed in a "gun battle" in which only one soldier had been slightly injured – a highly suspicious imbalance, especially since cartels are extremely well armed. En route to San Pedro Limón three days after the killing there, they stopped in each town to ask whether it was safe to continue and a man even gave them the name of a relative they could say they were going to visit if armed men stopped them on the road. The reporters made it and found plenty of evidence contradicting the official report, including bullet marks and blood spatters in a warehouse "giving the appearance that some of those killed were standing against the wall and were hit by one or two shots at chest level," and therefore likely executed.[6]

NO, COLONEL, I COUNTED THE BODIES

The imperative to count bodies – or, as in Stevenson's case, pools of blood – in an effort to establish accurate, truthful accounts of conflict has been one of correspondents' most universal, dangerous, and traumatizing routines. Its essential goal is earning the authority to cut through the official spin, as Anderson (4–5) did, twice, when covering how the million-strong southern Korean city of Kwangju rebelled in 1980 against the brutal put-down of antigovernment protests by chasing the army out of town and seizing it, until soldiers retook it with more deadly violence. Anderson and a photographer walked into the barricaded town – the taxi driver stopped a dozen miles short – and reported for nine days inside Kwangju, except for daily runs through the army perimeter to get to a working phone to file:

My first day was a day that actually caused me a lot of mental grief for a while. What does the AP do? It finds out things, basic stuff. How many people were killed? The army says three people were killed in the riots. How many people were killed? My first day, that morning, I counted 179 bodies which had been run over, beaten, dismembered, killed in various ways. I personally counted them, pointed a finger at one, two, three, four. I traveled all over the city counting as many bodies as I could find ... and I got out that evening, and I thought ... the government said – they're lying, there's not three people have been killed. I counted the fucking bodies.

Anderson was in a hotel next to Kwangju's provincial government building, the rebels' last holdout, when government troops stormed it – hitting the hotel too, and filling Anderson's room rate sign with bullet holes:

[W]e came out at dawn, scared shitless. ... Korean colonel came by in a jeep and I holler at him, "Colonel, Colonel, Colonel," and he stopped. ... "Colonel Kim, how many people were killed in the assault?" He looked at me and said two, one soldier and one rebel. We walked around the corner into the provincial government building and there are 17 people piled up in the garden. So a couple of other correspondents and I said okay, go find out what you can. We'll try to count bodies and come back, and we went out in different directions and we ended up with a total that was in the hundreds, that was our best guess. Nobody knows how many people died in Kwangju.

Anderson's story said as much – that the official figure was three in one battle but "reporters who entered the shell-battered building counted 16 bodies" and protest leaders were putting the total death count at 261: "Reporters had not seen that many corpses, but the students said many had been taken away by

---

[6] Mark Stevenson, "In Mexico, lopsided death tolls draw suspicion," The Associated Press, July 8, 2014.

families for burial and others were found in drainage ditches, vacant lots and construction sites."[7]

A few years later in Beirut, when death estimates varied from 400 to 15,000, Anderson and other correspondents counted casualties at hospitals, even cemeteries (like "Martyr's Cemetery" where, Tatro wrote, "flies covered the ground, and the air was thick with the smell of death")[8] – because "consistent and accurate reporting of this human suffering was our most important journalistic duty" (Fisk 2002, 275 and 2005, 1003). One AP reporter recoiled in horror at the taste of blood in the air, body parts protruding from plastic bags, and herself in the middle of the hospital room going "'One, two three,' . . . you have to do it with your fingers in order to concentrate. I said, 'One, two, three.' I don't know how many I counted – 30, 20. I said, 'I'm not going to do this.' I hated myself, just standing there and just counting these people's bodies" (AP Oral History, Faramarzi, 2009, 53–54). During the U.S. war in Iraq, AP reporters did the rounds of hospitals in Baghdad after bombings (or, when the security deterioration prevented it, took reports from stringers and acted as "secretaries at the morgue"), gathering evidence to back up their daily body counts even in the face of pre-surge U.S. military denials – "they always disputed our number because it put this war in a bad light" (Schemm, 1; Hurst, 8).[9]

Several correspondents gave AP a special responsibility in this gruesome task, because it functions as the "basis" that other media rely on. In the 1960s, Erbsen wrote for AP's internal magazine that his reporters in Rio de Janeiro "went to the morgue every day and checked for the highest number on tags attached to bodies of flood victims," giving the agency the only accurate death toll in the 1966 disaster.[10] In 1960s Saigon, AP correspondent Malcolm Browne penned a 24-page "short guide to news coverage in Vietnam" for the bureau that listed this tip: "in covering a military engagement, you must make every effort to count the bodies yourself before accepting any tabulation of results" (The Associated Press and Hamill 2014, 26). A young UPI reporter around the same time was badly reprimanded by legendary *New York Times* war correspondent Homer Bigart for a wire story about 200 Vietcong killed in a battle – when the two journalists went out to check, they found 12 bodies (Salisbury 1980, 39). Richard Pyle (15), who served as one of AP's Saigon bureau chiefs, said the U.S. military was willing to take journalists on helicopter rides to see the aftermath of battles – but there "were never as many bodies lying around as they said they'd killed," either because of "fudging the figures" or because they might have been "pulverized" in the destruction.

---

[7] Terry A. Anderson, "Government troops retake Kwangju," May 26, 1980.

[8] Nicolas B. Tatro, "Mass graves in a Beirut cemetery," The Associated Press, July 1, 1982.

[9] The AP also kept its separate tally of U.S. military deaths, with hundreds of short stories throughout the war.

[10] Claude E. Erbsen, "O que esta acontecendo na A.P. no Brasil," *The AP World* (Spring 1968): 16.

Beyond numbering, correspondents had to check out bodies for revealing visual details and some accuracy in how people had been killed. During Afghanistan's vicious war among mujahedeen groups, Gannon (16) saw a rocket blow apart a 5-year-old girl as she stepped out of an apartment and had evidence, literally at her feet, of the women who had been raped and scalped by one militia: "[T]his Hazara who was just in tears and threw this hair at me and – which was really gross – and then showed me the bodies." Gannon described the episode nearly 20 years later in an analysis of why Afghanistan's postwar collapse "shouldn't have surprised anybody."[11] Reporting on the women's killings in Ciudad Juárez, Stevenson (22) interviewed a local official – later to be murdered herself – working on skull reconstructions, who showed her workbook, with dozens of murdered girls: "invariably ... the last photo the family had was the girl at her coming-out party. So you'd have rotting corpse, sweet sixteen, rotting corpse. And by the end of that, you just wanted to weep."[12] After Iran's revolution, Doelling (14) went into downtown Tehran's morgue, where the coroner offered him a cup of tea and then showed him "four generals of the Shah's army who had been executed the day before, and they were naked, except for something over their groin, and their heads were being held up by some tomato cans. And the tomato cans, that was the end of the glorious Shah's army."[13] George Bria (5), who as a young child growing up in Italy had witnessed crowds hailing Mussolini, saw the broken bodies of the dictator and his mistress after they had been executed by a mob:

Gunned down, both of them ... hanged from the girders of a gasoline station in Milan. I didn't see that. I got there a day after ... we were shown the bodies in a [makeshift] morgue. Mussolini's body, bare, naked, with Claretta on the floor, like pieces of wood. Other bodies piled up next to them that had died in reprisal shootings. ... I remembered when I was 10 years old this figure on the balcony and all the shouting of joy and exuberance at this leader. There he was on the floor with his mistress. Quite a contrast. ... I wrote it like that. ... I didn't put myself in there. I should have.

Looking for evidence of cause of death in highly charged situations – Iraqi battlefields, Mexican cartel wars, or Central American guerrilla fights – has required even more dangerous and extended trips searching for bodies. At the height of the death squad killings in El Salvador, Frazier (23) accompanied a 27-year-old human rights worker who photographed the corpses, up to 40 on "a busy morning," before they were hastily buried in mass graves. One woman thus recognized her husband's picture and eventually got him exhumed – although

[11] Kathy Gannon, "Analysis: First-person view of Afghan collapse," The Associated Press, October 7, 2011.

[12] Mark Stevenson, "Grinning skull and four words: 'This is your daughter,'" The Associated Press, October 9, 1999.

[13] "Four Generals Executed in Iran; U.S. Begins to Evacuate Citizens," *International Herald Tribune*, February 17–18, 1979, p.1. The tea detail is in an internal AP log dated February 19, 1979, that Doelling provided to the interviewer.

when she was presented with "a piece of fabric and a jawbone from the reeking pit," she said to leave him where he was and she would get a refund on the coffin she had planned to take him home in.[14] Stevenson (10) found himself "in a weird situation of being in San Fernando looking for physically the mass graves," after hearing reports that many victims had been forced to fight each other with sledgehammers in exchange for a chance to be spared as cartel foot soldiers:

We went in and got a federal police escort, which took us to the secondary highway. They said, "The mass graves are down those dirt roads." "You're going down?" "We're not going down there. You want to go down there." So it was us and a carload of foreign journalists from some other media outlet, literally going down dirt roads looking for these mass graves, not being able to find them I think in part because (a) the feds didn't know where they were or they're no longer recognizable once they've been excavated. Hey, that looks like mass – it also looks like a quarry. So without someone on the ground to tell you, okay, that's where they excavated, you couldn't reasonably say that.

In Iraq, Reid (67–70) investigated two reports of wrongful killings by U.S. troops running against official accounts – and intense fact-checking paid off in both cases. In the first, the military said they had hit an "al-Qaida meeting." It turned out they had mistakenly killed more than 40 people at a wedding party:

[Y]ou accuse the United States government of lying like that and committing what could conceivably be a war crime, you better have your stuff in order. ... The [AP] stringer happened to find a guy who'd been making the wedding video ... he had like eight hours of tape, who wants to watch eight hours of tape? But, in the tape ... they had a wedding singer, the musician. His face, we found that same face, dead, in one of the trucks.[15] ... And then the U.S. military fell back on another line, which is: Even bad people get married. So we lived through that. They first tried to smear us, by presenting, "Oh we found these weapons in their possessions!"[16] ... [E]ven reporters who were trying to undercut our story, who would have loved to have seen our story get nailed, were saying things like, "That's not very many weapons, you got more?" ... [Coalition deputy chief of operations Brig.] General [Mark] Kimmitt says, "Well, this is not all. We're screening and we'll show more tomorrow." Next day they show the same weapons. ... And eventually, Kimmitt never apologized, never backed off, always maintained – but just quit talking about it, and the whole thing went away.

The second story started when a man told an AP reporter "hanging around the morgue" that U.S. troops from the 82nd Airborne had cuffed and shot in the back of the head his disabled brother in Fallujah during retaliation for a roadside bomb that killed a beloved sergeant. Since the story was not "all that preposterous," the reporter asked to see the body, but, unable to tell from the wounds, he found more witnesses who claimed they had seen it happen. After

[14] Joe Frazier, "Death's cameraman," The Associated Press, January 22, 1981.
[15] Scheherezade Faramarzi, "Officials say American aircraft kill more than 40 at wedding party," The Associated Press, May 19, 2004.
[16] Scheherezade Faramarzi, "U.S. airstrike along Syria border in Iraq reportedly kills more than 40; Iraqis say wedding party attacked," The Associated Press, May 20, 2004.

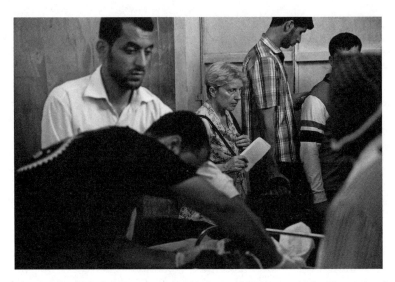

FIGURE 7.4. West Bank correspondent Karin Laub reports on the Gaza war from a morgue in the Beit Lahiya hospital in Gaza on July 24, 2014. (AP Photo by Lefteris Pitarakis)

more digging, with more details falling into place, AP called the military, who went "ballistic" but provided "nothing really conclusive, it's just their witnesses said this, our witnesses said that":

I had some calls with New York and talked it over with the senior editor, and basically we decided we were going to go with it, but we were going to wait until the next day and nail down ... one more little tiny detail to make this story airtight. So he goes back, he's hanging around the morgue ... talking to this one guy, ambulance driver ... [who] says, yeah that's the crippled guy. Selling cigarettes by the curb. He ... says he was there and "I was having trouble lifting him because his arms were flailing around in death, so I cuffed him." *So I cuffed him.* At that point, the story fell apart.

THE TRAUMA OF CORRESPONDENCE

Even for hardened correspondents, dwelling over bodies of victims of violence is a major cause of trauma, far more scarring than facing dangers – a shock dealt with for a long time without formal care mechanisms other than taking quick breaks in the "normal" world, and rushing back in. At his desk in the Tokyo bureau, newspaper clippings of his coverage of the twin natural and nuclear March 2011 disasters on the wall behind him, Talmadge (18) recalled following around a police search party looking for cadavers near the Fukushima radiation zone – they in "full white spacesuits" in the mud fields and the correspondent waiting in jeans:

I followed one of the search parties to a parking lot where they were pulling, they were bringing the bodies out of the mud, bringing them to this parking lot and hosing them down and putting them in a van to take them back to the morgue, which I had also just been to the day before. And I think after an afternoon of watching corpses get hosed down by people in radiation suits, that made me really wonder. It was really an unpleasant experience and when I went back to wherever it was that we were staying that night, I really wondered, "Why am I doing this? This is too much."

Like Talmadge, most correspondents saved their emotions for afterhours – protecting themselves at the scene, as it were, by carrying on with their job without leaving room for the horror to creep in until later. "Not then and there, there's work to be done, I had to go on. I had to continue what I was doing, and you leave the rest for later memories," said Max Desfor (4), whose photographs of human tragedies in the Korean War won a Pulitzer. Whether the disaster was a plane crash outside Paris or factory explosions in India, correspondents tried to run on adrenaline and block the tragedy while they were covering it, so that the very difficulty of finding sources and filing a story "puts a screen between you and the worst of what's happening" (Bryson, 33; also Doland, 4; Graham, 29). Despite losing several colleagues in the violent last days of South Africa's apartheid, Bryson (9) never went back to the bureau thinking "'Boy, I was almost killed today.' . . . I would come back and write a story."

When the scene gets to correspondents, work can become a coping mechanism. After the 2011 earthquake, Tokyo bureau chief Malcolm Foster (9) sent off his wife and kids to vacation in China, and he "just stayed at the hotel up here, above the bureau, and just worked nonstop, basically." In Baghdad when it became too dangerous to leave protected areas, the daily routine for one correspondent holed up in the heavily fortified AP house was: "the day would begin, I'd walk down to my desk, and I'd work until 1 or 2 o'clock in the morning, and I'd go to bed, and get back up" (Hurst, 6). Despair sometimes settles in, covering the terror of crushed Tiananmen protests in China (Kurtenbach, 3) or walking through the rain, mud, and open sewage of Jabalia in Gaza and realizing that generations of people have lived in that squalor with "so little hope of fixing this or solving this . . . that's very hard, to keep covering something that seems to be hopeless" – after all, "it makes it simply more fun to write about things that may have a happy ending," dashed as those hopes usually are (Laub, 9, 40).[17] Between the widespread violence, the killing of a colleague, and the inability to get help for a gravely wounded one, Smith (8, 13) briefly broke down his first days in Sarajevo during the siege. Years later, he remembered all the details except how many days he had actually been there:

It was – every day just seemed to blend into the next one. It was just really – it was one experience. . . . I really can't remember how many days it was, it must have been like 10

---

[17] Karin Laub, "Jabalia has become center of resistance to Israel," The Associated Press, December 19, 1987. The second paragraph reads: "Residents say they have nothing to lose by throwing stones at Israeli soldiers armed with submachine guns. Many here have lived in squalor for decades."

days, two weeks, something like that. .... And people have often asked me, "Do you feel like you're in danger?" And you don't really, it doesn't even register because you've got so much, you're too focused on doing what you've got to do. And so it's not every minute that you think, "Oh my God, I could be shot." Of course, like with the trip down sniper alley, then really you are heart in mouth, really. But all day every day you can't think about that, otherwise you shouldn't be doing this job. .... It's obviously not for you ... if you can't categorize things and put them to the back of your mind. Because if you really were to think about this, you just wouldn't be there, and you certainly wouldn't be going out and looking for stories and looking for danger, basically.

Some horrors are so visceral that correspondents can lose it at the scene – although hardly interrupting their work, the scars might never heal. In Beirut, Anderson (13) "watched a [3-year-old] boy die on an operating table from phosphorus burns all over his body and the doctor broke down. His twin infant brother and sister were in a bucket of water on the side of the emergency room, still smoking, and I wrote a story about it." Fisk (2002, 282–84, 128), who was in the same hospital a few hundred yards from the "Green Line" separating PLO-run West Beirut from the Israeli-occupied east side, remembered Anderson's crying as he typed in "suppressed fury." While being held hostage, Anderson wrote poems about the boy and about correspondence, about the hope against hope that covering such tragedy might make a difference "because the paper is dotted with our tears" – tears that are doubly "helpless" because there will always be another child to watch dying and another reporter who cannot emerge "unscathed" from "bathing in the world's violence" nor purge all feelings "in a thousand words or so" (Anderson 1993, 38, 29). Or 592 words, the length of Anderson's actual story:

Three-year-old Ahmed Baitam, his face and part of his chest covered with severe burns, was tied to a hospital bed with soft bandages. As Dr. Amal Shamma leaned over him to point out the injuries caused by a burning phosphorous shell, the youngster's heart stopped. ... The slim, intense pediatrician began pushing hard on the child's chest while the orderly breathed into his mouth. The nurse ran for heart needles and an electro-shock machine. Despite 20 minutes of effort Thursday afternoon, the boy could not be revived.[18]

Although in the past few years media organizations have begun to recognize the need to treat post-traumatic stress syndrome, correspondents were long left alone to deal with what they were witnessing. Some talked it out with colleagues (Schemm, 13), part of that intense team spirit that overcomes competition. Others craved solitude (Bartimus, 22), like playing Tetris in Sarajevo because "when the Serbs were firing mortars, there weren't a whole lot of other things you could do. And you didn't want to really think about the idea that one of these mortars could take you out at any time" (Alexander, 20). Correspondents just kept going, until they no longer could. Asked how he took care of himself

---

[18] Terry A. Anderson, "One phosphorous shell kills three children, burns 11 relatives," The Associated Press, July 30, 1982.

and his staff when covering daily carnage in Lebanon – not to mention the constant dangers of being killed in bombs and sniping – Tatro (15–16) chuckled and answered, "Well, I didn't. I drank too much probably. I don't know. I guess the bar was the solution for most journalists."

Then he listed a few episodes from Beirut: A veteran war correspondent, Alex Efty, walked into the bureau covered in the blood of people who had been killed while on a rooftop with him observing the airport's shelling; Anderson and another AP reporter went to a building collapsed by an Israeli strike[19] to talk with survivors and rescuers trying to get at victims trapped in the basement, when a car bomb went off. The explosion knocked both reporters down, and one woke up "covered with blood and body parts and I don't know what" from a pregnant woman he had been interviewing – a devastating trauma that "freaked out" the reporter, who had to leave. Ten weeks into the Israeli siege of West Beirut in 1982, Tatro wrote about the pregnant woman's killing, as well about a shell crashing next door to the AP office, in a terrifying analysis that argued the city had no winners and "nowhere was it safe."[20] When after nearly seven years Anderson (17, 19–20) was finally released by the kidnappers, AP provided him with two psychiatrists for daily counseling sessions – but 20 years later he bluntly said, "I am not sure that you ever can use the word recover for something like that":

I can never say that I'm healed, I'm a different person. All those things are part of who I am, all the damage is part of who I am. . . . And really the task has always been not to *heal* but to live my life, in a productive and decent way, which is what I have tried to do, not always successfully. But am I healed? I don't know. I don't want to go back to this counseling to find out. I am okay.

Although only a handful of correspondents endured trauma as profound as Anderson's, all refused to dwell on the tragedies they witnessed. When they needed to take a break from particularly overwhelming scenes, they quickly rushed right back in – because they believe in the significance of what they are doing, but also because if trauma and danger sink in, they might not function again. It is, simply, part of being a correspondent: "I never heard of anyone quitting the job because of their emotions, because of the misery and the terrible things that they have seen . . . not real journalists saying, 'Well, I can't go to that place because I know I'll see too many terrible things'" (Hanley, 14). After an 18-month stretch with five months in Somalia, three months in Bosnia, and a month in Rwanda, Alexander (3) took a year off – "I was sort of messed up in the head to a certain degree. I'd sort of lost my ability to trust people": "Everybody pays this price; it's just a matter of how you deal with it." At the end of the day watching corpses pulled out of radioactive debris, Talmadge (18)

---

[19] Fisk (2002, 313–314) gives a full account of the strike and car bomb, which he witnessed with Anderson.
[20] Nicolas B. Tatro, The Associated Press, August 21, 1982.

answered his own question as to why he did it: "I got my story, I wrote something that I thought was significant, and then woke up the next morning and did it again." After Hurricane Mitch killed thousands of people in Central America, Niko Price (18) spent 10 days wading through mudslides among bodies rotting in the sun, and eventually his bureau chief agreed to let him take a short break away:

I got on a plane and when I landed back in Mexico City, I remember getting a phone call from the international editor, saying, "I really don't think it was a good idea to come back." ... He was very nice about it. But he said, "Take your wife to the best restaurant in Mexico City tonight, charge it to me, tomorrow morning get back on an airplane." Which I was happy to do.

Even an assignment as threatening as Sarajevo kept pulling reporters back. After managing to carry his wounded and dead colleagues out of town, Smith (14) went to Great Britain to visit his father – who had last heard from him on a BBC broadcast that Sarajevo had been cut in half by bombing, since satellite phones were reserved for filing stories. After a week, he returned to the Vienna bureau and asked to be sent to Bosnia: "If I don't go back now, I'm never going to go back. ... I need to go back in. The story, I started the story, I want to continue the story, and if I don't do it, then I'm not too sure ... I will have the guts to do it later." His wife and two kids in Paris, David Crary (10–11) struggled with accepting his first assignment to Bosnia in 1992, where bullets whined over his head as he rode from the airport to the bureau. But after three weeks, he came to admire so much the bravery of both journalists and ordinary citizens there that "it just became something that I wanted to keep doing," even finding "almost bizarre" that he could come and go, "out of sorts and sort of like guilty" when back in Paris:

The first year at least there was no running water, there was very little electricity, it was real, real hardship for the people there, and you sort of experience that as a foreign reporter, you might have your fixer manage to get you food and water and stuff so you were maybe better off than the local people, but still suffering. But then you would come back to Paris, at whatever, Christmastime, and the city is full of luxury and gaiety and stuff. ... But the first couple times it was hard coming out as much as it was being scared the first time going in.

Similarly, Tatro (17) felt like walking "into Disney World" when he crossed from wartime Lebanon into Israel and "there were all these tourists there, these American kids, ice cream cones, short shorts. ... And I felt this big burden lift off my shoulders that I didn't even know it was there." Frazier (16, 35–37) also let out "this big pheeeeeeeeeew" when a Mexico-bound plane lifted off the ground of El Salvador, and flight attendants learned to leave the bottle instead of a drink: "We'd solve our problems [that way] on the way back up to Mexico – there was a lot of that, probably way too much." Still, despite blaming himself for his wife's death, feeling "full of adrenaline one day and ... depressed out of your mind the next," and knowing that a phone call to AP editors would have been enough for reassignment, he stayed on.

IS THE STORY WORTH YOUR LIFE?

To do that, to continue to work through the trauma and despite the dangers, correspondents have needed to dig deep to find the strength to carry on – not fearless, but facing down fears on a mission to tell truer, fuller stories that urgently needed witness (see also Shadid 2006, 69; Fisk 2005, 234–235). All correspondents have asked themselves whether a story is worth their life – and while all answered negatively, their practices suggest they meant the likelihood of death, not the possibility, since high risk is often unavoidable:

If, if I knew a story would kill me, I doubt the answer would be yes. But what you're really talking about is risk arbitrage. Every time you cross a street you're taking a risk, so if crossing the street is worth the risk to my life, if getting on the plane to go see, you know, the Super Bowl is worth the risk to my life, then without a doubt, participating in this unbelievable endeavor, which I really view as a mission and something of a dream come true also is, is yes. The risk – not the actual negative outcome, just the risk. (Perry, 37)

What Pyle (15–16) said about flying to combat scenes during the Vietnam War, and the four photographers who died when their helicopter was shot down over Laos, applies generally across time and place:

We spent an awful lot of time on helicopters going to places where nobody in their right mind would necessarily want to go. And I look back on that now and say, "For five years, doing that for *five years?*" The odds are going to catch up with you. And they did catch up with people, like the guys I wrote about,[21] but ... not one of those four guys would have stayed back when the opportunity came to take that trip into Laos in that helicopter. ... [N]one of them would have turned that down. ... [W]hen I left there after five years ... they had to drag me out of that place.

That does not mean that correspondents rush blindly into the line of fire. On the contrary, many dismiss "cowboy" journalism as needless and even conceited, since trouble has plenty of ways of finding the reporters without "trolling" for it (Frazier, 8). Korea and Vietnam reporting veteran George McArthur (3) deadpanned that frontline correspondence was "balderdash" – "I was cowering behind somebody," usually the radioman. In the late 1960s African independence wars, Larry Heinzerling (19) refused to chase a moving

---

[21] In 1971, four combat photographers, including the AP's Henri Huet, died when their helicopter was hit. The crash site was so remote that no investigators reached it until nearly three decades later, when Pyle and AP photo editor Horst Faas, who had also worked in Saigon, went to search for their friends' remains. None were found, though the site was identified. Richard Pyle and Horst Faas, *Lost over Laos: A True Story of Tragedy, Mystery, and Friendship* (Cambridge: Da Capo Press, 2003).

front line – "I didn't think it was worth it to get possibly shot. For what? To look at what? Some imaginary line that wasn't going to be there the next day" – and years later, after helping to negotiate Anderson's release and to lead AP's international desk, he argued that news organizations should discourage excessive risk-taking, as many AP editors did. Special correspondent Mort Rosenblum (31, 34) said he took only the risks he had to – not leaving Argentina after he was put on a hit list during the military dictatorship, for example, but sleeping in friends' apartments:

I was not going to leave, I was not going to say, these fuckers are going to run me out of the country. . . . But also . . . I'm a chickenshit. I didn't really want to get blown up, and I didn't want my wife or dog blown up.

Several correspondents weighed the imperative of "push and push and push, until you can get the story and get the truth" (Schemm, 15) versus their responsibility to their families, especially young children. After having pushed for an assignment to Iraq during the war, Sally Buzbee (8) put her fear in simple terms: "I had two kids at that point and I did not want to get blown up by a roadside bomb. And I basically tried not to think about it." Indonesia-based Robin McDowell (25) had a son under 10 when she took temporary post-9/11 assignments to Pakistan, and got on the plane asking herself, "Why did I make this choice? What's wrong with me? What is missing? Or am I just an idiot? . . . Fuck, am I really going there?" Another young reporter called a turning point in her career the moment she was asked to go to the desk in Pakistan shortly after *Wall Street Journal* correspondent Daniel Pearl was kidnapped and executed there, and she could not bring herself to do it (Doland, 12).

Each correspondent has had to make the individual decision of whether chasing a story was worth the risk of going around the globe, or even around another corner:

[A] big explosion . . . killed and injured 200, mostly women and children [in Beirut]. . . . [T]here were militiamen running up and down the street shooting in the air, the whole thing, they could have been just trashed by these incoming shells. And some people were afraid to go. And I went. And there was this big discussion after that, and it wasn't that you were a coward if you didn't go and you were brave if you did go, it's that I felt okay turning the corner and going down that street. Other people couldn't turn that corner, alright? . . . [Getting killed] never crossed my mind, but I did think when I turned the corner, where's the next doorway I can duck into in case it gets dicey. And that's what I did, turned a corner, got into a doorway . . . which we did very often because a neighborhood would explode and we'd be standing out there and we'd have to take shelter. If a family discovered that you were standing in their doorway, they would come down with coffee for you because you were a guest in their home. And they wanted to make you comfortable. So here you are, the streets blowing up or there's smoke all over the street, guys are shooting in the air, people are running back and forth, and you're standing in a doorway and someone is coming down with a hot cup of Lebanese coffee for you. (Powell, 4–5)

CONCLUSIONS

Deadly peril has been troublingly ubiquitous for correspondents as eyewitnesses to violence bent on a quest for accuracy and verification, down to counting corpses in morgues and hospitals across the world. Just being in battlefields is inherently dangerous, and even the protection of U.S. troops, such as in embeds, means reporters run the same risks as soldiers. Worse are fluid, fast-breaking civil wars, where close calls come anytime, anywhere, from a helicopter gunship overhead to an ambush, from sniper fire to kidnappings to being locked up in cells with blood smears on the walls and guards shaking guns in your face. Being a foreign journalist entails its own targeted violence, from angry mobs to beatings to death threats, the latter often coming from those in power. Correspondents are acutely aware of those dangers too – being told by Iranian officials that they cannot "guarantee their safety," awakened by "we know who you are" phone calls in El Salvador, or pulled out of the car by Syrian rebels who disliked an American journalist "moving around."

Over the years, they have taken increasing precautions to minimize risk, from wearing body armor (but never weapons) to ad hoc measures such as not traveling alone, taping a large "TV" on their vehicles (which some called a sign of more innocent times, since today in many countries that would be like painting a bull's eye), and checking their cars for explosives or themselves for radiation. Risk calculation sometimes put correspondents and editors at odds, especially in consistently deadly places like Beirut or Baghdad, and made some areas, such as Syria or Mexico's cartel-run states, no-go zones. Even there, however, correspondents continue to push, reassessing kilometer by kilometer how far to go, especially when they are on a mission to investigate suspicious deaths. Finding, numbering, and examining bodies is necessary to see through lies, especially since AP takes seriously its role as "basis" for other media. Told that three people had been killed, one correspondent went out and "pointed fingers" at 179 corpses. Before accusing the Pentagon of war crimes, others closely examined a crippled cadaver.

Obviously, the toll of "an afternoon of watching corpses get hosed down by people in radiation suits" traumatizes correspondents into wondering whether it is worthwhile – briefly, because on the scene there is too much work to do, and thinking too much about it later might keep them from what they really want, which is to go back out the next day and write more significant stories. Reporters do break down when faced with particular horror – infants killed by phosphorus still smoking in a hospital bucket, getting a dead colleague away through a gauntlet of sniper fire – but their cure is at most a short break into an ill-fitting "normal" world that seems unaware. All correspondents said that no story is worth a life, meaning the high likelihood of death, not its possibility, which shadows some of them for decades, and all of them when they run "where nobody in their right mind would necessarily want to go." They take those risks because it matters to tell the world the true stories of those who suffer far more than journalists – and who still bring them hot coffee while they huddle in a doorway during a gunfight. Another factor that pulls correspondents through danger and trauma is tight teamwork – and a dash of competition – with their colleagues, which Chapter 8 discusses.

Japan's Earthquake, Tsunami, and Nuclear Meltdown, 2011

Malcom Foster: Japan has an early warning system ... like 10 or 15 seconds. But we saw that [alert] and kind of like, "Whoa, that's scary." And suddenly it started shaking, like 10 seconds later. ... I could hear the building groan and squeak, and the blinds were rattling against the window. ... I'm texting – or using Communicator to text the desk saying, "There's a huge earthquake going on here." And I'm trying to start to type a news alert to say "Japan hit by a major earthquake and Tokyo buildings sway." [...] I wanted to say that we could feel, and so, bang, I sent that out, I think while it was still shaking. I remember having a hard time even typing that because [the keyboard] was literally still moving. And I thought for a second, "Maybe this building is going to come down." And then you think about your family and your life and you're like, "Wow, is this it?" Fortunately it subsided and the Asia desk sent out that alert, and we were proud of this because we were [one of the] first in kind of reporting it (Foster, 3–5).

Eric Talmadge: I was interviewing an innkeeper who was right on the shore, everything is just wiped out. Her inn survived but there was a car, it had been thrown by the tsunami onto her front yard. ... [A]larms go off and this police patrol comes by and says, "Get out of here! Get out of here!" We ignored them. And then another patrol came by, and then a third patrol – this time military – came by and they forced us to leave, to go to high ground. ... "A big tsunami has been confirmed, on its way. It'll hit within 20 minutes. It's going to be bigger than the initial tsunami was." ... We're sitting on this hill and pretty much everybody was a professional first responder, and us. And we're just looking out at the ocean, waiting for the tsunami to come, and all of a sudden, we hear this loud explosion, and it really reminded me of being back in Baghdad with the bombs dropping, and so I might have hit the deck, but I definitely did that kind of a response, and then we kind of look up again and we see some smoke and we're thinking, that tsunami must have hit something. The tsunami must be coming in. ...

[W]e waited a few minutes, and the chief fire department guy had a megaphone and he says, "The number three reactor just exploded." ... And we could see it, we could see that's where the smoke was coming from, when it blew up. And we felt it; we feel the vibration from the explosion. So we're all sitting up on this hill and now the reactor has just blown up. We had been told that a big tsunami is coming in, and the water line from the other one was just below where we were, so if it was bigger, you know, we're toast, but there's nowhere to go. . . . It was a . . . false alarm. And we're still sitting there, thinking, "Wow, we have no idea how much radiation we just took." That was a nuclear reactor that just exploded. And we could feel that explosion (Talmadge, 7–8).

8

Your Byline Today, Mine Tomorrow: Teamwork and Competition

Far from lone wolves, correspondents most often worked in teams, developing their closest ties with fellow APers, but also across the competition. Few examples illustrate the critical importance, and heartbreaking closeness, of this spirit better than what Tony Smith (10–12) faced with the handful of foreign journalists who had gone into Sarajevo as the siege began in 1992: AP photographers Santiago Lyon and David Brauchli, North Star photographer Peter Northall, and Jordi Pujol and Eric Hauck of the Catalan newspaper *Avui*. They had devised the strategy of splitting into pairs, each doing 90-minute patrols in different parts of the violent city to minimize risk and maximize newsgathering. One morning, Brauchli and Pujol did not come back. The two remaining pairs went out to mount a search and, after locals said they had seen them go up a road before a shell attack, tried calling the hospital. Getting no answer, they went there – and found Brauchli having shrapnel removed from half his body, without anesthesia, while 26-year-old Pujol, who had not been wearing a flak vest, had been killed on the spot.

"It was strange, really, because the coverage goes on, but you don't really notice it in a way,"[1] Smith recalled. In the next few "surreal" days, in addition to continuing to cover the news, Smith not only found someone to make a coffin (a high-demand but essential item, since with no electricity "it was all a little bit stinky") and bought a car with enough gas, but also waited for the doctors' okay that Brauchli, with no painkillers, could "risk" the trip out, and tried to arrange some transportation protection from international officials. After "breaking

---

[1] In Tony Smith, "Bosnian troops call off assault on army barracks," The Associated Press, May 17, 1992, Pujol's death came in the fifth paragraph: "Fighting overnight Saturday died down near daybreak, but an exploding mortar shell killed Jordi Pujol, a photographer for Spain's Catalan-language daily *Avui*, and wounded Associated Press photographer David Brauchli. He was operated on for shrapnel in the head, groin and arm. It was the first death of a journalist in the Bosnian war, which has killed 1,300 people and created 700,000 refugees in 10 weeks."

down" in the office – thinking "I can't do this . . . the goal post keeps moving, and it's not really, it's not fair" – Smith decided there was "no point in relying on the kindness of the UN because they couldn't find their arsehole with two hands and a roadmap." So the journalists made their own plan out of Sarajevo aiming for Split, about 100 miles away or a 12-hour drive then, with the "catatonic" Brauchli in the reclined seat of the "injured Toyota Corolla":

[W]e raced along the sniper alley. . . . It was probably the most scared I've ever been in my life . . . and you're thinking, "Well, okay, this is, this is it. We're trying, we're doing what we're supposed to do, this is the right thing to do and we've just got to try and do it." And so we got out of Sarajevo . . . there were roadblocks and [the more fanatical types of] militias and you really didn't know what was going to happen. . . . And we got to a point where it was just impossible to go any farther because . . . some civilian guys had told us, "Don't do that, don't go down there because they'll have you." And so the way to go past that was to go up the mountain . . . really bad, rocky, unpaved roads. With David in the state he was in . . . every time the pain got too much, he'd be singing "American Pie." I don't know why he did that. . . . And we finally came down the mountain, everybody in one piece, and . . . the Croatian police stopped us, said, "Where are your papers?" "Well, I don't have any. They've gone. . . . Our colleague here has just been wounded in Sarajevo, we've got a coffin in the other car. We need to get to the airport in Split, can we go please?" And he wouldn't, he just wouldn't. . . . [W]ith his walkie-talkie he goes off to the car, and I said, "Guys, we're going. Let's go." And so we just drove away, and the guy is like, couldn't believe it. And we were on the outskirts of Split already, so we just drove to the airport. . . . [AP editors] had arranged for the medevac plane to be there. And sure enough it was, so we hoisted David off onto the runway, put him on the plane . . . and off he went. And there was the whole thing to deal with the body. . . . And then I had to write this. They asked me to write it. It was the only time I did, I'd ever done a first-person.[2]

A day spent driving a severely wounded AP colleague and the body of another journalist through a vicious civil war and capped by writing about the experience on deadline is, thankfully, not typical, but the tightness of the bonds it reveals – and the ever-present necessity to feed the wire – does encapsulate the group dynamics of foreign correspondence. For a cooperative wire service like AP – which competes with everyone, including its members, but has a very low public profile for individual writers, whose bylines other publications often forgo – three interactions are crucial. Inside the bureau is, first, the unique wire-agency dynamic between the reporters "desking" (editing and often writing) and those out in the field, with bylines often a sign of teamwork rather than glory, and then the essential partnership between expatriate correspondents and "local hires." Outside is cutthroat competition but also comradeship with other foreign correspondents. The latter two

---

[2] Tony Smith, "Tearful farewell, then a drive past desperate refugees," The Associated Press, May 21, 1992. A writer for *The Guardian* also traveled out with Smith and wrote about the experience, including a blistering critique of the UN's inability to help; Maggie O'Kane, "Escape from Sarajevo," *The Guardian*, May 21, 1992.

interactions are undergoing significant changes today, with the industrywide reduction of foreign staff and the increasing reliance on journalists hired on-site. While "locals" tend to have better sources and more nuanced understanding of their country, not to mention language fluency, they have also brought different sensibilities to stories and are far more vulnerable to foreign government pressures. As longtime Middle East correspondent Eileen Powell (10) put it, "They have to live in Iraq when I go home. Okay? So these people put their lives on the line to report."

INSIDE THE BUREAU: SHARING BURDENS AND TRADING BYLINES

Teamwork is an essential and delicate routine, one in which the coordination necessary for a news wire "of record" leaves little room for egos. From Iraq's invasion of Kuwait in the summer of 1990 to the end of the Gulf War in spring 1991, roving correspondent and future Pulitzer Prize winner Charles Hanley (10–11) often wrote the main war story – in New York, under the bylines of the reporters in the Persian Gulf, Saudi Arabia, or accompanying U.S. troops:

Somebody at some desk somewhere may actually do the writing, but the byline will go to the person at the scene who, at times, actually files a full story but needs an extensive rewrite, and at times simply files notes or even just calls in a couple of fresh facts that a rewrite guy in New York, for example, can then put on top of older material, background material. ... It's sort of a point of honor that you are proud to do good work under somebody else's byline. ... [I]t's just a constant of the way we operate, is that there are anonymous people who are doing a lot of good writing under other people's bylines.

Especially on major events, such as a hugely popular pope's death (see this chapter's box) or wars covered on multiple fronts, reporters in the field feed news into central desks. There, editors – often other correspondents doing "desk duty," which one equated to "orchestra conductor" (Reid, 53) – put together stories, with bylines matching the reporting datelines and a combination of narratives that correspondents on breaking news assignments could rarely provide individually (Rosenblum 2010, 117). Sometimes the greenest reporters might get sent to cover breaking news precisely because they are too inexperienced to handle the desk, either its filing system or the deeper context. Donna Bryson (4) remembered an early story in apartheid South Africa, a township shooting where she "just got in the car with the photographer and went," barely knowing the layout:

I dictated the scene to more experienced reporters in the bureau, reporters who actually understood what was happening. I could tell them what I saw, what the consequences of the violence were, but I would take some time to learn what the roots of the violence were, what the real context was.

Angela Doland (4) similarly recalled her "first really big story," the Concorde crash outside Paris that killed 113 people in 2000. As "the most inexperienced person in the bureau and ... not experienced in banging out alerts," she provided eyewitness details of the "barely recognizable" fuselage, among the "scattered, smoking chunks" of the hotel it hit, for what turned out to be a team effort:[3]

I always felt very humbled by that experience, because there was this story about the Concorde crashing – it was my byline. When I woke up the next day, you see so many things and you realize how hard everyone else was working, and you just think, it's just amazing. It's really amazing.

Frictions do arise, as noted in Chapter 11, but most correspondents have worked at both ends and, while considering the desk job often thankless and far less stimulating than being on the scene, they appreciate the crucial selfless dynamic. In Kabul toward the end of the Soviet war, Maureen Johnson (19, 26) called material into the New Delhi bureau: "They would be there at 2 o'clock in the morning their time, taking some pretty incoherent dictation from me and turning it into a polished story ... for which I got all the glory.[4] ... There's nothing very exciting about sitting up at 2 in the morning getting somebody else's dictation, is there?" In some cases there is, as when David Crary (8), then news editor in South Africa, decided to send another correspondent "to be outside of the prison in Cape Town along with a couple hundred other reporters for that magic moment when [Nelson Mandela] walked out":

That would have been fun to be there, but I was actually the one who wrote the bulletin and got to press the button and send out the first few paragraphs, which was a thrill. I never regret making that choice to actually be the one who wrote that. Under somebody else's byline of course.

Where major breaking news broke, correspondents went in from around the world, both to "free up" bureaus by taking on "desking" and also to report, which gave more experienced writers enough time away from the nitty-gritty (and allowed the newcomers to discover angles that might have escaped those immersed in the scene). In the 1990s to 2000s, Paul Alexander (1–2) mixed dangerous reporting assignments, such as Somalia, with editing in South Korea, Pakistan, and Thailand during the 2004 Southeast Asian tsunami. From Cairo, news editor Donna Bryson (79–80) went over to Kosovo "just to kind of add my body to all the people working on the story" of the country's war – though her hope that she would at least be ready to handle names she knew in Arabic was quickly dashed: "You want to spell Mohammed like *what*?" In the mid-2000s, Bryson (50–51) became editor of the brand-new Africa desk, then based in London, having daily conference calls with reporters across the continent about story ideas, editing

[3] Angela Doland, "Concorde crashes outside Paris; at least 113 killed," The Associated Press, July 25, 2000.
[4] Such as this take on Kabul after the Soviets left: Maureen Johnson, "Food, fuel and optimism in short supply in beleaguered Kabul," The Associated Press, January 28, 1989.

features, and taking on the saddest managerial duty – going to Nairobi when one of the reporters based there, Anthony Mitchell, died in a plane crash. But in July 2005, when a series of suicide bombings on public transportation killed dozens, she "ran around looking for witnesses ... and calling in color from the crowds": "The London bureau needed people on the streets. And I said, well today I guess we're not going to have an Africa editor."

Major events or issues spread across multiple countries – from wars to the Arab Spring, from Europe's post–World War II reconstruction to the saga of young Cuban emigrant Elián González, from immigration to extremism – require different bureaus and central desks to coordinate even more closely. Covering the late-1940s beginning of the Cold War in Western Europe, Bria (11) recalled some irate correspondents whose stories, about refugees for example, would become a couple of paragraphs in the main daily update put together by New York. Six decades later, coverage of Iraq's sectarian wars – from the daily story count to the security arrangements – filtered through the Cairo hub (Buzbee, 2). In the 2000s, given the emphasis on longer, broader, more "impactful" and "big picture" stories (such as the one about unemployment driving unrest across North Africa discussed in Chapter 3) despite shrinking resources, regional coordination has grown, utilizing AP's unique network:

> Wherever you go, there's an AP office, and you can just basically send out what we call these "all pointers" and get the information, put it together, and it's a great resource. ... People really do pull together on these things. (Laub, 18, 39)

The benefits of mobilizing far-flung AP bureaus range from the mundane – getting a set of foreign ministers' quotes for a single story on some trend – to the dramatic. In the "triple disaster" of Japan's 2011 earthquake, tsunami, and nuclear meltdown, staffers were flown from around the world to keep Tokyo running 24/7, while bureau chief Malcolm Foster (7–8) was "managing and coordinating and being a traffic cop." He called it "a little bit frustrating," wishing he "could have been more involved" in actual coverage, but also important because he could keep focused on the "big picture":

> We had in the end six or seven teams rotating up there, doing different amazing stories about just the destruction they were finding, the search for bodies, the evacuees, how they're coping with it. ... And meanwhile, we don't know exactly what's happening at the [nuclear] plant. They're coming out with drips and drabs of information. So ... we assigned people to be basically camped out at Tepco – the Tokyo Electric Power Company, the owner of the utility – and at NISA, which was the government nuclear agency, because they were having briefings constantly. ... And then there was one person whose job [was] ... to kind of manage that and pick out things that were important and put it into paragraph form that the person that was writing the main bar could put in. And then Jeff [Donn] was sitting across from that person and ... his basic role was the resident expert to help us understand, to make sense of what was going on [with the nuclear crisis]. ... And then we brought an editor who actually filed it to the wire right there. So the writer and the editor and the expert are all within feet of each other and can talk about it. ... I think it

wasn't until the end of April that we kind of felt like we could kind of catch our breath a little bit.

The wars in Afghanistan and Iraq were another "team effort." During the latter, the "war desk" in Doha was manned by correspondents flown in from as far away as Mexico, while others embedded with different armed forces units or went in as independents. Veterans like Bob Reid took turns leading the reporting in Baghdad by correspondents rotating in and out for a few months and by local Iraqis. "Even the drivers were great journalists ... and they would lead us to stories time and time again," including one, later to become a political correspondent, who connected Hanley (23) with three Iraqi colonels for a story on "the Iraqi side of the fight ... great detail, great color, great tragedy from these three colonels and what they and their unit went through. They each had command of a battalion." Hanley's story described the three officers "at home, out of uniform, in the maze of narrow streets that forms north Baghdad's vast Shiite Muslim ghetto – a place of flies, heat, the stench of raw sewage," as they recalled their subordinates "deserting in droves in the night."[5]

Working as a Team, Even as Family

While tempers do occasionally flare during such huge efforts, all correspondents have considered fellow APers part of the essential team that gets the job done. As Reid (38) put it, "I really don't know that there is any [story] that I can say, I could have done this completely on my own," whether the help came from an interpreter coming up with the revealing question, "a sharp editor on a desk [who] says, you missed a lead but the fifth graph is perfect," or a colleague selflessly filing your story. During the Soviet war in Afghanistan, for example, Barry Shlachter flew from New Delhi to Kabul to join Reid (12–14), who had arrived there suddenly from Germany. Eager to get notes from his "fat little notebook" to the more experienced colleague, and the wire, Reid found him at the airport, held up by Afghan officials but already mining his sources, such as diplomats trying to leave:

We went up to this big coffee shop that was in a terminal building in Kabul. I started dictating my notes, because the assumption was that Shlachter would write stories – in fact he's the expert in the field, and I am just pitching in. So he's feverishly taking the notes, and there were a couple of other people at the table too, other reporters from Delhi. Then another guy walks up ... and he says, "Bad news. I was just downstairs and they decided to kick us all out. They're just trying to figure out what time the plane leaves." So I said, "Well, gentlemen, it's been a pleasure, but I have a visa stamped in my passport and I'm going to leave so I don't get caught up in this dragnet." So I shook hands with Shlachter and walked out the door, fairly comfortable and confident, because if they

---

[5] Charles J. Hanley, "Courage, despair, incompetence: The defeated look back on their war," The Associated Press, May 31, 2003.

did kick Shlachter out, he could file from Delhi. . . . [I]t was better that he left than two of us trapped in this no-communications place.

AP's capillary network gives globe-trotting correspondents an advantage that single reporters might not have. Even going on short notice to a treacherous, war-ravaged country like Somalia for the first time, APers found stringers, colleagues from around the region, a basic infrastructure already set up. That might be why, some wryly noted, even big-press correspondents tended to "mooch" around their national wire services, asking, "Hey, what's going on today? Hey, can we see what you've been writing?" and then came up with their own take, on a more leisurely deadline (Gray, 36; also Doelling, 22). The very nature of the wire service and the desk/field routines noted earlier foster collaboration among everyone, down to "those people who were hired without your knowledge and just walk in one day and start to work," as George McArthur (15) quipped.

In the Korean War, he had been the most junior of half a dozen AP reporters who wrote front-page stories while he picked up the leftovers. In wartime Saigon, he oversaw a staff of around 35, including various award-winning journalists with more than a decade's experience in Vietnam and the first woman on a long-term AP assignment there, Edie Lederer, who "was a surprise in the sense that wherever she went, she made her way. There's a saying in the wire service business: 'If they have to tell you to do it, it's already too late.' . . . You were not aware after the initial exposure to her . . . voice that she was a woman. She was a colleague, she was one of us" (McArthur, 17). Pyle (2), who took over from McArthur in Saigon, found that one key to oiling the teamwork wheels was that bosses came up from the staff, having earned their creds on the battlefield, "and we were all focused on the same thing. . . . And my best friends in the world today, in 2012, are the people I worked with in Vietnam."

Bureau routines, especially at times of mounting danger and professional demands, show that the dynamics often approximated those of friends or even families – drama-filled as those might be. The occasional meltdown between editors and writers was taken in stride when everyone was working 20 hours a day while mortar shells fell outside the office – even in the one case when a reporter and editor were married to each other, and having distinctly separate professional tasks was "the only reason that we didn't divorce or kill each other" in 18 years working together overseas (Powell, 1). Anderson (3, 15) recalled – fondly – how Pyle once slammed the wastebasket onto the wall in the Tokyo bureau after "somebody blew something on the wires," and how he himself in Beirut chased a reporter who had run into the bathroom after bursting into angry tears over an assignment:

I went and pounded over that door, "Scheherezade, write now, cry later." DELL'ORTO: How did that go over? ANDERSON: She came out. It . . . just was an enormously fascinating job. Again, I am not trying to minimize the toll it was taking on everybody – not just me, on everybody.

And just like in a big family, sometimes even pets became part of the team – levity amid horrifying occasions, as Mort Rosenblum's (36) dog, Odious Beast, or O.B., provided when he would not let his master sleep through a post-party night in Argentina after hearing an explosion:

Turns out that [former Chilean army officer] Carlos Prats, the guerrillas had put a bomb under his car and blown him so high that his car was like on the fourth floor and the steering wheel is on the 14th floor, and he was on all floors. . . . So, again, this was a story that I had in the middle of the night and by the time everybody else woke up, they were way behind. So in my expense account, I wrote, "chopped meat for stringer, $5."

Outside of wartime bureaus, former correspondents who had become news editors and bureau chiefs were recalled with admiration for always being there for brand-new reporters – like a "gracious" Debbie Seward when a 21-year-old correspondent in Paris called up late at night to ask, "What does this French legal term mean?" (Doland, 2) – and for getting out of the way of experienced ones. Local managers also acted as buffers between correspondents in their bureaus and editors in New York. Longtime London bureau chief Myron Belkind (18) knew that it was his phone that would ring if AP's president believed that London "had a fall-down on the news side," and, when major news broke, Brazil chief of bureau Claude Erbsen (10) "locked up the business files and . . . moved to the newsroom."

In Vietnam, Tad Bartimus (13, 16–17; 2002, 195) knew that AP president Wes Gallagher had charged her editors with keeping her – one of the first women assigned to cover war – alive, and so she was not supposed to be let out of Saigon. Soon enough, she and bureau chief George Esper reached an "unspoken truce that as long as I was sensible and I was operating with either a driver or a translator or a photographer, that I could go wherever." However, it took one big fight over a story Bartimus reported on limbless Vietnamese veterans who "considered it to be a blessing because they were Buddhists and they believed that because they had had so much suffering in this world, it would serve them well in the next." Esper could not believe it, Bartimus said, until he talked with the veterans himself:

From that moment on, I had [my] freedom. . . . George finally accepted that, okay, you're one of us. You're going to take your chances. If something happens, so be it. You're a big girl now. And it was the best compliment I could be paid. Because then, it was like I had the ankle bracelet off.

A few weeks later, Bartimus and Lederer – who had shared her resources with the new arrival, from her embassy contacts to her tailor – found themselves overseeing Cambodia coverage for several days. A "huge rocket attack" – whose progress they mapped using a Tampax in lieu of a ruler – had isolated Phnom Penh after they had been left in charge while the regular staffers took a day off at the beach (Bartimus 2002, 206). Eventually, to her enduring chagrin, Bartimus (23–24) had to leave Vietnam after falling seriously ill with an undiagnosed disease (later believed linked to Agent Orange) that left her unable to sit up and turned her tongue and eyeballs black. Undergoing tests for nearly a month in New York, she recalled how every day Gallagher "would come by that hospital and sit at the foot of my bed and talk to me for 15 or 20 minutes before he caught the train home."

Like Lederer and Bartimus, most correspondents also worked closely with – and relied for sources, experience, even protection on – AP photographers (and, later, videographers, who from the mid-1990s worked for APTV/APTN, the video news unit), whose bylines also occasionally appeared on the wire (as for Max Desfor [6] during the Korean War). In today's multimedia age, that coordination has increased from the traditional sharing of ideas followed by a belated "get photos for this story" to going together on most assignments and integrating all formats in the finished product.

EXPATS AND LOCALS: AN IDEAL TEAM

Often, photographers were "locals," natives of the country who worked for AP in a vast range of roles, from occasional fixers to one-country stringers to full-time, multi-decade staffers. The relationship between local and expatriate, mostly American, correspondents has been essential to newsgathering (not just at AP; Murrell 2015 details the centrality of fixers for TV correspondents, not only logistically but editorially). As one longtime Asia editor put it, "they were the backbone ... I don't think we could have done without them" (Liu, 21). "Locals" brought to the AP team unmatched knowledge of their area – its language, politics, culture, sensitivities, sources, and danger signs – and, in the case of experienced staff (working for the main English-language wire as well as affiliated ones in other languages), unique contextual and analytical insights, making them "unsung heroes" to many correspondents.

From El Salvador to Somalia, they also helped "parachuting" correspondents talk through checkpoints, track down black-market diesel, and arrange the necessary introductions for interviews (Alexander, 6–7; Frazier, 3). And they stepped in where Americans could not go, either because local governments would not allow them (such as during India's military operation against Sikh rebels in Amritsar or during the U.S.-Iran hostage crisis) or because of visa restrictions (such as in Afghanistan during some of the Soviet war) or because of the risk of violent anti-American feelings (such as in parts of Indonesia during the "war on terror") (Graham, 21; Johnson, 1–2, 18; McDowell, 15).

Today, the full-time local staff is getting more independent recognition as equal team partners instead of being seen as those sitting on breaking news until the Americans got there and could do the "deeper" investigations. The credit is well deserved for expertise, reporting skills, and news judgment developed in some cases over decades covering countries inaccessible to Westerners, like Burma. Oppressive governments, however, hardly foster local traditions of vibrant journalism, so newsgathering by less experienced local staff often requires substantial training before it adheres to U.S. correspondents' standards and techniques – such as basic objectivity, balance, and truly independent "vox pop." And then there are U.S. idiosyncrasies: Jean Lee (15) had to prepare new North Korean staff for Dennis Rodman's arrival in Pyongyang by showing them a picture of the former NBA star, with his tattoos, pierced nose, and dyed hair, "because I knew that it would be shocking."

At the bureau level, both rookie and experienced correspondents have long partnered up (Weissenstein, 3) with locals on story ideas as well as the logistical feasibility of reporting, and the differences in nationality are increasingly irrelevant. Newly arrived in Beijing to reopen the first post-Mao bureau, Vicki Graham (3, 9) first relied on an interpreter who scanned the local press for relevant news buried in the dense Party prose. Then, she made a daily habit – morning, afternoon, and again in the evening – of checking the posters that petitioners from around China put up on "Democracy Wall," which ran several meters along Xidan Street, along with Chinese AP photographer Liu Heung Shing – the two often traveling on a dark green motorcycle, Graham in the sidecar. One of her stories about the "fiery posters" that while "fading . . . still speak" contained Liu's translations of more than a dozen (ranging from soldiers wanting a job to a native of Hunan protesting the curses from a fellow poster writer) as well as of the signs atop the wall, warning "Lock your bicycle before looking at wall posters."[6]

Alexander (27), who covered treacherous conflicts across continents, including the Bosnian War, relied not only on the "leg work" done by fixers and interpreters, but on their sense of threat – learning not to press on or at least to take a break and huddle if they "started getting visibly antsy." Local staff at all levels has been fiercely protective of foreign correspondents. The former Yugoslav army officer who stood guard outside the AP Sarajevo office, eyesight failing but rifle at the ready, one evening refused to let in Bono and the Bosnian foreign minister – because the international pop star meant nothing to him, and, as he put it, "Everybody says they're the foreign minister and they come in here and they steal things" (Smith, 15).

In Saigon, Vietnamese staff and their families took under their wings both Lederer (7; 2002, 155) and Bartimus (22; 2002, 199), believing it was a "sacred trust" to look after "the greenie," even when it meant shielding her in a Mekong Delta ditch during a sudden firefight, as Nick Ut – who won a Pulitzer for the iconic photo of a girl burned by napalm – did for Lederer. When Saigon fell to the North Vietnamese, protection for Esper (1998, 546) and the other AP journalists who had remained behind came from an unlikely staffer – a longtime photo stringer who showed up at the bureau with two soldiers to announce he would "guarantee" their safety, since he was in reality a Vietcong spy. The group shared Cokes and "some leftover cake."

---

[6] Victoria Graham, "Today's focus: Voices from the wall," The Associated Press, April 24, 1979.

FIGURE 8.1. Beijing bureau chief Vicki Graham rides through the Chinese capital in the sidecar of the AP motorbike in the early 1980s, soon after helping to reopen the AP bureau. Pulitzer Prize–winning AP photographer Liu Heung Shing drives the bike, with Asia news editor Richard Pyle behind him. (Photo courtesy of Vicki Graham)

While the dangers for foreign correspondents are widespread and increasing, those for local staff can be even higher, because they are subject to far more pressure from foreign governments and groups in power, and they can be perceived as traitors for working for a U.S. organization. Anderson (16) recalled how he once, by mistake, took a Christian driver into a Druze village when the two sides where fighting during the Lebanese civil war: "he was just trembling, because if anybody … asked for his ID card, they'd haul him out and shoot him right on the spot." Another Beirut correspondent, Powell (5–6), described how the American reporters rotated on continuous four-hour shifts at the scene of the 1983 Marine barracks bombing, which killed nearly 250 U.S. troops. But they were "a little hesitant at that point to send some of our Arab reporters because we weren't sure how they were going to be

FIGURE 8.2. In winter 1993 outside the Hotel Belvedere, turned into the AP bureau, correspondents Tony Smith (second row, fourth from left) and Robert Reid (second row, second from left), with members of the AP Sarajevo staff, pose around one of the first "hard car" Land Rovers that made it into the besieged city, giving journalists a modicum of safety. (Photo courtesy of Tony Smith)

received ... [Marines] were pulling guys out, and some of them were alive and some of them were dead, and some of them had pieces – and of course the guys who were doing the rescue were frantic and upset." Her story on the attack described the "frantic Marines, some clad only in bloodstained underwear," combing "the blood-splattered ground littered with shattered glass, singed clothing, helmets and cooking pots" while others "stood and sobbed, stunned by the sight of the massacre."[7]

One 2007 story about the mounting horrors of Sunni-Shiite violence in the Hurriyah district of Baghdad, guarded by "teenage gunmen from the Mahdi Army" who hid among civilians to avoid patrolling U.S. soldiers, cited the precise observations of "an Associated Press reporter who lives in the neighborhood and whose name has been withheld from this story for security reasons. Journalists can be killed for recording the militia's activities." At the end, the story noted, "Material and reporting for this story was gathered by the AP staff in Baghdad. It was written by Associated Press Writer Sally Buzbee, the Chief of Middle East News, who is based in Cairo but frequently works in Iraq."[8] Nearly 40 years after the Khmer Rouge entered Phnom Penh,

---

[7] Eileen Alt Powell, "Grim search for comrades buried in rubble," The Associated Press, October 24, 1983.
[8] Sally Buzbee, "Mixed Baghdad neighborhood now firmly controlled by Shiite radicals," The Associated Press, January 31, 2007.

Gray (9) still mourned not having stayed with the Cambodian staff there, who had "intercepted messages from Khmer Rouge saying, 'You, Khmer, working for American journalists. We will kill you.'" In a story published on the 40th anniversary of his evacuation from Phnom Penh (together with the U.S. ambassador and almost all Americans), Gray wrote he counted himself among the foreigners "haunted to this day ... by the heartbreaking loyalty of Cambodians" who stayed behind, including "more than a dozen Cambodian reporters and photographers – about the bravest, may I say the finest, colleagues I've ever known. Almost all would die."[9]

For the AP "family" working in Israel and the Palestinian territories, facing constant dangers and intimidation forged intense ties between correspondents and locals "because we've all gone through so much together":

Mohammed [Daraghmeh], in the second intifada he lived in Nablus, which was like hell at the time. One time he got arrested by the army in a sweep of his neighborhood ... and after many, many phone calls we got him released ... he had to make his way back home in darkness and there were tanks everywhere and soldiers who were very nervous and afraid and might have easily opened fire on a figure in the dark, not knowing who it was. These were bad times for all concerned. That's the kind of thing that creates a bond for a long time. ... [W]e had written something about gunmen ... the next morning Mohammed found like five friendly gunmen from the neighborhood refugee camp in his office. Fortunately he's a charming guy and he managed to defuse the situation, but they face all kinds of pressures that as a foreigner you maybe do not face ... and they have families here. ... I don't remember any case where this kind of pressure actually worked. (Laub, 15–16)

All correspondents argued that having both expatriate and local staff is the best combination for quality as well as safety: "I might get deported, but I'm not going to disappear into a jail" (Bryson, 27). The mix also provides the variety of perspectives that can unearth fresh angles while contextualizing the story accurately. It ensures that the foreigner is not seeing a story that's not there, but can find stories locals might know so deeply they no longer see them (Rice, 8), like a feature about Tel Aviv's "big thick" phone directory showing "Israel's quirks":

[T]his was in socialist times, phones were hard to get, so there was a pecking order of who got phones. So he wrote about that ... and all sorts of other details – the advertisements that he saw in there, the little bits of the flag – and he wrote a feature about it. Now I would not have thought in a million years to write a feature about the phone book. ... But often he'd need my help. And so I was able to fill in some of the background for him, why is this category of person entitled to a phone ahead of that category of person, and there's always a reason for it. On history, on that sort of thing and the history of the place. ... I think it's symbiotic. (Eliason, 7)

---

[9] Denis D. Gray, "Ambassador: US handed Cambodia to 'butcher' 40 years ago," The Associated Press, April 10, 2015.

In addition to some useful distance, correspondents with a "foot in both worlds at all times" also have a better sense of how to frame a story so that it will interest and enlighten Americans (for decades the primary AP audience) and all readers outside the country itself – "how their story needs to sound for people far away" with little knowledge of the country (Porubcansky, 10; Crary, 17; also Erbsen, 4–5; Buzbee, 3–4):

Why do we call it foreign correspondence? Because it is inherently foreign. . . . [N]ever in our lifetime will we get to a position where regardless of their level of sophistication, regardless of their level of linguistic skills, a Chinese businessman in Shanghai will pick up a paper, or more accurately go to his tablet, read a story, and come away with the same ideas that his counterpart in Milwaukee will, or in any other part of the world. I think there is a delusion . . . that we are getting to the point where one story fits all. Now, that may be true for Twitter, but for anything deeper than that, it's not going to be the case. (Reid, 82–83)

Given U.S. geopolitical predominance, a few correspondents argued that being familiar with American policymaking helps contextualize foreign stories like Iraq's bloodied sectarian war – and gain access to American actors in it – while locals bring to the effort the ability to navigate the foreign country's own political landscape:

There was a military occupation, and U.S. military officials are more willing to deal with and talk to Western reporters – it's unfortunate, but it's true – than reporters who are even Egyptian. We had some excellent regional reporters, but at first we couldn't get them on embeds. . . . We had to have Iraqi staff who could go into Sadr City and hopefully bring a Western reporter along with them and make that work. . . . [W]e had to have people who could go out and see what the U.S. military was doing. And we needed the combination of people who could kind of get into both sides of the story, to get the full picture. (Buzbee, 5)

"Outsider" correspondents can also help keep wartime bureaus "on the straight and narrow" by encouraging local hires of all political stripes to recharge "both your involved batteries and your detached batteries," as one Tel Aviv local-hire-turned-correspondent put it (Eliason, 3). Whether in Iraq (Buzbee, 12) or the former Yugoslavia, resentments from the fratricide wars occasionally spilled over into disagreements in the bureaus, and correspondents had to step into charged conversations over stories, as one recalled doing between the staffers in Belgrade and those in Zagreb (not to mention Sarajevo) by saying, "Look, guys, we're not going to refight WWII here, who did what to whom in WWII. What we're doing here is sort of writing about what's going on today" (Porubcansky, 12–13). Middle East veteran correspondent Robert Fisk (2002, 201–202) of the London *Times* described how AP's Beirut bureau during the early 1980s functioned despite – and because of – staffers from all religious groups and even neighboring countries, who spoke in Arabic to each other and English to the Americans:

The AP bureau worked – unlike much of the country – because there was a mutuality of interest, trust, and friendship. The journalists there had to depend upon each other; there was no other way. Perhaps it was not by chance that the AP functioned so harmoniously; it was the only office I ever entered in Lebanon where almost every religious community was represented.

MY FRIEND, THE COMPETITION

Fisk's own relationship with AP in Beirut is indicative of the tangled ties that bound many foreign correspondents to the wire service, which would both scoop them and serve them. Making the bureau his first stop on arrival back in the Lebanese capital during the 1982 Israeli invasion, Fisk (2002, 197–200) was told to feel free to "go write [his] essays," but to keep out of the way of harried correspondents who were trying to shock into life the broken generator to get breaking news out. Once the international line restarted, he was allowed to sandwich his copy between AP stories for transmission, and, as Israeli tanks came so close that "their shells were smashing into the buildings around the AP office," Fisk returned the favor by alternating at the telex machine, "punching wire copy for the AP. . . . There were times, in the coming weeks, when I suspect my loyalty to these people outweighed my allegiance to *The Times*." Throughout the decades, the pressures of foreign newsgathering brought out both the fiercest competition and the most loyal collaborations among correspondents for AP and other media.

For most of the 20th century, AP's nemesis was United Press (later UPI), which had been explicitly founded in 1907 to do the "impossible – buck the Associated Press on a shoestring" (Morris 1957, 23), and the fight between "ROX" and "UNIPRESS" (to use the services' wire nicknames) echoed across hot and cold war battlefields (Prochnau 1995, 230; Daniloff 2008, 40). One Korean War correspondent chuckled at the recollection of how, eager to get to camp to transmit a story about the first day of truce talks, he jumped into a jeep just ahead of the United Press bureau chief and visiting president, and "they tried to pass me, and I took off, so they went into the ditch and I got a big beat" (Summerlin, 4–5). Lederer (9) remembered how reporters in Vietnam – no names mentioned – "didn't think anything about pulling out phone wires" after using a phone so that competitors could not make a call (on the intense wire competition in Saigon, see Ferrari 2003, 176). What drove George Bria (13) in postwar Rome was "to get the play" in U.S. media instead of UP, and still in the 1970s, one of his successors there said, "[O]ur job was to beat them, and their job was to beat us. Okay? And every day we were out there" (Simpson, 3).

Minutes mattered in the international wire competition. Taking an extra few to have "every Indian on the phone talking to every hospital" to confirm whether India's prime minister Indira Gandhi had died in an assassination attempt meant coming in second after Reuters, and "New York was beside

FIGURE 8.3. Korean War correspondent Sam Summerlin (to left of flash) waits with other U.S. reporters for the release of American prisoners of war. (Photo courtesy of Claire Slattery)

themselves. ... I don't blame them. We [in Delhi] were too" (Graham, 22). Having just succeeded in verifying reports that South Korea's president Park Chung-hee had been assassinated, Anderson (5–6) was phoning the news to editors in New York when a Reuters correspondent, locked out of his own Seoul office in the middle of the night, walked into the AP bureau, heard him and reached for a phone to call his editors. "I love you, but if you touch that phone, I'll break your fucking arm. Get out of my office now," Anderson recalled blurting at him. While covering the court martial in Somalia of a soldier who had fired at a thief in a crowd for grabbing sunglasses off his face, Alexander (11–12) decided not to join a Reuters colleague for lunch – "you didn't want to take any risk of missing out on a development" – and instead to wait for the verdict despite being told the jury would go on break. When they came back with the verdict right away, he got the story out and was back in court for the sentencing, scoring a three-hour beat.

With stories moving instantaneously online, today "it's very difficult to be surprised by what the opposition is doing, because you can see all the time" (Perry, 21). But before the digital era, back when the major newspapers were not on constant deadlines, big-time correspondents could focus only on the most interesting stories, leaving everything else "to the wire reporters" – who then still got messages from New York asking why they had not produced those analytical pieces too, further spurring competition. After John Roderick (1993, 56) and two New York journalists interviewed a deputy of Mao's in Yan'an in the 1940s, the AP man wrote his story immediately, but the others asked him to wait so they could all send copy together when the two returned to Beijing. Taking an extra day to rest there, they were jolted awake by angry cables from their papers, which had seen the story that Roderick had given to the journalists' pilot to deliver to AP "Beiping," which had forwarded it to New York. In China 30 years later, Graham (8) and Liu left the Peking Hotel telling an inquisitive reporter for the *New York Times* that they were "just going to walk around, it's so pretty around the canal" – only to run into that same reporter at their real destination, "the first hip, trendy café for young people," a revealing harbinger that "things were loosening up" whose story now the *Times* had to get out fast too, to compete with AP.

Competitors also knew when to bury the hatchet, and not just over late-night drinks in hotel bars, though plenty of that also happened: "we'd compare notes at the end of the day but not during the day," as Africa hand Larry Heinzerling (4) put it. Cooperation won the day when logistics made it necessary. Rosenblum (43; 2010, 111), desperate to get to Romania to cover its revolution, chartered a plane from Paris (after getting a half-asleep authorization from New York to invest the $5,000) with photographers from other agencies as well as two correspondents whose deadlines, and circulation, did not pose a real threat. In the 1980s Iran-Iraq War, Hanley (9) and a Reuters reporter, who had just arrived from another assignment in the Gulf in a three-piece suit, scrambled up a desert hill to verify exactly where the frontline action was (just as another colleague was doing along the Jordan-Syria border to "check reports of troop buildups").[10] Meanwhile the correspondent for a major U.S. newspaper stayed safely under cover, leaving it to the wire men:

[W]e went right to the very front because the Iranians wanted to demonstrate that they had taken back Iranian territory that had been lost to the Iraqis. . . . We looked up at one point and an Iraqi plane, a Mirage, had been shot down and we could see the pilot parachuting down and we see the plane plunging to the earth. So this was a real hot area. We pulled behind . . . the defilade of a little hill for protection. . . . [T]he Reuters guy and I went around the hill, climbed up the next hill, which still had trenches filled with Revolutionary Guards, and we crept up to the top of the hill. He's still in his three-piece suit. . . . And we look over this ridge, and all we could see is this flat plain just extending forever. And I knew. I turned to him and I said, "That's the Tigris and Euphrates plain. That's Iraq. So they pushed them back to the border." And he finally agreed, and meantime, we looked and we saw that there were two Iraqi tanks about half a mile from us, firing – that's where the shells were coming from, firing over our heads.

Sometimes dangers became so acute that survival depended on staying together, and mattered more than scoops. When mobs turned on journalists

---

[10] Nicolas B. Tatro, The Associated Press, November 28, 1980.

in Saigon during the Vietnam War, correspondents physically rescued one another (Arnett 1994, 118). In Mogadishu shortly after the Black Hawk Down incident, when Americans were targets for kidnapping and execution, CNN staffers distributed walkie-talkies for reporters to alert one another of "hot" areas; Alexander (8), who had been there longer than most, used one while on an "early recon mission" that took him among "all these guys walking with RPGs and AK-47s, just like they're walking to work, just trudging to work, towards the Green Line." AP burden-sharing had brought Alexander (4–5) to Somalia to begin with, since the regional bureau chief was back in the United States where his wife was about to give birth, the regular correspondent had been kidnapped on her last visit, and a local writer had had to retrieve the bodies of colleagues murdered by a mob. Just as he arrived, rumors started that the captured U.S. pilot was about to be released and Aidid would shortly give a news conference – events Alexander managed to get details on only because a cameraman with Worldwide TV News, whom he had befriended over his signature drink "Shithole Sour," let him see the footage, including some swapped with CNN: "So I had been on the ground like two and a half hours and I'm dictating on two urgent stories just because I was lucky and friends with somebody who could help me out." Decades earlier, another correspondent, newly arrived in Cairo with no experience of the Middle East, was greeted on his first day by the dreaded "rocket" cable message from editors in New York – "How, please?" – how had he missed a story about an archeological discovery:

[I] called the Reuters correspondent and introduced myself, freshly arrived from Hong Kong, and . . . I said, "I don't know a darned thing about sarcophaguses, and where did you get this? You know it's all very well to beat the opposition but it's always good to have company and if you're the only one they might doubt you, but I can trail in several hours later with a corroborating story." And he gave me the numbers to call. (AP Oral History, Essoyan 1997, 62)

Many other correspondents gratefully recalled how, arriving with no experience in unexpected postings, they had turned to the foreign press corps for "the fill" – "on what the story is, who the sources are" (Rosenblum, 18) – and as "sounding boards." Smith (5), who found himself in Angola though his academic expertise was in Yugoslavia, relied on a Yugoslav correspondent to check out rumors. Local media, which with their far larger staffs cannot count as competition, also helped orient correspondents – sometimes literally, as when smaller AP bureaus were inside a local newspaper building that subscribed to the wire (Olmos, 14; Hurst, 2) or when one correspondent traded car rides to press conferences for tips on guerrilla sources from Mexican reporters stuck on local transportation (Snow, 9).

Part of that truce in competition might be due to the unique nature of a cooperative wire service. Until the digital era, the public would only see AP news that newspapers or broadcasters put out, so stories were on the wire for other media to study hours before other correspondents' deadlines

(Cooperman, 18; Seward, 3). But some stems from genuine camaraderie, as when a group of white, male correspondents going to interview a pro-apartheid activist who had climbed a South African monument refused to be deterred by the suspicion that, with Bryson (16) in their midst, the activist might refuse to talk (he did not). In Moscow, AP's Alan Cooperman (14) managed to witness Gorbachev's signing his resignation – penning the end of the Cold War – and the folded-up USSR flag being taken off the Kremlin because CNN had shared with him their exclusive access. Perhaps the best description of the inextricable mix of ruthless competition over news and fierce personal bonds comes from Fisk's account (2002, 584–630) of his reaction when, stuck in a snowstorm on the way to Damascus for Anderson's anticipated release, he heard the BBC announce that his friend was finally free:

I banged my fist on the door of my frozen car and shouted "Goddammit!" Can such selfishness be forgiven? ... With every Shiite leader, I had pleaded for Terry's release. Not a month earlier, I had at last met Terry's own kidnappers face to face and asked them to show compassion for Terry. And now that one imperishable moment – of Terry's release – was to be shared by reporters in Damascus who refused even to travel to Lebanon, while I sat in the frost on Sannine.

The stimulating competition and the team spirit long meant that "if one of us got it wrong, the others didn't. And there was pressure on us not to get it wrong" (Rosenblum, 46). That is why several reporters said that their job has changed because of today's rapidly thinning ranks of foreign correspondents across the industry. In the words of roving correspondent Rosenblum (18), foreign correspondents ("trained people with expense accounts in bases that know each other") used to work as a pack of coyotes – one getting the first bite, the others catching up and leaving the bones picked clean. Now, they resemble a bunch of hyenas:

We all just skulk around, avoiding each other, and dart out of the bushes and grab whatever we can and pull it back into the bushes and gnaw as much as we can and then go away and leave the rest to rot. And so, that's the only way you can stay alive if you're totally independent, but moving out of the metaphor and into reality, that means that nobody knows the real story.

Going solo means more freedom to choose what to cover without worrying about "matching" what others (sometimes hundreds of others, as in wars) are doing, but also growing dangers for isolated reporters, as the gruesome beheadings of freelancers in Syria showed. Stevenson (17–18), who often ventures deep into Mexican cartel territory where progressively fewer others dare go, said he missed the drive to "get to the town before the *New York Times* did":

[I]t's very rare nowadays to meet another foreign correspondent out in the field. ... Even in ... this year's [2013] presidential election – and usually in presidential elections you'll see a pretty good gathering – I was down at the winning party's headquarters, this is the place you want to be, right? ... I saw two, three other correspondents there. ... Was it fun [before]? Yeah, there was a kind of crowd dynamic that made it fun. There was a sense of competition that kept you on your toes. Do I miss it terribly, terribly, terribly? No, because ... when you're in a pack of reporters, you're probably not breaking news. ... So there's more of an opportunity for us to break news. But we're not a pack anymore. There's not enough of us to make a pack.

CONCLUSIONS

The "pack" of foreign correspondents has always been marked by both ruthless competition and profound bonds – Smith raced down Sarajevo's sniper alley with a shrapnel-peppered, catatonic colleague in the passenger seat and another's body in the next car on a Tuesday, and by Thursday the escape story was on the wire. Inside AP bureaus, collegiality and ego-swallowing are prerequisites for correspondents who might be out in the field getting the front-page byline today and on the desk writing the story for someone else tomorrow. The collaborative give and take extends across regions, with correspondents pitching in around the world when major news breaks, affecting stories both by bringing in new perspectives and by allowing experienced staffers to focus on the big picture instead of daily updates.

As more news organizations increase their local hires, some question whether the future of foreign correspondence should continue to include expatriates. Journalists working in their own countries have the advantage of local knowledge, from language to sources, and can often go where and when Americans cannot – but they are also far more endangered by foreign groups in power, who can jail and exile them, and often they need training in the traditions of a free press. Correspondents believe that the audience wins where locals and foreigners are essential partners in newsgathering, mixing expertise with distance and the understanding of what will resonate with outside publics. They also regret that the overall tribe of foreign correspondents is dwindling, because even cutthroat competitors provided one another with crucial on-the-ground training and shared logistical hurdles and dangers – plenty of which came directly from foreign governments, whose relationship with correspondents is detailed in Chapter 9.

Death of Pope John Paul II, 2005

Victor Simpson: We had a death watch basically is what we had, you know? ... It came from the Vatican. We got it out first (Simpson, 38).

  Angela Doland: I was in Rome on and off for about six months, flying back and forth every time the pope got sick. They would fly everyone out, and then it looked like he was going to live, and then everybody would fly back again. ... For a while, when John Paul II was sick, I was doing the overnight shift, and it just basically involved sitting there and making sure there wasn't some announcement that the pope had died in the middle of the night. And I remember, every morning, at dawn, I would update the story with the same line: "The lights flickered on at 6:30 a.m. in the pope's bedroom at the hospital." ...

I was in St. Peter's Square, and I was just talking to people, and then there were a lot of people with candles lit ... and there was an announcement that suddenly came on that said, "The pope has passed." And I quickly called the office thinking, you know, this is news. [laughs] Little did I know that the Vatican had sent in a press release that wound up on somebody's Blackberry, and they had already filed all the alerts ... I guess that moment, just thinking of all the people in all the different places in Rome and Vatican City who were working on that story and doing different things on it, I really felt like being part of this team (Doland, 6–7, 11–12).

Alan Clendenning: I went to do a story in the Amazon, which involved a visit to an Indian reservation [the Munduruku tribe in Bragança]. And it was a very tough day, eight-hour trip or so, and we finally made it, and we didn't even know if the Indians were going to let us in too, because you have to get permission to go to an Indian reservation. ... [T]hey welcomed us in there and to stay ... and they said, "Did you hear the pope died?" ... They had radio there. We didn't have radio in our truck. ... [T]he next day in their tiny, tiny little church, where they didn't even have a priest – they just had like a lay pastor or whatever like that – they held their own service in honor of Pope John Paul. It was like 15 Indians in a church surrounded by palm trees in the Amazon jungle. And we had done already all the interviews we needed on the one story we needed, so we did interviews on the pope story, and we dashed like crazy for another eight hours back to the closest town that had communication, so we could file a pope death reaction story from the middle of the Amazon (Clendenning, 22–23).

[News from the Amazon made it into the main AP roundup story on the global reaction to the pope's death, and Clendenning's story also described how the Munduruku "mourned a pope they considered an ally of the Indians and the rain forest":

"Singing hymns to the beat of a single drum carved from rain forest wood, parishioners living along a tributary of the Amazon remembered John Paul as an advocate for agrarian reform key to the drive of Brazil's Indians to protect their traditional lands from encroaching loggers and soy farmers."][11]

---

[11] Alexander G. Higgins, "From great bell of Paris' Notre Dame to prayers in earthquake-stricken Indonesia, world mourns pope," *The Associated Press*, April 3, 2005; Alan Clendenning, "Indians near jungle highway fear pavement will destroy their way of life," *The Associated Press*, June 12, 2005.

9

Access, Censorship, and Spin: Relating with Foreign Governments

From Mao in the Yan'an caves to Nelson Mandela at a rally, from Pope John Paul II on his plane to rebel groups in jungles and desert hideouts, correspondents have interacted with all kinds of foreign leaders and opposition groups. This chapter explores how they obtained access to them around the world, from breaking through opaque bureaucracies to organizing meet-ups with insurgents by following trails of instructions hidden in tree trunks to negotiating the opening of bureaus in such closed regimes as North Korea. Governments have also used the denial of access as retaliation against negative coverage, in a widespread effort to control news. One of the most disturbing findings is the level of surveillance and censorship that correspondents have been, and continue to be, subjected to around the world, sometimes resulting in expulsions and detentions that block stories from reaching the wire, at least temporarily. Correspondents also face the opposite concern – how to avoid spin, staged access, and being manipulated for propaganda purposes, which leaders from Nicolae Ceauşescu to the Khmer Rouge all attempted.

GETTING ACCESS TO FOREIGN LEADERS

The earliest access conversation between AP and foreign leaders concerned the most basic logistical issue: can a bureau be set up? In Havana in the 1960s as in Pyongyang in the 2010s, correspondents (and executives) worked hard to obtain permission to open an AP office. Bilingual Ike Flores (1–2) was editing on the foreign desk and traveling through the Caribbean in the mid-1960s, shortly after the Bay of Pigs and the missile crisis, when he and "the AP brass," through "much give-and-take" via the Czechoslovakian Embassy in Washington, "succeeded in convincing the Cuban regime ... that they needed to speak to the world" – and that "we were objective, that we would give the good as well as the bad of the Cuban Revolution." Flores' first short visa kept being extended for almost two and a half years. Both Flores and his successor, John Fenton Wheeler, wrote analytical pieces on Cuba's basic struggles, including food shortages, sometimes juxtaposing the rosy regime predictions with matter-of-fact complaints by a Havana cleaner and a woman in a cattle-producing province.[1]

In 1969, however, the Castro regime kicked out all American resident correspondents, forcing AP to close its bureau. It was not until late 1998 that AP could try again, bringing top executives to Havana to meet with Cuban leaders. Among them was World Services director Claude Erbsen (1), who had often pulled all-nighters reporting on Fidel Castro's long speeches from the "bureau in exile" in Florida in the 1960s – all on overtime, for which the aging Cuban leader playfully demanded "a commission" at the later meeting. When Castro consented to the new bureau, Anita Snow (2) "was the lucky one who got to write the story about that"[2] – and was offered the correspondent job in the bar, over celebratory cocktails. Then the work began – building a staff and organizing the bureau while navigating both Cuban regulations, such as the months-long process of hiring Cubans through the required government employment agency, and the U.S. embargo, which prohibited direct money transfers.

In late 2010, Jean Lee (3) took advantage of a rare North Korean invitation to foreign correspondents (to cover "the debut of Kim Jong Un") to start approaching the government for permission for a Pyongyang bureau, which, after signing a sharing agreement with the official Korean Central News Agency, opened in early 2012. In the early 1990s, Israel wanted AP to move its Tel Aviv bureau to Jerusalem, along with the U.S. and other embassies, as de facto recognition of its capital status. While AP bureau chief Nick Tatro (20) also wanted to relocate, because it meant staying closer to the story and having easier access to Palestinian territories, he had to balance logistics and independence: "so that it wouldn't look like we were playing into Israel's hand, bowing to their policy needs, while still getting us into the right position to cover not only the Israeli ministries ... but also the Palestinian story."

Once inside a country, over time, access ranged from easy and privileged to hard to get and denied in retaliation, without necessarily following the country's relationship with the United States or its geopolitical status. The Communist Pathet Lao group, fighting a civil war against the U.S. government-backed

---

[1] Isaac M. Flores, "Cuba Hungry in 'Year of Agriculture'; Housewives Take What They Can Get," *Chicago Tribune*, September 19, 1965, B1; Fenton Wheeler, "Cubans Kept Busy Finding Enough Food," *Chicago Tribune*, June 18, 1967, A1.

[2] Anita Snow, "Cuban government approves re-opening of AP Havana bureau," The Associated Press, November 13, 1998. In 1997, the U.S. government allowed 10 American news organizations, including AP, to seek permission to reopen bureaus there.

Laotian regime, hosted an AP correspondent who got lost going up the Mekong and spent the night in their encampment:

I thought they would eat me and they didn't. I gave them the oranges and we ate oranges [together] ... this young Pathet Lao's English, the only thing he could say was a few words: Cold wind tonight. And yes, I said, cold wind tonight. And the next day [my colleagues and I] got back in the canoe and we went back downriver. (Bartimus, 20)

But in the friendly United Kingdom, Bob Barr (4–5), who worked in London for decades, recalled that in the Thatcher era, her spokesman did a separate weekly briefing for the American press, leaving correspondents to tape off her televised appearances or to wait for the UK's national news agency, Press Association, to deliver some breaking news – even momentous items like Thatcher's resignation: "we watched this great drama of Thatcher departing, but we weren't there."[3]

Governments in disarray rarely give correspondents the luxury of methodical news announcements, but they can be easier to reach. Jones (18, 31) recalled the chaotic days during the Tiananmen protests as an unparalleled window of press freedom in China. Not only did authorities not even try to censor the foreign press ("they could have confiscated transmission equipment, all the computers, the phones. And they could have stationed one or two soldiers at the bureau. And what could we have done?"), but Chinese reporting showed "astonishing" "frankness, speed and clear sympathy with protesters," as one story noted.[4] Foreign correspondents probed bluntly:

[W]e put the question to the Foreign Ministry: who was in charge of China? And the answer came back, it goes, "We cannot answer that at this time." And we didn't know if that meant that there were large swaths of sympathizers within the Foreign Ministry – I'm not sure there were – or if they were just too shackled and embarrassed to say anything beyond that.

Donna Bryson (17–19), who covered South Africa both in the volatile last days of apartheid and 15 years later, noticed the change as power politics settled:

In the '90s ... politicians in general, white or black, in South Africa knew the world was watching, and they really wanted to put their best foot forward, so it wasn't difficult to get access.... [A few years later] ANC was becoming more prickly about the press. They had been treated as heroes, as antiapartheid heroes, before the election, and now they were being treated like politicians, with the suspicion that comes with that. Reporters were asking sharp questions and asking whether you're leading in the right direction, and

---

[3] For example, Barr's story on "the most serious challenge to Prime Minister Margaret Thatcher" – the announcement by former defense secretary Michael Heseltine that he would "contest her position as leader of the Conservative Party, and thus prime minister" – quoted the statement Heseltine broadcast on Sky Television and noted that Thatcher had offered no statement; Robert Barr, "Thatcher rival challenges her leadership," The Associated Press, November 14, 1990.

[4] Terril Jones, "Press gives unexpected coverage to demonstrations," The Associated Press, May 18, 1989.

asking political questions. . . . [I]t became more formal and maybe more difficult to get to people in power. . . . But at the World Trade Center at the time [of negotiations to end apartheid], you just walked into the room where these discussions were being held, and if you needed to ask a question, you walked up to the person who had the answer. Looking now, I'm thinking, boy that was nice and easy.

After assiduous seeking, face-to-face meetings with leaders could still happen so suddenly that they caught correspondents off guard – and offered unexpected insights. In the middle of the 1980s Lebanese civil war, the day after the Phalangists had destroyed much of the rival Tiger militia in an attack on their headquarters, a spokesman for the latter "grabbed" Tatro (14) and took him to the apartment of Tigers' leader Dany Chamoun, who had survived, while he was having breakfast with his family, including his father, Lebanon's former president:

We just walked in and they were eating . . . there's a price on his head and he could catch a bullet any minute and he's just kind of having Wheaties. . . . [H]is wife starts to get hysterical and she starts yelling at him and she took off her shoe and started pounding on his chest . . . with the shoe and saying, "Where are we going to get money? We need money. We can't survive. What are we going to do?" . . . I was in the middle of this. . . . So this is access at the time.

Bryson (58–59) was attending a pre-election rally by Nelson Mandela – crowds so enormous that "you would get into them and your feet weren't on the ground, because you were being held up by the press of people around you" – when she was led to the recently released leader before having time to think of what to ask:

I came up with a question, probably something about the events of the day, and he looked at me and said, "That's not a very good question." [laughs] In his lawyerly patrician manner . . . I probably smiled and apologized and tried to think of another question.

Victor Simpson (8–9), who covered the Vatican for nearly four decades, and the rest of the traveling press corps were well known to John Paul II, who "never shied away" from questions and simply walked to the back of the plane, chatting with reporters in "airborne news conferences" that raised eyebrows "among Vatican officials who thought the exercise undignified." "Sprung from Vatican confines, airborne popes seem to feel freer to speak out," Simpson wrote in a story about his 92nd trip aboard a papal plane, this time with Benedict XVI, who congratulated Simpson on his announced retirement on February 26, 2013, without giving away any hint of news that would shock the world five months later – that Benedict too would resign, on exactly the same date.[5] (Simpson postponed his retirement, to cover the story.) It was not

[5] Victor L. Simpson, "Globe-trotting pope making his 100th foreign tour despite age, infirmities," *The Associated Press*, June 4, 2003; "Close encounters with the popes over 3 decades," *The Associated Press*, February 26, 2013.

the first time he had sat next to the pope in first class. One memorable day in 1986, Simpson (17–19) was invited to go up front and join John Paul II for an on-the-record dinner on the plane returning from a two-week Australia trip:

We got up at 4 o'clock in the morning, went to the Seychelles, where the pope celebrated a mass in … pouring rain and … on the last leg, we got back on the plane, and all I wanted to do was have dinner and go to sleep, right? When [Joaquín] Navarro-Valls, who was the pope's spokesman, came up to me and said, "Listen, the pope would like to have dinner with a journalist tonight and you've been selected. Would you like to go?" So I said, how could I say no, my God! … I was really unshaven, having shaved at 4 o'clock in the morning, and I was wearing like a terribly sloppy safari jacket that was soaking wet still from the rain … I was taken up to the Qantas upstairs first-class section, and I apologized to the pope for the way I looked, I said, "Excuse me, Your Holiness, these are my working clothes," and he grabbed … his white robe in his fist and said, "These are my working clothes." And put me at ease, right. And so it was wonderful and I got some great insights into the man, down to how he eats … I was hungry, you see, and that's the terrible thing. … The pope said he wasn't hungry, and I said, Oh my God, I'll never be able to eat. Right? But fortunately, we were joined by his chief organizer of papal trips, a Jesuit, who said I'm having lamb chops, he made a big announcement, and I said well that sounds good to me, I'll have the same. … I asked earlier, what are the ground rules [about the interview] and he said use your judgment.

No such freedom for Flores (3–5, 17; also Flores 2007, 48–53) when he found himself sharing a pizza in 1965 with Fidel Castro, who was "not generally available to reporters, particularly a Yankee like me." The Swiss Embassy, which Flores had cultivated as a necessary source in the closed regime, tipped him off one night around 2 a.m. that the ambassador and Castro were meeting "at a little pizza joint on the Malecón boulevard." Rushing there, among the "big cars" and security details, Flores was motioned to stay by a press officer, who, when the ambassador left, sent word that Flores wanted "a couple of minutes" with Fidel:

Fidel was sitting there, finishing off his pizza … and invited me to join him and sit down. So I did and tried to get him to answer some serious questions, but no, he was done by then. … He wanted to talk baseball. … I tried to set up … a personal interview where we would meet at some office or something. Again, he wouldn't say no, but he kept putting me off … told me that essentially I would learn what he had to say from his speeches. … I was called into the Foreign Ministry press information office by the censorship czar, in effect, and he said, "I understand you were at this pizza meeting with Fidel last night," and I said, "Yes." I knew he knew all about it. And he said, "Well, if you want to remain in Havana, you keep that for your memoirs. Okay?" And so I had to agree if I wanted to stay there.

Mao had been more open with John Roderick (AP Oral History, 1998, 8–14), though it still took a couple of months after the correspondent moved to Yan'an in the mid-1940s to cover the revolutionaries for Mao to receive him for dinner in his "hut," a "quite sumptuous meal" at which they discussed the future of China, including whether Sears might be willing to start a mail-order business there.

More dinners, Saturday night dances in tattered, padded woolen clothes, nights of Chinese opera, and occasional strolls through town followed, and while Mao "wasn't telling ... very much," Roderick could still write about what the Communist plans and hopes were for U.S.-Chinese relations. After the 1970 elections, which split popular support between Sheikh Mujibur Rahman and Zulfikar Ali Bhutto, thus precipitating East and West Pakistan toward war, Arnold Zeitlin (20–21) was invited first for a midnight interview by Bhutto, who, while getting a massage, told the correspondent he would boycott negotiations, but also that he thought Pakistan might have two prime ministers ("I wrote both stories," Zeitlin recalled). Then Mujibur asked him to his house, and, when Zeitlin said that Bhutto had talked about each side of the country having its prime minister, East Pakistan's de facto leader said he would agree. The correspondent, who had cultivated both sources tirelessly,[6] immediately cabled a story – and in the time it took to get back from the telegraph office to his hotel, the phone rang:

"You misquoted me." And I said to [Mujibur], "You know damn well I didn't misquote you." He said, "That story's going to hurt me in the West," meaning West Pakistan. "Can you withdraw it?" I thought to myself this guy may be the next prime minister of Pakistan. ... I said, "Okay, I'm going to go back to the cable office, and if that story hasn't gone, I'll pull it. But if it's gone to London, no way am I going to try to explain to London why it should be held up." ... The cable office was on strike. ... Next morning that story was replayed on All India Radio.

Following the mistaken perception of correspondents as American quasi-diplomats, leaders sometimes granted them access in an attempt to affect policy: all sides in the decades-long Israeli-Palestinian conflict, for example, with the political wing of Hamas seeing the foreign press as a "key element" in their efforts "to be recognized by the West" and granting frequent interviews (Laub, 21), and Israeli ministers traditionally eager to provide their narrative too, though some correspondents noted their desire to control the message.[7] Even Khun Sa, the nefarious opium warlord in Southeast Asia's Golden Triangle, invited correspondents to his jungle hideout to make a case that the United States should not put a reward on his head (Gray, 53).

But most governments can also make themselves difficult to reach – no small hurdle for correspondents bent on getting their side of the story, a comment, or even confirmation, no matter how hermetically sealed a country tries to be. In 1970s China, after the ping-pong overture but before the reopening, officials were impossible to get, so reporters in Hong Kong turned to their de facto

---

[6] For an example of Zeitlin's access, see Arnold Zeitlin, "Mujibur: Virtual Ruler of E. Pakistan," *Washington Post*, March 21, 1971, A26.

[7] *New York Times* correspondent Thomas Friedman (1995, 440), in Jerusalem in the late 1980s, also remarked on "this Israeli obsession with the American media," translating into access to "everyone from the Prime Minister on down within forty-eight hours of a request," but also in intense scrutiny of his articles.

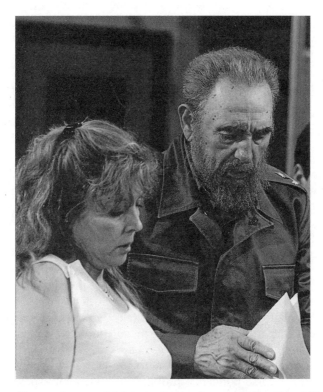

FIGURE 9.1. Havana bureau chief Anita Snow chats with President Fidel Castro in Havana in September 1999, after he appeared on state television to argue that Cuban athletes at the Pan American Games were framed for drug use and unjustly stripped of their medals. (Photo by Adalberto Roque, courtesy of Anita Snow)

representatives, *Xinhua* journalists, for "nibblets" of information (Liu, 12). For decades in Castro's Cuba, all correspondents could get on the record were the leader's public speeches, though in later years he might "chat with journalists a little bit" at the events (Snow, 19; also Wheeler, 4).

Italy's Silvio Berlusconi was hard to get for one-on-one interviews, perhaps because he felt ridiculed by foreign media (Simpson, 15), whereas many Arab governments, among them prominently revolutionary Iran, seemed to take journalists' "questions as challenges" from an unfriendly foe they had little incentive to tolerate (Bryson, 41). In fact, during Iran's revolution, when the Ayatollah Khomeini introduced his first prime minister at a press conference, reporters had "to climb over a tall iron fence to reach the auditorium" (Doelling, 12), and when the Shah left Iran, correspondents were told to leave the airport since the departure was cancelled – only to return to the office and hear the announcement that he was gone. But Tatro (10) was undeterred, sneaking on a felucca to a little resort island around Aswan, Egypt, inaccessible otherwise, where the Shah's plane first landed:

[T]his was probably the most adventurous I've ever been in my life, and it was, ultimately ... really stupid. ... [M]e and a photographer rented this felucca and we lied down on the bottom of the boat and told the felucca guy to take us to the island. ... [T]he Shah was walking around, we got to him, I asked him a question, and a bunch of reporters who were kept beyond, they saw us and so they ratted us out to the Egyptian security who, ultimately, threw us out. But I did get sort of a comment out of the Shah and fortunately was not arrested or shot.

Slow-moving bureaucracy challenges correspondents on deadline, who from India to France might resort to ambushing ministers right before or after they give a speech or briefing, trying to sneak in a question on the way in or out and hoping to get more than "wooden tongue," the pat party line delivered by the press office (Bryson, 30; Ganley, 6–9). In Mexico, the obstructionist lines from officials' secretaries – "he is not here, he has gone out to lunch, I could not tell you when he will be back" – became so routine that another wire agency's correspondent invented a rap song called "No sabría decirle, el licenciado salió a comer" (Snow, 12). In Nicaragua and Honduras during the Contra war, "if you wanted to talk to a Sandinista, it would take two weeks to get the clearance to do it. You'd have to sit by your phone till you got it, so you couldn't go out and work on anything else" (Frazier, 30–31).

Outright denial of access is also a time-honored tool by governments unhappy with the correspondents' probing. Although correspondents do not bow to the threat "Don't do this or I'll never talk to you again" (Stevenson, 20), they have to weigh the importance of publishing a story versus losing sources, credentials, travel permits, or even a necessary visa to stay in the country (also Prochnau 1995, 137–38; Frank 2013, 1). After quoting a member of the Palestinian Legislative Council calling an Israeli development program in Jerusalem "ethnic cleansing," Middle East veteran Karin Laub (16) was told by Prime Minister Benjamin Netanyahu's office that he would be available for an AP interview, but she could not be the interviewer, which led AP to decline the offer "because they do not dictate to us who's conducting the interview." In 2000s Indonesia, AP reporters wrote multiple stories investigating the country's antiterrorism efforts, including, most resented of all, the campaign to recruit former terrorists as informants. One story described a barbecue party hosted by the antiterrorism chief who "mingled" with his guests on his lawn as "convicted Bali nightclub bombers feasted on kebabs" – an "unusual gathering" that was "a striking example of what has emerged as a key plank in Indonesia's anti-terror campaign ... [and] also underscored Southeast Asia's progress in the fight against al-Qaida."[8] After it ran, the reporter "didn't get invited back," but the

---

[8] Chris Brummitt, "Indonesia says 'soft approach' yields dividends in Southeast Asia's war on terror," The Associated Press, October 12, 2007.

coverage was cited in the United States as an example of AP's "vital" international report (McDowell, 13; Ricchiardi 2008).

CONTROL TOOLS: COMPLAINTS AND THREATS OF EXPULSION

The correspondents' experience with a government's efforts to control its global image by muzzling them often started with being called in for a reproachful complaint about a story, followed by threats of expulsion that ranged from empty to forceful removal on the next flight. In many cases, the correspondents' firm line – defending the story's accuracy – enabled them to face down intimidation, as Claude Erbsen (10), Brazil bureau chief in the 1960s, did:

I got called from time to time to the foreign ministry, and they would have gotten a clipping from somewhere, from some Brazilian embassy, with a story that they didn't like, and I would listen politely and I would then say ... "please point out the inaccuracies." And they said, "No, no, no, we're not challenging an inaccuracy, but we wish you hadn't written it." I said, "Well, that's your prerogative to wish, but if you're not challenging its accuracy, then there's no point in continuing this conversation." By and large they agreed.

Nearly 40 years later in Brazil, another correspondent found ironic how the government would deign to answer requests for comment only barely before deadline, and then "mount a campaign against the reporter after the story came out" (Clendenning, 5). Complaints also backfired. Antonio Salazar's regime accused foreign correspondents "of filing dispatches detrimental to Portugal" – noted an article by AP's correspondent in Lisbon on Salazar's striking back at critics.[9] In Mexico in the 1990s, the complaints – which fizzled out when correspondents argued they were simply reporting the truth – could become that government's elusive quote:

They would complain and try to engage in a dialogue about representing their point of view, which was useful because then we have their point of view, which was not always something you could get. (Price, 19)

Other interactions, however, were both more sinister and more public, as when state media in the USSR lambasted AP reporting (Minthorn, 8). In El Salvador during its civil war, despite both the U.S.-backed government and the guerrillas having "their PR bit pinned down," the horrifying reality on the ground drove coverage, and Joe Frazier (13, 12) was "royally chewed out for stories ... that hadn't even been published yet, which tells you something." In Communist Poland, spokesmen questioned by other reporters about AP stories during weekly news conferences, broadcast on Polish TV, would assail them as "false and malicious statements" and "quickly dissemble or turn them

---

[9] Isaac M. Flores, "Scandal-Threatened Portuguese Regime Hits at Critics," *Washington Post*, December 25, 1967.

FIGURE 9.2. Warsaw correspondent John Daniszewski interviews Poland's Solidarity leader Lech Walesa in Warsaw in 1990. (Photo by Czarek Sokolowski, courtesy of AP Corporate Archives)

around, from the government's point of view," turning the conferences into a "public duel" (Daniszewski, 12). Correspondents there also had to face the foreign ministry official in charge of renewing their six-month visas, "who clearly was a secret police person who would exhibit great and detailed knowledge of the work you'd been doing and questioned about why are you always quoting these people and not us" (Daniszewski, 3).

From Poland to India, Egypt to Italy, government officials pressured AP's local staff. Simpson (35) wrote a story about how U.S. president Barack Obama had visited Italy's president on the way to the G-8 meeting in L'Aquila and "heaped lavish praise ... lauding his 'integrity,'"[10] which amounted to the U.S.

[10] Victor L. Simpson, "Obama praises ceremonial leader," The Associated Press, July 8, 2009.

president's "taking a stab at Berlusconi," who was enmeshed in sex and corruption scandals:

> Berlusconi's people went to the little office the AP had [at the G-8], and they screamed and yelled: "Simpson is really dangerous, how can he write this? He's trying to wreck the whole G-8." ... [AP writer] Alessandra Rizzo ... told me she said to them, "Call him! You have his number, I'll give you his number. You want to talk to him, call him." ... I never heard from them.

Bryson (71–72), news editor in Cairo around 9/11, recalled local reporters telling her that they had been called in by authorities to "answers questions" about stories, especially on "Christian-Muslim issues":

> And it didn't mean that they wanted to stop writing about these issues, and it didn't mean that I wanted them to stop writing about these issues. But the intent was to intimidate. ... They certainly would not call me in for writing the same kind of story.

India's government, "really furious" after an AP local writer reported not only that more than a thousand people were killed in the repression of the 1984 Sikh uprising in Amritsar, but also that some Sikhs "were found shot with their hands tied behind their backs, with their turbans," filed charges against him for inciting communal violence (Graham, 20–21).[11] Both he and AP stood by the story, because, as bureau chief Vicki Graham put it, "It was right ... it was the truth ... it was a big story":

> Now, whether that was the right decision, given all the flak and all the problems, I'm not sure. I mean, it's great to say, "To hell with everyone. We'll do this story." I think I'm glad we did. It caused a lot of problems, though ... it was very tense, a very unpleasant situation.

Also trying to blame its own actions on a perceptive reporter, Uzbekistan's government went after Kathy Gannon (2–3) when she wrote about how Andijan was "ready to explode" following the arrest of business leaders on charges of radical Islamism – just a couple of weeks before the military, responding to a massive uprising in the city, did kill hundreds of people.[12]

Over the decades, governments have followed through on their threats and expelled correspondents whose stories they disliked, sometimes shuttering bureaus for decades, as when Wheeler (8–9; 2008, 171) became the last resident U.S. correspondent ordered out of Cuba by Castro – with a 3 a.m. phone call telling him to be on a 6 a.m. flight, following a story that the projected crop of sugarcane was hugely inflated. (Wheeler had written periodically about the

---

[11] See Brahma Chellaney, "The battle at the Golden Temple," The Associated Press, June 18, 1984. For the government's reaction, see "Indian government criticizes AP reporting on Punjab," The Associated Press, June 19, 1984.

[12] In April 2005, Gannon wrote about the trial on charges of religious extremism of 23 members of the Akramia group in Andijan, Uzbekistan, arguing that they threatened to unleash demonstrations against the government; Kathy Gannon, "Religious business group in volatile Uzbek region represents everything rulers fear," The Associated Press, April 19, 2005.

projected sugar yield, casting doubt on Castro's goals;[13] nearly 40 years later, Castro "railed at" another U.S. correspondent "for reporting he had tried, but failed, to turn around a dismal sugar harvest"; Frank 2013, 3.)

In 1950s Moscow, a correspondent was given all of one week to leave after writing a "think piece" about Khrushchev's suffering a "public setback" following his visit to Beijing: "I figured I might have some trouble over this ... and it wasn't anything I had planned, just got carried away" (AP Oral History, Essoyan 1997, 40–43). After the 1971 coup, Harold Olmos (6) was expelled from his native Bolivia when he refused to stand trial for having received a letter from an exiled opposition general, which the government discovered by pilfering his mail. When the Iran-Iraq War broke out, Steven Hurst (5) fought for every scrap of information amid the official minders and denials – "We were just led around from filler to post" – until he wrote a story "about how much the Iraqi economy reminded me of the Soviet economy. And as soon as the story hit the wire, the Iraqis saw it and came and knocked on my door and said, 'There's a bus leaving for Jordan in the morning, and you'll be on it.' ... I had to go. I had no choice." In the week before Saddam Hussein's regime fell, 52 journalists were put on an Iraqi expulsion list (Shadid 2006, 136).

When they face hostile governments, correspondents know that they are "supposed to be reporting ... not supposed to be getting [themselves] kidnapped, ... not supposed to get [themselves] shot, and ... not supposed to get [themselves] expelled," said Reid (90, 14–15) – who over more than four decades was expelled from Czechoslovakia, Poland, and Afghanistan during the Soviet war, with the handful of Western reporters who had managed to sneak in. Having returned to his hotel after handing his notes to another AP reporter who had only made it as far as Kabul's airport before authorities sent him right back out of the country, Reid had just gotten into a taxi for one last reporting trip "down Jalalabad Road" before it got too dark to see whether any Soviet convoys were headed there, when the door flew open. The same Afghan official who had stamped his visa earlier that day pointed at Reid, said he had lied on his visa (Reid had put "writer," not "journalist"), and told him to come along to "a special hotel for the journalists":

I thought either this special hotel is jail or it's deporting. ... The guy from the information ministry I think is driving, big cop is in the shotgun seat, and two armed soldiers are there with me. ... [B]y the time we get to the airport, the sun is down and there are almost no lights on at the Kabul airport. ... I get out and he walks up to me and he says, "Let me have your ticket." I said ... I only flew one-way. ... So we divert from the departure lines in another direction to buy another ticket ... and then we hear "Mrrrrrr." That's the sound of the last plane of the day taking off for Delhi. ... "Okay, you can go back to your hotel and stay the night, but be here in the morning, at 9 o'clock." And the American diplomat turns to me and says, "Listen, I speak Dari. What he said in Dari was a lot less

---

[13] Fenton Wheeler, "Record Sugar Yield Is Cuba's '70 Goal," *Washington Post*, November 17, 1968, K4.

friendly than what he just said to you. Don't mess with this guy. Just be down here." I said okay. So he squirrels us back to the Intercon. . . . Woke up the next morning, looked out the window, and there was half a foot of snow on the ground. And I went downstairs and confirmed what I knew: Kabul airport was closed. We stayed there for almost a week before they finally got us out.

In some cases, expulsion from a country or parts of it might be the more benign alternative, given the threats correspondents also received from governments, as noted in Chapter 7. While in China "the threat of having officials interfere with your reporting is ever present," the kind of interference has changed over time, said Charles Hutzler (7, 23), who reported there since the mid-1990s:

[In the 1990s] we were supposed to get permission from the provincial authorities or the local authorities every time we went outside of Beijing to go to some area to report. Now, most of the time we didn't do that, but . . . it was a convenient excuse for the authorities to shut down any interviews that they didn't like. . . . [P]articularly on a sensitive story, you only had sort of a few hours within which to really have freedom of movement out in the provinces before you'd get detected and often busted. . . . [Then] the government or the police might barge in and . . . detain you and then escort you out of town, or maybe even escort you back to a hotel and make sure you get on a plane the next morning. Now the foreign media is more and more exposed to the same kinds of rough intimidation and violence that the Chinese media is.

In late 2014, a report by the Foreign Correspondents' Club of China found that the government was trying to manipulate coverage of "sensitive" topics, such as corruption and protests, through the whole gamut of threats: intimidation of both journalists and sources, keeping reporters away from large parts of the country, denying visa renewals and licenses to open new bureaus.[14] The report noted this trend was a reversal from the opening around the 2008 Olympics, when the Chinese government for the first time allowed journalists to travel around the country (except to Tibet) without the usual minders. Among enduring major geopolitical and economic powers, China sadly stands out for the level of surveillance and censorship it has imposed on correspondents – extreme control tools that continue to be stunningly widespread impediments to journalistic practices and, ultimately, coverage.

BUGS, BUGS EVERYWHERE: SURVEILLANCE

From bugs hidden in bedrooms to trailing cars to omnipresent minders, foreign governments have spared no effort to keep informed about correspondents' movements. In many tightly controlled countries, from China to Cuba to Iraq, accreditation came with official minders – sometimes cosmetically called "press

---

[14] "Position Paper on Working Conditions for Foreign Correspondents in China," September 12, 2014, retrieved from http://www.fccchina.org. Also Andrew Jacobs, "Foreign Journalists in China See Decline in Reporting Conditions," *New York Times*, September 12, 2014.

guides" or "translators" – charged with staying glued to correspondents and reporting on their activities, including their sources. After having waited weeks for permission to travel to Stalin's native Georgia to report on unrest there after Khrushchev's bombshell denunciation of the Soviet leader, the handful of correspondents allowed in were followed so closely that they "couldn't talk spontaneously to anybody. And everybody we asked said, 'No, nothing had happened.'" But AP's Roy Essoyan and a couple of others stuck around long enough that "the guards seemed to have stopped chasing" them, and got the story about the protest's brutal repression – earning them a dressing down by the foreign ministry (AP Oral History, Essoyan 1997, 23–26). On a visit to the North Korean border, Hutzler (11–12) managed a 15-minute unscripted interview with a Chinese farmer only because his minder, who had been ordering the driver not to stop when they saw regular people, had fallen into a hangover doze.

The relationship with minders was not always hostile: One correspondent bought "big boxes of Ramadan pastries" for the 17 soldiers assigned to "escort" her to a tiny Algerian village to interview the brother of the man arrested at the U.S.-Canadian border in 1999 for allegedly attempting to bring in explosives for terror attacks (Ganley, 44), while Moscow apartment guards occasionally rocked the pram of one correspondent's daughter (AP Oral History, Essoyan 1997, 30). (During the Cold War, correspondents and diplomats were often required to live in high-security government compounds or hotels where the guards doubled as monitors, which was an effective disincentive for any visitors; one correspondent in Beijing recalled that a U.S. Embassy officer, who was also a neighbor, would only answer questions in writing while at home; Graham 6–7; also Liu 2012, 275.) From Moscow to Havana to Beijing, correspondents suspected some of their local staff of spying on them:

Our interpreter, we had a cook and we had a driver, they all reported on us. And they all had to go to political study sessions, and I'm sure report on, "What did Ms. Graham do this week? Did she do a lot of shopping? What was she interested in?" I don't know what they wanted to know, but I think it put [these] Chinese people in a very uncomfortable position because we got to be friends and we respected them and I'd like to think they liked and respected us. (Graham, 5)

Did our employees spy on us? I don't know. Did the Cubans know what we were doing all the time? Probably. (Snow, 19)

Surveillance has also been more covert, though no less obvious, for correspondents in the Soviet Union, Eastern Europe, China, and a smattering of other countries. Correspondents in Moscow from the 1950s to the 1990s knew that they "lived under constant surveillance" (AP Oral History, Essoyan 1997, 29–30; Bassow 1988, 124; Bradsher 2013, 171; Daniloff 2008, 65). The KGB listened in on both their offices and apartments – several found bugs in bedroom lampshades – they were tracked wherever they went, and their

FIGURE 9.3. Moscow correspondent David Minthorn and his wife, Veronika, stand in Red Square in early winter 1981. (Photo courtesy of David Minthorn)

telephones were tapped. A typical call from a source desiring to remain anonymous would start with a Magrittesque "eto ne telefoniyi razgovor" [this is not a telephone conversation], meaning you should meet in person in an open space, although there the police might still show up and the correspondent be set up with possession of incriminating "secret documents" or participating in protests (Porubcansky, 3; also Minthorn, 2, 4; Cooperman, 9–10; Topping 2010, 199). In Pyongyang in the 2010s, Lee (6) assumed that all her communications and correspondence were being monitored.

Correspondents were also followed – one in Czechoslovakia wondered if the authorities wanted him to realize it, "because they put a very good-looking young blonde woman on my trail," and conceded that, to avoid being expelled and blacklisted from the country, he did not write "the really hardcore stuff, anti-Communist stories" until he was out of the country (Doelling, 6–7). In Ben Ali's Tunis, a correspondent would sometimes "walk down the street and I'd turn just to see if I could get someone fast, like he'd walk into me or something … it was always a spooky kind of feeling," which was accentuated by strolling along

tree-lined Avenue Bourguiba in the strong smell of jasmine and passing right by
the interior ministry, alleged to have housed torture rooms (Ganley, 34).
Electronic surveillance could be just as blatant, as John Daniszewski (10–11)
found in Poland:

> You could pick up the phone and hear the monitors talking in the background. I remember
> once in Poland having a phone call with somebody and then getting off the phone and the
> phone rang and – some kind of glitch – the previous phone conversation was being played
> back for me. . . . I also would be aware that different people had been in my flat while I
> wasn't there, and I think that was to check the eavesdropping equipment . . . it just was part
> of life then that you were being watched and monitored.

From minders to tails to electronic snooping, correspondents in China have
faced the gamut of surveillance ever since they were allowed back in 1979,
especially if they dared touch subjects like the suppression of Falun Gong, which
Hutzler (18–19) did in 2000. With a group of other foreign reporters, he was
tipped off to go meet movement representatives at a Beijing restaurant, from
there put in a series of taxis, driven around, and taken to a hotel nearly outside
the metropolis, where Falun Gong members held a news conference about their
torture and mistreatment. After the stories appeared in Western media –
including TV footage hand-carried out to Hong Kong since China controlled
broadcast transmission – the reporters' press cards were confiscated for two
weeks and aggressive surveillance began for six months:

> I was being followed from the moment that I left my home in the morning until the
> moment I got back at night. And we lived in one of these diplomatic compounds, and my
> kids were really very small back then . . . the Montessori school they went to was a few
> blocks away. And so I would walk them to school in the morning, and the minute that I
> would leave . . . holding my kids in each hand, they would follow us. . . . I never told my
> kids, at the time. Because they were small and you don't want them to get freaked out and
> think that China is some very scary and threatening place. And actually . . . they would be
> about 50 paces behind when I had the kids. The minute I dropped the kids off, they were
> about 30 paces behind me. And if I rode a bike, they were following me in a car. I did
> lose them a couple of times, not because I needed to lose them, but because it became kind
> of a game.

THIS STORY HAS BEEN APPROVED BY CENSORS

Many countries also tried their hand at outright censorship, particularly during
wars or national emergencies, though most targeted local media far more
oppressively than they harassed foreign reporters. While today the
requirement of prepublication censorship is a "red line" that correspondents
refuse to accept, such as Lee (6) in North Korea, most correspondents in earlier
times from Brazil to Israel to Cambodia had to submit their copy to censors,
usually installed at the post and telegraph offices that transmitted it overseas,
often after intentional delays.

Some restrictions, such as on describing troop movements, are generally accepted by war correspondents who simply note in the copy that the story has been reviewed by a censor. Several 1980s stories from the Lebanese war, for example, were prefaced by "This dispatch was submitted to the Israeli military censor who" – as the case may be – "did not order any changes" or ordered "several," even "significant" changes.[15] But correspondents opposed military censorship as mere message control, such as the story about two Israeli fighter jets colliding during the war with Lebanon that provoked Israeli officers into "threatening all kinds of terrible things . . . they wanted to have it all wrapped up their way before they released it even" (Tatro, 20; also Fisk 2002, 201). (Where U.S. troops have been involved, as in Korea or Indochina, American censors also reviewed copy, as noted in Chapter 10; also Hohenberg 1995, 253.)

Other restrictions were so blatantly unacceptable that correspondents tried all kinds of ruses to get around them, or directly confronted censors. In Central America during the guerrilla wars, one enterprising correspondent made it a habit to take the young lieutenant in charge of the Managua censorship office out for lobster lunches (AP Oral History, Aguilar 2009, 30). Both in the Vietnam War (Prochnau 1995, 383) and during Bolivia's 1974 coup (Olmos, 3–4), correspondents used photos to smuggle stories:

I picked out some old pictures, black-and-white pictures, with a basketball championship, and wrote captions in a couple of those pictures telling about the coup, in English, a few lines. And filed those pictures to New York, with the hope that somebody would be, "Okay, what is this? Why are we getting these basketball pictures from La Paz?" This was a way to let them know the office was interfered and that I was watched.

During France's Indochina war, a story about one battalion's defeat was entirely crossed out by a French censor – but the correspondent insisted it be sent anyway:

All he left was "Associated Press. Roderick . . . Six hundred words censored." I said, "Send it." . . . It went. The AP got it in New York . . . it was [a] box in almost every newspaper in the world to illustrate the censorship and the difficulties of reporting in Indochina. . . . One of the best stories I never, never wrote that got used. (AP Oral History, Roderick 1998, 40)

Myron Belkind (11–12) was watching the tape go through with his story about India's declaration of a state of emergency when he received a phone call from the government's former chief information officer advising him that he was now "chief censor" and that he would need to see all copy before transmission through approved circuits – all others would be cut. Belkind and AP editors in New York decided that he should stay, despite the censorship, explicitly saying in stories if they were redacted (e.g., "all news dispatches are now based on official government briefings and on other information cleared by

[15] For example, see Nicolas B. Tatro, "Israeli Army fights elusive guerrillas in South Lebanon," *The Associated Press*, January 13, 1985.

censors").[16] Eventually he and other correspondents managed to convince the information minister – by showing up at his house at 7:30 a.m. while he was taking his bath – to substitute the order with "guidelines" that included "make certain your dispatches are accurate," obviously not a problem for the journalists.

During Brazil's military dictatorship, Erbsen's "three-week game of cat and mouse with censors" began one late evening in 1968 when, with the telex tape of the latest story on democracy-crushing measures slowly making its way to AP, the phone rang and a Brazilian colleague warned that military censors were on their way. Erbsen telexed his editors that using his middle name would be the code signaling that the office was under censorship – which it became shortly afterward. Officers immediately ordered Erbsen to cut the line, but agreed to wait until after the standard confirmation of reception, so as not to arouse suspicion in New York:

RCVD OK came back the reply BIBIBI AND THIS IS CLAUDE ERNEST ERBSEN WISHING U GD NITE I tapped back. No more than a couple of minutes had passed when the incoming radioteletype circuit . . . fell silent. One of the majors strolled over and stared in astonishment at . . . an urgent Bulletin reporting that the Rio bureau of the AP had been placed under military censorship after two uniformed officials had arrived there shortly before midnight. . . . "But how do they know?" I smiled and replied "The Associated Press is well informed."[17]

Starting that night, censors, fluent in English, worked in the bureau in shifts to vet copy – though Erbsen (11–14) found creative ways to keep up coverage. When a major politician went on a hunger strike, the censor said not to mention arrests or strikes, so Erbsen wrote, "a guest of the armed forces has gone on a diet." The censor passed it, and New York filled in the blanks. Some of the censors even pitched in on news stories. When the bureau could not get an answer on reports about a shooting on Copacabana beach, the officer picked up the phone himself and called the local precinct captain: "This is Major So-and-so. We here at The Associated Press want to know . . . " and got a named source and a quote that somebody had just accidentally fired off a starter pistol. He was not the only "censor-stringer":

[W]hen they saw the trouble we would go to be accurate and to verify things, and go to two sources for most things that required careful sourcing, they sort of got sucked into it. I remember one night we had to cover two soccer games in the interior at the same time, and we covered them by radio. Basically we needed only to file about 100 words, such-and-such beat so-and-so, goals were scored by so-and-so at 13 minutes, 22 minutes, and 54 minutes. And our censor was listening to my conversation with my news editor: "We've got to bring in two stringers because one guy can't cover two games at the time." And the censor said, "You know, I was a sports writer in university. . . . If you want me to, I'll do it." So I said great! And showed him the format, and I showed him to sign his

[16] "Gandhi Grips Tight; Appeals Not Allowed," *Chicago Tribune*, June 28, 1975, 7.
[17] Erbsen provided the account of the first night of censorship to the interviewer in an email.

name at the bottom, and the next morning I got a message from New York on the wires saying who is so and so? And I said, "Our censor moonlighting as a sports writer."

In January 1970, AP reported a survey of 1969 news censorship from around the world, beginning with Cuba expelling Wheeler, and while arguing that now in Brazil there was "free flow of news," the story noted that Hong Kong and Tokyo remained "listening posts" for China, criticized Israel's military censorship that, while unevenly applied, had been in effect for more than 20 years, and called the front lines in the Nigerian civil war "virtually impossible to visit."[18]

PRESS MANIPULATION: DENIALS, SPIN, AND STAGING

To deny the evidence – the most blatant form of spin – and to allow access only to highly staged situations has constituted another form of de facto censorship and press manipulation by foreign governments. Some interactions become surreal, as Mark Stevenson (13–14) discovered in cartel-controlled, "no man's land" Tamaulipas when he went to interview a Mexican official investigating drug crimes:

There were MP vehicles parked outside his offices that were shot up. And I said, "Señor Ministerio Público, we heard reports that your offices were attacked." "No, not true. There hasn't been an attack here." The photographer is like, look out the back, the back window is shot out and there is blood. ... [T]his is a scared little man who was cowering in his office. And that gives you the idea of – the state is absent.

Covering the Libyan civil war, two correspondents who eventually rode along with rebels had also gone to Tripoli to cover the Gadhafi "government side of the story." They were forced to spend weeks in the luxury Rixos Hotel, allowed to leave only on escorted bus tours, and often roused in the middle of the night by a bell ringing on the loudspeaker announcing a news conference:

They would just give us the Libyan government position on things, like basically saying there was no siege on Misrata and so forth. ... Part of the job was to present the Libyan government position, because often I would just feed something to a bigger Libya story. ... [W]e had a trip with the government minders to the old city for shopping, so I got away from them for a bit and tried to grab some people, tried to do a little Tripoli mood story. ... [W]e all had a bit of a problem with this, trying to remain polite and respectful when the government officials were constantly telling us something we knew to be false. ... DELL'ORTO: Did you or the other journalists confront the government when you knew for example that something was just a blatant lie? LAUB: Yeah, yeah, of course. And they would just very smoothly then repeat the lie. (Laub, 26–27; also Schemm, 14)

---

[18] "News Censorship in 1969: A Checkered Map," *New York Times*, January 4, 1970, 14.

Readers of these Tripoli stories were given both the staged presentation – clearly labeled as such – and the real insights:

Journalists, especially in Tripoli, can only travel with government escorts, who stage shows of support for Gadhafi. Regime supporters, usually sporting trademark green scarves or headbands and chanting "Only God, Moammar and Libya," show up in remote locations precisely when reporters arrive there on government-sponsored trips. ... [A] 22-year-old woman approached a reporter in a clothing store. "Don't believe what these people say," the young woman said in English, after overhearing two middle-aged customers say in Arabic that life in Tripoli was normal. The young woman, a bride-to-be wearing a head-scarf and floor-length skirt, walked away from the other shoppers and pretended to be searching a rack of night gowns. Speaking in English, she said her brother has been missing since police opened fire on protesters last week. Clearly fearful that the other shoppers might report her, she then walked back to the front and said loudly in Arabic that the people are behind Gadhafi.[19]

Forty years earlier, the lead to a story from Conakry, Guinea, similarly used the difficulties of reporting to exemplify "the firm grip on everything" that the ruling party had in "black Africa's lone Marxist state":

"Interview the people?" repeated the official guide, incredulously. "That's impossible. I can't let you do it." Nor would he allow a group of visiting journalists to windowshop, walk on the beach, see a movie or go unescorted for a stroll down the capital's wide mango-lined boulevards or anywhere else. "We just want to talk to the people, look around, and see what there is to see," protested one reporter. "No," was the reply. "We'll find party officials to explain anything you want to know."[20]

Even when governments are not patently lying or hostile, journalists have to thwart their attempts to spin information to their advantage. Laub (4–5) argued that "the antenna for spin ... becomes very finely tuned ... experience [on the ground] is key" in the Israeli-Palestinian conflict, where both sides have grown increasingly "sophisticated" in their media strategies. After the second intifada, with terror attacks killing children on all sides, Palestinians – who had "worldwide sympathy" in the first intifada as "18-year-old kids in jeans and sneakers with the slingshot facing armed Israeli soldiers" – found it harder to stake a claim in the "competition for victimhood." So they became "as clever as the Israelis" in media management, down to fighting over which words reporters use:

[T]he Israeli areas in east Jerusalem. Do we call them settlements or do we call them neighborhoods? There was a longtime usage of calling them neighborhoods, but the Palestinian Authority or the Palestinians were saying, "Wait a minute, this is on occupied land; annexation was never recognized by the international community, and they're settlements just like settlements in the West Bank – you cannot differentiate." And ... we

---

[19] Karin Laub and Maggie Michael, "Growing discontent, armed attacks in Tripoli," The Associated Press, April 22, 2011.

[20] Larry Heinzerling, "Guinea: Life Under a Tight Lid," *Washington Post*, June 29, 1972, A16.

increasingly used the word settlement for these areas, or we say Israel built housing for Jews and then have the context or the background graph a little bit further down. ... [W]hen the barrier was built, separation barrier, the Palestinians called it the apartheid wall, the Israelis called it the security fence. Okay, neither are quite true, because sometimes it's a wall and sometimes it's a fence. What it does do, though, is it separates areas of the West Bank from Israel, Israel and parts of the West Bank. So we decided to call it the separation barrier because it is a barrier and it separates people. So it's not always possible to find this, but in this case it was an elegant solution because, as you see, with terminology and everything, the two sides always try to get their position across.

Trickier to evade than spin is the show foreign governments or groups put on for journalists who, often under surveillance and censorship, might have little recourse but to seek kernels of facts at staged events and interviews, and to specify on the wire that the stories have been arranged. During the Gulf War, taken "liked trained seals" by the Bahraini information minister to Saudi Arabia for an arranged speech by King Fahd, correspondents asked if they could interview the Saudi information minister – to which his Bahraini counterpart responded: "'Anything that I say to you, you may attribute to him.' Oh yeah? Not a chance, Jesus!" (Pyle, 15b). In the 1990s, one correspondent was taken on a highly controlled tour of a manmade river created by the Libyan government to reclaim desert land for farming: "Gadhafi shows up and he gets on a tractor, he's kind of performing for the assembled reporters, runs into a wall, gets off the tractor, and goes away" (Powell, 16).

Even guerrilla leaders in remote jungles can run sophisticated PR operations, beginning with treasure-hunt methods to get in touch. Denis Gray (48–49) traveled to meet Khmer Rouge leader Khieu Samphan, the main architect of the killing fields genocide, after pleading repeatedly with the Cambodian guerrillas' "ambassador" in Thailand for a chance to get their point of view. After a mysterious pick-up from Khmers in Bangkok – "a trip to the jungle camp of one of this century's bloodiest revolutionary movements begins with a woman's soft voice on the telephone and a stroll in the park," the story starts[21] – and a nine-hour overnight drive, soldiers met Gray and a couple of colleagues and escorted them over the border, or so they said:

I called my story guerrilla theater because from the very start I noticed – as we were walking along ... very out in the open, they had these, what they called punji stakes, they're bamboo stakes, sharpened with some sort of poison or usually cow dung, which is poisonous when you step on it. So evidently, these are jungle booby traps, that they had them sort of out in the open, totally pointless. Just to show us, just to give the idea that this was a real guerrilla camp under siege. ... These soldiers, all over the place; this sort of aura of danger and mystery. The whole thing was total stage. And then, of course, they really turn on the charm ... they threw a very nice dinner for us ... And they made sure they picked the nicest and most cultivated, charming guy who spoke excellent French and told us about going to school in France, and the culture. ... This whole thing, this

---

[21] Denis D. Gray, "Khieu Samphan Turns On His Charm," *Bangkok Post*, 1980.

whole camp, was made for a media show. But that's still not that unusual. But the thing that got me sort of personally was Khieu Samphan ... gave us a three-hour interview – not an interview, just a talk – about how the world misrepresented the Khmer Rouge and what they really did. And it was just the most surreal thing in the world ... I was trying to picture this human being, being responsible for the death of a million people, just like if you met Hitler – how do you react to somebody like that? You try to build up hate, in some sense, because he killed so many of my friends. But at the same time, he's a human being.

"Butterflies flutter around the briefing table and Khieu Samphan's low decibel voice competes with the chatter of birds and crickets and the roll of a distant thunderstorm," the story said, adding details of the Western dinner, the staged bamboo spikes, and musing on how difficult it was to connect the leaders' "lantern-lit faces" with the torture in Phnom Penh's Toul Sleng prison, "with a landscape of ruined pagodas and ravaged towns, with consistent stories of massacres, forced labour and dehumanising life in collectives."

In Mexico, Stevenson (5–6) followed an utterly managed trail of clues to leaders of the Ejército Popular Revolucionario, a small antigovernment guerrilla group organized in the aftermath of a 1995 police massacre, before realizing that it was only propaganda:

You'd get a phone call. Okay, go to a garbage can outside the Vips [restaurant] and you'll find a note, and that note will tell you to go to the parking lot outside Wal-Mart. Wait there for half an hour. Okay. You'll be observed. Okay. You'll get a cell phone call. ... You see that tree at the corner of the parking lot? Okay. In that first branch, there will be a note and that will tell you where to go next. And you will be watched during the whole journey ... which finally winds up you and your photographer in the mountains around Huitzilac, little secondary roads, and obviously they were observing you because ... they were so despairing that these hopeless journalists, that finally the sign in the road was actually a *mecate*, like twine tied across the road with a little red flag, and there was somebody standing in the trees off the road, jerking the red – stop.... You'd park the car by the side of the road. And they were doing a little propaganda actually, which was literally, okay, we'll all march out of the woods with our assault rifles, which probably had never been fired, and stop traffic and hand out leaflets. It's a total propaganda, and eventually we stopped doing that. Because we saw obviously presentation for the press. If we weren't there, it wouldn't have happened. So why do it?

During wars and rebellions, governments also controlled correspondents by allowing them to see only prescreened, tiny slices of ground where they could get interviews critical of the opposite side. During the Iran-Iraq War, Iraqi minders allowed one correspondent close to the front but only where "they had retaken an area and everybody was just happy and joyful that Saddam was back in control and that the marshes had been drained and that they had these spiffy new houses instead of those ugly old places that they had to live in before, before they got evacuated" (Rice, 2). At the same time in

Tehran, minders took a group of reporters to Evin prison, where the young counterrevolutionary prisoners, "to show their new loyalty to the Ayatollah, were taunting and chasing us through the corridors of the prison. ... I still can't believe they did this to us. In the end, we had to actually run a gauntlet of prisoners who were slapping us on the back. Nobody was injured, but they were striking us and chasing us, and we ended up barricading ourselves in a room" (Hanley, 8).

In Libya's civil war, Gadhafi's officials took reporters to see the aftermath of a NATO bombing, with massive unexploded ordnance still lying in the middle of the street: "the neighbors were all coming over and they were climbing over the thing and they were all excited about it, and we just said, 'We need to get out of here as quickly as possible'" (Laub, 27). In the late 1960s, the Congolese foreign minister once offered to fly the entire Kinshasa foreign press corps to visit Lubumbashi during the height of the postcolonial war – a "generous and open" move that had stunned correspondents until they realized upon landing that the motive was to get them out of town so they would not be able to report the end of a standoff with European mercenaries (Rosenblum, 8). When the Chinese government set to crush Falun Gong, the group's educated, PR-savvy members flooded Tiananmen Square with protestors on public holidays – alerting foreign correspondents ahead of time, "which led to a lot of really shocking coverage of plainclothes security people putting their feet on the heads of older women who they'd thrown onto the ground" (Hutzler, 17).

In 1979, Graham (30) went on the first post-Mao press tour to Tibet, managing to evade the scores of minders a couple of times when other journalists kept them busy showing "the happy Tibetans, really grateful for all the Chinese had done for them, and their lives are much better" – too bad that the correspondents also saw crowds of elderly faithful crying with despair as they circled around the Potala.[22] In the 1971 war when East Pakistan broke away to become Bangladesh, Mort Rosenblum (27–28), former APer Malcolm Browne (1993, 269), and others were taken by West Pakistani officials on a trip to show "the Potemkin village" where nobody wanted independence – an illusion protected by green bamboo netting on the side of the road that kept correspondents from literally seeing the carnage. Until, that is, they figured out a dodge: "There were five [escorts] and there were six of us ... so we worked it out ... the jeeps would stop and we would all run off in different directions, so these guys would have to chase five of us, and the sixth guy would find something out." The dodge is an old one – Max Desfor (11) had used it

---

[22] On July 19, 1979, AP published the first of a series of stories on Tibet, with this note: "For centuries, Tibet has been a land of mystery to the West, visited by only a few intrepid travelers, and communist control of it since 1950 has only made it less accessible. Last week, AP Correspondent Victoria Graham toured the three-mile-high land of the Dalai Lama with a party of foreign correspondents from Peking."

to shoot photos of Japanese diplomats destroying documents in their Washington embassy garden the day Pearl Harbor was attacked:

While two or three of them were burning papers, one guy was out there with a broom and a stick chasing the photographers, so ... we sort of separated, one group would go off and get chased by the guy with the broom, then he would turn around, come back and start getting after the rest of us who were standing by shooting pictures. And then he'd chase us and they'd come back and come in and make pictures.

Occasionally the staging backfired into revealing stories (as in Gannon's tumultuous access to Taliban leaders, in this chapter's box). One correspondent traveling to the cathedral in Esztergom to see the last plaque commemorating Hungary's Roman Catholic primate, József Mindszenty, found that the Communist authorities had rushed ahead of him to cover it with a wooden confessional: "my lead was then that Cardinal Mindszenty had become a nonperson in Hungary ... they're trying to deprive me of a story, but in effect they didn't realize that they were giving me a better story" (Doelling, 8).[23] Bob Reid (48) was taken on a Filipino tour to a Christian town burned down by Muslim extremists in the mid-1990s and, while waiting for his driver back at the Manila airport, the country's young interior secretary told him a "wild and outlandish story" that responsibility lay with the global jihad effort of a certain Osama bin Laden, a name Reid had never heard but dutifully reported.[24] During the 1973 war between a coalition of Arab states and Israel, one frustrated reporter was heard asking the Egyptian minder, "Where do you have the girl-and-pony show?" – which turned out to be at kilometer 101 on the road to Suez, cut off by Israeli soldiers who were up on a hill in full sight, along with the Tel Aviv press corps to whom reporters in Egypt threw TV cassettes for satellite transmission (Pyle, 28-29b). Years later, Pyle returned to write about the "rusting signpost ... at the barren spot where a historic Arab-Israeli peace began," where in 1973, in a show of power, "Israeli crewman played volleyball beside their parked tanks. A parade of Tel Aviv buses brought journalists and even tourists to see the sights. By contrast, no Egyptian tanks were in sight and days passed before Cairo-based foreign journalists were allowed to visit."[25]

Two of Romania's leaders, Nicolae Ceaușescu and his successor Ion Iliescu, even used interviews with correspondents as propaganda tools. In 1975, a photo of Otto Doelling (10) shaking hands with Ceaușescu made the front page the Communist daily *Scînteia* – though it was cropped and tilted so that the

---

[23] "Jozsef Cardinal Mindszenty has become a nonperson in his old archdiocese of Esztergom, the historic and now vacant seat of the primates of Hungary"; Otto Doelling, *The Post-Crescent*, July 20, 1974, p. 9.

[24] Robert H. Reid, "Saudi jailed in California may be key figure in extremist network," The Associated Press, April 16, 1995.

[25] Richard Pyle, "No marker shows where Egypt-Israel peace began," The Associated Press, May 11, 1987.

correspondent looked like he was bowing in deference to the actually much-shorter dictator.[26] Fifteen years later, Dan Perry (4–5) was ceremonially ensconced on an "enormous seat" in Cotroceni Palace and a large TV camera wheeled in. Perry, told it was for "presidential archives," did not object to the filming, nor did he challenge, live, Iliescu's answers, since they presented "very little of interest." Later that night, the interview was the main fare on Romanian television:

It's like "Stimat telespectatori [esteemed television viewers], we are proud to show you a meeting" – not an interview, a meeting – "between şef [chief] Associated Press and Preşedintele [President] Ion Iliescu." And there it is, like unedited, the entire thing – Iliescu giving me this disingenuous nonsense and me seeming to accept it. The ultimate seal of approval. [laughs] ... Today this would have been a monumental scandal, okay? I would have complained, I don't know what we would have done. AP in New York would have gotten involved, they can't just do this ... it'd be on the Internet – back then, you couldn't even make a phone call through Romania ... not easily. If I wanted to sort of tell New York what had happened, I couldn't get through. I'd have to send a telex. And somehow we just let it be.

If spin and manipulation have been a constant across time and countries, the "PR machine" has vastly increased in the digital era, further complicating correspondents' basic task when dealing with governments, as described by Gray (50):

[S]ometimes they'll bullshit you, and sometimes they ... are basically talking the truth, but they put on that extra layer of cream on the cake to make it sweeter and more digestible, and to make sure you report their side of the story so they'll treat you extra well, but it doesn't mean, necessarily, that they're totally pulling the wool over your eyes. ... [Y]ou have to try to make hopefully a fair judgment about what is pure, pure propaganda, pure lies, pure wool over your eyes, and what is just another PR.

CONCLUSIONS

In their quest to both gain reporting access and to portray all sides of a story, including the official government line however pat or even blatantly false, correspondents routinely interact with foreign leaders and officials, a vulnerable relationship in which the latter try to influence coverage through controlling access, surveillance and censorship, and ever-growing attempts at manipulation. A country's geopolitical situation, relationship with the United

---

[26] According to the diplomatic cables made available on www.wikileaks.org (accessed on January 17, 2014), the day that the interview was published in the Romanian press, the Bucharest embassy sent a cable to other Eastern European embassies as well as the secretary of state: "Ceausescu interview by AP correspondent Otto Doelling March 25, published today by Romanian press, contains first direct reference by Romanian leadership to MFN/emigration linkage in trade agreement negotiations." (Case changed for readability; original text had all-uppercase letters.)

States, and internal politics do not seem to predict correspondents' access. That ranges from privileged sit-downs with Mao or the pope – occasions that are made possible by pursuing them relentlessly on the ground – to hard or even impossible to get, since denying coverage, or even the ability to enter or stay in a country, are used for message control. Repeatedly correspondents have had to decide whether a particular story is worth being expelled for, since deportation is one effective tool governments use to retaliate after coverage they dislike. Defending a story's accuracy has sometimes been enough, but some journalists have had to face a secret police officer doubling as visa official who knows all about the stories, and does not enjoy them.

Surveillance has targeted correspondents long and wide, in the form of minders, electronic spying (universal in the Soviet Union and China), and tailing on the street – all of which also work to intimidate, especially sources. Overt censorship is rarer in peacetime, though some correspondents have had to deal with censors posted around the clock inside bureaus, but countries have tried to black out stories by providing only spin, denying the evidence – including blood smears or bodies – and allowing access only to areas where correspondents will meet only pro-government people, even if they have to

---

Taliban-Ruled Afghanistan, 1996–2001

Kathy Gannon: [W]hen the Taliban first took over ... [Taliban Prime Minister Mullah Mohammad] Rabbani ... wouldn't allow me at the press conference. I said that's fine. ... Amir Shah went, no problem. I went around with some other Taliban who were going through everything in the Palace and "Oh, look at this!" and I got a great story. ...

[A couple of days later, still in Kabul] I went to sit with a bunch of people at some brigade headquarters or something, and it was all these people sitting around and they're talking. And I'm asking them, "I don't understand about this, why you're sending women home? And what's this?" ... And then this guy [Mullah Nooruddin Turabi] comes in, big burly guy with one eye and ... a wooden leg ... and he was really angry ... and wanted to know what was going on. So [the acting garrison chief] stands up to explain, "No, I'm just trying to explain" – and he just went whoop to the guy, and slapped him across the face and pushed him on the chair, and said to my colleague, "Get out!" And ... I turned to him and I said, "Really??!!" [laughs] Just like that. And all he could say in Pashto, which I knew, was ... "go," and so I looked at him. I made the point of stopping and looking at him, and then turned away.

[Gannon used both episodes in highly revealing stories about what the new Taliban rule might portend, describing, for example, how Turabi's "arrival interrupted local Taliban leaders and clerics who had been trying to explain that the strict Islamic rule they were introducing in Kabul would be relaxed – allowing girls to be educated and other religions to be tolerated – once transportation and security matters were more settled."][27]

So there was a lot of hue and cry after the fact, when no one should have been surprised over the fact, because [the Taliban] didn't play any games. ... They didn't say, "Oh no, we're really moderate kind of guys," and then turned into these repressive – no, they were village mullahs then, now, and before (Gannon, 42–43, 19).

screen off everything else with bamboo netting along the road. From heads of state to jungle rebels, foreign groups have also been savvy at putting up shows for correspondents, events so staged that some refuse to cover them as news. Despite all these hurdles, correspondents continue to seek the official point of view as necessary to a balanced, objective story. Given the predominance of U.S. global power in the past eight decades, this quest has drawn them into a delicate relationship with the American government's representatives abroad too, which is described in Chapter 10.

[27] Kathy Gannon, "Taliban waste no time imposing its own brand of Islamic rule," The Associated Press, September 28, 1996; Kathy Gannon, "Out Front: Rebels use fear, punishment to impose strict Islamic law," The Associated Press, September 30, 1996.

Flacks, Spooks, GIs, and Objective Journalists: Relating with the U.S. Government Abroad

The relationship between American foreign correspondents and the representatives of the U.S. government abroad – from embassy-posted political officers to CIA "spooks" to soldiers – has undergone significant change. For decades, the U.S. embassy was the first port of call for most correspondents, and a cautious exchange of information was considered "innocent," as an old Africa hand put it. That ease waned after the Cold War and largely shut down after 9/11. From the "on the team" days of World War II and the Korean War to the freewheeling individualism in Vietnam, through the press manipulation in Central America and the Gulf War, and the "embeds" in Iraq and Afghanistan, AP correspondents' relation with the U.S. military has also evolved. Although correspondents whose reporting challenged the U.S. storyline experienced some political pressure, all clung to the ideal of objectivity, understood as lack of partisanship and efforts to present all perspectives, especially when covering scenes fraught with contentious politics and atrocious suffering.

THE EMBASSY LINE: U.S. OFFICIALS AS SOURCES

As Chapter 4 describes, U.S. officials long were essential, if obviously partial, tipsters, sources, and analysts for foreign correspondents. Diplomats and journalists often navigated the same expatriate social circles, though in established media capitals, like Mexico City, AP and other agencies, bent on feeding the wire, struggled to break into the group with elite newspapers whose more forgiving deadlines allowed for "on background" sessions (Price, 8). Even in Vietnam in the early 1970s, when the "dissemblance on details of what actually was happening" led to public clashes between veteran reporters and U.S. officials, one correspondent remembered that diplomats threw her a birthday party (Lederer, 5) – and when Saigon fell to the North Vietnamese and the U.S. Embassy was looted, an AP correspondent "retrieved" the bronze plaque honoring the U.S. troops who had died there during the Tet offensive (Esper 1998, 548). From a military coup in Turkey (Hurst, 3) to a devastating drought in Mauritania (Heinzerling, 2), embassy officials alerted journalists to news. Paul Alexander (12), who covered many unpopular conflicts featuring the United States in the 1990s, found that cultivating friendships with officials who hopscotched from one hot spot to the next elicited more information than being confrontational:

Rather than "How could you possibly have done this?" to "There are reports that say that this has happened. I'd like to give you an opportunity to comment on that." You try to build up a reputation for being fair and balanced so that people don't feel like they're going to get burned by you. . . . [I]n Kenya, you could buy three or four different kinds of liquor in, like, mustard and ketchup packs . . . [with] one shot in each one. And I would go out to the briefings with a handful of those, and it was amazing how much cooperation you could get from people who were really thirsty [in "dry" Somalia].

In wartime Saigon, George McArthur (19–20) also cultivated CIA sources – particularly "the top man" – with "a little bit of booze," while well aware of the dynamics in that information exchange: "the vast majority of his information comes from people like me and the likes of me, from the reporting bunch. . . . A spook . . . is not going to mislead you about a subject on which you are as well informed as he is. And so it's your job to be well-informed."

Thanks to a conscience-stricken officer attached to the U.S. Embassy in Buenos Aires, whom he knew through a network of sources and who risked his life to be a whistleblower, Mort Rosenblum (32–33) managed to get a scoop on Argentina's Dirty War, a time when people disappeared and "these mysterious bodies would just wash up on the shore in Uruguay" – victims of torture during secret police interrogations likely dumped still alive in the ocean:

So this [official] calls me and says, "Do you want to have lunch?" . . . He'd witnessed way too much torture. He'd go to this police commissary and he'd hear these people screaming in the next room, and . . . said, "I got to get out of here." Because he couldn't say anything to anybody, he couldn't tell, these were the people that he had to work with. So he decided to just tell a reporter. . . . [A] Uruguayan legislator and his wife had been killed, and they had these two kids. . . . And the government, which still had a compunction against killing babies then, tried to give them to the Americans. And that was kind of the tipping – because he said . . . "We were two days ago at that table, and they offered me these children." That's when he called me. So I wrote this story and . . . I called up my editors in New York and said, "Look, I'm going to write this story, and you're going to take a look at it and you're going to see really weird sources and stuff, but go with it here." . . . I . . . certainly couldn't say "Western diplomats" . . . I put together all the other stuff I'd had, and I had enough to be able to sort of write a story saying that the bodies, that sources, intelligence sources, you know, non-Argentine intelligence sources. . . . And then it was out. And then a lot of stories started coming out.

A month after leaving Argentina, Rosenblum wrote a widely published analysis of the reign of terror there that, as an illustration of "the atmosphere in Buenos Aires," cited the restaurant episode with the source identified only as "a police official," who told Rosenblum a government intelligence officer had described how the children's parents had been tortured and burned alive.[1]

More recently, however, officials have become tighter-lipped, embassies harder to access, and correspondents more skeptical that the time invested in "cozying up" is worth the meager return (Bryson, 62), especially when they have wider access to a variety of sources. A correspondent in South and Southeast Asia found U.S. diplomats less "forthcoming" and more defensive than other Western officials, in part because they have "more skin in the game" and recognize the larger impact that attribution to "U.S." versus "Western" officials would generate even for otherwise anonymous sources (Pennington, 16–17). The practice of informally pooling information between diplomats and journalists, both sides eager to have the other's knowledge particularly where foreign governments severely clamped down on Americans' movements – although AP journalists shared "nothing that we wouldn't report" (Gray, 15) – also fizzled out after recurring frequently during the Cold War. Then, it had seemed "a lot more innocent then than it does today," said Larry Heinzerling (5–6), who covered West Africa in the 1960s and ultimately helped lead AP's international coverage until the late 2000s:

We recognized this threat, this Soviet threat [during the Cold War]. And it wasn't that we were "on the team," but we were kind of cognizant of "this is serious business" and the U.S. is trying to do a thing that we agree with and support. ... [T]here was still sort of a partnership involved with the diplomatic community, which has evaporated, basically, today. ... I did a story about the USIS library that the embassy opened up in Soweto, which was a tremendous story because here was the Americans telling the South African government what they thought about apartheid. And the guy who did that ... proceeded with a black American diplomat, that was another push ... [to] together go into [an all-white] restaurant in Johannesburg, and I went with them, just to cover it. ... The owner saw the black diplomat, didn't blink an eye. Just took us to a back table. It was in the restaurant, but a table in the back. And fed us, and let us out. And that was it. But I did a story about it. It was sort of the first effort to integrate a restaurant in Johannesburg. [Heinzerling's story about diplomats' "activist program to stress American disapproval of South Africa's race policy" spotlighted the Soweto library.][2]

Aside from a few older criticisms about sources that smacked of efforts to "teleguide" coverage (Heinzerling, 14), most correspondents said that they suffered no "duress" from U.S. diplomats (Minthorn, 9) – something that might have stunned their wire agency counterparts from TASS or *Xinhua*,

---

[1] Mort Rosenblum, "The Harvest of Torture and Terror in Argentina," *Los Angeles Times*, October 24, 1976, E2; the same story was published in *The New York Review of Books* on October 28, 1976.

[2] Larry Heinzerling, "U.S. Presses Message of Racial Equality in South Africa," *Washington Post*, November 28, 1976, 20.

used to taking orders from their political elites (Belkind, 17–18). Being overseas shielded correspondents from political pressure more than their colleagues in Washington – because they looked at foreign realities more than at geopolitical or military relations (Seward, 10), and because their daily reporting tasks were often challenging and dangerous enough to take attention away from worrying, and even knowing, about "what concoctions were being stirred up in Washington" (Tatro, 5). As one correspondent with two decades of experience in the Middle East highlighted, the diplomats themselves in the field "are not necessarily saying the same thing you're hearing in Washington," and their "read on things" – especially "off the record" in their office – often aligned with the correspondents' more than with DC (Powell, 13).

Correspondents covering countries at the center of controversial U.S. foreign policies, however, have also been the targets of pressure, though most of it came not directly but either mediated by U.S.-based editors under fire by AP member media or straight from the audience, particularly in the digital age, as discussed in later chapters. In Cuba, Anita Snow (15–17), who reopened the bureau after nearly 30 years, had it coming from all sides – "somebody was always angry with you ... you can't win." The Cuban government summoned her to the press office for "loud arguments" over coverage of dissidents and the language use regarding Castro ("dictator" did not work), whereas the Americans wanted more coverage of the dissidents and lambasted that of Castro, and the exile community unleashed its fury on blogs (calling her "the C word" once, over a minor story). Covering Afghanistan post-9/11 or Mexican migration, correspondents faced an "insistent narrative" (Gannon, 46) coming from Washington, so that a story, when "not in line with what the U.S. government was saying ... required more effort to persuade editors that that was right" (Price, 14).

One real way that political pressure affected storytelling was the additional burden of proof required to write stories that gave the lie to U.S. government claims. One correspondent's story about the CIA's influence in Congo during Mobutu's early years never made the wire because he didn't have enough evidence to overcome official denials (Zeitlin, 12). The Pulitzer-winning story on the No Gun Ri massacre went through years of "struggle" – fact-checking but also acrimonious editorial discussions – before it was published, co author and special correspondent Charles Hanley said (14-19; also Port 2002). Bob Reid (42–44), who reported for AP for more than four decades, found Iraq a "classic" of politicized wrangling where the bar of proof was raised so high – to "absolutely certain" – that more prescient oppositional stories could never clear it:

We can't have the president, the chairman of the Joint Chiefs of Staff, the defense secretary, the head of the CIA, any number of them, other people saying black is white and we say no, black is not white [without compelling evidence]. ... There were stories that I saw, in the run-up to both the Afghan War and the Iraq conflict, that in retrospect were right on the button but were against the grain of American thinking. ... [One] had to do with weapons of mass destruction, which probably should have shown more skepticism on, but there was such fear that if we're going to go this route, there can't be a scintilla of doubt here, and never could get that final scintilla removed.

Hanley (20–22), who had developed a beat on arms control, found "the flaws in the reasoning and the gaps in the facts" in much that was discussed about Iraqi WMD as casus belli in 2002–2003 and, with AP editors' blessing, went to Iraq twice for UN inspections, something he had also covered in the 1990s. Although a couple of his "semi-analytical" stories were not used, plenty of other stories detailing what he found, or rather not, hit the wire in blunt terms. One January 2003 story from Baghdad stated in the lead: "In almost two months of surprise visits across Iraq, U.N. arms monitors have inspected 13 sites identified by U.S. and British intelligence agencies as major 'facilities of concern,' and reported no signs of revived weapons building, an Associated Press analysis shows." Making it crystal clear, Hanley wrote that the UN's work "seems thus far to support Iraq's contention that its old weapons establishment is not making new forbidden arms."[3] Such copy, however, hardly shook American resolve:

But they just weren't making the impact they should have made back home because the Beltway media were so focused on the U.S. sources rather than the actual hard facts on the ground in Iraq. ... [G]enerally, there is this deference to official U.S. sources, and

FIGURE 10.1. Roving correspondent Charles Hanley surveys the damage to Saddam Hussein's Great Movement Palace in Baghdad in May 2003, during a visit to the nearby U.S. WMD-hunting team. (Photo by Murad Sezer, courtesy of Charles Hanley)

---

[3] Charles J. Hanley, "Inspectors have covered CIA's sites of 'concern' and reported no Iraqi violations," The Associated Press, January 18, 2003.

particularly to the U.S. military. So ... I just kept plugging away, knowing that eventually they would find no WMD.

From army divisions to handfuls of "advisors," from land invasions to humanitarian missions, from five-star generals to mud-caked GIs, the U.S. military has been an inescapable feature of the global geopolitical landscape in the past eight decades, and correspondents have often encountered the U.S. government abroad in the person of its armed forces. Much has been written, usually critically, about the historical evolution of this relationship and of war correspondence (Sweeney 2006; Knightley 2004). Interviews highlighted four major aspects of the American military's impact on media content: logistical help in conflict coverage; efforts to control it, down to attempts at cover-ups; the controversial practice of "embedding"; and the historical GI-centric conflict perspective.

Hop Right In: Getting to War

Freely from World War II to Vietnam, and in the shape of tightly controlled press pools and embeds since, many correspondents have covered wars with the troops (see also Chapter 6). As most of the older generation pointed out, many correspondents had served in the armed forces and many military press liaisons had been newsmen, so trust came easier and journalists could get to the front on almost anything that floated or flew, and had room – especially in Vietnam, belying its reputation as a nadir in press-military relations (Desfor, 10; Behr 1981, 255; Prochnau 1995, 193). Already in the early 1960s, one AP journalist was invited by MACV (Military Assistance Command, Vietnam) to go on a mission against the Viet Cong – and when he wrote the story that the targeted village turned out to have none of them, the military promptly, but futilely, banned the press from similar trips (AP Oral History, Essoyan 1997, 49–50). Another correspondent later managed to accompany Marine helicopter pilots on a mission to rescue pilots shot down over North Vietnam, despite AP and MACV rules barring reporters from the North, after a sergeant offered to take him on what was supposed to be a test flight. The mission became a dramatic story when a pilot really was shot down and the reporter had to stay on as the helicopter was scrambled to the rescue. All went well, and while the rule-breaking story never made the wire, the correspondent had limitless free drinks reserved at the Da Nang officers' mess "because I had been aboard when they rescued this guy" (AP Oral History, Mulligan 2005, 18–19). Seeking to get pilots' reactions to Henry Kissinger's announcement that peace in Vietnam was at hand, Edie Lederer (2–3) went aboard the aircraft carrier USS *America*, the only woman among thousands of sailors. Even though she had to be "locked in prison sick bay overnight" for her own safety, she found a cheerful welcome and unusual insights:

[T]hese guys just loved talking to an American woman. And one of the things that I realized very early on was that you could ask these guys to explain anything, I think things that they would expect a guy to know. . . . I think that was one great advantage being a woman, and I used it.

Useful for getting to the scene, the military was also precious help for getting out, for example plucking two grateful AP reporters from the teeming, desperate crowd outside the U.S. Embassy in Saigon during its final evacuation (Esper 1983, 187). Arnold Zeitlin (23) was on the deck of a U.S. Navy cruiser as helicopters ferried in evacuees while the North Vietnamese closed in on the capital, though his thrill at being a privileged witness to the "incredible" conclusion of the war ended in an "anticlimax because I learned that all our stories were held up until the Pentagon released the news." In the late 1980s, Pyle (2b) reported aboard two dozen Navy ships to cover the "military escort operation in the Gulf" – battles that would have been entirely off-limits otherwise. Especially where violence made it too dangerous to roam around unaccompanied, such as during some stages of the Iraq War, some correspondents felt the need for "an information pipeline" from the military (Hanley, 23). In both Saigon and Riyadh, Pyle (12–14) found value in regularly scheduled military press briefings, especially for a wire service of record. He even wrote a story about how, despite wanting to avoid such appearance by refusing to push back the start time to 5 p.m., the Gulf War daily news briefing looked "more and more like its Indochinese ancestor," though without "gecko lizards scampering about the walls."[4] Vietnam's much-maligned "5 o'clock follies" were useful, he told me, because "whatever they said . . . was on the goddamn record so everybody knew what they said and they had to take responsibility for it" – especially when journalists confronted the military with conflicting information:

Something would be offered to us at the briefings, some information. And we would have somebody in the field who had already told us something that . . . contradicted that. And we would confront them with it. . . . That happened not every day but with some frequency, that somebody would have a "Wait a minute, Colonel, you said this but what about this, we have this." And they would have to make adjustments. . . . I've been told this by a couple of these . . . military guys, that in their pocket they would have a piece of information, a news release about something, that they would read if they were asked about it. If they weren't asked about it, it stayed in their pocket.

Command and Control the Stories

By providing selected information and logistical support, the military, correspondents said, also sought to influence and control coverage perceived as adversarial. Censorship ruled in World War II and Korea, and one Vietnam commander notoriously answered an AP correspondent's question about U.S.

---

[4] Richard Pyle, "Daily briefing seems more like Saigon 'Follies,'" The Associated Press, February 6, 1991.

casualties with a testy "Why can't you get on the team?" (Browne 1993, 163). Vietnam was indeed a paradox: Several correspondents remembered it for its ease of access and lack of censorship (as well as for the extremely high casualty count among journalists), with the U.S. military going "out of their way to help us" get to scenes, so that "by and large the American people got the straight skinny on Vietnam from the press" (Pyle, 3, 19). But to many U.S. officials, Vietnam was the turning point in press hostility. They tightly restricted or denied battlefield access in the smaller conflicts of the 1980s as well as the 1991 Iraq War. During the 1983 invasion of Grenada, correspondents were kept in a hotel on another island, only allowed into Grenada on "day trips" with U.S. military planes on missions. After the war ended, Ike Flores (14–16; 2007, 157, 162) spent a couple of weeks there, and the military "gave me helicopter tours and showed me around after the fact," including some of the camps where he sought out Cuban prisoners for information about just what they had been doing there – and how many of them had died.

Most journalists who covered the Persian Gulf War found it "terribly restrictive," even "canned" (Fialka 1991, 2; Fisk 2005, 599). Correspondents were forced to have escorts everywhere they went, and their ability to see any action depended on whether they were assigned to a pool "right in the heat" or one "doing nothing," since they could not escape unless they tried to sneak into Kuwait entirely on their own – according to Lederer (13), who "was at an air base in Saudi Arabia and got first word that the American warplanes launched the air war against Iraq."[5] The U.S. ground campaign was so short – lasting about four days – that reporters hardly got to see it (Ferrari 2003, 28). In the Iraq War, most correspondents noted the "huge pressure from people in the military to toe the line," to accept the war that they were selling, or the officers would either "start to freeze you out [including out of embeds], or they were constantly on your neck to try and change your mind" (Reid, 41). After the abuse at Abu Ghraib prison was publicized by other media, Hanley (25) wrote about how the military had "stonewalled" AP reporters six months earlier on the same story by not answering the half dozen questions they had – a denial that apparently came from a higher command than the MP unit involved.[6]

Correspondents like Gannon (10–12), who went out by themselves at great risk, not only found different stories but encountered some belligerence from U.S. officers who apparently felt they had lost control of the message. During an interview with the head of the Kirkuk council, U.S. soldiers came in with another journalist, and the Iraqi, who had been "very aggressive" telling Gannon what was happening, switched "night and day" to "things, they are

[5] Edith M. Lederer, "Allies' surprise attacks crippled Saddam and changed rules of war," The Associated Press, January 8, 1992.
[6] Charles J. Hanley, "Prisoners' early accounts of extensive Iraq abuse met U.S. silence," The Associated Press, May 8, 2004.

progressing."[7] Gannon quickly closed the interview – and later marveled at how advantageous AP's infrastructure was:

[T]he bureau in Baghdad is still working their asses off and doing the day-to-day and making sure that they get everything. The embed is there, somebody's doing the embed like this person, somebody else is doing something else, somebody's looking after this. And there's Kathy: "Thank you very much, I think I'm just going to go to Kirkuk." . . . They want to control you and everything, that's fine. If they want to, that's their business. It's our business to not let them.

Gannon (70) found the U.S. military reluctant to relinquish message control even after ceding nominal control to local troops: When she arrived in Gardez to embed with the Afghan National Army, she faced "a reaction, and it wasn't a positive one, from the U.S. military to independently going through the [Afghan] ministry of defense."

On occasion, efforts to control the message translated into cover-ups or even the "feeding" of a misleading story to a reporter, something that one Vietnam correspondent estimated "happened to everybody once or twice in their career" (Lederer, 11).[8] The "defensiveness" of many military spokespeople in the Iraq and Afghanistan wars (also described in Arraf 2009; Hoyt 2007; Katovsky and Carlson 2003) could be so clumsy that several correspondents could only get comments that "nothing bad was happening" (Hurst, 8) – or an innocent "What big bomb?" to which the exasperated reporter in Baghdad's Palestine Hotel retorted, "The one I can see right out my window" (AP Oral History, Reid 2009, 82). (In Saigon in the early 1960s, Browne had inquired about the U.S. aircraft carrier clearly visible at the end of the street – and the U.S. official's response was a "tongue-in-cheek" "I don't see anything"; Ferrari 2003, 95.)

Being on the ground to investigate gave correspondents enough material to break stories beyond the official line, uncovering abuses and sometimes contradicting U.S. accounts so irrefutably that changes were made in the field. A story on "perhaps the boldest and most sophisticated attack" against American troops in Karbala, Iraq, clearly stated in the lead that the U.S. military had finally confirmed the AP account of a violent abduction nearly a week after initially dissembling it as just another tragic but routine assault the soldiers had died "repelling":[9]

---

[7] Bassem Mroue and Kathy Gannon, "In northern Iraq, another war Kurd vs. Arab looms," *The Associated Press*, February 13, 2007. The story, datelined Kirkuk, noted: "Mroue reported from Baghdad and Gannon from Kirkuk. AP writer Yahya Barzanji in Kirkuk also contributed to this report."

[8] In a book chapter on Vietnam, Lederer (2002, 172) wrote that a U.S. officer told her he had been on a plane that had picked up three American POWs – but it was hoax, and the AP had to kill the story on its radio wire. Lederer wrote it was "one of the most painful lessons of my career."

[9] Steven R. Hurst, "AP IMPACT: Four U.S. soldiers abducted and shot to death last week in southern Iraq," *The Associated Press*, January 26, 2007.

[W]e kept saying, "Look, we're going to report this," and they kept saying, "We don't know anything more than what was reported." And once we had it on the wire, it was an enormous story. And the military here [in Washington] called the military there and said, "You guys better just tell the truth," and so they did. . . . [I]t shined a very bright light on the fact that what we were being told and what was happening were two entirely different things. Not every day, sometimes the truth was told. But when things really looked bad, it was covered up, as best as it could be covered up. (Hurst, 12)

In Afghanistan, correspondents traveled to remote and dangerous provinces to "do our best to nail down if civilians had died [in U.S. airstrikes] and then just put the military's side of the story as well": "I didn't get the impression that . . . we took heat for that in particular. And you can't do anything else, that's your job entirely" (Pennington, 10). In one case, reporting on an alleged retaliation shooting of civilians resulted in a military review and the removal of that unit from Afghanistan.[10]

Challenges and Opportunities of Embedding

The wars in Iraq and Afghanistan also saw the institutionalization of "embedding" journalists with U.S. troops, a strategy devised by the Pentagon to "protect operational security" for both soldiers and the media, and to counter Saddam's "lying" by having independent observers, which ultimately numbered 600 in Iraq alone, according to one of the policy's main architects (in Katovsky and Carlson 2003, 204–208). Most correspondents who went on repeated embeds in both wars found the often disparaged "in bed" experiences allowed them to report stories that would have gone undetected otherwise – such as "how everything ended up being about security rather than the actual aims of the war" (Buzbee, 9) – but that the same was true of independent coverage, so both were necessary to get the full picture "from every source possible" (Gray, 29; also Fahmy and Johnson 2007: 105).

Tokyo-based Eric Talmadge (9–10) covered Iraq and Afghanistan both independently and on embeds, and found an "amazing" "contrast of what you do and what you see," though both are "really, seriously dicey." The obvious disadvantage of embedding – the correspondents' movements were totally restricted to where their units went – was in many cases balanced by the advantage of relative safety, especially in the constantly moving front lines during the insurgency. The day Private Jessica Lynch's unit was ambushed, triggering one of the most high-profile and controversial stories of the war,

---

[10] Rahim Faiez, "Wounded Afghans say U.S. forces fired on civilians after suicide bomb; 10 killed," The Associated Press, March 4, 2007; Robert Burns, "Marines under investigation for firing on civilians; general orders them out of Afghanistan," The Associated Press, March 23, 2007. The Marines were ultimately cleared of wrongdoing.

Reid (56) took a call from a reporter assigned to follow behind U.S. troops as the area was cleared, to report on post-battle stories:

She said it's too dangerous to move forward, and it's too dangerous to move backward. What do we do? ... Basically we told her, "Find an American unit and beg them to let you go with them," which is what she did. And they took her all the way to Baghdad. ... [U]nits were all over the place, you could easily run into a hostile unit without knowing it, in an area that should have been okay, plus the friendly units were firing at you because they didn't know who was who.

Denis Gray (24, 27), who covered wars from Indochina to Iraq (both conflicts) to Afghanistan, compared the "free-for-all" of Southeast Asia with more than a dozen later embedded stints, in which for several weeks "you become almost part of the unit. You do everything that the soldiers do, basically, and you move along with them, you sleep with them, you do the rest of it, but they have you within their ranks, literally. The only thing you don't do, obviously, is fight." The long-term immersive experience gives a better feel for "the military life," especially if the assigned commander provides unfettered access, such as in Gray's latest embed in the Taliban's birthplace:

My last embed was with a fantastic colonel, with the 101st Airborne Division in Kandahar, who was outspoken, totally open, again very critical of what was going on. ... Very difficult, tough district, and they were there in the beginning [of a U.S. operation]. So, in a way, he didn't have to defend his record, for one thing; if he had been there six months later, he may have talked differently. But still, in the beginning, he said, "This place stinks, we've screwed up on our communications with the locals, there's no hearts-and-minds campaign, the local district government hasn't been seen here for months. We're in really deep, deep trouble."[11] So, extremely open-minded and allowed us to do anything we wanted.

Buddy System

For all the tension with Pentagon brass, correspondents have generally had warm, close relations with ordinary U.S. troops from World War II to today – not only to build up necessary sources and maintain access, but also because of shared dangers and a sense of responsibility, particularly in earlier wars and during tragic moments. George McArthur (3–5, 19; AP Oral History 2005, 6–7) covered both the Korean and the Vietnam wars, in the latter trying to keep out of his copy that he "wanted my side to win, [but] I knew damn well they weren't." (In fact, in one roundup story on conflict by year's end 1967, he wrote from Saigon that a "legal political structure" was "taking shape" there, but "the war is another matter.")[12] McArthur's first lesson was that "you don't want to go off to be a war correspondent to fight the fucking war, you went off

---

[11] Denis D. Gray, "Next US target: The birthplace of the Taliban," The Associated Press, August 23, 2010.

[12] George McArthur, "Southeast Asia," *Chicago Tribune*, December 31, 1967, 17.

FIGURE 10.2. Bangkok-based correspondent Denis Gray goes on a combat patrol with U.S. troops in the mountains of Zabul Province in Afghanistan, on one of his multiple embedded assignments, on April 9, 2007. (Photo courtesy of Denis Gray)

to see what was going on" – from the perspective of senior officers, whom he learned to respect, and the GIs he "always loved":

They're dumb and they're inarticulate and they're rough to get along with, but you find out easy enough that you mess with a guy and unless you're really stupid, you learn how they're thinking and feeling. And they're not serious at all, and they're not there to fight a war for the glory of the flag. . . . They had been sent there somehow, and they didn't quite understand it. . . . I hope there was some mutual respect. . . . Hell, I was so young [in his early 20s in Korea], I was a GI myself for all practical purposes. Had to learn how to open a mess can, for Christ's sake. . . . [A]long the demilitarized zone, you could camp out and make like a Boy Scout with the troops if you wanted to, and everybody did at least two or three times, sort of prove they had the guts to stay up there overnight.

Sixty years after the Korean War, Max Desfor (1–2) also remembered how he had traveled up and down the peninsula with American troops, landing at Inchon and fighting "our way" northward almost to the Yalu River and then being chased all the way back south. En route, Desfor, who was riding in an army photographer's jeep with two other journalists, saw a woman "wandering around" by the Taedong River and got out to see what she was doing – and the scene became his Pulitzer-winning photo of desperate refugees:

[T]here was this broken-down bridge, which I later found out of course had been bombed out of existence by American aircraft bombs. And I walked up to it and walked as far as I could, and I was on the top of the hillside ... what originally had been the approach to the bridge, and there I saw the people scrambling through the girders, broken-down girders, and scrambling with the few possessions that they were able to carry on their heads or wrapped around their body, but very, very little that they could possibly take with them. And I made the pictures of this scene, which was incredible to me. But I could not stay very long. ... First of all, it was pretty repetitive, if I continued shooting the same picture of the people crossing the bridge – basically it was the same picture over again. Besides which, in spite of the gloves I was wearing, it was freezing cold, and beside which, and more important, was that we were on the run and my jeep companions of course were getting pretty anxious and we had to continue our fleeing. I made eight exposures only; that's all I was able to do within that time and for these various reasons.

Either through their own military service or war reporting, several senior correspondents – male and female – found that knowing the "lingo" helped them earn troops' respect, earn access, and write better stories. Pyle (11–12b), who had been a company clerk in a Signal Corps company for two years, realized that when military brass talked, he "knew what the hell they were talking about. ... I knew how crazy some of it was, how nuts it seemed, but I knew why it wasn't nuts." Despite the "bad" restrictions on Gulf War coverage, Lederer (11–12) was asked by the chief military spokesman if she wanted to ask the first question at the first press conference – probably because he had a lot of "respect for the fact that I had been in Vietnam."

Whether covering an exchange of war prisoners at Panmunjom during the Korean War,[13] the Americans emerging "tired and hungry" (Summerlin, 4), or the 1983 bombing of the Marines barracks in Beirut, which killed 241 American servicemen, some correspondents, keenly aware of how many families hung on their words, "really felt for them":

You'd try to go talk to these guys, and they were "keeping the world safe for democracy." Well, no. They were sitting here on an airfield taking incoming from the mountains around them because a decision had been made that they were going to help reinforce what at that point they thought was a peace deal. (Powell, 3)

At especially tragic moments, such as after the media had published photos of the bodies of U.S. soldiers dragged through Mogadishu streets in the "Black Hawk Down" episode, Alexander (13–14) found himself doing a bit of explaining to soldiers "who weren't necessarily happy with us" – and some

---

[13] Among many, George McArthur, "42 Wounded and Ailing Cross Line to Freedom," *Washington Post*, August 6, 1953, 1.

FIGURE 10.3. Edith Lederer and other members of the AP Dhahran staff (from right to left: Sandy Higgins, George Esper, and Fred Bayles) piece together news of the Persian Gulf War from across the Middle East in early 1991. (AP photo by John Gaps, courtesy of AP Corporate Archives)

did understand that the media helped the world see "the type of brutality" they contended with. Alexander's reporting on the use of non-deadly force, for example, first worked with the military – and ultimately, unwittingly, against it:

There was one time when Fred Peck, who was the main military briefer, came up to me ... "Paul, you know, I hate to ask you this, but would you ask me about this issue during the news conference? I've been carrying around this can of pepper spray in my fatigues for the last week, waiting for somebody to ask." ... "So tell me, have you had any new developments as far as being able to deal with crowd control?" "Well, now that you mention it ..." And he pulls out the can. ... [I]t was a news-value issue. I actually felt badly once that, I went out on a patrol with a light-armored vehicle and ... as we were getting ready to leave ... several of the soldiers picked up rocks. And I was wondering, "What's going on here?" And we hit the street, and there were kids, and adults, throwing rocks at us. So they didn't want to shoot these kids, there's no way to use anything else long distance, so they would throw rocks back. So I reported that and suddenly there's a ban on throwing rocks at the populace. It's politically incorrect. I felt bad about that, because I thought it was sort of a clever way of dealing with it.

Alexander's story on the Marines and the rock-throwing Mogadishu children highlighted the bizarrely friendly dynamic:

They call him the king of crowd control. When Marine Sgt. Keith Credle shows up, the Somali kids start clapping and chanting "A-mer-i-can." His song-and-dance act is part of Company C's effort to bridge the cultural gap and convince people to turn in weapons to the troops, instead of pelting them with rocks. ... Lt. Mike Zeliff sports a Band-Aid that covers the six stitches on the bridge of his nose, broken by a baseball-sized rock last week. ... "There were 10 kids there waving, and one of them threw a rock at the vehicle. You should have seen the look of shock on his face when it hit me." ... When the patrol pulled out, a group of kids ran behind for a while. A couple of rocks landed harmlessly, and the Marines laughed and lobbed them back. Several adults rushed out and shooed the kids away.[14]

Throwing rocks back was one of the "nonlethal force" expedients that U.S. troops also used at the height of the Sunni insurgence in the Iraq War, getting them into trouble with the Pentagon, the *New York Times*' Dexter Filkins reported (2008, 162–163). Even in that vastly unpopular conflict, Filkins (207–213) wrote movingly of his relationship with troops – especially the Marine who was killed accompanying him and photographer Ashley Gilbertson to take a picture of a dead insurgent on top of a minaret in Fallujah: "Your photographer needed a corpse for the newspaper, so you and a bunch of Marines went out to get one. Then suddenly it's there, the warm liquid on your face, the death you've always avoided, smiling back at you like it knew all along. Your fault." An infantry unit Gray embedded with in Iraq also suffered casualties in a night ambush, so that the planned attack on Najaf gave way to a memorial service for a beloved sergeant whose wife was also serving in Iraq. Gray (60–61) began and ended that story with soldiers' tears, "unashamedly streaming down their sand-blown faces" and later recalled the ambush:[15]

[I]t was about a 24-hour trek because a lot of the bridges had been blown or mined, so we had to go around; it was endless, in the back of this crammed Humvee. And in the middle of the night, we were ambushed with regular fire and also an IED. And our Humvee was safe and the guy behind us was in a truck, fairly well armored ... was hit. ... [W]e had to run the gauntlet of the ambush; they were firing all over the place. That's one of the first times somebody handed me a gun, and of course, I said I'm not going to shoot, and then the soldiers didn't realize that we're not supposed to shoot. But anyway, we ran the gauntlet and we got through. And they stopped, and they had a helicopter land in the middle of the night. Very quickly, amazing. And they evacuated this guy, and everybody was down below saying, "Well, he's just been scratched, no problem." And they were joking.

[14] Paul Alexander, "Marines aim to bridge cultural gap," The Associated Press, March 11, 1993.
[15] Denis D. Gray, "Troops weep, remember friends as U.S. forces hold memorial services during bloodiest month in Iraq," The Associated Press, April 15, 2004.

JUST THE FACTS: SAFEGUARDING OBJECTIVITY

The inherent closeness of embeds – whether or not they ended with a soldier's blood splashing a reporter's face – could also tempt correspondents to "go along with their line ... you have to become very careful to maintain your objectivity" (Gray, 25). Throughout the decades, correspondents have assiduously defended objectivity as an essential practice, particularly for a wire service, in the face of major challenges to it, in U.S. wars but also when reporting on brutal enemies or unspeakable suffering. Walking the fine line of writing fair and balanced accounts of momentous occasions of national or even personal import, they sought to at least present most sides – and on only rare occasions let their outrage pierce through "just the facts."

Covering the Enemy

For much of the 20th century, America's enemy was Communism, and correspondents behind the Iron Curtain, in China, and in Cuba found it hard to ignore in almost any story they did. But they tried hard to avoid that as the frame, both to write more complete, neutral stories and to ensure that their host countries would perceive them not as Cold Warriors but as "an Associated Press reporter first and foremost" (Flores, 14). Moscow-based reporters strove to be non-ideological observers, giving a full picture of the challenges of daily life for ordinary Soviets without "presenting the life you came from as the only standard" (Minthorn, 7), and strictly keeping themselves and "an American point of view" out of the stories (Cooperman, 21). Alan Cooperman (22) "got called on the carpet" by AP managers for an interview with his first newspaper, the *Berkshire Eagle*, in which he said that the morning the 1991 coup was over, "caught up in the emotion of it," he had tears in his eyes: "You're an AP reporter. You're not supposed to have tears in your eyes. ... And, if you do, you don't talk about it." Nor was it the reporters' role "to shout from the hilltops, 'We've won!'" – not that he really felt such easy triumphalism when the Soviet Union collapsed, added Cooperman, who was in the room when Gorbachev resigned.

From late 1970s Beijing (Graham, 16) to 2000s Havana, correspondents also wondered how much they should reference Communism itself – surely not "neutral language":

We had to decide when was the fact that [Cuba] was a Communist state relevant, because maybe it wasn't always. If there was some government decision, yeah, it was relevant, but with some of the other things, perhaps not. ... You have to be fair, because ... [t]here are a lot of people in the world who don't think that Communism is a bad thing or might not know what it is. Well, a lot of people in the U.S. don't know what it is. ... You can't explain it in every single story out of Cuba. You explain that the government controls more than 95 percent of the economy or ... you use other things, like the only Cuban journalists authorized to work in Cuba work for the state media. Everybody else is working illegally. (Snow, 24–25)

Correspondents from El Salvador to Syria also sought to go beyond their sometimes instinctive siding with particular groups or narratives of the bad versus good guys. The "facts on the ground" of Syria's brutal civil war challenged the general Arab Spring feeling of being "quite positive towards the people who were revolting against the governments" – a feeling one reporter with more than a decade's experience in the Middle East said he came by "honestly," given that most governments were "frankly awful" and that "if you're going to make a judgment call, it should be the judgment call for the average person" (Schemm, 22). One unique test of AP objectivity came in covering the Lebanese war during the nearly seven years in which Hezbollah militants held hostage correspondent Terry Anderson (24; AP Oral History 1997, 22). A quarter century later, he recalled proudly how AP had not let reports of hostage killing influence its operations (except for pulling Americans out of Beirut, like everyone else, "because it was just too freaking dangerous"):

[N]obody can successfully look at the AP coverage of the Middle East while I was a hostage and say that they reported this or they didn't report that because Anderson was being held. And that's important. The AP ... is more than just a news organization. It is a social structure with values, and those values center around good journalism, objectivity, fairness, maintaining the highest standards you can at what you do. ... It would compromise our integrity, who we feel we are, if they had, say, gone light on certain things or covered certain things up or tried not to do their best to discover what the negotiations were about when there were negotiations.

In recent years, another profound test came for Gannon (61–63) in Kabul, writing about ordinary Afghans and even the Taliban during the war in the immediate aftermath of 9/11. Gannon's first wartime story datelined Kabul ran on October 25, 2001, with an incisive, instantaneous, intimate feel:

It's 9 p.m., and the Taliban have turned electricity off throughout the capital to make it harder for American attackers to find targets. Streets are deserted, silent. Dogs begin to howl and bark. Candles are lit. Dinner, usually eaten late, is now done by 8. ... Now: another jet. This one appears to be patrolling the city, perhaps trying to engage anti-aircraft guns on the ground. From Taliban positions comes an occasional boom, but they seem to be using their anti-aircraft weapons sparingly. Again, silence, for a while. And again, another roar, another jet – loudly, this time. Windows rattle. Six powerful explosions shatter the night, and bursting lights illuminate the night sky.[16]

Gannon later told me what it took to get stories like this on the wire (see this chapter's box for more on 9/11 Afghanistan reporting; also Reid, 44) – "long discussions" about how to word stories so as not to caricaturize the Taliban into a one-dimensional "evil entity," but rather to give "a sense of who they were" as

---

[16] Kathy Gannon, "Kabul's nightly routine: Jets, darkness, anti-aircraft fire," The Associated Press, October 25, 2001.

well as what "ordinary Afghans" were thinking – a test of journalistic integrity that she felt AP passed:

We had lots of people covering the other side with the Americans, with the Northern Alliance. ... But we had to be equally committed to that side of the story. ... [H]aving somebody in Kabul really I think gave AP the edge on the objectivity, because we had somebody who was covering that side of the story. We had somebody who was in there and talking to Afghans. And there was a lot of discussions before a story, a sort of a human interest–type story went on the wire, because there wasn't an appetite for it in America. But it was a story. There was a lot of debate – but it went. It went, and lovely things were kept in.

Telling the "Bad" Guys' Stories

Avoiding oversimplifying some groups or people as embodiments of "evil," no matter how vicious their actions, and probing for insight into motivations is also a necessary part of the objective practices that most correspondents, like Gannon (22–25), defended strenuously:

[P]eople who commit atrocities ... do I find that so difficult and horrible to deal with? Yes, what I witnessed down in Quetta in February going to the Shia areas where a huge bomb killed like a hundred people and it was just a week later, it was rainy and damp and there are still body parts, there are still people going around crying, mourning their loved ones, talking about what it was like.[17] But I might just be moved and feel that who did this is reprehensible? A hundred percent. Do I sit and talk to somebody and think, "You're evil"? No. ... I just want to know what you know. That's what I want. I'm a reporter. Not my job, really not my job to judge you. ... Our job really is to discover, understand as best we can, and report and we ask questions. That's what we do. Really at the end of the day. And the more knowledge we have, the better our questions.

While I was in Islamabad interviewing her, Gannon (23) was working on a story about Pakistan's minorities in advance of elections there.[18] She used her interview with the head of the Sipah-e-Sahaba Pakistan (SSP), "a banned organization devoted to declaring Shias non-Muslims and killing them," as an example of digging to get past pat answers and to try to grasp what might lie behind the "horrific" thoughts and actions:

This whole thing on "no, we don't want killings of Shias, we want to put an end to this sectarianism," which sounds very good and everything. And I said, "Oh really. But do you accept that Shias are Muslims?" And he says, "It's not about whether Shias are Muslims." And then I said, "But if that doesn't matter, then how come so many are being killed?" And you go on around, and around, and around, around it until eventually he comes down to, "We want legislation that makes it illegal to disrespect the companions

---

[17] Kathy Gannon, "Terrorized ethnic group to form force in Pakistan," The Associated Press, February 28, 2013.
[18] Kathy Gannon, "Pakistan's minorities have no faith in democracy," The Associated Press, May 7, 2013.

of the Prophet," which they say Shias do. So now you say, "So basically what you want to do is make it illegal for a person to be a Shia, and if they practice their religion as a Muslim, then they'd be open to the death penalty." But . . . you'd have to have evidence they say [that] . . . in the end that's exactly what it is, but it takes you like forever to come around. . . . [I]t's how you ask questions, but also that you *want* to talk to these people.

Correspondents who sat down with terrorists, mass murderers, and genocide leaders throughout the decades similarly focused on trying to elicit more information out of them, and then leaving it up to readers to judge. In postwar Germany, Otto Doelling (3–5) got to interview the originals of the stereotype of evil that would be attached to the worst perpetrators for the rest of the century and beyond – Nazis, some of whom were "eager" to be interviewed. "Putzi" [Ernst] Hanfstaengl, then 83, who had been Hitler's crony, played Wagner's "Liebestod" for Doelling, "resting his large head in his right hand" to imitate how Hitler had liked to sit while listening to his piano playing, which made him "relax." On the 25th anniversary of the Battle of the Bulge, the Wehrmacht assault's leader, General Hasso [Eccard Freiherr] von Manteuffel, complained about how "his superiors had failed to live up to the promised prerequisites for the battle" and "outlined his battle plan in pencil" for Doelling.[19] When writing about actual Nazi war criminals, Doelling (25) tried to be "balanced," but found it "pretty hard . . . when the guy, you know what he's done" – "you don't have to embellish that. Let the facts speak for themselves." Deep in the jungle interviewing Khieu Samphan, the Khmer Rouge leader later convicted for his instrumental role in Cambodia's killing fields, and some of his lieutenants (as discussed in Chapter 9), Gray (49) also highlighted the juxtaposition as he read to me from his story:

"Leaders hosted dinner with stuffed chicken and French fries, shish kebab and desserts. They are charming, sophisticated, and speak excellent French. And it's hard to connect their lantern-lit faces with the photographs of disemboweled children in Phnom Penh's Tuol Sleng prison." So, I tried to sort of juxtapose what I knew was a fact with these guys. But obviously I wasn't a judge, so I couldn't say, "These guys are guilty of this." Obviously they are, but right now, it's still being judicially decided.[20]

Where the violence might be just as brutal but far more evenly spread, with few sides convincingly claiming innocence, correspondents fought even harder to put themselves "in the other people's position, and trying to be fair to them and understand that" (Rice, 4). Covering religious conflict in Chiapas – with its "pretty horrifying" "torturing and burning" – John Rice interviewed one of the

---

[19] Otto Doelling, "Friend of Hitler, Advisor to Roosevelt: Memoirs of a Political Outsider," *Naples Daily News*, February 8, 1971; Otto Doelling, "German General Who Led Attack Tells Story – Battle of Bulge Occurred 25 Years Ago This Week," *Indiana Evening Gazette*, December 16, 1969, p. 14.
[20] In 2014, Khieu Samphan was convicted on charges of crimes against humanity by a UN-backed tribunal, almost 40 years after nearly two million people died from execution, starvation and disease during the Khmer Rouge regime.

caciques, who asked him in turn "how he might be able to sneak his way into the United States to get a good-paying job. And you start reading a little about their history and talking to them, and you realize that for 500 years, people have been trying to force them to assimilate and erode their culture" (Rice, 4–5).[21] Similarly, in Beirut Powell (3) saw the ferocious sectarian discrimination that might drive some to fight for a Shiite militia: "He ... was angry, okay? I can understand that. I would not have picked up a gun and shot Christians, but I understood his anger." In Zaire, Alexander (15) saw streams of refugees pour across the border from Rwanda:

[Y]ou want to feel sorry for them – there they are, they're carrying what few possessions they have on their backs. They're carrying their kids with them. They look poor, downtrodden. And then you go to the border and you see this huge pile of machetes there. How many of these were involved in the massacres? Is this, to a certain degree, what they deserve? How do you balance that into your reporting?[22]

Covering Central America's guerrilla wars over three decades, Joe Frazier (20–21) constantly faced the professional challenge and personal anguish of reporting a story with "very few white hats" and a whole lot of tragedy as "whole societies get reduced to a bloody cinder":

[Y]ou'd go into towns and talk to families where the guerrillas had taken their father away, and shot him in the head, because he dared try to hold political office. You had towns where the army had come in and burned out the town and shot all of them in. It's very hard to get on one side or the other of this. When you see what's going on, you realize that there's a lot of bad stuff going on out there, and everybody in one way or another has a role in it. And that was part of the story. And we spent a long time trying to make sense out of what was going on down there, and pretty soon we decided it didn't make any sense, so we started writing about that. That was the truth. ... You couldn't justify very much that went on down there. All you could do was report it.

The Objectivity Toolbox: Getting (At Least) Two Sides

To ensure that they would be "just reporting" traumatic wrongs and heart-rending ambiguity – often in the middle of great danger to themselves and with the twin imperatives of attracting audiences and breaking new ground while not misrepresenting the exceptional as routine or stereotype – correspondents relied on "basic tools" that virtually all reiterated: fairness, accuracy, and balance. That translated into not reporting what

---

[21] John Rice, "Religious conflict drives thousands from homes," The Associated Press, August 2, 1992.

[22] For the first among many stories, see Paul Alexander, "Rwandan refugees overwhelm border crossing, flood into Zaire," The Associated Press, July 13, 1994.

was not verified to the fullest possible extent, as discussed in Chapter 4. When the March 2011 earthquake and tsunami hit Japan late in the afternoon, both the damage and loss of life were hard to assess, leaving AP bureau chief Malcolm Foster (5–6) to urge caution among conflicting rumors, while mobilizing every resource to independently verify what had happened in the hard-to-reach devastated areas, rendered even more dangerous by the nuclear meltdown:

There were police who were reporting in the area along, near Sendai they were finding hundreds of bodies. And we always wanted to be careful about accuracy, of course, and not hype it too much. I remember, even the height of the tsunami, how high can we say it was? But we stuck very closely to the highest that we were seeing on the weather agency. . . . I'm more conservative; I really want to make sure it's factual, it's factual, it's accurate, rather than doing something fast and inaccurate. . . . [I]n terms of the numbers of casualties, the height of the wave, everything, I was making sure with my reporters that they were getting it. And then also with the nuclear plant, I remember early on . . . the government officials were very unclear about the extent of the damage. . . . But we had to rely on what they were saying. . . . And of course, it's radioactive, so you can't get close.

Straight breaking news – aside from the inherent interest bias of selecting to write about some events and not others – might still be the least challenging: The correspondents "just happened to be there, witness it, and write it up," as one put it self-deprecatingly (Cooperman, 22). A veteran of both the Middle East and Asia argued that while some non-wire correspondents "write and phrase it, shape it, like 'This is what you ought to know, you dumb shit' . . . you can't get by with that with the AP, thank God. . . . And it sounds corny, but it's true. Just facts, ma'am, please" (McArthur, 22–23). The challenge to maintain objectivity is steeper for analytical writing, especially from highly charged geopolitical areas like the Middle East. Perry and Tatro, two longtime correspondents and editors who, combined, have worked in the region from the 1970s into the 2010s, had strategies for keeping even analysis balanced – finding and portraying the straight facts (such as that "Israel is placing itself in a great demographic complication by occupying the West Bank") that will remain valid regardless of what policy implications others might derive (Perry, 17), and doing justice to diverging arguments:

I always told my reporters, "Find the best argument of both sides and use that in the story. Don't just take an offhand remark here that doesn't really define the position. Try to define what their position is. Try to give it the proper context so you're fair to both sides, and you give their best argument and not their worst argument versus the best argument," which is a really common way, I think, of angling a story towards one side or the other. (Tatro, 21)

For one of his own 1980s stories from "Nablus, Occupied West Bank," Tatro went on a patrol with Israeli soldiers, reporting the mixed reactions both among them and among the "Arab residents" who "accosted a reporter walking with the soldiers."[23] Trying to explain 1970s apartheid South Africa, Heinzerling (15-16) once wrote a long, 1,500-word "piece about why whites didn't like blacks in South Africa" – and got a call from longtime foreign editor Nate Polowetzky that became a lesson in getting all sides:

"Larry, I can't put this out on the wire ... it's racist." And I said, "Well, it's what people here say to anybody who asks them what they think about black Africa or black African–run countries." And he said, "Well, if we run this the NAACP is going to be up here raising hell with me because this is one side of it." So I said, "How about if I do a piece about what blacks think about whites?" So he said okay. So I did that and also got 1,500 words or equivalent. So then they put it out, the two stories. ... [AP] wants to make absolutely sure it's being equal, unbiased. And it was a good point to me too, because that one story would have inflamed a lot of people and not presented a counterview of things.

Correspondents believed in the effort to find multiple, contradicting voices, to avoid oversimplification ("You go from Lebanon around the arc, you're going to have as many different opinions as you have countries, and you're going to discover that there is no Arab side," McArthur, 11), and to produce a story that was not "tendentious." All, however, recognized that being fair, accurate, and balanced could not mean complete: "Everybody says, get both sides of the story. I've never seen, in my life, a story that had less than 10 sides" (Rosenblum, 15). One Vietnam correspondent described how she felt, as "a Mix-Master who has personal views. One day you felt this way, one day you felt the next. You were constantly [...] going around in a circle with the beat knocking you on the head. That's what the experience is like being in a war. You're whipsawed, instant to instant" (Bartimus, 16). Trying to balance accounts on deadline could mean portraying different sides who are all lying – and choosing which one to put first, with the correcting context, thus conveying differing impressions:

[I]n some of these conflicts, both sides had reasons to lie. So here you are, you've got ... lie A versus lie B, now how do I put this out? ... I bring my experience to something, and I weigh my biases in there by whom I choose to talk to, by which quotes I choose to use, by how I present the story ... but it is delimited by how skilled I am, delimited by how tired I am, delimited by where it was cut when it went into the desk, so it's not a perfect, it's never a perfect situation. (Powell, 17)

[Y]ou might have two sentences: "So-and-so says we're good people. They say you're bad people." Which order do you put it? And should there be a but? If you're consistently ... giving the one side's defense and then always following it with a paragraph that says "But ... ", as if to say, they're full of shit, right? So, you have to think about little things, like reversing the order often so that it doesn't create that. ... [Polowetzky] didn't just look at the daily report. He would take a month's worth of copy, on a big story, and go through it and go through it and go through it, and look at the cumulative effect of what we were doing. What kind of an impression were we building up? (Eliason, 6)

---

[23] Nicolas B. Tatro, "Soldiers become targets of Palestinian hatred," *The Associated Press*, January 12, 1988.

Even where correspondents' sympathies might lie with one side – dissidents behind the Iron or Bamboo Curtain, for example (Minthorn, 8; Liu, 9) – they resolutely sought to balance it with the official line, no matter how repetitious it got, as George Bria (14) recalled, sighing and chuckling, seven decades after returning from early Cold War Europe to be a supervisor on the foreign desk:

I remember [AP president Wes] Gallagher saying ... "If we can tell it from both sides and everything from both sides, what more can you do?" It might be three sides, four sides, but get them in, don't get in your point of view, and I think the AP has held to that pretty much. ... How did I cover both sides? You put in what the Russians were saying. ... I remember once ... the Marshal of the Soviet made a speech, and Gallagher said, "We've got to cover that." I said, "Jesus, he said that a million times." He said, "We have to cover the news as it happens."

Driven by the same desire to give a fair shake to the Communist side decades later, Debbie Seward (7) faced down Solidarity leaders who, after letting her in through a coal mine turnstile during their strike, told her she would no longer be allowed in if she also talked with the mine management:[24]

I always carried a radio with me, a shortwave radio. And it was really lucky because it was top of the hour, so I don't remember if it was VOA or BBC, but it came on. And it was my story. ... And I said, "Look, here you are. And we need the other side too." And they were stunned. ... It's not even a question of stamping your article so that you have this side or the other side. Because if you as a reporter are going to bring value to your reader, it is not simply being a scribe. It is to understand what actually is happening on that day and where the story is, how it is going to develop, and where you need to go. So if you don't take the opportunity to go talk to that other side, as unpalatable as you may find that as an individual, you're doing a disservice to yourself, to your readers, and to the other side.

Getting enough of each side's statements and opinions to give them "their due" did not always imply believing that there was no right or wrong, however, or a sense of moral neutrality, many correspondents pointed out. When "the other side" is a government's reason for brutal suppression, for example, all a story should do is present its case "fairly" – "try to express their case as they would do it" (Graham, 29) – without implying "on one hand this, on the other hand that," as David Crary (6) pointed out describing his coverage of the struggle to end apartheid in South Africa in the late 1980s:

I don't think we ever approached the broader story in terms of "Gee, maybe the black liberation movement is right, and maybe the white minority government is right, and we're going to write a 50/50 story." And I don't think we ever felt that we had to do that, and we didn't do that. And ... is that a violation of the kind of neutrality code? I don't think so. I don't think any of us feel that we were wrong to kind of write stories that were empathetic to the black liberation movement. ... [P]retty unique situation to be there, to be physically safe most of the time and yet sort of decide you're going to empathize with one side more than the other in a long-running political conflict.

---

[24] Deborah G. Seward, "Strikes shut down coal mines, Szczecin docks and transport," The Associated Press, August 18, 1988.

Objective Detachment – or One-Sided Sympathy?

When confronted by visceral human drama rather than ideological conflict, many correspondents struggled with keeping their detachment. And while some defended their role strictly as observers, others believed some stories called more for involvement than balance. Using famine in Biafra as an example, Rosenblum (23) described the high-wire act: "you have to get close enough so that you're relating with the reality you're looking at and you're understanding the people and trying to see who they are and what's happening, and therefore you have to get pretty close. But you've got to stand far enough back so that it doesn't turn you into" an advocate or your story's protagonist. Gray (10, 54), who wrote moving first-person stories about finding his relatives in Czechoslovakia after the Cold War and jogging past former Khmer Rouge residences on assignments, and whose "Seduced and Abandoned" story about U.S. actions in 1970s Cambodia left little doubt as to his personal feeling that "we didn't do good by" that country, regarded those as the exceptions to the rule that journalists should be "flies on the wall."

One specific exception emerged from many interviews, and from other correspondents' memoirs – the siege of Sarajevo. Balance and neutrality did not seem to fully apply to those writing from there, in part because many correspondents faced the same indiscriminate violence as Sarajevans at the hands of Serb militias, who were also hard to reach, and because it was the Vienna desk that filled in context and balance in the stories (also Bell 1995, 22, 127–128; Katovsky and Carlson 2003, 161):

Everybody's a shade of gray. And certainly you had a feeling that the Serbs were much darker than anybody else – for one thing because they were shooting at you too. There were reports of bounties out for shooting journalists. Every one of our armored Land Rovers was pocked with bullet marks. You'd come back and you'd get a big black magic marker and go out and circle the new ones. (Alexander, 17)

[T]he way that you ended up setting up operations in Sarajevo, meant that you really were part of, you were in a besieged city. And you were dependent for local staff on people who were willing to stay in a besieged city. ... [I]t does make a difference when you're sitting and eating a meal, whatever you can cobble together, in the Belvedere [a pizzeria and hotel turned AP bureau] at night, with Serbian TV on over there, and they're showing pictures of people who are shelling you. (Porubcansky, 12)

Then when you attempt to make overtures to the other side, they're hostile to you because they know you're living with the other side. It's a situation that feeds on itself. ... I went up in Serb areas a couple times, when they would let people in and invited them in, and there was palpable hostility. Not universally. One of the ways that we operated up there, because there were no hotels, the Serb staff in Belgrade made acquaintances of some private families up there, decent people, and so they would put you up for money. ... [T]he normal house we would use was full, but the woman had a friend ... it was a woman with a small boy. It was late, I didn't really talk to her very much, went into the bedroom, went to sleep, woke up the next morning, there was a picture of her and a man, arms around, and I asked her where her husband was or what happened to him. And she says, "Oh, he's fighting," needless to say with the Serbian militia. (Reid, 95–97)

CONCLUSIONS

Over the decades, correspondents have come to rely far less on U.S. officials, especially diplomats and intelligence officials, who used to be essential sources and information traders in many dangerous parts of the world. What has not changed is the high burden of proof required for correspondents who report stories contradicting official U.S. lines, such as accounts of the lack of WMD in Iraq – which did make it on the wire, albeit to no avail for U.S. policymaking. The closest interaction between journalists and the U.S. government abroad remains with the military. Although correspondents experienced the latter's efforts to control the message, both with movement restrictions and PR operations – alternatively freezing you out or breathing down your neck – as dramatically increasing after the Vietnam War, they continued to rely on the troops for logistical help, ranging from transportation to the front lines to on-the-record briefings. Paradoxically, being on the ground, sometimes embedded and other times independently, is what correspondents need most to muster facts unavailable through military filters but also what can endanger objectivity, since correspondents have long tended to feel for both the common soldiers and the civilian population under the gun.

Covering dangerous enemies of the United States can also test correspondents' standards of objectivity, defined as writing fair, balanced, accurate stories with only proven facts, no personal slants and a fair hearing for all arguments, even as the Cold War raged, the Twin Towers' rubble smoldered, or one correspondent wasted away hostage to terrorists. Getting all sides meant sitting down with mass murderers, war criminals, and genocidal killers – driven by the imperative to know, challenge, and tell, not to judge. "Balancing" stories did not imply moral equivalency, but rather the awareness of what perspective something as mechanical as word placement might privilege. After all this work on the ground, however, stories still needed to be filed and edited – an entirely different set of constraints, especially for policy-moving matters, discussed in Chapter 11.

9/11 and the Beginning of the U.S. War in Afghanistan

Kathy Gannon: I saw it once [the Twin Towers falling on television, prohibited during the Taliban regime], I thought, "Oh, that's so horrible, my goodness." And knew that life was over for us. And then the desk ... wanted some reaction because very quickly they pointed to al-Qaida. And so Amir Shah and I went out, went to different places that were open ... people were ... terrified. They had no idea what was going to happen. They didn't know what the World Trade Center was, but ... they had heard on the radio that ... these horrific things have happened and thousands of people are dead....

[M]aybe it was the next night or early the next morning, like at 3 in the morning. I guess there had been some rockets fired at the airport.... New York calls me [because of unconfirmed reports of a U.S. attack in Kabul] ... Me, I woke up, I didn't know what the hell was going on. So you had a curfew. The Taliban were there, it's not like you can say, "Well, we have to find out." ... "Are you under attack?" I hope not, I'm asleep. And so anyway I said, "Just wait before" – because really there's nothing that sounds that extreme, and so we went out as best we could and there were a few rockets had been fired on the airport. So I said, "The best we could say is that explosions have been heard." ... "But you know they're reporting ... " I said, "Honestly, I swear to you, explosions have been heard." So they did. They put explosions had been heard.[25] ...

And then on October 7th, they [Americans] launched the attack. Amir Shah ... and I did the story together.[26] So I would talk to him [from Pakistan] and he was whispering after that, because the Taliban turned off the lights, the electricity at 8:30 every night, thinking that if the Americans couldn't see them, they couldn't attack them. [laughs] ... So everything was dark and our sat phone has a little light, so Amir Shah would have to cover it (Gannon, 52–55, 58).

In the meantime, Bob Reid (49–50) had arrived in Islamabad to help with war coverage:

Bob Reid: [T]he phone rang and it was Amir Shah, our longtime local. ... Kathy could understand Amir Shah [with his "thick accent" on a bad phone line], so what she was doing was, when she was on the phone talking to him, she was repeating out loud what he was saying, I was typing it and filing it with the light from the screens because the power had gone out. And that was how we started the war.

---

[25] "Rockets flared and explosions could be heard north of the capital near the airport early Wednesday, hours after devastating terror attacks in the United States"; Kathy Gannon, "Explosions shake Afghanistan capital," The Associated Press, September 11, 2001. See also Kathy Gannon, *I is for Infidel*, 86–91.

[26] Kathy Gannon and Amir Shah, "Explosions rock Afghanistan as U.S. and Britain launch strike; bin Laden reportedly alive," The Associated Press, October 7, 2001. The story, datelined Kabul, provided many details from that city but also quoted many sources inside Afghanistan "reached by telephone from Islamabad."

11

Getting It Out, Getting It Edited: Filing News, Working with the Desk

> The [Japanese] surrender [signing] was onboard the USS *Missouri* . . . and I was
> well positioned for it, or thought I was. I was on an elevated part of the deck,
> looking straight down on the table where the signing of the peace treaty would
> take place, and I thought I was really all set because right in front of me was
> [Supreme Allied Commander] General MacArthur, Admiral Nimitz, [and General
> Wainwright], in order to witness the signing. But right at the last moment, just
> prior to the actual ceremony itself . . . a long line of very tall, high-ranking officers
> marched in on one side and then made a sharp turn and they filled up the gap
> between me and the table. . . . Yes, it was a terrible moment for me . . . I had to hold
> the camera over my head and shoot Hail Mary. I never knew, I never saw any of
> those pictures . . . I never saw the film. I never worried about it either. What could I
> do? (Desfor, 7, 11)

Chuckling at the memory of that blind shot of the final act of World War II
while we munched on French cheese left over from the party he had thrown for
his 99th birthday a few days earlier, Max Desfor told me how he had entrusted
the film to an officer to bring back to Washington before even knowing if he had
captured the historic images or not. No foreign correspondence practice has
changed more dramatically in the past eight decades than filing the news. For
the vast majority of the 20th century, correspondents who had chased sources,
braved dangers, and fought through spin and restrictions to write a story still
faced what was often the greatest hurdle: getting it out. Only in the past couple
of decades, instead of fighting over phone lines for dictation or ringing telex
bells hoping that some bureau somewhere in the world might be seeing the
story, foreign correspondents could be in constant contact from the front lines.
The increased connectivity, however, has subtly affected stories, especially by
minimizing the desk/field distance and by amplifying the time pressures on
reporting, putting at risk accuracy or depth.

The dynamic between correspondents and editors in New York has
sometimes been tense – at least as correspondents described it, since this

FIGURE 11.1. A few days after his 99th birthday in November 2012, Max Desfor stands in his Maryland apartment looking at two of his most celebrated pictures: the Japanese surrender aboard the USS *Missouri* that ended World War II (right) and refugees fleeing across a damaged bridge during the Korean War, the image that won him the 1951 Pulitzer Prize for Photography (left). The photo in the middle captured Desfor holding up his camera and shooting the "Hail Mary" surrender picture after sailors blocked his view. (Photo by Giovanna Dell'Orto)

research centers on them. While all correspondents said editors trusted them to determine their story lines, many still bristled at any unperceptive requests for coverage and second-guessing from afar, such as being asked to get confirmation of an attack when they were calling in the story under rocket fire. But their eyewitness knowledge, earned on the ground, virtually always prevailed in selection of coverage as well as the final edit that ultimately released news on the wire. This chapter examines how correspondents have handled their completed stories – how they got them out, and edited, over decades in a shrinking world.

MORE SOURCING, LESS BEGGING: TECHNOLOGICAL CHANGES IN REPORTING

Given that this book focuses on text correspondents instead of photographers or videographers, it is not surprising that their reporting practices were relatively little changed by the advent of television, computers, and digital media, though the latter did facilitate newsgathering – and saved time and hotel space traveling with photographers who no longer had to set up obnoxious-smelling dark rooms in bathrooms, as they did into the 2000s. The sudden influx of network and cable TV crews from Vietnam onward dismayed a few veterans, who, while admiring their courage in frontline reporting, regretted the way they could change the story ("the minute the cameras show up ... people start acting" [Pyle, 20]); oversimplify complex narratives ("sometimes there was some great video that may not have been representative of what was going on" [Alexander, 6]); and decrease the importance and impact of "the written word" even while increasing the pressure on print reporters to write off TV footage (Hurst, 13; also Porubcansky, 25). Several reporters from London to Caracas also disliked the first computers, massive, temperamental, and unforgiving machines that wiped out stories every time they broke down (Barr, 17; Olmos, 21). Where new and improved technologies, from walkie-talkies to Google search, from fax to Facebook, helped most was finding and developing sources.

In 1977, Nick Tatro (1, 23) walked into the Cairo office on his first day and saw all staffers "gathered around a big desk with the telephones, which were all different colors – there was green, red, black, and white, and maybe another one – and they were all off the hook and lying on the table." They were all waiting for dial tones, a rare commodity, though eventually the bureau obtained President Anwar Sadat's authorization to use walkie-talkies, "so we could go around town and report from the scene without worrying about those damn phones." In the Soviet Union, fax machines "opened up the ability to send information outside of the official channels" and a nonofficial news agency, Interfax, that distributed articles exclusively via fax became an "indispensable" "tip-sheet" for the Moscow bureau (Cooperman, 8–9).

Information online, from official budgets to dissident voices, allows for an unprecedented ease in reaching sources – before, "when you had to find a telephone number or something, essentially it was pleading, begging with a lot of people who might know people who might know people who might be able to get you a telephone number" (Stevenson, 3) – as well as a new level of detail in investigative reporting. In Beijing, over 10 years Charles Hutzler (3, 23–24) went from the background "annoying, early dot-matrix printer sound" of the wires to that "godsend to all reporters," Weibo, a microblog site. "Now the government has lost control of large parts of the narrative," he said; when an earthquake struck a remote Tibetan plateau prefecture in 2010, it took nearly two days to get reporters there, but social media provided contact numbers for aid groups already on the ground. Still, mining the wealth of online information required reportorial skills:

Within that information, what can you find that reveals the story in a unique way to a foreign audience? Also, then, can you find sources who aren't putting all their information onto Twitter? (Hutzler, 28)

Part of the dynamic between sources and correspondents has changed too, because sources wanting to reach a domestic or even international audience no longer need the press, as noted in Chapter 4, and correspondents no longer hold the technological upper hand, as one Mexico hand noted:

When you would cover hurricanes back in the old days, you'd literally be walking along the beach interviewing people taking shelter or putting plywood up, and everybody would be like, "Where's the storm? Where's the storm?" ... And today you do that same story, you walk along the beach and the people are there with their smartphones and they've already checked ... they can tell *you* where the storm is, because they've checked it more recently than you have. So where you used to be a sort of repository of knowledge and technology, that ... has flattened out entirely, which is good because now you're interacting ... with a more informed set of informants or interviewees. (Stevenson, 1–2)

The interaction with the audience after a story hits the wire also changed in the digital world, as discussed in Chapter 12, and correspondents in the 2000s increasingly have to think platforms and multimedia content as they conceptualize a story, especially with the growth of mobile formats. Developing the story about unemployment in the Middle East, for example, veteran reporter Karin Laub (13) decided not to focus on "lots of numbers that probably not a lot of people would read" but rather on the life story of one young man who set himself on fire in Tunis – "then break out little separate glances, short chunks of information that accompany it, and quote box ... to reach as broad an audience as possible" via mobile.[1]

FROM PIGEONS TO BGANS: THE FILING REVOLUTION

If reporting practices have adopted some new technologies, filing practices have been revolutionized by them, which, in turn, affects what kind of stories correspondents have the time, resources, and means to pursue. Today, copy transmits smoothly and instantaneously over wireless from Kandahar or Pyongyang, but until the early 2000s correspondents often had been at the mercy of willing "pigeons," fickle telex tape, and long lines at telephone booths, spending hours (and small fortunes) trying to get their stories out – and that was fast compared to photos. For the picture that won him the 1951 Pulitzer – one of only eight frames he shot of Korean War refugees as he himself fled enemy troops – Desfor (2–3) gave the film to an AP colleague he ran into at a remote runway while he continued to retreat with the GIs: "when I put it in his hands, that's the last I saw of it, the last I heard of it, and the last I knew about it." Until much later when, while taking a break from war reporting at an obscure Japanese inn, the owner told him to take a phone call, and an AP editor was on the line with news that he had just won the Pulitzer:

---

[1] Karin Laub, "Vendor's suicide reflects despair of Mideast youth," The Associated Press, May 11, 2013.

I said, "If you want me back to work okay, I'm ready to go and I will do it quickly, but don't give me a line of baloney like that." And I hung up on him. A couple of minutes later, the phone rang again and I again hear "denwa, denwa" – telephone – and I decided to take it. And the voice this time said, "This is Bob." It was Bob Eunson ... the chief of bureau. And he said, "This is Bob, and don't you dare hang up on me." And he said, "Just a minute." And he starts rattling off congratulations, all of the messages I received congratulating me, and that's how I found out that I had won the Pulitzer Prize. The other sign was that the innkeeper apparently found out what it was, and he came up with a tremendous plate of sushi, which I had not learned to like yet.

Not unlike Desfor 40 years earlier, Terril Jones (25–26) shot several rolls of film in addition to reporting on the Chinese army crushing protests in Tiananmen Square, and his editors, examining hastily developed negatives through a magnifying glass, did not see that in one, the tiny figure of the iconic "tank man" was already standing in the middle of the street, calmly waiting for the tanks that were still quite a distance away (see the box in Chapter 4).[2] Jones later realized it, and the photo was added to the historical record. But it is impossible to know what stories and nuances might have been lost because correspondents on the scene had primitive means of transmitting them – a final struggle that sometimes was the hardest of all, and the one they could least control.

When public phones or cable were the only way to transmit the news, correspondents got creative to handle the inherent censorship and beat the competition – U.S., foreign, or both (as in 1940s China, Roderick 1993, 41; and 1960s Vietnam, Browne 1993, 98). In Rome in 1944, the Allied press had offices in a palace where, at the end of a large room, an Allied censor stood waiting at a window for copy to scrutinize before passing it on via cable – so that on an urgent story, George Bria (2–3) and his competitors would write a couple of words on the cable form, run to get it in the censor's window slot first, then go back and write another few words on another cable form, until the whole story slowly emerged. To flash the news of the Korean War armistice, Sam Summerlin (2–3, 7), who weighed 120 pounds, "outran all the 200 other correspondents to the one telephone in Panmunjom" to dictate "'The war is over.' That was all I was able to say" to the Seoul correspondent, who "rushed it downstairs to the censor and the censor called AP in Tokyo and they had the flash ready" – beating the competition and making it "one of the best things that ever happened to me" (a single military phone line connected the press to the world; see Ferrari 2003, 66). Twenty years later in Phnom Penh, Denis Gray (12) had to first get past the Cambodian censor, then run to the teletype operator – "we always paid him a little extra. And then it went on, click, click, click, click, and then hopefully we prayed that we'd get a message, the next morning probably, saying, 'Hong Kong, we received your teletype.'" Gray also had to find a "pigeon" – a journalist or diplomat or "somebody at the airport who seemed nice" – to carry out 35mm film.

---

[2] See Patrick Witty, "Behind the Scenes: Tank Man of Tiananmen," *New York Times*, June 3, 2009.

For decades, "pigeons" carried politically sensitive stories and photos out of conflict-ridden societies ranging from Biafra (Rosenblum, 14; Behr 1981, 139) to Bangladesh to Bolivia – a stunningly trusting relay:

I had a story in Dhaka during the civil war, somebody alerted me to the fact that the village of a . . . judge who had gone rebel, was being attacked by the army. . . . There are rice paddies and they built bunds that were walking paths . . . I started to walk towards the smoke. . . . There was no one to talk to, I walked back. I wrote a story describing what I saw and what I knew about that village and . . . I knew there was no way I could go to the cable office and send this to them. I ran around, found somebody who was leaving by plane for Bangkok. I gave them the story, told them to get to the AP office in Bangkok and give it to them, and that's the last I heard on that (Zeitlin, 24–25). [When Dhaka itself was taken over by West Pakistan's army, Zeitlin's story was datelined "Colombo, Ceylon," and an editor's note read: "The writer of the following dispatch left East Pakistan yesterday. Censorship has prevented the dispatch of news from there."][3]

During one coup attempt in the 1970s . . . I rushed to the airport with the tape in a manila envelope, and gave it to a passenger . . . with a phone number written on it, the office of AP in Lima, which would go to the airport and pick up the tape and file it to New York. . . . I had to look at that person and see if that person looked reliable. So I took a chance, I had no other choice. So I gave it to him and said, "Listen, I'm giving you a tape with the full story of what happened in Bolivia over the past few hours. I have no means to file it, I have no means to get it to my office, but my office in Lima can. Can you please, upon arriving at the airport, call this number? And they will pick it up." (Olmos, 2–3)

In the first years of Castro's regime, Havana correspondents knew they could not trust monitored cable companies, where each story passed through a government "reader," for their vox pop or political stories, so they often relied on contacts at various embassies to ship their typewritten stories via flown-out diplomatic mail pouches (Flores, 5; Wheeler, 3–4, and 2008, 32, 38). In Laos with exclusive news of the 1960 coup, AP's Peter Arnett (1994, 55) found the telegraph office and the airport barred by soldiers, who were also patrolling river boats – so he waded across the Mekong to Thailand, the typed story clamped in his teeth. Bob Reid's efforts to get his breaking story of Iran's revolution onto the wire are detailed in this chapter's box. In Kabul in the early days of the Soviet invasion, Reid (78, 12) again "was on the world's biggest story, and I might as well have been yelling out the window" – though AP had been using as "secret stringer" an Indian Airlines station manager, who wrote on small pieces of paper information and rumors about the Soviet attack, then gave them "to the pilots just before they left for Delhi, and asked them to ensure that this got to The Associated Press." (Fisk [2005, 51], also in Afghanistan during the Soviet war, had an even more complicated pigeon relay involving a Pakistan bus driver.)

[3] Arnold Zeitlin, "Report E. Pakistan Revolt Crushed by West Troops," *Chicago Tribune*, March 29, 1971, 1.

Punching Out and Phoning In

When telex machines began to be installed in many overseas bureaus in the late 1960s, allowing correspondents to bypass the relay through often-censored, sometimes-bribable cable offices by punching their own stories on tape and feeding it directly to control bureaus across the world (although censors were still occasionally posted inside bureaus too), no wonder one called the clunky machine "the best invention since toilet paper" (AP Oral History, Aguilar 2009, 76; also Belkind, 3; Powell, 2). Thanks to a clanking teletype, Myron Belkind (10–11), alerted in the middle of the night by a local journalist that opposition leaders had been arrested, was able to get the news out of India's declaring a state of emergency in 1975 just before the censorship hit:

I kept that circuit going, quarter speed – the normal speed in those days was 66 words. This was a quarter, so if you wanted to say "bulletin," you had to say B ... U ... L. ... Mrs. [Indira] Gandhi went on the air at ... 8 in the morning, to announce that "Due to efforts by my opponents to hurt the economy and the country, I've declared a state of emergency." ... I got the text out, and I got a phone call ... "Myron, I've just been named chief censor, and I'm advising you that all copy has to be pre-censored before it is transmitting." And I was just watching that tape go through, and my last story went through, and the circuit stopped.

Two years later, still on that teleprinter, Belkind (13) "was able to write that Mrs. Gandhi today lifted the emergency that kept her in power and submitted her resignation as prime minister ... I always wanted, once the emergency was declared ... to be able to stay to see it through."[4]

But the monstrously time-consuming telex – "these big, humpy typewriters connected to a line, and you punched on them and you got this perforated yellow tape that came out, and you fed it to a tape reader, and that transmitted what you were writing to a machine up in Europe or wherever the hell you were connected to, if you were lucky enough to get a line" (Rosenblum, 4) – was no transmission panacea. His first experience with one made four-decade veteran Mort Rosenblum (4–5) wonder what he had gotten himself into as he started his first assignment to Kinshasa, during the Congolese war – when "bashing out" the cable on an unfamiliar French keyboard had been the least of his worries:

[T]here was this censorship and there was this guy behind me ... with this really grungy beard, this black, black shirt, kind of formal shirt with rolled-up cuffs that he hadn't washed in six months, and he was like stinking drunk, and he was reading over my shoulder as I typed and breathing on me and curdling the paper. ... And we had to write in French because he had to be able to read it. ... As this guy's looking at the copies, he's got this Belgian FN [gun] and he's dangling it ... and he drops it on the floor and the magazine bursts open and the cartridges are spinning on the floor and he's jumping up and down to stop them from spinning, laughing like this is really funny. And I'm looking

---

[4] Myron L. Belkind, The Associated Press, March 20, 1977.

while I'm typing and this is really garbled, and I'm scared shitless. This tiny, stinking small room, sweating like hell, and this guy's jumping on cartridges.

In China when the bureau was reopened in 1979, it took months to break through the bureaucracy enough to get machines into the AP office apartment (AP Oral History, Roderick 1998, 28; Graham, 3). In Beirut as in Moscow in the 1980s, a power shortage would mean recoding and resending the entire story, and even in the best circumstances, the typing, punching, and transmitting of tape could mean an hour and a half for a 200-word story – though that still beat trying to get an international phone call, which might take several hours (Hurst, 13, 3; Fisk 2002, 202–203). Eventually, "primitive" computers replaced typewriters (including one so "susceptible to static" that a blast of it would make the entire story disappear; Porubcansky, 23). Tandy laptops accommodated less than a dozen lines of copy on the screen, but could be connected to a machine that "would print out a long yellow telex tape" – AP's future international editor John Daniszewski (10) covered the uprisings in Lithuania at the end of the Cold War and "loved" that he could do that instead of "trying to type it yourself on the recalcitrant, heavy machines that were not forgiving of errors."

In the pre-digital era, the other way to file stories was by hunting for a telephone booth, dictating to an editor at the end of the line – if there was an open line, often a luxury in pre–satellite phone times. From the 1940s well into the 1980s, the mad dash and scramble for a pay phone and the ability to dictate a coherent story as it happened – even something as dramatic as the "flash" that the Korean War was over – were necessary routines. The cover of AP's history features correspondent (and future president) Wes Gallagher running ahead of the competition to report the 1946 verdict in the Nuremberg war crimes trial (Reporters of The Associated Press 2007). Twenty years later, Otto Doelling (4–5), outside the walls of Berlin's Spandau prison waiting for the release of the last two condemned criminals (except for Rudolf Hess, Hitler's deputy Führer), nearly saw his communication plan fail when the superintendent of an apartment complex next door got so drunk he wanted to renege on the arrangement to let Doelling use the telephone in the basement as the men were being let out of the prison. Another 20 years later, a correspondent in Chile covering demonstrations against Pinochet was not so lucky: "we would see somebody beaten by cops or shot, and no telephones around" (Gallardo, 20).

Phones were also precarious lifelines. With the AP Managua office engulfed in heavy fighting during the Nicaraguan Revolution, Joe Frazier (5–6) had to make do with the two public (and working) telex machines left in the city or wait for three hours for a line to Mexico, often to have it drop dead in the middle of dictating, off the top of his head, breaking war stories. Also in Nicaragua in the early 1990s, Anita Snow was in the town of Esteli, which had been retaken by former Sandinista rebels and was under attack by government forces, dictating stories in Spanish to the office in Managua, where staffers wrote them in Spanish, sent them to Mexico City, which translated them into English and sent them on to New York for final transmission. In Chiapas the following year covering the beginning of the rebellion against the Mexican government, Snow (4–5) arrived soon enough to see – and count – on the road a dozen bodies of slain rebels and interview survivors who "claimed they were from the Zapatista Army of National Liberation, a previously unknown group" (as her story specified):[5]

> But to file that story, it was crazy, because there were hundreds of people [journalists] then. . . . So that first day . . . I called collect on a pay phone, and there was this long line of journalists to file from a pay phone. And then after that, we found this pharmacy where . . . you could just pay them for . . . your long-distance call, and you could dial up to the AP server in Mexico City to connect via the Internet and file that way, sitting on the concrete steps going into the pharmacy. . . . And then after that, the Mexican government set up some sort of filing center, and it was just packed with people using it.

In 1989 Romania, Rosenblum (44) started off "dictating the revolution" to the Vienna bureau from inside the Romanian broadcasting station, when Ceauşescu's troops fired on it and the phone line went dead – the unusually long 2,322-word story mentioned that "Occupants of the TV building ducked as shots were fired toward the windows and the lights went out."[6] So he brushed off old skills by finding a telex machine: "I'm down on my knees, under the table, because I'm in the line of fire, from the open window. . . . There's no paper in the machine, there's just an empty rubber roller. And the keys are hitting the rolls, you can't read what it's saying . . . and I'm saying, 'Up space if you read this.' And it goes, chu-chu-chu." Earlier in Timişoara, where the uprisings against Ceauşescu were starting, Daniszewski (7) spent a night and day at the hospital and in the streets surrounded by "the crackle of automatic machine-gun fire and barrages from tanks," interviewing the wounded and their doctors – including a patient with a bullet hole in his leg who had asked for military aid, telling him "Send Rambo," but also requesting anonymity "in a reflection of the widespread anxiety that the revolution could be squelched and repression could return."[7] In the afternoon, Daniszewski holed up in the Yugoslav consulate, waiting for his turn, behind Yugoslav journalists, to use the only phone with an outside line to Belgrade – only to be told by an editor there had been more reports of gunfire, so Daniszewski went back out to check and got shot, nearly becoming one of the fatalities whose number he had been trying to verify.[8]

---

[5] Anita Snow, "Rebels clash with government soldiers, dozens reported dead," The Associated Press, January 2, 1994.

[6] Mort Rosenblum, "Romanians overthrow Ceausescu; hundreds dead in fierce fighting," The Associated Press, December 22, 1989.

[7] John Daniszewski, "Residents reclaim streets as rebel soldiers appear to control Timisoara," The Associated Press, December 23, 1989.

[8] John Daniszewski, "AP correspondent shot 3 times in early throes of Romanian revolt," The Associated Press, December 26, 1989.

Filing from the Scene: The Miracles of Sat Phones and Wireless

In the early 1990s, satellite phones and laptops ushered in the filing revolution, enabling correspondents to file directly from the scene, giving them more time for reporting from more, farther away places and conveying fresher, more immediate, often live details for their readers. Satellite phones really took off in the Somali civil war, where the "contraptions" weighed dozens of pounds and their delicate antennas had to be tweaked around until they caught a workable signal, at first connecting to a switchboard. They were far from reliable – one correspondent in Baidoa, trying to dictate his story to the Mogadishu bureau a couple of hundred miles away, got connected instead to an AP reporter in Sarajevo, who plaintively told him to get off, since she was in the middle of an interview as artillery pounded all around (Hanley, 12).

Sat phones quickly became indispensable tools, in besieged Sarajevo, powered by generators and the only link to the outside world (Porubcansky, 24) as in Mexico for coverage of the 1997 Acteal massacre of 45 Tzotzil indigenous Zapatista sympathizers – "Other reporters and NGOs and everybody would just look at you amazed as you set up ... the idea that you could fold up the computer top and catch a satellite signal with a sat phone in the middle of the outback of Chiapas was wonderful to people" (Stevenson, 2). In Central America, Price (19), flying in to cover Hurricane Mitch, crammed the user manual on the plane to "figure out how to use the thing" that, powered by a car cigarette lighter, he then relied on in the middle of mud fields to dictate stories of the devastation. In Afghanistan, Gannon (40) had to repeatedly contact mujahedeen commander Gulbuddin Hekmatyar after his people took her sat phone, three times, on the road from Jalalabad to Kabul, "and say, 'For God's sake, you guys have taken it again. Please?' ... And then we'd get it back."

Even in the remotest locations, sat phones and today's wireless cell phones have changed war correspondence. Gray (25–26), who covered both Iraq wars with U.S. troops, called the difference "night and day." In 1991, typewritten stories from the front lines, provided they passed military review, would be taken out by motorcycle messengers, and Gray ended up having to "throw into a ditch" his last (loaned) heavy typewriter on orders to "get light." In 2004, the military did occasionally confiscate Thuraya satellite phones, claiming Iraqis might use them to pinpoint U.S. positions; but otherwise the correspondents, embedded with computers, "were able to file pretty much what we wanted" – except, of course, for when either a commander's order or simply the impossibility of going outside an armored vehicle to get signal created "radio silence." Reid (58) recalled one reporter embedded with the Third Division who disappeared "for three or four days. We didn't hear a damn word from him. We had been relying on this guy to tell us what was going on ... we didn't hear from him until he got to Karbala ... that's like 50 miles south of Baghdad, for God's sake."

Gannon (81) covered Operation Anaconda, the 2002 U.S. mission to destroy a Taliban stronghold, with her "little bitty" sat phone: "I was sleeping on the floor in an old abandoned intelligence office and ... go and do my reporting, come back at night, throw up the thing, type my story and, Bob's your uncle, there, it's gone." And while she used to travel conspicuously in a minibus for all the communication equipment, she could now use her cellular phone anywhere between Islamabad and Kabul, and find wireless in Kandahar (also Pennington, 12). When NATO troops crossed the border into Kosovo in 1999, Donna Bryson (55) was on her cell phone ready to give the green light for AP to send "a news alert when the tires crossed the line. It was a war that we were covering from minute to minute." A little more than 10 years later, as bureau chief in South Africa, she had "stringers who can file a 500-word story on their cell phone – via SMS ... when the keyboard is ABC is 1."

Portable satellites with Internet capabilities, Internet cafés, and even good old landlines are still critical in war-torn places where the communication infrastructure is shattered, such as rebel-held areas in Libya's civil war (Laub, 30; Schemm, 12). But from Palestinian refugee camps (Laub, 12) to North Korea, where in 2013 3G service started and cell phones no longer had to be left at the airport on arrival, correspondents carrying nothing more than a smartphone can often file their stories (and tweets) directly and keep updating them as they are out reporting:

[T]o be able to use social media, like Instagram and Twitter, means that I'll be able to send images and snapshots of daily life [in Pyongyang] ... so that people can feel, on a real-time basis, that they're there with us and that they're seeing things. ... It might be something mundane like someone getting a haircut, but, actually, it's not easy for any foreigner to go to a local barber shop. So it's a small thing, and it's certainly not something I will write a story about, but I think that hopefully it will contribute to people's understanding of what daily life is like in a country that is so closed. (Lee, 13)

Lee's story about her tweet, "Hello world from comms center in #Pyongyang" – "the first sent from a cell phone using the country's new 3G mobile data service" less than a month before we met in Seoul – described the sea change it represented. It recalled a 2008 journey to the border city of Kaesong, when the bus curtains were drawn "to prevent us [visitors] from looking outside as we drove through the countryside, and through the cracks we could see soldiers stationed along the road with red flags. We were warned they'd raise those flags and stop the bus for inspection if they spotted a camera pointed out the window."[9]

---

[9] Jean H. Lee, "Tweets, pics give real-time peek into North Korea," The Associated Press, February 28, 2013.

PRESSURE'S ON: THE MILLISECOND DEADLINE
AND ITS TROUBLES

> The downside to this, the whole world is talking, and who's thinking? The whole world is writing, but who's reporting? And this has always been a problem, particularly at the AP, to balance the time it takes to report the story and the time it takes to prepare and update the story. ... [O]n every story, no matter whether it's a two-graph brief or big one, you have the advantages that the modern communications bring you. But on the really big ones, you also get the disadvantage, which is, they have to have enough people who have enough time to actually report the damn thing. And that's a difficulty. You're chained to that machine filing, when you should be out making contacts. (Reid, 79)

In his AP career spanning five decades, Reid had a full window on how the ability to file anytime, anywhere, competing every second, has turned every journalist into a wire reporter with a deadline each instant. The pressure to be first with news has always been there. To use only two extreme examples, in World War I, United Press reported the armistice, leaving AP frantic to confirm until the U.S. government announced it had not yet happened (Cooper 1959, 77–81; Hohenberg 1995, 117), whereas in World War II, a correspondent broke the Allied embargo to announce Germany's unconditional surrender, a scoop for which AP fired him, and apologized nearly 70 years later.[10] But new technologies have increased the demand exponentially, making stories more susceptible to errors and correspondents more susceptible to commands from editors. Many correspondents noted that the priority needs to remain "asking the right questions and listening to the answers. You can't tweet until you do that. You can't write a story until you do that ... nothing is more frightening to me than the idea of coming back to the office without the material to write a story" (Bryson, 62).

Before online publishing and its constant demand for updates, that fear of missing material on every-minute deadlines haunted wire correspondents far more than their newspaper or magazine counterparts, whom many envied for the extra time to report on the ground, to develop sources, to think through stories, and to write narratives, while AP reporters often had to rush back to the bureau to punch out copy. Still, AP correspondents carved out time for more analytical, in-depth stories, often called "enterprise," by relying on teamwork, as described in Chapter 8, and working around the clock during breaking news events. In South Africa, for example, Bryson managed to do a story on the first 100 days of Nelson Mandela's administration by going every couple of days to visit one family in Tokoza township, "a place where the worst of the country's problems are part of the landscape. From here, the view of South Africa is obscured by red dust and the smoke of the coal fires that warm the tiny shanties.

---

[10] David B. Caruso, "AP apologizes for firing reporter over WWII scoop," The Associated Press, May 4, 2012.

The joy at the assumption of power by a black-majority government is tempered by the daily fear residents still endure," the story noted.[11] "There was time for that, on top of everything else. It's hard to say why. I think just because I really wanted to do it," Bryson (23) recalled. In Central America during the guerrilla wars, Frazier (18) fed constant day-to-day updates, but used spare moments to write overviews explaining the larger issues, which he called "refreshing because I hated going out and getting the spot news all the time about 'So-and-so got ambushed and this town got taken and this town got taken back.'"

When Hurricane Mitch wiped out entire villages across Honduras, Niko Price (21–22) and a photographer spent several days shadowing a 3-month-old baby, her 17-year-old mother, Maria, and her banana-worker father, Jose, camped out on a highway above their flooded house.[12] Price's article showed them expecting, in vain, a food aid delivery on the scorched highway; Jose swimming through the inundated fields to gather a few bananas, their only meal for a week; and waiting for six hours at a clinic with the feverish, malnourished baby, 67 families ahead in line:

I think today that would probably be considered a bit soft for what we're doing and we would prefer to spend our time breaking news. And this was really just giving a flavor.... [A]s we got to know them better and as they began to open up to us, it became clear that there was some domestic violence in the family and that the husband occasionally would beat the wife. And that led to a lot of debate, which we had all the way up the chain, about how to handle this. I thought we should present it for what it is and write about it as a fact. It's probably not uncommon, and I thought we should just use the stories that they were telling as the stories they were telling us. And then some editors wanted to kill the entire story, because they said we shouldn't be making a poster child of somebody who beats his wife.[13] ... But yeah, that was the kind of ... deep dive into a very personal story that we did back then and that I think we do a lot less of now.... Our resources are more stretched now, and our priorities have changed. But I do think there's something to be said for that kind of story. I miss doing them.

Today's correspondents juggle the increasing demand for immediate, short updates with the need for distinctive, time-consuming coverage aimed at setting AP apart from the competition. In the early days of the Internet scramble, the emphasis seemed to be "feeding the monster." More recently, it shifted away from continually recasting stories for different deadlines around the world (including the end of the decades-old "AM/PM" cycle, with stories reworded for newspapers on morning and evening editions) and toward "impact" stories (McDowell, 17; Foster, 13). The challenge has often become doing the larger

---

[11] Donna Bryson, "Struggle for a better life just beginning in Tokoza," The Associated Press, August 17, 1994.

[12] Niko Price, "For newborn and others, Hurricane Mitch means sickness, hardship," The Associated Press, December 27, 1998.

[13] One paragraph in the story quotes Maria remembering the early days in their relationship, with Jose screaming "Trash!" at her and sometimes hitting her, and adds that he "said he didn't want to talk about it."

stories in less time. When Spain's economic crisis reached such gravity that several people facing eviction for unpaid mortgages committed suicide, it took three or four weeks, instead of days, to find one person who could be the center of the story and provide enough depth and context, as discussed in Chapter 4:[14]

What [editors and clients] really want, the story, okay, the suicides happen, you cover the suicides and three, four days later – no more than one week – here's the big take-out story that's TV, photos, a big text package. Well, what happened was it took me three to four weeks as opposed to one week, so it didn't get as much use as it would have. (Clendenning, 17)

Correspondents emphasized continuing to strive for credibility and accuracy, often gained only by eyewitness and painstaking checking, despite the mounting everyday tension "between getting things right and getting things out quickly," when "it requires courage to hold off when everyone else is reporting something" on major stories like the Arab Spring, in Laub's (14) example. She recalled being in the Cairo newsroom in 2011 when another news organization said President Hosni Mubarak had resigned. One of the Arabic-speaking reporters checked official statements and said she thought the translation was wrong:

I remember looking at our Mideast editor at the time, and he very calmly said, "Okay, we'll just hold off." And imagine the pressure, imagine that news organization was like hours ahead of the AP if it had been [right] ... those are the standards that often seem to be falling by the wayside now in this heat of competition, and they really have to be upheld.

Steven Hurst (13), who was bureau chief in Baghdad in the mid-2000s, recalled how in the face of the competition, "the demand for speed" could force one's hand to move "what is true of what you know, but it isn't the kind of story that you might've filed at the end of the day or the next day." Using the example of holding news of deaths until fully confirmed, even as other outlets are reporting them (also Barr, 18), Rosenblum (15) put it a tad more gruffly:

[T]his breaking news is bullshit. That's branding. That's a businessman's thing, breaking news. ... Someone shot a president, well, we should know this right away. But if we wait four minutes, to make sure it's right, that's pretty good. ... Today the mentality is, well, you can always fix it. Well, you can't. One, you can't fix it. And two, the deontology of it, the whole thing is, you don't get it wrong in the first place. It's not a question of whether you can clean up your mess.

Decades after making one such time-pressure mistake in his coverage of an IRA bombing in Northern Ireland, Marcus Eliason (9) was still smarting from not having taken the time to check his assumption before writing that it would

---

[14] Alan Clendenning, "Spaniards hope for eviction reprieve amid crisis," The Associated Press, December 10, 2012.

be a "feather in the cap" of the organization to hit a British marching band on Memorial Day:

If I'd waited a couple of hours, I would have learned that this was a major misfire. It ... killed only civilians, Protestant and Catholic to my memory, including a heartbreaking situation of a man whose daughter died under the rubble holding his hand. It was terrible, terrible! And everybody was shattered, and it was clearly a major setback to the IRA. ... I screwed up big-time; I should have waited. But I was under pressure, we needed analysis, we need to know what this means. I don't think I was being pressured from New York ... and I was wrong and then I wrote another one and correcting – I can't remember how I finessed my own bull – stupidity. ... [N]ow that I told you my screw-up, I'm very proud of the fact that that happened very rarely.

Eliason's next-day story led with the IRA claim that the bomb it planted was meant to kill soldiers and had only hurt civilians by going "off prematurely," and added, "The attack stirred a wave of revulsion on both sides of the border with the Irish Republic, from Protestants and Roman Catholics alike."[15]

Pressure for speed, and the editors' breathing down correspondents' necks demanding it, have only increased with instantaneous mobile connections. Victor Simpson (20) recalled how he was alone, working the night shift in Rome, when Pope Paul VI died on a Sunday in August 1978 – about as lonely as Rome can get. He sent out the "preparedness" – the obit on major figures that news organizations keep handy – New York relayed it, and eventually a colleague arrived: "in today's AP, within 30 seconds I'd have 20 requests. ... We need someone on the big stories just to handle the flow of questions and messages." In fact, John Rice (12) was in Cuba 20 years later covering – via broadcast, so he could file faster than if he had been on the scene – a speech in which Fidel Castro was expected to discuss the upcoming visit by Pope John Paul II. When the Communist leader spoke for three hours without a single papal mention, editors were "on the line screaming at me, 'What's he saying? What's he saying?!' Nothing. And so finally he started talking about the papal visit, and so you're listening to it on the radio and filing with your computer, as soon as he says two sentences ... I'm filing something in New York." Edie Lederer (4–5), a multi-decade AP veteran with a well-earned reputation for tirelessness – including squeezing in our interview in the middle of a Sunday during the UN General Assembly session, which she covered as AP's UN chief correspondent – recalled "the luxury of being able to take that extra time to check things":

The umbilical cord to your home office was not milliseconds away on a satellite phone, so you had a lot more autonomy to make decisions and sort of go with the flow of what was happening in the field, and not be micromanaged from 10,000 miles away. ... [W]e were competitive in trying to get things on the wire, [but] we weren't into 24/7 journalism yet.

---

[15] Marcus Eliason, "Bomb likely to revive IRA morale after setbacks," The Associated Press, November 8, 1987; Marcus Eliason, "Catholic revulsion and fear of protestant backlash over bomb," The Associated Press, November 9, 1987.

CORRESPONDENTS AND THE EDITING DESK

Most correspondents started out as desk editors before being assigned the coveted overseas posting, and became editors at other times in their careers – trying to use the previous experiences to ensure "that you're not asking [correspondents] to do things that are impossible ... and often being pleasantly surprised when they do things that are impossible," as top Europe editor Price (27) put it. But when reporting, all had to "deal with New York," the central international news command desk that made the final decision on what stories would hit the wire, and how worded, and that was replaced in the 2000s by regional desks in hubs like Mexico City and London. The editing process is beyond the scope of this book, which focuses on reporting practices; rather, this section explores the dynamic between "the desk" and foreign correspondents in the field concerning story selection and the final edit. (Other chapters detail more practices, including the teamwork and the logistical support that also affected correspondence – with editors' input ranging from stitching a story together from information gathered by reporters scattered around war fronts to sending in a medevac plane.)

I'm on the Story: Correspondents' Independence

The correspondents' ability to set their own agenda – to have to defend what to cover perhaps, but not be ordered a slant or perspective – has been a fundamental principle. All correspondents, regardless of era or location, said no editor had ever told them what to write along ideological, political, or nationalistic lines (e.g., Alexander, 33; Doelling, 17–18; Erbsen, 20; Gallardo, 21; AP Oral History, Gray 2005, 21; Price, 7; Pyle, 8b). Into the 1990s, as long as communication with New York meant jargon-heavy cables, slow telex messages, and hard-to-get, expensive, monitored international phone calls, correspondents were happily "pretty much on our own" (Tatro, 6; Gray, 37; Daniszewski, 5; Seward, 6; Price, 6), making their independent decisions on what to cover. While recognizing that outside input, background, and even close questioning are often helpful, most correspondents who worked in the pre-digital era valued the "autonomy to actually look at what was going on and not necessarily be influenced" (Lederer, 8). The massive increase not only in communication speed but in media outlets with live reporting, from cable television to social media, cut into the much-appreciated editors' attitude that one correspondent (Crary, 7) described as "you guys are there, it seems like a challenging situation, we're going to trust you to figure out what stories to do and how to do them." Correspondents long resented requests for a "match" from editors seeing something in major U.S. papers: "[O]ur biggest dread [in the Tokyo bureau] [was] that some correspondent would come and do this wide-eyed 'I'm new to Japan' story, 'and isn't this quaint?' ... And then we'd get what we called a rocket ... saying *Washington Post, New York Times, Wall Street Journal* has this story" (Jones, 10).

The 2000s shift from a centralized international desk in New York to regional editing hubs proved a game changer. The interaction with editors who now often sit across the room from reporters, or at least work in a similar time zone, means fewer last-minute calls from New York asking for a new story or a complete rewrite, and more local knowledge when the questions do come, as two correspondents (and editors) in the Middle East and Southeast Asia were happy to see:

[W]hen I was news editor, it's five o'clock here [in Israel] in the afternoon, I've already dispatched everyone to where they need to go and what to cover, and the day is pretty much set in stone, unless something dramatic happens. New York has just had their morning meeting and they said, "Wouldn't it be a great story to have this out of Jerusalem?" ... that's been reduced in a major way because of the regionalization. (Laub, 17)

"We should have had this angle!" "But we don't have that information. We don't have the quotes for that. We don't have the ..." "But we need this, we should have been on this. *New York Times* is doing this ..." ... That kind of stopped. So that was a good thing. (McDowell, 6; also Bryson, 20; Buzbee, 3; Kurtenbach, 5; Weissenstein, 17)

Correspondents usually had prevailed when they opposed some editors' occasional "big-footed" interventions requesting or questioning coverage that either reflected little understanding (including of the logistical hurdles) or directly contradicted what they saw on the ground. A correspondent wanted to write a feature on the future of South Africa right before Nelson Mandela's release from prison, highlighting that he "really could see a pathway now for South Africa to work its way out of this whole thing peacefully," and was met with "a lot of dubious skepticism from these bosses in New York":

It was one of the few where they sort of second-guessed me and said, are you sure you want to write this with an optimistic tone. And I said yeah, I really believe this. I've been here three and a half years. So that was sort of a struggle to get them to go along with that. And reading that story later I was really proud of it, because it basically came true. (Crary, 8)

Cooperman (22), covering economic disruptions during the disintegration of the Soviet Union, felt that the U.S. impact on them was minimal, but the questions kept coming from the desk "to say more about what it meant or might mean for the United States or ... what the U.S. input was in this." His story the historic day Gorbachev resigned, however, did not mention Washington until the 12th paragraph, and that was only to say that President Bush would make a televised address.[16]

---

[16] Alan Cooperman, "Gorbachev resigns, says has 'confidence' in Commonwealth's leaders," The Associated Press, December 25, 1991.

In the run-up to the 2003 Iraq War, Hanley (22, 24) wrote repeatedly about the utter lack of "firm evidence" of any WMD, the main casus belli. One story, put on the wire the week the United States invaded, ended on this note: "Now, with the [UN] inspectors gone, it will fall to U.S. military forces to locate any secret weapons programs and to convince the world they are the real thing."[17] Ironically, when the war started, Hanley's editors asked him to "join that WMD-hunting unit of the Americans" as it moved up Iraq, but he replied he would be wasting time since there were no WMD, and headed out to Baghdad instead (Hanley eventually visited the unit when they arrived, empty-handed, in the capital). In the Iran-Iraq War, another correspondent exploded to a longtime colleague, using his "vocabulary of expletives for editorial fools" before every other word – "How ... do I know if Saddam's ... son is fighting in this ... war when I'm on the Iranian front line getting shelled by the ... Iraqis?" (Fisk 2005, 235)

Correspondents did not win them all: In Somalia, Alexander (28) had to drive through fields for a day to write an update about an orphaned child whom others had written about months earlier, and he "felt kind of stupid going out to do this, just to chase down this one kid when so many other kids were suffering." Powell (9-10) went to Bangladesh in the late 1980s and wrote a story about "a quarter of the country ... made refugees by flooding. And my story was spiked ... and when I complained because I had risked my life in a Bangladeshi helicopter to get this story ... the reason they didn't use the story was 'It floods in Bangladesh every year.' ... It was discouraging."

Strategies for maintaining editorial independence over time included trying to "give them [editors] what they wanted before they knew they wanted it" (Clendenning, 11); fighting through initial refusals until editors relented and agreed ("if you really want to do a story and you're convinced it's a good story, it'll see light," McDowell, 22; "for every story they hashed up, they approved another one," McArthur, 12); and assuaging growing security fears, especially when pitching stories from volatile places like Afghanistan's Taliban-controlled provinces:

But now, to go to Wardak, you have to do a big spiel and you have to do this and you have to work your way around ... because of security. ... It's just imposed restrictions on us, the whole security issue, that we didn't, I never had before. ... I really do credit AP with respecting the fact of what I know and what I'm able to accomplish in terms of going out in areas that maybe other people won't go. (Gannon, 80–81)

Security concerns have driven many desk-field conversations. During the Korean War, Desfor (6) was told by his editor that he was not to join a group of paratroopers to jump with them – so he said okay, hung up the phone, and went. Regional and executive editors wrangled with reporters in Iraq when the country's civil war deepened throughout the 2000s, as Baghdad bureau chief Hurst (10) explained: .

---

[17] Charles J. Hanley, "As war unfolds, hard evidence of Iraq doomsday weapons remains elusive," The Associated Press, March 25, 2003.

We were as secure as we could possibly be. Rockets fell out in the front yard a couple of times. There's nothing you can do about that except not be there. But we had extraordinary security ... I think that they [editors and managers] kept us a little bit more locked down than we needed to be [for security concerns]. ... But that was their decision and they made the decision for reasons that are not available to me. So I don't dispute it.

Sally Buzbee (12), who was Middle East editor in Cairo around the same time, acknowledged the struggle over "our correct level of security," and over the correspondents' "very vivid sense" that desk editors did not understand their reporting challenges, which she tried to address by sending editors on two-week reporting stints to Baghdad. In some cases, it was up to local editors to raise security concerns, as one Paris-based correspondent did during the Algerian civil war when New York wanted the local writer in Algiers to get "out to talk to people in the streets": "It's one of the few times I really got sort of angry and I said I'm not going to tell this guy where to go and what to do. I'm impressed that he's still writing for us at all and can use his byline, and he's going to make the calls" (Crary, 15).

Again being on the ground carried the day – although several correspondents granted that the news could be so dramatically hard to believe, or hard to obtain from closed societies (Seward, 11), that the desk sometimes hesitated, understandably. Alexander (17) felt he "sometimes had to convince the bosses back in New York that I wasn't on peyote when I was doing some of this stuff [in Somalia]." Reid (70) sympathized with the editors making the final call on the accuracy of reports of alleged human rights violations by U.S. troops in Iraq from thousands of miles away, putting their own careers on the line too – though much less so with those whose distance from the field became nearly farcically evident, as when he was in Baghdad's Palestine Hotel and a U.S. shell hit it during the 2003 invasion. Wearing both a flak vest and his sports jacket with the AP bureau's $15,000 budget in cash in its pockets, and running up and down the hall trying to get signal on his phone to report the incident to the AP Cairo bureau, he had to call three times before a desk editor could hear him:

I just said without any introduction, "We are under attack." There is a long pause. He says, "Who is this?" Who is this? Who do you think it is, you know, Dubai? [laughs] Who else is going to call with a message like this? (AP Oral History, Reid 2009, 93)

In 1989 when the U.S. invaded Panama, another correspondent had a similarly surreal experience dictating the story of U.S. troops moving into Panama City as helicopters and rockets shook the hillside grocery store where he was on the line with the Mexico bureau:

[T]he natural question was, you know, "What's the source for the information?" I said, "Well, listen to the copters – the helicopters going by, and the ... rockets." And they said, "Oh, I guess there is." I said, "Believe me, it's on." (AP Oral History, Aguilar 2009, 52)

The Final Edit

> [In Tokyo in the 1970s] I got a message from one of the desk editors, foreign desk editors, that "suggest you rewrite story to emphasize this," and I sent him a message back, said "you rewrite it, put your name on it and a New York dateline," and they thought that was less than diplomatic. (Anderson, 2)

Virtually all correspondents shared Anderson's (7) dictum for desk editors – "Don't piss in my copy, don't change my story" – even though they knew their work was reshaped, even rewritten, on the desk (and, of course, that a good edit made copy stronger). Editors sometimes added information from other sources, in the early, slow-or-no communication days without necessarily asking correspondents first – "some of which I could have wrung their necks when I saw what Washington was saying," one Middle East correspondent said of the insertion of Washington's reaction to news she had reported on (Powell, 6). As Pyle (11) put it, he and his colleagues in Saigon "really didn't know what the hell the cable desk was doing with this stuff and how they were combining it and distilling it and homogenizing it with other copy." In South Korea, Anderson (7) had to be talked out of resigning after editors inserted the name of a U.S. military source to whom Anderson had promised anonymity in his story about the U.S. reaction to the military dictatorship that followed the assassination of President Park Chung-hee:

> I left this interview, and I went back and I filed a story quoting senior military sources, okay? The desk came back and said this is too important, we need better sources, and I said well I can't help you, that's the agreement I made, "senior military sources." ... The New York desk looks at the *New York Times* first-copy story, says he's got it by name, Anderson's got it by senior military sources, let's just put the name in. And they did, in my story. And of course the military went berserk because I violated the rules, and I said they do this in New York – they don't give a fuck and they don't want to hear about it. ... They didn't have the right to overrule me in the field, okay? If they had called me and explained what had happened, I might have been able to call the PR guy, the general's assistant, and said, "Hey, the *Times* has broken your name, can I use it?" Legitimate. They didn't have the right to overrule me and violate an agreement that *I* had made with military. ... They weren't compromising their integrity, they were compromising mine, and if you don't fight that, then you become a doormat.

But in the interviews covering eight decades, during which the correspondents collectively filed tens of thousands of stories, only one episode emerged when critical factual information was eliminated by the desk caving to political considerations or at least domestic sensitivities. During the height of the Vietnam War, Simpson (27–30; also Rosenblum, 1) witnessed it as he was getting started on the foreign desk, working an overnight shift. Peter Arnett in the Saigon bureau filed a story "about American troops going through a town [in Cambodia] and looting it." The foreign desk removed references to looting in the story for distribution in the United States, arguing that it was not "news" that troops could do this and that it would enflame public opinion (Arnett 1994, 267).

But the world desk, which was sending copy outside the United States and receiving stories separately from Vietnam, put it out. After Saigon went "wild" over this intervention, Gallagher ordered the story on the U.S. wire too – but also ordered the Vietnam copy to be filed only by the foreign desk, though a few months later that order was rescinded ("The Day ... " 1971, 30). Gallagher later admitted the interference was an error, and several Saigon staffers recalled him as backing the reporters despite pressures both from member editors and the U.S. government, and despite his own struggle to reconcile his experiences as a World War II correspondent with what transpired in Vietnam (Browne 1993, 179–81).

CONCLUSIONS

Filing copy is the foreign correspondence practice that changed the most over decades, becoming immensely speedier and easier, thus allowing for more time and breadth of reporting, but also for more control by editors at the receiving end. For text reporters, changes in communication technologies little affected newsgathering, though most took advantage of "new" media (from fax to Weibo) to find more and better-informed sources, and all must think multi-format today.

FIGURE 11.2. Baghdad chief of bureau Robert Reid does a standup for an AP Online Video report from the AP compound in the war-torn Iraqi capital in 2007. The minaret in the rear is from the 14th of Ramadan Mosque, on the square where U.S. Marines toppled the statue of Saddam Hussein during the 2003 invasion. (Photo courtesy of Robert Reid)

But when it comes to filing, the landscape is unrecognizable. Gone are the "pigeons" who carried news out of conflict zones and past censorship, the drunk censor jumping on gun cartridges as a reporter sweated at the telex machine (which even in the sanctuary of the bureau might waste hours for a few hundred words), and the endless waits at phone booths in the middle of wars and revolutions. Even at the remotest scene, correspondents armed with satellite phones and wireless connections no longer have to trade how far they can go for how fast they can transmit the news. Correspondents who, in the 1990s, lugged typewriters to Middle Eastern and South Asian deserts, by the 2000s might worry about the mujahedeen or the U.S. military confiscating their sat phones, but otherwise can be in constant contact from the front lines.

The downside is increased pressure to file faster, which leads to errors of both fact and interpretation, and to constantly feed the monster, keeping up with the flurry of online rumors and competing news while also, somehow, finding time to provide distinctive coverage behind the headlines, such as the perfect interview to illustrate Spain's eviction crisis, all in a couple of days. Lack of understanding of what correspondents faced on the ground has been the major source of conflict between reporters in the field and "the desk," with arguments that ranged from exasperation over clueless requests to grave news judgment disagreements, though even the most politically charged stories ultimately got the green light. Filed, edited, and on the wire, stories meet their audiences – and correspondents have long worried about how little readers seem to care about foreign news, how to attract them anyway, and the influence they have on coverage, which are the topics of Chapter 12.

Iranian Revolution, 1979

Robert Reid: [The translator, Ali] is running, "Bob! Run! The [Imperial] Guard is coming back!" And I looked up the street, and this Centurion tank had just made the corner and was coming down the street firing his machine gun wildly. . . . So we started running and running, and I noticed this construction site down the way, half finished. Perfect. . . . Jumped into the construction site, the tank comes by, the bullets hit the gravel that's there. And he stopped, he didn't go all the way to the base. Clears the Homafars out, they fall back. . . . And then from out of nowhere comes the guys who later became the Mojahedin-e-Khalq [Iran's leftist revolutionary organization]. . . . And they start pulling out the Coca-Cola cases of empty Coke bottles, fill it full of gasoline, and running out at the tank. . . . I thought, this guy is going to turn this machine gun around and he's going to kill us all. But it was too dangerous to move . . . and finally so many of these things had broken on the back of the tank that there was fuel and therefore it lights the fuel. . . . So the tank commander pulls the tank back and leaves, thank God. . . .

Ali finds me some merchant who's got a phone, so I call the office and the lines are crap, you could barely hear. The boss in the Tehran office picks up the phone, and I start to tell him, he says, "Get away, stop, get back. They've declared a 4 o'clock shoot-to-kill curfew" – by now it's after 3 – "You've got to get out." He doesn't want to hear anything I have to say. All this experience is never going to see the wire. [chuckles] ... So we run down the street, Ali stopping anybody in a vehicle, asking to take us out of there, but they won't take us out because of me. So meanwhile all the people are out making preparations for what they assume would be the inevitable return of the Guards in the streets. They are taking furniture out and making barricades and they are preparing Molotov cocktails. Everybody is running around like a rat on a speed. ... Ali says, "We have to go to my house. There's no way to get back [to the office]." ...

[The next morning] the boss says, "Take that stuff you called me with last night and try to file it." ... I'm sitting there punching out this magnetic tape, bit by bit. But we can't file it to anybody. The revolutionaries have cut most of the circuits. Tried New York, we couldn't get to New York. Tried London, we couldn't get through to London. Tried Nicosia, we couldn't get through to Nicosia. Nowhere. But we got through to Tokyo. Had figured they're still awake, so I'm filing this stuff, and by this time I was just punching, punching live ... and then it dawns on me: You know, it's a Sunday, I wonder if Tokyo is even there. So I hit the alarm key and punch it: Is anybody reading this stuff, question mark? A second later somebody punches back: Yes, the whole bureau. [laughs] ...

And all the sudden the local comes running in with this ferocious, wild look in his eyes. He says, "It's over, it's over!" "What do you mean?" "They all surrendered to Khomeini." ... so [punching sounds] banged that thing out through Tokyo.[18] And then that night ... some idiot imam got on state radio and said basically, "Hunt down and kill all the foreigners – they're spies." We had to shut off the lights, go into an inner room, and sit there until ... the level heads had heard this on the radio and sent somebody over to take control over the broadcaster to make sure he didn't continue to do this nonsense (Reid, 9, 28–32).

[18] See Thomas Kent, The Associated Press, February 11, 1979.

12

The Evolving Milkmen: Writing for an Audience

No connection is more critical, or more fraught, for journalists than that to their audience. Correspondents risk their lives to tell the stories of foreign peoples and countries to other peoples who should hear about them, while aware that only too often most readers would not care enough to find those countries in an atlas, especially after the first headline-making bursts of disaster. So correspondents conceptualize, report, and write stories with an eye toward attracting those distant eyeballs while unwaveringly staying true to their sources, the reality on the ground, and their ethical standards. When their subjects and topics do get great "play," on front pages or mobile screens, a child's life might be saved – or correspondents might be hit with a deluge of vicious accusations they have to waste precious time debunking. Thus, the omnipresent, imagined reader is a subtle but key shaper of foreign correspondence, affecting not only the storytelling but the story – a paradox for correspondents who can only hope that their hard-won eyewitness knowledge will eventually matter even to those disinclined to pay attention.

WHOM ARE WE WRITING FOR? (AND WHERE ARE THEY?)

For a wire agency that is a not-for-profit cooperative owned by its U.S. members but with hundreds of millions of readers around the world, defining who the audience is, let alone how to attract it, is inherently problematic: Will those unknown readers understand, need explanation, be offended, be engaged? Until well into the digital and globalization era, when wire stories only saw light in newspapers and on broadcasts, most correspondents wrote for "the milkman" in Kansas City or Omaha, in the words of AP's competitor United Press (Packard 1950; Morris 1957, 42; also Price, 12) – because if the middle-American, non-cosmopolitan middle class got it, journalism's fundamental democratic function worked. Correspondents envisaged as their readers their more curious family members – their busy but engaged parents in Missouri (Bartimus, 15) or grandmother in Florida (Bryson, 10) – and tried to give them a sense of "Here's what I see, this is what it tastes like, this is what it smells like, this is what it looks like," while acutely aware that on major stories, they were also "writing to officialdom, which added responsibility" (Heinzerling, 13). During most of the decades studied, AP ran stories both in the United States and overseas on different wires, and thus needed to cover both events that might be of stronger interest to foreign, regional audiences – that would score 10 paragraphs in Australia and a tiny "filler" in a U.S. newspaper – as well as the traveling Iowa senator whom nobody outside the Midwest cared about (Liu, 19; Erbsen, 18; Pennington, 13).

Nevertheless, conveying the news to Americans was long the "built-in consideration" in both story selection and storytelling (Desfor, 14; also Zeitlin, 9), particularly beyond the "obvious" breaking news stories. Roving correspondent Mort Rosenblum (21) tried to live by the advice given by a member newspaper's foreign editor: "Don't tell me what happens on a street in Chad. Tell me what a street in Chad looks like." Still in the 1980s, legendary foreign editor Nate Polowetzky encouraged correspondents "to write as if you're writing a letter back home," and future international editor John Daniszewski (4) took that to heart on his first assignment. He "tried to write about things that were different and unusual there, that stood out to me as an American living in Poland," even though his stories about challenges to Communism were often picked up, translated into Polish, and divulged back in Poland by Radio Free Europe (also Seward, 3).

By the mid-1990s, and increasingly in the 21st century, as correspondents themselves were more diverse and new technologies enabled reaching audiences farther away, the focus shifted toward global, multiple audiences of "international, intelligent, interested readers," including, though not primarily, those in the country being covered (Foster, 11; also Crary, 13; Bryson, 10; Buzbee, 3). Correspondents need to account for how millions of their readers might approach news with "a whole different load of emotional baggage" (Eliason, 3), and still often use themselves as the barometer to gauge the interest of such unknowable worldwide audience:

That was something that you sort of had to try to convey, very high up in the story, always, to let people know when you're writing what the French foreign minister said that day about the U.S. drive to war in Iraq, or whether you were writing about laws in France to ban burqas on the street or whether you were writing about a trading scandal at a French bank … "Why is this relevant to somebody in Chicago? Or somebody in Islamabad?" (Doland, 14)

"I make such a conscious effort not to write for an American audience, a Canadian audience, a Pakistani audience," Gannon (34) told me in Islamabad. "I try to really just tell the story." "Telling the story" is especially essential because audience interest is a moving and often fickle target. A hard-fought piece simply might not "ignite," while one that cost far less effort earns accolades, Daniszewski (6–7) reflected:

[I]n the field you seldom can be certain that what you're reporting is going to sort of catch fire that day. And sometimes it's surprising to you, when you've been covering a story in an ongoing way, which particular day it seems to really take off and go, what we would say today, "goes viral." And the challenge, I think, is try to tell the story day in and day out as accurately and forcefully as you can. And eventually people will hear it.

THE UNINTERESTED AUDIENCE, TURNING OFF STORIES AND COUNTRIES

Another difficulty in assessing audience interest is that, as correspondents (and public opinion polls) have repeatedly found, there is often painfully little of it. Even the most explosive foreign affairs revelations, such as the multiple ones by WikiLeaks, went largely unnoticed until major newspapers with "a predisposed audience" packaged them so as to attract attention (Beckett and Ball 2012, 154). There are a few, rare moments when correspondents knew the whole world was watching, such as the "split second" Nelson Mandela walked out of prison (Crary, 9), or stories of such magnitude that interest was taken for granted, such as the collapse of the Soviet Union, where "every small thing, if it could be put into the context of the larger story, was important" – although one Moscow correspondent added, "how much does the guy in Dubuque really care about these things, I don't know" (Hurst, 4–5). But as one south Georgia native and veteran of Korea and Vietnam war coverage put it, correspondents "quickly became aware of the fact that foreign news was not the paramount interest of the *Thomasville Times*" and that French presidents did not make for tableside conversation during most Americans' dinners – not that they would all be worth the time, he dryly noted (McArthur, 10). Even in Vietnam and Korea during the wars, some correspondents were "astonished" by the "little attention" Americans initially paid to their stories (Browne 1993, 98; Hohenberg 1995, 253).

Among the general lack of interest, several countries have been harder to spotlight, as discussed in Chapter 3, while others "generate some interest by definition" (Perry, 31). Among perennial reader favorites is Egypt, where in 1977 an unlikely story of a Japanese archeologist planning to build a new pyramid ran on the wire, and, 30 years later, "they did an autopsy on King Tut and figured out how he died ... probably the most-read story I ever did" (Schemm, 6; also Powell, 15; Bryson, 46–47).[1] Timbuktu also attracts, if nothing else "to say you had been there" – even a story about U.S. food drops during a vast Malian drought, datelined from the city described as "remote and

---

[1] Nicolas Tatro, The Associated Press, October 2, 1977; Paul Schemm, "A frail King Tut died from malaria, broken leg," The Associated Press, February 16, 2010.

FIGURE 12.1. Special correspondent Mort Rosenblum interviews a member of the Tuareg tribe in the dunes outside Timbuktu, Mali, in 1997. (Photo by Jerome Delay, courtesy of AP Corporate Archives)

legendary ... often a synonym for the end of the world," quoted one of the airmen as saying "I've heard of Timbuktu all my life ... but I never believed I'd get there" (Heinzerling, 12).[2] In Italy, "anything from Venice is going to be snapped up" (Simpson, 7). And Mexico is also an easier sell because "a lot of people know Mexico to a certain extent, have friends who do, their brother just got back from Cancun" (Rice, 4-5), although some observers of the devastating narco wars in the 2000s lamented the "scant attention" abroad (Ainslie 2013, 271). But beyond, geography often stumps readers, from Sri Lanka (Graham, 29) to Lisbon (Flores, 11) to the Congo, "which is a large group of land in Africa, which is south of Italy. I could get as far as Italy because people knew pizza, but ... people had absolutely no frame of reference," Rosenblum (21) quipped of his first foreign assignment.

Countries were also pushed off readers' radars by major news happening elsewhere and by the disappearance of well-known storylines. In Italy in the waning days of World War II, Bria (2) saw the "very heavy casualties, very rough fighting" there "forgotten" after Normandy, as all attention shifted to France and Germany. The 1969 helicopter crash that killed Bolivia's president made headlines for hardly a day before attention turned to French president Charles de Gaulle's resignation (Olmos, 7). A London correspondent found that interest in UK politics collapsed after Margaret Thatcher, because most

---

[2] Larry Heinzerling, "U.S. Flies Food to Parched West Africa," *Washington Post*, June 17, 1973, H1.

Americans actually recognized the British prime minister then, but after she was "chucked out in '90 ... the story just went down like a balloon, because I think we were back to nobody knew or cared" (Johnson, 14). On the other hand, Bryson (23, 52) noted that Nelson Mandela remained such a popular figure for decades (even talked about as "the President of Africa") that it made it "easier to sell a story about South Africa than almost anywhere else in southern Africa," which remained a challenge:

[I]t can be really hard to get people to pay attention to other stories in Africa when they begin to feel like they're all the same. ... [W]ar is still a big part of what's happening in Africa and the coverage in Africa, and I think the readers have a hard time differentiating from country to country. And readers have a hard time understanding why they should care.

Continuing stories like apartheid, wars, hostage-taking, and disasters can also turn off readers' attention by their repetitiveness, although they remain momentous. Even when correspondents feel that their story is "incredibly compelling" on its own, they need to keep their storytelling fresh, constantly find new sources and reactions, and focus on "incremental changes" and developments so that they do not appear to be "writing a version of the same story day after day, week after week" about South Africa's equal rights struggle, for example (Crary, 6). The same strategy applied to the hostage crisis in Tehran (Hanley, 3), the Lockerbie plane disaster (Barr, 2–3), Mexico's cartel violence (Weissenstein, 10), and the 2000s natural disasters in the Pacific. The Fukushima nuclear disaster was an exception, because it evolved "for a good three months before people, I think, elsewhere kind of got tired of reading about it," giving correspondents time to "do our job quite easily without worrying too much about, 'Do people still care?'":

[I]f you're not there, if you're not experiencing it, it does seem like, "Okay, I read about that yesterday. So what? It's the fourth day. They're still trying to recover from their earthquake." ... There's that trajectory with a natural disaster where it hits and people are interested, what's the magnitude, what's the death toll? International aid starts to flow in, and that's basically the end of the story. ... And that's really frustrating as a journalist because you know, when you're there, that these people are still suffering. There's a lot that you still really want to say. But you just have to be creative ... and express them in a way that people are going to care about. (Talmadge, 9)

Many war correspondents found it disturbing, even shocking, that public interest, perhaps "fatigued" by constant reports of violence and devastation, waned even in the middle of seminal, controversial, and U.S.-led conflicts like the wars in Vietnam (Pyle, 16) and Afghanistan. There Pennington (10–11) found that the civilian deaths became so routine that they lost "power in a way" for the audience:

I think you've got a basic kind of duty to report the facts of what goes down even if people are bored with it. ... I was always a little bit conscious of not wanting to [amp] up bombings because it's almost what jihadists want you to do, to have as big a media impact as possible. . . . [I]f an attack is egregious, then from what you write [that] will be plain. But . . . it's quite difficult to fight the fatigue syndrome. . . . My kind of attitude is . . . if readers had enough of it, if readers are bored of like death and destruction, well, tough, this is what it's going to be. This is what's happening.

One Baghdad bureau chief, sent to speak in Columbus, Ohio, about war coverage at the height of the mid-2000s insurgency, felt "an overwhelming disorientation":

[H]ere're the Americans who got, let's say, a hundred thousand troops, spending billions of dollars, maybe a hundred thousand or two hundred thousand Iraqis have been killed. And the country there is in the grips of civil war and here it is a Saturday in Columbus, Ohio. And there's no evidence of this even being on anyone's mind. . . . I liked my job as nasty as it was. Because I felt that it was important that we could tell the story. If anybody, who cared were the politicians who were either for or against the war. We were reporting to them and of course many, many, many citizens, thousands, hundreds of thousands, millions of citizens who did care. It was just for most people it was just that thing, that nasty thing over there. (Hurst, 9)

HERE, READER, READER: ATTRACTING A FICKLE AUDIENCE

All correspondents defended story selection as their prerogative, not the audience's (or the editors', as noted in Chapter 11), but many said they had to "to learn that what interests you intellectually is not necessarily what interests the reader" (Smith, 3), and therefore they had "to write it in a way that people are going to read it" (Talmadge, 13). The quest to attract the audience thus indirectly influences story-making and even newsgathering, with many correspondents "trying to get the story that will stick" and to package it so that it will have an emotional or intellectual impact on the largest number of readers (Ganley, 12). Aware that an ill-definable audience shows unsteady interest in foreign stories, unless already spotlighted by popular media or government, correspondents have tried a variety of approaches to draw readers in. Those have ranged from eye-catching details, even stereotypes, and common national references to analytical, contextual depth, and, most of all, "the human drama" – ideally in the lead:

You write your first paragraph in a way that sucks them into it. . . . And you give them the rest of it. And you try to explain why it's important, why you're writing it. And if you get that done in the first two or three paragraphs, then they'll read the rest. Or at least they'll know it's happened. (Erbsen, 15)

Tapa-sexos and Witch Doctors: Baiting with Stereotypes, Only to Puncture Them

If you are a correspondent in Brazil, you cannot not do carnival stories, because they are best-sellers every year, even if the only fresh angle is the latest change in the "tapa-sexo," "the tiniest G-string in the world that the Brazilian dancers wear" – "And yeah you kind of cringe at it, and say, 'Why are we spending all this time?' . . . But those stories sell" (Clendenning, 12). From France, the most-read stories highlight clichés, from "how much dog poop there is on the streets" to baguettes to, again, sex, creating a "constant struggle" for correspondents who know "that if you write a story about the Eiffel Tower, you'll get a lot of clicks. Knowing that if you write a story about French Roma children, you probably won't get a ton," said Angela Doland (9). She did visit a Gypsy squatter camp outside Paris to write about the struggles of integrating Gypsy children like her lead, 8-year-old Abel, who had never been taught how to hold a pencil or sit still.[3] But sex does sell better – so it can also be a way to attract readers to significant stories, about Italian politics for example. Without the raunchy antics of repeat Prime Minister Silvio Berlusconi, four-decade Italy veteran Simpson (14–15) said, "I wouldn't have written anywhere near the amount of stuff about politics that we do in other countries."

Does that baiting amount to "dumbing down"? Not if it helps make foreign political reporting interesting, accessible, and ultimately helpful to readers by "explaining complex things in plain language," said longtime China correspondent Charles Hutzler (9). When first assigned to Beijing in the mid-1990s, he stayed away from "Kremlinology" and tried to demystify China's peculiar Communist system through the lenses of tensions (and corruption) about migration, pollution, urbanization that would be familiar to any follower of the political processes in U.S. state legislatures – because "if the reporting is just dull, people are going to go elsewhere." On his first foreign assignment, trying to explain post-Communist Romania's sociopolitical changes in a way that stayed true to complexity but was also engaging, Dan Perry (7) did a story on something engagingly complex: how the Romanian language reflects its history of occupation, with Soviet-inspired bureaucracy imposing the "limba de lemn," wooden tongue, in which radio announcers would pontificate, "Valorile meteorologice să află pe o curbă ascendentă," or "meteorological values are present on an ascending curve" – it is getting hotter.[4]

The often stereotyped expectations that American audiences especially brought to certain countries both frustrated and helped correspondents, who sometimes dangled them near the lead to reel readers in, only to then contrast them with reality. Based in Kenya in the mid-1980s, David Crary (4) "really tried hard to draw people into the stories who wouldn't know kind of the rudimentary background":

I did one where I used the term witch doctor deliberately as a ploy to try to draw people in, and really the story was about how these aren't witch doctors, they're traditional healers, and write about the modern form of these traditional healers, who are still very

---

[3] Angela Doland, "Lack of schooling seen as root of Gypsy woes," The Associated Press, October 10, 2010.
[4] Dan Petreanu, "In Romania, doubletalk rolls off the 'wooden tongue,'" The Associated Press, March 28, 1993.

important, very diverse in the techniques and philosophies that they use. . . . That kind of decision, we would do that a lot. . . . Because I think there's a lot of danger for any foreign correspondent, maybe especially in Africa, to sustain stereotypes, to perpetuate stereotypes, and part of what we try to do is get away from that, but maybe use them to draw people in a little bit and then puncture them.

Crary's story from Nairobi about medicine in Africa began with numbers from the World Health Organization – one doctor for every 40,000 people on the continent, but one "traditional folk healer" for every 500: "What's more, some of their herbal cures have proved to be scientifically valid, providing a safety net for people who can't afford or don't trust modern healthcare. Don't call them witch doctors. Many of Africa's traditional healers contend they can cure bad luck and heartbreak as easily as a stomachache, but their remedies rely mainly on herbal formulas, not magic."[5]

Stereotypes and set narratives lacking nuance (and thus accuracy) abound in the popular imaginary for countries both near and from the spotlight. In South Africa in the early 2010s, writing about its cinema industry or Wal-Mart opening there, Bryson (10–11, 52) had to repeatedly explain that no, locals were not too poor to shop and go to the movies. In Cuba in the early years of Castro's regime, two correspondents labored mightily "to report the positives along with the negatives," but later realized little was published that was not bad, critical news:

When I wrote a piece that talked about healthcare, which Fidel Castro did move into rural areas, when I talked about education reforms, which he was about, those pieces somehow never made it into print because they weren't critical of the Cuban regime. . . . The AP would get this stuff on the wire so far as I knew, but I think American editors, U.S. editors in general, wanted pieces critical of Fidel Castro more than anything. It's easy to lay it out for the reader because that's what the editors thought that the readers wanted – just anything that criticized Fidel Castro. (Flores, 8–9; also Wheeler, 11)

Flores did write about how "independent observers" agreed that health services had improved in rural Cuba and even that "many Cubans still enjoy themselves despite Communist control over virtually every facet of daily living."[6] Central America veteran Joe Frazier (37–38) also fought against reducing most stories from the region to "we/they, good/bad" in the Cold War ideological framing: "I think an awful lot of the people in the States . . . were only worried that the Red Russian Communists were going to be on a beach the next foggy morning. And . . . they kind of got fed on that, and I think that helped fuel the interest of what was going on in Central America." As soon as that framing was over, "This place just quit existing . . . it went poof into thin air," as far as readers' interest.

[5] David Crary, The Associated Press, December 21, 1986.
[6] Isaac M. Flores, "Cuba Cites Big Gains in National Health Care," *Washington Post*, March 14, 1967, D11; Isaac M. Flores, "Havana Enjoys Itself, Despite Red Controls," *Los Angeles Times*, April 3, 1966, C16.

Hence the correspondents' fine line: "you grab people by what they know and sometimes you could play off of that and say it's not like that, or it's a lot more complicated than it seems," while being careful to avoid repeating racist ethnic stereotypes (Rice 6). In fact, correspondents sought to only use clichés "to destroy them or to challenge them or to affirm them, if they happen to be true":

But I think it's always easier to write about a place for a person who has some concept of it going in, even if that concept is wrong. Because then you can tell them actually that's not what it's like. But if it has a place in their brain, use that real estate. . . . I'm sure I did it on a daily basis. . . . [D]uring the election that led to [Vicente] Fox's becoming president [of Mexico in 2000], the ruling-party candidate, [Francisco] Labastida, I did a day with him. And for Americans, there's this mantra when you go to Mexico: Don't drink the water. So I challenged him on that. And he immediately basically made up a campaign pledge on the spot. He said, "If I'm elected, I will ensure that drinking water in Mexico is safe," which was (a) ridiculous; (b) he hadn't thought it through – it was just something he'd made up then. But I thought it was illustrative of the kind of campaign that it was, where he was throwing out promises left and right that he had absolutely no intention of making good on. (Price, 10–11)

The exchange made it into the story, which opened with Labastida at a rally in Oaxaca state, squinting "at the thousands of poor, mud-caked people surrounding him," and ad-libbing proposals, including one "born from a reporter's question about the U.S. stereotype of Mexico: 'Don't drink the water'" – "And thus another campaign promise is born."[7]

Well aware of the "cheap" storylines that confirm existing biases – "the only thing happening in Africa is illness and famine," for example – correspondents aim instead for stories with "counterintuitive facts" that, being unusual, might ultimately even generate a bigger following, said Daniszewski (17–18), who covered both South Africa and Eastern Europe. Middle East–based veteran Perry (13) echoed him, giving an example of how, to challenge the often one-dimensional portrayals of Jews and Muslims, he had written about controversial ultra-Orthodox Jews like Yehezkel Farbstein, a 26-year-old husband and father of two, who, the story began, "studies religion up to 15 hours a day, survives on a meager state handout and forgoes recreation. But he loves it, and yearns for the day when all Jews live this way":[8]

I actually went to the yeshiva [religious school], which most people don't do. . . . I spent a whole day with these guys. Now most Israelis, and also most foreign readers who trouble themselves to consider this issue, consider these guys, the ultra-Orthodox Jews, to be practically aliens of some sort. . . . If you spend enough time with them, you realize, in surprising ways they are becoming Israelified for one thing, and their desires and their

---

[7] Niko Price, "Mexico's front-runner campaigns with promise of a 'New PRI,'" The Associated Press, April 17, 2000.

[8] Dan Perry, "The black-hatted ultra-Orthodox: The real soul of Israel?" The Associated Press, October 6, 1996.

hopes and aspirations – this sounds a little clichéd but it's just true – are the same as that of the average Israelis and the average Western person. And I remember doing a story about that, which really confronted probably my own stereotypes about them as well as those of many of our readers and certainly, certainly Israelis.

To successfully spear myths and clichés, and inform misinformed readers, correspondents needed to truly own their subjects, whether Cuban politics or Japanese economics. Thus, they fulfilled the always-present responsibility of "getting people to be interested because they feel like they want to know," said Tokyo-based business correspondent Elaine Kurtenbach (13), adding that in the 2010s she needed to "put 'the world's third-largest economy' everywhere we can, as high as we can, whenever we can ... to get the point across that it matters. We're not telling you this just because we can tell you; there's a reason why you should know this, right?" That expertise and analytical skill can also attract a more discriminating audience, even when the story might not be front-page news. When Richard Pyle (16) covered the U.S. oil escort operations in the Persian Gulf before the 1991 war, he was keenly aware that he needed to write authoritatively, with all technical Navy details correct, including ship specifications, "or people who know about it are going to say, 'This guy don't know shit. We're not going to read this crap if you don't know what you're talking about.'"

What's in It for US? Is It a Home Run?

Another widely used strategy to attract readers has been to connect foreign stories to their impact on the United States, or the U.S. impact on them, although many correspondents cautioned against highlighting "our" angle at the expense of local reality, as noted in Chapter 3. Foreign coverage should help readers overcome the damaging "disconnect between what's happening out there and what's happening here [in the United States]" (Lederer, 14), while still focusing on revealing how interesting other countries are, not just how they might affect "us" in the global North/West. Regional desks editing copy and global online and mobile publishing have vastly decreased the emphasis on explaining in most stories how something relates to the United States, whether from London or Beijing, whether on rock and roll or diplomacy (Barr, 10–12; Jones, 6–7). Gone are the small stories requested by AP member newspapers that used to eat up correspondents' time – woe to the correspondent who did not file a story on the mayor of Philadelphia visiting Bangkok (Gray, 23) or the tourist from Harrisburg, Pennsylvania, who died mysteriously in a hotel in Nice (Ganley, 11). Also largely gone are idiomatic American English turns of phrase and cultural references – the "baseball analogies," the "Israel, a state the size of Delaware" (Perry 14, 33) – although if "in a story about 'Middle of Nowhere,' Costa Rica, when someone who lives in a village with no paved roads and it takes five hours to drive there, you see them wearing a Kentucky Fried Chicken

T-shirt," that vignette can not only draw readers, but illustrate "the weird way in which globalization has spread brand names around the world" (Price, 11–12).

Sometimes, however, the U.S. connection was the trick that got significant stories on the wire. A small revolution would have gone unnoticed "unless you could tie it to the Cold War" and its effect on the U.S.-Soviet balance of power (Reid, 20), while hundreds of oil well fires still burning in Kuwait landed on front pages across America for the description of one "called the longhorn, because when the Iraqis had blown up the wellhead, the flames were shooting up the side and coming up like this, like a longhorn" (Powell, 14). That metaphor made the story's lead: "Flames shot out 100 feet and curled up at the ends, just like the horns of Texas cattle. It was so hot that when doused on Friday, it 'felt like a cold front' had arrived, said one of the American firefighters who tamed it."[9] Many readers found themselves learning about agricultural politics in Burkina Faso after being captivated by a story about the "Ouagadougou Choo Choo," a train that connected the country's two largest cities (Rosenblum, 21). Still recently, Moroccan political change – "watching paint dry" to most people, albeit not to correspondents – made a story only if the first or second paragraph explained that the country was "a close U.S. ally in the fight against terrorism" (Schemm, 6). In order to interest international readers in the violent discrimination that the transvestite community suffered in Indonesia, Robin McDowell (8-9) decided to spotlight a person who not only had a significant story to tell, but whose U.S. connection was certain to grab attention – President Obama's childhood nanny:

If I just say, these guys have been beaten up in a bar . . . it's just not interesting. And then I remembered seeing a line in the story about – Obama used to live in Indonesia and his nanny, when he was a kid, was a transvestite. So it was like, we got to find this guy. Because if we can find *this* guy and tell *his* story, then it's interesting, right? Then it's not just interesting in Indonesia, it's putting a spotlight on this thing. This guy had this incredible story where . . . he would go out and wear women's clothes at night and stuff like that, and in the day, he dressed like a man. But that whole community is really persecuted, so the police would always come and . . . load them up in trucks or start hitting them and stuff like that. And he lost a couple of his friends that way . . . and at some point, he's like, "It's not worth it. I'm just going to start living like a man. I'm going to throw out my women's clothes and just –" which . . . it's like you're giving up your identity. . . . So it's a really touching story about this one guy and his experience and what he was doing now. . . . [E]ven [someone who is not interested in LGBT issues] . . . can actually hear the whole story, gets through the whole story, because it's not just some random person in wherever. . . . It's less singing to the choir that way, because you have to read about it, because it's Obama's nanny.

After some initial concerns that the story would be politicized out of context in the United States because the 2012 presidential campaign was under way, the

---

[9] Eileen Alt Powell, "'Long Horn' and 246 other oil well fires out, 510 to go," *The Associated Press,* July 27, 1991.

feature ran, with graphic details of the abuse Evie had endured. It noted that the White House had "no comment," but Evie certainly did about "Barry," who used to laugh when she would try on his mother's lipstick. The story ended: "Evie hopes her former charge will use his power to fight for people like her. . . . For Evie, who's now just trying to earn enough to survive each day on Jakarta's streets, the election victory itself was enough to give her a reason for the first time in a long time to feel proud. 'Now when people call me scum . . . I can just say: "But I was the nanny for the President of the United States!"'"[10]

Striking the balance between an engaging U.S. connection and still remaining true to the local reality is another fine line, especially for correspondents in areas that resonate strongly with U.S. policy or popular interest. In the Iraq War, reporters expecting readers' fatigue at "another story, another 200 people dead from a bombing," made an effort to explain "that this was a war that was initiated by the United States . . . [it] should be in the interest of the people who have moral questions about it, but also the people who are paying the bill, the taxpayers, and so we tried to contextualize it that way" (Hurst, 8–9). Bryson (11–12), who covered southern Africa in the early 1990s and late 2000s, found herself struggling with "the thing that everyone thought that they knew about South Africa," leading them to often faulty parallels – race relations. Few Americans paused to think that black South Africans are not a minority but a vast majority, she said, "so integration means something else entirely, for both sides":

There are some parallels, but basically, it's South Africa's story, and maybe you use the parallels to help explain things to American readers, but you can't leave it at that. And South Africans . . . are certainly tired of Americans making the comparison and of Americans offering solutions that are informed by our own experience, because that experience is quite different. And black South Africans . . . might not think of themselves as a black South African. They might think of themselves as a Zulu or a Xhosa or Colored, which Americans also don't particularly understand. . . . I don't know that I knew that when I first arrived, but South Africans were definitely quick to tell me so.

Kathy Gannon (36) used the example of her long-term coverage of Pakistani political leader Benazir Bhutto. A woman in a poor Muslim country with nuclear weapons and a conflict-prone border with the world's second-most populous nation was "easy" to make interesting – "but it was about how interesting Pakistan is," so Gannon also tried to explain Bhutto's relationship with her constituency and the slow reforms in health and education. In the same vein, Gannon told me she was "quite anxious, quite happy" to cover Afghanistan after the anticipated U.S. troops withdrawal, because "Nobody will be there. It will be a joy for me to be able to do my stories again." In an October 2014 interview, her first after being grievously wounded while reporting on Afghanistan's elections, she said she would return to cover the

---

[10] Niniek Karmini, "AP Exclusive: Obama's transgender ex-nanny 'proud,'" The Associated Press, March 6, 2012. McDowell contributed to the reporting.

country because "there's history still to be told there"[11] – and she always believed "people want to know. Really I do" (Gannon, 85).

Bring the Story Home: Real People, Human Dramas

The most time-honored strategy for telling that history in ways that readers can relate to is using a human drama – personal, close, sometimes shockingly rare and sometimes disturbingly universal. In this too correspondents knew they needed to strike a difficult balance – captivating without titillating, portraying without patronizing, serving their readers but being true to their sources. Bringing the news home to readers – letting "very small details" tell "the very big picture" (Laub, 9), giving "people a person to latch on to" (Bryson, 53) – is particularly necessary when the death count from wars, terrorism, and natural disasters is too enormous, or too constant, to grasp. In his first four months in Mexico, Niko Price (16) covered at least three hurricanes, and throughout his time reporting on natural disasters in Central America he searched for "people whose lives were accessible enough to make people care":

[T]he top of the stories would grab you before I had to introduce a name that sounded foreign . . . [I]f you can tell a story that, if it happened to your neighbor, you'd really want to know, then people, by the time they get to the foreignness of it, they're hooked and they want to read on. . . . [O]therwise it's just a death count and location and you're done. And that's not what we're there to do.

Price's stories about the devastation following Hurricane Mitch are spotlighted in this chapter's box. His report about the damage wreaked by Hurricane Pauline on Mexico's Pacific coast in 1997 did not name a local villager until the seventh paragraph and started this way:

Their clothes were muddy and tattered and they had eaten only a few tortillas in two days. Their houses – and everything in them – were gone. About 100 people huddled Thursday night around a single candle in the chapel – the only source of light in this town on Mexico's hurricane-ravaged coast.[12]

Similarly, in the weeks following Japan's 2011 triple disaster, the Tokyo bureau filed both "spot developments" and nearly daily features about, for example, the year opener in one school whose students had been washed away by the tsunami and a small village saved by its large, controversial "eyesore" seawall,[13] because, far more than with experts, "most people can resonate with . . . the upheaval it has brought to the people" (Foster, 9–10).

---

[11] David Crary, "Gannon vows return to Afghanistan," The Associated Press, October 15, 2014.

[12] Niko Price, "Pauline's path of destruction: Laying bare hundreds of poor villages," The Associated Press, October 10, 1997.

[13] Jay Alabaster, "Students return to school in Japan's disaster zone," The Associated Press, April 21, 2011; Tomoko A. Hosaka, "How one Japanese village defied the tsunami," The Associated Press, May 13, 2011.

To help readers wrap their arms around the height of Somalia's civil war, one correspondent described not only the "smell of death ... in the air everywhere," but also orphaned children in a UN camp who got one meal a day as recompense for not "running around the streets" and falling prey to militias. And yet he still felt it might not have been enough:

[I]f we'd done more of a daily diary of Somalia's struggle to feed itself and live on a daily basis, it would've been a more meaningful story in the long run than the political developments of the militia and the battle for control of Somalia, which nobody cared about then and nobody cares about now. They care about the struggle of the people. *That* has meaning to me. (Tatro, 24–25)

After Bhutto returned to Pakistan in 2007 and more than 100 people were killed by bombs at her homecoming rally in Karachi, Matthew Pennington first went to the morgue and described the grisly but dignified scene of volunteers cleaning the bodies and "putting up photos of corpses on the wall outside the morgue" to update relatives "hoping yet fearing they will recognize one of the battered faces staring blankly back." He then portrayed one young man's discovery that his 21-year-old madrassa student brother, Adnan, was among the dead, and the funeral, with relatives "gathered in the shade of a hastily-erected tarpaulin" and the father sobbing into his son's shoulder "after they placed the body in a grey cot for the mourners to view Adnan's sallow face peeking from the shroud."[14] "You can write about so many bombs and deaths and destruction to an extent that it doesn't really have an impact on anyone anymore. But if you can describe a bit more the ramifications of what it all means ... it's a valuable thing to do," Pennington (11) told me.

More than 30 years earlier, in what was then East Pakistan during the war that would create Bangladesh, Rosenblum (28) saw entire sections of towns "burned and bulldozed," and wells "full of people that they'd murdered and pushed in," amounting to possibly half a million Bengalis killed. First he had to contend with censorship: a story noted "Rosenblum was one of six correspondents admitted to East Pakistan after a five-week period during which foreign correspondents were officially barred. This dispatch was brought out to escape censorship."[15] Then he was stumped by how to explain horror on such a scale. One version of the story straightforwardly described "a civil war of staggering butchery and hatred" with damage "reminiscent of World War II." But this is the lead Rosenblum (28–29) remembered after decades, and why he composed it:

Vultures too full to fly perch along the Ganges River in grim contentment. They have fed on perhaps more than half a million bodies since March. Civil war flamed through

---

[14] Matthew Pennington, "Fearing the worst after bombing, relatives seek the dead at Pakistani morgue," The Associated Press, October 20, 2007.

[15] Mort Rosenblum, "Pakistan War Deaths Seen above 400,000," *Los Angeles Times*, May 13, 1971, 18.

Pakistan's eastern wing on March 25 [1971], pushing the bankrupt nation to the edge of ruin. The killing and devastation defy belief.[16]

I was trying to find a way to get across that ... horrendous breadth and depth of importance of this story, without saying, "Sources say ... *estimate* at least 500,000 people were killed by –" It's not that kind of story, you can't do that. ... You have to get across the enormity of it. ... Plus, they were Pakistani, Indians, and who gave a shit, you know, in America? That's the other problem. A dog bite in Brooklyn is bigger than a revolution in China.

Despite his best efforts, and the attitude that regardless of audience interest "any story worth covering is worth covering like it's the best story you've done in your life," Rosenblum (42) acknowledged that this was not the story that earned him the best play in media across the world. In 50 years of journalism (and counting, he kept a reporter's notebook in his jeans back pocket throughout our interview) that honor would go to, in his words, two "just fun" "bullshit" stories, one from Romania about Dracula and one from Kuala Lumpur about "frog wars." "Hardly a tear was shed for the hundreds who croaked in battle. But the weeklong amphibious war, fought by hopping and biting, unsettled soothsayers in this superstitious nation" because turf battles between different kinds of frogs were taken as omens of human tragedies, that story explained.[17]

In the best cases, however, humanized, personalized war zone stories can move audiences and change lives. A year into the continuing tragedy of the Bosnian War, which as news had thus "lost" its edge, Bob Reid (86, 84) zeroed in on Sead Bekrić, a 14-year-old boy evacuated from Srebrenica (then under siege and off-limits to journalists) to a hospital in Tuzla after "his eyes had basically been blown out." Three paragraphs in Reid's story about wounded children – portraying the boy "begging the nurses to assure him he will see again. He will not" – were enough to alter his fate:[18]

[T]his little boy, when I saw him, was lying in his underwear in a sort of a dirty bed – the sheets were dirty, the room was shabby ... and the boy was only semiconscious, if that. ... [T]here he was, blind, he really didn't by this point know that he would never get any better – a terrible situation. So as best I could, I wrote a little story about him. We got some pictures in the hospital bed. The story moved and it attracted a lot of attention among media in Tuzla. We were all stuck in this place ... scrounging around looking for stories, interviewing these refugees. Most of the stories were all the same, but this little boy's plight really kind of struck a nerve. So several other people did it. ... And ultimately, I believe it was a woman in California saw this, heard about the case, and adopted him. And I'd never seen or heard from this kid again until maybe 20 years later, I was watching a documentary on Sarajevo ... and they showed this tall, stocky, dark-haired young man with eyeglasses and a cane, speaking perfect California English,

---

[16] Mort Rosenblum, The Associated Press, May 13, 1971.

[17] Mort Rosenblum, "Hundreds of Frogs Die in War," *Daytona Beach Sunday News-Journal*, November 15, 1970; Mort Rosenblum, The Associated Press, October 2, 1983.

[18] Robert H. Reid, "Hospital copes with wounded children," The Associated Press, April 15, 1993.

talking about his life story and how, considering the situation that he was in that April [1993] morning when I saw him, life took a dramatic turn for him.

Correspondents have also sought to humanize, often in counterintuitive ways, characters whom the audience might easily see as "stick figures." A Palestinian refugee from Gaza becomes a University of Malta student whose great hope for Middle East peace is to get a passport, so that he can travel between family and school without being stuck in no-man's-lands at international airports (Eliason, 4). U.S.-bound undocumented migrants from Latin America can be only "desiccated" corpses in the desert unless correspondents "paint a picture of what the community is like that sent them there" and how the "pretty idyllic-looking little farm communities" with "maybe" some coffee or bananas really do not provide enough to make a living. Readers might learn more about U.S. counterinsurgency strategies in Afghanistan when the story focuses on a 39-year-old lieutenant colonel in Logar Province who, despite looking physically "like a gorilla," turns out to be an intellectual who reads Carl von Clausewitz's *On War* in the original German, "a self-styled maverick who has broken army rules and operates by his own rendition of counterinsurgency warfare" (Gray, 64).[19]

Complex or underreported issues, even countries, can also catch the audience's imagination if they get the personalized treatment. The economic impact of the 2010 World Cup in South Africa shines through Cecilia Dube, who moved from "frying doughnuts by candlelight," barefoot and before dawn, for workers building the inaugural stadium, to tending her own food stand for soccer fans and dreaming of one day opening a restaurant (Bryson, 53).[20] A feature about painters landed a rare AP byline in the *Washington Post* on the war in Angola:[21] "[D]ie-hard Angola followers . . . would read anything that comes out of Angola about the war, right? But then you would get the general public who really couldn't give a damn" (Smith, 4). British class distinctions literally find a voice in a young, uneducated Cockney broker whose fraudulent trades brought down the prestigious bank where he worked, but its aristocratic owners offered no comment to the press "because they're much too well-bred to do so" (Johnson, 15).[22] The rise of genital mutilation in Paris, itself a story about migration and Europe, was crystallized in "this little girl in her little frilly dress" (Ganley, 29), described unflinchingly in the story's lead:[23]

[19] Denis D. Gray, "Officer puts own spin on war," The Associated Press, December 20, 2009.
[20] Donna Bryson, "For one woman, a different kind of World Cup dream," The Associated Press, June 20, 2010.
[21] Tony Smith, "In Angola, Painting Perestroika," *Washington Post*, September 7, 1989.
[22] Nick Leeson, a 28-year-old broker, brought down Barings Bank in 1995 with fraudulent trades of over $1 billion in Singapore; Maureen Johnson, "Plasterer's son breaks blueblood bank," The Associated Press, March 3, 1995.
[23] Elaine Ganley, "Despite tougher laws, an ancient custom remains a secret horror for some girls in Europe," The Associated Press, September 7, 2007.

She remembers the new white dress with violet flowers, the lacy socks, the patent-leather Mary Janes. She was 6 years old and, she thought, off to a fete with her sister, her mother, three cousins and an aunt. Instead, she ended up naked in the basement of a Paris dormitory for immigrants, the air thick with the odor of garbage, incense and blood. She remembers the four women ... and how she struggled as one of them violated the most intimate part of her body with a razor blade. She remembers the searing pain that still makes her cry.

Covering the aftermath of the Soviet Union's collapse, about as momentous and difficult a topic to personalize as possible, Alan Cooperman (19–20) also zeroed in on "microcosms" of real people, such as the farmers at the Lenin Collective who "mope around the dusty barns." Their grumbling about the privatization that saved it from bankruptcy and fearing it would make them "slaves" to the entrepreneur owner were indications that the process of converting "the huge, inefficient collectives into private farms" would be "slow and painful."[24] Perhaps most prescient was a story about a 30-year-old Ossetian warehouse clerk, Marat Khaiti, who thought his Ingush Muslim neighbors "savages" he needed to "cleanse" out of his land, and who for six days had been doing just that, "with hunting rifles and gasoline bombs as they tried to burn each other out of their homes. But he also admits his family secretly sheltered an Ingush woman and child, probably saving their lives."[25] Cooperman wrote that the contradiction "reflects the political, ethical and emotional confusion in the Caucasus" – a confusion that puzzled Khaiti, who "could not explain" why he had kept his neighbors safe in his house, probably as the husband was out fighting Ossetians, and did not want fellow militants to know: "'It was only a woman and a little girl,' he said apologetically. Yet he was adamant that the two ethnic groups can no longer live together ... 'We hate them and they hate us,' he said."

THE AUDIENCE STRIKES BACK

Correspondents' ideas of what their audiences are interested in, and of how to make them interested if they are not but still need to know about foreign news, have an impact on both story selection and storytelling. But the audience is not just imagined – correspondents, and editors, have long studied which of their stories get the public's attention, and in the social media world, publicizing content has been added to the to-do list (making some media observers worry that it might detract from the already tight time for reporting and writing), while anonymous feedback can turn into chilling harassment. In the pre-digital era, New York (and occasionally other domestic bureaus) sent foreign bureaus

---

[24] Alan Cooperman, "Private farming in Russia: Bold reform or a new serfdom?" The Associated Press, August 24, 1992.
[25] Alan Cooperman, "In the Caucasus Mountains, a war that could tear Russia apart," The Associated Press, January 31, 1993.

"play reports" and clippings, indicators of what stories had landed on front pages across the United States, which had bested the competition, and whether, one correspondent said, they were doing "the right thing" at least as far as generating a following went (Doelling, 19–20; also Doland, 14; Kurtenbach, 7). The questioning from domestic editors, discussed in Chapter 11, as well as the occasional readers' letters, revealed how domestic audiences might lean, but the time lag used to buffer correspondents (Seward, 6; Bryson, 29).

With online and social media, the feedback has become instantaneous, massive, and ever more closely watched, often in real time, by many correspondents and editors studying everything from what is topping news searches to who is getting lots of tweets (even if only for a few hours, given the shortened attention spans), from readers' comments and emails to what is going viral and thus might merit a story, such as an obscure Spanish fresco that became an online phenomenon after a botched restoration turned it into an unlikely marketing icon (Clendenning, 20–21; Gray, 30; Kurtenbach, 8).[26] A new feature of the online world for AP is the ability to reach audiences unmediated by member newspapers or networks, especially through AP apps, as well as to publicize AP stories through social media and thus help drive interest online (Foster, 12). The facile interaction with readers has meant some useful corrections from engaged, knowledgeable interlocutors, occasional praise, and a deluge of recriminations and complaints of questionable truthfulness and value (Perry, 22; Talmadge, 12–13; Laub, 13; Bryson, 54; McDowell, 18) that several correspondents simply avoid reading.

Most correspondents said they could not let public opinion, no matter how flammable, influence their reporting choices, calling that a "violation of basic journalistic ethics" (Perry, 20). But some vocal audience members, directly or through member media, have long tried to exert pressure, and the new close contact might give them more power – if nothing else as a distraction when time is already tight – even against AP correspondents, who, writing for a wire service, used to be more shielded from harassment. Prominent newspaper correspondents in the Middle East, for example, grew accustomed to receiving hate mail, and The (London) *Times* Beirut correspondent Robert Fisk (2002, 419–420) recalled AP's Nick Tatro telling him, "These people are not looking for information ... they are trying to *inhibit* you from reporting information" (also Friedman 1995, 440; Geyer 1998, 314; Fisk 2002, 46). Eileen Powell (11), who had worked with them in Beirut and in the late 1980s transferred to Jerusalem, recalled the "vitriol" that coverage perceived as sympathetic to Palestinians generated in the United States, as well as in Israel.

That feedback, however, was still mediated by editors in New York who shouldered most of the anger and groundless rants – defending a Central America correspondent against accusations of supporting leftist rebels

---

[26] Alan Clendenning, "Disfigured Spain fresco rides global fame," The Associated Press, September 21, 2012.

(Frazier, 19) or a West Africa correspondent from complaints that, being a white American, he "could not possibly know what's going on in Africa" (Heinzerling, 15) – and left them alone to pursue their stories. But as that shield has largely disappeared because readers can easily track down individual correspondents, and respond in the anonymous free-for-all online, even war-hardened correspondents are stung by violent, often cruel feedback. In Vietnam to cover the 25th anniversary of the war's end, Paul Alexander (32) wrote about the thousands of people whom unexploded ordnance continued to kill, focusing on a boy badly maimed by a bomb that his friend had hurled against a rock, probably thinking it was a ball. "Ten-year-old Phan Huu Luan was 20 yards away watching over a water buffalo when a swarm of fragmentation pellets knocked him into an old bomb crater. Bleeding from head to toe, his leg badly broken, he crawled to the edge, saw his two friends dying and began crying for help," the story read:[27]

And I get a letter, an email from some guy [in Kansas] . . . "Oh, isn't that just so too bad? These people – they're getting what they deserve. And tell me, Mr. Alexander, do you roll over for the Vietnamese government because they pay you or because you like it?" And it's like, wow. To hear that anger coming over for a story that should be provoking the opposite emotions.

In the 2006 war with Lebanon, an Israeli strike killed scores, including at least two dozen children, in what Israelis insisted they thought was a terrorist hideout in Qana, and Gannon (7–9) got there "as they were still pulling the bodies out."[28] Her stories, and the pictures with them, touched off a furor online. Several bloggers alleged that AP ran photos of the same dead girl twice – while they were actually identical twins – and questioned the photographed presence of an emergency worker who had also been in Qana when Israel had hit a UN compound there in 1996. The online attacks, which even went after Gannon's Pakistani husband, were "such a surprise," she said, though their only outcome was to reinforce balance and meticulousness in reporting. Gannon's story about the relief worker rebutted the allegations directly, explaining that his "exhausting, heart-rending" recovery effort was witnessed "by an AP team that arrived at the scene along with other journalists":

After hours of digging in the blistering heat, Salam Daher emerged from the wreckage with the body of a 9-month-old baby, a blue pacifier still pinned to its nightshirt. He held the infant up and, click, an Associated Press photographer snapped another picture of Daher, in his trademark green helmet, displaying a civilian victim of Israeli bombs for the

---

[27] Paul Alexander, "25 years after war, bombs and grenades keep killing Vietnamese," The Associated Press, April 25, 2000. Later that year, Alexander covered a meeting in Hanoi between President Clinton and four boys from the same province who were maimed by unexploded ordnance.

[28] The bodies of 27 children were found in the rubble. Kathy Gannon, "Israeli missile strike in Lebanon kills at least 50; Rice asked to postpone trip to Beirut," The Associated Press, July 30, 2006.

world to see. Daher, a member of the civil defense for 20 years, has been photographed with bodies of the dead in two wars now. ... For that reason, some Web sites have ... accused him of being a member of the Hezbollah guerrilla group, and of showing off bodies as propaganda. "But that isn't true," he told The Associated Press. He is not affiliated with any party, he said. "I am just a civil defense worker. I have done this job all my life."[29]

Not that it was the first time the audience got viciously personal with Gannon. In Kabul at the beginning of the 2001 U.S. war, she had done a series of stories about the impact of bombing raids on civilians there, especially on children. "Darkness settles on the shattered city. Candles flicker in the windows. Everyone is waiting for the U.S. jets to come. 'When the planes come my daughter hides behind me,' said Mohammed Gul gesturing behind his leg. 'And my other small son hides behind the other leg,'" one story began.[30] "[N]asty hate mail" followed publication:

"Hey, Kathy Gannon, how would you like it if your mother was strapped to a plane and somebody smashed that into –" Well my mother was still alive then, but she had trouble getting around. I was going to write that but you don't have to – I didn't write back to any of them. ... It was a lot of it. And it was just, oh a story about some children hiding and there was a lot of stray dogs and kids in the street and just ordinary life. (Gannon, 61)

In at least one case, the online storm over a story was so destructively time-consuming to quell that one Iraq War correspondent questioned whether it had been worth writing it, a rare but dangerous sign of a truly malignant influence by audiences on news. In 2006, Steven Hurst (7, 11) wrote a story about six Sunni worshipers who had been "waylaid, doused with gasoline and burned" alive by Shiite militiamen as they came out of a Baghdad mosque, stating in the lead that the "gruesome attack ... dealt a new blow to diplomatic efforts to stop the violence and raised the pressure on President Bush days before his summit with Iraq's prime minister."[31] Hours later, one of the main sources, police captain Jamil Hussein, whom AP had visited several times over two years in his office at the police station, vanished and became impossible to contact, and the American military denied that he existed. Hurst wrote a story about that too, giving unusually detailed insight into how AP had reported initially and then found other local witnesses to the immolation (though some in the neighborhood "said they were afraid to talk about what happened"), and hinting tersely at the online and even official dissembling:

---

[29] Kathy Gannon, "Civil defense rescues the wounded, recovers the dead; one draws controversy," The Associated Press, August 12, 2006.

[30] Kathy Gannon, "At day's end, residents of Afghan capital hunker down for nightly air raids," The Associated Press, October 30, 2001.

[31] Steven R. Hurst, "Shiite militiamen burn Sunnis alive in revenge attacks for Sadr City slaughter," The Associated Press, November 25, 2006.

This account of one of the most horrific alleged attacks of Iraq's sectarian war emerged Tuesday in separate interviews with residents of a Sunni enclave in the largely Shiite Hurriyah district of Baghdad. The Associated Press first reported on Friday's incident that evening, based on the account of police Capt. Jamil Hussein and Imad al-Hashimi, a Sunni elder in Hurriyah, who told Al-Arabiya television he saw people who were soaked in kerosene, then set afire, burning before his eyes. AP Television News also took video of the Mustafa mosque showing a large portion of the front wall around the door blown away. The interior of the mosque appeared to be badly damaged and there were signs of fire. However, the U.S. military said in a letter to the AP late Monday, three days after the incident, that it had checked with the Iraqi Interior Ministry and was told that no one by the name of Jamil Hussein works for the ministry or as a Baghdad police officer. Lt. Michael B. Dean, a public affairs officer of the U.S. Navy Multi-National Corps-Iraq Joint Operations Center, signed the letter, a text of which was published subsequently on several Internet blogs. The letter also reiterated an earlier statement from the U.S. military that it had been unable to confirm the report of immolation. The AP received no comment Friday when it first asked the U.S. military for information. . . . The Iraqi Defense Ministry later said that al-Hashimi, the Sunni elder in Hurriyah, had recanted his account of the attack after being visited by a representative of the defense minister. The dispute comes at a time when the military is taking a more active role in dealing with the media.[32]

Then, for two "very, very awful" months, rightwing bloggers insisted that AP had invented the police officer, and the story. Finally, Iraq's interior minister admitted at a press conference that Hussein not only existed, but had said what Hurst had reported, and now faced arrest for speaking to the media. Hurst also reported this development, noting the accusations leveled against AP by both U.S. and Iraqi officials, "spread and amplified" by Internet bloggers, and stating that "Hussein appears to have fallen afoul of a new Iraqi push, encouraged by some U.S. advisers, to more closely monitor the flow of information about the country's violence, and strictly enforce regulations that bar all but authorized spokesmen from talking to media," in a move similar to Saddam's reign.[33] That ended the controversy, but damage was done:

I am confident of what we had reported and I am confident of the horror of what we reported. I'm not sure, knowing what I know now, that I would have reported it simply because . . . it was just another horror story in a very long horror movie. Right? A little more horrible perhaps because of the detail, but . . . It was a huge distraction, more so for the AP in the United States, I think, than for me. . . . [I]f I knew then what I know now, would I have reported it? I don't know. Or would I have written it a different way? I don't know. But it was a distraction that was not needed and . . . it was a waste of two months almost trying to battle against us.

[32] Steven R. Hurst, "Witnesses detail immolation attack on six Sunnis in Baghdad last week," The Associated Press, November 28, 2006.

[33] Steven R. Hurst, "Iraq threatens arrest of police captain who spoke to media," The Associated Press, January 4, 2007.

CONCLUSIONS

One fundamental question for correspondents has always been, who is the audience and how do we reach it? For decades, the answer was Uncle John, the milkman in middle America, although in reality he might also be sitting in the White House and in capitals around the world. Despite distributing stories on both a U.S. and a world wire, the primary focus always was on the American public, and although correspondents have had no intention of relegating to an imagined public their sense of news, they have tried to convey their sense of place. Part of the problem in guessing what interests readers is that it is not much, particularly about some countries. We will always have Paris, pyramids, and Middle East wars, but where in the world are Sri Lanka, Congo, and Lisbon? Interest in countries ebbs: Japan still has sushi and gadgets going for it, but as a major geopolitical and economic power and competitor, it has receded so far behind China as to be out of sight. Continuing stories are hard to maintain too, quickly becoming another suicide bombing, another rescue operation, another halting recovery, even when sizable U.S. interests are involved.

If it is happening, there will be stories about it, so tough for uninterested readers – but it is better if they can be made to care a little, at least enough to know that something happened, through both story elements and flow. Unfortunately, clicks and clichés go hand in hand, but a little sprinkling of the latter might draw readers into wholesome, nutritious stories like politics, and might even lead to debunk some stereotypes. Those Kenyan witch doctors are actually traditional healers, but hey, we made you look! The other way, also not without perils, to interest readers has been to highlight the connection to, parallel with, or impact on the United States: Who will read about the plight of Indonesia's transvestites unless told that Obama's nanny was one? What correspondents bet on the most, however, is to focus on the human drama – to sympathize and horrify, often at the same time, by sneaking in the "foreignness" under cover of real, relatable people. Then, it is no longer scores killed in another bombing, but families looking through body parts at morgues; it is no longer half a million dead halfway around the world, but vultures too full to fly perched on one of history's celebrated rivers. Thousand were massacred at Srebrenica, but one blinded boy's life would be changed by one story. Ditto for complex issues: European identity, migration, and genital mutilation become blood dripping down a 6-year-old's dress onto lacy socks and Mary Jane shoes in a squalid Paris banlieue.

For decades, except for occasional letters, editors' comments, and play logs, this was as far as correspondents had to imagine, and worry about, their audience's reactions. Today, the feedback is immediate, personal, viral, and often virulent, calling reporters traitors if they dare write about the suffering of Vietnamese or Afghan children, and liars if they give the lie to falsehoods. Given what a paradoxical obstacle the audience can be for correspondents, it is not surprising that most felt that their ultimate ethical responsibility lay with their sources, their stories, the realities they portrayed, not with what their readers did with it all:

I write to tell the story, not to an American. I think once we start to do that, we cheat ourselves, but we also cheat the story. So what, Americans are interested in this, or Europeans are, but what about the story? It's the story that's important ... it's about really enjoying the story and what is the story and telling the story and figuring out the story and meeting people so you can tell the story. It's not about the audience. If you're telling them the story, then there. ... If it's not an important story as a story, maybe you shouldn't be here. (Gannon, 34)

So why did correspondents think they should be there? Chapter 13 details their reflections on the purpose and influence of foreign correspondence.

Hurricane Mitch, Nicaragua, 1998

Niko Price: I remember it was Saturday night, Halloween – yeah, because we were all dressed up at a party – getting a call about three in the morning ... from a colleague in Mexico, saying ... "there are rumors that a village in Nicaragua has been covered by a mudslide. The mayor said something about thousands of people dead, and it's probably hyped, but we might want to check it out." The next morning, I went with a photographer that ... I worked with a lot, and we flew into Managua [from Mexico City]. We chartered a little prop plane to a town near where this mudslide had allegedly happened, rented a four-by-four and drove in, getting stuck many times along the way. And we made it. And it was as described: A mountain had basically fallen away and came roaring down and covered a couple of villages. And we spent the next 10 days basically wading through mud and fields of bodies that had been swept down the mountain and just rotting in the sun. It was an awful scene.

But again there were the personal stories that made it come home. [T]here was a body of a girl ... wearing a frilly little dress in the middle of the mud, on a plank of wood, rotting. And going back and saying, that's a pretty powerful image and let's figure out what happened here, and getting the whole story. ... But you don't have to know that you're in Nicaragua and you don't have to know who these people are to ... read that story and to get the emotional power of it. And that's how you could bring it alive to people very far away (Price, 16–18).

[One of Price's stories from the town of Rolando Rodriguez focused on the girl, Marta Pantaleon:

Two days after the mountain slid away, when the sea of mud had firmed enough to no longer swallow people up to their necks, Marcelo Narvaez Gonzalez and his neighbors waded into a peanut field, hoping to find his brother alive. They tried to ignore the bloated, blanched corpses twisted in fallen branches. They recognized each one as a friend or relative. Narvaez, 27, spotted a child lying on top of the muck and saw her chest move. It was 11-year-old Marta Pantaleon, a distant cousin. One neighbor slogged into the chest-high mud and dragged Marta to firmer soil. ... Narvaez and the others struggled on, pulling four more people from the mud before returning for Marta . . . her chest wasn't moving any more. They left her where she lay so they could carry the living to safety. On Thursday, with a light drizzle falling, she was still there, her frilly, pink dress pulled over her face and flies buzzing around her stomach. The stench was almost unbearable.][34]

[34] Niko Price, "OUT FRONT: Dying of thirst and infection amid mud, decomposing neighbors," The Associated Press, November 5, 1998.

13

Purpose and Influence of Foreign Correspondence

Middle East correspondent Terry Anderson spent most of seven years chained to the wall in a series of dark cells after being kidnapped by militants in Lebanon in 1985. Kathy Gannon covered treacherous conflicts in Afghanistan and Pakistan over three decades and, less than a year after our interview, was gravely wounded in an execution-style attack that killed AP photographer Anja Niedringhaus as they covered Afghan national elections. Given the dangers faced and the price paid on the job, Anderson's and Gannon's answers to my question of why they did what they did – what they thought were the purpose, influence, and significance of journalism – are especially striking:

[A]sk the people who kill them [journalists], beat them, and put them in prison, whether it's important, because they all know you cannot have a free society without a free press. Period. You cannot oppress the people, you can't steal from them, you can't take away their rights in the face of a free and active press, that's why they go after the journalists, that's why everybody hates journalists. No, we're not all wonderful people, we're not all even very good at the job we do, and there are constraints, institutional constraints, societal constraints that keep us from achieving this wonderful goal of finding and telling the truth, but most of the journalists that I know are highly idealistic people with a firm sense of outrage. They try to do that as best as they can. So yeah I think it was worthwhile. I think it was worth doing. (Anderson, 29)

I want to tell the Afghan story. The Afghans' story. I want to tell the Pakistanis' story. I want their voice as well to be told. ... To be able to get to villagers who are back of beyond, to be able to get to Pakistanis who are under threat ... it is for me a joy. ... I spend a tremendous amount of effort organizing it. ... Like when the story about ... the victims of the ... American soldier that is charged with killing those 16 people.[1] ...

---

[1] In summer 2013, U.S. Army Staff Sergeant Robert Bales was condemned to life in prison after pleading guilty to killing 16 Afghan unarmed civilians, mostly women and children, in their homes in 2012. Kathy Gannon, "Afghans tell of US soldier's killing rampage," The Associated Press, May 16, 2013.

[A crucial female witness] would never have been allowed to go to Kabul, so we went to Kandahar. And they took risks to come and talk to us, talking to foreigners, because there's of course Taliban around. We took risks because we wanted to go to them and tell their story. The little girl who, Zardana, . . . her grandmother was killed and she was shot in the head hiding behind her grandmother. And she remembered everything, and she had to come from her village to Kandahar. The poor little thing, her leg doesn't work right, and so sweet. . . . [I]f you don't hear their voices, you don't know them. If you don't know them, you don't understand them. If you don't understand them, you can't engage. That's the whole reason why we tell any story I think, or cover any area, is to know the people . . . not to know the people vis-à-vis us. . . . Yes, you have to embrace the larger questions. . . . But the conversation, the information has to be about – you have to get their voice. (Gannon, 76–77)

Six months after surviving the attack, Gannon vowed to return to report the Afghans' stories and the struggle they endured "and never succumbed to hopelessness": "Neither Anja nor I would ever accept to be forced out by some crazy gunman."[2]

While motivation is inherently personal and individual, all correspondents interviewed expressed a similarly self-effacing belief in their job as a public service, one they owed to their sources – often destined to remain voiceless if correspondents did not reach them – and to their publics, often relegated to ignorance and spin without independent, on-the-ground journalism. This chapter focuses on how correspondents defined their sense of purpose, on the assumption that what they thought they were doing would implicitly affect how they did it. Scholarship about normative theories of media in democracies has found "the provision of information" to be "the very core of journalistic professional practice" (Christians et al. 2009, 143, 120). All AP correspondents insisted that, as objective observers, it was not their job to influence foreign policies or international relations. They defined their responsibility as telling truthful stories first of all, and then in ways that would make people pay attention, see a new angle, maybe even feel the necessity for action, regardless of whether change or awareness eventually did come. Few pointed to examples of stories directly affecting others' lives or policy outcomes – but all talked about bearing witness and informing the public as the ultimate goal that made it all worthwhile, a perception unchanged over time.

BEARING WITNESS: FOR THE PUBLIC, FOR THE STORY

For several correspondents, the sense of purpose, of calling or vocation, starts with the basic bearing witness to what happened, the "fair and balanced" (Rosenblum, 15) reporting that creates a factual record upon which analysis and opinion can be based. Some described "doing their part" for democracy by spreading information (AP Oral History, Roderick 1998, 36), like bees or

---

[2] David Crary, "Gannon vows return to Afghanistan," The Associated Press, October 15, 2014.

perhaps wasps, as Anderson (1993, 285) wrote in a poem, whose "flirtation" with good and evil is not intended for personal satisfaction but to spread the pollen for others. *The Times'* Robert Fisk (2002, viii, xiv), who often worked with Anderson in Lebanon, also wrote that journalism was about "watching and witnessing history and ... recording it as honestly as we can ... so ... that no-one can ever say: 'We didn't know.'" "Perhaps we simply tell stories," wrote two-decade Middle East correspondent Anthony Shadid (2006, 12), who started his career with AP and died in 2012 on assignment in Syria for the *New York Times*. As veteran Bob Reid (77) put it, the on-the-ground, "nuts and bolts" function might be even more critical, if dangerously misunderstood, today:

[I]f you have got an environment now where any moron with a laptop and enough money to pay for his broadband connection can set him or herself up as a commentator on global affairs, no wonder no one has any interest in this [factual foreign news]. Or no wonder it's so hard to sell this stuff for a vast amount of money. ... We need to do the nuts and bolts reporting, because the others are relying on that.

From Central America to Eastern Europe, other correspondents felt that they were "monitoring" history in the making (Frazier, 17) – the raw, unscripted version. Mort Rosenblum (42–43), filled with emotion at witnessing an anti-Communist revolution sweeping Prague, found dissident leader Václav Havel coming out of a dinner and breathlessly asked him "Are you going into politics?" As the story noted, a "haggard" Havel replied, "I'm going to bed."[3] "On a bit of a lark," Mark Porubcansky (25–26) traveled with a photographer to Iaşi, Romania, shortly after the revolution against Ceauşescu, arriving at 3 a.m. in a train station with broken windows and no electricity. At the local government headquarters, where Ceauşescu's niece used to rule, he found chain-smoking Doru Tigau, a 43-year-old philosophy professor, speculating about "trying to run Romania's revolution in an out-of-the-way place like Iasi," as the story read, while acknowledging that "For the time being, this is a nightmare":[4]

[H]e was telling me ... how he and some of the other guys who were trying to run this thing had been out on the street a few nights before, at 1 or 2 o'clock in the morning, walking some place, and were nearly shot by soldiers, because the soldiers didn't know who the hell they were. It was just chaos. ... I remember thinking, this is what it's like to live through history. ... When we read history in history books, it's been tidied up for us. And a lot of stuff gets lost. A lot of stuff is deleted. But when you're living through that historical moment, there's a whole lot of confusion, a whole lot of uncertainty: "Well, what the hell is going on?"

---

[3] Mort Rosenblum, "Heady revolution pervades every corner of Prague," The Associated Press, December 4, 1989.

[4] Mark Porubcansky, "After the euphoria, Romania has bills to pay and jobs to fill," The Associated Press, January 16, 1990.

Dan Perry (36) recalled witnessing the day Moldova became independent, the joy spreading in the streets of Lvov a few days after Ukraine also declared independence,[5] and feeling that as a correspondent "you were the eyes of the world to a very large extent" because, pre-iPhones and social media, "there was no other way to bring the story out except via being a foreign correspondent." Wondering whether he would want his teenage children to become journalists, Perry (38) admitted some "caution" given the news industry's current wobbly finances and job security, but then added, "The pleasure and joy and satisfaction that you get is so incredibly profound that I'm still inclined to say yes, despite the difficulties."

Showing people far removed from it what the reality is on the ground fulfilled a double obligation, as two veterans of war coverage in Central America put it – to those living through the events and to the distant audiences whose assumptions about them might be entirely off (Frazier, 2):

> To tell someone in Kansas what is going on in Panama, and to give them the right kind of information and make him feel that he is being kept informed. And to be able to talk to someone in Central America – the woman who just saw her husband being shot – how they express their feelings and all that, and to attempt to convey that to people outside, instead of presenting political arguments. Just tell them what's going on, and they'll make up their own mind. (AP Oral History, Aguilar 2009, 78)

Informing the Public

The goal of informing the world through either eyewitness reporting or investigation has driven many correspondents, such as Debbie Seward (5, 14), who covered the collapse of Communism in Eastern Europe and the Soviet Union. She believed in "a civic purpose to journalism, to informing the public so that they are able to understand an issue and participate in, as citizens . . . I knew that the reality was different from both what the Soviets said it was and what the Americans said it was. And that was a driving factor behind the reason I decided to become a journalist." Special correspondent Charles Hanley (26), who reported from more than 100 countries, recalled how, while investigating the No Gun Ri massacre that won him a Pulitzer, there would be "moments when my hand would be shaking on the keyboard when I'm hearing what some guy's telling me on the telephone" – one can easily imagine that reaction since the story included quotes such as this from a former U.S. 1st Cavalry Division machine gunner: "We just annihilated them."[6] "You're just thrilled to be able to be the one to convey something to the rest of the world," Hanley told me.

---

[5] Dan Petreanu, "Moldavia declares independence," The Associated Press, August 27, 1991; Dan Petreanu, "Lvov, center of Ukrainian nationalism, wary of Russia," The Associated Press, September 1, 1991.

[6] Sang-Hun Choe, Charles J. Hanley, and Martha Mendoza, "After half-century's silence, U.S. vets tell of killing Korean refugees," The Associated Press, September 30, 1999.

To inform a global public appeared especially significant, and fulfilling, to wire correspondents whose output is rarely rewarded with bylines splashed across front pages. His sparkling sense of humor intact despite a brief delay by security at AP headquarters before our interview, retired executive Claude Erbsen (16) recalled his days "toiling in anonymity" from Latin America: "I felt that I was reaching more people than anybody else, so that was good enough for me." In his spartan, windowless office as *Stars and Stripes* Pacific news editor at Yokota Air Base outside Tokyo – but with his "midlife" dark-green two-seater parked outside – Paul Alexander (32–33), who covered many of the bloodiest 1990s conflicts for AP, also argued that "you feel like you've done your job" when your stories are published widely (although only once or twice "has someone actually known who I was" and remembered the byline). In the digital era of apparently infinite purveyors of stories, the role of foreign correspondents continues to be providing trustworthy, confirmed news, with an additional element of analysis and explanation that can guide the audience to the valuable information and put it in context. Those are the stories that "teach the reader something," said Robin McDowell (18, 27), giving as an example her controversial story about Indonesia's mistreated transvestite community (discussed in Chapter 12):

[A]n important role for a foreign correspondent is to kind of weed out all that other stuff and say, these are the things that I think are important in this country at this moment, or interesting, and really kind of give it a well-rounded look instead of just saying, "Oh yeah, Obama had a transvestite nanny. That's interesting, that's weird, isn't it?" And then cause some huge big debate that doesn't have anything to do with anything.

But today's media environment puts in even starker light the paradox in this definition of journalism's purpose: Not all stories do reach an audience, and those that do might not be the ones correspondents consider the most significant. Having always known that journalism is about the stories people "want to hear and know" (Simpson, 43), though people might be "watching Oprah" instead of paying attention to coverage of momentous happenings (Rosenblum, 13), correspondents today are better informed than ever on exactly what captures the audience. But play in other media and clicks online are only one measure of impact, and an imperfect one. Reflecting on a career spanning more than 40 years, Denis Gray (65–66) defined a great story as "after all, one that a lot of people read" – and then quickly added a critical qualifier:

If one of my stories gets 100 hits – I mean newspapers – and another gets 1,000, probably I would say, even though I didn't like writing the story as much, but I have to say that it was a better story. Because part of it is, if nobody reads your story, then what's the point of our job? ... So part of it is that we are servants of the worldwide – not just the American – but worldwide public. We are their servants ... and what I just said is totally nonsense in one sense. Because you write about, for example, Beyoncé's underpants, which AP did, I forget which star it was, ... that got a huge amount of play. ... But

I would say that for a serious story, if it is read by a lot of people rather than fewer people, then to me that is a good story.

Despite knowing with "crystal clarity" what kind of stories attract most readers online or on mobile apps, today's correspondents, as Perry (35) put it, cannot "pander just to what will be popular" or they would be "abdicating" their public trust:

Our mission, I think it's kind of a sacred mission actually, is to take what we believe as very informed observers is important for people to know and render it in such a way that it really will be interesting to people. Not so easy. Sometimes Sisyphean. And yes, I suppose one could argue that it's self-appointed and sanctimonious, but I don't think so. I think it's incredibly important as a public service and if done properly it should be a smashing business as well.

How to perform this public service of attracting readers to important stories is a constant quandary for most correspondents, as noted in Chapter 12. Mark Stevenson (34), who has often reported from deep inside deadly cartel-controlled Mexican provinces and matter-of-factly pointed out the latest mass kidnapping site as we walked to lunch in Mexico City, said self-deprecatingly that "What keeps me going is my core ethical principle of, I never bore my readers":

If I have one ethical principle, besides trying to tell the truth in one of its multiple forms, is that what I write is going to be edifying, interesting, entertaining. . . . It's not like I'm part of the entertainment industry. But it is that I really take it as . . . my job is to never bore my readers and to never make them sit through some schoolroom lesson. And because I'm here, this story becomes more interesting, more engaging, more revealing, more profound, or gets written at all. . . . Am I physically saving lives, or am I physically changing policies? You know, maybe that happens sometimes, but that's aleatory, that is completely aleatory. And usually these issues are so big that . . . if you went to bed every night with that idea, I don't think it would get you through it because it doesn't happen, so I prefer my ethical principle.

Letting the Voiceless Speak

For most correspondents, the essential purpose that took precedence was to tell the stories of those who could not speak to the world on their own, although all drew a clear line between their role and that of advocates. After all, sources did take often grave risks to interact with reporters. Gannon's story about the survivors of a U.S. soldier's murderous rampage, described at the beginning of this chapter, reported how one of them, Masooma, "defied tribal traditions that prohibit women from speaking to strangers to talk to The Associated Press." "Sitting on a dirty straw mat . . . inside a giant black shawl," Masooma's voice cracked "as she was momentarily unable to speak" when recalling the gunshots that killed her husband during the four-hour interview at her brother-in-law Baaran's house in Kandahar. The story explained that the two villages where the killings occurred "are too hostile for foreigners to visit. Even in Kandahar, some 150 kilometers (90 miles) away, the AP journalists sought to avoid being seen by Baaran's neighbors, who he feared would react negatively to their presence. ... The AP also spoke with several others who survived the attack or lost family members. To avoid putting the Afghans in danger should they be seen talking to foreigners, the AP arranged for those interviews to take place at a nondescript hotel in Kandahar. The Afghans drove the dusty, dangerous road from their villages to the hotel and then returned home" – including 11-year-old Zardana, who knew one English phrase only: "Thank you."

Calling a highlight of his career the grueling reporting from Nicaraguan villages buried by mudslides in the aftermath of Hurricane Mitch, Niko Price (26) said he felt that his presence "sort of was allowing the people who were there to be remembered and to be known about." In his heartrending first-person story, he described how some survivors in Rolando Rodriguez "spent half a nightmarish day guiding me through a canefield littered with rotting bodies, asking nothing in return. They figured the more people knew about the horror, the more likely they were to help" – and the stories vividly portrayed that horror.[7] Matthew Pennington (17–19) also found most rewarding the coverage of natural disasters – "being out there and kind of breathing it in, and sort of trying to understand how it affects people's lives":

There was a big earthquake in Kashmir in late 2005 ... killed 70,000 people[8] ... and so I spent a week or two, maybe 10 days pitching in a tent in Kashmir ... because there was nowhere else to stay, because most of the buildings were leveled or structurally unsound. And I remember doing a story about the mental health impacts of this earthquake and going to a hospital, and there was some woman who'd been found wandering ... and she was sort of frozen, and the doctor would lift up her arm and her arm would stay there, and she wouldn't put it down again. And it was like she was in this sort of shock, and that was a very vivid image.

One of Pennington's stories about the Kashmir disaster began and concluded with that "lone woman," whose name nobody knew and whose only words had been "Take me home."[9]

Eric Talmadge (12), who risked nuclear radiation to cover Japan's triple 2011 disaster from the hardest-hit areas, justified it as the only way to give that segment of the audience who might care "an accurate, full picture" of "what it's like, actually there, on the ground, not just for the journalist, but for the other people who are there on the ground ... who won't be going home when their assignment is over." Similarly, several correspondents across continents and

---

[7] Niko Price, "Reporter deals with rotting bodies, screaming children," The Associated Press, November 8, 1998.

[8] In October 2005, an earthquake struck Kashmir and northern Pakistan, killing more than 80,000 people and leaving 3.5 million homeless.

[9] Matthew Pennington, "Woman's plea, 'Take me home,' shows the suffering of quake survivors," The Associated Press, November 10, 2005.

decades said – a few with tears in their eyes, for the only time during the interviews – that they felt most satisfied in their job when shining a light on "a real human story" about long-suffering individuals. Jean Lee (16, 18) reflected that the new bureau in North Korea was creating access to, and getting answers about, a long off-limits people:

And that's what you have to do as a reporter, is trying to get those answers, try to understand what's going on – try to at least portray what's going on. . . . [H]opefully it will help broaden the understanding of how they think, what they want, why they do what they do. . . . Having daily interactions, these conversations with people that are so illuminating. . . . That's why we become journalists, because we're so curious about all of that. We want to find a way to share it. So we put up with the restrictions and the sacrifices because the story is worth telling. And to share that with the world is worthwhile. (Lee, 16, 18)

Of decades reporting in China and Japan, Elaine Kurtenbach (13–14) recalled two humble interviewees with extraordinary attitudes:

There was one story I did in Shanghai where I interviewed this man who has no arms, but he was winning piano competitions; he won this talent competition playing the piano with his toes. And I did a little profile of him – wasn't a big, huge work-up – but I really felt like that . . . was a meaningful story. . . . The story I did about the reconstruction, or lack thereof [in Japan after the earthquake and tsunami], there was this woman who we interviewed – an 83-year-old woman . . . beautiful, vibrant person, lost every single thing, and had such an amazing attitude. So when I meet these people and I get the privilege to

FIGURE 13.1. Pyongyang bureau chief Jean H. Lee prepares for a televised Q&A that was later broadcast live and beamed back to the United States from Kim Il Sung Square in Pyongyang, North Korea, on April 14, 2013. (Photo courtesy of Jean H. Lee)

talk to them and to learn from them – I mean, seriously – that's when you say, "Okay, how exciting!" You can't pay for this, right? I get paid to do it!

Kurtenbach's story described how the Chinese pianist, Liu Wei, whose arms were amputated after a childhood accident, "removed his shoes and right sock, carefully using his toes to place the sock in his right shoe. (He plays with his left sock on.)" It quoted him as saying, "What I demand is that my work be so good people won't notice my arms are missing." That spirit was not unlike 83-year-old Hide Sato's, who despite sleeping on cardboard boxes in chilly one-room temporary housing two years after the Japanese tsunami, told the correspondent, "This is our town and so we need to rebuild it using our own efforts. . . . We have to do what we are capable of doing, a step at a time."[10]

Tony Smith raced into Sarajevo with a tiny band of fellow journalists as most other observers left the city when the Serbian siege closed in. Shortly afterward he had to race out transporting a grievously wounded colleague and the corpse of another, only to return almost immediately to cover the war yet again. As we bumped down the idyllic country roads of Portugal's Douro vineyards in his Land Rover, Smith (16–17) argued that together with "professional pride," "idealism" was what had motivated those heart-in-mouth trips down sniper alley:

I really did believe that we had to help the people. [chuckles] It sounds twee, right? It really does, but I did believe that, and I believed that Sarajevo was really being dismembered and its people were really suffering and these were my guys because it was my story. . . . And if you put against that the fact that you could be killed, it doesn't really enter into the equation, because you decided you wanted to be a foreign correspondent, that's what you do. And it's not that I wanted to get shot or anything, of course not. . . . I owed it to myself and to my colleagues, to my boss, but most of all to the people, to the people in [the ex-Yugoslavia] . . . the whole situation was so bad and it was so ludicrously unjust that I felt that I had to. . . . [On an assignment] we ended up taking cover behind this building, this corner house, and you could actually, the cobblestones, I can still see it. You could see the bullets bouncing off the cobblestones. . . . That first contact, you think, oh, this is like real bullets, you know? And what am I doing here? And everybody has that reaction, everybody. But you just swallow it down and you've got to do it, that's what you're here for.

WILL IT MATTER? STORY IMPACT ON READERS AND REALITY

The irony of risking harassment, injury, even death to be there, to bring a foreign reality to a potential audience, is that correspondents have no say in what the consequences will be – and most argued that they would not want to anyway, agreeing with Donna Bryson's (64–65) sentiment that "what

---

[10] Elaine Kurtenbach, "Chinese man with no arms plays piano with toes," The Associated Press, August 27, 2010; Elaine Kurtenbach, "Tsunami-hit towns still barren as rebuilding lags," The Associated Press, March 8, 2013.

action [people] decide to take if their understanding is increased is not my business as a journalist." As we talked in her home filled with contemporary and folk African art, dinner slowly roasting in the open kitchen, Bryson was the only correspondent interviewed to tear up recounting a joyful moment: watching a family in Soweto lower and open their fists over their hearts as they watched Mandela do the same at his inauguration (see this chapter's box). Given how committed and engaged the correspondents demonstrated to be, and how they cherished the times when they knew they had made a difference, this widely shared profession of detachment seems better understood as a declaration of nonpartisan objectivity, of the separation of roles between advocacy and journalism, rather than actual indifference at the outcome of the controversies and tragedies they felt such a tremendous responsibility to cover:

I don't know how many people actually read what we produce. I don't know. I really don't. . . . It's something I can't change. All I can do is do the best I can to try to make this [Israeli-Palestinian] conflict in some ways accessible to people and try to explain what's going on in a productive way. I can't do more than that. . . . But I do take these things seriously. I often ask myself, are we doing this story justice, are we doing the best we can? . . . It is a big responsibility, because . . . we reach the largest number of people. It's just enormous. So if AP reports something from this region, it better be right and it better be fair and it better be good. (Laub, 11, 23)

Price (12–13) also saw a special role and even power for AP because of its broad and diverse reach, well beyond the "cultural, political, academic elite" comprising the audience of some of the more popularly recognized news organizations:

There's a very different kind of power that comes with the ability to teach ordinary people everywhere that people are actually less different than you might think in some ways, and more different than you might think in others – but help people understand the world around them, and I think it's sort of the most beautiful part of the AP's mission. . . . And our report, by helping people be better informed and understand better what's happening and to break through some of those stereotypes, I think that's a really, really powerful thing.

For some correspondents, such as veterans Rosenblum and Reid with more than 80 AP years combined, realizing how little most people did care and how rarely something changed was a hard lesson learned, but not enough to discourage them from continuing to write informative, revealing stories with the hope that someone would want to understand a bit more. Rosenblum (19–20) said he started off in the Congo believing "like a schmuck" that "if I could just . . . get across everything that was wrong, then people would fix it." The famine in Biafra disabused him of that: Correspondents "wrote and wrote and wrote about this, the starvation, the babies, and stuff like that," but it was one magazine cover photo of a starving child, by a parachuting journalist, that opened the world's eyes. Still, Rosenblum felt that there is "the section of the world which cares, which is significant ... they're worth talking to." Reid (81–82) also set a humbler but no easier goal for his reporting than "we make a difference":

I never brought down a politician, or felt I did. I never got anyone arrested who would not have been arrested anyway.... [I]f there was anything like a good or rewarding story it's to – at the end of the day, you feel like you took a complicated event or issue and put it into terms that people could understand and would find an interest in it. And would feel that it had been worth their time to at least look at the top of your story, if not the whole thing.

In his early days as hostage in Lebanon, Anderson (22) thought "all the time" about his job, including the "recurring fantasy" that, should his kidnappers just dump him on a street and let him go, he would "run ... walk into the AP bureau and ... file my own bulletin" on the release. But he also reflected on whether he had done anything as a correspondent that would make his own pain, and that of his family, "worthwhile." After his release, Anderson (28–29) received multiple awards – but the plaque he showed me when we met 20 years later as the honor he most treasured was the Associated Press Managing Editors' "reporter of the year," for "excellence in AP reportorial performance" just before he was kidnapped:

So I earned that. Now did I have any effect? There is nobody I can point to and no situation I can point to other than a very small way to say that I helped that person as a reporter, that I'd changed that situation, I helped find a solution. I don't believe I can do that. I don't believe very many journalists can do that, okay? So where is the value in what we do? What we do is find and tell the truth as best as we can in situations where everybody is lying and it's very difficult to do that and often dangerous to do that.... You have to believe in the inherent value of doing that, of telling the truth, of finding and telling the truth no matter what happens, whether people listened, whether things changed, whether anybody goes to jail, and sometimes they do, in order to understand and do this job, because then the ethics becomes simpler.

On some occasions, however, the correspondents' work did have a tangible, immediate effect on the lives of the people they covered – "and okay, we're not so self-righteous about not affecting things that I'm not happy that happened," as Perry (29) said of a story of his about "the incredible plague of AIDS and HIV in Trinidad and Tobago" that generated "calls from people wanting to help out some of the protagonists." The story stated – just below the lead vignette of an HIV-positive mother of two who used to slink "through back alleys to her job as a seamstress" because of the stigma – that AIDS advocacy groups in the Caribbean "hope to raise $35 million from the world's rich nations."[11]

"[O]ur job is not to change policy ... or to make people better or happier, but secretly, a lot of us, including myself, if there's proof that our story may have changed the world – this is a really, me getting way out there – either through policy or through some human action, for the better, then, to me, that's also a great

---

[11] Dan Perry, "Ignorance, fear, apathy, shame contribute to Caribbean AIDS spread," The Associated Press, August 26, 2000.

FIGURE 13.2. Terry Anderson, in the garden of his south Florida home on December 1, 2012, shows the plaque he was awarded "for excellence in AP reportorial performance" for his work from Lebanon in 1985, the year he was kidnapped. (Photo by Giovanna Dell'Orto)

[story]," Gray (66) concurred. He added that another way to measure the greatness of stories is whether some readers want to help their subjects – be they Vietnamese boat people or a nurse in Somalia or even Thai elephants – "even if maybe millions of people didn't read" the articles. Knowing he was the only foreign correspondent standing on a hill near Fukushima when the reactor exploded, and in the area for much of the crisis, Talmadge (6, 17) felt "like I was functioning as a journalist" because he got out "a good story that was important, that you knew people would pay attention to and they would then perhaps help the situation somewhat by maybe bringing more support, more donations – laying out what the problem was, so that people could focus more effort on dealing with it."

The practice of focusing on the suffering of a specific, ordinary individual – to personalize ongoing conflict stories so that readers will continue to pay attention – can change his or her life. It did for the blinded Bosnian boy whose plight Reid (86) covered and who would likely have been killed in the Srebrenica massacre if he had not been adopted, and also for a week-old orphaned Somali girl whom Alexander (28) discovered while reporting about a Swedish field hospital in Mogadishu:

I did a story, and I guess it was pretty good and it got a lot of attention.[12] And there were like hundreds of people trying to adopt this girl. . . . We had to do a follow-up story on that because people wanted to know what had happened to Mimi. . . . AP was getting letters about this little girl. How could people help? The rest of them, all these people dying of hunger and starvation – they didn't have a face. They didn't have an individual story to pull on the heartstrings.

Alexander's follow-up story's lead described Mimi as "the infant with the slashed throat whose plight has captured hearts worldwide," and an editor's note read, "Those wishing to contact Mimi's doctors may direct a fax to Dr. Goran Broden at the Swedish Field Hospital in Mogadishu, via satellite phone: 011-873-137-0537."[13]

Other stories can generate a policy or governmental response, at least temporarily. A father wrote Reid (87) that not a day went by when he did not feel grateful to the correspondent for saving his daughter's life. She had been taken hostage by a mob in Mostar while auditing a bank suspected of money laundering for the Croat militia and Reid, alerted by the father, reported on the ongoing story until the United Nations sent a reaction force to rescue the auditors.[14] David Crary (13), who covered both apartheid and the Bosnian War (see this chapter's box), felt that in the first case especially "the foreign press corps was part of a dynamic that did make a difference . . . made the Afrikaner government feel they were never going to be left alone to kind of do their own thing and drag out their oppression." Gray (32), who covered controversial U.S. conflicts from Cambodia to Iraq, said where he hoped "against all hope" to make a direct if "minute" policy impact was with stories about the environment and wildlife, such as an exposé on the smuggling of illegal elephant tusks through corrupt Thai airport controls. In Mexico, Stevenson's (28) stories stopped a hotel development on a sea turtle nesting ground and delayed by several years the government's plan to decriminalize drugs because "once the AP got ahold of that story, the U.S. reaction was such

---

[12] Paul Alexander, "Orphaned infant with slashed throat captures hearts," *The Associated Press*, April 22, 1993.

[13] Paul Alexander, "Infant with slashed throat may go to Sweden for treatment," *The Associated Press*, May 5, 1993.

[14] In an email that Reid shared with the interviewer, the father told Reid in 2012, 11 years after the events in Bosnia: "It was your quick response that put all the other events leading to her rescue into play. I don't believe I ever thanked you properly. There is not a week that goes by that I don't think of that day and your response to a desperate father's phone call. Thank you, Mr. Reid, for helping to save my daughter's life."

that they killed the bill."[15] The question of whether stories do – or should – change foreign policies in Washington, however, is far more nuanced.

MOVING WASHINGTON: SHOULD CORRESPONDENCE AFFECT FOREIGN POLICY?

Asked if they thought of the possible effect on evolving American policy as they wrote stories about volatile situations in Vietnam, Afghanistan, the Middle East, or Central America, correspondents always answered no – but they often still hoped that by fulfilling their goal of shedding light on realities on the ground, their reporting might ultimately make some difference. The tension between purpose and hope, between observing impartially and caring deeply, shows through these reflections by Karin Laub and Gannon, who since the 1980s have covered the Israeli-Palestinian conflict and Afghanistan/Pakistan, respectively:

On a personal level, I sometimes think if there's a certain story or something, "Oh, I hope the State Department decisionmakers read this one." ... But I don't know if they do and I don't know if it will make any difference at all, because policies are set in a different way and not based on news reports. Unless it's something really, really embarrassing or really problematic for the U.S., I don't have any illusions that they wait to hear our reports from the region and based on that they will figure out their policies. And I don't even know how much of this gets through to the readers or changes perceptions in any way. I have no idea; I really don't have any idea. (Laub, 10)

I'm a reporter who is really doing her best to question and question and question and question and question so that you have answers, to tell a story that you think is important because that's what I'm trained at. That's what I have a lifetime of doing. ... Does it make a difference to the reader? I hope that if I'm doing my job, it does, but do I waste any sleep over it? Not really, I mean not my business. (Gannon, 78)

In line with one correspondent's belief that "our job is not to shape policy, it's just to report what's going on" (Eliason, 8), all said that they reported what they observed without caving in to considerations about how it might look to Washington. They were also often too preoccupied with trying to figure out what would happen next right in the front lines, as one former Saigon bureau chief recalled:

We didn't sit around and debate this stuff, we didn't get into this esoteric shit. We were too busy worrying about what was going on in front of us. That was what the story was. We didn't look at things in the context of how this was being received on college campuses ... that wasn't our problem. Our problem was not the larger context of the war. Our job was to cover the war itself. What was happening there in front of us? What was going on in the rice paddies? What was going on ... in the DMZ, in the delta? This

---

[15] For the last story Stevenson wrote on the issue, see Mark Stevenson, "Three-year battle to save Mexican beach ends with defeat for Spanish hotel firm," The Associated Press, August 10, 2001; Mark Stevenson, "U.S. urges Mexico to rethink drug decriminalization as Mexico appears to step back," The Associated Press, May 3, 2006.

was the thing we were thinking about, the military. And diplomacy at that level. . . . And so we tried to cover it from that standpoint, not just the military, but the Vietnamese themselves. (Pyle, 10; also Lederer, 5; Erbsen, 3)

Several correspondents argued that their job was to interest and ideally enlighten the American public, or the global public, on important issues, not to inform the White House or other governments – though they also noted that reporting on stumbling U.S. efforts could possibly affect both public opinion and policy, from Pakistan to Venezuela to the Middle East. In Cairo in the early 2000s, Bryson (63–64) was keenly aware that she was covering a dictatorship that received major funding from Washington. Reporting, for example, on the trial of Saad Eddin Ibrahim, an American University sociologist jailed on the charge of having insulted President Hosni Mubarak,[16] Bryson "didn't think that, 'Oh this is going to make the U.S. government change its policy'":

But I did think that it could perhaps make the U.S., American readers understand more about what kind of government was being supported in the Middle East. . . . I don't think that I ever considered myself someone making policy or influencing policy. I just didn't think I had that kind of power, and certainly . . . didn't set that as a goal for myself. I wasn't an advocate. I was a describer. . . . [Opening people's eyes] is such a slow process and I think that's probably told over many stories. But I suppose I did, I tried to contribute to that slow process.

In Iraq, Sally Buzbee (6) felt that it was not her "job to tell [Americans] whether to be happy or unhappy with the war" – and she did not have "any belief of what policy should be." But it was the correspondents' responsibility to tell it as it was, which included, by the mid-2000s, "firsthand evidence . . . that the war was going much worse for the United States than people back home realized":

I did feel that what we saw when we were on the ground there was not what was being reflected back in terms of what the military leaders were saying at that point. . . . [I]t was a big shock to me, in 2006, that they were kind of saying, "Everything is okay and the media is making this worse than it is." And you were like, "Are you kidding me?" The city [Baghdad] was a freaking disaster. There was a full-scale sectarian war, and they were not admitting that, basically. And so I was worried that our reporting would essentially turn everyone off from the war, which is not really our point. . . . But it wasn't doing anybody any good to not be accurate about what was happening there. And we were obviously aware that it could just turn Americans off and want them to pull out of the war, but as a journalist, you have to reflect what is really happening, especially if you think that government officials are not quite capturing it.

While also adamant that Middle East correspondents were not "concerned with moving U.S. policy," Perry (16) added that "it's always nice when a story is so revelatory that it not only enlightens the reader but also the decisionmaker," especially by bringing attention to issues below the radar, "past the things that

---

[16] Bryson started covering Ibrahim during his imprisonment; Donna Bryson, "Egyptian activist speaks out from jail via cell phone," The Associated Press, August 6, 2000.

are said in public when you believe the things said in public don't really get at the heart of the matter." As an example, he cited a painstakingly reported story about how U.S. Secretary of State John Kerry's effort to bring Israelis and Palestinians "back to the negotiating table may well employ the moribund but strangely still existent 2002 Arab Peace Initiative" – which is exactly what happened less than a month later:[17] "So that obviously gave me enormous pleasure, because we were the only ones to focus on that, and that was the result of doing more than a stenography, but rather thinking."

Drawing attention to the unseen or unsaid, to the underreported, in the hope that it will add to the understanding of people elsewhere, whether ordinary citizens or executive policymakers, is also important in less well-traveled areas, or places entirely untraveled, such as North Korea, where Lee (16) helped open the first AP bureau in 2012: "I'm just there to try to broaden the understanding of the place, but if it ends up shaping policy and helping to inform the people who are shaping policy, that's great. But ... our main point is trying to flesh out the coverage of this place that is so badly covered." Reporting from Southeast Asia in the mid-1970s, and careful to avoid "editorializing," Gray (10–11) "started to think that besides just informing the reader about what was going on, perhaps, not necessarily Washington, DC, but the world should know what kind of suffering was brought about by certain foreign policy and military actions." His "proudest moment as a journalist" was being among the first correspondents "who went very hard after the story of the Khmer Rouge atrocities in Cambodia ... interviewed hundreds of refugees, came out with these horror stories."

From El Salvador to Bosnia, what drove coverage that had a hard-earned reputation for neutrality was "being witness to what you saw in front of you ... understanding on a very human level what the hell is going on here," said Porubcansky (18), who reported from Sarajevo and also oversaw war coverage in the Vienna bureau, and not a "'do something' impulse." That did not imply indifference: Joe Frazier (24) was "twinged" by the consciousness that Washington was supporting factions committing atrocities in El Salvador's civil war, "and all we could do was write about it. We couldn't do anything else. And that hurt, sometimes." One of his stories about the devastating impact of Nicaragua's civil war on children ended with this quote from a mother of eight at a refugee center "where 8,000 people live in tents and lean-tos, the children manage to smile and ask to have their pictures taken": "Take these children with you wherever you are going. ... There are so many flies the children all have dysentery. At night, we have to cover them over. There are so many flies ..."[18] One of John Daniszewski's stories from besieged Sarajevo included a similarly

---

[17] Josef Federman, "Decade-old Mideast peace plan re-emerges," The Associated Press, April 7, 2013; Josef Federman, "Arab League sweetens Israel-Palestinian peace plan," The Associated Press, April 30, 2013.

[18] Joe Frazier, The Associated Press, July 14, 1979.

South Africa, and their spillover in regional conflicts, might have spurred U.S. diplomats to put pressure on Pretoria.

Ultimately, human and political impact mingled. Tad Bartimus (14–15), who found herself and two colleagues accidentally running the Phnom Penh bureau during a rocket attack in the 1970s, felt the additional responsibility to absolutely "get it right" – "get the most you can, the best you can, the fastest you can, and get it out of there" – because the Cambodian capital was so isolated that news reports might well be factored in diplomatic, even military, actions. But she quickly added that other stories, like a day in the life of a war widow caring for her children, gave more lingering satisfaction:

Maybe I made somebody stop and think. ... [I knew stories would not] change policy at all, but maybe readers will read a story about this and understand that it isn't all just black and white. It isn't all bang-bang. It isn't all body counts. It's rather real people trying to live real lives.

Also during the Vietnam War, after AP scoops on Green Berets charged with killing a Vietnamese double agent, Richard Pyle (25–26) in Saigon heard that the Pentagon had dropped the accusations – and got to be the first to call and tell the sleeping soldiers, starting a "predawn barracks beer party" that made it into the lead of the story:[21]

"This is Colonel [Robert B.] Rheault speaking, who's this?" I said, "This is Richard Pyle of the AP in Saigon, Colonel. ... [W]e just have a report from Washington here that says that the secretary of defense has dropped all the charges against you and your men." He says, "Really, you don't say?" I said, "Yes, did you know about this?" He said, "No, this is the first I've heard that!" Wow, you know? And he said, "That's quite interesting, what else can you tell me?" "Well, it just says that they decided to drop the charges, they didn't explain why." ... I said, "Well, what are you going to do now?" He says, "I think I'll go wake up the other men, they may want to know about this." ... [T]hat was the sort of thing that happened, and every time something like that went on – this was real fucking journalism, this is what it was really about, if you were going to do this kind of work for a living ... the importance of it and the hands-on effect of doing it that way.

CONCLUSIONS

Ultimately, "people go into journalism because they hope to do some good in the world," said Daniszewski (5), who was shot while covering the Romanian Revolution, bullets penetrating his left arm "a few inches" from his heart and cutting "a gash" in his scalp.[22] Reporting on Eastern Europe's rebellion against

---

[21] "Green Berets Toast News at Beer Party," *Los Angeles Times*, September 30, 1969, 15.
[22] John Daniszewski, "AP correspondent shot 3 times in early throes of Romanian revolt," The Associated Press, December 26, 1989.

Communism had been especially meaningful to him – functioning as "a free independent press" in nations whose peoples "had had their voice taken away from them ever since Yalta." It is fitting to close this review of AP's foreign correspondence practices with a foundational question: What did correspondents think they were doing? The answers, borne out by their practices as described throughout this book, were variations of "finding and telling the truth," of wanting everyone's voices to be heard so that understanding of "what the hell is going on" might be increased. The essential purpose was to bear witness – others had to decide what to do with what correspondents told them. That goal has been uniquely strong for a wire service, both when it served as the only source of information and now when it aims to provide an accurate, enlightening record in the cacophony of today's media world. Reporters felt the responsibility inherent in reaching such a vast, diverse audience, though also aware that great public interest does not necessarily follow the most significant stories, so popularity is a weak indicator of a job well done.

A better guiding principle is giving foreign peoples a chance to be "known about," especially those literally nearly wiped off the map, as by mudslides in Nicaragua or earthquakes in Kashmir or violence everywhere, and muted, as in North Korea or besieged Sarajevo. Do correspondents think that bearing witness actually helps? Although most correspondents said that what people did with new knowledge was not their business, they still found themselves compelled to "swallow" their fears and brave major risks to be there to tell stories to at least the few who do care – a contradiction that speaks to how profoundly correspondents cared, but also how strongly they defended their role as observers and storytellers, not partisan actors. In fact, several said that they were not so "self-righteous" as to not rejoice when their stories moved others to action, whether that action meant offering help to AIDS sufferers in Trinidad and Tobago, Vietnamese refugees or a victim of Somalia's civil war, or turning on political pressure to right a wrong, from ending apartheid to protecting wildlife in Mexico or Thailand. As to political pressure on Washington, correspondents virtually unanimously said that influencing policy was not their goal – but. They did feel it was imperative to be eyewitness reporters to the consequences, and even failures, of American efforts – such as Baghdad being "a freaking disaster" wrecked by sectarian strife despite U.S. proclamations to the contrary. Some found it "hurt" when nothing happened despite a steady stream of reporting about massive suffering, as in the international community's slow response to the horrors of the Bosnian War. Still, they kept at it – reporting and writing in the hope that more knowledge and more visibility would make a difference in better understanding the world.

End of South Africa's Apartheid and the Bosnian War, 1990s

Donna Bryson: [I]t was the day [President Nelson Mandela] was inaugurated in Pretoria. ... I went to Soweto to do a sidebar about what this moment meant in South Africa's biggest black township, and the family had invited me in to watch it with them on television. It was a tiny little Soweto house and a tiny little Soweto television set, and it was just crowded with people watching. And when the national anthem was played ... it was "Lord Bless Africa," which had been a song of the freedom movement, and "Die Stem," The Call, which was the Afrikaner anthem. So it starts with "Lord Bless Africa," and when that song started playing, everyone stood up in this little room and they all raised their fists, which is what you would do at a rally, at an antiapartheid rally, and then you could see them, kind of one at a time probably, notice that Mandela had his hand over his heart. And they all, one by one, they lowered their fists and opened their hands and put them over their hearts. And for me to be there for that moment – I'm tearing up, but that was one of those moments when I thought this is what I've always wanted to do, to be able to witness this and to be able to see this, what Mandela means to people. And to see what hope there might be for South Africa (Bryson, 5–6, 75).[23]

David Crary: [T]o me there's a lot of commonality, the way the foreign press dealt with apartheid and the way the foreign press corps in Sarajevo dealt with that. In a way it was almost more pronounced in Sarajevo for a couple reasons. One, it was so clear to all of us that evil was being perpetrated on the city ... [and] there was no equivalent of the white minority government, there wasn't an authority that we had to say, Okay, let's get the other side of the story. ... There wasn't a second side, there was just this city and the people in it who were victims, and basically we all felt our role was to tell their story and ... keep the world informed of this very dramatic situation that was going on. ... I can think of no other running story that was quite that way, more so than South Africa, where you might not like one side of the story, but there were two sides. ... We never thought of these gunmen up in the hills as kind of a counterweight, a full-fledged other side of this story. ... [T]here were efforts at the beginning to explain why the Bosnian Serbs did what they did and our colleagues at Belgrade would write some stories

---

[23] Donna Bryson, "Mandela hailed in Soweto after decades of hopelessness," The Associated Press, May 10, 1994.

reflecting that, so it's not that AP as a whole ignored the kind of Serb nationalist side of the story. It was more, the people in Sarajevo, that was not our task. . . . I don't think during the three years of the war that anyone from the foreign media in general was that interested in, say, doing a feature story of spending a week up in the mountains around Sarajevo hanging out with these guys who were sending artillery (Crary, 11–12).

14

Eight Decades of Bearing Witness and Telling the World's Stories: Conclusions

This analysis of more than 1,700 years of work by AP foreign correspondents has documented their practices, as well as the array of constraints on them, to shed new light on the essence and impact of the bulk of foreign news content reaching the American public through eight decades of U.S. dominance in world affairs. The history of how and why correspondents wrote the stories that brought the world home – derived not only from the correspondents' candid and vivid descriptions, but by a few hundred of the stories themselves – provides the missing link in the understanding of the impact of foreign news on international relations. On the premise that journalistic content affects both public opinion and the range of policymaking options by building a certain set of images of foreign realities, the previous chapters have taken us, for the first time, on an unfiltered tour inside the construction site.

Much like the correspondents' reporting objective, the goal in telling their stories – in their own voices – is to understand not only what they do, and therefore the news that they produce, but also what the future might hold for both the profession and the content. To quote Kathy Gannon (23), "the more knowledge we have, the better our questions ... knowing what questions to ask is much more important than thinking you have all the answers" – and that applies just as well to scholarship as to interviewing Afghan villagers or Pakistani leaders. In this final chapter, then, the knowledge gained through the history of coverage of the world by The Associated Press informs questions about the possible future of foreign correspondence.

The timing for such query could not be more urgent. In the mid-2010s, a dangerous temptation for disengagement is spreading in both American foreign policymaking and journalism. The partial image of a world where power is diffused and fragmented, and information flows through connected social media citizens, can too easily become the convenient, and cheap, excuse for policy vacillation and media retrenchment. But the more we withdraw, the less we know; the more we ignore, the less we understand; and that lack of comprehension is bound to have devastating consequences when real events – land grabs, beheadings, environmental disasters, all impervious to our indecision – ultimately force policymakers, journalists, and citizens to engage. After all, despite "its definitional uncertainties" and widely divergent uses, power is "the cause of order," as one review of fractious contemporary international relations succinctly states (Zartman 2009, 4), and international order is a "global public good" that the United States continues to be uniquely positioned to provide (Nye 2011, 220). Coverage of the world's disorders, then, is so essential that the rapidly increasing murders of journalists constitute "a threat to global peace and security," as the executive director of the Committee to Protect Journalists argues (Simon 2015, 126).

And yet, on the topic of foreign news, this is the question resonating, increasingly loudly, in the corridors of academia and media management: With (dreamingly) worldwide connectivity plus multicultural citizen empowerment and (realistically) massive budget cuts plus fickle public interest, "are foreign correspondents redundant," as the title of a recent study by the University of Oxford's Reuters Institute for the Study of Journalism put it (Sambrook 2010)? The answer put forth by that study as well as others, sometimes triumphantly and sometimes in despair, is "perhaps yes" – foreign correspondents "may no longer be central to how we learn about the world" (Sambrook 2010, 1), "everyone can be a foreign correspondent" (Hamilton 2009, 478), and even "journalists have the ability to report on some events, particularly breaking news, without physically being there … 'being there,' meaning the hallowed belief that foreign correspondence had to come directly from the eyewitness reporter on the ground, was [by the mid-2010s] no longer the only reliable source for reporting from abroad" (Cooper 2014).

The answer provided by the history uncovered in this book could not be more different. Both the successes and failures of eight decades of foreign correspondence from Afghanistan to Zimbabwe leave little doubt that public discourse has been best served – the most accurate, in-depth, attention-grabbing stories produced – when international correspondents with professional training, time, and the invaluable partnership of a network of colleagues (especially "locals") have been in country long enough to amass the knowledge required to challenge pat narratives, call out the omnipresent lies, and stymie the frequently violent efforts of all those who would vastly prefer not to have the kinds of eyewitnesses who are capable of reaching, daily, billions of others with their credible accounts. That has not always been achieved, of course, or even possible, and it has entailed an extraordinary exposure to danger and trauma, but the logic is inescapable. "You have to be here to tell the story of here," and "If our mission is to report the truth, then we have got to be on the spot," correspondents said (Gannon, 85; Gray, 18) – and what they did (and could not do) from the 1940s to today proved it across the three foundational practices: recognizing what is a story, talking to everyone who might know something about it firsthand, and bearing witness.

THAT'S A STORY!

While hardly a household name, AP has played a crucial, and growing, role as agenda-setter in foreign news, though for the majority of the time studied here others decided how much the public would see of its content republished in newspapers and broadcast. Correspondents in the field have usually decided what to cover, merging their responsiveness to "obvious" breaking news (the wars and natural disasters long considered by others, erroneously, the sole specialty of "the wires") with analytical thinking that can uncover trends, and combining their empathy with "hard-headed realis[m] about the bigger picture" (Daniszewski, 19). Correspondents chose to cover stories ranging from the "truly extraordinary" to the endemically normal that reveals life on the ground, such as police corruption in Nigeria where a guard stole apples from a border-crosser's car (and forgot his machine gun in the trunk). But they also struggled with what they perceived as competing claims between the significant stories they could see – because they were in country – and those they knew would sell: Disney characters in North Korea, the latest G-strings at carnival, political love affairs (where the absurdity of the scrum of reporters staking out a Buenos Aires building for "the governor's Maria" also made a story), or, more soberly, a good old coup d'état.

Over time, correspondents have sought to dig deeper even in the coups d'état – or whatever other matter lights a country on fire – to ensure that a story has enough depth that readers will understand what it means and why they should care. In ongoing conflict, which does remain a staple of news but is the most liable to become a "paint by the numbers" set piece (one suicide bomb, one wailing victim, one disbelieving perpetrator's family, done), correspondents seek to portray the human impact – all this while being lied to, censored, and shot at. To get at the people translates into going past the general and into the ditch with the GI or the bar with the "girls," past the president's "zero hunger" initiative and into the dusty courtyard of the subsistence farmer who went from starving to affording a dinner table because of it. Story ideas have come from palace pronouncements, obscure items in the local press, and of course sniffing around (in person and online) for what makes a country tick or bares its essence – whether Chinese kindergarten morality plays or Cambodians dealing with killers in their midst, Polish citizens reclaiming their history from Russia's grasp or Brazil's unacknowledged racial tensions. But none of the reporting for this, obviously, can be done from afar.

Not that correspondents have been able to cover everywhere equally. As much scholarship has critiqued, some countries have mattered more than others, but in unexpected ways: Correspondents found it harder to produce stories from "quiet places" like Morocco, Europe, or Japan. Another criticism that superficially appears borne out is that many stories have spotlighted how a foreign reality might affect U.S. and global issues – but that has been in part a natural response to the United States' central role in geopolitics for most of the past 80 years and in part a strategy to find parallels and comparisons that grab the American reader, for decades the target audience notoriously uninterested in foreign affairs. Again, to break through this mold and provide a more nuanced, locally accurate perspective has required being on the ground in ways as challenging as embedding with Pakistani soldiers who, stuck on top of the mountains in knee-deep snow on the treacherous border with Afghanistan, wondered what more the West wanted from them, or as simple as writing about the reconstruction of a modest neighborhood mosque in Cairo that made Islam the center of its little community. The commitment to this kind of stories over time reveals a paradox: While the money and time needed to allow correspondents to explore are scarce today, competitive pressures to create original and "impact" reporting necessitate them.

So does perhaps the most difficult kind of story: The one about what *will* happen, which of course, within the "here to report and not to preach" (Laub, 12) constraints of professional journalism, is nearly impossible to write without "evidence," especially when challenging established narratives. After all, no correspondent predicted the way the USSR collapsed, or even that it would, but they did consistently write about small, illuminating everyday changes such as bread lines appearing in Moscow or enthusiasm for country music spreading in Poland. Readers might not find in a story the policy solution to the Israeli-Palestinian conflict, but because of correspondents who went beyond the obvious, they now can know and feel what it is like to study at a yeshiva or wait in line at a West Bank checkpoint. Such "evidence" of future direction can best be found, and reported as well as analyzed, in the choice of quotes and eyewitness detail – also necessarily gathered on the ground.

GET SOMEWHERE WHERE YOU CAN ASK SOMEBODY A QUESTION

The most critical reporting practice is "asking questions." That deceptively simple definition encompasses a tremendously time-consuming, even dangerous effort to find, develop, and protect sources among the highest and lowest strata of society, from the street (and inside the shops or houses lining it) to the ruling elites (always hard and not always pleasant to cultivate, since they might include an opium king or Taliban warlord) and the embassies (where the people in waiting rooms might be as revealing as those behind desks) – both of which were easier to reach in earlier times with fewer security concerns and PR entourages. Getting sources to talk has been easier when a country is falling apart – if one doesn't mind being shot at, detained by secret police, or led along a blind trail of clues into jungles – also because a wide range of dissidents from Poland to Libya have sought U.S. support and, on the common mistaken assumption that the media are a conduit to Washington, reached out to correspondents.

Digital communication altered that dynamic, with databases and search functions making it far easier to track down data and people, but with social media allowing many of those people to bypass journalists entirely. Correspondents monitor social media as assiduously as they have always studied local media, where anonymity prevailed anyway, from Soviet photographed underground sheets to state-run news agencies or even roadside banners from Mexican narcotrafficking cartels reacting to AP stories. The crucial difference, however, is that today's social media are "vox pop that is pushed" (Perry, 22), not pulled by journalists, and therefore automatically selective, purposive, and exclusive of large swaths of the population whose voice correspondents want to make heard. Reliance on social media, therefore, only exacerbates what has long been a dilemma: It is most dangerous for ordinary citizens to talk with journalists precisely in the most oppressive regimes where there are few other ways of getting their experiences and opinions out. That is why the story about the local impact of the U.S. drone campaign in Afghanistan, a crucial and highly secretive piece of international strategy in the mid-2010s, could only be told by arranging contacts accrued through years of presence and then crossing riverbeds in Taliban-controlled areas to reach villagers removed from all technologies.

To get the real opinions, the true stories and not only the stereotypical pithy quotes of the abused, the oppressed, the desperate, or just the ordinary, correspondents have especially needed time and patience, an endless quest for verification, and something else hard to convey if not in person: the belief that they actually care. The way they have proven they do is by waiting hours in an apartheid township while ANC activists hold an election to determine who shall be interviewed today, or riding a mule for 11 hours (one way) through the Burmese jungle, or climbing mountains with Afghan mujahedeen (those same ones who might then turn out to be friends with bin Laden's inner circle, thus providing the journalist with unique access, and the reader with unique stories), or even stopping to chat with the random crucial source you stumble upon because you are there and talk to everybody – in their language if you can. Fluency has hardly been the rule for correspondents usually circling the globe on assignments of various durations, but it has helped build trust as well as to check accuracy, especially since translators might order responses in authoritarian regimes or simply not translate enough nuance to actually understand, say, the horrors endured by survivors of the Cambodian killing fields.

The moral of the story – that it is necessary to visit as many sources as possible in person – has a moral dimension too: Many correspondents said that they owed interest, care, and protection to those who suffered or risked the most to tell their stories. Just as he was recalling his coverage more than 20 years previously of the Tiananmen Square protests, Terril Jones took phone calls from his seventh-grader daughter, who was upset over a cut-off Internet connection (not surprising, since the "great firewall" was particularly active in Beijing as the National Party Congress met), and then from his younger son, who wanted to say good night. Jones (32) told me he continues to agonize over not knowing "how lucky or fortunate I might be compared to what kind of misfortune I may have facilitated" by giving a worldwide voice – and full ID – to young protestors in the heady days before the wave of hope was brutally suppressed. From China to El Salvador, these legacies haunted correspondents who braved bullets, tanks, and trigger-happy security officers to allow to speak those "imploring" them to "report the truth" so that the world might see – and turned up as corpses hours after an interview.

In moral solidarity as well as to verify and investigate, then, correspondents have always needed to "go out and put [their] nose in it" (Frazier, 13), while constantly aware that they might be far from welcome, and that the way they are perceived, as foreigners and journalists especially, acts as filter on access to sources and scenes, and poses its own ethical dilemmas. None of the correspondents experienced systematic access or exclusion based on gender or race – not an African American correspondent in Africa nor female correspondents in Muslim countries, for example – an encouraging sign that dialogue is possible across those lines. But the same locale might host militias who want correspondents gone or dead because of what they might report, and people who want them to stay because they believe, often wrongly, that their presence means help is on the way. Mark Stevenson (33) has pursued human stories in one of the world's most lethal places, the parts of Mexico controlled by brutal drug cartels, and told me that what "feels like crap" is to be suddenly surrounded by a crowd of people asking him to write down their missing relatives' names and obtain justice, when he knows he cannot "do anything, other than give a general impression that there's a problem out there." (Of course, that in itself is a tremendous public service, because no problem can ever get solved if ignored.)

Pragmatically, to be perceived as journalist has been useful, mostly because it usually beats the perception of foreigner or American or spy (a distinction lost on many kidnappers and assassins) – until, as for Terry Anderson when the Lebanese war took a sudden, even more radical turn, it no longer does, and then the correspondent persona becomes even more dangerous, precisely because a terrorist might aim for those same advantages of high publicity and wide reach that media convey. For all the precautions and awareness, this is one unpredictable constraint that correspondents have had to bear, whether they waded through a street in Mogadishu (where "if the mood of the crowd changed quickly, that would be the last thing that you ever saw," Alexander [24] said) or entered a café in the dilapidated Paris banlieues. If they are perceived as foreigner first, they might enjoy the "foreigner discount," for example as unveiled women in male-dominated societies. Westerner/American also seems to have cut both ways (sometimes a positive, other times a reason to rant against U.S. policies), unless again mistaken for a government spy, a common and dangerous misperception throughout decades – who in the world else would go poking around and asking questions in hellholes? Its consequences ranged from, at best, maximum surveillance and attempts at entrapment to expulsion, kidnapping, even the very real threat of murder.

THE IMPERATIVE OF BEARING WITNESS

Aside from being targeted, most correspondents at some point have risked their life – taken a "reasonable" risk, not the quixotic certainty of death – as they sought to bear witness and tell the stories of wars, uprisings, and natural disasters, a particularly critical function for AP since it serves as the basis for many other organizations' reporting. The simple yet extraordinary reason why they have done it so consistently and willingly seems to be the strongest validation of why eyewitness reporting cannot be replaced: Beyond the depth and veracity it adds to the story, beyond the vividness that will attract readers to it, it is a moral imperative that most correspondents said they *owe* to the people who are actually going through whatever they are reporting – the people who bring the correspondent a hot cup of coffee as she seeks refuge in their doorway while the streets of Beirut blow up all around them in a vicious civil war (Powell, 4–5) and another correspondent is across town watching a 3-year-old die, burned alive by a phosphorous shell.

"Sometimes it feels like the very least the journalist can do, if those populations are facing those dangers, is to be there to show it and to tell people about it," said John Daniszewski (9), who was shot while covering the Romanian Revolution. "I had the feeling that if I wasn't there, nobody would care," said Niko Price (26), who spent days wading through thigh-high mud fields in Nicaragua counting dozens of bodies of a hurricane's victims. "I owed it . . . most of all to the people, to the people in [the ex-Yugoslavia] . . . the whole situation was so bad and it was so ludicrously unjust that I felt that I had to," said Tony Smith (16), who drove a tank trap–dented Toyota Corolla into Sarajevo because, if he had left with most other journalists and international observers, who would have told the story of the besieged city?

Some Sarajevan or Lebanese or Romanian or Nicaraguan with a Facebook profile or Twitter feed, one might answer today – but should we not be a little ashamed of delegating all responsibility? While local voices are extremely valuable, the techno-triumphalist narrative so popular in the privileged West tends to overestimate how connected or even functional the world actually is, and to obscure the old-fashioned constraints that governments everywhere, but particularly in the majority of the world not under mature democracies, increasingly use to censor journalism and expression (Simon 2015; Bennett and Naim 2015). Further, monitoring social media does not begin to touch the deeper moral and professional imperative that motivated correspondents to share some of the world's pain and joy, and that gave the necessary truthfulness and impact to their stories.

It is because they ran into mayhem, and would not be budged from it, that we have a reasonably objective, utterly comprehensible, and relatable record of what it was like inside the Russian White House during an expected coup in the waning days of the Soviet Union; or in the darkened streets of Kabul as the United States bombed it; or at a South African elementary school where life got back to normal on the second day of desegregation, after most of the police and the scrum of journalists who terrified the children were gone; or from the far too many places where the threat of violence looms every day, where before going to cover a war correspondents might need to take their children to school or help their mother dig a trench in the garden.

The risks are weighed for every story – is it worth traveling to a rebel-held town in Syria, another contender for today's most lethal place, to write about the lines at the bakery that do not disperse even for fear of bombing? The answer has been yes throughout the decades, as long as there is a reasonable chance of making it back out alive, because it will show how people there live, and they deserve the world to know and understand and, possibly, care. "If a reader sees another story about 'rebels took blah-blah-blah today' . . . people can't relate to it as easily as to a story from the ground that says, here is Mahmoud So-and-so and . . . this is what he's up against while he's living in this little town," said Karin Laub (36), who wrote that Syrian story. All correspondents considered essential to their jobs, and to the accuracy and impact of their stories, the ability to see with their own eyes – not just in covering breaking news but in roaming their countries searching for insights and for ways to show the grit, the dust, the smell of death, the still-liquid pools of blood, the tears of joy.

By being there as professional, trained observers and communicators, they can relate the unforgettable images, from a surrendering German general's outstretched, untaken hand to a Sandinista soldier proudly defending her stand with a rifle taller than herself and slurping a snow cone, since she is 14. Often, some striking observed details can reveal future trends and challenge preconceived notions – both for correspondents and readers – far more than thousands of words of analysis: the ripples of change in Communist Poland; the unshakable, defiant determination of Jewish settlers or of Central American migrants abandoned by their smuggler barely inside the Mexican border, with thousands of miles to go to the United States; the creative ways Cubans developed to survive on food rations decades after the revolution; the Soweto family who first raised fists and then opened their palms on their hearts as the South African anthem played during the first postapartheid presidential inauguration, a sign of "what hope there might be" (Bryson, 75); and the one helmet that 20 Afghan National Army soldiers shared at a dangerous outpost as they were getting ready to take over security from international troops, in a story that also included, through their voices, their mixed feelings. (In fact, all correspondents argued that no situation was simple or one-sided or even presenting only two sides, and that their expectations were rarely left unchanged by what they witnessed.)

The most irrefutable evidence of the crucial importance of bearing witness is the exceedingly long list of governments and people in power around the world and across time who have done their worst to keep correspondents away – using visas (handled by agents who might double as secret police and show detailed knowledge of correspondents' writings and life), open threats that their safety "cannot be guaranteed" and expulsions – as well as to show them only staged versions of reality, at their discretion. Given its powerful global presence, it is astonishing to note that China was pneumatically sealed off to American journalists less than two generations ago. Still in the 2010s, opening, and keeping, a bureau in foreign countries is not a given. Censorship and particularly surveillance have long constrained correspondents, who have found bugs in lampshades in offices and bedrooms, have been followed even when walking children to school, and are routinely assigned minders that track their every movement – and intimidate any potential sources.

The same interests have also vastly preferred that journalists only come into contact with the people they produce and the events they stage, to the point of putting up bamboo netting by the side of the highway in Bangladesh during its war of independence or taking reporters to pro-Gadhafi demonstrations that materialize in the middle of nowhere (too bad for them that the correspondents still had access to real conversations even in Tripoli, even if in whispers while pretending to look through a rack of nightgowns). Of course, the very denial of access can become an enlightening story, as in Gannon being kicked out of a news conference by a Taliban mullah who slapped his subordinate for having let a woman in, just as the local leaders were at pains to profess that the strict Islamist rules would soon be relaxed.

A growing constraint on correspondents' ability to bear witness has been the spread of no-go zones, where the only guarantee of safety is staying out. Again as testament of the determination to be present, correspondents continue to go as close as they can, up to a border road carpeted in cartel bullet casings, for example, where no one comes from the other direction for an hour and a "bullet-riddled army pickup truck" lies abandoned after a deadly ambush authorities deny happened, so that the story can conclusively say that "scenes witnessed by The Associated Press say something else" than the Mexican government's claim that all is under control and tourism should return.

The U.S. government has not been immune from the temptation to keep correspondents away or in line, although many of them noted a difference in the relationship outside the Beltway. Abroad, officers have courted news coverage of the opening of a USIS library in apartheid Soweto or the 2010s uprisings in Bahrain to put pressure on local governments, or even on Washington. Moreover, for decades, U.S. officials were invaluable sources – like the whistleblower attached to the embassy in Buenos Aires who gave Mort Rosenblum horrific insight on Argentina's Dirty War. The U.S. military also helpfully took correspondents along. Correspondents considered embedding, in all its forms, one valuable way to experience one part of conflict.

FIGURE 14.1. Mexico City correspondent Mark Stevenson talks with soldiers in Ciudad Mier, Tamaulipas, Mexico, on November 19, 2010, when army troops entered that border city after most of the residents had fled because of drug violence. (Photo courtesy of Darío López-Mills)

In Vietnam, the "5 o'clock follies" often peddled spin and sometimes lies (though at least on the record), but helicopter pilots routinely took journalists out into the battlefield, where they could see what the Pentagon might have preferred to keep hidden. The same close relationship between correspondents and soldiers on the front lines continued from Somalia (revealing soldiers lobbing small rocks to keep crowd control nonlethal) to Afghanistan (with "maverick" takes on counterinsurgency).

But the American government has grown increasingly keen on message control. Most evidently in Iraq, correspondents on the ground were often the only ones in the position to fact-check the pat lines they received with what they could see all around them, and present what was actually happening when "government officials [were] not quite capturing it," as Sally Buzbee (6) diplomatically put it. On the occasions when correspondents perceived that editors in the United States also were not capturing the situation, or were second-guessing them, they usually prevailed on the strength of their eyewitness knowledge, even when under extreme pressure as when other outlets, hours after 9/11, suggested that Kabul was under attack. Gannon braved the Taliban curfew and could establish that only a few rockets had been fired near the airport, so, on her authority, the story simply said "explosions could be heard" (it turned out, in fact, that they had been fired by the Northern Alliance, not the United States).

To all who received them, the notorious "New York requests" were further proof of the perception gap that distance can create, from simple logistics (why are you not there yet? it looks close on our map) to sourcing (why not just go out on the street and ask random Salvadorans what they think of the guerrillas?) to the basic accuracy of reporting (go look for WMD in Iraq again). Nevertheless, no correspondent said they were ever ordered a story based on political considerations and, over eight decades and tens of thousands of articles, one episode emerged where a story (about Vietnam) was stripped of important information because of them. Plenty of controversial, but painstakingly reported, stories got on the wire, from the revelation of U.S. soldiers killing refugees during the Korean War to straightforward descriptions of racial sentiments in apartheid South Africa.

Even provided that most stories require journalists on the spot, do they need to be foreign correspondents? Why not rely on the "locals," who have always been a crucial part of the team? The history revealed here helps answer that too. Teamwork by a diverse network of reporters on the ground, and an able "desk" of editors nearby, has produced the best stories, because, to put it simply, no single person can see the entirety of a complex situation, and both insider knowledge and fresh eyes offer crucial perspectives. Journalists working in their country have shared their superior linguistic and cultural skills, and more than once saved expatriates' lives even in unexpected ways, like the longtime photo stringer/Vietcong spy who promised to help the American reporters who stayed behind when Saigon fell. But the dangers they operate under can have a chilling effect on newsgathering – a foreign correspondent might get deported, but a citizen with no outside protection can far more easily disappear forever behind a jail door. At the height of Baghdad's sectarian carnage, a story carried an outsider's byline, stating that identifying the other reporters on the scene would expose them to deadly peril, just as it was lethal for Cambodian journalists after the Khmer Rouge took over, for example. In addition, particularly in long-oppressed or underdeveloped countries, local journalists have often needed training in professional standards, particularly objectivity, which correspondents treasure even though they are far from naïve about it.

Take Denis Gray and his jungle camp interview with Khieu Samphan, the Khmer Rouge leader later convicted of crimes against humanity in the deaths of more than a million people. Newly PR-conscious former guerrillas welcomed Gray with shows of both friendliness (French fries, anyone?) and fearsomeness (careful with the punji stakes!), and Gray's story revealed both the staged charm offensive and the difficulty to reconcile his hosts with the murderers of so many of his Cambodian friends and colleagues. Repeatedly, correspondents sought to put aside their feelings, to gather information, and to present even repellent perspectives for what they are, defining their job as asking questions, probing, and reporting, not covering one's ears and screaming "evil!" That was especially helpful where the reality they met turned out to be more shaded than they anticipated: The heart bled for downtrodden Rwandan refugees – who were leaving behind at the border masses of machetes; Salvadoran villages were "reduced to a bloody cinder" – by both government forces and the guerrillas that opposed them, so that soon correspondents "decided it didn't make any sense, so we started writing about that" (Frazier, 21). Most correspondents also felt that some stories did not need balance – bombing civilians to smithereens or apartheid, for example – but as much as possible should be seen, verified or challenged with their own eyes.

THE UNSPOKEN TOLL

A strikingly routine and traumatic part of that verification task has been examining and counting bodies at scenes of violence, from Mussolini's execution to the 2010s Arab revolutions. In bloody morgues, reeking mass graves, and smoldering battlefields, correspondents have literally pointed fingers at one, two, three – dozens of corpses in an effort to establish at least that modicum of truth, and often far more than that. In an analysis of why nobody should be surprised that post-Taliban Afghanistan again descended into ethnic fighting and lawlessness, Gannon recalled the blood-dripping hair that, during the Afghan civil war, an old man threw on her feet before showing her the bodies of five women raped and scalped by the same forces now back in

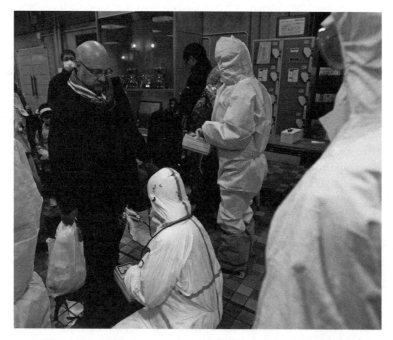

FIGURE 14.2. Tokyo news editor Eric Talmadge gets a radiation check on March 15, 2011, in Oriyama City, Fukushima Prefecture, Japan, four days after a massive earthquake and tsunami struck the country, causing meltdowns at the Fukushima nuclear plant. (Photo by Wally Santana, courtesy of AP Corporate Archives)

power. While leading the Baghdad bureau, Bob Reid oversaw two investigations in the alleged killings of Iraqi civilians by U.S. forces, and the days spent looking through truckloads of corpses were necessary in both cases – one was proven beyond doubt and the other unraveled just before the story hit the wire, when a reporter made one more trip to the morgue and found an ambulance driver whose evidence disproved the contentious detail allegations centered on. Reporting from Japan's tsunami-devastated provinces, Eric Talmadge (18) was waiting out another storm alert when he heard a blast and felt its vibration – which turned out to be the Fukushima reactor exploding nearby. Soon after, "an afternoon of watching corpses get hosed down by people in radiation suits" made him "really wonder" why he was doing this. His answer? "I got my story, I wrote something that I thought was significant, and then woke up the next morning and did it again."

Throughout history, correspondents were aware of the costs that bearing witness entailed for them and for their families, but made the decision to swallow down their fears and consciously avoid focusing on them, mostly because they perceived what so many others were experiencing as so much worse that being there and telling the stories was the "least" they could do. That is an extraordinary perspective, especially where correspondents also saw the hatred and hostility toward them. There was some pride but also some modest discomfort in the fact that often they would not think of being anywhere else than a place where "normal" people would not think of being at all – but then again, locals were stuck there, and correspondents served the story more than anything else.

In wars, correspondents have advanced with combat troops, taking the same sniper fire and rockets (nothing like being sprayed with shrapnel to see through the headquarters' assessment that all goes well), but have also reported from enemy capitals under U.S. bombardment. In civil wars and revolutions, the danger was exponentially multiplied by governments or those against them specifically targeting journalists because of coverage, so that the traditional giant "TV" taped or painted on media cars has alternatively functioned as a safety measure and for target practice. Paul Schemm (19) had a very narrow escape in Syria when "a lot of dudes with guns" – hard to pinpoint factions – tried to take him, the American, away and the attempt was thwarted only because it happened in his driver's village, around people he knew.

Part of what gets correspondents through dangers and trauma is feeling they belong to a likeminded team, both within AP but also among correspondents in general, sharing the sense of mutual obligation that made Smith (11) race, heart in mouth, along Sarajevo's sniper alley with a wounded photographer and a corpse because "this is the right thing to do and we've just got to try and do it." Foreign correspondence has plenty of cutthroat competition, running to be first on the phone when not also cutting the wires. But the story that transpired from interviews is one of collaboration, especially for AP, which serves its members, not just scoops them, and in dangerous assignments, when many rushed in "just to add a body" and free up some of the permanent correspondents, particularly by helping on the desk. Most vastly preferred being on the scene to doing desk duty, but all recognized how crucial it was to get the story on the mark. Multinational bureaus appeared to have often functioned as families with profound bonds forged under fire, with shared values that trumped the occasional editorial yelling match. As dangers rise but correspondents' numbers dwindle, this coping mechanism is also increasingly faltering.

THE BITTER PARADOX

The most cynical question of all to ask about the future of foreign correspondence is this: Even given all of the above – the appallingly dangerous efforts to bear witness to the world's travails against the best efforts of all those with something to hide – has it actually made a difference? Has it had any impact on the audience or on the peoples whose stories correspondents go to such lengths to tell? After all, AP correspondents have not written (only) to inform policymakers and aid workers – their audience is us, the general public, in particular in the United States, not only because historically it was the primary audience but because American actions (and inaction) continue to play a uniquely large role in global dynamics. From the 1940s into the 2000s, reaching an audience – filing stories – was one of the most arduous hurdles to overcome. While in almost all other aspects of text-based foreign correspondence new technologies have had a relatively minor impact, the digital age has revolutionized filing.

It is astonishing that foreign news flowed as it did when to transmit it reporters had to punch telex tape with armed censors standing over them or kneeling under windows in the line of fire, or find "pigeons" to carry frontline or sensitive stories out from the airports in Dhaka or La Paz, or spend hours bent over a machine, praying against static and power outages. From the 1990s, with sat phones first and wireless later, correspondents could file from jungle outposts, mujahedeen-overrun roadsides (provided the stolen phones are returned) and from the middle of U.S. columns advancing up Iraq (provided they can get out of the armored car long enough to get signal). With the ease of filing has come even more pressure for speed, which can mean another form of enslavement to machines and, more worrisome for wire reporters who have long had to fight against this, even less time to check facts before publishing a story that turns out to be wrong, such as the consequences of an IRA bombing. Some stories would not see light at all unless substantial time is devoted to them, such as a detailed take-out on a family camped up on a Honduran highway among hurricane devastation.

Digital media have also changed and diversified the perceived audience, who used to be principally U.S. newspaper readers to whom correspondents should send the equivalent of "letters home" and now could be anybody around the world with a smartphone and the AP Mobile app. Just as the audience thus becomes harder to identify for the purpose of attracting it to content, digital media also provide plenty of easily quantified evidence that most people do not care about foreign news beyond Timbuktu, Venice, and the pyramids. Clicks, tweets, and most-emailed lists prove that the same dubious news judgment choices that scholars have long blamed on journalists actually apply to audience preference: It flits from disaster to disaster and threat to threat, so that poor Japan is stuck with sushi as its chance for global attention, since the big Asian story is now China, while Africa is "a large country" with all the same stories of starving children, and on the fourth day after an earthquake anywhere, they are still pulling out bodies, so what?

Except, of course, that geopolitics are constantly shifting, that static discourses and blind spots hurt policy debates, and that those ravaged by disasters continue to suffer, which correspondents know because, again, they are there to see it happen. Hence we return to the question of the "duty" that they feel to the truth, to the stories, to the people more than to the audience, in what is ultimately a bitter paradox: "If readers had enough of it, if readers are bored of, like, death and destruction, well, tough, this is what it's going to be. This is what's happening," as Matthew Pennington (11) put it – but correspondents still have to try to attract those readers. Even stereotypes can serve their function when they attract attention only to be then debunked: Want witch doctors? Try the latest WHO report on traditional healing. With the blend of persistent realism and humble idealism that all correspondents appeared to share, Daniszewski (6) proffered this suggestion: "try to tell the story day in and day out as accurately and forcefully as you can. And eventually people will hear it." It just might be what the best foreign correspondence has provided: the real stories of the people of here, enlightening through the human connections that transcend clichés and grand narratives, and that correspondents care the most about anyway.

Occasionally, connecting through shared humanity does make a difference. One blinded child in Bosnia might get a new chance at life because of three paragraphs in a wire story that was picked up by all other journalists, stuck in a small town trying to go elsewhere. Serendipity – the sudden insight, source, or image found by just being there and alert – is perhaps the biggest casualty in an overwhelmingly mediated world. Many other times, it is harder to imagine that that human connection is working when correspondents' loyalties, personal lives, and even eyewitness accounts are attacked in the wake of stories about children maimed by unexploded ordnance in Vietnam or killed by bombing in Lebanon, or Iraqis burned alive in displays of religious hatred. Public trust in media continues to decline, and a growing number of news consumers appear unable to tell the difference between professional correspondents, regardless of the format they work in, and what one of them uncharitably called "any moron with a laptop" – or far most frighteningly, between the stories they each produce.

The history of foreign correspondence practices in this book has shown that stories became indeed "more interesting, more engaging, more revealing, more profound, or [got] written at all" (Stevenson, 24) when correspondents were there, when they managed, against daunting odds, to fulfill their mission "to take what we believe as very informed observers is important for people to know and render it in such a way that it really will be interesting to people" (Perry, 25).

At a time of uncertainty over the role and the future of foreign correspondents, this book seeks to inform our understanding of how news content has been created over eight decades by professionals working, despite major obstacles, with the twin aims to "find and tell the truth as best as we can in situations where everybody is lying and it's very difficult ... and often dangerous to do that" (Anderson, 28), and to "know the people," through their own voices, so that others, far away, can understand and engage (Gannon, 77). People like Masooma, a widowed mother who survived a deadly rampage and risked another one by fellow Afghan villagers had she been spotted while talking for four hours with two Western journalists. She was not on Facebook – in fact, she kept her face hidden inside a giant shawl.

When they overcame danger, threats, and obfuscation to meet their goal of accurately finding out and engagingly portraying what was happening to the

FIGURE 14.3. Kathy Gannon, special regional correspondent for Pakistan and Afghanistan, interviews Masooma (sitting against the wall, fully covered in shawl), whose husband was one of 16 villagers killed by a rampaging American soldier, and chats with Masooma's children and nephews, in Kandahar, Afghanistan, on April 20, 2013. (Photo by Anja Niedringhaus, courtesy of Kathy Gannon)

world's peoples, from faceless villagers to popes and presidents, correspondents gave the public, and policymakers, crucial, eye-opening material on the majority of vital foreign issues confronting them. Could they have done it without bearing witness, despite all its risks and tolls? No. Does it ultimately make a difference? That is for us – the public who could do something with the information we are given – to ponder. The correspondents are too hard at work finding and telling us the stories.

Bibliography

Ainslie, Ricardo C. *The Fight to Save Juárez: Life in the Heart of Mexico's Drug War.* Austin: University of Texas Press, 2013.

Anderson, Jon Lee. *The Fall of Baghdad.* New York: Penguin Press, 2004.

Anderson, Terry. *Den of Lions: Memoirs of Seven Years.* New York: Crown Publishers, 1993.

Archetti, Cristina. "Journalism in the Age of Global Media: The Evolving Practices of Foreign Correspondents in London," *Journalism* 14/3 (2013): 419–436.

Arnett, Peter. *Live from the Battlefield: From Vietnam to Baghdad 35 Years in the World's War Zones.* New York: Simon & Schuster, 1994.

Arraf, Jane. "Disappearing Iraq," *Columbia Journalism Review* (September/October 2009): 29–31.

The Associated Press, The Associated Press Corporate Archives, "AP Technology, 1846–2013" (unpublished reference guide, The Associated Press Corporate Archives, New York), 2013.

The Associated Press, The Associated Press Corporate Archives, AP 20, Oral History Collection. Containing the cited interview transcripts for: Eloy Aguilar (interviewed on January 24, 2009, by Luis Alonso); Terry Anderson (interviewed on September 30, 1997, interviewer unknown); Roy Essoyan (interviewed on December 22, 1997, by Janice Magin); Scheherezade Faramarzi (interviewed on May 29, 2009, by Valerie Komor); Denis D. Gray (interviewed on May 1, 2005, by Kelly Smith Tunney); George McArthur (interviewed on October 16, 2005, by Richard Pyle); Hugh A. Mulligan (interviewed on June 23, 2005, by Valerie Komor); Robert Reid (interviewed on April 27, 2009, by Valerie Komor); John Roderick (interviewed on July 17, 1998, by James Lagier); Sam Summerlin (interviewed in November 2004 by Kelly Smith Tunney).

The Associated Press. *A New Model for News: Studying the Deep Structure of Young-Adult News Consumption.* The Associated Press, June 2008.

The Associated Press, and Pete Hamill. *Vietnam: The Real War: A Photographic History.* New York: Abrams, 2014.

Bartimus, Tad. "In-Country," in Tad Bartimus, Denby Fawcett, Jurate Kazickas, Edith Lederer, Ann Bryan Mariano, Anne Morrissy Merick, Laura Palmer, Kate Webb, Tracy Wood, eds. *War Torn: Stories of War from the Women Reporters Who Covered Vietnam.* New York: Random House, 2002.

Bassow, Whitman. *The Moscow Correspondents: Reporting on Russia from the Revolution to Glasnost*. New York: William Morrow and Company, 1988.

Baum, Matthew A., and Philip B. K. Potter. "The Relationships between Mass Media, Public Opinion, and Foreign Policy: Toward a Theoretical Synthesis," *Annual Review of Political Science* 11 (2008): 39–65.

Baum, Matthew A., and Philip B. K. Potter. *War and Democratic Constraint: How the Public Influences Foreign Policy*. Princeton and Oxford: Princeton University Press, 2015.

Beckett, Charlie, and James Ball. *WikiLeaks: News in the Networked Era*. Cambridge, UK: Polity Press, 2012.

Beckmann, Matthew, and Richard L. Hall. "Elite Interviewing in Washington," chapter 10 in Layna Mosley, ed. *Interview Research in Political Science*. Ithaca and London: Cornell University Press, 2013.

Behr, Edward. *Anyone Here Been Raped and Speaks English? A Foreign Correspondent's Life behind the Lines*. London: Hamish Hamilton, 1981.

Bell, Martin. *In Harm's Way*. London: Hamish Hamilton, 1995.

Bennett, Philip, and Moisés Naím. "21st-Century Censorship: Governments around the World Are Using Stealthy New Strategies to Control the Media," *Columbia Journalism Review* (January/February 2015): 22–28.

Benson, Rodney. *Shaping Immigration News: A French-American Comparison*. New York: Cambridge University Press, 2013.

Bernstein, Carl. "The CIA and the Media," *Rolling Stone* (October 20, 1977): 55–67.

Bloch-Elkon, Yaeli. "Studying the Media, Public Opinion, and Foreign Policy in International Crises: The United States and the Bosnian Crisis, 1992–1995," *Harvard International Journal of Press/Politics* 12/4 (2007): 20–51.

Boczkowski, Pablo J., and Eugenia Mitchelstein. *The News Gap: When the Information Preferences of the Media and the Public Diverge*. Cambridge, MA: MIT Press, 2013.

Bollinger, Lee C. *Uninhibited, Robust, and Wide-Open: A Free Press for a New Century*. Oxford: Oxford University Press, 2010.

Boyd-Barrett, Oliver. *The International News Agencies*. London: Constable, 1980.

Boyd-Barrett, Oliver, and Terhi Rantanen. "News Agencies as News Sources: A Re-Evaluation," chapter 1 in Chris Paterson and Annabelle Sreberny, eds. *International News in the 21st Century*. New Barnet, UK: University of Luton Press, 2004.

Bradsher, Henry S. *The Dalai Lama's Secret and Other Reporting Adventures: Stories from a Cold War Correspondent*. Baton Rouge: Louisiana State University Press, 2013.

Broussard, Jinx Coleman. *African American Foreign Correspondents: A History*. Baton Rouge: Louisiana State University Press, 2013.

Browne, Malcolm W. *Muddy Boots and Red Socks: A Reporter's Life*. New York: Times Books, 1993.

Chang, Tsan-Kuo. "All Countries Not Created Equal to Be News." *Communication Research* 25/5 (1998): 528–563.

Chang, Tsan-Kuo, Brian Southwell, Hyung-Min Lee, and Yejin Hong. "A Changing World, Unchanging Perspectives: American Newspaper Editors and Enduring Values in Foreign News Reporting." *International Communication Gazette* 74/4 (June 2012): 367–384.

Chapman, Jane. *Comparative Media History: An Introduction: 1789 to the Present*. Cambridge, UK: Polity Press, 2005.

Christians, Clifford G., Theodore L. Glasser, Denis McQuail, Kaarle Nordenstreng, and Robert A. White. *Normative Theories of the Media: Journalism in Democratic Societies*. Urbana: University of Illinois Press, 2009.

Cohen, Akiba, ed. *Foreign News on Television: Where in the World Is the Global Village?* New York: Peter Lang, 2013.

Cole, Jaci, and John Maxwell Hamilton. "The History of a Surviving Species," chapter 12 in Bob Franklin, ed. *The Future of Newspapers*. London and New York: Routledge, 2009.

Cooper, Ann, and Taylor Owen, eds. *The New Global Journalism: Foreign Correspondence in Transition*. New York: Tow Center for Digital Journalism at Columbia University, 2014.

Cooper, Kent. *Kent Cooper and The Associated Press: An Autobiography*. New York: Random House, 1959.

Dahlby, Tracy. *Into the Field: A Foreign Correspondent's Notebook*. Austin: University of Texas Press, 2014.

Daniloff, Nicholas. *Of Spies and Spokesmen: My Life as a Cold War Correspondent*. Columbia: University of Missouri Press, 2008.

"The Day GI's Looted and AP Blinked," *Columbia Journalism Review* (May/June 1971), 29–30.

Delli Carpini, Michael X., and Scott Keeter. *What Americans Know about Politics and Why It Matters*. New Haven and London: Yale University Press, 1996.

Dell'Orto, Giovanna. *American Journalism and International Relations: Foreign Correspondence from the Early Republic to the Digital Era*. Cambridge, UK: Cambridge University Press, 2013.

Dell'Orto, Giovanna. *The Hidden Power of the American Dream: Why Europe's Shaken Confidence in the United States Threatens the Future of U.S. Influence*. London and Westport, CT: Praeger, 2008.

Duffy, Matt J. "Anonymous Sources: A Historical Review of the Norms Surrounding Their Use," *American Journalism* 31/2 (Spring 2014): 236–261.

Esper, George. "Communists Enter Saigon," in *Reporting Vietnam, Part II: American Journalism 1969–1975*. New York: The Library of America, 1998: 546–548.

Esper, George, and The Associated Press. *The Eyewitness History of the Vietnam War, 1961–1975*. New York: Ballantine Books, 1983.

Fahmy, Shahira, and Thomas J. Johnson, "Embedded versus Unilateral Perspectives on Iraq War," *Newspaper Research Journal* 28/3 (2007): 98–114.

Feldstein, Mark, "Kissing Cousins: Journalism and Oral History," *Oral History Review* 31/1 (2004): 1–22.

Ferrari, Michelle, ed. *Reporting America at War: An Oral History*. New York: Hyperion, 2003.

Fialka, John J. *Hotel Warriors: Covering the Gulf War*. Washington, DC: Woodrow Wilson Center Press, 1991.

Filkins, Dexter. *The Forever War*. New York: Alfred A. Knopf, 2008.

Fisher, Marc. "Who cares if it's true? Modern-day newsrooms reconsider their values." *Columbia Journalism Review* (March/April 2014): 26–32.

Fisk, Robert. *Pity the Nation: The Abduction of Lebanon*. New York: Thunder's Mouth Press/Nation Books, 2002.

Fisk, Robert. *The Great War for Civilisation: The Conquest of the Middle East*. New York: Vintage, 2005.

Flores, Isaac M. *Stories to Tell ... History-Making People and Grand Adventures in a Small World.* New York: iUniverse, 2007.

Frank, Marc. *Cuban Revelations: Behind the Scenes in Havana.* Gainesville: University Press of Florida, 2013.

Frazier, Joseph B. *El Salvador Could Be Like That: A memoir of war, politics, and journalism from the front row of the last bloody conflict in the U.S.-Soviet Cold War.* Ojai, CA: Karina Library Press, 2012.

Friedman, Thomas L. *From Beirut to Jerusalem.* New York: Random House, 1995.

Gannon, Kathy. *I Is for Infidel: From Holy War to Holy Terror: 18 Years inside Afghanistan.* New York: Public Affairs, 2005.

Gans, Herbert J. *Deciding What's News: A Study of* CBS Evening News, NBC Nightly News, Newsweek *and* Time. New York: Random House, 1979.

Garber, Megan. "The AP: Intimations of Politico." *Columbia Journalism Review* (October 16, 2009).

Garibaldi Rogers, Caroline. *Habits of Change: An Oral History of American Nuns.* New York: Oxford University Press, 2011.

Geyer, Georgie Anne. *Buying the Night Flight: The Autobiography of a Woman Foreign Correspondent.* New Brunswick, NJ: Transaction Publishers, 1998.

Gilbert, Allison, Phil Hirschkorn, Melinda Murphy, Robyn Walensky, and Mitchell Stephens, eds. *Covering Catastrophe: Broadcast Journalists Report September 11.* Chicago: Bonus Books, 2002.

Gross, Peter, and Gerd G. Kopper, eds. *Understanding Foreign Correspondence: A Euro-American Perspective of Concepts, Methodologies, and Theories.* New York: Peter Lang, 2011.

Hahn, Oliver, and Julia Lönnendonker, "Transatlantic Foreign Reporting and Foreign Correspondents after 9/11: Trends in Reporting Europe in the United States," *International Journal of Press/Politics* 14/4 (2009): 497–515.

Hamilton, John Maxwell. *Journalism's Roving Eye: A History of American Foreign Reporting.* Baton Rouge: Louisiana State University Press, 2009.

Hamilton, John M., and Eric Jenner, "Redefining Foreign Correspondence," *Journalism* 5/3 (2004): 301–321.

Hannerz, Ulf. *Foreign News: Exploring the World of Foreign Correspondents.* Chicago and London: The University of Chicago Press, 2004.

Hayes, Danny, and Matt Guardino. *Influence from Abroad: Foreign Voices, the Media, and U.S. Public Opinion.* Cambridge, UK: Cambridge University Press, 2013.

Heinzerling, Larry. "A Rare Breed," in Reporters of The Associated Press, *Breaking News: How The Associated Press Has Covered War, Peace, and Everything Else.* New York: Princeton Architectural Press, 2007: 257–305.

Hess, Stephen. *International News & Foreign Correspondents.* Washington, DC: Brookings Institution, 1996.

Hohenberg, John. *Foreign Correspondence: The Great Reporters and Their Times.* 2nd ed. Syracuse, NY: Syracuse University Press, 1995.

Houghton, Kate. "Subverting Journalism: Reporters and the CIA," Special Report of the Committee to Protect Journalists, 1996 (retrieved from http://www.cpj.org/attacks96/sreports/cia.html).

Hoyt, Mike, John Palattella, and the staff of the *Columbia Journalism Review*, eds. *Reporting Iraq: An Oral History of the War by the Journalists Who Covered It.* Hoboken, NJ: Melville House Publishing, 2007.

Jensen, Klaus Bruhn, "The Qualitative Research Process," chapter 14 in Klaus Bruhn Jensen, ed. *A Handbook of Media and Communication Research: Qualitative and Quantitative Methodologies.* 2nd ed. (London and New York: Routledge, 2012): 265–282.

Katovsky, Bill, and Timothy Carlson. *Embedded: The Media at War in Iraq.* Guilford, CT: Lyons Press, 2003.

Kennedy, Ed. *Ed Kennedy's War: V-E Day, Censorship, & The Associated Press.* Baton Rouge: Louisiana State University Press, 2012.

Knightley, Phillip. *The First Casualty: The War Correspondent as Hero and Myth-Maker from the Crimea to Iraq.* Baltimore: Johns Hopkins University Press, 2004.

Koh, Heungseok. "International news coverage and issue relevance to the U.S.," unpublished paper presented to the International Communication Association, June 2013.

Ladd, Jonathan M. *Why Americans Hate the Media and How It Matters.* Princeton and Oxford: Princeton University Press, 2012.

Lederer, Edith. "My First War," in Tad Bartimus, Denby Fawcett, Jurate Kazickas, Edith Lederer, Ann Bryan Mariano, Anne Morrissy Merick, Laura Palmer, Kate Webb, Tracy Wood, eds. *War Torn: Stories of War from the Women Reporters Who Covered Vietnam.* New York: Random House, 2002.

Liu, Kin-ming, ed. *My First Trip to China: Scholars, Diplomats and Journalists Reflect on their First Encounters with China.* Hong Kong: East Slope Publishing, 2012.

Loory, Stuart H. "The CIA's use of the press: A 'mighty Wurlitzer,'" *Columbia Journalism Review*, September/October 1974: 9–18.

MacKinnon, Stephen R., and Oris Friesen. *China Reporting: An Oral History of American Journalism in the 1930s and 1940s.* Berkeley: University of California Press, 1987.

McChesney, Robert W., and Victor Pickard, eds. *Will the Last Reporter Please Turn Out the Lights.* New York and London: New Press, 2011.

Miller, Derek B. *Media Pressure on Foreign Policy: The Evolving Theoretical Framework.* New York: Palgrave Macmillan, 2007.

Morris, Joe Alex. *Deadline Every Minute: The Story of the United Press.* Garden City, NY: Doubleday and Company, 1957.

Mosley, Layna, ed. *Interview Research in Political Science.* Ithaca and London: Cornell University Press, 2013.

Mulligan, Hugh A. *No Place to Die: The Agony of Viet Nam.* New York: William Morrow and Company, 1967.

Murrell, Colleen. *Foreign Correspondents and International Newsgathering: The Role of Fixers.* New York: Routledge, 2015.

Neuenschwander, John A. *A Guide to Oral History and the Law.* New York: Oxford University Press, 2009.

Newman, Nic, and David A. L. Levy, eds. *Reuters Institute Digital News Report 2013: Tracking the Future of News.* Oxford: Reuters Institute for the Study of Journalism, 2013.

Nye, Joseph S., Jr. *The Future of Power.* New York: PublicAffairs, 2011.

Packard, Reynolds. *The Kansas City Milkman.* New York: E. P. Dutton, 1950.

Paterson, Chris, and Sreberny, Annabelle, eds. *International News in the Twenty-First Century.* Eastleigh, UK: John Libbey, 2004.

Paterson, Chris. "News Agency Dominance in International News on the Internet," chapter 7 in David Skinner, James R. Compton, and Michael Gasher, eds. *Converging Media, Diverging Politics: A Political Economy of News Media in the United States and Canada*. Lanham, MD: Rowman & Littlefield, 2005.

Patterson, Thomas E. *Informing the News: The Need for Knowledge-Based Journalism*. New York: Vintage, 2013.

Patton, Robert H. *Hell before Breakfast: America's First War Correspondents Making History and Headlines, from the Battlefields of the Civil War to the Far Reaches of the Ottoman Empire*. New York: Pantheon Books, 2014.

Pedelty, Mark. *War Stories: The Culture of Foreign Correspondents*. New York and London: Routledge, 1995.

Perlmutter, David D., and Hamilton, John Maxwell, eds. *From Pigeons to News Portals: Foreign Reporting and the Challenge of New Technology*. Baton Rouge: Louisiana State University Press, 2007.

Pew Research Center. *State of the News Media: Overview*. March 2014.

Port, J. Robert, "The Story No One Wanted to Hear," chapter 9 in Kristina Borjesson, ed. *Into the Buzzsaw: Leading Journalists Expose the Myth of a Free Press*. Amherst, NY: Prometheus Books, 2002: 201–213.

Prochnau, William. *Once upon a Distant War*. New York: Times Books, 1995.

Pyle, Richard, and Horst Faas. *Lost over Laos: A True Story of Tragedy, Mystery, and Friendship*. Cambridge, MA: Da Capo Press, 2003.

Reporters of The Associated Press. *Breaking News: How The Associated Press Has Covered War, Peace, and Everything Else*. New York: Princeton Architectural Press, 2007.

Reynolds, James. "Correspondents: They Come in Different Shapes and Sizes," *Nieman Reports* 64/3 (Fall 2010): 8–11.

Ricchiardi, Sherry. "Covering the World," *American Journalism Review*, December/ January 2008.

Richburg, Keith B. *Out of America: A Black Man Confronts Africa*. San Diego: Harcourt Brace and Company, 1998.

Ritchie, Donald A. *Reporting from Washington: The History of the Washington Press Corps*. Oxford and New York: Oxford University Press, 2005.

Ritchie, Donald A., ed. *The Oxford Handbook of Oral History*. New York: Oxford University Press, 2011.

Roderick, John. *Covering China: The Story of an American Reporter from Revolutionary Days to the Deng Era*. Chicago: Imprint Publications, 1993.

Rosenblum, Mort. *Little Bunch of Madmen: Elements of Global Reporting*. Millbrook, NY: de.Mo design, 2010.

Rosenblum, Mort. *Who Stole the News? Why We Can't Keep Up with What Happens in the World and What We Can Do about It*. New York: John Wiley & Sons, 1993.

Salisbury, Harrison E. *Without Fear or Favor: The New York Times and Its Times*. New York: Times Books, 1980.

Sambrook, Richard. *Are Foreign Correspondents Redundant? The Changing Face of International News*. Oxford: Reuters Institute for the Study of Journalism, 2010.

Schanberg, Sydney. *Beyond the Killing Fields: War Writings*. Washington, DC: Potomac Books, 2010.

Schiff, Frederick, "The Associated Press: Its Worldwide Bureaus and American Interests," *International Communications Bulletin* 31/3–4 (Spring 1996): 7–13.

Shadid, Anthony. *Night Draws near: Iraq's People in the Shadow of America's War.* New York: Henry Holt and Company, 2006.

Simon, Joel. *The New Censorship: Inside the Global Battle for Media Freedom.* New York: Columbia University Press, 2015.

Spencer, Graham. *The Media and Peace: From Vietnam to the 'War on Terror.'* New York: Palgrave Macmillan, 2005.

Stacewicz, Richard. *Winter Soldiers: An Oral History of the Vietnam Veterans Against the War.* New York: Twayne Publishers, 1997.

Stephens, Mitchell. *Beyond News: The Future of Journalism.* New York: Columbia University Press, 2014.

Sweeney, Michael S. *The Military and the Press: An Uneasy Truce.* Evanston, IL: Northwestern University Press, 2006.

Terry, Wallace. *Missing Pages: Black Journalists of Modern America: An Oral History.* New York: Carroll & Graf Publishers, 2007.

Terzis, Georgios, ed. *Mapping Foreign Correspondence in Europe.* New York and London: Routledge, 2015.

Thomson, Alistair, "Memory and Remembering in Oral History," chapter 5 in Donald A. Ritchie, ed. *The Oxford Handbook of Oral History.* New York: Oxford University Press, 2011: 77–95.

Topping, Seymour. *On the Front Lines of the Cold War: An American Correspondent's Journal from the Chinese Civil War to the Cuban Missile Crisis and Vietnam.* Baton Rouge: Louisiana State University Press, 2010.

Usher, Nikki. *Making News at* The New York Times. Ann Arbor: University of Michigan Press, 2014.

Waugh, Evelyn. *Scoop.* London: Chapman & Hall, 1938.

Westwood, Sean, Rebecca Weiss, and Shanto Iyengar. "All the News That Is Fit to Print? Gatekeeping Effects in Newspaper Coverage of International Affairs," unpublished paper presented to the International Communication Association, June 2013.

Wheeler, John Fenton. *Last Man out: Memoirs of the Last U.S. Reporter Castro Kicked Out of Cuba during the Cold War.* Spokane, WA: Demers Books, 2008.

Wilhoit, G. Cleveland, and David Weaver, "Foreign News Coverage in Two U.S. Wire Services: An Update," *Journal of Communication* 33/2 (1983): 132–148.

Williams, Bruce A., and Michael X. Delli Carpini. *After Broadcast News: Media Regimes, Democracy, and the New Information Environment.* Cambridge, UK: Cambridge University Press, 2011.

Willnat, Lars, and Jason Martin. "Foreign Correspondents – An Endangered Species?" chapter 36 in David H. Weaver and Lars Willnat, eds. *The Global Journalist in the 21st Century.* New York and London: Routledge, 2012.

Wu, H. Denis, and John Maxwell Hamilton, "U.S. Foreign Correspondents: Changes and Continuity at the Turn of the Century." *Gazette: The International Journal for Communication Studies* 66/6 (2004): 517–532.

Zartman, I. William, ed. *Imbalance of Power: U.S. Hegemony and International Order.* Boulder, CO: Lynne Rienner, 2009.

Zelizer, Barbie. "On 'Having Been There': 'Eyewitnessing' as a Journalistic Key Word," *Critical Studies in Media Communication* 24/5 (2007): 408–428.

Index